CONVERSANT ESSAYS

EDITED BY JAMES McCORKLE

CONVERSANT ESSAYS

CONTEMPORARY POETS ON POETRY

WAYNE STATE UNIVERSITY PRESS   DETROIT

LIBRARY OF CONGRESS CATALOGING-IN-PUBLICATION DATA

Conversant essays : contemporary poets on poetry / edited by James McCorkle.
p. cm.
ISBN 0-8143-2099-6 (alk. paper). —ISBN 0-8143-2100-3 (pbk.: alk. paper)
1. American poetry—20th century—History and criticism—
Theory, etc.
2. American poetry—20th century—History and criticism.
3. Poetry—Authorship. 4. Poetics.   I. McCorkle, James.
PS325.C68   1990
809.1—dc20   *89-32152*
CIP

PERMISSIONS

CONTENTS

1

THE SUFFICIENCY OF LANGUAGE

2

QUESTIONS OF FORM

3

READINGS

4

TRACING THE PERSONAL

5

HISTORIES

6

SPECULATIONS

ACKNOWLEDGMENTS

I would like to express my deepest gratitude to all the poets who responded to my invitation to contribute essays to this collection—to those who offered essays and to those who, though unable to contribute essays, offered helpful suggestions. Hobart and William Smith Colleges and the English Department were essential in providing the necessary support to undertake this project. I would especially like to thank Ann Hovey and Pati Mattice for their assistance and, more importantly, their irrepressible and irreplaceable good humor. I am grateful for the support and thoughtful comments by Donald G. Marshall. Lee Ann Schreiner, my editor at Wayne State University Press, was more than supportive: without her enthusiasm from the very beginning this collection would not be. I am also grateful for the care and assistance provided by Paulette Petrimoulx at Wayne State University Press. I would especially like to thank Claudette Columbus. Her comments concerning my introduction were extremely helpful; I only fear I have muddled them. More importantly, her teaching and friendship have been sustaining—to her this book is dedicated.

INTRODUCTION

THE PROSE OF THE POET

What can a poet tell us in prose that is not already found in the poetry? The poet's prose asks this same question, but it is asked in the excess of the act of writing, in the face of failing to write, and in the necessity of reading. The poet reminds us of the difficulty of both writing and reading, or ontological difficulties that, as George Steiner states, cannot be resolved by being looked up or through a readjustment of sensibilities, for they "confront us with blank questions about the nature of human speech, about the status of significance, about the necessity and purpose of the construct which we have, with more or less rough and ready consensus, come to perceive as a poem" (41). The modernist tradition of the poet as the sole arbitrator of the word is something we may wish to preserve and yet may also fear, in part because of its exclusiveness and in part because of the power ceded to the word and our own anxieties concerning this century's history of power. We remain under the shadow of Pound and Eliot, and, though this is not the place for questioning the canon, that shadow is narrow and divisive. The reduction of modernist poetry and criticism into that of a few individuals and a restricted selection of their own work vindicates and extends marginalization and neglect in the readings of our contemporaries.

This collection presents as diverse a group of poets writing critical and personal prose as possible. The collection maps an array of voices discussing poetry and its intersections with the world. These essays propose far less separation of the world and the poem; between the poet's prose and poetry a space opens, analogous to the littoral zone of oceans and bays.

Having grown up on Florida's gulf coast, I almost by nature resort to this geographical and biological site as a means of thinking about what the poet's writings—prose and poems—offer us. The littoral zone is tidal, awash with daily shifting habitats: air; sea or bay or gulf; the mud or silica and finely ground shell; the sun and moon. This is a place where change is also dynamic equilibrium. This is a place, also, of flooding over, of erasure, of absorption. Although I hesitate to argue that the poet is solely an autochthon, the final celebrant of the earth, the poet's prose does investigate the poem as a phenomenon of the world: the poem is an object to be investigated as well as an ecology of interrelated and interdependent elements. The *investigation* of the poem denotes that the poem is the site of a transaction or a transgression—waves against beach, the figurative reshaping the familiar. *Investigation* derives from footprints or tracks. The poet's prose forms tracks or the record of someone's contact with a poem. To read the poet's prose is to witness the process of reading and unveiling.

Likewise, the poet's prose recognizes words as having the physical presence of prints, traces, tracks. This ecology fills with presences both vital and mnemonic.

But what do the poets offer us in prose not found in their poetry? Simply, they teach us how to read and, by extension, how to perceive. These essays record the acts of intimate reading, reading that enjoys repetition, that takes joy in moments of mulling, chewing, tasting. The poet's reading, unlike that of most others, brings us to the sheer physicality of words; the poet's prose reminds us of the connection—atavistic or desired—between the world and the word. Poems teach us this firsthand, as in Galway Kinnell's "Blackberry Eating":

> *I love to go out in late September*
> *among the fat, overripe, icy, black blackberries*
> *to eat blackberries for breakfast,*
> *the stalks very prickly, a penalty*
> *they earn for knowing the black art*
> *of blackberry-making; and as I stand among them*
> *lifting the stalks to my mouth, the ripest berries*
> *fall almost unbidden to my tongue,*
> *as words sometimes do, certain peculiar words*
> *like* strengths *or* squinched,
> *many-lettered, one-syllabled lumps,*
> *which I squeeze, squinch open, and splurge well*
> *in the silent, startled, icy, black language*
> *of blackberry-eating in late September.*

Kinnell's poem forms his own *ars poetica* as well as one for the prose of poets because the poem directs our attention to the density of words and the material for meditation. The poem's one sentence holds the words like the clustering seed-globes of the berry while revealing to us how Kinnell reads that "black language" or magic that is finally the connection between world and word. The poem records the pleasure of language: the physical movement of pronouncing words is at root of the desire for words to be interchangeable with the things themselves. By becoming self-aware of the enunciation of words, we become possessed by them. There is a double movement of absorption: we consume the word in all its fullness while simultaneously being absorbed into the body of the word. Poems are the records of the poet's reading of the world, of the self, of language. The poet's prose is didactic and exemplary, for it is an essaying or weighing of writing.

Jane Cooper has written that poetry "is the soul's history and whatever troubles the soul is fit material for poetry" (55). The poet's prose recounts the making of that history and in so doing affirms both the poem and the soul. The poet's prose, moreover, locates the poem in our history and our peculiar discourses, whereas the poem specularly and synchronically moves through histories. The poem gauges our salvation and abandonment, primarily as a statement of condition; the poet's prose readdresses this for our particular moment. This collection of essays is a map of readings, a history of how the poets are reading, a speculation of why their concerns are what they are now (especially if they differ from the past), and a questioning of how we both read and essay our souls.

To ask what can the poet's prose tell us is to ask what the poet can tell us, or, more essentially, what is a poem. The poet's prose is always defining what a poem *is*—what it might be in a moment of reading and in moments of rereading. As the poem is a history (of the soul), the reader brings to it histories, and the poet's prose suggests or demonstrates an orchestration of those histories. The poet's prose, moreover, notices and insures the ongoingness of a poem and the open-ended, nonteleological speculation as to what a poem (or soul) might be. In his essay, "The Figure of the Youth as Virile Poet"—with what wonderful odd echoes of those venereal soils of Florida!—Wallace Stevens writes,

> Aristotle said: "The poet should say very little *in propria persona."* Without stopping to discuss what might be discussed for so long, note that the principle so stated by Aristotle is cited in relation to the point that poetry is a process of the personality of the poet. This is the element, the force, that keeps poetry a living thing, the modernizing and ever-modern influence. The statement that the process does not involve the poet as subject, to the extent to which that is true, precludes direct egotism. On the other hand, without indirect egotism there can be no poetry. There can be no poetry without the personality of the poet, and that, quite simply, is why the definition of poetry has not been found, and why, in short, there is none. (45–46)

Stevens locates a central condition for poetry—personality. Voice and ethos are constituents of personality, not substitutes. The realization of personality comes when the poet has placed himself or herself in the congruent weathers of the mind and the world and when the reader recognizes the profound force of will by which the poet writes.

Soul and personality—these necessitate poetry, for it is their only tracing. Stevens argues that poetry is "the imagination of life" or a "special abundance and severity of abundance" (65–66). Thus, the poet's personality informs; it is necessary for the process of transformation and illumination manifested by the poem. The poem materializes the process by which a personality comes to be voiced and inscribed however conditionally or momentarily. As a record of that process, it forms the only communication of the idea, potential, or truth of a personality. The poem and the poet represent the possibility of personality, hence of the intimate and the personal. In a culture that denies these possibilities—or cynically commodifies them—these are no small claims. Moreover, Stevens' argument is that the virility of the poet is the soil, the world, or the "visible is the equivalent of the invisible," where the "imagination . . . is the sum of our faculties" (61), not divided from this world. As a reification and a conjunction of the self, history, and myth, the poem mirrors the promise of the prose of the poet. The force of writing itself—when does a poet, while writing, stop being a poet?—carries the poet's personality elsewhere, sometimes into the domains of prose. This is not a conflation of poetry and prose but a questioning of the boundaries of the poet's personality in regard to the act of writing. Perhaps in the poet's prose, in ways unlike other prose, we also see what we desire, a momentary constellation of a self in script. The poet's prose reminds us of the poem's empowerment and examines its transformative presence.

Stevens' poetry and thought has Emerson as one of its anchors. Emerson can be considered the central voice—or at least the voice that has set out the typical concerns—for both the poetry and the criticism offered by poets in the United States. Emerson writes in "Poetry and Imagination" that "the poet listens to conversation and beholds all objects in nature, to give back, not them, but a new and transcendent whole." Similarly, one of our most important poet-critics writing a century later, Adrienne Rich, states that "Poetry is above all a concentration of the *power* of language, which is the power of our ultimate relationship to everything in the universe" (248). Both Emerson and Rich place themselves in the universe and, in Emerson's words, listen for "the spirit of the thing" to give it back in the form of language. Emerson's concerns with nature, the transcendent and the historical, the perception of objects, the relation of the senses to poetry and poetic language, and the masking of the autobiographical describe the embedded conventions of the prose of poets now writing.

Of course, Emerson's writing is a transaction between American intellectual history and European romanticism and transcendental thought. His willed desire for the ideal, utopian, or transcendent, however, is shadowed by both a utilitarianism and a skepticism. This mix marks Emerson as peculiarly of the New World, staining all subsequent poet-critics. Emerson writes in "Poetry and Imagination" that

> Poetry is the *gai science.* The trait and test of the poet is that he builds, adds and affirms. The critic destroys: the poet says nothing but what helps somebody; let others be distracted with cares, he is exempt. All their pleasures are tinged with pain. All his pains are edged with pleasure. The gladness he imparts he shares.

By personal urgency and will, Emerson desires the poet to be transforming himself or herself while also invoking the utilitarian process of the poet as one who builds and adds and, like Whitman and Dickinson, literally heals. Healing, one of the most ancient functions of language as Frazer, Cassirer, and Malinowski have pointed out, empowers the word in myth, magic, and metaphorical thinking. The poet is also communal: "The gladness he imparts he shares." The doubling of the verbs of giving enforce the aspect of the poet as healer, one who reminds us of the community in which we live.

Obliquely affirming Whitman, we find Emerson stating that "there is no subject that does not belong to him [the poet]—politics, economy, manufacturers and stock-brokerage, as much as sunsets and souls; only these things, placed in their true order are poetry; displaced, or put in kitchen order, they are unpoetic." Emerson's statement is a prelude to modernist poetics; although it does not prescribe the form such poetry should take, it does, critically, swerve us from the generic. Although it follows a traditional role of taxonomy and explanation, it also subscribes to a peculiarly North American vision established in writers such as Franklin and Thoreau. The poet's prose has underscored the pragmatic by often concerning itself with the nuts and bolts of poetic composition. Thus, the poetry of the New World becomes a experiment in the vital and the inclusive, yet also, ironically, a pragmatic transcendentalism.

Emerson's prose seeks to instill the rigor of a personal intelligence—as distinct from a philosophical intelligence—in the poetry written in the United States. His disdain for the critic has remained a part of the sensibility of poets as has his sometimes prescriptive voice. His use of such phrases as the "true order" are found in such current expressions as "honest" and "authentic." In this, the poet-critic writes evaluative criticism, of which Robert von Hallberg, in his essay "American Poet-Critics since 1945," rightly is suspicious because it can easily lapse into a narrow and moralistic tone employing such terms as authentic, honest, or genuine to describe only certain poems, implicitly leaving others unauthentic and dishonest (292–293). These terms have little evaluative criteria to support them not because no poetic decorums function in our culture but because they do not correspond to evaluative decorums. Although Emerson grounds his rhetoric in particular aesthetic traditions, particularly that of Coleridge, and identifies his intellectual and cultural adversaries as the natural and applied sciences, without partaking of a simplistic oppositional rhetoric, more current applications of this Emersonian vocabulary by poet-critics are not as thorough in establishing their grounds for such aesthetic and cultural criticism. Emerson's prose then marks a function that persists: the poet's prose offers a prescriptive vision of the poet's place in society and of the forms the poet's expression will take; it also celebrates, affirms, or validates the role of poetry in a society of "manufacturers and stock-brokerage." Ultimately, Emerson asks us to read a poem as a moment of transcendence revealing the order of the world. Obliquely, then, to ask of the function or role of the poet's prose is to be answered by the poem. The poet's prose returns us incessantly to the poem; this is its function. Most radically, and no matter how brilliant the writing, the poet's prose demonstrates the inadequacy of criticism or of prose discourse.

A poet's essay belongs to a genealogy that addresses issues of *poesis* as well as reveals the poet's strongest convictions. Dante's letter to Can Grande, typifying the critical theories of his age, and his *De vulgari eloquentia,* arguing for a vernacular poetry, could be seen as prototypes for many current debates, much as Eliot, Olson, and Merwin, for instance, have echoed Dante's sinners "in cold hell, in thicket." Like images recast for the temperament of the age and the poet, the poet's essay is part of a convention. The genealogy of the poet's essay unfolds interminably like that of the modern long poem, or more exactly like writing itself. The essays shadow poetry, making poetry substantial in the historical moment; they locate the specific experiments of writing and renew or re-vision those experiments. Unlike poems, the poet's essays are solely artifacts of their times; for this reason they demonstrate their insufficiency and their necessity. Nothing can replace the poem, the poet's essay implies, if we are to maintain a belief in either the soul or poetry.

In *The Bow and the Lyre,* Octavio Paz distinguishes between poetry and the poem: "A magnetic object, a secret meeting place of many opposing forces, the poem gives us access to the poetic experience" (14). Continuing, he writes that "the poem is just this: a possibility, something that is only animated by the contact with a reader or a listener." The poem is the revelation and the mediation of the poetic, and tautologically the poet's essay and subsequent criticism form further mediating scrims. In that moment of reading—active and visionary reading—that "instant contains every instant. Without ceasing to flow, time stops, overflowing itself." Paz's exuberance reminds us of our own experiences of the poetic, but the question persists: Given the power of the poetic moment, why has there come into being a genealogy of poets' essays?

I expect fear generates the necessity of the poet's essay. Darkly, perhaps, even the poem comes out of fear. This fear could be the relinquishing of one's identity to what seems another voice, an archaic voice against which one is powerless and which takes us outside the domain of "sense" or sensibility. As Paul Valéry writes,

> It must not be forgotten that for centuries poetry was used for purposes of enchantment. Those who took part in these strange operations had to believe in the power of the word, and far more in the efficacy of its sound than in its significance. Magic formulas are often without meaning; but it was never thought that their power depended on their intellectual content. (74)

The poem comes out of fear because the poem is both the record and the perpetual recording of the violent sundering of language and the world. In poetry, we recognize most fully that the division between subjective and predicative has created the self-conscious structures of time and history: poetry recalls and names our mortality. And in it the self—the poet and the reader—is momentarily memorialized. Perhaps there is fear because we must write and listen to the history of the soul, for without such histories we lose the possibility of the soul, of personality, of intimacy. Poetry remains a register of a speculation on the conditions of one's own soul, of humanity's or the world's soul. Although potentially anagogical, this is not a religious task but a question of being. If poetry marks the soul or personality, then we may fearfully recognize the condition of ourselves as diminished and eroding; the poem is then the last record of the self. If the poet, as Adrienne Rich has written, "is endowed to speak for those who do not have the gift of language, or to see for those who—for whatever reasons—are less conscious of what they are living through" (181), then there is an institutional fear of the poet and poetry. If poetry is a revelation about nature, and thereby marks our separation from nature, there is a fear of acknowledging being bereft, or knowledge of abandonment, as in the closing lines of Mary Oliver's poem "The Shark":

> *Whoever He is, count on it: He won't answer.*
> *The inventory is like the hunter—each*
> *in the crease and spasm of the thing about to be done*
> *is lost in his work. All else is peripheral,*
> *remote, unfelt. The connections have broken.*
>
> *Consider the evening:*
> *the shark winched into the air; men*
> *lifting the last bloody hammers.*
> *And Him, somewhere, ponderously lifting another world,*
> *setting it free to spin, if it can,*
> *in a darkness you can't imagine.*

The poem itself is a fearful object: it generates language; it is part of an ever creative language. It spins on its own once I have left it with some shadow of myself. While prose attempts to harness language's energies, poems gather them into an ongoing force, violent and irreducible to a conclusive order.

The writing of prose by poets remains a curious affair, for it also marks relinquishing the metrical tensions of language in what has become the acceptable form of self-expression. Metered language—loose, banal, tight, highly stressed, or complex—remains the sole form of interconnection with the world of others. Unmetered language does not necessitate enactment; it allows a widening cultural solipsism that describes a culture's growing bureaucracy, divisiveness, and subjectivity. Our definition of time as moments needing to be spent or as a commodity to be negotiated is antithetical to the time offered in a poem—metered, rhythmical time. Poetry—poems, dance, or pictorial—is the place of the festival, which Hans-Georg Gadamer calls "'fulfilled' or 'autonomous' time" (42). The festival unites us in the intention of the celebration: we renounce ourselves or our privacy when hearing the song of the poem. The poem's rhythm is what we listen for in order to be in the festival's own time. The emphasis here is on the intention of listening and being in the festival rather than arriving or crossing into festive time. Characteristic of the festival is the "specific, rhythmical recurrence that elevates it above the flow of time. In a kind of cosmic rhythm, it assures that not all times pass by indifferently in the same homogeneous way. On the contrary, in the course of festive time, the heightened moment returns" (60). The festival, as the rhythm of poetry, subverts the disciplined partitioning of time. Gadamer's festival parallels Bakhtin's dialogic imagination, viewing language as a shared event outside individual possession. While Bakhtin argues for a social heteroglossia in the novel as opposed to poetry, Gadamer argues for a more radical vision of language that offers a community of enacted time. Poetry's autonomous time, that of rhythm, creates a community that we disciplined souls fear, for such a shared and enacted time is outside the comprehension of bureaucracy and hence is unnatural.

The neglect of meter or rhythm in discussions of poetry reflects a pull toward disassembling the festive. The decision by poets to write in prose may reflect two approaches to festival or rhythm. The poet may seek shelter from the demands of the festival's otherness. Prose becomes a momentary narcotic or a necessary camouflage. Alternately, the poet may write in prose either to re-vision prose or to expose its deadening effects. Prose, not being part of enacting the otherness found in the rhythm of poetry, avoids fear; after all, prose is the medium of our sociability, not of our soul. Rhythm in poetry is world-building or world-naming; in addition, we experience renunciation by the cosmos. Poetry does not belong to us, unlike prose, and its rhythm marks that otherness. Rhythm offers the recurrence of the festival's community and the terrifying experience of the always inscribed disaster of the termination of rhythm or, conversely, the overriding awareness of our mortality by rhythm's inexorable interminability. Poetry becomes inhuman; the festival terrifies. Poetry's rhythm enacts an ordering outside the conventions of social and literary decorum: the enactment of rhythm refuses our definitions of the human condition.

Violence is a sensational word, but one that is justified because the poem always eludes the captivity of prose. This elusiveness—or freedom—perhaps is what is terrifying: it is sublime; it is outside the domain of state or law. The uncoiling of language can represent madness and chaos; the poem reveals chaos and our need for order. Not surprisingly then Czeslaw Milosz closes *Unattainable Earth* with a prose entry:

> To find my home in one sentence, concise, as if hammered in metal. Not to enchant anybody. Not to earn a lasting name in posterity. An unnamed need for order, for rhythm, for form, which three words are opposed to chaos and nothingness.

A poem's play between order and chaos describes our historical, cultural, and individual conditions in the successive moments of reading the poem. In *The Witness of Poetry*, Milosz writes that "only an awareness of the dangers menacing what we love allows us to sense the dimension of time and to feel in everything we see and touch the presence of past generations" (4). The poet's prose provides an exterior viewing—distinct from an interior, empathic, homeopathic meditation—on the dangers confronting our epoch and on time and the dimension of the past.

The poet's prose is a final act of naming, for there poetry is named; there Milosz can turn and argue that poetry witnesses us. The poet's prose actively participates in the increasingly severe contemplation of our history and culture by artists, writers, and theorists. Caught in a double-bind, we fear both order and its loss. The poet's prose provides us with order or meaning like all interpretations; however, in its implicit demand to return to the poem because exegesis cannot succeed or fulfill, the poet's prose points to an object that means yet also overflows with and outlasts meaning.

As a necessary form of conservation, the poet's prose reflects a withdrawal from those energies that drive a poem. The poet's prose refigures how the poet ventured into such speculation and, as such, describes the creative process. The poet must stand witness to the history of the soul and to the making of the poem: the poem witnesses the soul's history while the prose testifies to the making of the poem. The poet's prose takes the reader into the poem's interior and the poet's psyche. Prose creates a critical space where the conditions of choice—metaphor, arrangement, and sound—are studied. The poet may focus on what appears to be technique where technique is a figure for aesthetic judgments that inevitably point to the problem of good and bad, issues of ethos, and questions of understanding. In his essay "The Inward Muse," Donald Hall suggests that the discussions of technique by poets describe their ways of overriding the constraints the conscious mind erects to control the creative process. Hall argues that questions of technique help censor the demands for constraint and bring into coincidence two modes of thought: "To write (or to cross out) a word was simultaneously an act of judgment and of imagination, of the critic and of the creator" (119). Hall concludes that the division between critic and creator is a fallacy because the two modes are in continual internal dialogue throughout the creation of a poem.

To discuss the poet's prose is to discuss the place and function of criticism: the poet's prose implicitly questions criticism's endeavor to provide complete readings. In some ways, the poet's prose takes a deconstructive turn, for the very gesture of the poet's prose recognizes the endless, ongoing, or interminable sway and shift of language. The poet's dwelling in the word and its habitations parallels Jacques Derrida's work. For instance, in his *Signéponge,* Derrida undertakes a playful, cornucopic dwelling in the name of the poet Francis Ponge so as to dwell metonymically in the body of Ponge's poetics. Both poet and critic employ self-reflexive turns: the critique always and already problematizes itself. Although there are arguably shared impulses, the rhetorical scales differ. Without proposing any connections between the criticism written by poets and deconstruction, Robert von Hallberg notes that, unlike scholarly criticism, that by poets has a far greater rhetorical range, "to vary their tone or rhetoric to suit a particular occasion," often in order "to hold open their options at the poles opposite to earnestness, judiciousness, and civility" (290). The poet-critic decries the methodical; the unorthodox approaches offered by recent poet-critics instate the improvisational and personal. Given the currency of "crisis" in critical vocabulary—crisis of meaning, crisis of language—the totalizing effects of a criticism based on demanding explanation, rather than speculating and essaying, fulfill the demands or parameters of each crisis. The criticism of circumstance avoids the absolutism of systematized criticism exemplified by the works of Harold Bloom and Northrop Frye and compels the reader to return to the poem, to the place where the experiment with language is at its greatest.

Nonetheless, the term poet-critic underscores the connections the poet shares with the critic. The term represents the division and the union of these two figures. One term defines and makes present the other. It further describes the potential interchange between the two; the hyphen bridges one domain with another. Separation is necessary; but drop one term, and the whole flies out of balance. This is not to argue that either all poets must be critics or all critics must be poets. The interchange between the poet and the critic increasingly is necessary because both are engaged in a process that, as Geoffrey Hartman in *Criticism in the Wilderness* writes, "*reinscribes* us, to use a current expression; and the expression is good, because life in culture is a palimpsest that can only be deciphered by a species of 'thick description.'" Swerving us from the Arnoldian position, Hartman argues, "It is a mistake to think of the humanist as spiritualizing anything: on the contrary, he materializes us, he makes us aware of the material culture (including texts) in which everyone has always lived" (301). Hartman's defense and description of the critic fairly describes that of both the artist and the poet-critic. As perhaps one of the most sensitive and agile readers, Hartman argues persuasively that culture is material and palimpsestic and significantly that the poet and the critic are the combined makers and rememberers of this live archaeology. Hartman will not risk, hence the conservatism of criticism, suggesting what remains always beyond critical definition, what Cooper, Paz, Rich, and Stevens have risked describing and enacting.

The poet's criticism, however, occupies a singular position among possible forms of critical writings; the poet's criticism, in its double guise, marks a threshold. Outside, or perhaps against, the poet's criticism is Frye's argument in *The Anatomy of Criticism* that literary criticism is, or should be, an analytic, scientific endeavor: "If criticism exists, it must be an examination of literature in terms of a conceptual; framework derivable form an inductive survey of the literary field" (7). Frye's methodology sets up counters of opposition within the critical frame; additionally, it excludes the impulse that decries a unified theory or expression of meaning, poetics, or poetry. Frye's task arises out of a rage for order as well as a need for validating the enterprises of teaching literature and practicing criticism, whereby literature itself marks normative social structures. Literary criticism then invokes the vague subjective term "scientific"—with its overtones of the social sciences, materialism, and empiricism—as its defense for demystifying literature and, by extension, poetry. The poet's criticism is both in and against the grain of such endeavors, for it describes the choices and movements of a poet's examined reading of language—the charity of the word—while also reinscribing the mystery of the word.

To read the poet's prose is to investigate both the condition and the power of language. One can further read the criticism by poets as exposing the rifts among disciplines: the growing insulation of disciplines and the transformation of poetry into an institutionalized or accredited discipline with its own specialized vocabularies describe but one instance of a growing fear that we will no longer be able to talk with one another in any substantive manner. In fact, the writings of poet-critics tend to go against the divisiveness among disciplines; the most technical essay, say on meter, typically demonstrates the lack of rhetorical distance the poet-critic places between his or her position and that of the reader. The poet-critics, as the term implies, are among the most synthesizing of writers; in their writings we can find preliminary examples of crossdisciplinary investigations.

The poet and the critic share a common task; the work of each involves a form of memory or a recovery of memory. Frye argues that "a public that tries to do without criticism . . . brutalizes the arts and loses its cultural memory"(4). Frye's argument grows from Eliot's arguments that sought a discrete literary tradition for conserving culture and argued against impressionistic criticism that was unsatisfactory given the limitations of poetry's traditional functions in a scientific epoch. In "The Social Function of Poetry," Eliot writes that the poet's "direct duty is to his *language,* first to preserve, and second to extend and improve" (9). Eliot's argument is one of both nationalism and pragmatism, but this is modified with his observation that poetry is a "reminder of all the things that can only be said in one language, and are untranslatable" (14). Eliot describes, here, the "*spiritual* communication between people," which, arguably, can be found only in the reading of poetry. In the very late essay, "The Frontiers of Criticism," Eliot states that poets have "other interests beside poetry— otherwise their poetry would be very empty: they are poets because their dominant interest has been in turning their experience and thought (and to experience and to think means to have interests beyond poetry)—in turning their experience and thinking into poetry" (129–30). The critic, like the poet, must be "whole," to use Eliot's term; interestingly this contrasts with his desire for the invisibility of the poet (and the world) in relationship to the poem. The poet and the critic, for Eliot, share in the responsibility to language that means to generate and revise a collective identity, one of differences within a whole. That language constitutes self and world would seem to be Eliot's intuitive argument: poets and critics share in both examining and extending this argument.

Eliot, nonetheless, defined a growing schism between the role of the poet, the critic, and the poet-critic. In fact, he placed a nearly anthropological cast to the discussion of poetry by insisting upon national, social, and local *functions* for poetry. Far from integrating discussions of language, he insisted upon a transcendental and removed position for poetry as well as the critical responses to poetry. Eliot is not the cause of such a schism, as is often asserted, rather he, almost anonymously, marks a sea change in the relationship of poet, critic, and audience. Disciplining the world, dividing knowledge into special competencies and functions, can easily throw barriers against curiosity and work against the belief of the function of poetry. The uneasiness, which may become a general neglect, with the poet's role as critic no doubt is anchored uneasily with contemporary poetry itself. In the current formation of public education, which has essentially resisted complete and radical restructuring, poetry, like the arts in general, remains a luxury in a system that only reinforces division of class and race while warehousing what has become an expendable and transient labor pool. The teaching of literature has become *used* explicitly as a form of disciplining or stipulating social conformity exemplified by the packaging of textbooks for literary studies. Reading and writing are taught as disciplines, and often in such a way they are easily turned into punishments. Despite this, poetry has proliferated—given the undergraduate and graduate programs in creative writing, the contests and grants, the numbers of readings and magazines—while arguably it has also been commodified by these same agents and, simultaneously, has come to be considered expendable or antiquated, hence subject to dismissal.

The point is not that there are too many or too few poets, or that poets have withdrawn themselves from the intellectual scene, but rather that, whatever the superficial reasons, an abiding necessity remains for the release and the experience of the poetic. More important, the prose of poets suggests ways, though not explicit pedagogies, of reading. The prose of poets reminds us of the difficulty of the poem, the choices that the creative process provoke, the thick pleasure of language, and the entwining of the word and the world. Typically, we read against the corporeality of the word and against the pleasure of the text; analogously, our culture has feared the body, nature, and the other, and hence it has written against or upon them. Such French theorists as Michel Foucault, Jean-François Lyotard, and Jean Baudrillard argue twentieth-century Western culture, in its relentless pursuit of realizing the simulacral sign, breaks apart knowledge and radicalizes meaning by eliminating or threatening to eliminate players in the language game in order to maintain a homeostasis of power and knowledge in the system. Cosmological and ecological beliefs as well as their revisioning are threatened by the "dominant existence today of techno-science, that is the massive subordination of cognitive statements to the finality of the best possible performance, which is the technological criterion" (Lyotard, 76).

In the 1960s, with the swelling of the population of college students, there was a concurrent dispersion of poets geographically and stylistically. Sandra Gilbert has written, during the expansion of the university, the poet has become a technician in an institutional program. The poet is now part of the disciplinary modality of education—one that demands conformity and the abstraction of individuals into social roles. Conversely, the poet's poem and prose potentially subvert such an enterprise. The fear of poetry—and I use the term "poetry" in the large sense that Octavio Paz has described—has necessitated poetry's containment. It questions the power and control of language for those who maintain the economy of power. This sounds sensational, but on the literal level the containment and extinction of languages has taken place on every continent in recent human memory. Language is part of the ecology, an Amazonian tribal language is part of the same rain forest that is being ripped away:

> *Just so the Christians, hard as nails,*
> *tiny as nails, and glinting,*
> *in creaking armor, came and found it all,*
> *not unfamiliar:*
> *no lovers' walks, no bowers,*
> *no cherries to be picked, no lute music,*
> *but corresponding, nevertheless,*
> *to an old dream of wealth and luxury*
> *already out of style when they left home—*
> *wealth, plus a brand-new pleasure.*
> *Directly over Mass, humming perhaps*
> *L'Homme arme or some such tune,*
> *they ripped away into the hanging fabric,*
> *each out to catch an Indian for himself—*
> *those maddening little women who kept calling,*
> *calling to each other (or had the birds waked up?)*
> *and retreating, always retreating, behind it.*

This final stanza of Elizabeth Bishop's poem of controlled anger, "Brazil, January 1, 1502," illustrates languages, gender, and environment as interwoven threads that belong to the same vast tapestry. Bishop outlines a threshold of a history that continues, but she also describes the unwillingness—or refusal—to recognize the other except as an object to be subjugated. Bishop's poem, and arguably all poetry, is part of this violated fabric. As obvious as this is, the significant point is that the processes of education incessantly deny interconnection, the other, and hence poetry. The poem, as Bishop's poetry marvelously demonstrates, *travels* in all the figurative *senses* of the word. Her geographic "primers" do not merely instruct; they illuminate. The poet, in prose and in poems, insists upon a traveling curiosity, a topophilia. Curiosity maintains the life of the soul, as any true teacher knows.

The prose of poets teaches us again how to read or redirect our ways of reading. We could look at their prose as notes on the possibility that reading is an act of translation. The prose then provides notes toward a reading, an accommodation of poetry and the reader, yet with the understanding that the translator or the reader not the text, was ephemeral. In *Convergences,* Octavio Paz notes that among the Chinese and Tibetans, traveling and translating were parallel activities that encompassed a lifetime, the "school of translators was a school of travelers and explorers. . . . Their hardships were yet another proof of their capability as translators. More specifically, this capability was at once an intellectual ability and a moral worth" (21–22). If writers as diverse as Cassirer, Derrida, and Paz argue that we constitute the world solely through langage, then language is both our inevitable object of contemplation and our abode for it. Paz describes the linguistic theories of the American linguist, Benjamin Lee Whorf:

> The archetypal configurations of language (the forms that bind and group the different elements together so as to construct words and sentences) "are basic

in a really cosmic sense" and "form wholes, akin to the Gestalten of psychology, which are embraced in larger whole in continual progression." Language is a fabric made of the patterns, from the simplest to the most complex, formed by the different linguistic elements. Although this fabric is continually changing and moving, the patterns that appear, disappear, and reappear are variations of a few archetypes or models, inscribed, so to speak, in the laws of motion that produce the different combinations. The verbal patterns reproduce in some way the forms of perception (*Gestalt*), the map of the cosmos, the musical score, the page of equations, and the forms of geometry. The idea that the fabric of the universe appears in language was one already familiar to other civilizations, as Whorf himself points out. (*Convergences*, 44–45)

If language is a configuration of viewpoints, then should we follow Paz's enthusiasm for Whorf's theories? Plurality is then a linguistic condition that necessitates examining and conversing among the multiplicity of viewpoints rather than confining oneself to the narrows of a single perspective. Plurality hinges on a willingness for curiosity, which, in turn, depends upon accepting Keatsian negative capability as the modality of critical contemplation. The poem is the direct expression of such a poetry. The poet's prose is indirect and surveys; the poet's prose exemplifies contemplation and how much we are language. Their prose links reading and contemplation; the world and the word are then connected.

The contemplation of language is not a nihilistic task but one of necessity which defines who we are. To refuse this contemplation would be, as Lyotard describes, "to wallow together in the 'anything goes,'" where "it remains possible and useful to assess the value of works of art according to the profits they yield," for such "realism accommodates all tendencies, just as capital accommodates all 'needs,' providing that the tendencies and needs have purchasing power" (76). Meaning does not vanish into tautologies demonstrating meaninglessness, but Whorf's "patternment," Chatwin's "songlines," Buddhism's *sunyata,* the Greek *melos,* the Sanskrit *cinoti:* a matrix, or geography, of pure form's emptiness and plenitude. The poet's prose implicitly addresses the desire for recognizing language's recombinatory energies, which extends past Whorf's "patternment" and rejects the terrifying chain-reactions of interminable displacement and replacement found in most contemporary discussions of language. The transcendent and alienating verticality of metaphor and the inexorable horizontality of metonymy are questioned by the activity of *poiesis.* The poet's prose suggests that poetry arises from an understanding of radical possibility and that reading is an engagement in such a contact with recombinatory possibilities.

In 1917, the Spanish poet Antonio Machado wrote:

But language is already much *less mine* than are my feelings. For after all I have had to acquire it, learn it from others. Before being *ours*—because it will never be *mine* alone—it was theirs; it belonged to that world which is neither subjective nor objective, to that third world to which psychology has not yet paid sufficient attention, the world of *other I's.* (168)

The poet's prose records this world of other I's; it is a dialogic document that provides connections between texts and readers. The poet's prose reminds us of the pleasure in reading, of the pleasure of connection, of recalling this is a shared world. Although poetry may possess us, Machado insists that it denies we can be possessive. "Any uttered word requires some sort of continuation," Joseph Brodsky writes. Language can be continued in various ways—logically, phonetically, grammatically, in rhyme—but "what has been uttered is never the end but the edge of speech" (186). The continuation of language insures a continuous remodeling of time and our human presence: "Song is, after all, re-structured time, toward which mute space is inherently hostile" (137). The poet's prose asserts this continuity. It reinforms us of time, and poetry is the most profound expression of time. The poet's prose must also record the attempts to forestall loss by desiring to hold this quicksilver language.

The passage from Machado describes the domain of language as a meeting place, as genealogical, for language is passed down, and other—*theirs.* For the critic and the poet, the experiment is language. But unlike the scholarly critic who often tends toward method and closure, the poet-critic ponders the choices in language and seeks to uncover the paths the energies of poetry's interconnection offer us. The poet's prose is the record of contemplation's traces, the record of a reader (the momentary coming-into-being of a self) enlivened by the poem's *abode-ing* spirit.

The arrangement of this collection creates resonances among essays, rather than filling categories. Usually, we read individual entries to collections and occasionally a whole section, if it suits our immediate purposes. Reading selected discrete essays is one approach to this collection, but the essays can also be read as interconnecting clusters. The six sections operate in several ways. Although the essays included would naturally fall into place, other essays are also included that readdress the definition of the section. Consider two examples from the first section, "The Sufficiency of Language." John Taggart's essay on the poetry of Robert Duncan could certainly belong to the "Readings" section. The essay explicitly investigates the sufficiency and power of the word; thus, it is included in this first section. William Logan's essay on Geoffrey Hill's prose, which might be read as another opening to this collection, could fit into several sections, but it probes the thorny charity of language envisioned by Hill as well as enacted and subsumed in the scholasticism of Hill's prose. The arrangement of essays is an act of reconsidering or "essaying." The collection's closing essay, by Stanley Plumly, reinforces this speculative "essaying" by proposing thresholds that return us to both the poems and the essays. I should also note that the opening essay of each section acts as an introduction to reinforce as well as expand the terms implicit in each section's title. Each section's concluding essay works as a resonating vessel to the section's initial essay, swerving us again into further speculation. In this bracketed grouping there are self-evident pairs and triads of essays, consciously placed but without any baroque symmetry or contrivance, my desire has been to initiate conversations between the essays and to draw the reader into the conversing.

The collection can be read as a group of implicit *artes poeticae.* The essays on individual poets reveal as much about the poetics and sensibility of the essayists as they do about the essay's subject. Moreover, the collection is both a place of interchange and a means of suggesting various ways of working with the form of the essay. Thus, the collection contains personal narratives, close readings of poems, collages of language, meditations, and speculations. There is no single form of an essay or of the ways toward knowledge. These essays are the shadow-work of the poems of the essayists; the variety of the essays mirrors the variety of poems now being written. In the collection I strove to attain as wide a range of poets writing in prose as possible. Some expected figures are missing due to the demands of time and timing, and some, no doubt, are missing due to my ignorance. Collections and anthologies also work, sometimes insidiously and sometimes innocently, to validate the work of those included. I would like to think no one's work needs this form of validation; nonetheless, it is true that many voices in this collection, either the essayists themselves or the work of those written about, are outsiders, seldom heard and not easily found in print.

The ambition of this collection is to present essays that map the diverse critical concerns of poets now writing. Additionally, it suggests the variety of poetry being written and the demands each of these poets confront in their poems. I hope this collection will both inspire the writing of criticism by poets and draw attention to the essays by poets that appear regularly in such journals as *American Poetry Review, Antaeus, Critical Inquiry, Field, Ohio Review, Parnassus: Poetry in Review, Sulfur,* and *Tremblor,* to name only a few. Here it is important to note the eclectic and invigorating quality of essays the no longer published journal *Ironwood* always demonstrated. Although journals are usually guided by an editorial voice that believes in a particular poetics, a collection such as this assumes another role. Assembling this collection has been an exercise in withdrawing my personal aesthetics, except in what may be discerned in this introduction, in favor of and as a deep commitment to the possibility of many dialogues. The collection has as its shape its division into specific sections, what I have found to be continuing topical constellations. Ideally, these essays will suggest other critical directions without replacing those now favored. The schism between the poet and the critic has become either profound or recognized as being always and already abyssal; however, this collection opens the possibility for exchange. These essays also significantly demonstrate that scholarly criticism and poets' criticism participate in the same critical debates, despite their differing approaches.

To return to the earlier analogy of the littoral or tidal zone, the anthology is such a place. It is an ecology, and like the tidal zone there are great interchanges, amazing shifts of sea current and wind and sand. Life is microscopic and giant; the very planet is animate, and language—far from being a shrouding—is part of these shifting, living, spaces.

REFERENCES

Bishop, Elizabeth. *The Complete Poems: 1927–1979.* New York: Farrar, Straus, and Giroux, 1983.

Brodsky, Joseph. *Less Than One: Selected Essays.* New York: Farrar, Straus, and Giroux, 1986.

Cooper, Jane. *Maps and Windows.* New York: Macmillan, 1974.

Derrida, Jacques. *Signéponge/Signsponge.* Trans. Richard Rand. New York: Columbia University Press, 1984.

Eliot, T. S. *On Poetry and Poets.* New York: Farrar, Straus, and Giroux, 1961.

Frye, Northrop. *Anatomy of Criticism.* Princeton, N.J.: Princeton University Press, 1971.

Gadamer, Hans-Georg. *The Relevance of the Beautiful and Other Essays.* Ed. Robert Bernasconi; trans. Nicholas Walker. Cambridge: Cambridge University Press, 1986.

Gilbert, Sandra. Review of *A Field Guide to Contemporary Poetry and Poetics,* by Stuart Frie-
bert and David Young and *Goatfoot, Milktongue, Twinbird* and *To Keep Moving,* by Donald Hall.
American Book Review 3, no. 6 (September-October 1981): 3–4.

Hartman, Geoffrey. *Criticism in the Wilderness.* New Haven, Conn.: Yale University Press, 1980.

Hall, Donald. *To Keep Moving.* Geneva: Hobart and William Smith Press, 1980.

Hallberg, Robert von. "American Poet-Critics since 1945." In *Reconstructing American Literary History,* ed. Sacvan Bercovitch. Cambridge, Mass.: Harvard University Press, 1986.

Kinnell, Galway. *Mortal Acts, Mortal Words.* Boston: Houghton Mifflin, 1980.

Lyotard, Jean-François. *The Postmodern Condition: A Report on Knowledge.* Trans. Geoff
Bennington and Brian Massumi. Minneapolis: University of Minneapolis Press, 1984.

Machado, Antonio. "From Notes on Poetry." Trans. Reginald Gibbons. In *The Poet's Work,* ed.
Reginald Gibbons. Boston: Houghton Mifflin, 1979.

Milosz, Czeslaw. *Unattainable Earth.* Trans. the author and Robert Hass. New York: Ecco Press,
1986.

————. *The Witness of Poetry.* Cambridge, Mass: Harvard University Press, 1983.

Oliver, Mary. *Dream Work.* Boston: Atlantic Monthly Press, 1986.

Paz, Octavio. *The Bow and the Lyre.* Trans. Ruth L. C. Simms. Austin: University of Texas Press,
1973.

————. *Convergences: Essays on Art and Literature.* Trans. Helen Lane. New York: Harcourt,
Brace, Jovanovich, 1987.

Rich, Adrienne. *On Lies, Secrets, and Silence.* New York: Norton, 1979.

Steiner, George. *On Difficulty and Other Essays.* New York: Oxford University Press, 1978.

Stevens, Wallace. *The Necessary Angel.* New York: Random House, 1951.

Valéry, Paul. *The Art of Poetry.* Trans. Denise Folliot. In *The Collected Works of Paul Valéry.*
New York: Pantheon, 1958.

PART
ONE

THE SUFFICIENCY OF LANGUAGE

THE ABSOLUTE
UNREASONABLENESS OF GEOFFREY HILL

WILLIAM LOGAN

I do not think anyone would read Geoffrey Hill's essays for pleasure, any more than one would read for pleasure the political tracts of John Milton. Milton's pamphlets are part of an oeuvre and illuminate transiently, or transversely, a mind that composed great poetry. Hill is not a great poet, at least not a poet as great as Milton; but he is often a poet as inconveniently intelligent and as exercised by the demands of dogma: an epic poet scaled to the corridors of the country house, an epic poet of cloister or interior.

Even interiors have their demanding and bloody philosophies. The critical writings of poets are irritable affairs in a tradition of belle-lettres, not scholarship. They range in our century from the exquisite pulse-takings of Eliot to the haphazard theorizing of Empson, from the journalistic smash-and-grab of Randall Jarrell to the cranky domesticity of John Crowe Ransom. What unites the varying temperatures of their prose is the degree to which critical method justifies poetic manner. The prose is an unguarded back door to the designs of the poetry. A critic as self-devouring as Geoffrey Hill must realize, when he accedes to another critic's proposal that "Ransom on Milton . . . is also Ransom *as* Milton, or Ransom on Ransom," that such a concession may be turned against him. A critic who gnaws his own entrails may even want it to be.

If poets must create in their prose the taste that will celebrate their poetry, Hill has made every attempt to thwart that celebration. Thick with their own purposes and heavy with apparatus, one hundred and sixty pages of text dragging the slow length of forty pages of notes, the result of twenty-five years of meticulous scholarly practice, *The Lords of Limit: Essays on Literature and Ideas* could be the work of a professor anxious to publish no line not already buttressed with three quotations, able to pass the most stringent inquisition and satisfy the nicest scruple. At their worst Hill's essays parody the academic manner and bring to their subjects none of the élan we expect when a poet treats literature. Hill considers his prose, like his poetry, too much a discipline to admit any reaction as fatal as pleasure; nevertheless, his seriousness is not the seriousness of the professors. These are not professings but deep engagements with the nature of language and literature, the wrestlings of someone fatally enwrapped with the Word.

Most poets approximate the condition of man before the Fall, content to name the beasts as if the beasts had never been named before and to practice their craft in Edenic innocence. There are no real snakes in such imaginary gardens. Hill's opening essay, "Poetry as 'Menace' and 'Atonement,'" reveals how far into the post-Edenic wilderness he has traveled and with what guilts. Justifications are self-justifications, just as criticisms are self-criticisms, and the essay, in establishing poetry as an act of atonement, itself atones for poetic practice. Theologically justification is the divine absolution of guilt for sin: as Hill wittily recognizes, it is enormously difficult to confess a sin if no one but oneself believes a sin has been committed.

That is a transgression typical of Hill, to usurp the prerogatives of religion in a secular atmosphere, borrowing the burdens without making obeisance to the faith. In his prose as in his poetry he drains religion of its fact in order to clothe himself in its fiction, unable to immerse himself in its healing unions, whether transcendant and mystical or formal and baptismal. This would mark him for the damnation of expedience if it were not the mark of a deeper damnation, a self-damnation recognizing that only the faith in which it is impossible to believe provides the myths, and more importantly the acts, that respond metaphorically to his predicament.

Poetry becomes atonement only by the adroit and repentant translation of etymology, which returns atonement to at-one-ment. To Hill language is inertial and coercive, and to overcome that inertia and that coercion in the act of composition is to achieve a momentary sense of fulfillment and concord. That sense is attested to not least by the reader's instinct and Hill's own practice, where the inertias of language, however dominant and determining, are line by line overcome to reach a temporary accord, an agreement or understanding. Reading, though Hill does not acknowledge it, is the act of atonement that recapitulates the act of composition. Not content to trust instinct or practice, Hill finds that moment of fulfillment phrased by two poets more than usually sensitive to the transcendant potential of language: Yeats for whom "a poem comes right with a click like a closing box" and Eliot in his "moment of exhaustion, of appeasement, of absolution, and of something very near annihilation." It may be noted wryly that the mystic's definition is resolutely practical and mundane, while the banker stutters toward a meaning unreliably mystical, one that in failing to reach that moment of fulfillment provides instead, or very nearly, an example of annihilation.

Those two definitions are severely different, as Christopher Ricks has noted, but that does not prevent Hill from imposing on them the silence of reconciliation. If poetry is to atone, it must atone for something, and it cannot be the mere anxiety or guilt that afflicts ordinary mortal existence, for which literature is the troubling and troubled conduit. It must be something harsher and more intractable, "a sense of language itself as a manifestation of empirical guilt." When the unnamed beasts approached, Adam could name them immediately and without reflection, again and again achieving effortlessly the concord that is at-one-ment. As Milton recognized, or as Milton as Adam articulated, that concord is the binding of comprehension: "I named them, as they passed, and understood / Their nature." But what if Adam had gotten their names wrong? Hill can approach the guilt inherent in language only through a shrinking that is not a shrinking from, through the knowledge that one can repent a sin but not a mistake.

It is not the last instance of Hill's mordant humor that the propriety is social, and that the aptest quotation is Chesterton's: "There are ways of getting absolved for murder; there are no ways of getting absolved for upsetting the soup." Hill can approximate the mortal sins of language, generally acts of omission, of failing to set the words and the things at one, only by cataloguing the venial sins more culpably committed and more easily reproached: "*faux pas,* the perpetration of 'howlers,' grammatical solecisms, misstatements of fact, misquotations, improper attributions." Although these are only minor acts of oversight, of failing to set the words at one with themselves, they are no less reprehensible. They are crucial betrayals of the writer's responsibility, the worse because once set wrong they can never be set right. Retrospective correction never alters the original commission of error or the "empirical guilt" that attends it. To enforce the notion that such error is a matter of ethics, not accident, Hill quotes Simone Weil, another mystic able to demand definition of the mundane: "anybody, no matter who, discovering an avoidable error in a printed text or radio broadcast, would be entitled to bring an action before [special] courts."

One can then imagine, with only the brief flickering of a smile, the writhings to which Hill might be subjected on discovering that in this very essay he has misdated the letter in which Yeats marks the closing click of a poem. It makes no difference to the argument that he wrote the letter to Dorothy Wellesley in 1935, not 1936, though it makes an ethical difference that a critic in quoting Hill has already repeated his *faux pas:* from such innocent transmissions whole rotting branches of scholarly error derive. The sin lies not in the duplication but in the original transgression: as a symbolic act it represents the disharmony, the unfulfillment, the discord of the words set against themselves. This is only the shadow of a larger guilt and a deeper despair, the poet's discovery of the moral demands of language.

Hill is aware of the disproportion of setting careless proofreading (Péguy, it will be remembered, was "a meticulous reader of proof") beside the more monstrous guilts to which language is subject, to which the world itself is subject. The case of the knitting editor who says "if I make a mistake there are jerseys all over England with one arm longer than the other" is ludicrous and almost insignificant measured against the life and death of Mandelstam, against the world of torture and political murder over an idea. In making the comparison Hill strengthens his argument by seeming to strangle it. The anxiety over *faux pas* is only a "comic subplot," a mimesis of a larger anxiety that must be established in a world of moral idea and moral scruple: "in the act of 'making' we are necessarily delivered up to judgment." That is not merely the judgment of critics.

If the "menace" is the poet's discovery that language has a moral nature, the "atonement" must take place in the satisfaction of moral demands, in the setting at once of not just the mean particular with the mastering plan, the language of feeling with the life of the form, but even the act said and the act done. In that acknowledgment is the argument of *The Mystery of the Charity of Charles Péguy.* Hill honors and atones for that world of moral action by his own private rectifications, the rectifications in the poetic act: "local vividness" set at one with the "overall shape," the "sense of language" with the "feeling for the ways of life," the "density of language" with the "specific gravity of human nature" are the terms he employs, some borrowed and some merely brokered. The burdens are the burdens of language, but they are not what they seem.

Hill must return to Eliot, that figure always lurking beneath the horizon of his prose and verse, for a phrase that implicates the poetic act even while it means to implicate something else: "the unmoral nature, suddenly trapped in the inexorable toils of morality." Though the relation is imperfect and accidental, it allows Hill to admit what he would prefer to deny, and in so self-denying a nature the admission must come, as always, through a quotation by someone else, in this case Wallace Stevens: "After one has abandoned a belief in god [*sic*], poetry is that essence which takes its place as life's redemption." The scrupulous [*sic*] is Hill's, at once diplomatic to God and undiplomatic to Stevens, the appropriate priority for a poet whose anxiety must be that his "agnostic faith" is indelicate to divinity and overdelicate to poets.

The burdens, then, are accepted in lieu of religion by a nature whose longings cannot master its reason, if reason is not too dry and ennobling a term for the sickness of hesitation and the cowardice of irresolution, not presence of mind but absence of will. The judgment is harsh but not harmful. Hill has too many times admitted the desire unfulfilled, the hunger unsatisfied, for there to be any doubt about the tension between possibility and practice; in the interview with John Haffenden: "one is trying to make lyric poetry out of a much more common situation—the sense of *not* being able to grasp true religious experience." Where poetry substitutes for faith, the agnostic, alive to his own disability, his suppurating wound, receives his measure of menace and atonement. But, as Hill has also said, "I would not wish to describe myself as an agnostic."

This leads to an irony and an escape. The irony is that "a man could refuse to accept the evident signs of grace in his own work; that he himself could never move beyond that 'sorrow not mingled with the love of God' even though his own poems might speak to others with the voice of hope and love." Hill's poems are not likely to risk speaking to others with hope and love, but the point holds. No man can be his own reader. A poet is forever foreclosed from the pleasures other readers take from his work, whatever the difficult satisfactions of composition. No man can read innocently what he has guiltily composed. These satisfactions, however, contrive his escape. The poet subject to the guilt of language, the moral demand in the medium he would master, is consequently afflicted with the shame and despair of the "irredeemable error in the very substance and texture of his craft and pride." What he cannot enslave he must be servant to, living with the affliction as a vocation, Adam after the Fall, Philoctetes in his cave: "in the constraint of shame the poet is free to discover both the 'menace' and the atoning power of his own art."

Hill is often engaged not by specific poetries as much as by specific moral acts construed through style. To such men as the martyr and poet Robert Southwell he can only stand in allegorical relation, reasonable in the face of "The Absolute Reasonableness of Robert Southwell." The poet is not a martyr—he is more often the penitent knitting editor than the persecuted Mandelstam—but certain conditions of the poetic act can be more easily comprehended in the martyr's constraint of language. The comparison is grotesque and attractive: most poets would flatter themselves as persecuted or even prosecuted outsiders, sacrificing to bring the black letter, the true word, to countrymen starved of religion. The pressure on language that a sense of moral responsibility occasions, whether fantasized or simply aggrandized, is a tension of style. It is not the only time in these essays that the tension of such relation uncovers some anxiety in Hill's own poetry.

Style is not merely the measure of speech but the manner of silence, and behind Southwell's eloquence, in speech or in silence under torture, lies "violence and coarse preciosity and disgust." What Southwell achieves is an equity, a reasonableness that transfigures the violence ranged against him. Even the possibility of disembowelling may be transformed, acknowledged, and accepted by conceit: he writes to a colleague in Rome, "You have 'fishes' there greatly wanted here, which, 'when disembowelled, are good for anointing to the eyes and drive the devils away,' while, if they live, 'they are necessary for useful medicines.'" If poetry makes nothing happen, it need not collude with the violence the world outside it offers. That is the religious vocation Hill would command for poetry: to accept injustice and atrocity and return moderation if not mildness. The martyr understood both the reparations such a course required ("how well verse and vertue sute together") and the cost of such equity in sacrifice. The cost is sacrifice, but the reward is serenity achieved through acceptance and trans-figuration, "achieved in the full awareness of the realities of spiritual and legal vio-lence."

The poet is often at odds with his time, with the circumstances his time has con-trived, and this may be an estrangement felt or a division recognized. It is not as a moralist that Hill, after establishing the guilts inherent in language, speaks of the poet "necessarily bearing his peculiar unnecessary shame in a world growing ever more shameless." Here the estrangement is shamelessly embraced (as the "renewed sense of a vocation"), and no one who has twisted in the coils of Hill's poetry will fail to detect the sinuous self-gratifications in such a remark. Any poet may take pleasure when he has convinced himself that what he has said can be said no better, but the pleasure takes a caustic wash of pride when the poet relishes, however thinly, the travails of his difficulty.

Such divisiveness is internal and subjective, however external and objective its effects. Against it must be set the public divisions that may menace the poetry and even the poet himself. Southwell was martyred but not for being a poet. Jonson's thumb was branded for murder, and only benefit of clergy saved him from the scaffold. Still, it is well to remember that he almost lost his nose and ears over the libellous statements in *Eastward Ho!* and that he was imprisoned for his share in *The Isle of Dogs*. The question that most deeply afflicts Hill's criticism, the disturbance at the heart of much of his poetry, is whether the poet can respond to his time without either compromising with or being compromised by it. The essays on Southwell, Jonson, Shakespeare, and Swift trace the strategies of reaction and restraint used by these poets to transfigure different circumstances of menace.

The poet who does not face death may face something worse than inconvenience, and art may serve a public discretion whatever its private serenity. Southwell may have tried to evade capture because evasion was a moral duty; but he was not trying to evade the penalty of his Catholicism. The transfigurations of his prose and verse were inner notations against an outer threat, a threat whose death sentences no sentences of his could make worse. Jonson and Shakespeare were forced to practice their craft under the dangerously shifting claims of Elizabethan and Jacobean politics. In both dramatists the subversive is voiced but usually under the restraint of characters evil, corrupted, or betrayed. In a medium hemmed in by official censors, the subversive must be subverted if it is to challenge official myths. The playwrights are allowed the tension of a confrontation between ideas without the risk of being called to account for them. The tactfulness of this art ensures that ambiguity is not damned as equivocation, but as Hill notes the dramatists "contract out of direct commitment" when the commitment would be to sedition. The compromise is not compromising, unless we believe that playwrights should sacrifice their ears and noses to the waywardness of their tongues. The artist can be true to his art without being untrue to himself: Jonson spent a decade composing court masques. It is a matter of great importance to both Hill and his work that the artist not be confused with the ideas he manipulates. Certain effects and certain understandings may only be achieved through artistic detachment. His model is the artist, like Jonson, who "redeems what he can." The reader who believes in the official myth of freedom of speech may find this nonsense, even subversive nonsense. He might study with instruction the libel actions that have been so expensive to *Private Eye* or the official prosecution within the past decade of a "blasphemous" poem. The incidents are English, but in England *Romeo and Juliet* is not censored in secondary schools. In any society there are things that cannot be said and times when an artist like Hill must quote Pisanio: "Wherein I am false, I am honest; not true, to be true."

Swift's problem was different but no less dangerous. There were £300 on his head after *The Public Spirit of the Whigs* and another £300 after *Drapier's Letters.* The printer of *A Proposal for the Universal Use of Irish Manufacture* was prosecuted. For an upholder of public order Swift did his best to undermine it. Hill isolates in him the tension between Tory stoicism and wanton destructiveness, not as ideas whose force the artist contemplates but as contraries his imagination embodies. If he enlisted as an artist what he loathed as a moralist, it would explain what Hill defines as his ambiguous attitude to anarchy: "In principle he abhorred all its aspects . . . ; pragmatically he played along with it to some extent; poetically he reacted to it with a kindling of creative delight." One could define in Hill a similarly ambiguous attitude to order.

The artist is often attracted to what might destroy him, whether anarchy or an excess of order, and it is the responsibility of his art to transfigure that destructive element, an element that may be responsible for the art itself. The art must transfigure not just the warring tendencies of the artist's imagination, but the dissonant divisions of his life. The disorders of the imagination may be discomfiting, perhaps even maddening, an estrangement felt; but the external disorders, or excesses of order, endanger the artist's life with his livelihood. Hill, always alert to the daily conditions of an artist's hazard, locates Swift in the governing class of an Ireland that did not want to be governed. Shakespeare and Jonson among the censors, Southwell among the priest-catchers: the circumstances of difficulty released the creative energies they were transformed by. In this way defeat (and Swift felt Ireland a defeat) may be converted, just as, in those poems where defeat is the poet's condition, "wit converts the necessary failure into moral and rhetorical victory." Hill aspires to the reactionary poetry of which he has often been accused only in the sense that he uses "reaction" of Swift: not as "a supposedly 'retrograde tendency' in politics or . . . a 'revulsion' of feeling" but "the capacity to be at once resistant and reciprocal." To redeem the time is to redeem oneself.

Hill's essay on "Redeeming the Time" is nominally "An enquiry into the nature of rhythm," the rhythm of speech disrupted in the nineteenth century. The concessions a century would require force those who oppose them to adopt certain methods of resistance in the language itself, and these resistances are evident in the poetry and the prose, raw speech and arguments cooked in speech. The essay opens in opposition to an assertion by Iris Murdoch that "the nineteenth century, where the disruptive forces were not only dispossessed and weak, but incoherent, disunited, and speechless, could think itself a single world." Hill thinks this is nonsense, not even seductive nonsense, but the form of his opposition is peculiar and sidling: "Faced with such a statement by so manifestly intelligent a writer one looks nervously for a hidden language-game." To call someone "manifestly intelligent" is to call that intelligence into question. And "nervously," even in a writer as nervous as Geoffrey Hill, offers more than a suggestion of Uriah Heep squeezing his hands. It is the nervousness of someone about to be caught in the act, for no sooner is the possibility of a language game in Murdoch rejected than language games begin furtively to infiltrate the essay.

Such games are not usually worth notice, but for motives that are only gradually clarified Hill prefers, in this as in the opening essay, to argue through a perversely coiled and indwelling mimesis. It is not for pleasure that the rhetoric prepares to mirror the reason, though pleasure may issue from the small recognitions and reciprocities these games entail. The pleasure, say, when praise of "a brief comic masterstroke in counterpoint" is immediately counterpointed by an example of failure, or when Engels' description of England as "the classic soil of . . . transformation" is transformed to serve a description of an English orator: "The 'classic' oration of a tribune of the people suffers a grotesque 'transformation,' 'soiled' by the outflow of a fractured tradition." The pleasure, say, of a tenuous transition between paragraphs immediately followed by Coleridge's suggestion that *The Spectator* had "innocently contributed to the general taste for unconnected writing" or of the key phrase "recurrent responses" in George Eliot parroted by this attack of recurrent responses in Hill: "'familiar rhythm' is both liturgical and extraliturgical, telling of a rhythm of social duties, rites, ties and obligations from which an individual severs himself or herself at great cost and peril, but implying also the natural sequences of stresses and slacks in the thoughts and acts." One would be ready to dismiss such appealing torments as, well, tormented appeals, if Hill had not written that "It should not be thought, however, that in referring to the possibility of a 'language-game' one is being lightly dismissive."

The explanation lies in the arguments about rhythm. "[R]hythm," Hill writes, "is . . . more than a physiological motor. It is capable of registering, mimetically, deep shocks of recognition." If rhetoric is rhythm, or obtains rhythm, it too is capable of rendering these deep shocks as part of the drama of reason. The "drama of reason" is Coleridge's term for his parentheses, devices that contradict and condition the growth of argument, preventing argument from sliding into the subsidies of self-agreement. Staging that drama requires, as Hill makes clear, the "antiphonal voice of the heckler," the "cross-rhythms and counterpointings which ought, for the sake of proper strategy and good faith, to be part of the structure of such writing." There is danger in such drama: to take account of such conflicting forces, to allow oneself to be sensitive to the disjunctions of argument and not merely the cozy proprieties of the age, may be "to risk convolution and incommunicability," whatever one's admiration for plain speech.

The issue for Hill is a sacrifice, the sacrifice of "a powerful and decent desire, the desire to be immediately understood by 'a common well-educated thoughtful man, of ordinary talents.'" The structure of the style that results is peculiar and peculiarly familiar: "a recognition and a resistance; it is parenthetical, antiphonal, it turns upon itself." It is of course the style of these essays. Hill must turn to Hopkins, that figure of resistance to nineteenth-century rhythmical life, for what may fairly be regarded as a justification of his own long toils in verse and prose, both opaque to the common well-educated thoughtful man:

> Plainly if it is possible to express a sub[t]le and recondite thought on a subtle and recondite subject in a subtle and recondite way and with great felicity and perfection, in the end, something must be sacrificed, with so trying a task, in the process, and this may be the being at once, nay perhaps even the being without explanation at all, intelligible.

Such prose, periodic to the point of Jamesian annoyance, full to satiety with "recurrent responses," coldly smothers its own simplicities. The prose is unfortunate, but the perception is not. The alternative for Hill is a different and more disagreeable sacrifice, the sacrifice to "a certain laxity in the use of language" that John Stuart Mill found "must be borne with, if a writer makes himself understood." Although the dichotomy is hardly convincing, it has a convincing application to the critic who asserts it and whose work assents to it. Hill's fear, as critic and poet, is that surrendering to the laxities of the time, to "the very inertia of general taste," would be surrendering the complexities that might redeem it.

Coleridge, Hill believes, "surely foresaw the obligation to enact the drama of reason within the texture of one's own work." "Surely" is surely a plea, and the sly insinuation of "one's" for "his" ought to remind us, if the language games do not, that Hill seizes the obligation as his own. The language games, however frivolous, are the minor mimesis of a major enterprise: the drama of reason the verse and prose are elsewhere attempting. Self-indulging and seemingly irrelevant, they form a template for reinforcing ideas in the identity of a style. They echo in rhetoric the moment of rhythm on which the essay turns: the "change of time signature" that quickens the opening of the ninth stanza of Wordsworth's "Ode: Intimations of Immortality from Recollections of Early Childhood":

> *O joy! that in our embers*
> *Is something that doth live. . . .*

Hopkins thought the change magical; Hill believes it "perhaps the greatest moment in nineteenth-century English poetry." By breaking the rhythm the poem has previously settled upon and settled into, by registering a shock in a change of speech, it acknowledges that disturbance these meditations on an antiphonal, resistant style derive from. The lines respond not just in their rhythm but in their reason to the argument that language must provide these recognitions, whatever the sacrifice. Only through such sacrifices may the time be redeemed.

Or so the poet would like to believe. It is comforting and even consoling to be forced ethically to the very choice one's inclination would make. No time can be redeemed through the ethical intuitions or rhythmical grumblings of its poets. To make this redemption a vocation, as Hill claims for Hopkins and as I claim for Hill, is to accept the terms of one's own defeat. That defeat may be the poet's reasonable and even acceptable condition is a proposition that might command Hill's assent: "There are triumphs that entrap and defeats that liberate." As poet and as critic, Hill has consistently flinched from the triumphs that entrap, if triumph entails conditioning one's language to the taste of others. However, his unctuous and insincere hand-wringing (the apparition of Uriah Heep again appears) over the sacrifice of that "powerful and decent desire," to be understood by the ordinary reader, reminds us that defeat can be all too eagerly relished.

The subtheme of "Redeeming the Time" is the danger of compromise, and the two companion essays offer cautionary examples in John Crowe Ransom and T. H. Green. Green, the Victorian idealist philosopher, succumbed in the conflict between "writing to be received, and . . . conducting a running battle with the premises of current receptivity." Because he ignored language *as* moral action in favor of language *about* moral action, his ideas are no longer alive in his language and "his lectures now seem heavy with the diffuseness of paraphrase rather than tense with the bafflements of communication." A less fastidious critic might say that Green simply could not write well, but Hill would isolate in that *well* a moral sickness only the precise use of language can cure. The problem is as difficult as its probity: the compromised use of language offends its moral nature. By ministering to the desires and derangements of his audience the writer places himself, or at least his work, beyond redemption, and becomes the negative example of a positive obligation.

The essay on Ransom requires the most exacting formulation of that demand: "the double consequence of a poet's involvement with language is complicity and revelation." When this formula is repeated, however, "double consequence" becomes "double-consequence," suggesting by renovating accident or cunning revision that complicity and revelation may be brought into malignant equilibrium, may even disastrously intermingle, a complicity to revelation, a revelation in complicity. That is the particular and telling failure of John Crowe Ransom: his revelations were purchased at the cost of complicity. Although Hill is never slow to admire a virtue, he will not tolerate a writer's "coy indulgence of the 'humble reader.'" There are errors, even knowledgeable errors, but there can be no forgiveness (not even by the most 'umble person) when a writer, even a writer as uncompromising as Ransom, "has been led . . . to mistake compromise for communication." To indulge the reader out of whatever generous motive or genuine mistake is license, and against this Hill erects the standard of an implicit regard if not an explicit belief: "[I]t is possible for a poet to serve the integrity of thought and language in the exemplary nature of his constraint."

That constraint may be observed wherever the poet is tempted to abandon it, most conveniently in the laboratory of his revisions. There Ransom occasionally found it possible to "clear his meaning," even after a lapse of decades and the failure of intervening experiments. This was the rare fortune in an unfortunate tendency, for otherwise he was "gripped by a 'mania' which drove him . . . to the ruinous rewriting" of earlier work. Hill's own restraint may be measured in the fussy integrity of the small adjustments scattered through his *Collected Poems.* Except to correct some unfortunate hyphenation in the prose stanzas of *Mercian Hymns* (in one case clearing the ambiguity of certain "male-/factors" who ought to have been more prosaic "mal-/

efactors"), he has rarely tampered with his later books. The minor revisions betray an intelligence afflicted with coercive responsibilities, coercions no more evident than in his admission of change: "I have felt impelled to alter words and phrases here and there. I have changed only those details which have become a burden over the years."

Burdens that impel are not opportunities grasped; the amendments disclose a moral resistance more than an aesthetic renewal and express belated penitence rather than timely possibility. "Words and phrases" is perhaps an aggrandizing phrase; of some sixty textual changes only seven concern matters more grave than punctuation or spelling. That is not to take lightly the details that weigh heavily upon Hill: a small change of punctuation may signify a great change of heart. Even so, these adjustments mostly modify a rhythm or remove an eyesore. The separation provided by a parenthesis, that drama of reason, rarely needs to be reinforced with external dashes, and a mature directness has chastened whatever youthful delicacy was responsible by dropping the dashes or removing the parenthesis. Still, there is a distinction, perhaps even a magnifying difference, in the detachment that "Shrunken, magnified—(nest, holocaust)— / Not half innocent and not half undone" surrenders to "Shrunken, magnified (nest, holocaust) / Not half innocent and not half undone" ("Of Commerce and Society"). Dashes are elsewhere denied, the awkward precision of "From bitter—as from sweet—grapes bled" becoming the more comfortable blurring of alternatives, "From bitter as from sweet grapes bled" ("The Bidden Guest"). Some gulfs are widened, some narrowed: a dash or a semicolon promoted to a period; a semicolon demoted to a comma. In "Funeral Music," what was the World becomes the world.

One does not have to admire the individual changes to admire the meticulous nature that has found them necessary. The sober critic corrects his youthful indiscretions most stringently by tempering to dour statements a number of spirited exclamations: "Those varied dead" are deader now than when they were exulted as "Those varied dead!" ("Metamorphoses"); "O visited women, possessed sons!" are more solemnly invoked as "O visited women, possessed sons" ("Annunciations"); the expectation of "Love, oh my love, it will come / Sure enough!" now adopts the resignation of "Sure enough" ("The Songbook of Sebastian Arrurruz"). A change of heart.

Elsewhere a change of mind. Lowell might have made seven grave alterations in one edition and changed them back again in the next. Hill's nature does not adapt easily to correction because correction always admits an original mistake. He would shudder at any aesthetic practice that eagerly contemplated a shifting range of potential additions and contractions, alterations and corrections. The burdens must impel: the unhappy note of plump vulgarity (or the grim solecism of tautology) in "By day I cleansed my pink tongue" must be narrowed and cleansed, must become more nastily vulpine as "my thin tongue" ("Three Baroque Meditations"). The passively functional "railway-sidings" in "An Apology for the Revival of Christian Architecture in England" are exchanged for the more actively dangerous "railway-crossings," resonant with the central crux to which Hill is always attracted. The submissively leaden "accrued," in a hymn on Offa's coins (Mercian Hymns XII), is transmuted into the more visually aggressive "raked up": "I have raked up a golden and stinking blaze." Blazes are not usually accrued. It would not do, in "God's Little Mountain," to have the devil's cloven hoof silently associate with "And yet the sky was cloven." The poem is about the absence of gods, not the presence of devils. The association has already been prepared by "a goat / dislodging stones" and a mountain that "stamped its foot." The sky must therefore be "riven," not "cloven."

The burdens of beginnings weigh more heavily. It is perverse and perversely attractive that of all his poems Hill has been impelled to alter most severely the one that stands first, the myth of artistic creation, "Genesis." It may be a sensible act of violence to maintain that the "tough pig-headed salmon" are "Ramming the ebb, in the tide's pull." Critics can rarely question confidently a voice so confident in its ambiguity, but the change invites the doubt that the salmon were ever sensibly "Curbing the ebb and the tide's pull," unless they were very large salmon. The "glove-winged albatross" has lost its gloves, become the more prosaic "long-winged albatross." Hill may have finally seen an albatross in flight and thought better of his metaphor, or he may have been annoyed to find "glove" in this poem, "cloven" in the next, and "glove" and "cleave" in the one after that. The final change is also the first, not amendment but deletion. Where there was once:

> *Against the burly air I strode,*
> *Where the tight ocean heaves its load,*
> *Crying the miracles of God.*

there remains:

> *Against the burly air I strode*
> *Crying the miracles of God.*

The contraction expels an influence, the Lowell whose "Where the heel-headed dogfish barks its nose" is still archly present in the "tough pig-headed salmon." It expels an influence and accepts for the speaker a deepened isolation, his labor stripped of setting, no longer doubled and dramatized by the ocean's struggle against its own weight. The sea is first brought to bear only in the second stanza, as if the speaker had a hand in its creation. A burden has been removed: the ocean no longer heaves its load. The acknowledging pun does penance for the excision.

The scarcity of these changes registers a difficulty, not a complacence. That difficulty in turn measures the penitence of an earlier alteration, the reprinting in *King Log* (1968) of a poem from *For the Unfallen* (1959), then out of print. Hill's note read: "I dislike the poem very much, and the publication of this amended version may be regarded as a necessary penitential exercise." The poem was "In Memory of Jane Fraser," and aside from a few trivial changes in punctuation the amendment consisted of altering the final line from "And a few sprinkled leaves unshook" to "Dead cones upon the alder shook."[1] Some authorial discomfort with the verb "unshook" is understandable, but the wording of the corrective note is odd, even strikingly odd: Hill seems to say that he is reprinting the poem *because* he dislikes it, a form of penance for having written it. If this seems to go too far, "I dislike the poem very much" goes well beyond disagreement with a line and seems to carry dislike even into the amended version. The new version carried the subtitle "An Attempted Reparation," which may seem to conclude the matter more simply; but the act, whether simple or complex, advertised self-flagellation. Perhaps Hill felt the need to make amends for a bad line, but not at the cost of allowing readers to think he admired the poem. Another poet would have revised the poem and reprinted it without comment. The reparation, its punctuation repaired, is now silently entered in the editions of *For the Unfallen* and *Collected Poems.*

In the great burden he places upon changes, however minute, Hill shows the strength of purpose he would muster against those who cannot take seriously the moral obligations of poetic language. The burden may be no less sharply felt even if such changes are neurotically motivated or dramatized. The epigraph to Hill's final essay, "Our Word Is Our Bond," reads in part: "[W]e can issue an utterance of any kind whatsoever, in the course, for example, of acting a play or making a joke or writing a poem—in which case of course it would not be seriously meant." The philosopher so irresponsibly responsible is J. L. Austin. Hill would rescue poetry from those empiricist philosophers who believe it a parasitic use of language, but to defend poetry against some of its enemies he must protect it from some of its friends. Empiricists like Austin cast poetry beyond the "actual languages" that alone deserve study into the outer dark of the "ideal languages." The bias against poetic language and in favor of plain speech or plain prose unites, Hill argues, even such seventeenth-century philosophical adversaries as Hobbes and the Cambridge Platonists. Poetic language, that infected medium of metaphor, will not serve the philosophers: first, it clouds the supposedly transparent discourse philosophy requires; and second, although it can speak, it cannot enact, cannot mean seriously what it seriously says. It forms easily but imperfectly performs, and for Austin "a performative utterance will . . . be *in a peculiar way* hollow or void if said by an actor on the stage, or if introduced in a poem." The poems cannot stand by their words, cannot say *our word is our bond.*

Against such antagonists, poetry cannot maintain its claims when even its friends are prepared to cede its position. Sidney meant to defend poetry when he said, "Now for the *Poet,* he nothing affirmeth, and therefore never lieth." It is not unreasonable to suggest, though Hill does not suggest it, that a language which cannot lie cannot tell the truth. This would hardly perturb most poets, who have an elastic and expedient regard for truth, though that does not make them politicians, or priests. The retreat may be galling to some, but it is galling to Hill in that intensely personal way that suggests the infection of public argument with private motive. We are returned to Stevens: "After one has abandoned a belief in god, poetry is that essence which takes its place as life's redemption." It cannot redeem if it is falsified in its very nature, falsified by not ever being false. It cannot even ransom a poet from the academics, and these essays in part attempt to redeem him on their ground and in their terms.

Sidney's proposition temptingly relieves the poet of responsibility to the world, if not the imagination. The status of poetry is secured, but at the cost of the poet accepting "that his art is a miniature emblem or analogy of res publica rather than a bit of real matter lodged in the body politic." That will not satisfy poets who require redemption from their art, though Hill does not deny that an art which accedes to such limitations can be real and responsive. It knows its place, but what he requires is an art that does not, that wrestles with "dark and disputed matter." The views are incompatible and mutually incomprehensible, felicity vs. perplexity, cure vs. infection, wit's providence vs. wit's anarchy. The comedians claim that "the undoing of language is . . . the making of it"; the melodramatists mutter that "its very making is its undoing."

Hill appreciates that temperament may incline a poet to a certain view and the constraints of a practice, in his case the melodramatic view and practice that "In a poet's involvement with language, above all, there is . . . an element of helplessness, of being at the mercy of accidents, the prey of one's own presumptuous energy." Someone "at the mercy of accidents" (and even "a meticulous reader of proof" may fail to notice the quotation mark inadvertently dropped from *Mercian Hymns* XX in *Collected Poems*) may be unnaturally sensitive to the intent and designs of others. The matter of his defense is the manner of his reconciliation, and in conciliatory manner he notices first that, despite their intentions, the philosophers cannot keep infection from their language. They indulge in "nuanced play," oblige the poetry inherent in prose, and measure their words not precisely to their uses but in excess of them. The infection is inherent in words cooperatively employed, in "ordinary circumstances" and "ordinary language," and so what might have merely been registered must be insisted upon: that there is "'dark and disputed matter' implicated in the nature of language itself." The comedians and the melodramatists realize separate halves of a complex relation: *our word is our bond* as "reciprocity, covenant, fiduciary symbol" vs. "shackle, arbitrary constraint, closure of possibility." If language is a reciprocal shackle, an arbitrary covenant, it discovers its possibilities at the very moment it seems closed off from them, whereas Ransom noted "the density or connotativeness of poetic language reflects the world's density." Where the world is poised against the word, it is poised in the word: it was perhaps by "the mercy of accidents" that in the *Poetry Book Society Bulletin* (Autumn 1968) recommending *King Log,* the first line of "Annunciations" read, not "The Word has been abroad, is back," but "The World has been abroad, is back."

To recognize a substance is not to recover a status. Poetry can impose no sanction for its statements: they lack the essential "hereby" that converts the words proposed into the act accomplished (the "comic subplot" of the essay is Ezra Pound's entanglements with the verdicts of criticism and the verdicts of courts). If modern poetry is to satisfy its desire for a "sense of identity between saying and doing," a desire no less admirable whether it reflects a general demand or a particular need, it must return to those understandings that implicate verbal obligation with moral necessity, verbal precision with moral exactness. A working formula for Hill, one which accounts for the moral appeal within the appearance of language, is Kenneth Burke's definition of "workmanship" as "a trait in which the ethical and the esthetic are one." The status of poetry cannot merely be asserted, as Pound could assert that "all values ultimately come from our judicial sentences"; it must be won instance by instance and line by line. The obligation Hill embraces leaves the poet under continual threat, every word a risk, every rhythm a warning: "The status fought for, and accomplished, within the comedy and melodrama of this sequence, is, therefore, that of standing by one's words in a variety of tricky situations." The sequence is *Homage to Sextus Propertius,* but the application is to *The Mystery of the Charity of Charles Péguy:* "Must men stand by what they write."

If the status of poetry can be recovered in prose, Hill secures his claim not by his shrewd examples but by his shrewish style. The prose erects the standard it can otherwise only assert, by its strict attention to the possibilities of language within the medium of argument. The position of poetry is an ancient matter, an ancient matter "dark and disputed," and its defense takes place in such charged provisions, "stratagems of the out-manoeuvred man, / the charge and counter-charge." But prose is never wholly sufficient to the necessity of poetry. It is no merciful accident that the only poetry to prove this status is the poetry of atonement, redemption, and bondage Hill has reserved as his domain, the poetry for which Péguy is a sacrificial figure. Martyred for his words, he provides the concluding Passion to the mission of artistic creation begun in "Genesis": "To ravage and redeem the world." The new testament completes the old; the death for words repays the beginning that was the Word.

It is difficult to feel warmth for such difficult splendors or for the moral obligations that prescribe them. The demands made are also denials, the restorations also restrictions. Geoffrey Hill stands by his words by standing apart from everything else, proud of an authority no one wishes to dispute because no one cares to be lord of such limited wasteground. The brilliance of his poetry cannot go unmarked, however limited its effect, however stunted its appeal. It judges the time, and the time stares back blankly. Geoffrey Hill's magnificence is the magnificence of a refusal, and if the poetry, with its tormented recognition of the ethical matter within an aesthetic manner, has been the unacknowledged legislator of the prose, the prose has slowly argued for just such sacrifice and just such fulfillment. To ask otherwise would be absolutely unreasonable.

NOTES

1. There is error even in correction: Peter Robinson in "Reading Geoffrey Hill" unrepentantly renders the line as "Dead leaves upon the alder shook" (Peter Robinson, ed., *Geoffrey Hill: Essays on His Work* [Philadelphia: Open University Press, 1985]).

HOW EMERSON AVAILS

DOUGLAS CRASE

He seemed to encourage us wherever it might count, and even a partial record will suggest his success—and stamina. "With the Kingdom of Heaven on his knee," observed Emily Dickinson, "could Mr. Emerson hesitate?" Yet for much of the present century it was possible to ask if his own works weren't fatally dated. It was possible, that is, until a reviewer in 1984 proved the question obsolete by posing it in *The New Yorker*, a forum to demonstrate how timely Emerson had again become. By now you may have seen the name Emerson brightening the book reviews, like Barthes or Foucault or Virginia Woolf. I have even seen, in a college alumni magazine, remarks by a sophomore who referred in passing to his "Emersonian self" as if that needed no explanation, as if he had used a world-class signifier to disclose one of his more desirable attributes.

It is not the first time Emerson has served this way. His *Essays* were once in everybody's hands and everybody's thoughts; you could find them in John Muir's hang-nest at Yosemite or in bed the morning of January 18, 1895, with Marcel Proust. (My own secondhand copy first belonged to a high school senior of 1902 in Galesburg, Illinois.) So I think our renewed attention to Emerson could be hardly more significant. It means from now on that the scholar, not just the American Scholar, will be less easily disinherited. It means we have the luxury now to worry that the inheritance might become an embarrassment of riches, that we might actually make an authority of this writer who in his first published sentences equated biographies, histories, and criticism with sepulchres, and who asked, "Why should not we also enjoy an original relation to the universe?"

Exactly, why shouldn't we also? If the textual Emerson, too, now stands with the great apparition, the nature that "shines so peacefully around us," then the recourse is to inquire, to what end is Emerson? The inquiry is being put by some awfully smart critics and philosophers.[1] What I'm proposing is that you and I inquire, as poets, how Emerson avails.

"Avail" was one of Emerson's favorite words, a good word to use on him because it implies that he is not just a theme park to wander around in, but a transitive, updatable input for poetry. He would have liked that, or that's one way to read his hope in that last sentence of "Experience":

and the true romance which the world exists to realize, will be the transformation of genius into practical power.

His genius, our power: not really a far-fetched romance because there's a whole procession to testify how his genius has availed. There was Whitman, who said he was simmering until Emerson brought him to a boil. There was Frost, who said never to forget Emerson. And there was Gertrude Stein, who said, "and I said there was Emerson, and there was Hawthorne and there was Edgar Poe and there was Walt Whitman and there was, well, in a funny way there was Mark Twain and then there was Henry James and then there was—well, there is—well, I am."

We could cite the evidence at length, except trails of influence, like money trails, are apt to leave the impression that writers are exchanging something on the sly. I think it's more honest than that. In his book *The Selfish Gene*, ethnologist Richard Dawkins suggested a word for ideas and phrases that are replicators in biological evolution the way genes are replicators biologically. By analogy, and with a root as in mimesis, he came up with "memes." From what I know about poets and writers, "memes" make at least as much sense as saying that "mature poets steal." Steal implies intent, but when you end up hosting powerful phrases isn't it because you can't get them out of your head? There are countless memes, replicating in poetry this way, that we can track to Emerson.[2]

My own prejudice is that when so many poets host memes from an identical source, it raises the presumption that the source is another poet. The problem is, most of the influences traceable to Emerson aren't from his verse but from his essays. Or maybe it isn't a problem, but a clue. Because I think all you have to do is ask whether the essays are really poems, or contain hidden poems, to take possession of the Emerson truly there.

> *Vast spaces of nature, the Atlantic Ocean, the South Sea,—*
> *Long intervals of time, years, centuries,—are of no account.*
> *This which I think and feel underlay every former state of life*
> *   and circumstances,*
> *As it does underlie my present, and what is called life, and*
> *   what is called death.*

That is actually not Whitman, even if it does sound like "Crossing Brooklyn Ferry." And of course I've cheated to show that you can demonstrate how Emerson's essays are like poems just by setting them like poems. Those lines were from "Self-Reliance," and these that follow them are better known, more beautiful.

> *Life only avails, not the having lived. Power*
> *Ceases in the instant of repose; it resides*
> *In the moment of transition from a past to a new*
> *State, in the shooting of the gulf, in the darting*
> *To an aim. This one fact the world hates,*
> *That the soul becomes. . . .*

But the prosody isn't the point. The point is, when you set Emerson's words this way the lines themselves reveal how someone can love the essays even if they refuse to come clear as criticism or philosophy. They don't have to come clear, not as poetry.

Emerson has a reputation for memorable images and analogies, partly because that's what he said good writing consisted of. "Wise men pierce this rotten diction and fasten words again to visible things," is just one way he put it. So which are the visible things in "Life only avails?" There is a thing called power and one called a moment of transition, a gulf, an aim, and states both past and new. Talk about abstract diction.

Yet that is finally how Emerson's power is conveyed, in a diction that doesn't fasten words to things so much as it lets ideas loose in sounds. Those roomy vowels in *Life only avails* (even roomier as the *l*'s stretch them out) are vowels that make space and time in the very pronouncing of them, enough to reconnoiter his typical inversion. Does he mean "only life avails" or "life but avails only?" *Life only avails,* is what he writes, and listen to how it reverberates over the lesser vowels that are brushed aside: "not the having lived." These measure the inutile flipside of life, and there's no way to pronounce them expansively. It's not an image but sounds that make the "idea" of this line, the constricted syllables of past tradition being blown away by the hosanna at the beginning and that sforzando coming at the end: *Power.*

This is not to say you won't find in Emerson plenty of things: "swine, spiders, snakes, pests, madhouses, prisons, enemies"—though even that list is trying to vaporize into abstractions. Which pests or enemies? These are less things than enabling images. They permit you the liberty of moving on to visible things of your own, and liberty, yours and his, is something Emerson is scrupulous about. In "Nominalist and Realist" he writes that the world is so full of things it's good you can't see them all. If you could, you would be immobilized.

> As soon as the soul sees any object, it stops in front of that object.

He doesn't mean just paused, he means transfixed, taken prisoner. This is the exminister who wrote elsewhere that every thought, even every heaven, is a prison. Translate into poetic practices, and you see why he so seldom beats you over the head with some X-is-like-Y analogy. Powerfully good or bad, an image can bring you to a stop.

The analogies Emerson prefers are the kind that emphasize how you can get free of one heavenly prison and enter the next—how something moves, becomes, how it avails.

> Power ceases in the instant of repose. It resides in the moment of transition from a past to a new state, in the shooting of the gulf, in the darting to an aim. This one fact the world hates, that the soul *becomes.* . . .

And if in the face of the world's hostility the idea is to keep your soul becoming, to keep it on the move, then we have a clue to why Emerson's real poetry is in the essays and not so much in his verse. Because if the soul stops in front of an object, it may also stop in front of a rhyme.

In an early lecture on English literature, Emerson came close to saying he admired George Herbert, for example, in spite of his rhymes. (After conceding that Herbert's poetry was initially "apt to repel the reader," Emerson went on to argue that its thought nonetheless had "so much heat as actually to fuse the words . . . and his rhyme never stops the progress of the sense.") In a later lecture he claimed the finest rhythms of poetry were yet unfound, "compared with which the happiest measures of English poetry are psalm-tunes." It was March 5, 1842, in the Library of the New-York Society on the corner of Leonard Street and Broadway. Here is what else he said.

> I think even now, that the very finest and sweetest closes and falls are not in our metres, but in the measures of prose eloquence which have greater variety and richness than verse.

Then he added, "In the history of civilization, Rhyme may pass away." If that sounds familiar I don't have to tell you who was in the audience in Mannahatta that day.[3]

What's significant, of course, is not whether traditional or nontraditional form is better. That's not an argument poets should want to settle. What's significant is that Emerson's distrust of rhyme points, like a shadow to the sun, to what he thought poetry was for. It was liberty, liberty of perception: "The senses imprison us, and we help them with metres as limitary,—with a pair of scales and a foot-rule and a clock."

The paradox was that while meters might infringe on your perception they offered one liberty that prose withheld, the freedom to tell the truth. For the rest of what was said to the twenty-two-year-old Walter Whitman and the others in New York that March day was that rhyme might pass away, but it would always be remembered as a "privileged invention possessing . . . *certain rights of sanctuary.*" It seems inevitable in hindsight. But if your problem is to invent a form that permits you that liberty to perceive which belongs to prose, together with that privilege to speak which belongs to rhyme, you do what Waldo Emerson did. You invent the prose-hidden poem.

So what is the truth a lapsed minister, an aspiring poet, cannot put into ordinary prose? You can't tell father, mother, wife, and brother flat out in prose that the tropes, the metaphors of their society are a prison. You might say it, but you can't tell them, because logic is powerless against their metaphors. "I fear," wrote Emerson when he was only twenty, "the progress of Metaphysical philosophy may be found to consist in nothing else than the progressive introduction of apposite metaphors."

Today we have whole literatures and philosophies to point to our imprisonment by trope and language and media's prime time, so much pointing you have to wonder how far this fascination has become our apposite metaphor of the hour. But Emerson did more than point, and it would be interesting to know how he would proceed against the tropes of today. We know his pleasure was to subvert trope with trope. Of society, even more a male club then than now, he focused back on it the anxiety that male bonding is supposed to alleviate in the first place. "Society everywhere is in conspiracy," he wrote (and we have learned to supply the italics), "against the *manhood* of every one of its members." Of getting rich quick, too often called the American Dream, he labeled it a "bribe." Of gender vanity, he wrote (and here the emphasis is his own) that there is "in both men and women, a deeper and more important *sex of mind.*" Of divine absolution, he simply referred us to a divinity closer at hand: "Absolve you to yourself, and you shall have the suffrage of the world."

I would like to say these examples amount to recombinant memes. I can certainly say along with Charles Ives that Emerson, in his essays, was "lighting a fuse that is laid toward men"—and I could hardly say it better, except to add how it was laid toward women to the same impolite effect.

So where as poets does that leave you and me? If the old metaphors are blown away it leaves us right where Emerson wanted us, in the position of having to choose metaphors, turn tropes, that express our original relation to the universe. It's a heresy that may seem too much to ask, and there were times in Concord he must have thought so too. "Despair is no muse," he once wrote in his *Journals,* a formulation that makes you aware of the extent to which Emerson's so-called optimism is a strategy for writing: self-help for poets.

In life, he had plenty of practice. When his five-year-old son died in 1842 Emerson lost his first and, as far as he knew then, his only son. "I am and I have: but I do not get," is what he would write in "Experience" two years later, "and when I have fancied I had gotten anything, I found I did not." He had not even begotten a biological future for the name Emerson. "Never mind the ridicule, never mind the defeat": he writes bravely, "there is victory yet for all justice." But what kind of victory can compensate for the failure of heirs to carry your name in the world? You can still beget memes named Emerson.

> and the true romance which the world exists to realize, will be the transformation of genius into practical power.

Considering how he left us face to face with the universe, we could use some of that practical power. Because no matter how good you are with words, it's hard to turn new tropes until you newly perceive, and the redemptive power of the trope will be proportional to the redemptive power of the perception. This is bedrock poetics, and it is this ratio that is behind Emerson's consistent emphasis on the eye-ball, on vision: "We are never tired, so long as we can see far enough." The implication is that how you manage your perception will determine how much energy there is in what you write, which does sound like the start of a self-help course for poets.

My guess though is that the course will seem compromised in its first lesson, *Nature.* You are probably not convinced by Emerson's analogy there that the poet who turns nature into tropes is like the savior who rides in triumph into the holy city, an analogy which taken to its conclusion can only mean that salvation itself depends on the tropes you mount. We don't make big claims like that for poetry. There are a lot of bat-boy ideologues and vigilante divines in public life, and they make claims. But among poets and scholars there still flourishes the notion that poetry makes nothing happen and can be written accordingly. I have a hunch that if Emerson were around he would see that as a metaphor for *our* imprisonment.

Chances are, the tropes you turn on nature just might support salvation. When Emerson was reading astronomy, in 1833, he noted in his *Journals* that "God has opened this knowledge to us to correct our theology & educate the mind." Yet more than 150 years later, when the space shuttle had exploded and slapped into the Atlantic Ocean, the best the president could do was to paraphrase a bad sonnet: the astronauts, he said, had "slipped the surly bonds of earth and touched the face of God."[4]

Forget the God part, and it is still unbearably dissonant. What can it mean to refer to the surly bonds of earth?—bonds not slipped at all since gravity brought the astronauts and their cabin into contact with the surface at 200 miles per hour. And what is surly about the bonds that hold the atmosphere, that make this planet the only breathing, protected paradise we know of and keep it from being, for instance, Mars?

You're wondering if I'm really serious, if it matters that an ill-managed president broadcasts a piece of mimetic vandalism grabbed up by a speechwriter. But tropes that make the earth unlovely make humans who do not love the earth. If theirs is the species that also has the bombs, or just the subdevelopment rights, then I think poetry has quite a lot to do with salvation. You don't have to be so impersonal about it, though. "For the value of a trope," or so Emerson left the issue, "is that the hearer is one: and indeed Nature itself is a vast trope, and all particular natures are tropes."

Clever enough, except it still leaves for us the problem of nature, which as a source of poetry can seem like one painful anachronism. Walking in the Walden woods, the woods he owned, Emerson thought nature was "sanative," a remedy for everything false in human culture. It was a standard by which inconstant culture could be measured, re-troped. But who can study nature now, except with a broken heart? There's a hole in the ozone, isotopes in the reindeer, and a mile to the west of Emerson's woods are the waters of the Sudbury River which flow into the Concord River, go under the rude bridge that arched the flood, join the Merrimack and pass Plum Island into the Atlantic—all this after having first taken the outflow from a little tributary called (of all things) Chemical Brook, in Ashland, Massachusetts. There is where the river picks up the mercury, lead, chromium, cadmium, arsenic, trichloroethylene, nitrobenzene, and chlorinated benzenes that have made its contamination, according to the EPA, permanent.

Emerson thought there was nothing, except losing his sight, no calamity that nature could not repair. A mile from where he stood, nature cannot even repair itself.

It's no wonder, considering what has been done to North America, that the American Scholar would rather contemplate frescoes in Italy than benzenes in Massachusetts. And yet what were American scholars up to in 1837 except Italian frescoes?—or Emerson would have had no subject for his famous talk. The difference is that they complained the continent was too empty, too untouched for art, and here I am complaining it's too full and too messed up. But since they felt despair because nature was too empty and we feel despair because it's too full, is it possible the fault is not in nature but in despair?

> The ruin or the blank, that we see when we look at nature, is in our own eye. The axis of vision is not coincident with the axis of things, and so they appear not transparent but opake.

He never said it was easy to perceive what nature was about. "It is easier to read Sanscrit," is what he did say. But you and I have this advantage: somebody tried the axis of vision before and left records, essays on how to proceed.

A peculiar thing about the *Essays* (and another way they are like poems) is their titles, titles that don't reveal the subject so much as protect it. Of these, none has been less forthcoming than the most famous one, "Self-Reliance." Partly as a consequence, there is no masterpiece in our literature that has been more capriciously maligned. Emerson does insist on liberty, it's true, while the world seems to offer endless illustrations that humans can't always live up to liberty. Why this should make anyone feel smug is beyond me, but it does. More than one person of letters has felt compelled to note how irrelevant "Self-Reliance" is to a wiser culture that now recognizes the errancy of the individual as opposed to the steadfast guidance of. . . . But that's just it. No two agree on what the alternative authority is, though each must have one in mind even if, too bad for the other, it's not the same in both cases.

Of course, there is creative reading as well as creative writing. Because despite its title the famous essay is not really about the selfish self at all. On the contrary: if we are to have our original relation to the universe, then the self, the one with the instilled appetites and the learned desires, this self must stand aside—which makes sense when you remember what the problem was.

> The ruin or the blank, that we see when we look at nature, is in our own eye.

So if not the self, who do we rely on? Like any poet, Emerson suggests his answer in a writerly way, by qualifying his terms. Not halfway through, and he has renamed self-reliance to be self-trust, in order (while reminding his reader that trust has a fiduciary meaning) to ask: "Who is the Trustee?" It is, he writes, "that science-baffling star, without parallax."

No parallax, so it never appears to change position, even though he also described it at the outset as flashing from within. You can see Emerson liked riddles, since the light that never changes position yet is carried hither, thither and elsewhere within you is—our "common origin." Instructed, as we are supposed to be, in the dimensions of our inheritance, in the starbursts that deliver the elements that twist themselves up into things that replicate, we can better appreciate the justice of this answer, our common origin. It's a meme he elaborates at length.

> We first share the life by which things exist, and afterwards see them as appearances in nature, and forget that we have shared their cause.

Nice, but. Taken to its logical conclusion what does it mean? That you put your trust as a poet in the Big Bang?

Intelligent people like to think intelligent thoughts, not wacko ones, so those people will be happy to hear the word "cause" in Emerson's sentence. "Cause" will remind them of nineteenth-century Idealism and its has-been philosophers, and, if Emerson is like those philosophers, then his sentence is a has-been too. No wonder Emerson believed a thought was a prison, when what his words really add up to is a sentence that wants to release us where it will, just like poetry. So what if we forget philosophy and read "Self-Reliance" as natural history?

We apparently do share, in DNA for instance, the life by which things exist. We apparently do share in the maintenance of the biosphere but for centuries thought earthly things were natural appearances instead of dependents in a common cause. Here is Emerson's sentence in its place.

> In that deep force, the last fact behind which analysis cannot go, all things find their common origin. For, the sense of being which in calm hours rises, we know not how, in the soul, is not diverse from things, from space, from light,

> from time, from man, but one with them, and proceeds obviously from the same source whence their life and being also proceed. We first share the life by which things exist, and afterwards see them as appearances in nature, and forget that we have shared their cause. . . . We lie in the lap of immense intelligence, which makes us receivers of its truth and organs of its activity.

What fascinates me in those lines is the assumption, in slow and equal iambs, of equal status among the five reliers in the one consortium. Being human doesn't separate you, not from things, from space, from light, from time, from man. With a list like that, the mind reaches farther back than DNA. Far enough to raise the question again: What do we do, rely on the Big Bang?

We *were* looking for an original relation to the universe. And the Bang does promise a new twist on the axis of vision, especially if we could perceive our rights to be but coequal in evolution with those of space, of time, of light, of things.

Emerson let self-reliance in for a lot of trouble when he wrote on the lintels of that doorpost, *Whim*. People have come out of the woodwork on account of *Whim* to condemn him for everything from bran flakes to poets who lust after the Big Bang. What they are really condemning in the process is your liberty as a poet to perceive. "Thoughtless people . . . fancy that I choose to see this or that thing," he writes, beginning one of those qualifications you learn to keep reading for. "But perception is not *whim*sical, but fatal." I added the emphasis because the secret of "Self-Reliance" is that it proposes no whim, but a release of objectivity, the objectivity to honor facts as perceived from the axis of our common origin. In that case your perception itself is a fact, "as much a fact," says Emerson, "as the sun."

The catch is what happens when the soul sees a fact. It stops in front of that fact. The soul stops, and, to adopt the figure of "Circles," it is encircled. Lucky for us if our Virgil knows an escape. "The way of life is wonderful": he explains, "it is by abandonment." Brilliant as your perception was, the thing to do is to abandon it.

Maybe this won't sound so frivolous if you consider what we've learned from quantum physics about the uncertainty of measurements. Heisenberg's uncertainty relation is taken in popular terms to mean you can't measure simultaneously the momentum and the position of any particle, though this is apparently not quite right. What you can't know simultaneously are the average of many moments and the average of many positions for any particle. To know one completely you would have to abandon completely your measurement of the other.

Heisenberg argued that you could not draw moral or practical analogies from quantum nature. Niels Bohr argued that you could. To an Emersonian self like mine, it seems inevitable. For example, if as a poet I measure for pollution at Chemical Brook, then I will perceive either more or less pollution. If less, I will be gratified by the better fit with our fashionable metaphor, ecology. If I perceive more pollution, I will be in pain, my axis of vision out of whack with the axis of things.

But what if I were to abandon ecology and measure instead by that lesson from our common origin?—evolution. From the first contamination of protons after the Big Bang to the chlorinated benzenes in Chemical Brook, the project of the universe seems to have been to make big molecules and to mix things up. Given the record, you might wonder if humans aren't specifically here to mix things up, if we shouldn't as poets write that Chemical Brook, for degree of evolution, was never so beautiful as when it ran with a trichloroethylene sheen.

Maybe that's what he means in *Nature,* about how sordor and filths will no longer be seen.

I agree it's a perverse perception, and I am duly embarrassed. Embarrassed enough to be the example for Emerson's second remedy for encirclement. In order to write, you not only abandon your first perception, but you must also abandon yourself to love of the new one.

People don't often regard Emerson as a lover, but he was at least once or he couldn't use love as the standard for how far you have to go in order to write. Think of love as the time when we forgive ourselves all embarrassment and later never remember that we were ridiculous but only that we were in love. If in the act of writing you turn Chemical Brook into a freshet of the new Eden, you could stop in embarrassment or keep writing and go all the way. After all, "Life is a series of surprises"—or so begins in delight that passage from "Circles" that is one of Emerson's most beautiful and that ends, after its writer has cast away his "hoard" of knowledge, in a relief of wisdom.

> The simplest words,—we do not know what they mean, except when we love and aspire.

Turn that inversion around and it says, to love is to know what words mean. To perceive is to know what words to write.

Today you may be justly suspicious of any presumption in favor of new perceptions, as if anybody needed more of them, as if they didn't crowd in on us already from film, television, from printed things and things unprintable—so many of them, there are days the world seems nothing but rumors, everything less and less for real. Yet it's largely due to the present experience of data overload that Emerson's complaint in "Experience" can sound, not fatally flawed, but as modern and postmodern as our own.

> All things swim and glitter. Our life is not so much threatened as our perception. Ghostlike we glide through nature, and should not know our place again.

It isn't fair. You follow all his self-help counsel, and he informs you at last that experience will undo your perceptions, once by denying them outright and again by not being true enough to have ever made them real.

A measure of how this troubled Emerson himself is that "Experience" is the most overtly organized of his famous essays. Eight parts, though if you subtitle them according to his own summary it's more like seven, plus a coda. (This puts part four at the essay's center, even more clearly its focus than before.) In the first three parts, Emerson names those sensations, all too real, that seem to deny his best begotten perceptions. In the last three, preceding the coda, he counters with generalizations to mend or embrace the denials. Nowhere does he suggest the generalizations are real enough to make up, say, for losing his son: "The amends," he writes elsewhere, "are of a different kind than the mischief." But the essay's structure does suggest how hard he was trying and how compelling this makes the resolution he has balanced there in its fourth section, on "the equator of life, of thought . . . of poetry." There, in a kind of purgatory between the inferno of sensation and the paradise of generalization, his solution is: "add a line every hour, and between whiles add a line." His solution is to write.

To say inferno, and so on, is close to accusing Emerson himself of hosting some famous memes. (He once noted that if he taught writing he would use Dante as his textbook, so the speculation isn't wild.) Of those three beasts Dante confronts after he wakes, lost in midlife, it is the wolf of envy that finally destroys his hopes. Predictably, or so Virgil tells him, because envy lets no one pass and you must take another way. In the first sentence of "Experience" Emerson likewise wakes ("Where do we find ourselves?"), is likewise lost in midlife, and having suffered the death of his son he too has an envy to confront. His martyrdom has been insufficient, the griefs of others more romantic than his own.

Not martyred enough. On one level this sounds like some vestigial religious envy of those who have suffered more than we have. On the level of Emerson's concern it is envy of those persons, those systems even, that we fear have perceived more than we have, that have seen all the data in the world or, worse, seen through it all. It is especially envy of data itself. And it's to counter this romance of envy that he offers what he calls the true romance: turn the genius of your own perceptions into practical power. "Thou art sick," he writes, not mincing the word, "but shalt not be worse, and the universe, which holds thee dear, shall be the better."

I'm not sure how the universe will be better if everybody sits down tomorrow and writes a poem. It's possible, if the project of the expanding universe is to evolve, to become something else, then the more memes, the more poetry, the better. What I want to know, especially since I thought the anthropic cosmos was a conceit peculiar to the new cosmology, is whether Emerson really believed the actual physical universe would be better.

Eight years after "Experience" was published, Waldo Emerson, forty-nine, laments in his *Journals* that just when you get to be a good writer you get old. Your physical energy has begun to fail. Then he reminds himself that whatever he has already perceived and written was thanks to the universe, and thanks to the universe he, and any of us after, writes again.

> In you, this rich soul has peeped, despite your horny muddy eyes, at books & poetry. Well, it took you up, & showed you something to the purpose; that there was something there. Look, look, old mole! there, straight up before you, is the magnificent Sun. If only for the instant, you see it. Well, in this way it educates the youth of the Universe; in this way, warms, suns, refines every particle; then it drops the little channel or canal, through which the Life rolled beatifically— like a fossil to the ground—thus touched & educated by a moment of sunshine, to be a fairer material for future channels & canals, through which the old Glory shall dart again, in new directions, until the Universe shall have been shot through & through, *tilled* with light.

Like nature as he hoped nature could be, it is Emerson's motive that is revealed as sanative, a remedy for what is false in our culture. As an incitement to write and guide for doing so, it is unbeatable. It indicates now, and will indicate deep in the twenty-first century, how Emerson avails.

NOTES

This essay was first delivered as remarks to the Literary Roundtable of the American Academy of Poets, New York, January 12, 1987.

1. Especially important to me are the reclamations of Emerson made by Harold Bloom, Barbara Packer, Stanley Cavell, and Richard Poirier.

2. Replication of Emersonian memes is not confined to poems. The last line of *Walden* ("The sun is but a morning star") descends from Emerson's "Politics": "We think our civilization near its meridian, but we are yet only at the cock-crowing and the morning star." Dickinson's apologia ("My Business is Circumference") refigures "Circles": "There is no outside, no enclosing wall, no circumference to us." William James's reality ("Life is in the transitions as much as in the terms connected") recalls "Self-Reliance": "Life only avails. . . . It resides in the moment of transition from a past to a new state." Frost's figure a poem makes ("For me the initial delight is in the surprise of remembering something I didn't know I knew") retraces "Intellect": "What you have aggregated in a natural manner surprises and delights when it is produced." Stein's argument in "The Making of Americans" ("It is hard living down the tempers we are born with") repeats "Experience": "Men resist the conclusion in the morning, but adopt it as the evening wears on, that temper prevails over everything of time, place, and condition." Stevens' aphorism ("Money is a kind of poetry") improves on "Nominalist and Realist": "Money . . . represents the prose of life." And, as Richard Poirier points out, Eliot's quotable wisdom ("mature poets steal") is itself derived from Emerson's "Shakespeare": "It has come to be practically a sort of rule in literature, that a man, having once shown himself capable of original writing, is entitled thenceforth to steal from the writings of others at discretion."

3. "Rhymes and rhymers pass away, poems distill'd from poems pass away," is the first line of section 13 from "By Blue Ontario's Shore," which echoes similar words from the 1855 preface to *Leaves of Grass*.

4. The sonnet, "High Flight," was written by John Gillespie Magee, Jr., a nineteen-year-old American airman who, as a volunteer in the Royal Canadian Air Force, was killed in the defense of Britain on December 11, 1941.

OF THE POWER OF THE WORD

JOHN TAGGART

Is anything more exciting and more dangerous for the
poet than his relation to words?

—Heidegger

Poetics allows the poet to stand outside
the poem. In that position it can be determined not only how well the job has been
done, but also the basis for the act of composition itself may be investigated and the
future direction of the work, necessarily intwined with that investigation, decided
upon. Poetics allows the poet to stand outside the poem with something like the active
engagement and responsibility of composition. In this allowance, perhaps addressed
to no one but the poet himself, to a doubting friend, or to anyone who would pause
in walking through the park, reticent or ardent, poetics remains conversation.

The poetics of a major poet, however, does not simply invite us to join the conversation. Rather it forces us to reconsider our own poetics. We are forced to reconsider
the nature and value of craft, the underlying basis of composition, and the future of
the poem. The poetics of a major poet throws everything into question.

Robert Duncan is such a poet, a "big poet" in Charles Olson's description. His
bigness, like that of Olson, reflects the degree to which he would put everything concerning poetry in doubt. Good, even interesting poets work within their generation's
understanding, within the assumptions of that understanding of what the poem should
be. Good poets consider this question essentially once, as young poets, and work
thereafter within the answer established at large by their contemporaries. A major
poet continues to consider not only the past or present generation's answer, in reaction; he continues to consider all answers and their assumptions. He opens up the
range of what the poet might be; he keeps the poem's range of possible definition
open. By putting everything in doubt, the major poet makes the poem always possible.
We are called on, at times commanded, by a major poet to respond. We must either
respond—even to the point of interruption—or go down in his wake. And our response should be in kind. Let our questions bestow honor on this poet, and keep up
our end of the conversation.

I take as the text for my questions a single passage from *The Truth & Life of Myth*
essay.

Speaking of a thing I call upon its name, and the Name takes over from me the story I would tell, if I let the dimmest realization of that power enter here. But the myth we are telling is the myth of the power of the Word. The Word, as we refer to It, undoes all the bounds of semantics we would draw in Its creative need to realize Its true Self. It takes over. Its desire would take over and seem to put out or to drown the individual reality—lonely invisible and consumed flame in the roaring light of the Sun—but Its creativity moves in all the realities and can only realize Itself in the Flesh, in the incarnation of concrete and mortal Form.

First sentence: words are two things, or fulfil two functions. They are the means by which things are summoned, brought to conscious definition, a kind of counting, and they are things in themselves. As names, they enable the speaker to call things not present into awareness for the purpose of telling the speaker's story; they aid the storytelling but are subservient to it. With words as names, our attention is given to what is said to be there, what is said to happen in the story. Words as names give the poet an apparent power over things, a power to move things about in the interest of his story. As things in themselves, they are empowered to dictate their story to the speaker; they transform the poet as speaker to the bespoken. The story becomes an account of words. They are the actors in their own story which the speaker reproduces. It would seem that both functions can be active simultaneously or that the poet can be aware of both simultaneously. The Homeric singer invokes the muse and is at the same time responsible for the word-to-word order in the moving line of his song. The poem, by extension, is a balancing, a maintenance of tension between the two. The word as name of a thing encourages accounting and manipulation (plot). It does not acknowledge the intrinsic properties of the word; it acknowledges form only insofar as that can be brought about by the list and its elaborations. The word as Name has a power capable of making our relation to the physical world tenuous, complicating our sense of any center, frustrating the communication of emotion or of action in response to such communication. The word as Name reduces men and women to isolate respondents without means of a like energy or off-setting response. It's desirable, to say the least, to find a balance between the upper and lower case word.

Second sentence: myth means story. The headnotes to Duncan's essay build up a composite definition that corroborates and expands this meaning: myth is the making of a sound (Liddell & Scott); myth is the development from such interjectional utterance to narrative, the plot of the dromenon or ritual action (Jane Harrison); myth is an expansion of empirical reality (Ernst Cassirer); myth, when a real event may be the enactment of a myth, is the truth of the fact and not the other way around (Kathleen Raine). The headnotes prepare for the essay's opening definition of myth as the story told of what cannot be told, of what cannot be revealed or known. This would seem to give us myth as spiritual story. I write "seem" because the not-there is hardly an exclusive property of the spiritual. Myth, in Duncan's definition, can be either spiritual story or the story of absent empirical reality, real events or facts; the two can also be combined, interpenetrated. What is told is not simply the power of the Word, but also *the story* of the Word's power. The reality of the word in itself and its ability to transform the speaker to bespoken, to "take over" is confirmed. Yet this is only a story, one among others. There could be other stories, other myths which we might relate at some other time.

Third sentence: an indication of the Word's power is that it somehow transcends the limitations human speakers would impose upon it by their definitions (bounds of semantics). This power is demonstrated in the story we (are made to?) tell. The motivation for its demonstration is need; the Word needs to realize Its true Self. This Self is apparently understood by that which is other than, if not antagonistic to, the impositions of the speaker's intended story (as the nature of the Word's need may be taken as other than the need of its speaker). As to how the Word can have such need in the first place, that's subsumed in the declaration of Self. If the word is granted an intrinsic existence (Name as opposed to the name of a thing), then it may be thought to have a self and thus a need to maintain that identity. Having a self creates need.

Another way to conceive of the word's self is as its ultimate etymological root, a sound. This develops from our sense of the self as somehow inside us, distinct from the outer body, an interior, the essential as opposed to the accidental. The word is spoken and the self as root is carried, sounded, within our speech. Once this occurs, the word enters an endless branching process, which properly had its beginnings long before our usage, by way of its combination with other words and the speaking of others which continues to carry or recall and yet deviate from the root. The process is creative in that the root is parent to the branching out to include other words and usages. The self as root, despite the on-going nature of this process, is not lost, but further manifested. Each time the word is spoken, the root is sounded, carried, and displayed. Root reminds us of plants and flowers. A flower may contain its own seeds, it may be self-seeding. The speaker is true to the word's self so long as he attends to its root sound. That attendance gives him a source of melody line and inclusive form. In speech the self as root is planted, blossoms, and in the natural decay of sound is replanted as seed waiting to bloom once again in "returned speech" by others who respond. The entire anthology depends upon a single root. The word is felt to have power, but only as it is sounded in our telling.

Last sentence: the desire of the word is its need to realize its "true" self, which may be understood as an interior etymological root which, as a usage and a sound, is always being manifested whenever the word is spoken. If the speaker becomes increasingly aware of the word as a thing in itself, there's the feeling of having become a passive vehicle, a subject courier for the word's story. The realization of the word's self means a corresponding obscuring of the speaker's self. "To put out or to drown." This is given in the subjunctive by Duncan because the word's self-realization is active in "all the realities" and merely seems to obscure the individual speaker. For this realization can only take place in the flesh, in the resonating human interior. The closing terms of this last sentence bring into play specifically Christ story associations. The myth of the word that Duncan would have us tell is any word in itself and the word as Christ incarnate, the Logos. The myth of the power of the word, as with the opening definition of myth, is given a playing ambivalence. It is any word, the Logos, or both at once.

There is much in Duncan's sentences that is disturbing. While the Aristotelian may object that there can't be an action without an actor to begin with, and thus to speak of the word's need to realize itself is beside the point, anyone engaged in composition will readily admit, I think, that words are experienced both as the names of things and as things in themselves. In fact, composition makes us aware of the latter as ordinary usage, which seeks to convert language into something else, does not. This is not a matter of theory. Whatever the nature of his form, inherited or found, the poet quickly discovers he must stay awake to the words' history of usage and sounds if the poem is to attain its form in any active way.

Readily enough we move from our experience of the form-aiding potential of the word to the upper case absolute power of the word. The ease of the move is betrayed by the elaborate figure of the extinguished individual reality in the description of the word's desire to realize its true self. I'm aware that the figure derives from the story we have supposedly chosen to tell about the power of the word. Yet it is not simply one among equally possible others. This is particularly so when it's entangled with the Christ story, the old old story of Jesus and his love that has been told to the exclusion of others since the "beginning" of time. One way of reading the work of our fathers, the modernists, and of their fathers, the romantics, is as a struggle against the hegemony of any single story, any single vision, which is also a single definition of what the poem can be.

Duncan's poetics prompts us to consider the range of our choices, if any, and by what means that range can be assured, if it can be assured, in the face of the word's power.

Choice is available when the speaker has a story to tell. How and where is a story to be found? The most common solution has been to retell an already existing story, to find what we would tell in what has already been told. As Duncan notes, this recognizes mythology as poets' lore. The problem is that, while we are given something to say, it is necessarily derivative, secondary, and inessential. One story displaces another only to repeat it.[1] This process works to undermine the reality of our own lives in poetry in its suggestion that we exist only as we reproduce or represent the images of previous stories. We are made parts of a consuming process of repetition through our appropriation of the past. We are made readers and rereaders. And the more we read the more we feel the need to read still more. The poet, who is first a reader, makes no original discovery in reading; instead, he becomes only more aware of the spider-web connectedness of his sources and of the innumerable ghostly speakers still beyond them. At best, our displacements might operate as clever enough variations on previously laid down themes. But what is finally repeated is an absence. The search for the originating source of an experience in language—in effect, for its first telling—is honorable, but futile. It only serves to expose the arbitrariness of the enterprise. The first recorded usage is all too obviously not the first. And if it is not the first, then there can be only a repeating of what is already a reproduction.

It may be, as Stevens writes, that "There was a myth before the myth began, / Venerable and articulate and complete." But what precedes both ourselves and the myth before myth is "a muddy centre." That center, the physical universe, is silent. When we would make our way back to the myth before myth, it leads us there, to silence and absence. (Even Heidegger, who attempts to establish an ontology for language, Saying instead of Being, is forced to propose a place of arrival created by the calling of naming; called forth in the calling, this "place" is a "presence *sheltered in absence.*") The center is silent; presence is absent. Words, which we would trace back past the myths to the center as a final nontextual, nonlinguistic reference, are its representations. Words are carriers of absence. The first muthos, conjectured in the Jane Harrison note, is relevant. What did this utterance interject with? It could only be silence. Duncan's opening definition of myth—which can be taken as a definition of the poem—emphasizes the *not-there*. The definition suggests there could be other stories about other things. It would say that, whatever their seeming subjects, they are also always "about" something else.

Earlier I sought to conceive of the word's self as its ultimate etymological root, a sound. I speculated how that root is engendered through our speaking. The implied ethics were that the poet should try to remain true to the word's self by attending to its root sound. Such attentive speaking was to encourage the root to blossom and, in the decay of sound, to bloom repeatedly in the returned speech of others. I would have the entire anthology depend on a single root. All of this may be so. Yet it strikes me now as dangerous in its invention. For that root is attached to the center. What, consequently, it attaches all its related words and their speakers to is that same center, its silence and absence. Per Celan, its flowers are niemandsroses. The danger is that we forget this attachment, its final reference. Caught up in composition, aware of the care of our predecessors, we forget that reference and are tempted to formulate laws based on our stories. The expectation grows that there ought to be a primal story teller, a primal creative agency responsible for all our smaller, individual stories. We will believe in this agency, try, like Klee, to divine its will and put ourselves in right relation to it. The idea of a range of choices becomes fruitless. It is dangerous to forget that the little boy and girl lost are found, given parents, only *within* Blake's songs.

This leads to a further question of whether it's possible for the poet to observe a condition of silence and remain a poet, active in the use of language and even interested in what his voice sounds like.

The answer is yes and a catalogue of techniques of resolution might be drawn up. What we would have is the history of what we are learning to call postmodernism. But let us consider the answer contained in Duncan's poetics. Perhaps surprisingly, what I would draw from the passage quoted from *The Truth & Life of Myth* is also in the affirmative. Yet it is distinct from the typical postmodern resolution. That is based on ellipsis, collage of disparate vocabularies, contradictory or suspended syntaxes put in juxtaposition, cancellation, or erasure. These techniques acknowledge silence through the contrived failure or frustration of statement. (Whether these techniques, which would forcibly induce silence in the poem by way of failure or frustration, are actually sympathetic with a poetry concerned with the recognition of a silent center, of silence as the final reference, is a good question.) It might be asked how they differ from what we find in old "poetry is a destructive force" modern poetry. Modernism struggles against what is perceived as univocal authoritative statement to open up a range or field of choices, which the postmodernist inherits as one available choice, a way in itself of speaking: not to fragment a previous symbolic whole, but to speak directly in fragments. The techniques should probably not be considered as inherently different. How the poet is able to come upon them is: the postmodern poet inherits the choice of nonstatement as a way of speaking. His voice can sound like it isn't there. This is not to be confused with what we hear in Robert Duncan's poetry and poetics. That voice is radically present, non-stop, insistent to the point of irritation for the reader accustomed to both modernist and postmodernist not-saying; it is the voice of a believer for whom none of the gods—and none of the words—is dead.

What makes me answer yes for Duncan is neither his use of taking-out techniques (he would want to bring everything in) nor, clearly, his voice. What makes me answer yes is play. Previously, I noted a playing ambivalence in Duncan's definition of myth and in his telling of the power of the word. If we object, disturbed by the weaving of poetics in terms of the spiritual—and the reverse—; if we object, disturbed by our sense that such power is threatening and might very well take over, his likely reply would be that *it is the myth that's being told now*. Others can be told which, given one's ability to realize form, to listen to each sound in turn, would be just as true or actual, just as compelling. Assuming that all the stories of all the words may have such potential, then none need dominate over any other or its speaker. Like a bricoleur child, Duncan would play with all the words, tell all the myths. And in this constant smiling (not simply "positive") play, in which everything is make-believe and at the same time declared *to be* with all the resources of the skilled adult voice, operative upon us here and now, the silence is nonetheless observed. For the playing with each sound of each word, each possible story, means the "distractability" of all. To make the poem a ground for play does not deny the muddy center as its foundation.

In the fairy tales of George MacDonald, the older a man is the younger he is. MacDonald's old man of the fire is to be truly identified as a child. Robert Duncan is a major poet, a poet with fire, by virtue of the constancy of his smiling play. We learn from his poetics that we need not deny the power of the word, as we need not deny the silent center, for fear of our realization as speakers and poets. We learn that our choices are governed not so much by incidental technique as by a willingness to listen to the root-self-sound of every word, that, therefore, the range of our choices is as limited or limitless as the number of words themselves.

NOTES

1. I am indebted for this idea to Edgar A. Dryden, whose essay "The Entangled Text" has been pivotal to my thinking; see *Boundary* 2 (Spring 1979).

MILOSZ AND THE
MORAL AUTHORITY OF POETRY

EMILY GROSHOLZ

What authority does poetry have in the present age? Czeslaw Milosz often poses this question in his essays on literature and poetics, history and philosophy. He sees humankind threatened by proliferating universals, the necessities of scientific and social theory which seem to negate the integrity of the individual, as they usurp the claims of poetry to truth. Thus as a theoretician he is attracted to metaphysical systems like those of the Russian philosopher Lev Shestov and the French philosopher Simone Weil, which pose the human soul as a radical particular allied to a transcendent good in opposition to social and natural necessity. He can then ground his practical concerns as a poet in a kind of poetic nominalism. The authority of poetry stems from its courageous witness that necessity does not engulf us; poetry is the voice of the individual free to pursue the good, which in fact establishes the good by speaking.

Milosz was raised in the forests of Lithuania, began his studies in the provincial capital of Wilno, and moved to Warsaw, where he spent the war years as a member of the Polish Underground formed in resistance to the German occupation. He survived the Warsaw Uprising (in which the Red Army waited and watched the Polish resistance destroy itself in futile combat with the Germans before entering the city), was caught up by the Russian takeover of postwar Poland, and defected to the West five years later. After a decade in Paris as an itinerant man of letters, he accepted a professorship at Berkeley, where he has remained since, an emigré and exile.

Some poets in the United States have regarded Milosz with a strange mixture of admiration and jealousy. They blame the peripheral status of poetry in this country on the surface calm, the decadent affluence and tolerance of a society where all values are relative. Anyone can say anything, and no one pays much attention. By contrast, Milosz was privileged to live in the midst of great events, war, the collapse of civilizations, repressive occupation, in which writing a poem could be an heroic gesture, a genuinely moral act, the expression of objective value. In such situations, when poetry claims the authority of truth, it can become as necessary to the populace as bread, and the romantic-modernist isolation of the poet is abolished.

Milosz cannot be blamed for this naive assessment of his example by people who have never suffered the disruption of the entire fabric of their society. His ironic and hopeful account of the relation of poetry to our moral and political interests belies such naiveté. Yet his animosity toward the universal is so intense, and his insistence on the particular and transcendent so radical, that his advice to us is less useful than it might be.

In this essay, I would like to engage Milosz's moralizing poetics with my own alternative account, which relates poetry to the social, everyday activity of moral deliberation and makes it easier to see the possible authority of poetry in ordinary as well as cataclysmic situations. Though I will make reference to a number of his books, I will concentrate on his Charles Eliot Norton Lectures, *The Witness of Poetry*, a full-dress statement of his poetics published by Harvard University Press in 1983, and to some of his poems available in English translation in his revised *Selected Poems* (The Ecco Press, 1980).

Briefly, I agree with Milosz that "scientific" social theories which pretend to reduce particular cases to necessary universal principles endanger our moral education and impugn the status of poetry. But I see our best recourse against the tyranny of necessity not in the radically particular and transcendent, but in social discourse and the spirited embodiments of everyday life. Poetry can be authoritative to the extent that it helps us discover the good. But discovery of the good is an unending social process of deliberation about values, which are always, in the phrase of W. B. Gallie, essentially contestable. The very meaning and import of values are worked out in the offensives and defenses which modulate and regulate each other in practical deliberation. As we deliberate about what to do, we are constructing social reality. We are also involved in a process which continually adjusts universal principles to particular cases, without the domination or disappearance of either. When poetry in the United States fails, its inadequacy is then best understood as a failure of eloquence and phronesis, prudential wisdom. Nonetheless, poetry can play an important role in moral deliberation, and in what follows I will examine this role more closely.

I

In *The Captive Mind*, a book written shortly after his departure from Poland, Milosz discusses the effect of the Russian-controlled Marxist regime on Polish writers of his acquaintance. "Alpha the Moralist" was a haughty, austere personality who admired purity and wished to be recognized as a moral authority. He tended to write novels of ideas, insufficiently rooted in experience and observation of life. In underground Warsaw, his writings on the ethic of loyalty and self-sacrifice inspired many of the young people who were to be among the two hundred thousand slaughtered in the Warsaw Uprising. Milosz relates that Alpha's first postwar novel contained oversimplifications at odds with his richly ambiguous experiences in the war. The Communist regime imprisoned large numbers of resistance fighters who had been allied with the London government-in-exile; although they had been fighting Hitler, they were now called class enemies. (Precisely the same fate awaited Communist resistance fighters in Greece.) Yet Alpha depicted them in his novel merely as lost souls, incapable of hearing the good news offered by the protagonist, a fearless old Communist.

"Beta the disappointed lover of humanity" made his literary career in postwar Poland by writing a chilling account of his experience as an "upper-caste" prisoner in

Auschwitz. (The Party welcomed all anti-Nazi literature at the time.) He described how the less clever and aggressive perished, while he managed to keep himself warm and well-fed. Life in the camp appears as Hobbes' state of nature, each individual pitted against all the others, without sympathy or conscience, stripped of the illusory habits of civilization. And yet, Milosz points out, fellow-inmates who knew Beta in Auschwitz say that he often acted with courage and compassion. The extreme brutality of his stories disguised his principle of selection.

Milosz accuses Alpha and Beta of failing both as artists and as moralists. Indeed, the two kinds of failure cannot be disentangled. Because they didn't capture the depth and complexity (the moral *reality*) of the characters, their work is morally unedifying and also bad art. They have reduced their characters to angels, demons, or animals. We have nothing to learn from such types, which are intrinsically good, incorrigible, or simply amoral and so incapable of enlightenment or degeneration. They cannot be used to think through the meaning of moral principles brought to bear on difficult situations. Neither do they compel our attention or compassion; as works of art, they are inert. We are not tempted to inject ourselves imaginatively into these adventures, rounding out the story in reflective hindsight: What if she had acted otherwise? What would I have done in that situation? If only . . . No genuine moral tension calls us back into the story; we simply do not care enough to return to it. Our evaluation of an author's display of moral imagination is at once an aesthetic and an ethical judgment.

The long terrible silences of the war incited a whole generation of postwar Polish writers, Milosz among them, to give expression to what they and others had experienced. Dialectical materialism was a theodicy which provided rationalization a priori: the enemy (the exponents of capitalism in its most virulent form, fascism) deserved to die, and the innocent . . . Well, they could die with the satisfaction of knowing this conflagration was needed to clear the way for the Communist millennium. Shestov, if he had lived to hear the pronouncements, would have repudiated Marxist necessity as he repudiated the whole philosophic tradition springing from Greek metaphysics for which, he complained, only the necessary and general were important. But why should we respect a necessity that has no respect for us, radical particulars, and in fact violates our intensest desires? We must not accept even one tear shed by one innocent child; reason masks the absurdity of existence; suffering is the key to truth. In his collection of essays, *Emperor of the Earth* (University of California Press, 1981), Milosz devotes a whole chapter to expounding Shestov's refusal.

Yet even Milosz must find it difficult to make sense of Shestov's rebellion against not only mathematical and natural necessity, but historical necessity as well. Shestov demands of God that He unmake history. We cannot accept, for example, that Socrates died at the hands of the Athenians. But with this demand, the self, the radical particular, also demands to be itself unmade. We are what we are because of our origin in a certain cultural geography, a moment in history, with all its injustice and suffering. Shestov tries to extract the self from the determinations of historical necessity, but in so doing he empties it of content.

Is there then no middle ground between the necessity of the Marxist and Shestov's radical but empty voluntarism? Are we condemned to complacent rationalization or impotent and uncomprehending rage? A middle ground does exist; it is the place where we deliberate about the past, where poets compose poems, about the past as part of that process. Aristotle said we only deliberate about the future, but there he was mistaken. We are continually engaged in constructing the moral truth of the past as well as of the present. The reality of the past is in part how it influences us now; as we deliberate about it, our characterization of it changes, and it acts on us differently. What can a poet do for the past? Engage the dead in conversation; mourn; forgive. Like all deliberation, this is a long and difficult process, with no certain outcome.

How lucky Milosz is, the American poets say, to have the experience of such great suffering, which yields such depths of moral insight. What Milosz recounts, however, about the witness of poetry in reaction to war and genocide does not bear out this foolish romanticism, akin to the myth that the best poets are madmen. The human conversation itself suffers when society breaks down, and with it our moral discriminations and our poetry; often the damage can hardly be repaired.

In Chapter 5 of *The Witness of Poetry,* Milosz makes clear that cataclysms provide neither necessary nor sufficient conditions for profound moralizing or great art. During the war years, poetry was the main genre of underground literature, since a poem could be contained on a single page. A recently published anthology of such work, called *Poetry of Fighting Poland,* contained almost two thousand pages of poems and songs. But most of them, he concludes, do not have much aesthetic worth: only a few show much familiarity with poetic craft; most were too blatant in their calls to battle. In general, they were filled with moral and aesthetic commonplaces. And this is not surprising, since "people thrown into the middle of events that tear cries of pain from their mouths have difficulty in finding the distance necessary to transform this material artistically." War presents the least favorable conditions for prudence, the ability to see an issue from all angles, in all its ambiguity. It is unlikely that a soldier or prisoner will consider the lofty ideals, the stupidity, pain, and grief of the enemy firing at him.

If the trauma to social life has been thorough enough, even the cessation of hostilities will not restore the conversation. Milosz reviews the work of a half-dozen postwar Polish poets and finds them all to one degree or another misologic, hostile to and distrustful of the word. They reproached culture with being a tissue of illusion, "a network of meanings and symbols as a façade to hide the genocide underway" and were therefore attracted to various forms of reductionism. Their imagery tends to assimilate people to animals and physical objects, action to motion, human relations to the push-pull of forces. Their diction and vocabulary is simple and even slightly decomposed; they eschew obvious figures, stripping their poems of "eloquence."

I find such poetry both crippled and moving, half in retreat from discourse and half engaged; its expressiveness belies its distrust of expression. True despair is silent; these utterances of despair are hopeful insofar as they are uttered. Yet their moral usefulness is impaired, for the retreat from discourse which they represent is the source of the suffering they protest, not its solution. Eloquence can certainly be abused. But moral wisdom must be eloquent, for it must be effective, and virtue is worked out in social discourse. We must be able to persuade others about their own interests in order to get anything done. The cure for the abuse of eloquence is more eloquence, more efficacious wisdom.

Milosz

Milosz quotes two poems, the first by Zbigniew Herbert, the second by Aleksandor Wat, in which the writers take stones as being worthy of emulation. The duplicity of the message is revealed by the fact that both poets provide their stones with eyes:

> *Pebbles cannot be tamed*
> *to the end they will look at us*
> *with a calm and very clear eye.*

> *. . . With the eyes of a stone, myself*
> *a stone among stones, and like them sensitive,*
> *pulsating to the turning of the sun.*

On the one hand, this conceit is morally unhelpful; the fixity and silence of stones is simply unattainable for human beings (though not for corpses). On the other hand, neither poet can resist anthropomorphizing the stones, investing them with the virtues of self-possession, nobility, honesty, and sensitivity. But virtue is social and is created by people who talk about themselves and each other.

Even Milosz sometimes seems infected by such misology, when, for example, he wishes for fixed and "objective" values, like those removed, disembodied monoliths, the forms of Plato; or when he excuses the reductions of the foregoing poets as a kind of realism. Yet Milosz himself managed to write poems about his ruined country which are eloquent and mournful and which address both the dead and the living. Those silenced by catastrophe really do need us to speak for them, to forgive them; sometimes poetry is equal to the demand. "Dedication" was written in Warsaw in 1945.

> *You whom I could not save*
> *Listen to me.*
> *Try to understand this simple speech as I would be*
> *ashamed of another.*
> *I swear, there is in me no wizardry of word.*
> *I speak to you with silence like a cloud or a tree.*
> *What strengthened me, for you was lethal.*
> *You mixed up farewell to an epoch with the*
> *beginning of a new one,*
> *Inspiration of hatred with lyrical beauty,*
> *Blind force into accomplished shape.*

> *Here is the valley of shallow Polish rivers. And an*
> *immense bridge*
> *Going into white fog. Here is a broken city,*
> *And the mind throws the screams of gulls on your grave*
> *When I am talking with you.*

> *What is poetry which does not save*
> *Nations or people?*
> *A connivance with official lies,*
> *A song of drunkards whose throats will be cut in a moment,*
> *Readings for sophomore girls.*

That I wanted good poetry without knowing it,
That I discovered, late, its salutary aim,
In this and only this I find salvation.

They used to pour millet on graves or poppy seeds
To feed the dead who would come disguised as birds.
I put this book here for you, who once lived
So that you should visit us no more.

Only in the first stanza does Milosz resort to the reductive commonplaces of his generation and its curious inversion of the pathetic fallacy. "I speak to you with silence like a cloud or a tree." Admittedly, there is something paradoxical about the way in which elegiac poems address the dead person directly. Yet we often have unfinished business with the dead, and thus they enter into our deliberations; we talk to them so they will not haunt us into repetitions of revenge or grief. For they both are and are not beyond salvation.

"Dedication," like all successful deliberating, exhibits a delicate enmeshment of universal and particular. It begins with a situation which is both concrete (the shallow rivers, the bridge, the broken city involve "Warsaw, 1945") and general (everyone at one time or another must turn to their dead, and their defeats). This context has brought Milosz to certain realizations about poetry and about himself as a poet and moral agent. Poetry cannot serve univocal theory, which becomes the official lie; it cannot be the instrument of mere passion; it must go beyond the naiveté of inexperience. Milosz gives himself, and any poet, this admonition and concludes the poem with a resolve to do a particular act in fulfillment of universal principles. The act is writing the poem, settling with his dead; and it fulfills the injunction that poetry must save nations and people. For maintaining our conversation with the past, with each other, is our best hope; and forty years later, in another country, even in translation, this poem still questions us.

II

Milosz often complains about nature and the necessities with which it threatens us. His extended, sympathetic discussion of Blake's opposition to the strictness of Newtonian physics in *The Land of Ulro* (Farrar, Straus & Giroux, 1984) can be summarized thus: "The problem that engaged Blake would loom increasingly larger, in both range and magnitude, up to the present: The fact that the Particular has been consumed by the Universal." In *Visions from San Francisco Bay* (Farrar, Straus & Giroux, 1982) he announces, "[I do not like] the natural order, which means submission to blind necessity, to the force of gravity, all that which is opposed to meaning and thus offends my mind. As a creature of flesh, I am part of that order, but it is without my consent." And in Chapter 3 of *The Witness of Poetry,* called "The Lesson of Biology," he writes: "Nature in its incredible prodigality, producing the billions of creatures necessary to maintain the species, is absolutely indifferent to the fate of the individual. Once integrated into nature, man also changes into a statistical cipher and becomes expendable." I think there are really two issues here, which Milosz doesn't always distinguish in his arguments. As a poet and a moralist, Milosz is worried about the hegemony of scientific theory. As a mortal creature with a Catholic upbringing, he is also worried about embodiment.

The hegemony of scientific theory intrudes on our lives in more than one way. Reductionist theories of human nature pretend that people are like blocks and pulleys, that their actions are motions subject to physical laws and thus determined, inevitable, amoral. Moral responsibility as a category drops out of the description of human affairs. Thus, moral disputation (and poetry) are simply by-products of our confusion about ourselves, which we can ultimately do without. Theories about human nature cannot dispense with values, however, and in fact such theories bring values in again by the back door. But then their practical effect is pernicious: for their authority as "theories" discourages practical deliberation, and their pretense of being value-free theories masks the way they impose values in rigid and often inappropriate ways. Here we recall Milosz's complaint about the deployment of Marxist theory.

Even if one grants, however, that the application of scientific theory to people is inappropriate (as Milosz surely does), one might wonder what to make of its application to other creatures and entities. If the "rest" of nature is accurately described by science, then it is merely a realm of necessity, where things cannot be otherwise, and therefore is not subject to deliberation. If it has no moral dimension, then we have no responsibility toward it. The hegemony of scientific theory then dictates that we take only a theoretical, not any moral, interest in the rest of nature. And this also disturbs Milosz.

But Milosz tends to deal with this disturbing issue in too simple and dichotomous a fashion. He often argues as if our only choices are to construe nature as a machine with the scientists or to construe it in magical, anthropomorphic fashion as did the peasants of his native Lithuania. In a poem "To Robinson Jeffers," protesting Jeffers' portrayal of nature as "an inhuman thing," he concludes: "Better to carve suns and moons on the joints of crosses / as was done in my district. To birches and firs / give feminine names." Neither alternative satisfies him.

Milosz (and all lovers of poetry and nature) would do well to recall that nature, science, mechanism, and even necessity are themselves essentially contested concepts. The testimony of science is more complex than he allows, and besides, it is not the only source of reliable testimony. First of all, science is not a single theory, but a patchwork of heterogeneous domains, each with its own characteristic items, problems, methods, and theoretical components. The objects of some parts of science (say, physics and mathematics) indeed behave predictably, as if they could not be otherwise, and an important part of our cultural coming of age was to recognize clearly how these levels of existence do not act like people. But all the objects of biology (and biology itself is an internally heterogeneous collection of domains) have a cognitive as well as a causal dimension. Sentient, self-reproducing organisms are already, in a rudimentary way, expressive and social. Words like information, communication, error, and correction are as central to the vocabulary of biology as are molecule and cell.

Piffle, scoffs the reductionist; these structures are all "really" described by chemistry. The reductionist, however, has failed to deliberate properly, by not meshing global pronouncements with attention to cases. Those who study the history of science, the actual practice of scientists came to regard "reduction" as a plurality of special strategies for relating the results and methods of various sciences. The description of, for example, genetic phenotypes in terms of biochemical processes is one such (highly successful) strategy. But in fact and in principle no one-to-one correspondence exists between the descriptive terms of macroscopic genetics and the chemistry of DNA and RNA; the items and problems of the more highly organized domain do not collapse into that of the simpler one. Two distinct sciences remain, with a new pathway between them.

Science enters into moral deliberation on two levels. (So there is no good reason why we do not write more poems about science.) First, even if the objects of scientific study are plausibly described as subject to necessary laws, the practice of science is a human activity which always requires deliberation (by both scientists and laity). The debate about the meaning of "reduction" is a good example of this. Second, the heterogeneous plurality of the sciences testifies to the variety of natural kinds; the more highly organized of these exhibit genuine intentionality, which already springs the trap of the classical conception of cause and effect. Thus at least part of nonhuman nature shares with us sentience, choice, expressiveness. We may debate about how extensive this part is and how morally compelling we find this mutuality, but even science does not preclude some fellow-feeling with the rest of nature.

Finally, science is not the only source of evidence relevant to the latter debate. Scientific knowledge does not exhaust our experience of nature, even if we want to disallow some aspects of the peasant or tribal worldview. The subordination of the theoretical interests of the sciences to the practical interest of deliberation gives priority to our ethical and aesthetic understanding of the world. A great deal of social reality escapes the nets of science; and we have no reason (either moral or scientific) to deny the sociability of other creatures. The sad irony of the second part of Milosz's "Three Talks on Civilization" admits as much:

> Yes, it is true that the landscape changed a little.
> Where there were forests, now there are pears of factories,
>   gas tanks.
> Approaching the mouth of the river we hold our noses.
> Its current carries oil and chlorine and methyl compounds,
> Not to mention the by-products of the Books of
>   Abstraction:
> Excrement, urine, and dead sperm.
> A huge stain of artificial color poisons fish in the sea.
> Where the shore of the bay was overgrown with rushes
> Now it is rusted with smashed machines, ashes and bricks.
> We used to read in old poems about the scent of earth
> And grasshoppers. Now we bypass the fields.
> Ride as fast as you can through the chemical zone of the
>   farmers.
> The insect and the bird are extinguished. Far away a bored
>   man
> Drags the dust with his tractor, an umbrella against the
>   sun.
> What do we regret?—I ask. A tiger? A shark?

> *We created a second nature in the image of the first*
> *So as not to believe we live in Paradise.*
> *It is possible that when Adam woke in the garden*
> *The beasts licked the air and yawned, friendly.*
> *While their fangs and their tails, lashing their backs,*
> *Were figurative and the red-backed shrike,*
> *Later, much later, named* Lanius collurio,
> *Did not impale caterpillars on spikes of the black thorn.*
> *However, other than that moment, what we know of nature*
> *Does not speak in its favor. Ours is no worse.*
> *So I beg you, no more of these lamentations.*

The only real way to reduce (in the Comtean sense) a biological entity to chemistry is to kill it. If we do this enough, we will kill all our delights and then ourselves. Yet Milosz is not simply making a point here about the environment; he also reminds us, in the last six lines, of the amorality and inhumanity of nature. The shrike impaling its living food on a thorn recalls another strain in the conversation: our membership in nature brings with it not only gratification but also pain and death.

The topic of science frequently prompts Milosz to discuss the metaphysics of Simone Weil, as it does at the end of "The Lesson of Biology." He regards her as a thinker who "could cope with great reduction, but who at the same time would offer a new opening and a new hope." Weil extended determinism to all the phenomena of this world, including the psychological. This world was then the domain of the Prince of Darkness, evil when it diverts us from the good, evil because the good is wholly absent from it. Our plight does not however impugn the goodness of God, but rather proves it: He withdrew from his creation out of love for his creatures, to make way for them. Weil called reality the veil of God.

Weil's ethic is wholly colored by her repugnance to corporeal existence; our only hope of salvation is renunciation. All gratification is destruction; we must refuse to eat the objects of our desire, loving not them, but our hunger. If we can keep ourselves empty, grace may enter, but that is God's free gift and has nothing to do with us. Indeed our only hope is to disappear into him, paradoxically to be eaten by God. Thus Weil, like that other paradoxicalist. Shestov, so admired by Milosz, ultimately fails to preserve the integrity of the self. My objection to Weil, which could be lodged against her master Plato (or at least a certain brand of Platonism), is that she wholly subordinates gratification, gratification relevant to particular embodied human beings, to renunciation, and fails to connect the good with the everyday. Specifically, she grants no positive role to the messy, pedestrian business of moral deliberation, which gets us from one day, one task to another, and which, not inessentially, requires that we delay some gratifications in the interest of identifying and enacting others.

Though his interest in Weil is so strong that he translated her *Selected Works* into Polish, Milosz does admit that her neoplatonic intellectuality was too much for "a romantic nature lover who in the Ponary Mountains collected specimens for a herbarium and who hunted with Jozef Maruszenski on the outskirts of the Rudnicki Wilderness," who could not, in short, renounce the pleasures of hunting, eating, descriptive science, friendship, or the peculiar claims of a locale. Yet on some level he retains, like Weil, a mistrust of the body and of discourse; and so he often fails to oppose her more extreme opinions, without quite going to extremes himself. At the end of "The Lesson of Biology," he quotes uncritically her castigation of the surrealists, who, she felt, "expressed the frenzy of total license, the frenzy which takes hold of the mind when, rejecting all considerations of value, it plunges into the immediate." Weil is of course blind to the virtue of the surrealists, which was their appreciation of the sensual imperfect abundance of experience. And she reproaches them for not having values; on her terms, they could not have values, for they were searching for them in the wrong place (this world). On the contrary, their failure was a lack of eloquence. The myth of automatic writing left their work gnomic, private, and opaque; they failed to clarify and thus make effective their values for themselves or anyone else.

Neither science nor religion can furnish values a priori, which can then be applied automatically and without ambiguity to all cases. The pretense that such values exist leads to a dangerous silencing of deliberation. Values are essentially contestable. But we need not therefore despair that "the frenzy of total license" will ensue. For we always deliberate and write poems under severe constraints. We begin with a situation which is both universal and concrete, both local and typical, and resolve to take some action in fulfillment of certain principles. Our locality presents us with specific problems and gratifications and limits our perspective, beliefs, tastes, means, and sphere of action. Universal principles are limited by the requirements of deliberation itself; we cannot choose principles which entail silence. (This meta-principle is itself subject to deliberation; yet however it is locally determined, it constrains.) The process of deliberation is the construction of an imperfect, orderly social reality, governed by a flexible but still determinate system of rules. Deliberation is constrained because we must come to conclusions and act; poetry is constrained because it must be relevant to moral deliberation. Indeed, the worst kind of chaos (like that which Milosz suffered and exorcised) results in the wake of attempts to impose one rigid construal of values, allowing one voice in the conversation to drown out all the rest.

III

Obviously, writing a poem is not the same kind of contribution to the human conversation as taking part in a school board meeting, a strategy session of the Opposition, a judicial process. Like Milosz, I want to say that poetry has a role to play in our moral improvement, and I share his hope that such improvement is possible. But in my concern to exhibit the moral function of poetry, and to segregate and chasten *theoria*, I have risked assimilating *poesis* too strongly to *praxis*. Poems, as art, are distinguished from practical deliberation by their freedom and form.

A poem need not refer to an actual situation or propose a specific course of action. It may contain such reference, and it will always be grounded in the poet's locale and the concerns which arise there, but a poet is free to construct exotic and historical situations, utopias, and antiworlds. Part of moral education is the cultivating of moral imagination, learning to think through how principles might bear on lives and dilemmas different from our own. Fictional cases enrich and round out our fund of experience, rendering it more systematic and cosmopolitan. Of course, it is also in part the poet's responsibility to make these exotic constructions accessible, to exhibit their analogy with the experience of a possible audience. To this end he may use specific strategies, like Homer's use of the simile to relate the heroic world to the domestic, agrarian world of his audience, or rely on the universality of the principles embodied in the story. The reader too is responsible for applying his cosmopolitan, historical, and systematic critical abilities to the poem, in order to bring it close to the sphere of his own experience.

The freedom of poetry is thus always useful, but its usefulness takes on a special poignancy in times of trouble, when silence rules. People caught up in social catastrophe (anarchy or a too-rigid order) have reason to recoil from their circumstances; a good poem offers an alternative reality, critical insofar as its analogies and disanalogies with the present are clear, hopeful insofar as it presents a reality which is plausibly human. When circumstances are so cruel that one hardly knows how to begin to deliberate about them, poetry may offer an interim means of expression. Poems are repeated by the solitary prisoner to affirm the conversation now lapsed, the gratifying world now in abeyance. Poems are often told about the silenced, so that they won't be forgotten, nor the moral significance of their lives left out of the conversation. And the defensively self-righteous, shamed, and frightened aggressor may also sometimes be haunted by poems persuading him to listen. Poetry does not replace practical deliberation, but may instigate, deepen, and protect it.

A good poem must also have enough formal integrity to make it worthy of being repeated and memorized. Part of a poet's education is technical; he or she must listen to the classics and do enough five-finger exercises to master the rhythmic and phonic resources of the language and tradition. In this respect, poetry, like music and painting, does have its experts. And such expertise is somewhat independent of moral sense. But even this area of mastery shades imperceptibly into moral terrain. What counts as euphony cannot be disentangled from clarity. For example, Strunk and White teach that passive constructions most often constitute bad style in English; they "sound" awkward. At the same time they obfuscate by masking attributions of agency, an unclarity with direct moral bearing. Moreover, prudential wisdom must be eloquent to be effective; eloquence is persuasive. And part (but not all) of eloquence is an attention to form: balanced periods, colorful figures, symmetry of argument and counterargument.

A poem is compelling and preserved because it is beautiful. The aesthetic appeal of a poem itself has a moral dimension, allying it to an ethic of gratification. Reading a poem should provide the joys of aesthetic satisfaction. It should refine our ability to hear and see, our delight in a particular language, in the sensual presence of life in a particular locale. And thus it persuades us of the pleasures and intrinsic value of this world. This point is worth emphasizing, since I have been focusing so much on the critical, mourning, and forgiving functions of poetry. But a poetics in which they are foremost would be morbid; rather, these functions are justified and motivated by our sense of the goodness of existence. If we are not persuaded of the goodness of existence, there is no hope in whose service we can responsibly act; there is no point in living, or talking, or writing poems. Eloquence can be abused, but the cure for that abuse is not silence and deformity but more eloquence and more beauty.

In Chapter 4 ("A Quarrel With Classicism") of *The Witness of Poetry,* Milosz worries that the freedom and formality of poetry impede its ability to testify to the real. He cites Erich Auerbach as pointing to a certain lack of reality wherever a convention is used: "where the poet creates as beautiful a structure as possible out of topoi universally known and fixed, instead of trying to name what is real and yet unnamed." And he further remarks: "The world exists objectively, despite the shapes in which it appears in the mind. . . . That objective world can be seen as it is; yet we may surmise that it can be seen with perfect impartiality only by God. Intent on representing it, the poet is left with the bitter realization of the inadequacy of language."

On the contrary, language, concepts, conventions, topoi, et cetera, reveal reality. They describe the parts of reality "which could not be otherwise" (though they reduce its complexity), and they construct social reality, the issues we deliberate about (though they can be criticized and revised). Milosz's "bitter realization" is due in part to his misology and in part to his detour into an epistemological blind alley. This blind alley, which has trapped some but been avoided by most Western philosophers, is the supposition that ideas are the immediate objects of experience, proxy-objects which stand *between* us and things. The best way to avoid this error is to recall that all our interaction with the world is cognitive; to have an idea about something is to understand it. We do encounter the world directly, and our access to it is by means of ideation. Where else could we live but in the world, and how else could we experience it except through consciousness? This epistemological stance excludes divine intuition and causal interaction as models for the way we know.

For most utilitarian purposes, we can describe medium-sized dry goods, rocks, and top hats, in fairly exact and unambiguous terms; other people understand the descriptions right away and we don't need to deliberate about them. (I am here bracketing certain difficult issues raised by scientific description of physical phenomena not directly accessible to the senses.) In such cases, the naive notion of mimesis seems plausible; language accurately represents reality. Milosz sometimes argues as if all a poet need do in pursuit of the real is to describe more medium-sized dry goods, in more detail; this picture accords with his nominalism in an odd way. Thus he characterizes the poet's confrontation with the real as "that elementary contact, verifiable by the five senses, [which] is more important than any mental construction. The never-fulfilled desire to achieve a mimesis, to be faithful to a detail, makes for the health of poetry." But then why should we complain about the inadequacies of mimesis? Milosz's complaint arises when he shifts examples in midstream without admitting what he is doing. He shifts from things to events of great moral complexity, and then rightly observes that mimesis, simple and complete description, cannot capture the ambiguous reality. Instead of blaming the intervention of the "veil of ideas," he should see that deliberation, the construction of social reality, and not mimesis is the relevant poetic activity. The demands of realism and the employment of conventions, ordered forms, are not incompatible.

Consider the poem "No More" which he quotes in the course of this chapter:

> *I should relate sometime how I changed*
> *My views on poetry, and how it came to be*
> *That I consider myself today one of the many*
> *Merchants and artisans of old Japan,*
> *Who arranged verses about cherry blossoms,*
> *Chrysanthemums and the full moon.*

If only I could describe the courtesans of Venice
As in a loggia they teased a peacock with a twig,
And out of brocade, the pearls of their belt,
Set free heavy breast and the reddish weal
Where the buttoned dress marked the belly,
As vividly as seen by the skipper of galleons
Who landed that morning with a cargo of gold;
And if I could find for their miserable bones
In a graveyard whose gates are locked by greasy water
A word more enduring than their last-used comb
That in the rot under tombstones, alone, awaits the light,

Then I wouldn't doubt. Out of reluctant matter
What can be gathered? Nothing, beauty at best.
And so, cherry blossoms must suffice for us
And chrysanthemums and the full moon.

The erotic metaphor is centrally important here. It depends on the old convention that women and matter form a metaphoric unity and stand in opposition to man-spirit. Milosz has chosen not only women but prostitutes, especially prone to reduction to the flesh. This convention allows him to employ the sleight-of-hand which I have just noted in an especially elegant way. He suggests that the woman-thing can be plausibly mimed and then, recalling that she is a person in a moral context of great complexity, announces that mimesis must fail to capture her reality. Thus the poet must rest content with mere convention.

If this poem were only an epistemological mistake, it would not compel our attention as it does. For we can see that the poem engages reality despite the disclaimer, and its success is not merely the accurate recording of detail. What I find so attractive about the poem is the richness of nuance in the poet's depiction of the courtesans and of his relation to them. Milosz initially presents them as languid beauties, trafficking in pleasure. The entrance of the skipper of galleons reveals them as both agents and commodities in an economic transaction and also, where the red weal marks a belly like a little wound, women who must make their privacies public. Their vulnerability results from the special risks of their trade (disease, sterility, death; the stigma of sin) and the general burden of mortality. In their final appearance, they are literally reduced to a collection of bones, mixed up with a comb that alone commemorates vanished beauty. Like Carpaccio, to whose painting the poem makes reference, Milosz balances the demands of aesthetic paganism and Catholic asceticism; he mourns and celebrates these women who, like him, endure their mortality even as they (paradoxically) await the light. The tense, erotic sympathy which exists between artist and human subject applies as well to Carpaccio and his original models and, no doubt, to the artisans of Old Japan who commented on human affairs when they used the convention of flower and moon.

Evidently, I resist the convention which structures this poem and for so long has consigned women to passivity, impurity and self-enclosure. I am disturbed by the unconscious ease with which Milosz deploys the convention, even though in the end he manages to undermine and complicate its usual import. Having once reduced the courtesans to matter, he then reanimates matter, making it reluctant, resistant to amorous possession by the word. I might conclude that a better way to think about the relation between enspirited matter and the word is not rape but marriage.

In this summary comment, I have tried to show how the conventions in Milosz's poem contribute to the conversation in which we are all engaged. Speaking out of his local concerns as a poet and his cosmopolitan acquaintance with history, painting, and religion, he uses conventions authoritatively to construct and reveal moral realities. These conventions are always subject to further evaluation and revision. His poem constrains and illuminates, but does not dictate, the reader's appropriation of it as part of a moral education. Entering into a painting by Carpaccio, or a poem by Milosz, reveals that moral education is not just an undertaking of great seriousness; it is also an opportunity for affirmation and delight.[1]

NOTES

1. I would like to acknowledge my debt in this paper to essays by Eugene Garver and Joseph Schwab on practical reason, by Judith Van Herik on Weil and by Yves Bonnefoy on Shestov.

"POSTMODERNISM":
SIGN FOR A STRUGGLE, THE STRUGGLE
FOR THE SIGN

RON SILLIMAN

Asked about "the vagaries of a term such as 'post-modern,'" the late Roman Jakobson responded, "I try not to use even Modernism, because what is Modernism, it depends on who writes it and at what moment."[1] This exchange is emblematic of an environment that presently confronts these concepts, which may or may not be opposites but which are both confused and confusing. Jakobson's answer suggests literally a fusion *with:* to invoke postmodernism is already to possess an idea not merely of the modern but of moder*nism* as well. More than just a series of states, postmodernism suggests a largely realized cultural analysis, historically placed. Yet *postmodernism*'s a term that has only lately begun to acquire, as if through sheer repetition, something approximating an intelligible body of meanings. Far from providing ground for consensus, these are points of contention in an increasingly visible academic debate. What is being contested is control over a discourse whose task it is to conceptually (and politically) integrate the arts of our time into society. As such, the debate over postmodernism stands over every artist (including every poet) both as opportunity and threat: at stake is the framework through which our activity and its products will be received, "understood," and, most of all, explained.

While the adjective appeared at least as early as the title of Joseph Hudnut's 1949 "The Post-Modern House,"[2] it did not begin to evolve toward the status of a category until used a decade later by literary critics Harry Levin and Irving Howe, each bemoaning an entropy they felt had fallen over modernism proper.[3] The term *modern* itself hardly represented a clearly defined phenomenon, having only during the previous twenty years evolved from a general characterization of anything written or produced since the dawn of the industrial revolution to something more specific: a version of aesthetic history that identified its origins in the Europe of the 1850s (for example, Baudelaire), arriving in English with Pound and Joyce.[4] As the depiction of a broad program, modernism, as understood thirty years ago, was vast and internally contradictory, containing everything from the Catholic symbolism of T. S. Eliot to the Yankee nominalism of William Carlos Williams. The term itself was never a name adopted or espoused by any literary or art movement[5] but was, rather, imposed (somewhat retroactively) upon them all, borrowed from American art criticism, particularly through the writings of Clement Greenberg. Thus Lawrence Alloway writes: "In America the term *Modernism*, at least in the visual arts, has been largely pre-empted by Clement Greenberg to refer to a particular kind of painting,"[6] a position echoed by Donald Kuspit: "*Modernism* . . . most of all . . . has been identified with Clement Greenberg's idea of Modernism, which is essentially that the work of art is a self-referential object which is in a self-critical relation to itself, particularly to its medium."[7]

The idea of the modern, a much broader category, has been traced by Hans Robert Jauss to the late fifth century, where it "was used for the first time . . . in order to distinguish the present, which had become officially Christian, from the Roman and pagan past."[8] From then on, the concept reappears whenever an epoch has sensed the need to articulate its difference from the period immediately preceding. According to Jürgen Habermas, there is a decisive shift in this lineage of recurrences during the French Enlightenment. All previous instances had conceived themselves as *reestablishing a broken connection* to the supposedly universal and timeless truths of classical antiquity—back to the basics—while this new version cast itself in the paradigm of science, a linear model of progress without limit. In this view, that modernism which was initiated by Baudelaire is characterized most prominently by its sense of time and of time's relation to society. "Make it new" thus meant "make it better." This attitude was codified by Harold Rosenberg, the most influential of Greenberg's peers, who called his first substantial collection *The Tradition of the New*. The dominance of linear progression is perceptible throughout Greenberg's career, for example in this sentence composed thirty-two years after the death of Cézanne: "Cézanne's art may no longer be the overflowing source of modernity it was thirty years back, but it endures in its newness and in what can even be called its stylishness."[9] Even as modernity and newness are given as values, Cézanne's painting is subsumed, its worth both determined and limited, by the greater clock of aesthetic time.

Interestingly, the term *modernism* does not appear in Greenberg's 1939 aesthetic credo "Avant-Garde and Kitsch."[10] The project here is not unlike that of Walter Benjamin's essay "The Work of Art in the Age of Mechanical Representation"—to account, socially, for changes within the arts that had become evident when the specter of Hitler was manifest and a new European war in the offing. Benjamin and Greenberg, both Jews of German descent, were also Marxists radically at odds with Stalinism. "Avant-Garde and Kitsch" is presented as a Trotskyist perspective, with Trotsky's own 1924 *Literature and Revolution* serving as source and inspiration. Like Trotsky, Greenberg takes two elements of bourgeois life, education and leisure time, as the necessary prerequisites of all culture. The promise of communism lay not merely in its democratization of the economic benefits of the industrial revolution but also in the universalization of literacy and learning, in the full and free development of the post-bourgeois individual.

Benjamin and Greenberg concur that, in Trotsky's words, "Every ruling class creates its own culture, and consequently, its own art."[11] A major result, therefore, of the transformation from feudalism to capitalism lay in its transfer of cultural hegemony from a minuscule aristocracy to a much broader, although still small, bourgeoisie. One might say that, according to this view, the spread of learning under capitalism was achieved less by an increase in the total quantity of education, not to mention knowledge, available to society as a whole, than by a parceling out of ever smaller amounts to a wider range of subjects.

While many of Greenberg's assumptions in "Avant-Garde and Kitsch" approximate Benjamin's, his ultimate motive is different. Benjamin's concern for the relations of production and consumption cause him to focus closely on technological innovations that might alter the structure and consequences of such dynamics, so much so that some have accused him of a McLuhanist technocratic determinism. Like Trotsky, Greenberg, however, proceeds not just from the concrete evidence of existing works of art but also with an already intact analysis of society in which, for each class, the relationship between economic base and cultural superstructure stands as a given:

> There has always been on one side the minority of the powerful—and therefore the cultivated—and on the other the great mass of the exploited and poor— and therefore the ignorant. Formal culture has always belonged to the first, while the last have had to content themselves with folk or rudimentary culture, or kitsch.[12]

Both Trotsky and Greenberg are committed to the belief that the first portion of the twentieth century is the "last phase for our own culture," capitalism. Where Greenberg differs from the Russian revolutionary, however, is in his lack of confidence that this last imperialist epoch is about to be replaced by any higher, or better, stage of human development. If "kitsch has in the last ten years become the dominant culture in Soviet Russia," and the sole other alternative to capitalism is Hitler, the prospects for "formal culture" are bleak indeed. Trapped between these two dead-end streets the rise of Tin Pan Alley,[13] the paintings of Maxfield Parrish, and the verse of, as Greenberg calls him, Eddie Guest represent the clear and present danger within the West that art itself might soon suffer the fate facing the Jews, gypsies, homosexuals, and communists of Europe:

> Capitalism in decline finds that whatever of quality it is still capable of producing becomes almost invariably a threat to its own existence. Advances in culture, no less than advances in science and industry, corrode the very society under whose aegis they are made possible. Here, as in every other question today, it becomes necessary to quote Marx word for word. Today we no longer look toward socialism for a new culture. . . . Today we look to socialism *simply* for preservation of whatever living culture we have right now. (21)

Greenberg associates culture with those two aspects of political and economic privilege that render, in his view, the ruling elite the class of cultivation: education and leisure time. Education differs from training in that it is not instrumental or, as contemporary educators might phrase it, vocationally relevant. Likewise, leisure time differs from any other because it is also noninstrumental. Each is a dimension of human life that, if and whenever it can be separated out from the purposefulness of daily existence, raised to no other goal than the psychic satisfaction of the individual, might then create the grounds for a consensus of human values that could transcend class, gender, ethnicity, history, etc. For it is the instrumentalization of such necessities that fragments society into competing and hostile sectors. *If* the concept of transcendent values is anything other than an idealization, and *if,* by being the sector of society whose daily needs are least subject to instrumentalization per se—two very big ifs—then bourgeois *culture* would necessarily be the least distorted, even if it is the bourgeois economic program that directs this very process of regimentation and alienation, deciding which aspects of life are to be incorporated into it, and how. These are assumptions that underlie Greenberg's assertion that

> all values are human values, relative values, in art as well as elsewhere. Yet there does seem to have been more or less of a general agreement among the culti-vated of mankind over the ages as to what is good art and what bad. Taste has varied, but not beyond certain limits. . . . There has been an agreement then, and this agreement rests, I believe, on a fairly constant distinction made be-tween those values only to be found in art and the values which can be found elsewhere. Kitsch, by virtue of a rationalized technique that draws on science and industry, has erased this distinction in practice. (13)

When we examine his historical presentation of the development of these transcendent values, we find that they rest upon a conception of progress that models itself after scientific method. The crisis that provokes his formulation of modernism is nothing less than the problem of instrumentalization turning upon its masters. Implicit is the fear that human values might not be transcendent after all.

As the title suggests, "Avant-Garde and Kitsch" articulates a bifurcated vision of the aesthetic domain.[14] Deprived of real artistic values, the masses must, in Green-berg's words, "content themselves" with ersatz imitation, "folk culture." Even now, Greenberg is remembered as the American propagandist for the avant-garde in paint-ing, and as the theoretician of the historic role of abstraction. Just as his praise for Cézanne subsumed the French painter into a larger historical structure, so, as late as 1958, Greenberg is capable of blaming—the word is his own—Hans Hoffman for a failure to *go beyond* "Late Cubism":

> Hoffman's overriding weakness . . . lies in . . . the endeavor to achieve, it would seem, an old-fashioned synthesis. . . . But that part of the "new" American painting which is not Late Cubist distinguishes itself further by its freedom from the quasi-geometrical truing and fairing of lines and edges which the Cubist frame imposes. This freedom belongs with Hoffman's open surfaces as it does not with de Kooning's or Kline's, and his hesitancy in fully availing himself of this freedom—despite the fact that he himself had such a large hand in winning it—must be attributed to his reluctance to cut himself off from Cub-ism as a base of operations.[15]

The privilege that Greenberg affords to abstraction is inseparable from the sense of temporality he views as an inherent element in art itself, different facets of a single logic. The rise of "avant-garde" culture in the nineteenth century represents a recog-nition by one sector of the bourgeoisie that its then hegemonic values were, in fact, not universal but simply the consequence of history, and of a particularly corrupt and transitory phase at that:

> Hence it developed that the true and most important function of the avant-garde was not to "experiment," but to find a path along which it would be pos-

sible to keep culture *moving* in the midst of ideological confusion and violence. . . . The avant-garde poet or artist sought to maintain the high level of
his [*sic*] art by both narrowing and raising it to the expression of an absolute
in which all relativities and contradictions would either be resolved or beside
the point. (5)

What Greenberg does not explicate is why culture inherently *must* move. The answer
of course is progress. Prior to the French Revolution, painters were forced economically to subsume the aesthetic concerns of their work beneath portraits of the aristocracy and its privileged landscapes. Severed from this elite by history—Greenberg calls
it "the first bold development of scientific revolutionary thought"—and comprehend-
ing the limits of the new capitalist class, painters and other artists were freed of any
political requirement for the representation of surfaces, just as, in science, the development of micro-, stetho-, and telescopes had freed the individual researcher of the
perceptual constraints of her or his own senses. Yearning for the rigor of the empirical,
aesthetics is viewed as tending always toward an ideal of complete knowledge, a goal
that is inexorably approached (if never to be arrived at) through the mechanisms
developed by a freed discipline. The analogy to "pure poetry" is thus "pure science."

It has been in search of the absolute that the avant-garde has arrived at "abstract" or "nonobjective" art—and poetry, too. The avant-garde poet or artist
tries in effect to imitate God by creating something valid solely in its own
terms, in the way nature itself is valid. . . . But the absolute is absolute, and
the poet or artist, being what he is, cherishes certain relative values more than
others. The very values in the name of which he invokes the absolute are relative
values, the values of aesthetics. And so he turns out to be imitating, not God
. . . but the disciplines and process of art and literature themselves. This is the
genesis of the "abstract" (5–6).[16]

If one agrees, as it is clear Greenberg does, with the "decision" of poets and artists
not to align themselves with the bourgeoisie, it then follows that, in the scientific
search for aesthetic truth, what is of greater value is what is more abstract. Thus, to
the degree that Hoffman's paintings do not "free" themselves from the illusionistic
planes and framing that were the residue of an earlier cubism's own flight from representation, then to this degree his paintings are flawed.

But Greenberg's characterization of the modern is couched in a rhetoric that, following the distinction made by Habermas, is not modern *in the contemporary sense*.
Unlike the modernism of the French Enlightenment, but like earlier instances of it,
Greenberg's call "for the preservation of . . . living culture" is an attempt to reestablish a connection with values whose very existence has been threatened. The values
carried forward by modernism are endangered by the same instrumentalization of
culture that made their progress possible. Education and leisure time, embodiments
of "surplus value," are essential if the individual is, like the researcher using prosthetic
tools, to extend perception beyond what is superficially obvious to the untrained,
unreflexive eye.

One can, of course, delineate the ways in which this presumption that the ultimate
reality is invisible parallels concepts within Marxian dialectics, Darwinian evolution,

Freudian psychology, Saussurean linguistics, and contemporary physics, not to mention several religious doctrines. A more crucial recognition is that this doctrine of modernism itself was first articulated as a *classical* defense against what, if only Greenberg had had access to this word, he might have called postmodernism. *From its inception, the dominant model of cultural modernism is, both ontologically and epistemologically, dependent upon the postmodern.* Modernism, as we shall see, is but the moment in which the postmodern becomes visible.

Greenberg's doctrine spread pervasively across critical discourses in the United States and England. This permeation has been so complete and, within literary criticism, so unchallenged that when Cyrena Pondrom, in an article on "H. D. and the Origins of Imagism," uses *modern, modernism,* and *modernist,* singular and plural, twelve times in her first three paragraphs, the effect is hardly noticeable.[17]

Not surprisingly, Greenberg's dominance has been documented most fully by those by whom he has been most directly attacked, left critics of the visual arts.[18] These writers go after Greenberg principally through a historical and an economic critique of abstract expressionism, whose "overriding weakness" is identified as an inability or unwillingness to separate itself from its perceived audience and champions, the liberals of corporate capital, as in this passage from Serge Guilbaut's *How New York Stole the Idea of Modern Art:*

> Avant-garde art succeeded because the work and the ideology that supported it, articulated in the painters' writings as well as conveyed in images, coincided fairly closely with the ideology that came to dominate American political life after the 1948 presidential elections. This was the "new liberalism" set forth by Schlesinger in *The Vital Center,* an ideology that, unlike the ideologies of the conservative right and Communist left, not only made room for avant-garde dissidence but accorded to such dissidence a position of paramount importance.[19]

Thus Greenberg's 1939 Trotskyism is viewed as "the beginning of a piecemeal rejection of Marxism itself."[20]

The documentary evidence supplied by these critics is extensive, complete with such lurid episodes as secret State Department funding for overseas exhibitions of abstract expressionism by the Museum of Modern Art.[21] What is less sharply defined, however, is the aesthetic (and political) stance in whose name this critique is being made. The "working class" is far too broad a category into which to dissolve the diverse ethnic, gender, cultural, class, linguistic, religious, and regional experiences of multilayered societies. At its worst, the neopopulism inherent in Eva Cockroft, Serge Guilbaut, Carol Duncan, and others, advocates a renewed instrumentalism in which images are conceived as symbols, coded and subsumed by a narrowly political version of an imagined *pueblo unido* that is no less a homogenizing construct than is its opposite.

The issue of autonomy is important in the debate over postmodernism. Writing out of a framework that owes more to Adorno than to Greenberg, German critic Peter Bürger makes a sharp division between modernists and the avant-garde based on their different attitudes on the integrity, self-sufficiency, and/or object status of the individual work of art. Modernism is defined as that art which arose during the capitalist epoch, in which daily life was being increasingly absorbed into the rationalized strata of a hierarchic logic whose overrriding goal was to maximize profit. Art's social function was to be the realm into which whatever might exist only in and for itself could then retreat. When no thing nor any person could be said to retain autonomy, writers and artists began to speak of "art for art's sake" and "the self-valuable word." This, for both Adorno and Marcuse, is the kernel of art's utopian potential. The avant-garde, by which Bürger means the dadaists, surrealists, and, to some degree, the Russian futurists, recognized that art's autonomy was achieved precisely by means of its removal *as an institution* from everyday life, and thus at the cost of its social effectiveness. The aesthetic, that site for the abstract expressionists' search for the absolutes of form, is not possible until "art has wholly detached itself from everything that is the praxis of life."[22] Avant-garde activity is an attack not on art conventions but on art as an institution within society, upon which hinges its claim to autonomy. Duchamp's display of a urinal signed "R. Mutt" in a museum points not only to the social context of a sacramental high-art framing for this most profane of ready-mades but also to the importance of the signature in any work's assertion of uniqueness and value.

Bürger's thesis would seem to displace, if not negate, Greenberg's argument for abstraction as a critical impulse. Failing to address the situation of art as an institution, rather than as a process, Pollock and company never "sold out" only because they were never in any position to sell. Their incorporation as evidence into corporate liberalism's campaign for the American way during the 1950s represented neither a reversal nor an abduction; it was in fact implicit in their practice from the start. Their fetishization of autonomy is manifestly evident in the romantic and heroic individualism that characterizes so many of their large canvases.

There are numerous problems with Bürger's theory, not the least of which is the primary role assigned to the avant-garde's assault on art as an institution. Yet, when contrasted with the neo-instrumentalism proposed by Duncan and Cockroft, his depiction of the fate of the historical avant-garde movements is worth heeding:

> Once the signed bottle drier has been accepted as an object that deserves a place in a museum, the provocation no longer provokes; it turns into its opposite. If an artist today signs a stove pipe and exhibits it, that artist certainly does not denounce the art market but adapts to it. . . . Since now the protest of the historical avant-garde against art as an institution is accepted as *art,* the gesture of protest of the neo-avant-garde becomes inauthentic.[23]

If all context, and indeed all allusion, is necessarily social, as Bürger implies, the distinction between abstraction and any mode of representation lies not in the question of "Does the work refer?" but "To where?"

There is, in fact, a difference between a painting hanging in a women's clinic and the same object in a SoHo artist's bar or in the Museum of Modern Art. This is precisely its interaction with its social context, which may be more or less active depending on the work. Abstract expressionism denied the instrumentalism of materials and process, opening a vast terrain to exploration concerning the relations between color, mass, line, depth, and shape, issues which are at once both cognitive and social. Indeed, it was their general romanticism with regard to size and mass that made the abstract expressionists' work both attractive and vulnerable to corporate reinterpretation in the 1950s—not the lack of content but the presence of a specific one.[24]

The major impact of this critique of modernism has been the reaction it provoked from neoconservatives such as then *New York Times* art critic Hilton Kramer who, in a piece entitled "Muddled Marxism Replaces Criticism at *Artforum*" that called Carol Duncan a "Maoist," wrote: "It will be interesting to see how long the magazine's Bourgeois advertisers—mainly art dealers plying a trade the magazine now seems to regard as a crime against humanity—will support its new line."[25] Kramer extended his red-baiting into a reactionary defense of modernism per se when he founded *The New Criterion.* The unsigned manifesto that initiates the first issue echoes concerns of Greenberg's forty-three years earlier: "The very notion of an independent high culture and the distinctions that separate it from popular culture and commercial entertainment have been radically eroded."[26] Only now the origin of the problem is found elsewhere than in the rationalization of culture that appeared with the rise of capitalism:

> A very large part of the reason for this sad state of affairs is, frankly, political. We are still living in the aftermath of the insidious assault on mind that was one of the most repulsive features of the radical movement of the Sixties. The cultural consequences of this leftward turn in our political life have been far graver than is commonly supposed. In everything from the writing of textbooks to the reviewing of trade books, from the introduction of kitsch into the museums to the decline of literacy in the schools to the corruption of scholarly research, the effect on the life of culture has been ongoing and catastrophic.[27]

This state of affairs, "has condemned true seriousness to a fugitive existence," a theme that Kramer takes up again in the same issue in a piece entitled "Postmodern: Art and Culture in the 1980s": "What is primarily at stake is the concept of seriousness."[28] Kramer's analysis is a curious inversion of Bürger's. Making no distinction between modernism and avant-garde, he argues that the transformation of modernism from radical opposition to dominant cultural force undermined both it and the society into which it had been assimilated: "Something very odd happened to the culture of modernism while it was achieving its unexpected ascendancy over our institutions and our tastes. It was, so to speak, subverted from within. . . . It acquired a yearning for what had been destroyed" (37). Kramer shows no affection for premodernist "bourgeois art" and openly disdains such "postmodernists" as Andy Warhol, John Cage, John Ashbery, Donald Barthelme, and Philip Johnson. Yet he is aware that "Modernism was born, after all, in a spirit of criticism and revolt" (36). More than any individual artists or even principles of modernism, what Kramer laments is a loss of tension between oppositional works of art and "official culture," a clash in which it is the social prerogative of the critic to mediate:

> This pattern of challenge and assimilation was bound to alter the outlook of both parties. Each came to have a stake in the power and vitality of the other. . . . Bourgeois culture, for its part, acquired a finely developed sense of what could be absorbed and what deferred. For this process of selection and adjudication, it created special institutions—museums and exhibition societies, schools, publications, foundations, etc.—which functioned, in effect, as agencies of a licensed opposition. This was something new in the history of Western culture—bourgeois liberalism's most distinctive political contribution to the life of culture. (36–37)

The end of modernism is not the succession of action painting by Pop Art but the end of the myth of a homogenous audience in a neutral relation to absolute standards that must be articulated, mediated, and defended by the guardians of seriousness—in short, the end of the cultural dominance wielded by Greenberg. Kramer underscores his view of modernism as art governed by criticism when he identifies as a key perpetrator of the postmodern Susan Sontag's piece "Notes on 'Camp'":

> This important essay . . . severed the link between high culture and high seriousness that had been a fundamental tenet of the modernist ethos. It released high culture from its obligation to be entirely serious, to insist on difficult standards, to sustain an attitude of unassailable rectitude. It relaxed the tension that had always existed between the fierce moral imperatives of modernism—its critical conscience—and its appetite for novel aesthetic gratifications. "The whole point of Camp," Miss Sontag wrote, "is to dethrone the serious," thereby defining the special temper of postmodernist culture. (40)

This argument between left-populist and neoconservative polemics might have been relegated to a footnote in the history of art criticism were it not at just this point that Jürgen Habermas initiated a second, overlapping debate, covering similar territory with virtually parallel terminology. Like Kramer, Habermas' intent, presented in a paper with the combative title "Modernity Versus Postmodernity," was to separate these terms in order to resurrect the former. But Habermas' modernity is the inverse of Kramer's modernism.

Habermas' context is that of the Frankfurt School. Adorno's modernism rather than Greenberg's. Thus, modernity is more broadly conceived. The analysis proceeds

> by recalling an idea from Max Weber. He characterized cultural modernity as the separation of the substantive reason expressed in religion and metaphysics into three autonomous spheres. They are: science, morality and art. . . . Each domain of culture could be made to correspond to cultural professions in which problems could be dealt with as the concern of special experts. This professionalized treatment of the cultural tradition brings to the fore the intrinsic structures of each of the three dimensions of culture. . . . As a result, the distance grows between the culture of the experts and that of the larger public. . . . The threat increases that the life-world, whose traditional substance has already been devalued, will become more and more impoverished. . . . This splitting off is the problem that has given rise to efforts to "negate" the culture of expertise. But the problem won't go away.[29]

The description here differs from Greenberg's insofar as the separation out of the arts is not elevated to the level of a courageous decision. Specialization, the concentration of education and instrumentalized professions, is thus carried out at the cost of underdeveloping our daily lives in any area in which each of us is not an expert. Yet modernity is not simply equated with this process of underdevelopment. As Weber's three domains became autonomous, their relationship to society itself changed:

> By the time of Baudelaire . . . the utopia of reconciliation with society had gone sour. A relation of opposites had come into being; art had become a critical mirror, showing the irreconcilable nature of the aesthetic and the social

worlds. . . . Out of such emotional currents finally gathered those explosive energies which unloaded in the surrealist attempt to blow up the autarkical sphere of art and to force a reconciliation of art and life. (11)

Like Bürger, Habermas identifies surrealism's assault on the institutionality of art as its defining element, a position that fails to square with such evidence as the manifest object status of the typical text by Eluard or Breton, Man Ray's photography, or the paintings of Dali and Ernst.[30] Habermas views the attack on autonomy as a central moment *within* the program and history of modernism itself. The postmodern decline can be traced to the failure of attempts to eradicate the barriers between life and art.

In Habermas' eyes, such thwarted reconciliations serve to reinforce the separation of domains. For example, barely a dozen years after Robert Smithson's death, his earth-works, far from dissolving aesthetics into nature, appear as instances of a monumental formalism. Conceptual art, whose strategies of dematerialization attempted to liberate visual aesthetics from the iron grip of the gallery system, demonstrated instead that materiality was the art object's primary bridge to the nonart world, resulting in the ironic production of marketable documentation.

For Habermas, the failure of the surrealist revolt is the consequence of two "mistakes." First, in attempting to dissolve boundaries, it eliminated the very categories through which its assault was manifested; so that its "contents" were "dispersed."[31] The surrealists' second error lay in not considering the broader scope of modernity, leading to a sort of Stalinoid aestheticism that proposes "socialism in one cultural domain" and attempts to reunite art with life without addressing science and morality.

Following Habermas' logic, it would seem that virtually any project such as the political modernism posed in 1939 by Greenberg would be vulnerable, some forty years hence, to the type of critical reversal suggested by the neopopulists *and*, sadder still, to a defense such as that provided by Kramer. In order to avoid this trap, modernity itself needs to comprehend that "the reception of art is only one of at least three aspects. The project aims at a differentiated relinking of modern culture with an everyday praxis. . . . The chances for this today are not very good" (13). Missing is the mechanism through which this relinking could occur: "Communication processes need a cultural tradition covering all spheres" (11). Were it even remotely possible, such an ideal process would require the universalization of both education and leisure time.

Habermas concludes this gloomy analysis by distinguishing between three varieties of modernism's enemies, "the *anti*modernism of the 'young conservatives' . . . the *pre*modernism of the 'old conservatives' and the *post*modernism of the neoconservatives" (14). The category of premodernism, the "old" conservative line, common enough in recent Anglo-American poetry, stems from a rejection of the same fragmentation of knowledge that Habermas's modernity would seek to reunite. If the premodernist utopia lies in the past, like the eternalized Victorian epoch of a Richard Howard dramatic monologue, it nonetheless parallels Habermas' ideal future.

The "young" conservatives are even more problematic because the names cited are not universally conceded to be examples of reaction: Foucault, Derrida, Bataille—poststructuralists who, according to Habermas, appropriate the segmenting drive of modernity ahistorically, finding within the autonomy of cultural spheres a "decentered subjectivity" that allows them, on "the basis of modernistic attitudes," to "justify an irreconcilable antimodernism" (14).

The "neoconservatives" are postmodern precisely because they do welcome modernity's benefits: "technological progress, capitalistic growth and rational administration. [However,] they recommend a politics of defusing the explosive content of cultural modernity. . . . What remains . . . is only what we would have if we were to give up the project of modernity altogether" (14). While Habermas cites Daniel Bell and Wittgenstein's *Tractatus* as instances of this postmodernism, the diagnosis certainly fits Hilton Kramer. Thus Kramer, the self-announced defender of modernism, is, by this paradigm, a *post*modernist. Habermas warns that the real danger facing modernity today, flawed and incomplete though it may be, lies in the potential for alliance between the old conservatives of premodernism with the neoconservatives of postmodernism, a coalition that can be found in *The New Criterion.*

Habermas offers as another example the inclusion of architecture in the 1980 Venice Biennale: "Those who exhibited . . . formed an avant-garde of reversed fronts. . . . They sacrificed the tradition of modernity in order to make room for a new historicism" (3). Architecture has supplied the greatest definition to date of postmodernism, an actual body of work that has more or less adopted the name. Its most complete presentation has been in *The Language of Post-Modern Architecture* by Charles Jencks, a member of Paolo Portoghesi's committee which organized the Biennale. There are numerous features to architectural postmodernism, of which historicism is merely one. Equally important are a preference for eclecticism over simplicity and uniformity, a conception of architectural language that is symbolic rather than functional or formal, and, often, a sense of wit or irony that stands out in sharp contrast to the glass-curtain highrises that typify the modernist high seriousness of the International Style. One type of postmodern architecture would be an urban renewal program in which new homes are built to match existing brick row houses, rather than to maximize land use or take advantage of recently developed methods of construction. Another would be a strategy used to counter the restrictions imposed on new construction by historical designation status of older buildings in central cities, where a nineteenth- or early twentieth-century façade is retained as a "cornerstone" or "base" to an otherwise late-modern glass-wall highrise. A third example, popularized as a model of democratic architecture by Robert Venturi and his partners, is the Las Vegas strip. A fourth would be the highrise or public building that utilizes the features of the International Style in an ironized fashion. Then there are the grandiose projects, such as the Sydney Opera House in Australia or Eero Saarinen's TWA terminal in New York, calculated to attract attention and provoke comment.

Postmodern architecture is thus many things, primarily (and loosely) united by a rejection of the functional formalism of Mies van der Rohe and company. Yet a commitment to formal progress was only half of Greenberg's definition of modernism, the other being an essential autonomy. Both by its utilitarian social requirement to provide shelter for residential, industrial, commercial, public, and other uses, and by its inescapable relation to capital, architecture is *the* nonautonomous aesthetic discipline.

Nowhere is this more evident than in Venturi's paradise, Las Vegas. Here we find that, contrary to postmodern theory, social function does indeed dictate architectural form, once we acknowledge that the determining activity is the circulation not of humans but of capital, a process raised suspiciously close to an autonomous meta-level through the trope of gaming. It is not that the "decorated sheds" of the large casinos disavow symbolism but that their use of it is intended to occlude the individual's experience of surrendering money in the search for wealth.

Thus, even if we read on the jacket of *Learning from Las Vegas* that the text is "calling for architects to be more receptive to the tastes and values of 'common' people," we find its authors citing Morris Lapidus, architect of the Fontainebleau, which suggests that such "tastes" are heavily conditioned:

> People are looking for illusions; they don't want the world's realities. And, I asked, where do I find this world of illusion? Where are their tastes formulated? Do they study it in school? Do they go to museums? Do they travel to Europe? Only one place—the movies. They go to the movies. The hell with everything else.[32]

With the exhibition in Venice and publication of Habermas' and Kramer's essays in less than two years, soon followed by a response to Habermas by Jean-François Lyotard (an antimodernist in the Habermasian paradigm, but answering in the name of *post*-modernism), critical mass was achieved: the debate exploded. The *New German Critique* has devoted three issues to the subject, *Telos* one; it has become an ongoing topic in the *New Left Review;* Hal Foster has edited one anthology while Mike Davis is at work on another; and cultural critics such as Fredric Jameson, Edward Said, Rosalind Krauss, Terry Eagleton, Jean Baudrillard, and Martin Jay have leapt into the fray. In the compartmentalized field of aesthetics, this much concentrated publication on a single, if complex, topic is phenomenal. Something is happening here.

At one level, this activity represents an attempt on the part of Habermasian Critical Theory to wrest the center of European intellectual discourse, the academic narrative of the humanities, away from the deconstructionists, a power play that becomes both confused and infinitely more suggestive when combined, in a contradictory fashion, with the American dispute between neoconservative and neopopulist art critics *and* superimposed over an evolving tendency in architecture. Beyond this muddle, the debate has made clear, even within universities, that a wide gap exists between contemporary artistic production in all media and the critical vocabulary and constructs that attempt to account for its results. There is as yet no consensus as to what constitutes postmodernism. Part of the reason for this has been that, until recently, academic discourses have failed to pay close attention to contemporary developments in the arts save in piecemeal, fragmentary fashion (for example, in the theories of camp and confessional poetry).

Of necessity, the "evidence" to which critics are now turning includes current artwork, other theoretical writing, *and,* as a means of comparison against a presumably stable background, theories of cultural modernism. Here, however, the lack of consensus as to the basic aspects of postmodernism should be a signal that this common framework may itself be a contributing factor to a larger incoherence. Without an adequate, shared articulation of that from which, by all accounts, postmodernism arose (or descended), attempts at a new critical construction are simply futile.

We need to turn back to Greenberg's initial conception and ask ourselves again, "Did modernism exist?" and, if so, what was it? Because the theory extended from a formal analysis of the visual arts, it is useful to examine this model within a different context. Literature provides us with a domain grounded in a substantially dissimilar medium. Language is possessed by all peoples and literacy by many. Words, unlike oil pigment and brush strokes, possess an immediately recognizable referential dimension. Greenberg himself notes this distinction, seeing it as a difficulty not for his theory, but for writing: "If it were easier to define poetry, modern poetry would be much more 'pure' and 'abstract'" (7). Although he acknowledges the existence of sound poetry, the major literary genres are alleged to be blocked by the inherent nature of their medium from the "pure" formalism of the modern and must content themselves with a second-order abstraction, self-referentiality:

> Aside from the fact that most of our best contemporary novelists have gone to school with the avant-garde, it is significant that Gide's most ambitious book is a novel about the writing of a novel, and that Joyce's *Ulysses* and *Finnegans Wake* seem to be, above all . . . the reduction of experience to expression, for the sake of expression, the expression mattering more than what is being expressed. (7–8)

Given the implication that writing could only produce an echo of the period's dominant aesthetic effect, Greenberg's paradigm met with surprisingly little resistance from poets, novelists, and their critics. While writers such as Williams had used *modern* in a general, nontheoretical way, it was exactly the problematic aspects of Greenberg's formulation that enabled it to be extended to so many kinds of writing emerging prior to 1960. Consider the contour of American poetry during the early and mid-1950s. Greenberg's identification of the avant-garde as the preservers of high-art cultural value suited the *classical* impulses of academic verse: Robert Lowell declared himself to be the true heir of Ezra Pound. A commitment to formal innovation could be seen as related to the theory of the New Critics, an opportunistic interpretation Greenberg himself promoted, even as their interest in formal analysis concealed a deeper hostility to change. In its elevation of the avant-garde prior to the Second World War to a series of classic monuments, the partisans of Pound and Williams were given a mechanism by which not only to rescue Pound from the consequences of his disastrous political choices but also to claim for Williams a centrality that he had not always been accorded. Poets whose work appeared to be experimental, such as Olson, Duncan, or Creeley, were continuing the important tradition of formal progress. And the poets of the New York School, after all, not only subsumed their own poetics into a larger aesthetics that openly conceded a privileged position to painting, their name itself was appropriated from a Greenberg coinage for abstract expressionism. Finally, contributing to the prominence of the Beats was the difficulty that critics had fitting a heavily foregrounded romanticism into this model.

The test of an aesthetic theory needs to be more than that its internal inconsistencies be available to all agendas. Even with the difficulty that confronted Greenberg's attempt to apply his construction to literature, and the virtual disinterest in the historic development of forms that typified the New Critics, the modernist paradigm permeated the field of writing even as it was hardly able to identify anything more specific than a broad period of time. Although he does not acknowledge it, this is the problem that causes Fredric Jameson to write that

> it may be conceded that all of the features of postmodernism . . . can be detected, full-blown, in this or that preceding modernism (including such astonishing genealogical precursors as Gertrude Stein, Raymond Roussel, or Marcel Duchamp, who may be considered outright postmodernists, *avant la lettre*).[33]

Postmodernism, in this view, is therefore not to be conceived as a style or stage of formal development in aesthetics but rather as a "cultural dominant . . . the presence and coexistence of a range of very different, yet subordinate features."[34] This phenomenon, characterized by elements whose point in common is the lack of a family resemblance, might itself be called a postmodern effect, and it is not surprising that much of what Jameson then identifies fits the decentered universe of the poststructuralists, Habermas's *anti*moderns. But Jameson's Marxism insists that even this antisystematic entity be historicized, its relation to social dynamics be made explicit. This he crudely attempts by referring to the economic periodization put forward by Belgian economist Ernest Mandel. The three stages of capitalism are each initiated by the machine production of a new mode of power: the steam engine in 1848, electric and combustion motors in the 1890s, and, finally, electronic and nuclear "apparatuses" in the 1940s. According to Jameson, "my own cultural periodization of the stages of realism, modernism and postmodernism is both inspired and confirmed by Mandel's tripartite scheme."[35]

Yet if the model of literary modernism is problematic, and if, as Jameson himself concedes, postmodernism is perceptible only insofar as it differs from aspects of this earlier paradigm, then his overall three-part construction, one that leads him to no less extreme a conclusion than that humanity is on the brink of a "mutation," finds itself on the shakiest of grounds. The fact that poets like Blackburn, Duncan, and Creeley, whose process-centered aesthetics and concept of "composition by field" caused them, since the late 1950s, to be treated as a rough literary equivalent to action painting, can now, in the title of the revised edition of the Donald Allen anthology, be called *The Postmoderns,* or that individual poets of that era such as Olson and Spicer can be argued to have been deconstructionists *avant la lettre,*[36] suggests that postmodernism—and particularly those symptoms that Habermas attempts to contain by categorizing as antimodern—must be investigated as something at least other than simply an ensemble of "subordinate features."

What is required is a formal description of the postmodern. But before this can be attempted, the problematics that envelop modernism itself need to be redrawn.

What Greenberg started with in 1939 was a term rich with connotations that had been in continuous use for nearly a century. *Modern* is an adjective Marx and Engels apply to "bourgeois society" in the *Communist Manifesto.* What Greenberg lacked, in extending his scheme beyond painting, was a model of form for the literary arts *predicated upon the dynamics of the medium itself,* which are linguistic rather than visual. The fundamental Saussurean demarcation between *signifier,* the word as a complex of sound or letters, and *signified,* the word as a concept, could have led him to a very different analysis of the relationship between form and content.

Greenberg credits the turn toward form to the withdrawal of the avant-garde from the value system of the bourgeoisie: "A superior consciousness of history—more precisely, the appearance of a new kind of criticism of society, historical criticism—made this possible" (4). This explanation parallels Habermas' own that modernist art, from Baudelaire on, is an essentially critical project. Yet neither addresses those achievements which set the stage for this moment. Realism was that dream within the arts of a completely transparent form, of an identity between the signified or an aesthetic communication and its ostensible referent in the material world. In the realist art object, conceived as a sign, all aspects are subordinated to the signified. It is worth reminding ourselves of this because of Roman Jakobson's observation that in the poem all the functions of language are turned in just the opposite direction. Thus, from the perspective of linguistics, *realism is that program which attempts a unity between signifier and signified in a manner that conceals the presence of the signifier.* In fact, the successful realist effect is a transfer of whatever presence inhabits the signifier onto the signified: the characters, we say, come alive.

There has never been a realism, of course, that was not thoroughly stylized, constructed, and artificial. It is possible today to see this project merely for its limitations and to moralize, as does Jean-François Lyotard, that the task which has been assigned to realism is to "preserve various consciousnesses from doubt."[37] Yet it is critical that we understand realism for the prodigious technical accomplishment it was—this attempt to unify two different features of the sign made visible to writers the entire spectrum of functions at play within the linguistic act, foregrounding in particular that which was to have been suppressed, the signifier. Consider this complaint of Flaubert to Louise Colet, concerning the composition of *Madame Bovary:* "This book, which is all style, is constantly threatened by the style itself. The phrase goes to my head and I lose sight of the idea."[38] The step from here to works in which it is precisely "the style" and "the phrase" that are up for consideration, whether by this we mean Stein and Joyce, or even Emily Dickinson, is not large. Realism, far from having been just the instrumentalization of technique, constituted an assault on the privilege of the signified.

What this brought up for writers, however, was not merely a reconsideration of the signifier's role, for the linguistic sign, unlike the bifurcated model Greenberg derived from painting, does *not* divide neatly into form and content, signifier and signified. There are, as Jakobson discovered, a minimum of four additional functions, a total of six factors necessary for the simplest linguistic act to take place. The others include an addressor, an addressee, the code or system of language itself which is being used, and the method of contact, "a physical channel and psychological connection between speaker and addressee."[39]

This differentiation of functions would have transformed Greenberg's simpler polarity. The dominant role Jakobson assigns to form, the signifier, implies that the turn in this direction on the part of an avant-garde was less a heroic decision to withdraw from the philistinism of bourgeois values than simply the extension, within the aesthetic realm, of the same instrumental reason that was active not only in the sciences, law, and business but within realism as well. This suggests, further, that the social organization of an individual's sight may be no less heavily coded than the structure of his or her language. Greenberg's conception of form, the basis for his theory of the modern, excludes factors essential to the consideration of either a painting or a poem as a significant, communicative act. Had his model been sufficient, the pure "abstractions" of the Russian *zaum* poets, the sound poetry of Kurt Schwitters and Hugo Ball, or the visual work of the Concretists should have had far greater an impact.

The inclusion of these omitted factors suggests a very different paradigm for modernism. We should bear in mind that the distinction between writing and the visual arts is not that language is social and sight is not, but rather that language is *admittedly* social. Even though writers had no more information concerning the academic investigation of linguistics, this inescapable recognition forced upon them exactly those issues that are absent from Greenberg's system.

The utopia of realism was not merely one of the transmission of unmediated signifieds but also of a language rendered pure by just this process: "Nobody has ever contemplated a kind of prose more perfect than what I have in mind," Flaubert wrote to Colet.[40] But transcendence on this order dissolves in the same instant it is achieved. Searching for the signified, the realists discovered the signifier. Seeking to abolish style, they empowered it, in all of its partiality, multiplicity, and omnipresence. Intending to create, at long last, the whole word, the unified sign, they instead blew it apart. This is the deeper significance of the phrase "revolution of the word."

One possible response to such circumstances is denial, and varieties of realism continue to be produced. In fact, virtually all types of writing that have come into existence over the past 150 years are still being practiced in some form, to some degree. Rather than dismissing any as "old-fashioned" or "reactionary," or relegating them, as did Greenberg, to that category beyond art, kitsch, it is far more useful to consider what their orientation to the issues posed here actually is, and especially how their relationship to an audience or constituency reflects that sector's own cultural history. If one of the major effects of realism was the creation of awareness in the reader of a particular kind of subjectivity, along the lines of what Jameson calls "the subject as a monad-like container," without which the conceptual benefits of instrumental reason remain opaque, and with all of the implications for power or powerlessness that are thus inscribed, what then is the function of realism for a constituency that has only been the object, and never the subject, of history?

A response similar but not identical to denial would be to attempt the reunification of language through other means. This, in essence, is what Jameson and many others mean by the term *modernism,* as evidenced when someone like Stein is then cited as an instance of the postmodern. An early and important example of this attempt to reestablish the lost balance of realism would be symbolism. A symbol, after all, is a signified that functions as a signifier.

This yearning to recapture a lost unity in the functions of language plays out on another level a parallel breach, equally the consequence of instrumental reason, that had been evolving for decades through the elaboration of "organic" form, and it is intriguing to observe the tension of a longed-for closure in the work of writers who themselves were responsible for the very techniques that rendered any artificial holism impossible. The starkest instance may be Pound's call for a "splendour" that would cohere where *The Cantos* do not, but the problem is that of any innovator, really, unwilling to concede that *the inherent consequence of any evolutionism in aesthetic form is the dissolution of unity itself.* This is what accounts for the inevitable decline of every project over the past century that has been predicated on establishing a unification of the sign—the end of modernism was inscribed at its origin.

Equally present in that same moment is the possibility of writing itself, minus that impossible dream. It is this which is so clearly manifest in the work of Gertrude Stein that Jameson cannot acknowledge her as a modernist. It is a major distinction, if not so sharply drawn, between a work such as *The Cantos* and Louis Zukofsky's "*A*". It is, once we extend it from writing to the broader category of art, that which underlies the surrealists' attack on the institutional sanctity of high art and on the division between art and life itself. Now we can see why modernism is so riddled with postmodernist "exceptions." Modernism in this sense is even less than the announcement of the post-modern. It is merely a lingering hangover from the previous realist paradigm.

The central place of the dramatic monologue, the use of persona or "personism," in so many conservative poetics, anti- and postmodern alike, can now be described. These aesthetics attempt to reunite the sign by asserting an identification between signifier and addresser. The presence within the signifier, which in the realist text was displaced onto the signified, is here transferred to an ostensible speaker. The reading subject thus constituted is no longer the passive spectator of the realist scene, but is no less immobilized. In its most extreme articulations, this program denies the possibility of evolution within linguistic-aesthetic form, even though development is implicit in the impulse to act, to create, to write.

The importance that conservatives place on the immobilization of their readers through the use of "unified speakers" suggests the critical role that both the subject and subjectivity play in the social and historical elaboration of these issues. From the perspective of the triumph of instrumental reason, the creation of this subject (the individual of individualism) is the dominant aesthetic *and social* effect. The breakup of realism was not experienced by writers or readers as a problem of linguistics but of the credibility of the text. The path of the "monad-like container" of this subject was blocked by the gradual emergence of the signifier, cluttering and disrupting what was supposed to have been the domain of the signified. It is no accident that the post-structuralists should uncover the "death of the subject" in the same moment that the myth of a reunification of the sign ceased to carry great weight with many poets.

The lessons for poets here are many. The debate over postmodernism is far from complete, and there is no guarantee that it will yield any increased comprehension of the arts. This does not mean that it will not, however, reorganize, both conceptually and politically, art's institutional relation to society, and consequently our perceptions of poetry's inner terrain. While it is evident that, for those of us whose class may have, in fact, been the subject of recent history, a resurrection of the realist or pre-modern paradigm can only represent our despair at our own impact on the world, any retro-modern reunification of the sign merely reduplicates this backward-facing utopianism in a different guise.

The postmodern debate has shown a marked resistance to even coherently posing such questions. What is the nature *and history* of a writing that no longer yearns for a unified sign? What, once the presence of an addressee is admitted into our model, bringing in society, can be intelligibly said of literary genres, let alone individual poets and poems? The future of poetry is certainly to be determined by how poets conceive of the relationship of their activity to society. Yet until these issues have been confronted and deeply explored, and until the aesthetic history of the past one hundred years has been rewritten from their perspective, this relationship can only remain opaque.

NOTES

A talk given originally at Canessa Park Gallery, San Francisco, May 1985, and subsequently revised and presented at the New Poetics Colloquium, Vancouver; at St. Mark's Church, New York; and in the Lines series at the Detroit Institute for the Arts.

1. "Roman Jakobson interviewed by David Shapiro (June 1979)," *Sulfur* 12 (1985): 171.

2. Charles Jenks, *The Language of Post-Modern Architecture,* 4th ed. (New York, 1985), 8.

3. Andreas Huyssen, "Mapping the Postmodern," *New German Critique* 33 (Fall 1984): 11.

4. This conception is far from a consensus, even within the confines of a single discipline such as the visual arts. Lawrence Alloway, for example, following Adorno, identifies it as "the first wave of the avant-garde, starting early in the 20th century." Peter Bürger, however, makes a sharp distinction between the avant-garde and modernism, predicated on the former's alleged attack on the autonomy of art and the latter's defense of it.

5. The nearest approximation might have been The Modern School, a day school for children founded in Harlem in 1911 under the direction of Will Durant. The school, which also provided adult education classes, combined anarchism with the arts of the time and featured such lecturers as Emma Goldman, Margaret Sanger, Jack London, Clarence Darrow, Lincoln Steffens, and Upton Sinclair. While they published a journal called *The Modern School,* the noun here specified "education" rather than "movement," and the venture's ambivalence to the term *modern* led them to alternately use The Ferrer School as their name. See Francis M. Naumann and Paul Avrich, "Adolf Wolff: 'Poet, Sculptor and Revolutionist, but Mostly Revolutionist,'" *The Art Bulletin* 67, no. 3:486–87.

6. "Necessary and Unnecessary Words," in *The Idea of the Post-Modern: Who Is Teaching It?,* ed. Joseph Newland, first published as *The Idea: At the Henry,* no. 2, Henry Art Gallery, University of Washington (Seattle, 1981), 7.

7. "Postmodernism, Plurality and the Urgency of the Given," in ibid., p. 13. Indeed, the success of Greenberg's usage of the word was essential to the impact of Adorno's own work in the United States when it first became widely available here in the 1970s, even as it offered a different paradigm.

8. Jürgen Habermas, "Modernity: An Incomplete Project," in *The Anti-Aesthetic: Essays on Postmodern Culture,* ed. Hal Foster (Port Townsend, Wash., 1983), 3.

9. "Cézanne," in *Art and Culture* (Boston, 1961), 50.

10. *Modern* appears just once in the piece, applied not to painting but to poetry.

11. *Literature and Revolution,* trans. Rose Strunsky (Ann Arbor, Mich., 1960), 184.

12. "Avant-Garde and Kitsch," in *Art and Culture,* 16. Future citations from this essay are embedded parenthetically in the text.

13. Tin Pan Alley represents the instrumentalization of music through the capitalist control over production and distribution of new technologies for its *re*production, the radio and phonograph.

14. The title of Greenberg's collection parallels this only slightly more subtly. In both instances the word *and* means "versus."

15. "Hans Hoffman," in *Art and Culture,* 194–95. It is worth noting here that the phrase "New American," which played such a major role in shaping poetic discourse in the fifties and sixties, is itself an application of just this usage by Greenberg.

16. The prescriptive rhetoric here is worth reiterating: content *is to be* dissolved, and aesthetics itself is said to possess values without reference to any audience or community in which these might be situated.

17. In *Sagetreib* 4, no. 1 (Spring 1985):73–74.

18. These include Max Kozloff and John Coplans, during their editorial reign over *Artforum* from 1973 through 1976, contributors of theirs like Carol Duncan and Eva Cockroft, plus others who have worked with, and learned from, them, such as historian Jane de Hart Mathews and Serge Guilbaut.

19. *How New York Stole the Idea of Modern Art: Abstract Expressionism, Freedom, and the Cold War,* trans. Arthur Goldhammer (Chicago, 1983), 3.

20. Ibid., 36. Guilbaut is quoting James Burkhart Gilbert's *Writers and Partisans: A History of Literary Radicalism in America.*

21. Eva Cockroft, "Abstract Expressionism, Weapon of the Cold War," *Artforum,* June 1974, 39–41.

22. Peter Bürger, *Theory of the Avant-Garde,* trans. Michael Shaw (Minneapolis, 1984), 23.

23. Ibid., 52–53.

24. The instrumental imagery advocated by Cockroft, et al., merely reverses the problem. What is so often absent from such images is a capacity to comment critically not just on the formal mechanisms of perception put into play through the viewing process but the actual social context of the work itself. The image of Judy Grahn that can be seen in a mural under an overpass in Oakland's Grand Lake district is thus at once a statement both of the pride and possibility within lesbian culture and of those larger social relations that render homosexuality marginal, "deviant," and open to hostile state intervention. What this mural does not address is how such an image, complete and ambivalent as it might be, serves to justify, culturally, and to distract one's attention from, the state infrastructure whose primary socioeconomic purpose is to deliver the transportation needs of human beings to a handful of automobile corporations. Art such as this is hardly more free from compromise and the potential for cooptation than was that of the abstract expressionists.

25. December 1975, section 2, p. 40. The editors did not make it through 1976.

26. "A Note on *The New Criterion,*" *The New Criterion* 1, no. 1 (September 1982):1.

27. Ibid., 2.

28. Ibid., 40. Further citations of this article are embedded parenthetically in the text.

29. Subsequently published as "Modernity: An Incomplete Project," 9. Further citations of this article are embedded parenthetically in the text.

30. Cf. Richard Wolin, "Modernism vs. Postmodernism," *Telos* 62 (Winter 1984–85):15.

31. This "anticipates" the fate that met both the French Lettrists when they transformed themselves into the Situationists and the Anglo-American Art-Language tendency.

32. Robert Venturi, Denise Scott Brown, and Steven Izenour, *Learning from Las Vegas: The Forgotten Symbolism of Architectural Form* (Cambridge, Mass., 1977), 80.

33. "Postmodernism: or The Cultural Logic of Late Capitalism," *New Left Review* 146 (July–August 1984):56.

34. Ibid.

35. Ibid., 78.

36. Joseph Riddel has made this argument with regard to Olson in "Decentering the Image: The 'Project' of 'American' Poetics?" in *Textual Strategies: Perspectives in Post-Structural Criticism,* ed. Josue V. Harari (Ithaca, N.Y., 1979), 322–58. Even more well known is Robin Blaser's essay on Spicer, "The Practice of Outside," in *The Collected Books of Jack Spicer,* ed. Blaser (Los Angeles, 1975), 271–329.

37. "Answering the Question: What Is Postmodernism?" trans. Regis Durand, in *The Postmodern Condition: A Report on Knowledge* (Minneapolis, 1984), 74.

38. "The Novelist on His Art: Excerpts from Flaubert's Correspondence," trans. Helen Weaver, in *Madame Bovary* (New York, 1981), 326.

39. Linda Waugh, "The Poetic Function in the Theory of Roman Jakobson," *Poetics Today* 2, no. 1a (1980):57–58. In what follows, I have applied Saussurean names to some of Jakobson's categories in order to avoid further convoluting the line of my argument.

40. "The Novelist on His Art," 318.

METAPHORS IN THE
TRADITION OF THE SHAMAN

GLORIA ANZALDÚA

We are all prisoners of our own self-images.
—Andrew Kaplan, *Scorpion*

Right after *Borderlands/La frontera*[1] came out, I focused on what was weak or lacking in it and all the stuff that was "wrong" with my life. I repeatedly represented (with pictures and words in my head and with internal feelings) how things were in such a negative way that I put myself in a disempowering state and eventually made myself sick. As is true with all humans, the working of my imagination acted upon my own body. Images communicated with tissues, organs, and cells to effect change. Once again it came home to me how powerful the image and the word are and how badly I needed to control the metaphors I use to communicate with myself. *Si, la imaginación es muy poderosa.*

And now eight months after *Borderlands/La frontera* hit the bookstores the answer to the questions interviewers keep asking me—Just what exactly had I written and why—came to me. I realize that I was trying to practice the oldest "calling" in the world—shamanism. And that I was practicing it in a new way. The Sanskrit word for shaman, *saman,* means "song." In nonliterate societies, the shaman and the poet were the same person. The role of the shaman is, as it was then, preserving and creating cultural or group identity by mediating between the cultural heritage of the past and the present everyday situations people find themselves in. In retrospect I see that this was an unconscious intention on my part in writing *Borderlands/La frontera.*

To carry the poet-shaman analogy further, through my poet's eye I see "illness," *lo que daña,* whatever is harmful in the cultural or individual body. I see that "sickness" unbalances a person or a community. That it may be in the form of disease, or disinformation/misinformation perpetrated on women and people of color. I see that always it takes the form of metaphors.

La curación—the "cure"—may consist of removing something (disindoctrination)—of extracting the old dead metaphors. Or it may consist of adding what is lacking—restoring the balance and strengthening the physical, mental, and emotional states of the person. This "cure" leads to a change in our belief system, *en lo que creemos.* No longer feeling ourselves "sick," we snap out of the paralyzing states of confusion, depression, anxiety, and powerlessness, and we are catapulted into enabling states of confidence and inner strength. In *Borderlands/La frontera,* I articulate the debilitating states that women and the colonized go through and the resulting disempowerment. It is not easy to get out of these states. All cultures and their accompanying metaphors resist change. All Mexicans are lazy and shiftless is an example of a metaphor that resists change. This metaphor has endured as fact even though we all know it is a lie. It will endure until we replace it with a new metaphor, one that we believe in both consciously and unconsciously.

We preserve ourselves through metaphor; through metaphor we protect ourselves. The resistance to change in a person is in direct proportion to the number of dead metaphors that person carries.[2] But, we can also change ourselves through metaphor. And most importantly, we can *share* ourselves through metaphor—attempt to put, in words, the flow of some of our internal pictures, sounds, sensations, and feelings and hope that as the reader reads the pages these "metaphors" would be "activated" and live in her.

Because we use metaphors as well as *yierbitas* and curing stones to effect changes, we follow in the tradition of the shaman. Like the shaman, we transmit information from our consciousness to the physical body of another. If we're lucky we create, like the shaman, images that induce altered states of consciousness conducive to self-healing. If we've done our job well we may give others access to a language and images with which they can articulate/express pain, confusion, joy, and other experiences thus far experienced only on an inarticulated emotional level. From our own and our people's experiences, we will try to create images and metaphors that will give us a handle on the numinous, a handle on the faculty for self-healing, one that may cure the depressed spirit, the frightened soul.

En posreción de la palabra. Despite language, class, and identity differences and conflicts there exist strong cultural links among Chicanas, Native, Asian, *mexicanas,* and other women. We can safeguard and strengthen these links through communication. People in possession of the vehicles of communication are, indeed, in partial possession of their lives.

NOTES

I want to thank Betsy Wootten and Barbara Lee of the Steno Pool at Kresge College, and Nicolette Czarrunchick, Women's Studies UCSC, for their help in typing this essay.

1. Gloria Anzaldúa, *Borderlands/La frontera: The New Mestiza.* San Francisco, CA: Spinsters/Aunt Lute, 1987.
2. William J. Gordon, T. Poze, and M. Read, *The Metaphorical Way of Learning and Knowing.* Cambridge, Mass.: Purpoise Books, 1971, p. 224.

DRAWING IN NETS

JUDY GRAHN

Thinking about drawings, the meaning and purpose of drawings, always leads me in two directions with two related stories at their ends, like currents at the ends of a forked divining rod.

One story is based in the word "drawing" itself, the literal meaning, "to draw toward oneself," to create a magnetic field that draws something to it. "I am drawn to her."

"I felt irresistibly drawn to a particular house on that street," a storyteller may begin, proceeding then to describe in detail the plate glass window, beige drapes, gleaming peak of chandelier; or conversely, the seven looming gables, murky windows, hostile chimney—all the carefully chosen images within the magnetic field that particularly "drew" the artist to her/his description and that hopefully will also preoccupy the viewer or reader.

This magnetic-field description of the word "drawing" further entices me to remember a story to which I am repeatedly and irresistibly—drawn. It seems that in certain sects of India, I suspect Hindu, the mistress of the house, every Friday evening, takes up chalk or other marking material, and after carefully sweeping her threshold until its surface is smooth and clean as new-bought poster board, she draws on it a very particular geometric figure whose purpose is to protect her household.

The drawing power of this geometric image lies in its ability to create a field that is irresistible to particular kinds of guardian spirits, one of which while on its usual rounds about the village, is certain to become entangled in the householder's web. The configuration is further designed in such a way that, once tangled in it, the guardian spirit cannot escape as long as the lines remain fixed and clear, and it is thus forced, like a raven in an ancient Roman entryway, to sit in front of the artist's door for the entire week protecting her house from all evil doings that might otherwise enter.

And it is also true that everyone in the village sees the crisp design at her doorway and knows from long traditional use of it that she has protected herself. Their mutual knowing draws them into a collective vision of the art, so they, too, with the image in their minds, protect her doorway. Malevolence keeps away from her.

This meaning of drawing, to draw by means of clever and knowledgeable construction of one's imagery, so irresistibly that a power otherwise loose in the free-form universe is now captured and exerting its force in the context of human lives, never ceases to engage me whenever I think of art and how it works. That it works like a vessel or plumbing system with which we capture water. That it works like a hexagram on a barn wall to repel unwanted forces. That it works like the barn to secure the cows of our desiring. That it works like a dolly on whom we pour our expectations, hurts and love, and in whom we stick our pins of anger and repulsion.

Yes, all that and much more is involved in imagery and magnetism. However, very often an image, in poetry, say, works like a spirit-drawing by using the geometry of language to capture the power of some force in the natural world to materialize the thought-form of the poem. "The moon, and my heart, stood still."

This is a great and terrible power, this poetic power of geometric imagery, and it utilizes at least three different ways of looking at the spirit conjured or trapped in the metaphoric net. If I say in a poem: "You have wolf eyes," this wolf first exists in the language of our brains as we imagine "wolf" when we read the word; second, all the symbology collected by our literature, films, cartoons, folk tales, jokes, dreams, and habits of speech with regard to "wolf" is in the net. And lastly, I am calling on a genuine power and person of nature, the wolf. I am using the qualities displayed by wolf culture to amplify some human understanding or experience. Genuine flesh-and-blood wolves out in what little terrain is left them are in the net of metaphor I have made.

If I say: "This man, whom I wish would drop dead because he is bothering me sexually and I am afraid of him, is a wolf," I am wishing that wolves would drop dead, for as I believe—metaphors always work both ways. If I am like the moon, the moon is also like me. If my eyes are a wolf's eyes, then a wolf's eyes are my eyes. If I wish for the death of some quality in human behavior that I also say is "wolf," I effect the death of wolves.

This is why it is so important to construct imagery with great precision and care, with the accuracy of geometry, with accuracy of emotion and thought, lest the artist catch something in her drawing that she really did not intend to catch. Exactly which spirit is it that I am trying to capture? Which moon is it that stands still when my heart does, and which wolf has eyes like my eyes?

To finish out the other end of my divining rod, one of those used by dowsers who can detect water when the rod is suddenly drawn down toward the earth from the power of the magnetic currents (or spirit) of whatever they are seeking, I want to tell a last story.

I once wrote a long poem, so long and so meticulous that it has captured a number of spirits. Some of them are good, I guess, and some not so good. This poem, "A Woman Is Talking to Death," doesn't use imagery that calls on powers from the natural world, rather it describes women's history and experience in a context of a masculine-defined, patriarchal, world. It begins with a long description of a fatal motorcycle accident on the Bay Bridge in Northern California and then meanders through women's history and my own lesbian history.

I expected the poem to be something that gave heart to women who were going out into the world and taking stands about their right to be there rather than cloistered at home. And I did hear stories about that particular power of the poem, also that it has helped women in mental hospitals get through breakdowns, and other things like that. But I was disturbed that a number of women told me that they were now frightened every time they had to drive across the Bay Bridge, that my poem returns to them each time. The power of the description has burned the memory of the accident into the Bridge, and there it is trapped, crying out "Fear, Fear" to all who are tuned into this entire construct.

This disturbed me for a time, until I heard another story of the poem and got over my own fear. A woman named Anita, who had worked with me in the press I founded so I could get poems like that one into print, took a trip to Southeast Asia to find her grandmother. She was staying in a hotel room in Shanghai when a man broke in and tried to rape her. When she fought back, he continued to attack her and chase her until finally she was exhausted and he had his hands around her neck choking her. She was still resisting, so he bent her neck back and to the side, until it was as close to snapping as it could get without her losing consciousness.

"I thought for certain I was going to die," she told me months later when she returned to California, "all he needed was one more second of that terrible pressure on my neck. And then I remembered "A Woman Is Talking to Death," the poem and the warrior feeling of the poem just came into my mind. And then I had a flash of all of you here at the press, and I let out a death cry that you wouldn't believe. I just howled it out. And he was so freaked out, he dropped me and ran out of the room."

Her eyes must have been a wolf's eyes at that moment.

Because there is a collectivity of agreement about the form of the net, I can tell this story even though it is about my "own" poem.

Although I seem somewhat arrogant to myself talking about my own work, I am very humble before this netted power; that is true of art, and that comes through the artist out of the collective imagery and experience (metaphors) of some entire body of people to whom she belongs. Like the household artist of India, I too make configurations to protect the houses of the women in my modern—fragmented—farflung—but nevertheless—village.

THREE CHAPTERS FROM "NOVICES"

CLAYTON ESHLEMAN

8

WHAT YOU SHOULD KNOW TO BE A POET

all you can about animals as persons.
the names of trees and flowers and weeds.
names of stars, and the movements of the planets
                    and the moon.

your own six senses, with a watchful and elegant mind.

at least one kind of traditional magic:
divination, astrology, the book of changes, *the tarot;*

dreams.
the illusory demons and illusory shining gods;

kiss the ass of the devil and eat shit;
fuck his horny barbed cock,
fuck the hag,
and all the celestial angels
                    and maidens perfum'd and golden—

& then love the human: wives   husbands   and friends.

childrens' games, comic books, bubble-gum,
the weirdness of television and advertising.

"Novices" is a twelve-chapter essay that addresses the initial chaos as well as the potential coherence involved in making a commitment to poetry and argues that blocks and chasms are not to be avoided but are to be worked through and assimilated. It presents and critiques "curriculums" by Gary Snyder, W. H. Auden, Robert Graves, and Charles Olson and views Harold Bloom's "Revisionary Ratios" as stages of a single archetypal poetic labyrinth; it also ponders the alchemical, psychological, and sexual ramifications of making contact with origins and makes a case for an old-fashioned apprenticeship to the art of poetry. It is written for the young independent writer who desires that impossible state identified by Artaud in the asylum of Rodez: "The great total dimension is to become as a simple man strong as all infinity."—CE/February 1988

> *work, long dry hours of dull work swallowed and accepted*
> *and livd with and finally lovd.   exhaustion,*
> > *hunger, rest.*
> *the wild freedom of the dance, extasy*
> *silent solitary illumination, enstasy*
>
> *real danger.   gambles.   and the edge of death.*
> > —*Gary Snyder*[1]

The lack of capitals and the presence of periods give this page of Snyder's a modest notational quality, a man sharing his thoughts with you, without broadcasting their importance. At the same time, "What You Should Know" is a tool kit, a Poetic Curriculum,[2] a several-year study program in nucleus that if followed, in disciplined "ordered derangement" on one's own, might represent a meaningful compromise between the oversocialized university writing programs and Artaud's stark command of no enlightenment other than oneself on oneself, no initiation *period*. Artaud made this statement after having put himself through his own equivalent of Snyder's Curriculum, and after he had been incarcerated in asylums for nearly nine years, where he had been "initiated" by therapy and electroshock.

I would like to draw three nodes from Snyder's piece—*experience, research, self-regulation*—and suggest that becoming a poet is involved with working out a balance, or rhythm, between these three multiradial activities—

Experience: having the courage of your own impulses, getting in "water over your head"; acting out curiosities and responsibilities whenever possible—confronting a friend, telling off an unfair superior, having the abortion, etc., rather than nonaction that subsequently possesses or leaks into poems.

(In Kyoto, 1963, Snyder seemed to me to live like a monk during the week and like a libertine on the weekend—he rose at 4 A.M. and had a day's study and writing done by late morning; as I recall, afternoons were given to chores, shopping, teaching English as a foreign language. Early rising, probably Zen practice, permeated but did not curtail—)

Snyder at a ranger station in Mt. Baker National Forest, twenty-one years old:

> Discipline of self-restraint is an easy one; being clear-cut, negative, and usually based on some accepted cultural values. Discipline of following desires, *always* doing what you want to do, is hardest. It presupposes self-knowledge of motives, a careful balance of free action and sense of where the cultural taboos lay—knowing whether a particular "desire" is instinctive, cultural, a product of thought, contemplation, or the unconscious. Blake: if the doorways of perception were cleansed, everything would appear to man as it is, infinite. For man has closed himself up, 'til all he sees is through narrow chinks of his caverns. Ah.

> the frustrated bumblebee turns over
> clambers the flower's center upside down
> furious hidden buzzing
> near the cold sweet stem.

In a culture where the aesthetic experience is denied and atrophied, genuine religious ecstasy rare, intellectual pleasure scorned—it is only natural that sex should become the only personal epiphany of most people & the culture's interest in romantic love take on staggering size.[3]

Research: is, of course, a kind of experience, too, but here I stress finding contemplative territories that have not been mined (or strip-mined) by other poets and making them your own, bringing them into contemporary writing, by poetry or by prose, in order to increase its range of responsibilities.

This should involve travel, when such territory is visitable. Olson could have gone to the library and read up on Maya research. In fact, he did but was so dissatisfied by what was available that he became all the more obsessed with going to Yucatan on his own; however, nearly penniless, he went to Merida and picked up shards rather than merely examining photos of them.[4]

Penelope Shuttle and Peter Redgrove write that they went to their college librarian seeking information on menstruation because of Shuttle's cramps and depression. They found nothing that they could use and thus began their own research on an area of every woman's experience that has become an endless lode of discovery for both of them.[5]

There is something embedded in the nature of poetry itself that yearns to travel and to translate, not merely a foreign text, but the experience of otherness. "The most sublime act," Blake wrote, "is to set another before you." Thus Bashō's physical urge to get roving one spring morning in 1689 led to his famous *Oku-no-Hosomichi,*[6] the last of several haibun-haiku hiking journals, a model of layered cultural awareness, acute observation, and a heart open to transiency and "the modest proportions of human destiny." "What Bashō doesn't say," writes translator Cid Corman, "moves at least as much as what he does. One knows his silences go deeper than reasons. And when his eyes plumb words for heart—when the heart holds the island of Sado, locus of exile, at the crest of a brimming sea, and the eye lifts from that pointed violence and loneliness on the horizon to the stars flowing effortlessly up and over and back into the man making vision, who has not at once felt all language vanish into a wholeness and scope of sense that lifts one as if one weighed nothing?" (Here it is appropriate to note especially in the context of *Novices* the distance Corman has traveled from being an apprentice pounded by Olson's injunctions to the author of the just-quoted sentence.)

In 1965 I hitched, bused, and flew to Lima, Peru, to study the worksheets for the poetry of César Vallejo that I had been attempting to translate from error-riddled editions. Although the Vallejo part of the trip was utterly frustrating (his widow denied me and all others access to materials that would have enabled translators and scholars to make his achievement available on an international scale), the spirit of Vallejo led me into days of wandering in the worst of Lima's barriadas and my need to pay my way into experiencing USIS censorship of a bilingual literary magazine I was hired to edit. The context in which poetic research takes place can become as valuable in regard to learning as the project itself.

To only have yourself as subject, novice, is undermining, and it will tend to push you toward an "academic" (that is, conventional, diminutional) imitation of other poetries. If your attentions are not partially given over to the non- or foreign-literary, the temptation is to read, with blinders, the work of friends and teachers and to operate under a single canopy of current literary taste.

At twenty-four, Snyder saw experience and research ultimately as irreconcilable opposites:

> Comes a time when the poet must choose: either to step deep in the stream of his people, history, tradition, folding and folding himself in the wealth of persons and pasts; philosophy, humanity, to become richly foundationed and great and sane and ordered. Or, to step beyond the bound onto the way out, into horrors and angels, possible madness or silly Faustian doom, possible utter transcendence, possible enlightened return, possible ignominious wormish perishing.[7]

In "What You Should Know," written when he was in his mid-thirties, Snyder implies that such opposites are contraries (a Blakean perception: two-way traffic without collisions).

It is risky to go to college and remain there more or less for the rest of one's life and expect to write significant poetry. For the poet, the library is a more intimidating place than a foreign city, and to spend one's life nursing in a library is not only to remain an "eternal adolescent" as far as the alleys of Calcutta are concerned but to become so overwhelmed by what one does not know—can never know—that what one intuits, or does at least deeply feel, gets trashed. Great writing involves protecting one's intuitions, even one's ignorance. Knowing, as such, is not always an advantage to making significant art. Acknowledging one's ignorance and learning to respect personal as well as human limitations, *while* one works with the welter of fantasies that tumble between certainty and helplessness, is not learnable in school and can probably best be dealt with in what I would call "neutral solitude" (Rilke's little château in the Swiss mountains, Blake's flat in "fourfold" London, Artaud's cell at Rodez). For a poet, ignorance is as deep a well as knowing, and lifelong adherence to institutions of higher learning (with travel contingent upon awards) not only wrecks any possible balance between the two, but puts the poet, daily, class-wise, office-wise, library-wise, before the dragons of respectability and caution.[8]

The poetry and prose of William Bronk is a testimonial of the extent to which ignorance can be fugally held in an imaginative frame.

Again, Artaud (he is contemplating Van Gogh): "No one has ever written, painted, sculpted, modeled, built, or invented except literally to get out of hell.

And I prefer, to get out of hell, the landscapes of this quiet convulsionary to the teeming compositions of Brueghel the Elder or Hieronymous Bosch, who are, in comparison with him, only artists, whereas Van Gogh is only a poor dunce determined not to deceive himself."[9]

Self-Regulation: I take the term for this third "node" from the psychology of Wilhelm Reich, who believed that "the function of the orgasm" was to enable an individual to respect and take responsibility for his own energy household. Reich envisioned a world that did not need regulation from without (the police, the state, the nation) but a world in which people enjoyed their work because they had chosen it as an outgrowth of what Snyder refers to as "the discipline of following desires" (in contrast to negative self-restraint). In contemplating an ideal world made up of self-regulatory people, Reich was elaborating one of the core perceptions in Blake's poetry (1793):

> What is it men in women do require?
> The lineaments of Gratified Desire.
> What is it women do in men require?
> The lineaments of Gratified Desire.[10]

—a way of erotically grounding the Golden Rule, as it were; physical gratification as a *requirement* (note how trenchantly this word clings in the line, in contrast to "want" or "need") of the human, identical for both sexes, a reciprocity. Neither Blake nor Reich saw Gratified Desire or self-regulation as an end in itself—both saw it as a requirement for giving oneself wholeheartedly to one's work, whether that work be farming or sculpture. In my own life (partially through two years of Reichian therapy, 1967–1969), I have discovered that there is an "antiphonal swing" (I coin the phrase off the last line in Hart Crane's *The Bridge*) between gratificational love making and imaginative release, that these two "acts" are contraries, not opposites, and that as in the alchemical image of the "double pelican" they both feed each other in contrast to sapping strength from each other.

That which helps us define what we are also marks out boundaries. What we are not, artistically speaking, is a limitation. The challenge is to create a self that is up to and imaginatively includes all the selfhood and selves one has experienced. Even if we are able to allow contradiction and a flow of contraries in our work, each assertion, each placement, carries, like an aura, its unstated qualification or exception. In my own case, this challenge is: how accommodating can I be to material that flies in the face of my "antiphonal swing"?

Crane's "Havana Rose" recalls a conversation with the bacteriologist Hans Zinsser over dinner at a restaurant in Havana, 1931:

> And during the wait over dinner at La Diana,
> the Doctor had said—who was American also—
> "You cannot heed the negative—, so might go on

> *to undeserved doom . . .   must therefore loose yourself*
> *within a pattern's mastery that you can conceive, that*
> *you can yield to—by which also you*
> *win and gain that mastery and happiness which*
> *is your own from birth."* [11]

For thirty years, I have thanked Crane for having the savvy to write down Zinsser's words (whose "undeserved doom" Crane met within a year of that dinner), which offer yet another image of the labyrinth, as a pattern one masters and works (dances) within (Olson's: "how to dance/sitting down"). My own attempt at a "pattern's mastery" is sounded by the three words I have been mulling over in this section, words that make up a kind of web, or trampoline, I have constructed between sky and earth, and on which, against which, by which, I have lived and worked since the late 1960s. To these three words, I would now add a fourth: *Experiment,* the poetic engagement with the sustaining mesh of experience–research–self-regulation. One's eyes bouncing off one's sheet of typing paper, one's mind against the trampoline, hurling one's self-in-process at it again and again, aware that often one smacks and loses balance, falls through a hole and probably wrongly scrambles to get back to what one knows—

> *work swallowed and accepted*
> *and livd with and finally lovd.   exhaustion,*
> *hunger, rest.*

9

Snyder's "What You Should Know" is the child of post–World War II interdisciplinary, experimental, experience-oriented poetics, a new American poetry, open to (and often weakened by) crosscultural appropriations. In his broad and thoughtful essay, "The Poet and the City," (1962), W. H. Auden proposed a more traditionally Western curriculum, what he called his "daydream College for Bards":

1. In addition to English, at least one ancient language, probably Greek or Hebrew, and two modern languages would be required.

2. Thousands of lines of poetry in these languages would be learned by heart.

3. The library would contain no books of literary criticism, and the only critical exercise required of students would be the writing of parodies.

4. Courses in prosody, rhetoric and comparative philology would be required of all students, and every student would have to select three courses out of courses in mathematics, natural history, geology, meteorology, archaeology, mythology, liturgics, cooking.

5. Every student would be required to look after a domestic animal and cultivate a garden plot. [12]

Auden's "College," with its emphasis on memorization that has become archaic in our time, is a model for poet as Man of Letters, a Jack-of-All Literary Trades, who elaborates his life in poetry, letters, reviews, essays, possibly editing and translating, and so on. Relative to Snyder's "What You Should Know," it is ivory towerish; at the same time, it implicitly believes in a continuity of Western literature and humanities that have become suspect to Snyder with his Eastern focus aligned with Zen Buddhism and underscored by a belief in a usable shamanic deep past. Snyder's program is thus more tied to present-day consumer society and to the deep past than is Auden's, which spreads out in the immense Western "interval" between. Snyder's poet is a ronin (a masterless samurai) with his house on his head; Auden's a broadcaster at the console of the great Western library, with a house or cottage to stroll home to in the evening. Broken down into the most rudimentary forms, Snyder is a hunter, Auden a planter.

While pondering poetic curriculums, I recalled Robert Graves' *The White Goddess,* a scholarly Fantasia on the nature of "true poetry," in which Graves' picture of ancient Celt and Irish poets not only carries Auden's erudition but also Snyder's shadow of "the dancing sorcerer," the Upper Paleolithic shaman of 15,000 B.C. (a figure involved with the whole rope of a clan's knowledge and ability to survive, in contrast to the contemporary American poet who at best represents one strand of a rope unraveled throughout the humanities, medicine, magic, and law):

> The ancient Celts carefully distinguished the poet, who was originally a priest and judge as well and whose person was sacrosanct, from the mere gleeman. He was in Irish called *fili,* a seer; in Welsh *derwydd,* or oak-seer, which is the probable derivation of "Druid." Even kings came under his moral tutelage. When two armies engaged in battle, the poets of both sides would withdraw together on a hill and there judiciously discuss the fighting. . . . The gleeman, on the other hand, was a *joculator,* or entertainer, not a priest: a mere client of the military oligarchs and without the poet's arduous professional training.

> In ancient Ireland the *ollave,* or master-poet, sat next to the king at table and was privileged, as none else but the queen was, to wear six different colors in his clothes. The "bard," which in medieval Wales stood for a master-poet, had a different sense in Ireland, where it meant an inferior poet who had not passed through the "seven degrees of wisdom" which made him an ollave after a very difficult twelve-year course.

> Who can make any claim to be a chief poet and wear the embroidered mantle of office which the ancient Irish called the *tugen?* Who can even claim to be an ollave? The ollave in ancient Ireland had to be master of one hundred and fifty Oghams, or verbal ciphers, which allowed him to converse with his fellow-poets over the heads of unlearned bystanders; to be able to repeat at a moment's notice any one of three hundred and fifty long traditional histories and romances, together with the incidental poems they contained, with appropriate harp accompaniment. . . . to be learned in philosophy; to be a doctor of civil law; to understand the history of modern, middle and ancient Irish with the derivations and changes of meaning of every word; to be skilled in music, augury, divination, medicine, mathematics, geography, universal history, astronomy, rhetoric and foreign languages; and to be able to extemporize poetry in fifty or more complicated meters. That anyone at all should have been able to qualify as an ollave is surprising; yet families of ollaves tended to intermarry;

and among the Maoris of New Zealand where a curiously similar system prevailed, the capacity of the ollave to memorize, comprehend, elucidate and extemporize staggered Governor Grey and other early British observers.[13]

Graves will go ahead through his charming, questionable, vexing, and thoroughly labyrinthine work to argue that all "true poetry" celebrates some incident or scene of a particular story, identified in "The Single Poetic Theme" chapter:

> Originally, the poet was the leader of a totem-society of religious dancers. His verses—*versus* is a Latin word corresponding to the Greek strophe and means "a turning"—were danced around an altar or in a sacred enclosure and each verse started a new turn or movement in the dance. The word "ballad" has the same origin: it is a dance poem, from the Latin *ballare*, to dance. All the totem-societies in ancient Europe were under the dominion of the Great Goddess, the Lady of the Wild Things; dances were seasonal and fitted into an annual pattern from which gradually emerges the single grand theme of poetry: the life, death and resurrection of the Spirit of the Year, the Goddess's son and lover.

> Poetry began in the matriarchal age, and derives its magic from the moon, not from the sun. No poet can hope to understand the nature of poetry unless he has had a vision of the Naked King crucified to the lopped oak, and watched the dancers, red-eyed from the acrid smoke of the sacrificial fires, stamping out the measures of the dance, their bodies bent uncouthly forward, with a monotonous chant of: "Kill! kill! kill!" and "Blood! blood! blood!"

> Constant illiterate use of the phrase "to woo the Muse" has obscured its poetic sense: the poet's inner communion with the White Goddess, regarded as the source of truth. Truth has been represented by poets as a naked woman: a woman divested of all garments or ornaments that will commit her to any particular position in time and space. The Syrian Moon-goddess was also represented so, with a snake head-dress to remind the devotee that she was Death in disguise, and a lion crouched faithfully at her feet. The poet is in love with the White Goddess, with Truth: his heart breaks with longing and love for her. She is the Flower-goddess Olwen or Blodeuwedd; but she is also Blodeuwedd the Owl, lamp-eyed, hooting dismally, with her foul nest in the hollow of a dead tree, or Circe the pitiless falcon, or Lamia with her flickering tongue, or the snarling-chopped Sow-goddess, or the mare-headed Rhiannon who feeds on raw flesh. *Odi atque amo:* "to be in love with" is also to hate. Determined to escape from the dilemma, the Apollonian teaches himself to despise woman, and teaches woman to despise herself.[14]

If poetry did begin in a matriarchal age, and if the first poets were women, how could their source be the Muse Graves identifies as *the* Muse for the heterosexual male poet? Graves would, of course, argue that regardless of cultural gender-priority the first poets were male; in fact, he goes a good deal further, by stating that "woman is not a poet: she is either Muse or she is nothing."[15] But since men are the guardians of attitudes and laws in a patriarchal culture, it is reasonable to assume that women would be the guardians, and shamans, of what appears to be ancient Indo-European matriarchal culture.

I suspect that the matter is much more complex than this and offer the following suggestion: in an Upper Paleolithic seminomadic hunting-based clan, the magic of the kill would be primarily man-determined and the domain of a male shaman. On the other hand, the magic of generation (fecundity, birth, the hearth) would be primarily woman-determined and the domain of a female shaman. The gender emphasis of Upper Paleolithic image-making is clearly matriarchal, and is associated with cave shelter (the so-called Venuses were found in rock shelters, either as a carved part of the shelter, or stuck into the shelter-floor) or deep-cave sanctuary; it stresses fecundity and the "Demeter delta," or yonic triangle. There are, however, male images too: more often than not animal-garbed, dancing figures whose animal attributes or associations appear tied up with the hunt and power over hard-to-kill beasts.[16]

Graves' book is, in fact, an amazing mish-mash of personal projections and ollave-like research, and I would not reject all of his detailed evidence for a view of poetry based on a White Goddess, who at one time may have been as cogent a source for imagination as Jesus-Christ was for Renaissance painters. But always white? Whiteness is but a portion of the spectrum attributed to The Triple Goddess (the precursor figure for the Christian trinity):

> a Goddess in three aspects—as a young woman, a birth-giving matron, and an old woman. This typical Virgin-Mother-Crone combination was Parvati-Durga-Uma (Kali) in India, Ana-Babd-Macha (the Morrigan) in Ireland, or in Greece Hebe-Hera-Hecate, the three Moerae, the three Gorgons, the three Graece, the three Horae, etc. Among the Vikings, the three-fold Goddess appeared as the Norns; among the Romans, as the Fates or Fortunae; among the druids, as Diana Triformis. The Triple Goddess had more than three: she had hundreds of forms.[17]

In the margin of the "Fates" entry page of Barbara G. Walker's *The Woman's Encyclopedia of Myths and Secrets,* I scribbled various attributes of the three phases of The Triple Goddess:

1. lily   dove   white   purity   spinner   frog   spider   silver fish   white stag   silver wheel   white-flower   virgin   creator

2. rose   passion   red   measurer   heifer   serpent   dragon   perserver

3. darkness   black   cutter   sow   vulture   sphinx   black bitch   maresdestroyer   [Homer's black ewe which Odysseus sacrifices in order to speak with Tiresias in the 11th book of the *Odyssey*]

Relative to the amazing rainbow of The Triple Goddess, to simply call her White is to remove her from the dimensionality of red and black (the Venus of Laussel, carved in the prow of a tiny rock shelter in the French Dordogne at around 20,000 B.C. was originally painted red). And might there not be Brown Goddesses? Yellow Goddesses? Blue Goddesses? "The White Etc. Goddess," Olson is said to have commented.

And the homosexual poet? In Graves' categorical patriarchal (matriarchally veiled) thinking, he is Apollo-bound and without a "true" source, or figure, of inspiration. Yet for both Garcia Lorca and Robert Duncan, to mention two homosexual *and* Dionysian poets, the source is neither Muse nor angel, but the figure so compellingly described by Lorca as the "duende," the daemonized thought of the blood.

And lest Apollo be implicitly dismissed by Graves' dismissal of him from the "truth" of poetry, the novice should consider Walker's entry on "Abaddon" in her *Encyclopedia,* which describes the first spirit-pits, which seem to float in time between the Upper Paleolithic cave-sanctuaries and the pagan temples, of which medieval cathedrals and modern churches appear to be the final "installments":

> The god Apollo was a solar king in heaven during the day, and a Lord of Death in the underworld at night. His latter form became the Jewish Apollyon, Spirit of the Pit (Revelation 9:11). Apollo-Python was the serpent deity in the Pit of the Delphic oracle, who inspired the seeress with mystic vapors from his nether world. The Greek word for Pit was *abaton,* which the Jews corrupted into Abaddon—later a familiar Christian synonym for hell.
>
> Also called a *mundus* or earth-womb, the *abaton* was a real pit, standard equipment in a pagan temple. Those who entered it to "incubate," or to sleep overnight in magical imitation of the incubatory sleep in the womb, were thought to be visited by an "incubus" or spirit who brought prophetic dreams. Novice priests went down into the pit for longer periods of incubation, pantomiming death, burial, and rebirth from the womb of Mother Earth. Once initiated in this way, they were thought to gain the skill of oneiromancy: the ability to interpret dreams.
>
> The Old Testament Joseph earned his oneiromantic talent by incubation in a Pit. The "brothers" who put him there seem to have been fellow priests. He could interpret Pharaoh's dreams only after he had submitted to the ritual. Assyrian priests derived similar powers from a sojourn in the Pit. They then assumed the priestly coat of many colors, signifying communion with the Goddess under her oneiromantic name of Nanshe, "Interpreter of Dreams." It seems likely that Joseph's coat of many colors would have been given him originally not before the initiation but afterward, by a "father" who was actually the high priest.[18]

The Irish ollave in his six-colored garb, priest Joseph in his many-colored coat, against the backdrop of a primordial spore in which clear skies and the moon, night and the bottomlessness of source, fire and the blood of renewal as well as the blood of destruction, are "the deeds done and suffered by light."[19]

11

The poet's resistance to psychoanalysis is a resistance to discovering his unconscious motives for writing poetry—as if discovering is severing—a witch with a long nose intruding into the playhouse window, discovering what the children are "really" doing, there. The fear that more information is the end of information is Blake's enemy, "doubt which is self-contradiction," and it hamstrings the novice through developing a reluctance to investigate Psyche—to investigate *anything.*

But I want to cut across what I believe here and let a poet who rejected analysis and who went ahead to write magnificent poetry after doing so, speak: Rainer Maria Rilke to Lou Andreas-Salomé, 1912:

> I rather shun this getting cleared out and, with my nature, could hardly expect anything good of it. Something like a disinfected soul results from it, a monstrosity, alive, corrected in red like the page of a school notebook.[20]

> I do feel myself infinitely strongly bound to the once begun, to all the joy and all the misery it entails, so that, strictly speaking, I can wish for no sort of change, no interference from without, no relief, except that inherent in enduring and final achievement. . . . It seems to me certain that if one were to drive out my devils, my angels too would get a little (let us say), a very little fright and—you do feel it—that is what I may not risk at any cost.[21]

Rilke would agree with Auden about allowing no books of criticism in a College for Bards, and like Rimbaud, is concerned with the monstrous but from a differing angle: Rimbaud intends to *infect* himself to undermine the starched domesticity of Charlesville and make contact with the chthonic powers of poetry. Rilke fears the *disinfected* soul that might result from analysis, as if it could empty him back to the military-school classroom where he was at the mercy of a master's formulaic revisions. By offering his devils (hardly daemons here; more likely neurotic habits) to a Freudian analyst, he fears that he will be removing an essential alchemical component from the compost he needs to nurture his angels, or flowering. For disinfected Rimbaud, ensouling is a reinfecting; on the other hand, Rilke, probably more abused and disoriented by education than Rimbaud, now seeks to protect what he has been able to save of himself. Infection and disinfection coil like snakes about the caduceus of a healing that for the poet is never clearly one or the other.

In 1922, having weathered this critical period of his life without succumbing to analysis, Rilke wrote to another correspondent:

> I believe that as soon as an artist has found the living center of his activity, nothing is so important for him as to remain in it and never go further away from it (for it is also the center of his personality, his world) than up to the inside wall of what he is quietly and steadily giving forth; his place is *never,* not even for an instant, alongside the observer and judge. . . . Most artists today use up their strength in this going back and forth, and not only do they expend themselves in it, they get themselves hopelessly entangled and lose a part of their essential innocence in the sin of having surprised their work from outside, tasted of it, shared in the enjoyment of it! The infinitely grand and moving thing about Cézanne . . . is that during almost forty years he remained uninterruptedly with his work, in the innermost center of it—, and I hope someday to show

how the incredible freshness and purity of his pictures is due to this obstina-
tion: their surface is really like the flesh of fruit just broken open—, while most
painters already stand facing their own pictures enjoying and relishing them,
violating them in the very process of the work as onlookers and recipients. . . .
(I hope, as I say, someday convincingly to point out this to me absolutely defin-
itive attitude of Cézanne's; it might act as advice and warning for anyone seriously determined to be an artist.)[22]

Artaud: "I don't want to eat my poem, I want to give my heart to my poem."[23]

For Rilke, the labyrinth of the creative process is a walled monastery, out of which fans
the heretical world of analysis, worldly fame, hubris, enjoyment, and relishing. While
the present is not walled off from the past, inspiration is to be protected from its
correctives, as if it takes its orders from a source that regards forays into its inver-
sions, opposites, and caricatures as blasphemous (elsewhere Rilke praises Cézanne for
not losing an afternoon of painting even to attend his only daughter's wedding).

Rilke's words are profound and brave and speak from an ability to sustain himself in a
solitude that most American artists would find pathological (so gregarious are we, or,
in alchemical terms, such "leaky vessels"). However, I see a long-standing problem in
removing the poet from a realm that includes correction, self-observation, and judgment. As a European poet born in the nineteenth century, who made good use of some
of the last aristocratic patronage, Rilke participates in a removed, high romantic image which regards the poet as spontaneous and visionary, a receptacle through which
a primordial frenzy speaks itself. In a "classic" statement of this viewpoint, Jung, in
1922 (the same year Rilke wrote his mature masterpieces), declared: "as long as we
are caught up in the process of creation, we neither see nor understand; indeed we
ought not to understand, for nothing is more injurious to immediate experience than
cognition."[24]

But there is a shadowy side to this viewpoint: if the poet does not "see" or "understand" while writing, such seeing and understanding will have to be done for him. As
one with "special access to the beyond, he is from a societal viewpoint put in the same
category with the child, the insane, and the primitive and, at one time, women,"[25] and
thus ultimately in need of correction or criticism. He is only to be trusted at the point
his writing is rationally framed, canonized, and thus sheared of the fangs that made
him special in the first place. Living poets, from this viewpoint, are better off dead,
when the irrational and disturbing aspects of their writing have been drained off. A
second shadow is this: those who do the draining and evaluating cannot be creative
because spontaneity and self-involvement would weaken critical judgment. For several
hundred years, poets and critics have been snapping at each other across a narrow but
deep river. The living presence of the poet vexes the critic who is unsure of what to do
with him as he has no historical perspective on him. Moreover, the poet not only finds
it disgusting that someone outside his "divine frenzy" should be allowed to judge him
(and in effect decide whether he is to be read or not by future generations) but also
suspects that the critic is a "closet" poet who does not have the guts to strip and bay
naked at the full moon.

In 1984, I recorded several hours of conversation with the archetypal psychologist James Hillman, whose thoughtful and creative books I have been reading for the past decade. We wanted to start to build a bridge across the river I have briefly described, feeling that poetry and psychology can make use of both banks. Neither of us believes in what Hillman refers to as "a certain court model, which splits consciousness from unconsciousness, reason from unreason, creation from criticism." He responded to the Jung passage:

> I wouldn't agree with that. I would say that when you're in the midst of the process of—I don't want to use the word "creation" either, it tends to get in-flated—but in the midst of writing, or speaking a poem, or whatever, let's just say writing, there is a seeing going on in the hand and in the heart, and in the eye, which is not the kind of seeing Jung is talking about which is detached outside seeing, but the fingers have an eye in them. E-Y-E. An eye that knows to put this word and not that word and to cross that out suddenly and to jump to the next thing. That's all seeing. It's not blind. That's a romantic sense that there's natural creativity and then there's detached scientific observation.

In regard to his own practice of analysis, Hillman commented:

> I think most of these alternatives come into the analytical room, especially the one of being a scientific detached judge/critic/observer. Certainly that is a fa-vorite stance one takes in being an analyst. But it is not the only story at all. There's also the talking from that place Rilke is talking about, when you're absolutely inside the image, or inside the emotion or complex that's in the room with the two of you, maybe it's come out of a dream, maybe it has just come out of sitting there and what is said is very free. And now: *is* it blind? . . . Are we where Jung said you don't know what you're saying and you don't see what you're doing? I don't think that's the case. I think it's very much like I said. Your fingers have eyes in them. And when you're reacting emotionally and imag-inatively to the dream, you are doing the same thing as Rilke is talking about. There is a poesis. You are making a whole new construction, which is not an interpretation. It's a new construction that's closer to what you do when you translate. . . . But let's get rid of that word "interpretation," and maybe even "translation." For the moment, that isn't what I want to do with this dream that is coming. I don't want to *interpret* the dream. I want to talk to the dream, talk about the dream, restate the dream, imagine from the dream, but I don't mean a free-floating fantasy. And I sure don't mean a bunch of subjective reactions and feelings and associations: "This makes me think of . . ." You are there, I believe, to *respond* to the dream, and that forces you to stick pretty close to it, much as you have to with a poem that you are translating. The dream is your master, let's say. It provides the limits, the discipline. What you say to it is in service of the dream. Yet, all along the response comes from the imagina-tion."[26]

THE SUBJECTIVE

is not the opposite of the rigorous.
It is the most rigorous, the most difficult.

The precise subjective *is what philosophers are too
lazy & too generalizing to labor, scientists too
frightened to search out.*

The Objective is p.r. for the Generalization.

*Objective Order, so-called, is mental artifact,
   consensus, "collective consciousness,"
   "lethargy of custom (STC"*

*The 'objective' is a consolation prize for those
   who've lost the real.*[27]

        —Robert Kelly

NOTES

1. Gary Snyder, *Regarding Wave* (New York, 1970), p. 40.

2. In February 1968, Olson wrote out a two-page "Plan for a Curriculum of the Soul" and mailed it to George Butterick, then an editor of an occasionally appearing magazine, *Institute of Further Studies,* in whose fourth issue, the plan appeared. Because of complicated typography, I have reproduced it as an Appendix to *Novices.*

3. Snyder, *Earth House Hold* (New York, 1969), p. 19.

4. For Olson in Yucatan, see *Letters for Origin,* and vols. 5 and 6 of *Charles Olson and Robert Creeley: The Complete Correspondence* (Santa Barbara, 1983, 1985), as well as the essay "Human Universe," in *Human Universe* (New York, 1967).

5. Penelope Shuttle and Peter Redgrove, *The Wise Wound: Menstruation and Everywoman* (New York City, 1988).

6. *Back Roads to Far Towns,* Bashō's *Oku-no-Hosomichi* (New York, 1968). A landmark in the translation of Japanese haibun and haiku. For improvisations on haibun in English, see the six Haibun in John Ashbery's *A Wave* (New York, 1984). Direct imitations of haiku in English are generally of little interest; however, many of Corman's very short poems are keen workings off haiku sensibility and form. For example,

> *The cicada
> singing isnt:
> that sound's its life*

(from *for granted* (New Rochelle, N.Y., 1967). Haiku suggests that all event is spontaneous and that dramatic narrative is an accordion-expansion of a shakahachi flute-shriek moment.

7. Snyder, *Earth House Hold,* p. 39.

8. In his *The Life of John Berryman* (London, 1982), John Haffenden wrote: "He belongs to what has become known as the Middle Generation of American poets, a group that includes Delmore Schwartz, Robert Lowell, Randall Jarrell, and Theodore Roethke." While "confessional" (a term I believe coined by poet and critic M. L. Rosenthal) is a fuzzy identifying term for these poets, much of their writing is characterized by personal trauma felt as *the* centripetal force that whirls all other considerations of myth, learning, and daily observation, into its vortex. Refusing la vie bohème, expatriotship, and engagement by non-English European literary movements— Berryman it seems might have improved his lot by becoming a Dadaist—these poets stayed home, looked up to Yeats, Auden, and Frost, and established the image of the American poet as

a teacher sharing an office with his academic colleagues, a very tactile member of a middle-class professional community. Because of the congruity of these poets to the teaching profession itself, and because their writing for the most part does not provide any challenging difficulties, it is natural that they have been taught a great deal, identified by teacher-critics as *the* poets of their generation, and are presented in the majority of textbook poetry anthologies as the creators of post–World War II American poetry.

9. *Antonin Artaud: Selected Writings* (New York, 1976), p. 497.

10. *The Complete Writings of William Blake* (London, 1957), p. 328. For Reich on self-regulation, see *The Function of the Orgasm* (New York, 1961), pp. 143–161.

11. *The Poems of Hart Crane* (New York, 1986), pp. 200–201.

12. Auden's essay is from *The Dyer's Hand and Other Essays* (New York, 1962); it is reprinted in *Poetry and Politics* (New York, 1985), pp. 36–51.

13. Robert Graves, *The White Goddess* (New York, 1969), pp. 21, 22, 457.

14. Graves, *The White Goddess,* pp. 422, 448. Graves' dancers, turning and twisting as we poets intend our lines to imaginatively turn and twist, are also figures of the labyrinth, an open version of its interior action: after the elevation of Dionysus and Ariadne as a divine couple into the night sky, Theseus and his companions are said to have danced a swirling in and out dance around a horned altar, which recalls the actual bull horns through which Cretan bull-dancers flipped in a sacred marriage of the sun-king and the moon-goddess.

15. Graves, *The White Goddess,* p. 446.

16. S. Giedion's *The Eternal Present,* Vol. 1: *The Beginnings of Art* (New York, 1957), is an excellent introduction to Upper Paleolithic imagination. See also Olson's lectures in *Olson* 10, and my *Fracture* (Santa Barbara, 1983).

17. *The Woman's Encyclopedia of Myths and Secrets* (New York, 1983), p. 1018.

18. *The Woman's Encyclopedia,* pp. 2–3.

19. Goethe is said to have stated: "Colors are deeds done and suffered by light."

20. *Letters of Rainer Maria Rilke, 1910–1926* (New York, 1969), p. 44.

21. Ibid., p. 51.

22. Ibid., pp. 273–274.

23. *Artaud Anthology,* p. 101.

24. Jung, "On the Relation of Analytical Psychology to Poetry," *The Portable Jung* (New York, 1972), pp. 301–322.

25. "Part One of a Discussion on Psychology and Poetry," by Clayton Eshleman and James Hillman *Sulfur* 16, p. 58.

26. Jung, "Psychology and Poetry," pp. 58, 72–73. At other points in our discussion, Hillman unpacks such loaded terms as "divine frenzy" and "primordial," terms whose ultimate effect is as negative as it is charismatic.

27. Robert Kelly, "On Discourse," *Io* 20 (Biopoesis), p. 18.

PART
TWO

QUESTIONS OF FORM

"THE SUPERIOR ART":
VERSE AND PROSE AND MODERN POETRY

TIMOTHY STEELE

In the last and longest section of his *Orator*, Cicero takes up the subject of prose rhythm; and, speaking of the earliest writers to attempt rhythmical arrangement in prose, he says of Isocrates:

> The enthusiastic admirers of Isocrates extol as the greatest of his accomplishments that he was the first to introduce rhythm into prose. For when he observed that people listened to orators with solemn attention, but to poets with pleasure, he is said to have sought for rhythms to use in prose as well, both for their intrinsic charm and in order that monotony might be forestalled by variety. (174)

This passage reminds us that ancient prose writers, in developing their art, emulated the older art of poetry. From the fifth century B.C. on, orators and rhetoricians were centrally concerned with establishing quasi-metrical procedures for prose that would give it a structural integrity and attractiveness comparable to that of verse. Gorgias, reputed to have been Isocrates' teacher, is generally considered initiator of rhythmical prose; Cicero himself, shortly after making the comments cited above, argues that both Gorgias and Thrasymachus preceded Isocrates in the innovations with which the younger man was sometimes credited. And Diodorus Siculus makes clear (12.53.2–5) that when Gorgias made his famous embassy and speech to the Athenians in 427 B.C., he had already developed a prose style that incorporated devices—isocolon, homoeoteleuton, parisosis, and the like—suggestive of poetry. In a similar vein, Demetrius observes (*On Style*, 12–15) that, before Gorgias, prose writers employed a loose, disjointed style (*lexis eiromemē*), whereas Gorgias and his followers fashioned a more tightly organized, periodic style (*lexis periodos*) in which, Demetrius says, "the periods succeed one another with no less regularity than the hexameters in the poetry of Homer."

To be sure, ancient writers never insisted that prose actually be composed in meter, that is, in the regularly measured rhythmical units of verse. Yet all major writers on oratory and rhetoric treat prose rhythm as a principal aspect of their subject. And, as Cicero's observations indicate, it was agreed that rhythmical arrangement was a chief means by which poets enchanted their listeners and that something of the same kind of organization would similarly benefit prose writers.

Quite a different phenomenon, however, characterizes recent literary history. Rather than prose emulating the order of verse, verse emulates the freedom of prose. Whereas in earlier times prose writers experimented with cadences suggestive of verse, in the modern period many poets forgo conventional versification in favor of looser rhythms traditionally associated with prose.

One reason for this development concerns the modern novel. Although traditions of prose fiction go back at least as far as Aesop, until fairly recently in literary history the fiction of prestige is mostly in meter. This point is noted by Ezra Pound, who observes in his essay "How to Read" that "from the beginning of literature up to A.D. 1750, poetry was the superior art." But in the late eighteenth and the nineteenth century, the situation changes. Many of the finest fiction writers compose in prose instead of verse, and the novel acquires a popularity and respectability formerly accorded to epic, verse drama, and lyric. In fact, by the end of the nineteenth century, the novel is the dominant form of fiction. Many modern poets—among them Ezra Pound, Ford Madox Ford, and T. S. Eliot—urge that poetry has lost much of its material to prose fiction and that if poetry is to recover that material, it must assimilate characteristics of the novel. Prose, in short, replaces poetry as the superior art.

This situation contributes to the most unusual aspect of the modern movement in poetry: the abandonment of traditional versification in favor of free verse. Wishing to reform their medium, modern poets were forced, as earlier reformers were not, to come to grips with an impressive body of prose fiction. They were forced to compare their art, which was metrical and which appeared in a state of decline, with an ascendent form of fiction produced without meter. In this context Ford and Pound asserted that, as Ford put it in *Thus to Revisit* (an underappreciated volume of reminiscences published in 1921), "verse must be at least as well written as prose if it is to be poetry." In view of the attenuated character of much late Victorian verse, and in view of the contrasting vigor of the novel during this time, one can understand and applaud Ford's sentiment. Yet the sentiment could be, and in fact was, transmuted into the notion that verse should be written as the novel was written—without meter.

Three additional factors contributed to the singular situation of modern poetry and to its moving away from traditional versification and toward prose. First, as I have observed elsewhere ("Tradition and Revolution: The Modern Movement and Free Verse," *Southwest Review* [Summer 1985]), the modern movement's leaders identified the dated idiom of Victorian verse in particular with meter in general and assumed, in consequence, that to overthrow the dated idiom it was necessary to overthrow meter. Previous revolutions had involved, as the modern revolution did, an attack on antiquated style. By identifying metric with idiom, however, and in associating metric with the obsolete mannerisms to which they objected, the leaders of the modern movement created a climate of literary opinion distrustful of versification itself.

The second factor concerns the doctrine, which originated with eighteenth-century aesthetics, that works of art are autonomous entities whose essential virtues reside in their internal, "organic" self-coherence as opposed to conformity with external, "mechanical" convention. If one applies this doctrine to poetry and regards each poem as an autonomous entity, one will naturally be led to believe that every poem may or should create its own prosody. Related to this is the belief, also developed in aesthetic theory, that poetry should aspire to the suggestiveness of music in form as well as meaning. These ideas underlie much modern dissatisfaction with explicit metrical arrangement and much modern desire to loosen the medium of verse. And the ideas can be seen working together in, for instance, Eliot's "Music of Poetry" lecture, in which he suggests that poetry should have a musical rather than a metrical structure and states that free verse embodies "an insistence upon the inner unity which is unique to every poem, against the outer unity which is typical."

The third factor involves modern science and the influence of the concepts of "experiment" and "progress." Because modern science has achieved many advances by refining the apparatus and discarding older procedures, certain modern poets— Pound is representative in this respect—have hoped that poetic breakthroughs and discoveries might result from analogous poetic refinements and discards. And just as the aesthetic doctrine that the poet is autonomous has undermined traditional rules of versification, so the idea that he ought to seek technical novelties has called into doubt standard metrical practice and has moved poetry toward prose. To these observations I may add that, from the founding of the Royal Society of London in the second half of the seventeenth century, and from the time of the reforms in English style urged by Thomas Sprat and other leaders of the Society, prose is widely considered the language of scientific exactitude, poetry the language of metaphoric fancy. Because many modern poets aimed at exactitude and chafed at poetical ornament, it is not surprising that they would be drawn in the direction of a style prosaic not only in diction but also in rhythm.

Given these circumstances, one should not be surprised that the Ford-Pound maxim—verse must be as well written as prose if it is to be poetry—was converted into the idea that verse might profitably be written, as was the novel, without meter. I would like to demonstrate how the conversion was made; more important, I would like to point out the ways in which modern poets, developing a free verse designed to compete with prose fiction, employed concepts that ancient writers had employed in developing an artistic prose designed to compete with poetry; and I will also examine how some modern poets, arguing that free verse was more natural and sophisticated than (and consequently superior to) conventional verse, were sounding ideas that ancient prose writers had sounded during their attempts to establish artistic prose as a legitimate rival or successor to the older art of poetry.

Before we continue, however, it may be helpful to say a few words about the concept of "free verse" itself. Poets did not self-consciously write free verse until the mid-1880s, when Gustave Kahn, Jules Laforgue, Édouard Dujardin, and others began to publish *vers libre* and articles expounding it in Parisian journals such as *Vogue* and *Revue Indépendante*. In his *Premiers Poètes du Vers Libre,* Dujardin gives 1886 as the year of the seminal publications. To point out this fact is not to deny the importance of earlier figures, from the translators of the King James psalms to James Macpherson and Novalis to Martin Tupper, Walt Whitman, and Arthur Rimbaud; it is well to remember, however, that these earlier writers did not call their work "free verse."

It is well to remember, too, that English and American poets did not immediately translate the term *vers libre* into English. It took a while for the term to be naturalized. For instance, when, in the 1910s, Eliot discusses the medium, he speaks of *vers libre;* when he discusses it in the 1940s, he speaks of "free verse." Delays in adopting the Anglicized term may partly be explained by the fact that "free verse" sounds, as Eliot and William Carlos Williams noted, self-contradictory. This difficulty seems to have been less felt in France, perhaps because *vers libre* derived from and was homophonic with *vers libres*, a type of classical French poetry, exemplified by La Fontaine's *Fables* and Molière's *Amphitryon,* which was perfectly metrical. *Vers libres,* that is, are not "free verses" in the twentieth-century sense; they merely feature a mixture of different but conventional meters and a mixture of differents sorts of rhymes—*plates* (couplet), *croisées* (crossed), *embrassées* (enveloped), and so forth. For a comparable kind of versification in English, we might think of works such as Abraham Cowley's Pindaric odes or Matthew Arnold's "Dover Beach."

When the French experimentalists dropped the "s" from *vers libres,* they did so to advocate a new kind of poetry, a poetry which, in Dujardin's words, "pushing liberation to its extreme limit, admits an indeterminate number of syllables." Yet because of its resemblance to and aural identity with the traditional term, the French *vers libre* did not jar the ear and mind in the way that the English term did.

The conversion of which I spoke a few moments ago is evident in a "formula" that Ford drafted in the 1890s, when he began writing *vers libre.* In *Thus to Revisit,* Ford sets forth this formula, the individual articles of which, he tells us, were

> that a poem must be compounded of observation of the everyday life that surrounded us; that it must be written in exactly the same vocabulary as that which one used for one's prose; that, if it were to be in verse, it must attack some subject that needed a slightly more marmoreal treatment than is expedient for the paragraph of a novel; that, if it were to be rhymed, the rhyme must never lead to the introduction of unnecessary thought; and, lastly, that no exigency of metre must interfere with the personal cadence of the writer's mind or the pressure of the recorded emotion.

Beginning with the notion that poetry should address real life and should be written in the same vocabulary as that which one would use if one were writing prose, Ford ends with the idea that meter must not be allowed to interfere with poetry.

If poetry is not metrical, a question arises as to how it can, in compositional terms, be defined. Although "poetry" is a concept that has been over the ages susceptible to many constructions, writers and readers have, historically speaking, associated the art with metrical composition. This is true even of readers such as Aristotle, who have sensibly insisted that a poet should do more than simply write in meter. Does free verse represent a species of what has been traditionally regarded as prose? This question cannot be definitively answered. One can say only the following. On the one hand, free verse is certainly poetry, so far as accepted by custom as poetry. "Poetry is the kind of thing poets write," Robert Frost once remarked; and if poets write free verse, it stands to reason that free verse is poetry. On the other hand, free verse resembles prose, so far as the principles with which the leaders of the modern movement explain free verse are principles customarily elaborated with regard to prose. And we can best appreciate this latter aspect of free verse by scrutinizing several of these principles.

The most common and comprehensive principle that the modernists of our century advance is that free verse is, though not metrical, rhythmical. It is significant that the earliest popular work of what we now call free verse, Tupper's *Proverbial Philosophy* (First Series, 1838), was designated by its author as "Rhythmics." Similarly, William Ernest Henley, the poet whom Ford cites as his most distinguished British predecessor in *vers libre*, uses the term "rhythms" to describe the free verse poems he composed in the 1870s during a long illness. Prefacing his collected *Poems*, Henley speaks of this verse as "those unrhyming rhythms in which I had tried to quintessentialize, as (I believe) one scarce can do in rhyme, my impressions of the Old Edinburgh Infirmary." Ford himself reflects this aspect of free verse theory when, in the "Vers Libre" chapter of *Thus to Revisit*, he constructs a linear diagram, one extreme of which is represented by the factual prose of civil service documents and the other extreme of which is represented by highly rhetorical and musical verse, such as the *Marseillaise*—the intermediate area being occupied by forms of prose and verse that are increasingly "creative" as they verge toward the midpoint and each other. And of the diagram overall, Ford writes:

> And so the case for *Vers Libre* is made.
>
> It is made for even the least intelligent reader. For who in his senses will deny that, between the entrenched lines of Prosaists and Versificators lies a No Man's Land that is the territory of Neither-Prose-Nor-Verse? And few who have given the matter any attention will deny that this is the oldest, the most primitive, the least sophisticate form of all literature. It is the form of incised writing, of marmoreal inscription, of the prophets—rhythm!

In essence, Ford is defining rhythm in terms of the opposition Isocrates uses when he says in a surviving fragment of what is evidently a lost *Art of Rhetoric:* "[P]rose must not be merely prose, or it will be dry; nor metrical, or its art will be undisguised; but it should be compounded with every sort of rhythm." The same opposition appears in that section of the *Rhetoric* that Aristotle devotes to prose rhythm:

> The form of diction should be neither metrical (*emmetron*) nor without rhythm (*arrhythmon*). . . . If it is without rhythm it is unlimited, whereas it ought to be limited (but not by metre); for that which is unlimited is unpleasant and unknowable. Now all things are limited by number, and the number belonging to the form of diction is rhythm (*rhythmos*), of which the meters (*metra*) are divisions. Wherefore prose (*logon*) must be rhythmical, but not metrical [i.e., in a specific meter such as a trimeter or hexameter], otherwise it will be a poem (*poiēma*). Nor must this rhythm be rigorously carried out, but only up to a certain point. (3.8.1–3)

Isocrates and Aristotle define, in other words, the same no-man's-land that Ford defines, and for Isocrates and Aristotle, as for Ford, this territory is rhythm. However, for the ancient writers, the territory is occupied by artistic prose, for Ford by *vers libre*.

If free verse generally embodies rhythm rather than meter, free verse embodies particular principles that earlier periods have associated with prose. One is the principle of suggesting, while at the same time avoiding, meter. With regard to free verse, this principle is most clearly expressed by Eliot in his "Reflections on *Vers Libre*":

> [T]he most interesting verse which has yet been written in our language has been done either by taking a very simple form, like the iambic pentameter, and constantly withdrawing from it, or taking no form at all, and constantly approximating to a very simple one. It is this contrast between fixity and flux, this unperceived evasion of monotony, which is the very life of verse.

To illustrate his remarks, Eliot quotes T. E. Hulme's "The Embankment" and a passage from Pound's "Near Perigord," and comments: "It is obvious that the charm of these lines could not be, without the constant suggestion and the skilful evasion of iambic pentameter."

These observations resemble those that Demetrius makes when he says (*On Style,* 183) of Plato's prose: "Plato in many passages owes his elegance directly to the rhythm. . . . His members seem to glide along and to be neither altogether metrical nor unmetrical." Eliot's observations also resemble those Cicero makes when he urges (*Orator,* 198) that "in spoken prose, a passage is regarded as rhythmical not when it is composed entirely of metrical forms but when it comes very close to being so." Furthermore, Eliot's argument that, in writing free verse, the poet should move between affirmations and denials of metrical expectation recalls a suggestion that Quintilian, following earlier writers such as Aristotle and Cicero, offers in his *Institutes of Oratory.* A good oration, Quintilian urges, should have rhythmical qualities. Nonetheless, its rhythms should not be too consistent or definite, and "[i]t will therefore be desirable from time to time that in certain passages the rhythm should be deliberately dissolved" (9.4.144).

With respect to this last point, one should note that ancient Greek and Latin, in elements such as pitch and stress, differed from modern English and for that matter from each other: the aural effect of rhythmical dissolution in an oration would not be exactly the same as the effect in an English free verse poem. The principle, however, is similar. One might also note that, although the practice of ancient prose rhythm was never uniform, all the available evidence (e.g., Aristotle, *Rhetoric,* 3.8.1; Dionysius of Helicarnassus, *On Literary Composition,* 11; Cicero, *De Oratore,* 3.195–196) indicates not only that almost all prose writers took rhythm seriously but that even uneducated audiences could appreciate skillful rhythm in an oration and could be irritated and put off by inept rhythm.

Another principle advanced by leaders of the modern movement is that, in free verse, the poet is concerned with the overall movement of the poem rather than the metrical structure of the individual lines. In free verse, this argument runs, conventional versification is sacrificed in the interests of broader rhythmical arrangement. Pound succinctly expresses this principle in his review of Eliot's *Prufrock and Other Observations:* "Prosody is the articulation of the total sound of a poem"; he subsequently remarks, "There is undoubtedly a sense of music that takes count of the 'shape' of the rhythm in a melody rather than of bar divisions." Eliot himself, in his "Music of Poetry," expresses this principle when he contends that "the music of verse is not a line by line matter, but a question of the whole poem. Only with this in mind can we approach the vexed question of formal pattern and free verse." And the principle can be traced in Williams' argument, in his entry for Free Verse in the *Princeton Encyclopedia of Poetry and Poetics,* that some of Milton's work resembles free verse because

Milton, like the modern experimentalists, exhibits a "tendency to make the verse paragraph rather than the line his basic unit."

Again, the principle thus expounded is one earlier expounded with respect to prose. In fact, with this principle Quintilian distinguishes prose from verse: "[R]hythm has unlimited space over which it may range, whereas the spaces of meter are confined. . . . Further it is not so important for us to consider [in prose] the actual feet as the general rhythmical effect of the period. . . . Therefore rhythmical structure will hold the same place in prose that is held by versification in poetry" (9.4.50;115–116). That is, just as some of the modern experimentalists suggest substituting, in prosodic theory, *rhythmos* for *metron,* so they suggest substituting, in practice, *compositio,* the general putting together of a written composition, for *versificatio,* the specific arrangement of speech into metrical lines.

Another concept sometimes advanced by free verse poets is the possibility to establish, in free verse, an indeterminate unit of versification. This concept is anticipated by Gerard Manley Hopkins in his Preface to his *Poems (1876–1889),* in which he discusses "Sprung Rhythm," involving "feet from one to four syllables, regularly, and for particular effects any number of slack or weak syllables." It is interesting that Hopkins cites the paeonic foot, about which I will say more, as being particularly appropriate to sprung rhythm and that he favors sprung rhythm partly because he believes it prosaically free of affectation: "Sprung Rhythm is the most natural of things. . . . It is the rhythm of common speech and of written prose, when rhythm is perceived in them." In practice, Hopkins' verse, with its heavily accentual quality, its frequently insistent alliteration, and its rhyme seems in some ways remote from the work of the twentieth-century free versers. Hopkins himself compares his procedures to those of the older, purely accentual tradition of *Piers Plowman.* Yet so far as his theory of sprung rhythm appeals to prose rhythm and proposes an expandable metrical foot, a foot that can accommodate "for particular effects any number of slack or weak syllables," he prefigures certain modern experimentalists.

Robert Bridges, Hopkins' friend who edited and published in 1918 Hopkins' poems and preface, developed along different lines ideas like those Hopkins pursued. The best-known exponent of an indeterminate metrical unit, however, is Williams, who, late in his career, developed a theory of what he termed "the variable foot." Though Poe invented this term in his "Rationale of Verse," his "variable foot" is not truly a foot but a "caesura"; and Williams appears to have adopted the term for his own purposes, without being influenced conceptually by Poe. Indeed, in his discussion of the variable foot in his entry for free verse in the *Princeton Encyclopedia,* Williams neither refers to Poe nor mentions Poe's essay in the bibliography attached to the discussion.

Williams' variable foot is a sort of prosodic accordian. One can squeeze it down to a syllable or two or draw it out to eight or nine or more syllables. Williams sees in Hopkins a suggestion of this new type of poetic foot. "Hopkins, in a constipated way with his 'sprung' measures, half realized it but not freely enough," says Williams in a letter to Richard Eberhart. And in another letter to Eberhart, Williams discusses his theory, citing the following lines:

> (1) The smell of the heat is boxwood
> (2) when rousing us

> *(3) a movement of the air*
> *(4) stirs our thoughts*
> *(5) that had no life in them*
> *(6) to a life, a life in which . . .*

and then commenting: "Count a single beat to each numeral. You may not agree with my ear, but that is the way I count the line." Thus, six successive feet ostensibly possess metrical equivalence to each other, with their equivalence consisting of their each having one beat. But the feet are also variable because their variability consists of their accommodating different numbers of unstressed syllables.

An interesting feature of both Williams' and Hopkins' variable feet, and of indeterminate units of versification generally, is that they recall the ancient prose writers' interest in paeonic feet and *clausulae.* The paeon was the foot that various writers on rhetoric felt especially appropriate to prose. Its basic form was the first paeon ($- \smile \smile \smile$ or its inversion $\smile \smile \smile -$); it was recommended because unlike the dactyl, spondee, trochee, and iamb, the paeon was not linked with any particular poetic meter, such as the hexameter, tetrameter, or trimeter. Thus, prose writers could make the paeon their own, using paeonic rhythm without too great a risk of sounding overly poetical. Aristotle, who spells the word, in contrast with later custom, with an alpha instead of an omega as the fourth letter, puts the matter this way (*Rhetoric,* 3.8.5): "[T]he paean should be retained [for prose], because it is the only one of the rhythms mentioned which is not adapted to a metrical system, so that it is most likely to be undetected [i.e., likely to sound rhythmical without too much calling to mind this-or-that verse form]."

As for *clausulae,* they were cadential units designed to highlight the conclusions of clauses and periods and consisted of different combinations of feet. For instance, three *clausulae* favored by Latin orators were the cretic spondee ($- \smile - - \asymp$), the double cretic ($- \smile - - \smile \asymp$), and the cretic dichoree ($- \smile - - \smile - \smile$).

The point to note about paeons, *clausulae,* and variable feet is this: in both the modern and ancient cases, units are longer than normal poetic feet, and, in both cases, writers explore such units because they have no association with conventional meters. The comparison does not extend beyond a point. Even those writers most interested in the paeon seem to have believed that paeonic rhythm was applicable only to the beginnings and ends of clauses and periods and that *clausulae* marked simply grammatical pauses, whereas a poet writing in indeterminate feet uses them throughout his poem. Furthermore, even the *clausulae* were relatively well defined and appear recognizable to the ear, whereas the modern variable measures are just what they are said to be—variable—and they discourage perception of any but the roughest proportional relationships.

There is a related matter. Though orators desired to speak movingly and memorably to their audience, and though rhythmical arrangement helped them achieve this end, they also recognized that conspicuous stylistic refinements might prove counterproductive, especially in forensic oratory, where an impression of sincerity was crucial. Therefore, the paeon was favored by prose writers largely because it offered the opportunity for rhythmical arrangement without too great a risk of poeticality. And prose writers in general tried to strike a balance between being organized but not too organized. Quintilian says of prose rhythm, "Above all it is necessary to conceal the care expended upon it so that our rhythms may seem to possess a spontaneous flow, not to have been the result of elaborate search or compulsion" (9.4.147).

In the same spirit, modern critics often warn poets to go in fear of metricality. It is often said that meter should be shunned because it is too artificial to accord with the effective expression of feeling. Ford, for instance, in his "Notes for a Lecture on Vers Libre" (a lecture delivered in the 1920s in New York City, the notes having been preserved by Frank MacShane in his *Critical Writings of Ford Madox Ford*) says: "[T]he worst of verse forms is that they lead almost inevitably to imitation and almost inevitably to insincerity." And the fear of many modern poets that they will be convicted of affectation if they write metrically is like the fear among ancient orators that they will lose persuasiveness if, in legal or political debate, they do not appear sufficiently spontaneous.

Another interesting circumstance is that, just as some ancient orators argue that their art is more demanding than verse, so some advocates of modern free verse contend that their art is more taxing than metrical composition. Moreover, in both cases, the argument turns on the same idea: the poet working in meter has a pattern to assist him in organizing his material, but the writer not working in meter must create his structure *ex nihilo*. For example, Cicero voices this argument when he urges (*Orator*, 198) that "prose is harder to write than verse, because in the latter there is a definite and fixed law which must be followed. In a speech, however, there is no rule except that the style must not be straggling or cramped or loose or chaotic."

Similarly, Eliot contrasts, in his essay on Kipling, straightforwardness of meaning and metric with a poetry based on "a musical pattern of emotional overtones." Eliot suggests that poetry which is, like Kipling's, metrically direct is merely "verse," whereas work musically elusive in structure belongs to "the more difficult forms of poetry." A related idea underlies Eliot's view, expressed in his "Reflections on *Verse Libre*," of rhyme: "The rejection of rhyme is not a leap at facility; on the contrary, it imposes a much severer strain upon the language." In brief, it is as if the age-old debate about the relative difficulty of the two literary arts—poetry with the constraints and at the same time support and sensuous appeal of meter, prose with the freedom from and at the same time need to approximate order—is transposed in the modern period into a debate about the relative difficulty of metrical as opposed to free verse.

There is another interesting aspect of the situation we have been examining. In antiquity and the early Middle Ages, there was a sense of a single *ars dictaminis*—if there was a sense of discourse that embraced both poetry and prose—that art involved to some extent the study of metrical and rhythmical arrangement. At times in this century, there seems a single art of discourse, but the art is based on the absence of such arrangement. For instance, in a letter to Parker Tyler, Williams remarks, referring to both his use of prose passages in his verse and Wallace Stevens' characterization of it as an "antipoetic" device:

> It is *not* an antipoetic device, the repeating of which piece of miscalculation makes me want to puke. It *is* that prose and verse are both *writing*, both a

matter of the words and an interrelation between words for the purpose of exposition, or other better defined purpose of *the art*. Please do not stress other "meanings." I want to say that prose and verse are to me the same thing.

And in a letter to Horace Gregory, Williams discusses the presence of prose correspondence in Book One of *Paterson*, and says:

> The purpose of the long letter at the end is partly ironic, partly "writing" to make it plain that even poetry is writing and nothing else—so that there's a logical continuity in the art, prose, verse: an identity.

> Frankly I'm sick of the constant aping of the Stevens' dictum that I resort to the antipoetic as a heightening device. That's plain crap—and everyone copies it. . . . The truth is that there's an *identity* between prose and verse, not an antithesis. It all rests on the same time base, the same measure.

Earlier writers would have agreed with Williams' contention that prose and verse are related. But they would probably have treated that relationship, first and foremost, with respect to poetry and its metrical order. For Williams the relationship seems to involve first and foremost prose and the freedom of its rhythms.

The modern appropriation, for theories of verse, of ideas traditionally associated with prose appears unconscious. In the entry for free verse, which Williams wrote for the *Princeton Encyclopedia* late in his life and which in fact was not published until 1965, two years after his death, Williams refers to Eduard Norden's *Die Antike Kunstprosa*. This landmark work, first published in 1898, has since remained a standard study of ancient prose rhythm. Otherwise, there is no evidence that the experimentalists realized the sources of their ideas. This should not surprise us perhaps because much early scholarship about ancient prose rhythm was in German. Nevertheless, George Saintsbury's *History of English Prose Rhythm*, published in 1912, makes note of the German work, though Saintsbury himself is more concerned with the development of English prose than with matters related to prose rhythm in general. Moreover, most of the relevant classical texts were available, in their original languages and in translations; one would think that Eliot and Pound, both of whom expressed interest in classical literature, might have known some of the material. As it is, their not knowing the material would not matter, except that an important point is made throughout earlier discussions of meter and rhythm: speech can be ordered generally by rhythm, particularly by meter; take away meter, and you have nothing left but rhythm.

Equally important is the point, stressed by even those ancient writers who believed prose superior to verse, that rhythmical organization has meaning only with reference to a literary context in which meter is practiced. Meters are specific types of the more general quality of rhythm, and one cannot do much in the way of discussing general rhythmical effects, except against the backdrop of the more particular structure of meter. Interestingly enough, Eliot makes this point in his "Reflections on *Vers Libre*" when he says that "the ghost of some simple metre should lurk behind the arras in even the 'freest' verse: to advance menacingly as we doze, and withdraw as we rouse." The problem is that the poet may draw his sword and with the cry of "How now? A rat?

Dead for a ducat, dead!" make a pass through the arras and finish off meter once and for all. This is, in fact, what has happened with much verse since the triumph of the modern movement. Many poets cease to "withdraw" from meter. They simply ignore the question of meter entirely.

I must mention a related development. When the experimentalists abandoned traditional meter in hope of emulating qualities of prose fiction, they were responding to a particuar literary situation. Poetry had fallen on hard times; the novel was flourishing. Maybe the experiment of writing poetry without meter had to be tried. Maybe what Williams termed, in a letter to Kay Boyle in 1932, "a formless interim" was necessary. Yet that interim has since been repeatedly extended until many poets, following the modernists' procedures, yet remote from the context of their revolt, have taken the view that, if one tries to work in meter and has trouble expressing what one wants to express, one should turn to free verse, rather than trying patiently to improve and broaden one's skills in conventional versification.

An example of this attitude is provided by one of the most influential poets of the second half of the twentieth century, Robert Lowell. Although he wrote his early verse in meter, he became dissatisfied with it because, as he says in an interview with the *Paris Review* in the 1960s, "I couldn't get any experience into tight metrical forms. . . . I felt that the meter plastered difficulties and mannerisms on what I was trying to say to such an extent that it terribly hampered me." This feeling was related to another feeling, to wit, that "Prose is in many ways better off than poetry. . . . [O]n the whole prose is less cut off from life than poetry is." Lowell remarks that he attempted for a time to write in prose but "I found it got awfully tedious working out transitions and putting in things that didn't seem very important but were necessary to the prose continuity." Faced with these problems, Lowell moved into free verse and into what he terms "breaking forms."

One appreciates Lowell's feeling. At the same time, one cannot help imagining Homer telling the *Chios Quarterly*, "When I began the *Iliad*, I had this crazy notion that I would write it in hexameters. Can you believe that? Well, I soon learned that there was no way I was going to fit the passions of Achilles and Hector into those rigid six-feet lines. The only thing to do, I realized, was to break down my forms." What is it that Dionysius says (*On Literary Composition*, 20) of Homer? "This is the practice of Homer, that surpassing genius, although he has but one metre and few rhythms. Within these limits, nevertheless, he is continually producing new effects and artistic refinements, so that actually to see the incidents taking place would give no advantage over our having them thus described." One could apply similar tribute to Dante or Shakespeare or Emily Dickinson or almost any excellent poet. We admire them in part because they write distinctively and vitally in meter.

There is another issue. Lowell may well feel, as he says in his interview, "It's quite hard to think of a young poet who has the vitality, say, of Salinger or Saul Bellow." Yet, in making this statement, Lowell might have considered that Salinger's and Bellow's fictions move and entertain us partly because Salinger and Bellow were willing to undertake the "awfully tedious working out of transitions and putting in things that didn't seem very important but were necessary to the prose continuity." An unfortunate aspect of Lowell's attitude is that it entails dispensing with something of great value— poetic meter—without securing in return the discipline of prose fiction. It leaves poetry between verse and prose, offering the poet the challenges of neither art and the reader the appeals of neither. And this is not the end that Ford, Pound, and Eliot envisioned when they initially insisted that poetry should become more like the novel.

In most respects, prose is more favorably situated than verse. Prose is the more accommodating medium. It is more fluid and variable; it more readily tolerates different kinds of expression. Nonetheless, throughout most of literary history, readers and listeners have more loved and venerated verse, and verse has served as the primary literary art. Its primacy has derived from meter. The intellectual and aural beauty of fine metrical arrangement has, by itself, outweighed the manifold advantages of prose. In concluding this essay, one can do no better than to cite Samuel Johnson's observations, from *Rambler* 86, on this point:

> [V]ersification, or the art of modulating his numbers, is indispensably necessary to a poet. Every other power by which the understanding is enlightened or the imagination enchanted may be exercised in prose. But the poet has this peculiar superiority, that to all the powers which the perfection of every other composition can require he adds the faculty of joining music with reason, and of acting at once upon the senses and the passions. I suppose there are few who do not feel themselves touched by poetical melody, and who will not confess that they are more of less moved by the same thoughts as they are conveyed by different sounds, and more affected by the same words in one order than in another. The perception of harmony is indeed conferred upon men in degrees very unequal, but there are none who do not perceive it or to whom a regular series of proportionate sounds cannot give delight.

Author's Note. In this essay, I have referred to editions of works that are for the most part standard and easily available. I have used the Loeb Classical Library editions of nearly all of the ancient writers discussed. However, references to Dionysius of Helicarnassus's *On Literary Composition* are to W. Rhys Roberts' edition (Cambridge, 1910), which also contains (pp. 192–193) the fragment of Isocrates' lost *Rhetoric* cited in this essay. The cited essays and reviews of Pound can be found in his *Literary Essays* (New York, 1968). Eliot's "The Music of Poetry" and his essay on Kipling appear in his *On Poetry and Poets* (London, 1957) and his "Reflections on *Vers Libre*" in his *To Criticize the Critics* (London, 1965). Williams' letters appear in John C. Thirlwall, ed., *The Selected Letters of William Carlos Williams* (New York, 1957).

VERSE AND VOICE

CHARLES O. HARTMAN

"Singing is just sustained talking."
—The Music Man

The point about verse, by now, is not con-
tention between free and metrical verse. That choice is important for each poet, vital
for each poem; but it is not a choice between formlessness and form, or fresh and
trite form, or the old and the new, or responsibility and anarchy. The point about verse
is prosody, in a sense—not a particular prosodic choice, but the presence, for both
poet and reader, of a fully imagined shape in time.

I began to write poetry after I began to play music, and poetry seems to me more
instructively like music or dance than like painting. It deepens our awareness of being
in time. Time is linear, just one damned thing after another; yet our experience of
time is also layered and multiple. Einsteinian physics says that simultaneity, not to
be found in the universe at large, is born of our view of the universe. The set of things
we see as simultaneous defines precisely where and when we exist—our point of view;
that is, who we are.

This complexity in our temporal experience bears on a theory of the arts like Morse
Peckham's in *Man's Rage for Chaos.* Much of our mental equipment is devoted to
selectively closing out the plenitude of sensation the world offers us, to avoid what
William James called "a bloomin', buzzin' confusion." This adaptive insensitivity makes
a surviving adult out of the infant Auden describes, who "cannot / Stop the vivid
present to think" and must spend considerable time learning what to pay attention to
and what can be safely ignored—learning, as our guardians admonish us, *to do one
thing at a time.* Yet as we perfect our habitual methods and methodical habits, we
stagnate. This is true for a day and a lifetime, for a decade and a whole culture. Our
problem as a species, Peckham says, is to introduce ourselves always to a little more
multiplicity and confusion than we can comfortably stand. The arts disturb our habits
of perception, calling our attention to aspects of the world we didn't think we needed
to know about, making more of our experience available to us. This counterbalance to
routine is adaptive also, since it trains us for the inevitable job of coming to terms
with something new.

In *Free Verse* (Princeton, 1981), trying to indicate how poets writing nonmetrical
verse make us experience their work as layered and plentiful while paradoxically it

unfolds moment by moment in time, I used the word "counterpoint." When Bach wrote his almost-final work, the *Art of Fugue,* he called each piece in it a *contrapunctus.* In that style (nearly dead by the time his sons sold the engraved plates to pay for the funeral), two or three or four or even six voices, all independent and each carrying a singable and highly integral melody, are set against or beside each other in such a way that they come together, almost as if by accident, in a continuous stream of momentary harmonies, a coherent whole. This contrapuntal style embodies a remarkably hopeful vision of social being. Critics have uscd this metaphor before; I adopted it to substantiate a definition of prosody as the poet's method of controlling the reader's attention to the temporal experience of the poem. This version of "prosody" neither excludes free verse (like some older theories) nor valorizes it over metrical verse.

Many free verse poems use counterpoint, especially between the *line* and the *sentence,* as the basic principle of prosodic organization—the main vehicle of our heightened sense of layered experience in the reading. When the line ends in the middle of a sentence, or the sentence in the middle of a line, we hear two kinds of things going on at once. But the importance of counterpoint is not confined to free verse. Here is the first stanza from Andrew Marvell's "A Dialogue Between the Soul and the Body." The Soul is complaining about the illnesses and temptations and sensory distractions that the Body presents:

> *O who shall from this dungeon raise*
> *A soul enslaved so many ways?*
> *With bolts of bones, that fettered stands*
> *In feet; and manacled in hands:*
> *Here blinded with an eye; and there*
> *Deaf with the drumming of an ear:*
> *A soul hung up, as 'twere, in chains*
> *Of nerves, and arteries, and veins;*
> *Tortured, besides each other part,*
> *In a vain head, and double heart.*

In these clear iambic tetrameter couplets, what is counterpointed? First, the same interplay between line and sentence that sustains many free-verse poems is at work here. We call any single instance of this "enjambment": Marvell's fifth line enjambs or runs on into the sixth. We speak of strong and weak enjambments, or light and heavy ones: "and there / Deaf" is strong; we *know* something else is coming, and we wait in suspense; the line-break makes a "sharp cut" in the syntax, as John Hollander puts it (see *Vision and Resonance* [Oxford, 1975]). The break between the last two lines of the stanza exemplifies a weak enjambment; the syntax permits a cleaner division after "other part," and the lines pose with greater independence.

But enjambments are not isolated events. They are points at which the system of the sentence intersects and interferes with the system of the lines, where verse and syntax cross each other. When the two coincide—when they agree about where the voice should divide the stream of speech, as here at the ends of couplets—we hear a "weak enjambment" or none. Where the continuity that one system makes us expect is interrupted by the other system, what we call the "strong enjambment" makes us much more conscious of the presence of both systems. Marvell devotes one line to an image, "a soul hung up . . . in chains," and the next line to a list: "nerves, arteries and veins." But "chains" is linked to "nerves" and the rest by the word "of." This syntactical and metaphorical linkage crosses the line boundary. We hear the articulation of the sentence and the contradictory articulation of each line simultaneously.

In some ways, this kind of counterpoint is even more readily available in metrical verse than in free verse because the system of the line is more obviously systematic. The steadiness of the meter strengthens the feeling of enjambment. Consider Marvell's second couplet: The syntactical inversion allowed in seventeenth-century poetry could make the first of its lines stand alone; "With bolts of bones, that fettered stands" could equal "That stands fettered with bolts of bones," and "bolts" seem close enough to "fetters." The regular iambs encourage us to hear the isolated line that way. But the sentence continues, and the couplet is incompleted: "In feet, and manacled in hands."

More systems come into play in this couplet than the metrical line and the sentence that runs across it. There's also the rhyme; our expectation of an answering rhyme helps tell us that the sentence is going to continue. There's also alliteration, within and between lines. There's also the assonance of "stands" and "manacled," again crossing the line-break. There's also the pair of etymological puns, "fettered in feet" and "manacled in hands." Those puns depend on the ambiguity of the little word "in." Marvell plays frequently on prepositions and other particles; and in this way he seems—like Williams—to uncover potential counterpoints growing out of the littlest elements of our speech.

There are counterpoints within lines, as well as between them. The most basic counterpoint in metrical verse is the relation between the meter, which is abstract and regular, and the rhythm, which is always particular and unique to a single line. In some poetry, the counterpoint shows up as metrical variation (substituted feet); Yeats is full of good examples. In Marvell as in most poetry of the century after him, aside from a few telling trochees and ionics, the main counterpoints in the line come from the shifting position of the caesura and the varying weight of the stresses. His four stresses can sound like three or even two; and they can divide themselves into one and three, two and two, three and one, four separate units—patterns that we hear against the four-square solidity of the basic meter.

The point is not pretty geometrics but our multiple simultaneous awareness. We listen to language in sentences; that is how we know what's being said. We also listen to lines and their rhythms and meters; as fundamentally musical animals, we find our attention caught by catchy sounds. We hear Marvell completing a statement, and we hear him completing a rhyme. These events, utterly different in kind, happen at the same time and seem to have something to do with each other.

Throughout Marvell's stanza, we're aware of the distress of the Soul—and of pleasure in the neatness of sound and wit in the expression of that pain. Furthermore, the language is the language of paradox—"blinded with an eye" and so on. What is paradox, we could wonder, but a counterpoint between two trains or two modes of thought? You get an eye, you expect to see; but no, it simply makes you blind to what can only be seen without eyes. We could speak of a counterpoint between possibility and actuality, as well.

One can overextend any supple and powerful critical idea; as it colonizes the available territory of thought, everything becomes contrapuntal, or metaphorical, or ironic. The sooner this happens, the shorter the useful life-cycle of the critical term. But one question about the limits of "counterpoint" helps to clarify the fundamental continuity between prosody and meaning. The largest formal rhythm of Marvell's poem is the alternation of stanzas. It would be possible, recalling Bach, to speak of a counterpoint literally between the two *voices,* the Soul's voice and the Body's, which is a counterpoint between two personalities, two visions of human life, and so on. Yet the Soul speaks, and *then* the Body speaks. Should we call such a dialogue contrapuntal or not?

It hardly matters. But complex counterpoint is certainly created when a dialogue is collapsed into simultaneity. One example would be Ashbery's long poem in two columns, "Litany." A smaller example is Simon and Garfunkel's "Scarborough Fair/ Canticle," in which a new song of anger against war is entwined with an old song of bitterness in love. Both these examples are emphatically *oral* works. The Simon and Garfunkel piece, like any song (any music), has its full existence only in live or recorded *performance.* This means that the pace at which the audience receives the work is determined by the performer. The artist (in one role or another) has unusually direct control over our temporal experience of the work, over the density and layering of that temporal experience, what we hear in conjunction with what. Ashbery's poem is printed in a book; but I find I can't read it at all unless I work continuously to reconstruct a simultaneous, more or less fugal relation between the two voices in the two columns. In any case, the title, "Litany," calls attention to the idea of mutually responding voices.

II

The word *voice* runs through all our discussions of poetry—in the classroom, in reviews, in critical studies. An idea about voice seems to involve an idea about personality. We ask for *genuine* and *authentic* voices, and we urge students to find their own *individual* voices. All these ideals seem to demand that the voice be somehow *single*—and I wonder if it ever is.

It's a rare poem that contains any original words; and most of those that do we call nonsense poems. Coleridge said poetry is the best words in the best order; and in a way the poet's job is simply to select words from the dictionary and compose them. On that basic level, *authorship* becomes a fuzzy concept. Again, as Lewis Hyde points out (see *The Gift* [Random House, 1979]), almost every poet reports the peculiar experience of having written a poem without having been the writer of it—as if the poem were a gift that passed through the poet without leaving any pride or responsibility behind it. It's hard to take credit as the author of a poem like that (though of course we manage). And something of that anonymity seems to attach to every poem. In one degree or another, it may attach to everything we say and hear, poems being structures of language arranged so as to bring out this resonance.

Suppose you overhear a few words of conversation at a party: "the things you are, my favorite things." You might feel a moment of interesting, perhaps uncomfortable dividedness of, attention—not between these words and whatever you were listening to before (though that is another counterpoint), but within these seven words your ears picked out. As I put it earlier, this bit of language brings with it or evokes or demands or participates in at least two *systems* or contexts—the stream of some-body's speech and the set of all popular song titles. There are other contexts, as well. Since it isn't a complete sentence, you might suspect that it's part of one—a clause and an appositive phrase. You might hear it as a little orchestration of sounds—the repetition of the word "things," the variations of "th" and "r" sounds, the transition from short vowels to long back to short again. On an ethical level, there is a two-part movement, out from the speaker and back again, in the shift between "you" and "my." And of course there may be a second quoted song title, "(All) the things you are." There might even be a metrical context, since the words scan easily as an iambic tetrameter. Metrical or not, it has an internal rhythmic neatness—the two pairs of stresses, with the repeated word chiasmically crossing the pairs.

At least potentially, all these versions or associations of the bit of language would be simultaneously available to you. Presumably, you would try to sort out which ones were relevant—or rather you would do the sorting automatically, probably by means of the question, "Is that something the speaker meant?" You might wonder whether the quotation was deliberate. If so, is the speaker's listener supposed to recognize it, or are you hearing someone like the young English poet in Waugh's *The Loved One,* who woos a young woman from Los Angeles by sending her unattributed Keats?

On the other hand, if you find these words in a poem, they belong furthermore to an *invented* stream of speech, the speech of a person more or less artificial, less or more identical with the poet. Now the question of how the quotation is meant be-comes even more complex—did the poet mean to quote that song title, or was it a coincidence of common words? Did he or she want us to think that the invented speaker meant to quote it?

ANTHEM[1]

> I remember Bird, I remember
> Clifford, I remember Django.
> I remember you.
>
> Says my heart, What is this thing
> Called love? My foolish heart. People—
> People will say we're in love, say it
> Over and over again; it's the talk
> Of the town. Who knows? How am I
> To know? How about you? In your own
> Sweet way, you don't know what
> Love is, what a difference
> A day made, what's new, what now,
> My love. What is there to say?
> I hear music. The song is you.
> . . . .
> You're my everything. How long
> Has this been going on? Always
> It's the same old story: Out of nowhere
> It could happen to you, all over again.
> Everything happens to me—all

> *The things you are, my favorite things;*
> *All of you, all of me; all day long, all through*
> *The night; all too soon, too close*
> *For comfort, too marvelous for words. All*
> *Or nothing at all. Sometimes*
> *I'm happy, sometimes I feel*
> *Like a motherless child—but*
> *Beautiful, careful, falling grace, bouquet,*
> *Bewitched body and soul. Come*
> *Rain or come shine, we'll be*
> *Together, we'll be together*
> *Again, again, time after time, moment*
> *To moment, cheek to cheek.*
> *Close your eyes, I'll close my eyes.*
> *I feel a song coming on. The song is you.*

When I wrote that poem, I had been noticing how close the table of contents in a fake book came to making sense. The titles were like the words of a metasong that Americans had been singing to each other for sixty years. I carried myself through the work of writing the poem by thinking it was an exercise: Could I make plausible sentences using nothing but the titles of songs? But when I had finished, something had happened that surprised me. It seemed that I had written a love poem, and one in which the emotion felt genuine.

This paradox—the earnest poem that is wholly plagiarized—recalls an example used by Barbara Herrnstein Smith for somewhat different purposes (see *On the Margins of Discourse* [Chicago, 1978]): You go into a store and buy a card with a bit of doggerel about getting well; and you sign it; and you give it to somebody. (Or Andy Warhol signs a Campbell's soup can—see Hugh Kenner, *The Counterfeiters* [1968; Anchor, 1973].) Is what you do with the greeting card dishonest? Toward the author of the doggerel? Toward the person you give the card to?

For Eliot, this is the counterpoint between "Tradition and the Individual Talent": "We shall often find that not only the best, but the most individual parts of [a poet's] work may be those in which the dead poets, his ancestors, assert their immortality most vigorously." But my example poem reminds us that the voices entering in may not be confined to those of "the dead poets." The voices available to poems are Joyce's "cry in the street," or "the speech of Polish mothers" that Williams lovingly attended, and they are voices that belong to all of us. A great discovery of American poetry is that the voice of a poem, the voice of genuine and perhaps original feeling, is not really *a* voice at all, but a chorus of voices. "Counterpoint" becomes a name for the way in which a poem can have many voices and yet be one thing and express one self.

Any doubleness of speech, including meter, allusion, metaphors, and puns, naturally makes us question the sincerity of the speaker and the authenticity of the speech. But unless we are the proverbial bumpkin who wonders why the people on stage don't notice the missing wall or complains that folks don't really talk in blank verse, we learn to tolerate instructive duplicities. Works of art owe part of their greatness to originality; but the arts owe their existence to conventions. What turns artificiality into art is its ability, when sufficiently fresh, to import another voice into the work.

The secret of being "free in whatever form," in Wallace Stevens' phrase, is not to exclude the hobbling, hampering voices around and within us, but to find some way of inviting them in and bringing them, somehow, on some level, into agreement. Some of these voices come from the past—from recent decades of popular music history, or from centuries of prosodic experimentation. Others come from around us in the human world, especially at times when the language of poetry needs to be revived. Still others come from inside us, and in a loose way we speak of them as our *own* voice. The question of authenticity can hardly be reduced any further.

III

Auden's "In Memory of W. B. Yeats" is a great and familiar poem about which I want to say only a couple of things. Its three sections use different prosodies, and each section presents a different central voice; the voice and the prosody are always related. To review:

The first section is in free verse—the sort of rhetorical or oratorical free verse in which longish, end-stopped lines rather loudly renounce any intention of being "poetic" or artificial. The tone here is casual and urbane, and quite detached from the reported death.

The second part is in a loose iambic hexameter; and as always, the hexameter brings with its murmurs from the ghosts of Homer and Virgil. Here the speaker essays a loftier and more formal declaration about the death of Yeats—so lofty, in fact, as to recall the ideal of generality which the eighteenth century saw in the epic modes of Homer and Virgil.

The prosody of the third section is another matter entirely. A headless iambic tetrameter, it's a measure which hymns and children's songs and prayers have made the property of the whole English-speaking people. The tone in this section becomes too complex to summarize briefly, and I'll have to come back to it in a moment; but part of my point is that this tone comes to include, and transcend, the tones of the earlier parts.

It's not that Auden's ambivalence toward Yeats has dropped away in the third part. The distance that let him speak casually in the first part about Yeats "disappearing," and that led to flat metaphors about "the mercury . . . in the mouth of the dying day," continues in the stanzas in part III about time forgiving Yeats along with Kipling and Claudel, despite their objectionable politics. (I'm referring to the original version, available in the paperback *Selected Poems.*) The objection has not been dropped; but it has been subsumed in something larger.

In structure, this poem seems to go back to the same kind of interplay of voices as Marvell's "Dialogue"—the three voices are sequential, not simultaneous. But they are not the voices of three separate speakers; they are unmistakably stages through which a single speaker moves. And the movement isn't simply from one voice to another to another, but an *accumulation* of multiple voices or tones. The gathering of voices, I suggest, represents a discovering of authenticity.

Near the end of the first, free-verse section, the verse becomes more regular and actually moves through some boisterous anapestic pentameters and a hexameter: "When the brokers are roaring like beasts on the floor of the Bourse / And the poor have the sufferings to which they are fairly accustomed / And each in the cell of himself is almost convinced of his freedom." It is not true, as some early critics of free verse claimed, that impassioned language naturally rises toward meter. But in this poem, as often for Auden, meter represents an engagement with the subject. Where the speaker imaginatively joins the roaring beasts in the marketplace, he begins to take part in the ritual meal that will transfigure Yeats from a mere personality into a multifarious, efficacious self: "The words of a dead man / Are modified in the guts of the living." This first admission into the poem of a fervent tone, disrupting the calm of the oratorical voice, helps to explain why, a few lines later, the repetition of a couplet that fell very flat earlier takes on a new force: "O all the instruments agree / The day of his death was a dark cold day." We may hear another, much older voice here—that of the Anglo-Saxon bard, with his alliterative four-beat line, extolling a fallen leader.

The second secction seems at first like a retreat. It was the last section to be written, not included in the first magazine publication of the poem, and there's still something a little gratuitous about it. But it does perform one vital transformation on the first voice: Here the detachment is not from Yeats into "the importance and noise of to-morrow" and the rest of daily life; rather, it's an historical detachment that includes the poet, Auden himself, in its irony. Because "poetry makes nothing happen," Yeats' conservative politics in the end had little effect—no more than Auden could expect his own (1939) radical politics to have. We can ignore Yeats' merely personal convictions in reading his poems; but in doing so, we know that in the same perspective it will be necessary to ignore our own as well. The loftiness of tone in this section allows the ground to shift toward the lasting greatness of the work, away from the invidious engagement of a young, radical personality with a conservative personality from a previous generation. In that sense, the second section makes the resolutions of the third possible.

One of the voices we hear in the chorus of the third part is Yeats' own: He had used this meter several times, as in "To Be Carved on a Stone at Thoor Ballylee," which begins "I, the poet William Yeats," and moves toward the looser iambic prayer, "And may these characters remain / When all is ruin once again." All may be ruin, as Auden insists on the eve of World War II, long before the natural crumbling of stone and wood brings down Yeats' tower. "In the nightmare of the dark, / All the dogs of Europe bark." But "Time" that "Worships language" will help see that "these characters remain."

It's not that Auden achieves (or aspires to) the grand simplicity of Time or the gods in his opinions. The first sction offered that chilling modern image, first presented in *The Waste Land*, "And each in the cell of himself is almost convinced of his freedom." The last section ends by celebrating the poet's power in transforming the same image: "In the prison of his days / Teach the free man how to praise." This is the language of paradox again, spread all through this section—"a rapture of distress," the "healing fountain" in "the deserts of the heart." The brittle voice of part one demonstrates one way of dealing with the horror of 1939—by holding it as arm's length; but the voices of part three can include an unanesthetized vision of that horror and still praise the poet who can "persuade us to rejoice."

Are these separate people arguing with each other? Of course not—this is one person, doing what we all do when we allow ourselves to become engaged in important problems, which means problems that don't have simple solutions: he's contradicting himself. As we tease out the various strands of that contradiction, we hear the many voices that go to make up a single mode of belief; and when we hear the counterpoint among those voices, we hear what unites one speaker in himself, and with us. If what we hear as simultaneous defines our point of view and thus our selves, then when we hear the same thing at the same time we become, for a moment and insofar as we are listening, the same person. When we are the same person with the poet, then the poet can speak for us.

NOTES

This essay began as a lecture sponsored by the Grolier Book Store in Cambridge, Mass. (Nov. 3, 1983).

1. The third, fourth, and fifth stanzas of "Anthem" have been omitted.

ON WILLIAMS' TRIADIC LINE;
OR HOW TO DANCE ON VARIABLE FEET

DENISE LEVERTOV

Although so much critical literature on William Carlos Williams has accumulated & continues to proliferate, that part of it which concerns his prosody typically applies a tin ear, or no ear at all, to the sounds of his poems & to the relation of sound, & especially rhythm, to the nuances of significant expression. The common reader who approaches Williams without the intervention of critical mediators frequently resonds with instinctive understanding; but a great many persons first encounter him in the classroom, where—if the instructor assigns or is strongly influenced by the secondary material—mistaken concepts, confidently asserted, too often lead them astray.

The old evaluation of Williams as a homespun Imagist dies hard: the red wheelbarrow is trundled on stage at every "Introduction to Modern Poetry" course, year after year, at college after college. And "The Yachts," admired by the academics of twenty or more years ago less for itself than for its atypicality, which enabled them to patronize Williams with a "can do good work if he tries" school-report, retains its contrasting place in the anthologies. In recent years, his stock having risen so far above what it was in his lifetime, the focus has shifted to his prosodic theories & to the poems, from *The Desert Music* on, in which he demonstrated them. But just what constitutes a "variable foot" evidently puzzles the critics, often to the point where it is dismissed, after a brief *pro forma* attempt to define or describe it, as an obsessive illusion of his old age.

I have not read the entire body of Williams criticism, but from the books and articles I have read I derive the impression that this bafflement is due primarily to a failure to recognize that the variable foot is a matter not of stress patterns but of duration in time.

Reed Whittemore for example[1] seems to come closer than many to understanding this measure when he quotes Yvor Winters on "the foot in free verse"—

> "one heavily accented syllable, an unlimited number of unaccented syllables, and an unlimited number of syllables of secondary accent,"

in a context which assumes that this clustering of a variable number of syllables around a central beat, which was to be found in poems written long before Williams proclaimed the variable foot as a discovery, nevertheless describes the phenomenon. But this formulation is at best only a partial description; and Winters' assumption that the focus of such a cluster was the central heavily-accented syllable, while applicable to 'free verse' and perhaps (as I shall set forth later), to Williams' earlier poems, does not apply—as Whittemore tries to make it do—to the consciously written variable foot and triadic line of the later Williams. Winters, in his 1947 *In Defense of Reason* to which Whittemore was referring, had chosen to scan Williams' "The Widow's Lament in Springtime," from the early 1920s; he did so by marking what he heard as its strong stresses (which to his ear turn out to be consistently two to a line). Whittemore comments that by 1955 the major change Williams would have made in those lines "would not have been in the syllable count but the spacing" (into triads) because by the 1950s Williams "was not thinking syllable by syllable[2] but unit by unit so that each triad was really a threesome of ones." And he then proceeds to more or less dismiss this "spatial" arrangement, as he calls it, as less significant than Williams liked to think. But whether or not Williams' concept and practice of the variable foot are or are not of vital importance for modern poets and poetry in general, their significance is *not* "spatial" (and thus visual) but temporal and auditory. Perhaps that's what Whittemore means by saying Williams was "thinking unit by unit" but I don't think he makes it clear.

Again, Alan Stephens, as quoted by Louis Simpson,[3] said that though there was "no definite and recurrent combination of stressed and unstressed syllables" and therefore no possibility of that "measurement" Williams desired and claimed, yet Williams' line "is a line because, relative to its neighboring lines, it contains that which makes it in its own right a unit of the attention" and beccause it "has a norm against which it almost constantly varies . . . the formal architecture of the sentence." Simpson comments, "He [Alan Stephens] goes on to say that this principle also underlies verse in meter; 'audible rhythm' is not the 'supreme fact' of the line of verse, and so 'Dr. Williams will have been working in the tradition all along.' . . . Dr. Williams would not have been happy to hear it," says Simpson, "for he insisted on the variable foot's being a measurement in time . . . a unit of rhythm, not a form of sentence structure." But Simpson does not commit himself further; instead he switches, at this point, to the question of whether or not there is indeed an "American measure."

Williams himself tended to cloud the understanding of his prosodic ideas by linking them too closely to his own emphasis on notating American, not English, speech patterns; but the variable foot itself is a principle equally applicable to other idioms, not only to American speech. Simpson, however, a page or so earlier, *had* reiterated some of Williams' own clearer definitions of the measured line he was after—the phrases "auditory measure" and the assertion that "the passage of time (not stress) is the proper . . . key to the foot." In the face of such evidence it is particularly distressing to read that as astute a critic as Hugh Kenner, whose close reading of "Young Sycamore Tree" and the little poem about the cat stepping over the jam-pot are models of what such analyses can be (and rarely are), could write to Mike Weaver[4] that Williams' use of the triadic line was merely a visual aid to reading aloud after strokes had affected his visual coordination. Perhaps Kenner was merely trying to account for why the variable feet were arranged in three's rather than four's, let's say. I would find no argument with that attempt: it's a good question; but Kenner's remarks *can* be read as a relegation of what was a deliberate auditory notation to the level of merely visual typographical convenience; and in *The Pound Era* he does say the term "variable foot" suggests "a rubber inch."

As for Marjorie Perloff, she claims that Williams scored his lines for the eye, not the ear[5]—something I know, from my own conversations with him and his approval of my way of reading his own work back to him (at his request), was not the case. Unfortunately, Flossie Williams was the only witness to those occasions, so you have only my word for it. Among the writers on Williams whose expositions of the variable foot I've read, only James Breslin approaches clarity and understanding, for he does write[6] of "uniform intervals of lapsed time," with variable syllable count and "pauses used to fill out the intervals in the shorter lines"—but even this does not seem to adequately acknowledge the variations in *speed* which I hear in these units, nor, to my mind, are pauses merely fillers—they are not *resorted to,* as it were, but have expressive functions to fulfill, for example, waiting, pondering, or hesitating.

What then is my own sense of how to read the variable feet in their (usually) triadic line-clusters? It is so simple, if I am right, that one wonders at all the confusion and mystification. Each segment of a triadic cluster is a foot, and each has the same *duration.* Thus a foot (or segment) with few syllables, if it is to occupy the same amount of time as one with many, must by the reader be accorded, in the enunciation of those syllables, a slowness (or marked "quantity"); or else, if that would, in any particular instance, distort the words and impart a weird mouthing effect, then the reader must give full value to the spaces between the words, especially those where syntax and expression, punctuated or not, call for some degree of pause in any case. Conversely, a foot (or line-segment) of many syllables must be uttered with whatever rapidity will give it equal duration with a few-syllabled line. What sets the norm? Just as the tempo at which a piece of music will be played is established in the first bar (so that if, in practising the piano, one starts very fast, one will be obliged to play the designedly quickest passages all the faster!) so, in reading aloud a poem of Williams' written in this relative mode, the opening segment (many- or few-syllabled) is a determinant. As one moves through a poem, the consistency of *duration in time,* though not absolute, can be felt, registered, experienced—not in a blatant or obtrusive way, but in much the same way that the consistency of traditional metric patterns is felt: as a *cohesive* factor. In *The Pound Era* Kenner records a conversation with William Carlos Williams[7] in 1957. Kenner asks (conversant as he was with Pound's definition of rhythm as "a form cut in TIME" he would, one might suppose, have had no real need to enquire), "Did he mean . . . each line to take up the same time?" Williams, he recounts, "at once said Yes; then he said, More or less."

That "Yes" is clear and unequivocal; nor does the added "more or less" take it back, but simply qualifies it in the same degree that any traditional prosodist would note that an absolutely unvarying rhythm, with no inverted feet, no departures of any kind from a rigid norm, is deadly dull and inexpressive: some "give," some "more-or-less-ness" is required.

If duration in time, not number of syllables nor of stresses (or accents), is the simple, open secret of the variable foot, what determines which words go into which foot? that is, *why* are some words—being few or of few syllables, or even single monosyllables—stretched, or their surrounding silences given more than average importance, so that they may, taken together, form a foot or segment as long as another which contains a larger number of polysyllabic words, which in turn are uttered with rippling rapidity? Why should not some of the latter have gone into the preceding few-syllabled segment? The answer is in this case no different from that with which the same question would (by my lights) be met had it been asked concerning any modern poem written in nontraditional forms: the ultimate determinant of what goes into a line is the totality of the demands of expressiveness, comprising intellectually comprehensible syntax, sensuous and expressive musicality (including variation of pace), and above all the emotional charge—delicate or forceful and intense—of content. Each of these interpenetrates the others. The more fully wrought the poem, the less discrete each of its strands.

This assertion leads me to consider in what way the poems written before the triadic line became Williams' prevailing mode differ from the latter in rhythmic organization. If duration in time was not, in these, the cohesive structural factor, what was? One finds in them that "pulse"—a rhythm experienced underneath all else, yet rarely "heard," just like our heartbeats—which is essential to any good poem (and which distinguishes nontraditional, nonreuseable forms from mere formless free verse, though the latter term is widely employed to allude to poems which deserve a better definition). And it is my conviction that the source of this pulse, this subliminally registered ground-bass, this verbal analogue for such unifying elements in visual art as an unobtrusively recurring hue or a subtly echoing series of diagonals, is a *dominant* (not a relentless) number of strong stresses per line, often with an alternation—usually irregular in frequency of ocurrence—of another number of strong stresses. So that rather than the steady march of two strong stresses in each line that Winters, juggling natural enunciation a bit to demonstrate his point, claimed for "The Widow's Lament in Springtime," we get in one poem, if we count strong stresses only, a definite dominance of three, let's say, with a goodly number of two's and a *sprinkling* of one's or four's or even more disparate numbers per line; or in another poem, five's may dominate, with three's a strong second and here and there the odd six or four; and so forth. The shorter the poem the less variation, otherwise a sense of dominant stress will have no chance to accrue. And in a longer poem the balance may shift, gradually, to a different figure.

This unifying pattern of stresses is written by ear and out of the feeling-tone of the content, not by conscious scansion; but the vigilance of ear and sensitivity are as "crafty" as in the work of syllable-counting or the maintenance of traditional meters. In the case of Williams, his aural alertness was toward the speech around him, but this focus of his attention as listener and as maker was held in tension with a peculiarly distinctive high rhetoric very different from common speech; and I think this contributes greatly to the abiding interest of his diction, rhythm, and syntax, which are both more intense and more lofty than so much contemporary work supposedly influenced by him but which is flat and flabby, devoid of that aristocratic and eccentric inner voice Williams engages in counterpoint with the notation of external voices. His typical use, into a generally demotic phraseology (which is unobtrusive as *diction* even when its images startle) of such turns as "save only" (e.g., "lifeless / save only in / beauty, the kernel / of all seeking"); "by what" (e.g., "passionately biased / by what errors of conviction" or "heedless of what greater violence"); "were it not" (e.g., "Were it not for the March within me, . . . I could not endure" etc.), contribute, along with other syntactic idiosyncrasies, to this important stylistic tension.

An example—not outstanding but representative—can be found in the poem "Approach to a City,"[8] which begins with the vernacular "*Getting through with* the world" (my italics), and moves through four stanzas of images, simple in diction but giving, in their precision, the "shock of recognition"; then, in the last stanza, though without recourse to a recherché or abstruse vocabulary, he gives the whole poem a culminating lift into the language of the inner voice as he says,

> *'I never tire of these sights*
> *but refresh myself there*
> *always for* there is small holiness
> to be found in braver things'
> (my emphasis, quotation marks added)

To demonstrate the kinds of stress-dominance I've spoken about I've chosen a poem which does not clearly manifest this peculiar counterpoint since it is an intimate conversation between Williams and his ancient mother—two very articulate people.

THE HORSE SHOW[9]

4   Constantly near you, I never in my entire

5   sixty-four years knew you so well as yesterday

4   or half so well. We talked. You were never

3   so lucid, so disengagaged from all exigencies

4   of place and time. We talked of ourselves,

4   intimately, a thing never heard of between us.

5   How long have we waited? almost a hundred years.

3   You said, Unless there is some spark, some

4   spirit we keep within ourselves, life, a

4   continuing life's impossible—and it is all

4   we have. There is no other life, only the one.

4   The world of the spirits that comes afterward

5   is the same as our own, just like you sitting

4   there they come and talk to me, just the same.

4   They come to bother us. Why? I said. I don't

4   know. Perhaps to find out what we are doing.

3   *Jealous, do you think? I don't know. I*

4   *don't know why they should want to come back.*

2   *I was reading about some men who had been*

3   *buried under a mountain, I said to her, and*

4   *one of them came back after two months,*

3   *digging himself out. It was in Switzerland,*

3   *you rememember? Of course I remember. The*

4   *villagers tho't it was a ghost coming down*

2   *to complain. They were frightened. They*

3   *do come, she said, what you call*

3   *my "visions." I talk to them just as I*

4   *am talking to you. I see them plainly.*

4   *Oh if I could only read! you don't know*

3   *what adjustments I have made. All*

4   *I can do is to try to live over again*

3   *what I knew when your brother and you*

4   *were children—but I can't always succeed.*

2   *Tell me about the horse show. I have*

3   *been waiting all week to hear about it.*

4   *Mother darling, I wasn't able to get away.*

4   *Oh that's too bad. It was just a show;*

4   *they make the horses walk up and down*

3   *to judge them by their form. Oh is that*

3   *all? I tho't it was something else. Oh*

4   *they jump and run too. I wish you had been*

4   *there, I was so interested to hear about it.*

Here I find four to be the dominant number of strong stresses per line: twenty-three out of forty-two lines; three is the secondary dominance, with thirteen lines, and there are three each of five and two.

Read the poem aloud without any thought of traditional prosodic feet or of counted syllables, but paying minute attention to *what* is being said and in what mood, in this poignant dialogue; and I hope the logic of my scansion will then be apparent.

It may be helpful, in studying the rhythms of this or other poems, to mark off with a musical "phrasing mark" those cadences which override syntactic units, especially those which "swallow" some words, that is, give them minimal emphasis. Such cadences do in fact, in common speech as well as in poetry, run counter to syntactic logic, or coincide with it only incidentally. Here for instance are a few examples of this method:

Note that, though I've marked four strong stresses for this line, it has three cadence units.

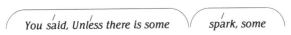

Again: three stresses, but only two cadence units.

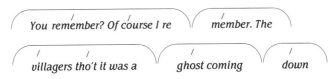

Note that the speech cadence break in the penultimate example cuts right through the word "remember," in the same way that a line-break occasionally divides a word in modern poems. A principle that emerges from this phrase marking seems to be that what I designate as the end of the unit occurs just before one of the strong stresses and just after a "swallowed," minimally stressed syllable, in other words, when that particular combination—of the extremes of unstressed and strong-stressed—appears. Not all strong stresses follow notably unstressed syllables.

Unless the poem is given physical embodiment—voiced reading—it is not possible to fully evaluate, that is to weigh and measure, the components of its sonic character. This does not imply that silent reading (if "sounded out" in the mind) should be abandoned as inferior; but its limitations (and virtues) need to be more clearly recognized by most readers. Both silent and voiced reading are needed for the fullest experience of a poem.

How do Williams' pretriadic line poems differ from the triadic ones? An effect of the triadic line seems to me to be a certain stateliness of pace, even though individual line-segments may move swiftly. Thus they seem peculiarly appropriate to his late years and to express formally a hard-earned wisdom. But wherein lies the principal difference between the two kinds of Williams poems when we consider them with a view to better comprehension of his theories? Clearly the cadences I have pointed out partake of the character of what he later named the variable foot; but rather than the organizing principle being parity of *duration,* as in the triadic lines, the earlier poems depend upon the less conscious phenomenon of focal stresses around which the syllables cluster in variable, or, as Winters called them, unlimited, numbers. But this does not imply that the "pulse" provided by focal strong stresses is absent from the triadic, duration-organized structures. Williams did not abandon it but absorbed it into the triadic mode. An examination of that process is not within the scope of this essay. My hope for the preceding pages is simply to clarify a subject which has been considered more difficult than it is or else contemptuously dismissed as illusory. Williams *did* know what he was doing, and it worked.

NOTES

1. Reed Whittemore, *William Carlos Williams: Poet from Jersey* (Boston: Houghton Mifflin, 1975), p. 316.

2. Williams never *had* been a counter of syllables, and a pattern of *stresses* is not the same as syllables anyway!

3. Louis Simpson, *Three on the Tower* (New York: William Morrow & Co., 1975), p. 305.

4. Ibid., p. 305.

5. Marjorie Perloff, "To Give a Design": Williams and the Visualization of Poetry, in Carroll F. Terrell, ed., *William Carlos Williams: Man and Poet* (Orono: The National Poetry Foundation, University of Maine, 1983).

6. James E. Breslin, *William Carlos Williams: An American Artist* (New York: Oxford University Press, 1970), p. 266.

7. Hugh Kenner, *The Pound Era* (Berkeley: University of California Press, 1971), p. 542.

8. William Carlos Williams, *The Collected Later Poems* (New York: New Directions, 1963), p. 177.

9. *The Collected Later Poems*, p. 185.

THE BREAKING OF FORM IN
LORRAINE SUTTON'S *SAYcred LAYdy*

LUZ MARIA UMPIERRE

Although Latina women writers in the United States have made many important contributions to both "American" literature as well as the literature of their home countries, the truth is that they have yet to receive serious consideration from mainstream critics.[1] Many reasons could be cited for this neglect; some include the fact that many of these women writers are not associated with academia and the fact that their writings have either appeared in small presses or been self-published. Another reason for the neglect is the fact that some of these writers publish part of their works in Spanish or refer to Latina culture. Thus, mainstream critics of U.S. literature have tended to further ignore their literature because of language barriers and monoculturalism.[2]

A notable example of why this group of women deserves further recognition is that of Lorraine Sutton, a pioneer in the nuyorrican or neorrican poetry movement.[3] This movement, of the 1970s, included mostly literature written by second-generation Puerto Ricans in the United States, first appearing in Miguel Algarín's anthology, *Nuyorican Poetry: An Anthology of Puerto Rican Words and Feelings.* Even though Algarín attempts to define the term "Nuyorican" in his introduction, the term still remains highly controversial.[4]

Lorraine Sutton was born in Caguas, Puerto Rico, and raised in New York. She published her collection *SAYcred LAYdy* in 1975; however, her collection has been left out of anthologies and has yet to receive an in-depth and lengthy study from critics of U.S. and/or Puerto Rican literature. The collection is composed of fifteen poems with the epigraph: "These poems belong to all women who dare struggle for what is rightly theirs."[5] From that first line we realize that one salient aspect of the text is its feminist intention. And the reader quickly notices that one of this text's most striking displays of feminism is its breaking of form. One could argue, perhaps, that all poetry supposes such a break. However, the breaking of form I refer to here deals with not only form and content of the text but also the broader idea of breaking boundaries and stereotypes referring to Hispanic life and women, a break that had not been seen before to this extent in the literature of Latinas and, I would dare say, Latinos in this country.

Perhaps one of the best pieces to capture this "breaking of form" is "Temptation," poetry breaking not only literary form but also social form. The poem begins with the female speaker's wish to reach out of enclosure, represented here by a bathroom, and grab snowflakes from outside: "i want to reach thru the bathroom window and grasp flying flakes" (14). We, as readers, immediately confront what is symbolically seen as the epitome of alien for an islander—snow. But the speaker is interested in defining via the concept of snow visions as readers of life in the United States in a white society. Thus, when the speaker mentions that she would like to feed herself with snow it is an effort to change that element inwardly by placing it within her. Elsewhere I have called this "cannibalism"—eating what is foreign to change it and make it different.[6] Consuming the snow, of course, would melt it. However, being a Latina woman, consuming the snow, swallowing in whiteness and U.S. culture, would not provoke a change in the speaker—she would not become Snow White but rather turn "snow black." The speaker realizes that grabbing U.S. culture (snow) will not change her racially. The specks (spiecks) of snow in her black hair would only be a "Glistening Brilliant crown" (14). A second part of the poem, which begins with the line "beyond the Lavoris/Colgate/ Ultra Ban 5,000" (14) shows us an angrier female speaker. The commercialism in her bathroom, her prison, the sale of "White Snow" as something pure and good, the sale of U.S. culture as products, provokes an angry reaction—she wants to smash her fist over the window and fuck every snow flake. The act of violence is dual: the poem seems to suggest by its ending that the only way to arrive at a new concept—to blend a foreign substance (U.S. culture)—snow—with the self to generate a new image of change is through violence: suicide and rape.

In spite of what could be perceived as a negative ending in light of what I've just mentioned, the poem is still called "Temptation," suggesting that the woman/speaker can fantasize about her self-immolation to generate a new concept—the Pink Puerto Rican Snow woman—but that this remains only in the realm of wishes. The woman speaker understands that racial and capitalistic boundaries need to be broken but not at the expense of her/self. She can break and create a new form through her writing, not necessarily through self-destruction like so many Latin American women poets have.

The poem that gives title to the collection, "SAYcred LAYdy," is almost a primal scream of self-assertion for Puerto Rican nationhood. The title is a play on words making reference to both the statue of liberty—the saycred lady—and the rape of the Puerto Rican nation—the saycred lay. The speaker in this poem becomes the image of her nation—a woman who equates a march to Washington for Puerto Rican political prisoners with a rape of her selfhood.

On a first level of meaning, the poem could be read as a political scream to those who take a march as a *fiesta* or a celebration: those, she says, "who think freedom / will come from / a faster merengue / a slower bump/bump/bump/bump" (19). This posture is unacceptable to the speaker who feels that while they laugh she wants to cry. On a second level of meaning the poem, through stressing words like "body," "scream," "out," "coming," "flesh," "womb," becomes before our eyes the image on the page of the rape of the Puerto Rican nation. Puerto Rico is seen as a woman who has been asked to serve as prostitute—a saycred lay—and who wishes the "NOBODY," the Puerto Rican sell-out-man and the U.S. pimp, "out"; out of her/self, out of her island nation. This woman refuses to cry because "SOY UNA BORICUA LLENA DE CORAZON" (19). The poem is like an act of extrication from her/self of those who just want to Bump, Bump, Bump (fuck) her island/her/self and come. The poem ends with the assertive word "OUT" but in the form of a question. The female speaker is uncertain if her defiant cry/scream "OUT" has made a difference, has provoked a change in some way.

Nowhere is women's rage more vividly portrayed and their empowerment through writing stronger than in the poem "The Burning." The speaker begins by referring to papers, overdue assignments, and incompletes for which she could get an *F*. But instead of succumbing to fear and to compliance with these mechanical forms demanded from students, she decides to let her typewriter play with words and express her torment. How can she bother herself with mechanical/academic assignments when "my Hermanas r dying / burnt / tornnipples / raped / raped / reaped / while MENstrual BLOOD / goes / flows uncovered" (20–21). The poem expresses the ways in which women die through hemorrhage, either by giving birth or by being raped or used for experiments, and how they bleed to death without joining as women to provoke a change.

Toward the end of this poem, the speaker is confronted by her man who wants her to stop her "shitty typin" (22), in other words, her own creation, her own birth, to cook him supper. The final part of the poem makes us realize the meaning of the title of the poem: women should burn the food, burn the images of themselves as victims, burn their roles in society and serve these to the HER MANO, the patriarch. The poem ends brilliantly when the speaker serves him his "supp HER" (22)—the burnt plate of images of women—her old self.

The play on words in "The Burning," carried with both cleverness and brilliance, generates the destruction of female roles and builds a new "cook" image instead—a woman who destroys traditional images of herself through the masterful use of her writing and the power of her anger and serves this as "supp HER."

The female speakers in other poems realize that "cunt-frontation," (confrontation) of their images/roles within society and the affirmation of their selves, means coming face to face with nationhood and motherhood.[7] Not only is the nation the "saycred lay"—that is, the mother, nation as woman, the reverence for motherhood—but also this nation/woman has been asked to perpetuate the image of woman as venerable mother. Sutton seems to propose in "The Head is Clear" a new type of motherhood that arises from this cunt-frontation—from perceiving and being aware of sexual politics. Women should decide to be *real* mothers: mothers to their own selves.

But how can this come about? In another poem, "Inside (again)," the speaker, as in "The Burning," suggests that in writing—playing with words, solving the puzzles of the names used to oppress us—lies women's own birthing of themselves. Sutton's collection is thus truly re-volutionary, for she proposed and executed for us Latina women readers a clear blueprint, as early as 1975, of what lay ahead and what still lies ahead of us if we wish to end the "saycred lay," our rape by patriarchal words and actions. As both women and as writers we have to strive for breaking form—the breaking of alphabets—for words and language present one of our greatest imprisonments. Dismembering words, searching for new meanings, untangling the knots of the alphabet and syntax will give us a clearer image of who we have been led to believe we are—whores, mothers, guardians, keepers of nationalism, virgins, ladies—and will help us generate a new writing, a cunt-frontation with sexual, social, linguistic, and cultural definitions in order to break them. By breaking form, syntax, and words, Lorraine

Sutton brilliantly shows us the way, as Latina women writers, for a truer definition of nationhood, one that really includes us in truth and essence, not as symbols. Sutton also defines our new role within society: creating new, daring, defiant, and exciting remakings of ourselves in our *own* words, our own meanings, and a new alphabet of freedom, a female body of literature that truly says who we are.

NOTES

1. I am not in accordance with using the term "American" to describe the literature produced in the United States or its mainstream culture. América is an entire continent: both North and South. I prefer to use the term U.S. literature or U.S. culture.

2. Monoculturalism is linked to the "melting pot" policy of the United States as a nation, and it provokes a lack of knowledge and comprehension of other cultures as well as having the effect of nullifying the culture of the minorities that come to the U.S.A. as immigrants. I have an unpublished lecture on this subject "Resolution or Acceptance? Authoritarian Discourse vs. Artistic Expression," which I presented at the conference on Conflict and Conflict Resolution, held by the West Virginia Consortium for Faculty and Course Development in International Studies in October of 1985.

3. In an interview I held with Sandra María Esteves, this neorrican poet, also a member of this generation of writers, says: "Lorraine Sutton was a strong influence. She was probably the only woman around that time, other than Suni Paz, that I was very much influenced by." See "I Want What I Write To Be Necessary: An interview with Sandra María Esteves," *Conditions: 14* (1987):103–17.

4. I recommend reading, in regard to the nuyorrican or neorrican movement, the introduction to Algarín's anthology published by William Morrow (New York, 1975) as well as Edna Acosta Belen's "The Literature of the Puerto Rican Minority in the United States," *The Bilingual Review* 5, nos. 1 and 2 (1978):107–15; Efraín Barradas' "Introducción" to *Herejes y mitificadores* (Río Piedras: Ediciones Huracán, 1980), 11–30; Margarita Fernández Olmos' "From the Metropolis: Puerto Rican Women Poets and the Immigration Experience," *Third Woman* 1, no. 2 (1982):40–51; Luz María Umpierre's "La ansiedad de la influencia en Sandra María Esteves y Marjorie Agosín," *Revista Chicano Riqueña* 11, nos. 3–4 (1983):139–47.

5. Lorraine Sutton, *SAYcred LAYdy* (New York: Sunbury Press, 1975), 2. All other references will be to this edition, and the page numbers are cited parenthetically in the text.

6. Article in progress for an anthology of essays on Spanish American women writers to be published by Greenwood Press.

7. The term "cunt-frontation" is taken from Sutton herself.

WORD ROOTS: NOTES ON FREE VERSE

MARK RUDMAN

1

For Pound "to break the pentameter . . .
was the first heave," and the same was true for Ginsberg, Merwin, most of the Black
Mountain poets, and many of the generation of American poets born in 1926 and
1927. To escape the anxiety that comes from a poet taking a larger role in the community, the "return to form" has occupied itself almost exclusively with verse technique, with what can be measured against content. This is neutral ground. I remember
Auden telling me how I missed a beat in the villanelle Paul Nemser and I wrote for his
seminar, and that's all he concerned himself with. (We were the only students to do
his assignment. Metrical poetry was out of fashion then.) It wasn't a debatable point,
and that's why external form is so attractive now: you resurrect "standards" without
any reference to moral or ethical imperatives. I always remember that it was Wittgenstein who in the *Tractatus* insisted on the necessary unity between ethics and aesthetics: Ethics and aesthetics are one. Wittgenstein, Trakl's anonymous patron, who was
willing to back him while claiming not to "understand" (whatever that means) his
work. . . . There is no poetry without form. Some poets' imaginations thrive on the
specific boundaries of rhyme and meter. I do think that free verse opened up possibilities for language that have only begun to be explored, much less exhausted, and that
it is retrograde to write primarily in fixed forms. These "forms," from the regular use
of rhyme and meter to the production of pantoums and sestinas and villanelles, are
to my mind a simplification, and an escape from deeper formal issues.

2

The risk involved in writing free verse carries a lot of responsibility and anxiety. Any
laxness on the part of the poet and it becomes its dreaded counterpart, prose. It is
understandable, in their anxiety that poetry should not be prose and that poetry
should be easily separable from prose, that some poets would have us abandon free
verse to clear up the boundary. Good prose can be very good. Or is it poetry?

Pound's obsession with that which was carved in stone. The Acmeist obsession with the same. "Romance of the precise." Movements bearing false analogies to give its practitioners footholds in something they imagined to be real.

Suspicion of free verse among its practitioners. Williams' insistent search for definitions, as though the need for breathing room in the poem needed to be given greater credibility.

From Mandelstam's essay, "The Morning of Acmeism": "What sort of idiot would agree to build if he did not believe in the reality of his material, the resistance of which he must overcome? . . . We do not fly: we ascend only such towers as we ourselves are able to build."

Mandelstam wrote only one poem in free verse, "The Ode to the Horseshoe," and it is a kind of *ars poetica.*

> *Where to begin?*
> *Everything cracks and shakes.*
> *The air trembles with similies.*
> *No one word is better than any other,*
> *the earth moans with metaphor*
> *. . . . .*
> *Human lips,*
> *   that have nothing more to say,*
> *keep the shape of the last word uttered,*
> *and the hand keeps feeling the weight*
> *even though the jug*
> *   splashed itself half empty*
> *   while being*
> *carried home.*
>
> *What I'm saying now isn't said by me,*
> *it's dug up out of the ground like grains of petrified*
> *   wheat.*
>
> *(translated by Clarence Brown)*

His "Conversation About Dante" is the most farsighted, penetrating, and profound essay I've ever read about poetry. One could quote from it endlessly. . . .

Joyce and Proust are always more "poetic," in the old sense, than Williams and Pound. Because what is poetic has nothing to do with poetry as such anymore but belongs equally and indifferently to poetry and prose.

Emerson in "The Poet": "We need not metres but a metre-making argument." (What more is there to say?)

Basil Bunting's *Briggflats* seems to me to be good example of how free verse can be seen as an advance over the strictly metrical. "A mason times his mallet / to a lark's twitter / listening while the marble rests," rhythm drawing its sound from the world's body.

> *The solemn mallet says:*
> *In the grave's slot*
> *he lies. We rot.*
>   . . . . . .
> *Brief words are hard to find,*
> *shapes to carve and discard:*
>   . . . .
> *It is easier to die than to remember.*
> *Name and date*
> *split in soft slate*
> *a few months obliterate.*
>   . . . .
> *Starlight quivers. I had day enough.*
> *For love uninterrupted night.*

Free verse—with rhyme? The rhymes have been dictated by the materials, the "solemn mallet" repetitions. "Uninterrupted" equals an inconceivable time of endless duration. A wordless word.

3

Other examples: Roethke's "The Meadow Mouse," "Now he's eaten his three kinds of cheese and drunk from his bottle-cap watering trough—" and "The Geranium." His identification with "all things innocent, hapless, forsaken" gives the rhythm a gravity and finality that the subject would otherwise belie. And, in many of his other poems, an Elizabethan bittersweet toughness, a range and complexity of tones and sonorities.

Williams' "The Drunk and the Sailor" is another poem rooted in a powerful recognition about the self through an encounter with another heretofore buried, invisible part of the self. The psychological connection between the imagined scene and the pain alongside it imbues the language with a mysterious power. I want to quote the Williams poem in full because it is less well known than the others and, though it is quite memorable, its virtues are less obvious.

> THE DRUNK AND THE SAILOR
>
> *The pretty fury*
>   *that disrupts my life—*
>   *at the striking of a wrong key*
> *as if it had been*
>   *a woman lost*
> *or a fortune . .*
>   *The man was obviously drunk,*
>   *Christopher Marlowe*
> *could have been no drunker*

> *when he got himself*
> *   stuck through the eye*
> *with a poniard.*
> *   The bus station was crowded.*
> *The man*
> *   heavy-set*
> *   about my own age*
> *seventy*
> *   was talking privately*
> *   with a sailor.*
> *He had an ugly jaw on him.*
> *   Suddenly*
> *   sitting there on the bench*
> *too drunk to stand*
> *   he began menacingly*
> *   his screaming.*
> *The young sailor*
> *   who could have flattened him*
> *   at one blow*
> *kept merely looking at him.*
> *   The nerve-tingling screeches*
> *   that sprang*
> *sforzando*
> *   from that stubble beard*
> *   would have distinguished*
> *an operatic tenor.*
> *   But me—*
> *   the shock of it—*
> *my heart leaped in my chest*
> *   so that I saw red*
> *   wanted*
> *to strangle the guy*
> *   The fury of love*
> *   is no less.*

Williams' whole psychic life is embodied here, where the doppleganger motif takes place in the light of day: he sees his past and present self reflected in both the young sailor and the old man, "about my own age / seventy," he wants to strangle. The drama of the poem is in how it builds toward that recognition. It's difficult to imagine a more potent "flat" line than "The bus station was crowded." It arrests the action and functions like a stage direction to open up the way for the power of "he began menacingly / his screaming," which is the way to say it—when there's something wrong but you don't know what—yet.

4

Where does free verse take its cue? One place is in Hotspur's opening jag in *Henry IV.* The actions he describes and the emotions behind them seem to invoke the rhythm of the language that ensues:

> But I remember, when the fight was done,
> When I was dry with rage and extreme toil,
> Breathless and faint, leaning upon my sword,
> Came there a certain lord, neat, and trimly dress'd,
> Fresh as a bridegroom; and his chin new reap'd
> Show'd like a stubble-land at harvest home;
> He was perfumed like a milliner;
> And twixt his finger and his thumb he held
> A pouncet box, which ever and anon
> He gave his nose and took 't away again;
> Who therewith angry, when it next came there,
> Took it in snuff; and still he smiled and talk'd,
> And as the soldiers bore dead bodies by,
> He called them untaught knaves, unmannerly,
> To bring a slovenly unhandsome corse
> Betwixt the wind and his nobility.

Hotspur has his own language, yet *Hotspur does not exist.* The matter at hand to be conveyed generates the words, the magnificent yet immediate piling up of qualifiers and clauses. Each of these exists due to an emotional pressure, a specific agitation, the matter, the material, at hand. And later in the play this man of action says, like an antipoet, to refute the moonstruck "romantic" Glendower, in words that are almost prophetic of the manifestos to come:

> I had rather be a kitten and cry mew
> Than one of these same metre ballad-mongers.

5

After Shakespeare, Wordsworth is the precursor of free verse in getting poetry to expand its capacity to integrate materials. The most memorable passages in *The Prelude* are also concerned with *movement:* skating, boating, climbing Snowden. Free verse, once it broke clear of imagist imperatives, a limitation become a distraction, concerned itself with movement: And then went down to ships, set keel to anchor. There was always information being conveyed, as if in synchronous concurrence with Husserl's "Consciousness is always consciousness of something."

6

Free verse, of course, is a misnomer. "No verse is free. . ."

Free verse: a poetry in which, to put it crudely, something is happening. To break away from nostalgia.

Free verse, by now, is a classical mode. The inscriptions on cave walls, the psalms.

One cannot account for the power of free verse without recourse to the novel. Cross-fertilization and interplay of forms. Prose began to take over the domain of the long poem and the epic.

Pound's *Mauberley* speaks for this: "His true Penelope was Flaubert. . . ."

Free verse attempts to set the prose of the world to music.

It is not far from "the language of men" to free verse. And each step forward is an attempt to integrate and quarry more material from the real. Impurities boost the paradigm.

But much modern poetry follows in the footsteps of the novel: Pound and Eliot take the milieu and an attitude toward subject matter of their early work from James; Akhmatova, Mandelstam, and Pasternak, from Tolstoy. It has to do with how to embody the commonplace, how to employ detail.

(This is also the thrust of a book I wrote about Robert Lowell, being reluctant to restate here what I said there. . . .)

"But what do you mean by detail?"

The metonymic imagination: With Stevens and Pasternak it is the weather, the season, thistles, or the trees at a meeting that speak, as in "The Sublime Malady":

> *Poverty-stricken February*
> *groaned, coughed blood,*
> *and tiptoed off to whisper*
> *into the ears of boxcars*
> *about this and that,*
> *railroad ties and trucks,*
> *the thaw, and babbled on, of troops*
> *foot-slogging home from the front.*

7

The world, Bronowski insisted, following Leakey, cannot be grasped by meditation. The new formalism arose just after the so-called poetry of voice began to dominate the scene and is almost welcome as a corrective to that lax "I," as against eye-oriented, indulgent stuff. Poetry seeks tension and release from tension. Some of the people writing in form today are reacting to that poetry which is at once formless and for-mulaic. What we lament in much of the "free verse" being written today is the absence of sound.

There's a danger of reductiveness in all schematic inquiry. (Even Bachelard can be reductive.)

Rhythm, rather than rhyme, is the goal of any poetry, and yet when Mayakovsky talks about rhyming in order to remember his own poems which he composed as he walked, who can quarrel with that? Many poets are stimulated by formal constraints. And it's a mistake to underestimate the purely ludic factor.

8

Oppen's comment on why Reznikoff was so slow to gain the recognition he deserved (the same being true of himself); that his poetry is "*merely* perfect and profound and infinitely moving" (my emphasis) and "that he is of little use to those who would teach or explicate a poem. . . . The least of Rezi's one line poems says more—does more—than anything one can say about it."

> *Once a toothless woman opened her door,*
> *chewing a slice of bacon that hung from her mouth*
>   *like a tongue.*
>
> *This is where I walked night after night;*
> *this is where I walked away many years.*

In passages such as this poetry has made a giant step forward, and its relation to prose is not a thing to be despised.

9

Reading Bronk's *Careless Love*. Something poems leave unsaid moves me: "a face / a leaf, a certain light which prompts us to see, / as in a mirror's *blank*. . . ." A reluctant eloquence. Being able to breathe in the interstices of what is left unsaid. In such dislocations as "The stove is out" in "Worlds and Changes" which recapitulates a life's experience in its context. Maybe the point is that the lyrical statement can never be taken literally. What is free about this verse?

Title of the book that brought Oppen back to poetry after a silence of twenty five years: *The Materials*.

The pressure should be everywhere and invisible.

The question of syntax.

10

How one takes refuge in form as in a harbor, "hugging the shore," to borrow Updike's phrase that is as applicable in terms of a distinction between poetry and verse as it is in terms of criticism versus fiction. Diminished risks.

Leopardi: "For men are willing to suffer almost anything from each other or from heaven itself, so long as *true words* do not touch them."

But when anxiety surrounds us as the night used to, why not pull the blanket up over our heads and return to form?

Leopardi: "Men are miserable by necessity, yet determined to think themselves miserable by accident."

Is this the same as the return to the figure and the image in painting? Or the swing back toward straight narrative in film after the discontinuities (non-narrative) work of Antonioni, Resnais, Godard, Bergman, Altman, and others?

There is no point in "returning to form" because there is no external form to return to, no fixed neutral element waiting to be reactivated by the well-intentioned poet.

I hate the separation of poets into formal camps. Poetry transcends attitudes and predilections, even sensibilities. The best poets never fit into any camp.

The animus we sense in the air transcends the peccadilloes of individuals. Mandelstam gives substance to this in "Some Notes on Poetry," an essay/review of Pasternak's *My Sister—Life:* "In poetry, war is always being waged. It is only in periods of social imbecility that there is peace or a peace treaty is concluded. Like generals, the bearers of word roots take up arms against each other. Word roots battle in the darkness, depleting each other's food supplies and the juices of the earth."

11

Larkins' *Required Writings.* With what shrewdness and drollery does he toss off some outrageous maxims. One statement in particular activated my interest and ire: "Writing poetry is playing off the natural rhythms and word-order of speech *against the artificialities of rhyme and meter,*" (my emphases) as though *that* were all there were to the matter. The answer lies in our senses, not in our aesthetics. A poet is not a phenomenologist, though he may equate seeing with being. And if he doesn't have a music in his head, and an idea of what he wants to do that is higher than the realm of restrictions that would constrain him, why would he bother? And yet it is only the context creating second part of Larkin's sentence I disagree with. Are rhyme and meter the *only* "artificialities," objective, intractable, against which a poet can play off the natural rhythms and word-order of speech? Or is not this rhyme and meter that which is embedded in the tradition, as a pressure that is everywhere and invisible as basic structure, as well as in the poem being made.

John Hollander speaks to the idea of false distinctions in the *Paris Review* (1985): "I find free verse very, very difficult to write; in the past, when I've written free verse, I've felt the constraints some people must feel trying to write couplets. I don't know why some people have an ideology about form—"open," "closed," "whatever." "Each poet evolves individually."

12

Absence of trust in the unknown quantity, in the unmeasurable aspect of form. Robert Frost's characteristically witty and vicious line about free verse being like playing "tennis without the net." My rejoinder to that is that it's much more difficult to have to imagine the boundaries.

Playing Kadima (or "smash ball") on the dock while waiting for the ferry on Swan's Island, an island on the Maine coast, I thought, this is harder than tennis because there is no net. The free verse poem is played off against the genre and tradition, familiar lines, touchstones. The form responds to the poet's sense of what is possible. Frost was an innovative poet; his use of speech rhythms and casual diction was radical. Frost is subtle where Hardy is bold, and there was enough in these tensions and contradictions for him to explore throughout his life. He was threatened by the idea of nonmemorable lines, and he had every right to be. History may show "The Death of the Hired Man" (and other of Frost's dramatic poems) to be as innovative a poem as "Zone." His lyrics ask to be memorized:

> *I have been one acquainted with the night.*
> *I have walked out in rain—and back in rain.*
> *I have outwalked the furthest city light.*

And yet we can memorize Apollinaire's poem too, which rhymes in spite of its cubist construction, radical juxtapositions, and unpunctuated lines.

> *Et tu observes au lieu d'écrire ton conte en prose*
> *La cétoine qui dort dans le coeur de la rose*

and even in Samuel Beckett's translation:

> *And you observe instead of writing your story in prose*
> *The chafer asleep in the heart of the rose*

Death is what gnaws at the core of the poet's work.

But does a poem like Williams' "The Desert Music" ask to be memorized? When I think of it I see it on the page and remember only words like *Juarez, sequins, flange, girder.*

> *Now the music volleys through as in*
> *a lonely moment I hear it. Now it is all*
> *about me. The dance! The verb detaches itself*
> *seeking to become articulate*

13

The straight genres have been exhausted, and we need a radical yet revisionary spirit to "make it *live*" (rather than "new").

THE CONFINEMENT OF FREE VERSE

BRAD LEITHAUSER

I hope to vanish, with a modest flourish, from this essay in a moment. Since my interest here lies in universal literary questions, I suspect that any appearance of the first-person singular may well be obtrusive or misleading. And yet, given my thesis (that free verse at the moment shows signs of exhaustion), and my own relationship to it (as the recent author of a book whose poems all employ some variety of systematic rhyme, I would like to be thought of as a formalist), perhaps I might usefully offer a few simultaneously self-exculpating and self-expunging words.

To speak of exhaustion in any art form is a notoriously perilous undertaking. So I proceed gingerly, apologetic in advance, and well aware that any such impression of fatigue may spring from all sorts of dubious emotions extrinsic to the art itself—peevishness, prickliness, intolerance, inflexibility. In some cases, what looks like fatigue may simply be a reflection of inner depletion; in others, it may serve as one of those helpful illusions by which a writer reduces the world's helter-skelter to a manageable size and form. But in any case, and whatever the motivations behind them, notions of artistic exhaustion often prove misguided.

For the fact is that poetic genres over the years prove exceptionally hardy. One recalls that T. S. Eliot at the outset of his career expressed doubts as to whether the sonnet was still practicable. In "Reflections on 'Vers Libre,'" an essay that sought to explain and justify the new free verse movement, he hypothesized that the heroic couplet, although dormant, had "lost none of its edge since Dryden and Pope laid it down"; it merely awaited the awakening touch of the true satirist, than whom "no man of genius is rarer." But "as for the sonnet," he added, "I am not so sure." These judgments were offered in 1917, at a time when Frost, surely one of the great sonneteers in the language, was just coming into his own. Whether Eliot was right about the heroic couplet remains uncertain, since the new Pope has not yet arrived, but about the sonnet he was spectacularly wrong. How heartening it is to contemplate the bounty and range of magnificent sonnets composed in the decades since Eliot's pronouncement. Frost's triumphs were succeeded by those of John Crowe Ransom, W. H. Auden, Louise Bogan, Patrick Kavanagh, Robert Lowell, Elizabeth Bishop, James Merrill, Malcolm Lowry, Philip Larkin, and Seamus Heaney. Obviously, one must be wary in calling any form exhausted.

Yet literary forms do on occasion grow tired—as Eliot's own career, with its brave abandonment of much that had become enfeebled and formulaic, so inspiringly demonstrates. Although much good poetry was produced by Eliot's conservative contemporaries, especially within that motley gathering known as the Georgians, their work does in retrospect look rather staid—as though it needs a real roughing up. Eliot came at a good time.

But poetic forms may do more than grow tired: they may actually perish. English alliterative verse of the sort that flourished from *Beowulf* down into Chaucer's era at some point apparently crossed that bourne from which none return. Even Auden, who worked successfully in more poetic forms than any other English-language poet, could not quite, in his monumental *Age of Anxiety,* pull off its resuscitation. And one cannot rule out the possibility that various literary forms alive today will eventually become extinct. (One notes in passing that the masque, despite Frost's heroic efforts, doesn't seem these days to enjoy the flush of health. . . .) And while I don't mean to suggest that free verse is dead, or will ever die, it does seem to me (to work my exit behind a pun) that free verse, its energies having peaked some time ago, is nov looking rather peakèd.

Formal or free, every poem offers the reader in its first few lines what might be called a prosodic contract. These lines necessarily serve a multiplicity of functions—they are simultaneously lure, inquiry, and pledge. They ask, in effect, *Do you like what you've seen so far?*, and pledge, in effect, *Well, there's more to come.* . . . The true poet takes this pledge with utmost gravity, since he is asking for what is (from the poet's point of view) the most precious commodity in the world: a moment of the reader's attention. In the public imagination, poetry is viewed without fail as a solitary enterprise—which it is, of course, in its composition and its eventual consumption. But this stereotype obscures an inescapable element of salesmanship (one not even escaped by the poet whose work is published posthumously). Whether he writes in a cabin in the tundra or in the telephone-jangled offices of a New York City literary magazine, the poet at some point becomes a hawker at an increasingly crowded fair—that which is represented by the poetry anthology—and must seek with every cunning to make his own wares look irresistible. The prosodic contract serves as one of his prime enticements.

How the poet chooses to meet the terms of his prosodic contracts will in many ways define his artistry. He may decide to keep to their terms punctiliously. On the grandest prosodic scale, this is what Milton accomplishes in *Paradise Lost.* The epic's first few lines advise the reader that what will follow is not only an evocation of man's fall from grace but also a colossal procession of immensely vigorous, freely enjambed, and yet stringently decasyllabic blank verse—and this is, from the prosodic standpoint, precisely what Milton delivers, with no let-up or let-down, for some ten thousand lines. In the humbler arena of the lyric, Frost was a great one for upholding his prosodic contracts. He delighted in a little game in which he would pose contractual terms of such strictness that they looked destined to be broken—and then would carry the thing off to the letter. The opening of "Provide, Provide" offers a choice instance:

> *The witch that came (the withered hag)*
> *To wash the steps with pail and rag*
> *Was once the beauty Abishag,*
>
> *the picture pride of Hollywood.*
> *Too many fall from great and good*
> *For you to doubt the likelihood.*

The terms of the prosodic contract could not be clearer. Frost is pledging to supply exactly rhymed iambic tetrameter triplets. The reader may reasonably conjecture that the rhyme, pressured by thematic necessity or the mere threat of musical monotony, will eventually take refuge in off-rhyme, or that the meter may have to relax itself. But the rhymes remain exact throughout the poem's seven stanzas, and the meter, though here and there relying on the common substitution of a trochee for an iamb, stays strictly octosyllabic and absolutely taut.

Some of the best poets believe that prosodic contracts were made, like records, to be broken. Auden's "The Lesson," for example, lies on the page like a short, modified sonnet sequence (one in which octave and sestet have been transposed), and in many ways it feels like one, too. And yet each of these "octaves" proves short by one line; they produce, uncomfortably, thirteen-line sonnets. The resultant disequilibrium enhances the tale the poem tells of confused wanderings and squelched expectations.

Or the poet may seek to snare the reader by offering a contract whose terms are mysterious. What in the world, the reader must ask, is Robert Graves pledging when he constructs an initial stanza like this one?

> *You, love, and I,*
> *(He whispers) you and I,*
> *And if no more than only you and I*
> *What care you or I?*

With all lines within each quatrain rhyme with each other? Or is Graves going one step further and actually warranting that each stanza will have but one end-word? The reader, challenged, bemused, is pulled magnetically into the second stanza:

> *Counting the beats,*
> *Counting the slow heart beats,*
> *The bleeding to death of time in slow*
> *   heart beats,*
> *Wakeful they lie.*

Only now can the reader safely say what the convenant is: the first three lines of each stanza will conclude with the same word; the fourth (serving as refrain) will offer a rhyme on *i.*

Whether the formal poet chooses to uphold the prosodic contract, or to break it, or initially to conceal its terms, his or her poem addresses the reader on two levels. The underlying reassurances and occasional trickeries that the poem's prosody engineers are related to, but ultimately detachable from, the poem's content. Prosody is a game played with the reader's legitimate expectations, and the more firmly these are established, the more fruitfully can the game's designer meet or upset them. And free verse, if it would engage the reader as entirely as the best formal poetry does, must supply an analogous series of satisfactions and frustrations—since prosody is a game of such liberal rewards that few poems can afford to disregard it altogether. One must ask, then, what is the prosodic contract that free verse makes?

The answer, which not surprisingly is complex, depends partly upon when the poem is being read. In an earlier age, perhaps, an appearance of formlessness on the page might in itself have delivered a small shock and an intimation of freshness. But that time has long since departed. Formlessness has become the norm in our country; notwithstanding Eliot's warning that "there is no freedom in art," the "free-est" of free verse has been adopted as our orthodoxy. Admittedly, to be the orthodoxy is not necessarily a bad thing (despite what certain reflexive, and hence at bottom conservative, rebels might cry to the contrary). It's a role that offers plenty of compensations, among them a heartening sense of community. And one need only consider the Georgians to see that an era's orthodox poetry may be durably lithe and lively. But the orthodoxy, by definition, relinquishes most of its ability to shock. Today, those free verse poets whose prosodic contracts announce *I Pledge the bracing surprise of inconsistency* are presenting no surprise at all. To entrance the modern reader, a free verse contract must be more novel than that.

If one selects a poem at random from a contemporary "little magazine," the result will likely be something in free verse that makes no prosodic pledge beyond this promise of irregularity. The opening lines will engender no feeling of accumulation, no sense of gathering melody. Naturally, the typical poem of any age will be at best a mediocre affair: excellence is always the rarity. But the prevalent species of badness may prove instructive as to why the good poets of the age wrote as they did and why, when they failed, they failed as they did. Taken in moderation, and in the right spirit, the reading of typical bad poems may repay study.

One sort of typical bad poem of our time is, thematically, a distinctive blend of personal jadedness and self-congratulation. Structurally, its lines usually vary from six to nine syllables; its diction is flat; and its vocabulary is drastically narrowed—often more so than that to which a writer of children's verse would restrain himself. The poem may occasionally slip into rhyme (that hoary convention has an interesting way of surfacing when the free verse poem strives after a powerful conclusion), and line breaks—enjambments—tend to be extremely dynamic.

Enjambment plays a central, even a defining, role in contemporary American free verse. Its prominence is that of the sole survivor; with so many prosodic devices having been cast aside, enjambment remains as one of the few "tricks" to be pulled from the crumpled black silk hat of the free verse writer. The harmonies of rhyme, along with all the vitalizing dissonances of off-rhyme, have been largely silenced. So, too, the heartbeat of meter, and the tugging counterpoint that speech rhythms create against it. And so, too, the caesura, most of whose verve arises from the contrast between its own darting mobility and the stable grid of a metrical substructure. The final result, when coupled with a lack of interest in new, compensatory prosodic devices, is a poetry that seeks to build most of its energy by breaking its lines at whatever points appear most confusing or disruptive. One sees again and again an attempt, in Richard

Wilbur's words, to "throw a monkey / wrench into the poem." The effect sometimes *is* a kind of energy, but of a transitory and often unpleasantly bumptious sort. This is freneticism masquerading as power—a sort of jittery, caffeine high. And given the narrowness of its source, one is not surprised when its stamina collapses and all energy drains from the poem on a second or third reading.

This perception of prosodic bankruptcy clarifies some aspects of that puzzling phenomenon known as "confessional verse"—an unfortunate term, and one usually resisted by those to whom it would be applied (Berryman reacted to it "with rage and contempt"). If used to encompass Berryman's work, or those autobiographical free verse poems Lowell assembled in *Life Studies,* it is a term tinged with honor. Nonetheless, and whatever its glorious roots, confessional verse has come to designate a body of work whose subject matter is as intimate, and often as grisly, as possible, and whose style appears an attempt to render style irrelevant. This sort of verse regards the employment of any "artifice" (rhyme, meter, elevated diction, and so forth) as evidence of insincerity, and from the prosodic point of view it tries to "heat up" the poem to a point where craft, or the lack of it, becomes extraneous. And to some extent it may succeed in doing so. The critic is apt to feel churlish, anyway, in pointing out that a poem which chronicles, say, the gruesome bullying the poet underwent in junior high school happens to be devoid of music, artistry, and intelligence. Although its makers would hardly regard it in these terms, confessional verse can often be viewed as a not always conscious attempt to overcome the besetting problem of contemporary free verse: the running impoverishment of a genre whose prosody is limited to enjambment.

Some of the difficulties the free verse poet now confronts may be clarified by analogy to the writer of what is known as either syllabic or pure syllabic verse—poetry, that is, organized around the number of syllables occurring per line without regard to where or how often stresses fall. The two genres have much in common. Both free verse and syllabic verse are children of this century. Both were born in a spirit of revolution. Both attempt to escape the long-standing hegemony of accentual-syllabic verse, as epitomized by the dominance of the iamb. And both would oust the iamb through the establishment of a line that has no metrical feet. In addition, syllabic verse provides a useful analogue because it, unlike free verse, has the "advantage" of relative unpopularity; with so few poets writing or having a stake in it, syllabic verse offers an opportunity for disinterested inquiry.

The development of syllabic verse in English stems from the concurrent but independent explorations of two women, Elizabeth Daryush in England and Marianne Moore in America. Daryush was furthering the prosodic explorations of her father, Robert Bridges, the poet laureate. Marianne Moore's antecedents remain unclear. But in any case, each was writing syllabic verse by the late 1920s, although their work otherwise shows little similarity of tone or feel or subject matter. In Moore's hands, syllabic verse generated wildly variable line lengths, including, most strikingly, very short lines of five, three, two, and even one syllable. The potency of her effects often depended upon the foiled expectations of a reader accustomed to iambic units. Daryush no less than Moore played with iambic expectations, but more quietly. Her choice of line length was usually a five- or four-syllable line, although on occasion she wrote a decasyllabic line that drifted charmingly in and out of iambic pentameter. Partial freedom from the iamb fostered in both poets an agreeable informality; Daryush chose, significantly, to capitalize the first word of each line in poems written in traditional metrics but to use lower case for syllabic verse. And (though sometimes more in theory than in practice) freedom from the piston-pulse of the iamb released a subtle and hitherto unheard music. A kind of prosodic egalitarianism was to be instituted, through which the unaccented syllable, traditionally subordinate, would become an equal partner with the grandee that bore a heavy stress: each would contribute evenly toward the new music of the syllable-cluster.

Yet as its relative unpopularity testifies, syllabic verse in English offers a bare-bones prosody. Its primary, and irresolvable, problem remains the flimsy building block with which it would erect its monuments. The syllable in spoken English leads a somewhat precarious existence; if unstressed, it tends to be "swallowed up" by any proximate stress, thereby rendering very troublesome any determination of the number of syllables a word actually possesses. Does "different," say, have two syllables or three? In actual speech, as opposed to the clean divisions a dictionary might impose, how many syllables do "comfortable" and "temperature" and "reference" have? When such words appear in metrical verse, the reader has the firm clue of the prosodic foot as a guide to the writer's intention. In traditional iambics, for example, "heaven" may be monosyllabic in one line and disyllabic a few lines later; the meter instructs us even where a mark of elision ("heav'n") has been omitted.

Those languages that have nurtured a long-standing prosody based upon syllabics tend to have sharply demarcated syllables differentiated by relatively light stress. In Japanese poetry, for example, one is never in doubt as to how many syllables a word should be accorded. But when, as in English, the syllable count is disputable, the reader finds it impossible to sense viscerally whether or not a line conforms to its norm; and without the active participation of the viscera, no prosody can flourish. Marianne Moore often worked with an extremely expansive syllabic line—sometimes as long as seventeen syllables—but there is simply no way in which the reader can know (without benefit of counting) whether a line not subdivided into metrical feet actually contains seventeen syllables or veers slightly above or below that figure. Not surprisingly, syllabic verse often inclines toward the short line and the minified subject matter and treatment which a short line encourages. No sane soul will ever write an epic in syllabic verse.

Syllabic verse in English has been around long enough—more than half a century—for us to speak with some assurance about its intrinsic shortcomings. There can now be little question that, notwithstanding its considerable charms, it lacks a generous enough prosody to evolve and to go on evolving, as accentual-syllabic verse has done for more than half a millennium. One suspects, in fact, that it will never fully extricate itself from the iambic line; today, no less than at its inception, syllabic verse scores many of its points by "playing off" traditional metrics. If evaluated as an alternative to accentual-syllabic prosody, syllabic verse must be deemed a failure—but one in many ways analogous to that glorious Elizabethan failure which sought to liberate English verse by means of a quantitative system. Those attempts (which, incidentally, as Derek Attridge shows in his *Well-Weighed Syllables: Elizabethan Verse in Classical Metres*, published in 1975, were based on somewhat faulty conceptions of classical versification) sought to create in English a consciously musical prosody based upon syllabic duration. Sidney, Spenser, Campion, and a host of lesser writers had a go at it before this cul-de-sac was given up. But if it had spawned no other poem than Campion's "Laura," one would have to look kindly upon this misguided endeavor. Similarly, when one contemplates the "failure" of syllabic verse, one must note that the lyric in our century would be a much diminished thing without felicities like Moore's "Bird-Witted," Daryush's "Still-Life," Sylvia Plath's "Man in Black," Ted Walker's "By the Saltings," and Auden's "Lullaby."

If syllabic poets suffer from the innate limitations of their prosody, writers of free verse face still more formidable trials, since they must contend with prosodic tools which by comparison are in many ways even more attenuated. A good argument might be made (perhaps expanding upon Daryush's brief explanatory preface to her collected poems) that syllabic verse enjoys the primary advantages of free verse—ease, informality, flexibility, and, perhaps most important, a flowing naturalness—while also commanding the significant further asset of its own distinctively patterned music. Clearly, free verse poets labor under an extreme handicap. Clearly, as well, to labor under a handicap can be a salutary experience; the poem may be better for the difficulties thrust upon it. (The writer who embarks on a Petrarchan sonnet in English labors, too, under a sizable disadvantage—the necessity of meeting a demanding rhyme scheme in a language that can be niggardly with its rhymes; much of our literature's best poetry is severely "handicapped" in some way.) Given the inherent difficulties of free verse, one is not surprised that Eliot wrote, in "Reflections on 'Vers Libre'":

> The rejection of rhyme is not a leap at facility; on the contrary, it imposes a much severer strain upon the language. When the comforting echo of rhyme is removed, success or failure in the choice of words, in the sentence structure, in the order, is at once more apparent.

Theodore Roethke echoed this sentiment in a short personal critique entitled "Some Remarks on Rhythm":

> We must realize, I think, that the writer in freer forms must have an even greater fidelity to his subject matter than the poet who has the support of form. He must keep his eye on the subject, and his rhythm must move as a wind moves, must be imaginatively right, or he is lost.

Poets and critics customarily greet such remarks with a sort of approving skepticism, regarding them as understandable overstatements meant to illustrate that this business of free verse is not so easy as it looks. But the longer one lives beside free verse, and surveys the field of its achievement, the more evident it becomes that such pronouncements deserve to be taken uncondescendingly—that is, at face value. Eliot was not only generally correct, but particularly, literally so: it is harder to write truly excellent free verse than excellent metric verse.

Once this truth is accepted, the extraodinarily anomalous condition of contemporary American poetry reveals itself. Nearly all of the verse now being composed in our country undertakes a severely taxing genre. From the evening workshop at the community adult education center to the advanced writing seminar at the Ivy League university, most everyone has chosen to scale Parnassus from its most slippery and treacherous face.

Among poets, critical analysis of the relationship between free verse and prosody has been scanty. This lack stems partly from the recognized problem of applying prosodic analysis, with its troublesome blend of ambiguity and nicety, to the dispersive, category-eluding entity that is free verse. Any orderly attempt to bring the discipline of prosody to a literary genre often perceived as disdainful of all order and discipline may seem faintly perverse—although neither William Carlos Williams nor Charles Olson, two of the spiritual fathers of free verse, shied from the task. In their different (but unfortunately equally hazy) ways, each sought to unearth the solid theoretical underpinnings of free verse. Williams' scattered observations on the "variable foot" and Olson's on "projective verse" both acknowledge a need for some coherent exposition of their chosen genre.

This is a need which has been little served or even recognized by the academic community, as Charles Hartman points out in his excellent book, *Free Verse: An Essay in Prosody* (1980). Hartman begins with an investigation into the origins of free verse, managing in the process to disinter a good many fresh quotations, and moves from there to a look at why free verse behaves as it does. If his tone at times is overly defensive (free verse surely requires no apologia at this point), one excuses this as a ground-layer's impulse to take little for granted. And if his role as defender curbs Hartman's willingness to discuss the problems free verse now confronts, the reader nonetheless comes away from the book feeling that a difficult subject has belatedly been readied for discussion.

The problem of free verse in 1917, when Eliot wrote, and even more pressingly in 1987, is the necessity of discovering sufficient rewards to compensate for those lost with the abandonment of traditional prosodic devices. And in 1987 it grows evident that if free verse is ever to go forward and forge a body of work comparable to that cultivated under the iamb, it will require fresh tools. It must "make new" what was made new before.

Attempts to broaden the range of prosodic tools in contemporary verse have come from various directions and have brought a variety of successes and failures. Three cases seem noteworthy. Ted Hughes has sought to restore to verse some of the harsh, "primitive" rhythms of chant and imprecation. Others have attempted this before (one thinks of Vachel Lindsay and his "Mumbo-Jumbo will hoo-doo you. / Beware, beware, walk with care. / Boomlay, boomlay, boomlay boom"), but rarely with Hughes' power, as displayed in the opening of *Crow:*

> *Black was the without eye*
> *Black the within tongue*
> *Black was the heart*
> *Black was the liver, black the lungs*
> *Unable to suck in light*
> *Black the blood in its loud tunnel*
> *Black the bowels packed in furnace*

James Merrill, expanding on the work of Wilfred Owen and W. H. Auden, has imported into American verse an unusual sort of rhyme in which (as in "live" and "love," or "sun" and "soon") consonants remain fixed while internal vowels are altered. This is sometimes referred to as consonantal rhyme, although Edmund Blunden's coinage, "pararhyme," seems vastly preferable. When used as extensively as Merrill somehow manages, the effect can be new sorts of harmonies:

> *Gliding to a halt, the prodigal stirs.*
> *Pays the driver. Gives himself up to home.*
> *His mother, a year younger, kisses him.*
> *Maids are wafting suitcases upstairs. . . .*

Or, later in the same poem:

> *Another underground*
>
> *Chamber made ready. If this one was not*
> *Quite the profoundest or the most ornate,*
>
> *Give it time. The bric-a-brac*
> *Slumbered in bonds that of themselves would break*
>
> *One fine day, at any chance unsealing . . .*
> *("The Will")*

And James Dickey struggled for some years to write a verse whose basic foot was not the iamb but the anapest, whose basic inversion was not the trochee but the dactyl.

Dickey's exertions were interesting for a number of reasons. Although they found an obvious kin in Longfellow, who inclined toward rustic subjects and a systematic alternative to the iambic foot (Longfellow favored the falling meter of the trochee: "Forth upon the Gitche Gumee, / On the shining Big-Sea-Water . . ."), they had links to Swinburne as well, who likewise sought to expand our poetry not by destroying but by supplanting its reigning metrical foot (Swinburne experimented with modified classical feet). Dickey's eventual abandonment of the anapestic line and his failure to enlist other poets in its cause illustrate the peculiar staying power of the iamb. It was not about to depart merely because bidden to do so.

J. D. McClatchy, writing in *Poetry* magazine, made a useful point about poetry's general stubbornness, its resistance to change:

> Poetry is the most conservative of the arts. When one thinks of the difference between Bach and Cage, or of the range of styles available to the visual artist, then poetry's resources seem limited indeed, and its very possibilities for change narrowed to them. A poem—any poem—written yesterday will seem closer to Homer and Sappho than the buildings in which those poems were conceived would resemble each other. Why? I don't know. Perhaps the nature of language itself, perhaps the channels of imagination, perhaps an abiding response to a few themes and stresses.

The durability of the iamb in English is but one manifestation of this conservatism. If one pauses to consider the revolutions the world has undergone in just the last few decades, to say nothing of the last few centuries, one comes away astonished to perceive that iambic pentameter—in the hands of a Richard Wilbur, anyway—thrives today in a form Chaucer would feel at home with.

Some further answers to that sharp *Why?* which McClatchy raises are sketched in a fascinating chapter called "The Neural Lyre" in Frederick Turner's *Natural Classicism.*[1] Turner not only has done an enormous amount of reading into the body's physiological responses to verse but also has helped carry out some technical research. His analyses extend those of I. A. Richards, whose writings seem now to have a before-their-time "hardness," a "high-tech" quality. Richards repeatedly stressed that poetry, for all its ethereality, must ultimately be understood as a force that opeates upon the chemistry of the human body. What Turner has done is to advance this view by incorporating into his theories recent revelations about human physiology and the brain.

One of his most interesting discoveries concerns what he calls "the fundamental unit of metered poetry" and designates by the term LINE. He continues: "We distinguish it by capitalization from the normal use of the word, because some orthographic traditions do not conventionally write or print the LINE in a separate space as we do; and in other traditions there are examples of a long line divided into two sections by a caesura, which would, in terms of our classification, actually constitute a couplet of LINES. Metrically experienced poets can readily recognize the LINE divisions of poetry in languages they do not know, when it is read aloud." In a great many literatures, apparently, ranging from English and French to Japanese and Chinese to Ndembu (Zambia) and Eipo (New Guinea), the LINE tends toward a duration of between 2.5 and 3.5 seconds. A LINE in a tonal language like Chinese may have only eight syllables and the French Alexandrine twelve, but relative differences of syllabic velocity ensure that in recitation each requires between 3 and 4 seconds. It is impossible to sketch here the range of ideas and data which Turner advances in "The Neural Lyre"—without which, unfortunately, his theories are apt to sound rather shaky or thin. But his preliminary findings strongly suggest that something innate within the matrix of the human body—some complex concatenation of heartbeat, respiration, and, especially, synaptic firings within and between the two hemispheres of the brain—contrives to impose on any sort of poetry demands that run deeper than the language of their composition. It implies that there is nothing random or adventitious about the prosodic systems that evolve over time. Poets will gravitate toward those prosodies amenable to the demands that the body brings to the task of assimilating a line of verse; and these prosodies must change when changes in the language render them unfit to go on meeting those demands. Therefore, any attempt to "free" English verse from old patterns of line construction may run into constraints far less tractable than those of mere literary convention. Fundamental changes in prosody, such as those which occurred in English in the fourteenth century, may not be the product of artistic innovation so much as of adaptation: it may be the shifts of its language, and not the temperaments of its poets, which largely shape a culture's prosody.

The research Turner documents in *Natural Classicism* will no doubt be modified as refinements are made and further experimentation carried out. Regardless of how these may compel us to alter our perceptions, however, they can only confirm that no theory of poetry can afford to ignore the functioning, and the inbuilt limitations, of the body. And whatever new directions American poetry embarks upon in the next few decades, or for that matter in the next few centuries, these must supply, if they would prove artistically enduring, what Turner calls the "endorphin payload"—a term encompassing what the Greeks called "catharsis." When Emily Dickinson praised poetry that made her "feel physically as if the top of my head were taken off," she was calling for deeper endorphin payloads.

Given the demands and restrictions of the human body, it may well turn out that free verse is inherently barred from the very grandest heights of poetry. Great free verse poems have been written in America and will likely continue to be written, since many of our best contemporary poets work chiefly with free forms. But it is almost inconceivable that any free verse creation will ever be penned, or even word-processed, which could be placed beside *Paradise Lost* or *The Tempest.* (Admittedly, one need proceed on tiptoe when discussing what can and can't be done in literature. If Milton had never written *Paradise Lost;* had it been he who drowned in 1637 and not that distant friend Edward King whose death occasioned "Lycidas"; then university shelves would surely sway under the heft of treatises showing precisely why English and England proved inimical to the composition of an epic. . . . Doing the impossible is just one of the things that literary genius delights in.) For page after page after page, *Paradise Lost* engages the full powers at the top of the reader's mind, where one's logic and learning are lodged, while serving up to a lower, less intellectual sector of the brain an endlessly entrancing music plucked from the five-stringed lyre of the iambic pentameter.

But perhaps this conventionally vertical depiction of the mind, with its division into top and bottom, is inappropriate. Turner's "Neural Lyre" suggests that the story which *Paradise Lost* unfolds would automatically, as a string of language, be processed by the left temporal lobe of the brain, while the music of its meter would be assimilated by the right. "If this hypothesis is accurate," he continues, "meter is, in part, a way of introducing right-brain processes into the left-brain activity of understanding language; and in another sense, it is a way of connecting our much more culture-bound (and perhaps evolutionarily later) linguistic capacities with the relatively more 'hard-wired' spatial pattern-recognition faculties we share with the higher mammals." The reading of *Paradise Lost,* then, or any other densely metrical poem, would be an ongoing act of neurological synthesis. And the centrality of this synthesis would also help explain poetry's curious conservatism. One understands the poet's reluctance to forego the oldest, and perhaps richest, means he has of "making himself whole."

The English language, and the bodies and brains of those who read and write it, may well be lmited structurally so as to ensure that not only free verse, but every other poetic genre as well, will never match the breadth and vigor of the iambic line— particularly the pentameter. As developed and refined by Chaucer, Wyatt, Spenser, Shakespeare, Marlowe, Donne, Milton, Pope, Keats, Tennyson, Yeats, and countless others—some great, some good, and some only occasionally good—the English iambic pentameter line represents one of the grandest collective accomplishments of humankind. It is one of those apical achievements—like the discovery of perspective in painting, or the development of the cathedral in architecture—that forever redefine their medium.

Where does this leave the contemporary American poet? Probably in a state of some disquiet. An impatience with the iamb is understandable and in many ways admirable—we should be hungry for new methods, and the freedom and brio and joy that the genuinely new brings with it. On the other hand, free verse is hardly new any more, and over the years it becomes (as Pound predicted it would by century's end) increasingly exhausted. What is needed, ideally, is some mode as multiplex as that iambic model which free verse has constantly sought to subvert and supplant—some mode whose potential might still be disclosing itself after a couple of hundred years. And time alone can reveal to us whether in fact this new mode has been waiting for us all along, folded and encoded simultaneously in our everyday language and in the storehouse of the brain. But as we wait for this uncertain revelation, we do ourselves no good—quite the contrary—by supposing that we possess what we don't possess, or that the problems afflicting free verse are secondary. Skepticism of free verse is, after all, not only a fully defensible attitude but a surprisingly long-lived and honorable one. It was only a couple of years after "vers libre" had made its forcible entrance into English poetry that Pound and Eliot began to fret that its original aims and energies had been waylaid. Recalling this moment in a 1932 issue of *The Criterion*, Pound wrote:

> That is to say, at a particular date in a particular room, two authors, neither engaged in picking the other's pocket, decided that the dilutation of *vers libre*, Amygism, Lee Masterism, general floppiness had gone too far and that some counter-current must be set going. Parallel situation centuries ago in China. Remedy prescribed in 'Emaux et Camé' (or the Bay State Hymn Book). Rhyme and regular strophes.
>
> Results: Poems in Mr. Eliot's *second* volume, not contained in his first 'Prufrock' (Egoist, 1917), also 'H. S. Mauberley.'

This pilgrimage from the prosodically straitlaced to the unfettered and back again will doubtless go on until—if? when?—something better comes along.

John Berryman once remarked that "the artist is extremely lucky who is presented with the worst possible ordeal which will not actually kill him." It's the sort of horrific notion one instinctively turns one's back on—even while noting, over one's shoulder as it were, how much of our greatest poetry sprang from overwhelming personal tragedy. But whether or not Berryman's dictum is valid, it suggests a corollary applicable to the poem rather than the poet: *A poem should undergo just as much prosodic suffering as does not actually kill it.* Most poems benefit from being made to "suffer" (through their toiling makers) the rigors of prosodic demands. These demands must in some cases be very light. There are poems whose charm resides in their looseness, their unlabored ease—and to force them into the carapace of an elaborate pattern of meter or rhyme or rhythm would likely prove fatal. (Although one must contrarily note that Cummings often managed effects of great spontaneity and nonconformity in poems that only with rereading reveal themselves as sonnets; it is amazing how "free" the formal poem can be.) Those poems, however, whose subject matter or tone allows for prosodic intricacy, whether of a traditional or an innovative sort, should be made to bear it. A poem needs to proceed on as many levels as possible—intellectual, melodic, rhythmic—if it is to quarry from the mine of the body that "payload" which accompanies excellence.

Difficult though it may be to envision what a worthy replacement for the iambic pentameter line might actually look like, one can safely speculate that it would be at once strong and yet supple enough to embrace a range of expectations equivalent to those traditionally borne by metrical verse. In the introduction to one of his last books, *Dr. Brody's Report,* Jorge Luis Borges observed that "each thing implies the universe, whose most obvious trait is complexity." His own career, with its incessant mixings of the traditional and the innovative, provides convincing testimony of the powers of art to reflect that complexity and an incentive to continue creative investigations into a zone that appears to grow more mysterious the farther we push. If free verse is to keep pace with our increasingly complex lives, and is to continue healthily serving us—through this century, into the next—it will need to gather to itself a broader collection of effects, a denser music.

NOTES

1. Frederick Turner, *Natural Classicism* (New York, N.Y.: Paragon House, 1986).

NOTES ON THE NEW FORMALISM

DANA GIOIA

1

Twenty years ago it was a truth universally acknowledged that a young poet in possession of a good ear would want to write free verse. Today one faces more complex and problematic choices. While the overwhelming majority of new poetry published in the United States continues to be in "open" forms, for the first time in two generations there is a major revival of formal verse among young poets. The first signs of this revival emerged at the tail end of the 1970s, long after the more knowing critics had declared rhyme and meter permanently defunct. First a few good formal books by young poets like Charles Martin's *Room For Error* (1978) and Timothy Steele's *Uncertainties and Rest* (1979) appeared but went almost completely unreviewed. Then magazines like *Paris Review* which hadn't published a rhyming poem in anyone's memory, suddenly began featuring sonnets, villanelles, and syllabics. Changes in literary taste make good copy, and the sharper reviewers quickly took note. Soon some of the most lavishly praised debuts like Brad Leithauser's *Hundreds of Fireflies* (1982) and Vikram Seth's *The Golden Gate* (1986) were by poets working entirely in form.

Literature not only changes; it must change to keep its force and vitality. There will always be groups advocating new types of poetry, some of it genuine, just as there will always be conservative opposing forces trying to maintain the conventional models. But the revival of rhyme and meter among some young poets creates an unprecedented situation in American poetry. The new formalists put free verse poets in the ironic and unprepared position of being the status quo. Free verse, the creation of an older literary revolution, is now the long-established, ruling orthodoxy; formal poetry the unexpected challenge.

There is currently a great deal of private controversy about these new formalists, some of which occasionally spills over into print. Significantly, these discussions often contain many odd misconceptions about poetic form, most of them threadbare clichés which somehow still survive from the 1960s. Form, we are told authoritatively, is artificial, elitist, retrogressive, right-wing, and (my favorite) un-American. None of these arguments can withstand scrutiny, but nevertheless, they continue to be made so regularly that one can only assume they provide some emotional comfort to their advocates. Obviously, for many writers the discussion of formal and free verse has become an encoded political debate.

When the language of poetic criticism has become so distorted, one needs to make some fundamental distinctions. Formal verse, like free verse, is neither intrinsically bad nor good. The terms are strictly descriptive not evaluative. They define distinct sets of metrical technique rather than rank the quality or nature of poetic perform-ance. Nor do these techniques automatically carry with them social, political, or even, in most cases, aesthetic values. (It would, for example, be very easy for a poet to do automatic writing in meter. One might even argue that surrealism is best realized in formal verse since the regular rhythms of the words in meter hypnotically release the unconscious.) However obvious these distinctions should be, few poets or critics seem to be making them. Is it any wonder then that so much current writing on poetry is either opaque or irrelevant? What serious discussion can develop when such primary critical definitions fail to be made with accuracy?

2

Meter is an ancient, indeed primitive, tech-nique that marks the beginning of literature in virtually every culture. It dates back to a time, so different from our specialized modern era, when there was little, if any, distinction between poetry, religion, history, music, and magic. All were performed in a sacred, ritual language separated from everyday speech by its incantatory metrical form. Meter is also essentially a preliterate technology, a way of making language memorable before the invention of writing. Trained poet-singers took the events and ideas a culture wanted to preserve—tribal histories, magic ceremonies—formulated them in meter, and committed these formulas to memory. Before writing, the poet and the poem were inseparable, and both represented the collective memory of their culture.

Meter is therefore an aural technique. It assumes a speaker and a listener, who for the duration of the poem are intertwined. Even in later literary cultures meter has always insisted on the primacy of the physical sound of language. Unlike prose, which can be read silently with full enjoyment, poetry demands to be recited, heard, even memorized for its true appreciation. Shaping the words in one's mouth is as much part of the pleasure as hearing the sounds in the air. Until recently education in poetry always emphasized memorization and recitation. This traditional method stressed the immediately communicable and communal pleasures of the art. Certainly a major reason for the decline in poetry's popular audience stems directly from the abandon-ment of this aural education for the joylessly intellectual approach of critical analysis.

Free verse is a much more modern technique that presupposes the existence of written texts. While it does not abandon the aural imagination—no real poetry can—most free verse plays with the way poetic language is arranged on a page and articu-lates the visual rhythm of a poem in a way earlier method verse rarely bothered to. Even the earliest known free verse, the Hebrew Psalms (which actually inhabit a middle ground between free and formal verse since they follow a principle of syntatic but not metrical symmetry) were created by "the people of the Book" in a culture uniquely concerned with limiting the improvisatory freedom of the bard for the fixed message of the text.

Most often one first notices the visual orientation of free verse in trivial ways (the lack of initial capitals at the beginning of lines, the use of typographical symbols like "&" and "7," the arbitrary use of upper- and lower-case letters). E. E. Cummings spent his life exploiting these tricks trying to create a visual vocabulary for modern poetry. Eventually, however, one sees how the visual field of the page is essential to the organization of sound in free verse. Rearranged in prose lines, a free verse poem usually changes radically. Its rhythms move differently from their original printed form (whereas most metrical verse would still retain its basic rhythmic design and symmetry). This visual artifice separates free verse from speech. Technological innovation affects art, and it is probably not accidental that the broad-scale development of free verse came from the first generation of writers trained from childhood on the shift-key typewriter introduced in 1878. This new device allowed writers to predict accurately for the first time the *look* of their words on the printed page rather than just their sound.

All free verse deals with the fundamental question of how and when to end lines of poetry when there is no regular meter to measure them out. The earliest free verse matched the line with some syntactic unit of sense (in Hebrew poetry, for instance, the line was most often a double unit of parallel syntactic sense):

> 1   *Except the Lord build the house, they labor in vain that build it:*
> *Except the Lord keep the city, the watchman waketh but in vain.*
>
> 2   *It is vain for you to rise up early, to sit up late,*
> *To eat the bread of sorrows: for so he giveth his beloved sleep.*
> *Psalm 127*

Once free verse leaves the strict symmetry of sacred Hebrew poetry, there is no way for the ear to judge accurately from the sounds alone the metrical structure of a poem (unless the reader exaggerates the line breaks). Sometimes one wonders if even the poet hears the purely aural pattern of his words. Most critics do not. For instance, it has never been noted that the most famous American free verse poem of the twentieth century, William Carlos Williams' "The Red Wheelbarrow," is not free verse at all but two rather undistinguished lines of blank verse:

> *so much depends upon a red wheel barrow*
> *glazed with rain water beside the white chickens.*

One reason that these lines have proved so memorable is that they are familiarly metrical—very similar in rhythm to another famous passage of blank verse, even down to the "feminine" endings of the lines:

> *To be or not to be that is the question*
> *Whether 'tis nobler in the mind to suffer . . .*

That Williams wrote blank verse while thinking he was pioneering new trails in prosody doesn't necessarily invalidate his theories (though it may lead one to examine them with a certain skepticism). This discrepancy, however, does suggest two points. First, even among its adversaries, metrical language exercises a primitive power, even if it is frequently an unconscious one. Second, the organizing principle of Williams' free verse is visual. What makes "The Red Wheelbarrow" free verse is not the sound alone, which is highly regular, but the visual placement of those sounds on the page.

> *so much depends*
> *upon*
>
> *a red wheel*
> *barrow*
>
> *glazed with rain*
> *water*
>
> *beside the white*
> *chickens.*

Here the words achieve a new symmetry, alien to the ear, but no less genuine. The way Williams arranged the poem into brief lines and stanzas slows the language until every word acquires an unusual weight. This deliberate visual placement twists a lack-luster blank verse couplet into a provocatively original free verse lyric which challenges the reader's definition of what constitutes a poem. Much of the poem's impact comes from catching the reader off guard and forcing him to reread it in search of what he has missed because nothing of what Williams has said comprises a satisfactory poem in a conventional sense. The element of surprise makes this type of poem a difficult trick to repeat and may explain why so much of the minimalist poetry written in the Williams tradition is so dull. The poetic experience comes in the rereading as the reader consciously revises his own superficial first impression and sees the real importance of Williams' seemingly mundane images. Just as Williams' imagery works by challenging the reader to see the despoiled modern world as charged with a new kind of beauty, so too does his prosody operate by making everyday words acquire a new weight by their unexpectedly bold placement on the page. No aural poem could work in this way.

3

The current moment is fortunate for poets interested in traditional form. Two generations now of younger writers have largely ignored rhyme and meter, and most of the older poets who worked originally in form (such as Louis Simpson and Adrienne Rich) have abandoned it entirely for more than a quarter of a century. Literary journalism has long declared it defunct, and most current anthologies present no work in traditional forms by Americans written after 1960. The British may have continued using rhyme and meter in their quaint, old-fashioned way and the Irish in their primitive, bardic manner, but for up-to-date Americans, it became the province of the old, the eccentric, and the Anglophilic. It was a style that dared not speak its name, except in light verse. Even the tri-nominate, blue-haired lady laureates now wrote in free verse.[1] By 1980 there had been such a decisive break with the literary past that in America for the first time in the history of modern English most published young poets could not write with minimal competence in traditional meters (not that this failing bothered anyone). Whether this was an unprecedented cultural catastrophe or a glorious revolution is immaterial to this discussion. What matters is that most of the craft of traditional English versification had been forgotten.

Since 1960 there has also been relatively little formal innovation done by the mainstream either in metrical or free verse. Radical experimentation like concrete poetry or language poetry has been pushed off to the fringes of the literary culture where it has been either ignored by the mainstream or declared irrelevant. At the same time most mainstream poets have done little of the more focused (and less radical) experimentation with meters or verse forms that open up new possibilities for poetic language. Since 1960 the only new verse forms to have entered the mainstream of American poetry have been two miniatures: the double dactyl and the ghazal, the latter usually in a dilute unrhymed version of the Persian original.

Indeed, the most influential form in American poetry over this quarter century has been the prose poem, which strictly speaking is not a verse form at all but a stylistic alternative to verse as the medium for poetry. In theory the prose poem is the most protean form of free verse in which all line breaks disappear as a highly charged lyric poem achieves the ultimate organic form. In recent American practice, however, it has mostly become a kind of absurdist parable having more to do with the prose tradition of Kafka and Borges than the poetic tradition of Baudelaire and Rimbaud. As poetry literally became written in prose, was it any wonder that verse technique suffered?

Likewise, although the past quarter-century has witnessed an explosion of poetic translation, this boom has almost exclusively produced work that is formally vague and colorless. Compared to most earlier translation, these contemporary American versions make no effort whatsoever to reproduce the prosodic features of their originals. One can now read most of Dante or Villon, Rilke or Mandelstam, Lorca or even Petrarch in English without any sense of the poem's original form. Sometimes these versions brilliantly convey the theme or tone of the originals, but more often they sound stylistically impoverished and anonymous. All of the past blurs together into a familiar tune. Unrhymed, unmetered, and unshaped, Petrarch and Rilke sound misleadingly alike.

This method of translating foreign poetry into an already available contemporary style also brings less to the language than the more difficult attempt to recreate a foreign form in English (as Sir Thomas Wyatt did for the Italian sonnet or the anonymous translators of the King James Bible did for the Hebrew Psalms). New verse forms and meters can have a liberating effect on poetry. They allow writers to say things that have never worked in poetry before or else to restate familiar things in original ways. Many of the most important forms in our language were once exotic imports—the sonnet, sestina, ballade, villanelle, triolet, terza rima, pantoum, rubaiyat, haiku, ottava rima, free verse, even the prose poem. Recent translation has done little to expand the formal resources of American poetry. Ironically it may have done more to deaden the native ear by translating all poetry of all ages into the same homogenous style. Studying great poetry in such neturalized versions, one gets little sense of how the forms adopted or invented by great writers are inseparable from their art. Not only the subtleties are lost but even the general scheme.

This assessment does not maintain that metrical innovation is necessary to write good poetry, that successful poetic translation must always follow the verse forms of the original or that prose is an impossible medium for poetry. It merely examines some current literary trends and speculates on both their origins and consequences. It also suggests that the recent dearth of formal poetry opens interesting possibilities for young poets to match an unexploited contemporary idiom with traditional or experimental forms. Indeed the current moment may even offer poets an opportunity for formal innovation and expansion unprecedented in the language since the end of the eighteenth century, for no age since then has been so metrically narrow or formally orthodox as our own.

4

For the arts at least there truly is a *Zeitgeist,* especially at moments of decisive change when they move together with amazing synchronization. We are now living at one such moment to which critics have applied the epithet "postmodern," an attractive term the meaning of which no two writers can agree on precisely because it does not yet have one. The dialectic of history is still moving too fast, and events still unforeseen will probably define this moment in ways equally unexpected. One day cultural historians will elucidate the connections between the current revival of formal and narrative poetry with this broader shift of sensibility in the arts. The return to tonality in serious music, to representation in painting, to decorative detail and nonfunctional design in architecture will link with poetry's reaffirmation of song and story as the most pervasive development of the American arts toward the end of this century.

No one today can accurately judge all the deeper social, economic, and cultural forces driving this revival, but at least one central motivation seems clear. All these revivals of traditional technique (whether linked or not to traditional aesthetics) both reject the specialization and intellectualization of the arts in the academy over the past forty years and affirm the need for a broader popular audience. The modern movement, which began this century in bohemia, is now ending it in the university, an institution dedicated at least as much to the specialization of knowledge as to its propagation. Ultimately the mission of the university has little to do with the mission of the arts, and this long cohabitation has had an enervating effect on all the arts but especially on poetry and music. With the best of intentions the university has intellectualized the arts to a point where they have been cut off from the vulgar vitality of popular traditions and, as a result, their public has shrunk to groups of academic specialists and a captive audience of students, both of which refer to everything beyond the university as "the real world." Mainly poets read contemporary poetry, and only professional musicians and composers attend concerts of new music.

Like the new tonal composers, the young poets now working in form reject the split between their art and its traditional audience. They seek to reaffirm poetry's broader cultural role and restore its parity with fiction and drama. Poet Wade Newman has already linked the revival of form with the return to narrative and grouped these new writers as an "expansive movement" dedicated to reversing poetry's declining importance to the culture. These young poets, Newman claims, seek to engage their audience not by simplifying their work but by making it more relevant and accessible. They are also "expansive" in that they have expanded their technical and thematic concerns beyond the confines of the short, autobiographical free verse lyric which so dominates contemporary poetry. Obviously, the return to form and narrative are not the only possible ways of establishing the connection between the poet and the broader public, but it does represent one means of renewal, and, if this particular "expansive movement" continues to develop successfully, American poetry will end this, its most distinguished century, with more promise to its future than one sees today.

5

One of the more interesting developments in the early 1980s has been the emergence of pseudo-formal verse. This sort of writing began appearing broadly a few years ago shortly after critics started advertising the revival of form. Pseudo-formal verse bears the same relationship to formal poetry as the storefronts on a Hollywood backlot do to a real city street. They both look vaguely similar from a distance. In pseudo-formal verse the lines run to more or less the same length on the page. Stanzas are neatly symmetrical. The syllable count is roughly regular line by line, and there may even be a few rhymes thrown in, usually in an irregular pattern.

Trying to open the window on a Hollywood façade, one soon discovers it won't budge. The architectural design has no structural function. Pseudo-formal verse operates on the same principle. It displays no comprehension of how meters operate in English to shape the rhythm of a poem. Though arranged in neat visual patterns, the words jump between incompatible rhythmic systems from line to line. The rhythms lack the spontaneity of free verse without ever achieving the focused energy of formal poetry. They grope toward a regular rhythmic shape but never reach it. Ultimately, there is little, if any, structural connection between the look and the sound of the poem.

There are two kinds of pseudo-formal poem. The first type is the more sophisticated. It tries to be regularly metrical. The first line usually scans according to some common meter, but thereafter problems occur. The poet cannot sustain the pattern of sounds he or she has chosen and soon begins to make substitutions line by line, which may look consistent with the underlying form but actually organize the rhythms in incompatible ways. What results technically is usually neither good free verse nor formal verse. Here, for example, is the opening of a poem by a young writer widely praised as an accomplished formalist. (Most poetry reviewers call any poem that looks vaguely regular "formal.") This passage wants to be blank verse, but despite a few regular lines, it never sustains a consistent rhythm long enough to establish a metrical base:

> *From this unpardoned perch, a kitchen table*
> *In a sunless walk-up in a city*

Of tangled boulevards, he tested
The old, unwieldy nemesis—namelessness.
Forgetting (he knew) couldn't be remedied
But these gestures of identity (he liked to think)
Rankled the equanimities of time:
A conceit, of course, but preferable to
The quarrels of the ego, the canter of
Description or discoveries of the avant-garde.

At first glance this passage appears to be in blank verse. The poem's first line unfolds as regular iambic pentameter (with a feminine ending). The second line has ten syllables, too, but it scans metrically either as awkward trochees or pure syllabics. A regular iambic rhythm appears again in line three, but now it falls decisively one foot short. Line four begins as regular blank verse but then abruptly loses its rhythm in word play between "nemesis" and "namelessness." Line five can only be construed as free verse. After a vague start line six plays with a regular iambic movement but dissipates itself over thirteen syllables. And so it continues awkwardly till the end. Good blank verse can be full of substitutions, but the variations always play off of a clearly established pattern. Here the poem never establishes a clear rhythmic direction. The lines never quite become blank verse. They only allude to it.

The second type of pseudo-formal poem is more common because it is easier to write. It doesn't even try to make a regular pattern of sound, however awkwardly. It only wants to look regular. The lines have no auditory integrity, as free or formal verse. Their integrity is merely visual—in a gross and uninteresting sense. The same issue of *The Agni Review,* which published the previous example, also contains a poem in quatrains which has these representative stanzas:

When at odd moments, business and pleasure
pale, and I think I'm staring into space,
I catch myself gazing at a notecard propped
on my desk, "The Waves at Matsushima."
. . . .
and wider than the impossible journey
from island to island so sheerly
undercut by waves that no boot could find
a landing, nor a shipwrecked couple

rest beneath those scrubby pines at the top
that could be overgrown heads of broccoli,
even if they could survive the surf, tall
combers, more like a field plowed by a maniac . . .

These line lengths seem determined mainly by their typographic width. Why else does the author break the lines between "pleasure" and "pale" or "tall" and "combers"? The apparently regular line breaks fall without any real rhythmic relation either to the meter or the syntax. As Truman Capote once said, "That's not writing—it's typing." There is no rhythmic integrity, only incompatible, provisional judgments shifting pointlessly line by line. The resulting poems remind me of a standard gag in improvisational comedy where the performers pretend to speak a foreign language by imitating its approximate sound. Making noises that resemble Swedish, Russian, Italian, or French, they hold impassioned conversations on the stage. What makes it all so funny is that the actors, as everyone in the audience knows, are only mouthing nonsense.

The metrical incompetence of pseudo-formal verse is the most cogent evidence of our literature's break with tradition and the lingering consequences. These poets are not without talent. Aside from its rhythmic ineptitude, their verse often exhibits many qualities that distinguish good poetry. Even their desire to try traditional forms speaks well for their ambition and artistic curiosity. How then do these promising authors, most of whom not only have graduate training in writing or literature but also work as professional teachers of writing, not hear the confusing rhythms of their own verse? How can they believe their expertise in a style whose basic principiles they so obviously misunderstand? That these writers by virtue of their training and position represent America's poetic intelligentsia makes their performance deeply unnerving—rather like hearing a conservatory trained pianist rapturously play the notes on a Chopin waltz in 2/4 time.

These young poets have grown up in a literary culture so removed from the predominantly oral traditions of metrical verse that they can no longer hear it accurately. Their training in reading and writing has been overwhelmingly visual not aural, and they have never learned to hear the musical design a poem executes. For them poems exist as words on a page rather than sounds in the mouth and ear. While they have often analyzed poems, they have rarely memorized and recited them. Nor have they studied and learned poems by heart in foreign languages where sound patterns are more obvious to non-native speakers. Their often extensive critical training in textual analysis never included scansion, and their knowledge of even the fundamentals of prosody is haphazard (though theory is less important than practice in mastering the craft of versification). Consequently, they have neither much practical nor theoretical training in the way sounds are organized in poetry. Ironically this very lack of training makes them deaf to their own ineptitude. Full of confidence, they rely on instincts they have never developed. Magisterially they take liberties with forms whose rudimentary principles they misconstrue. Every poem reveals some basic confusion about its own medium. Some misconceptions ultimately prove profitable for art. Not this one.

6

In my own poetry I have always worked in both fixed and open forms. Each mode offered possibilities of style, subject, music, and development the other did not suggest, at least at that moment. Likewise experience in each mode provided an illuminating perspective on the other. Working in free verse helped keep the language of my formal poems varied and contemporary, just as writing in form helped keep my free verse more focused and precise. I find it puzzling therefore that so many poets see these modes as opposing aesthetics rather than as complementary techniques. Why shouldn't a poet explore the full resources the English language offers?

I suspect that ten years from now the real debate among poets and concerned critics will not be about poetic form in the narrow technical sense of metrical versus nonmetrical verse. That is already a tired argument, and only the uninformed or biased can fail to recognize that genuine poetry can be created in both modes. How obvious it should be that no technique precludes poetic achievement just as none automatically assures it (though admittedly some techniques may be more difficult to use at certain moments in history). Soon, I believe, the central debate will focus on form in the wider, more elusive sense of poetic structure. How does a poet best shape words, images, and ideas into meaning? How much compression is needed to transform versified lines—be they metrical or free—into genuine poetry? The important arguments will not be about technique in isolation but about the fundamental aesthetic assumptions of writing and judging poetry.

At that point the real issues presented by American poetry in the 1980s will become clearer: the debasement of poetic language; the prolixity of the lyric; the bankruptcy of the confessional mode; the inability to establish a meaningful aesthetic for new poetic narrative; and the denial of musical texture in the contemporary poem. The revival of traditional forms will be seen then as only one response to this troubling situation. There will undoubtedly be others. Only time will prove which answer is the most persuasive.

NOTES

1. The editors of *The Hudson Review* ask, as perhaps they should, if this statement is a sexist stereotype. I offer it rather as investigative journalism based on painful, firsthand knowledge of the work of such important contemporary poets as Sudie Stuart Hager, Winifred Hamrick Farrar, Maggie Culver Fry, Helen von Kolnitz Hyer, Louise McNeill Pease, and the late Peggy Simson Curry (the official poets laureate of Idaho, Mississippi, Oklahoma, South Carolina, West Virginia, and Wyoming respectively). When such poets write in free verse, how can that style not be said to belong to the establishment?

OF FORMAL, FREE, AND FRACTAL VERSE: SINGING THE BODY ECLECTIC

ALICE FULTON

For the past three years, there's been a critical outburst against the "formlessness" of much contemporary poetry. This critical bias defines and defends a narrow notion of form, based largely on a poem's use of regular meter. J. V. Cunningham defined form more generously as "that which remains the same when everything else is changed. . . . The form of the simple declarative sentence in English is the same in each of its realizations." Hence, by changing the content of any free verse poem while retaining (for example) its irregular meter and stanzaic length, one can show its form. And if a poem's particular, irregular shape were used again and again, this form eventually might be given a name, such as "sonnet."

It seems to me that good free and formal verse have a lot in common. In fact, I'd venture to say that both are successful in proportion to their approximation of one another. Often, a metered poem contains several lines so irregular we might as well call them free. The poems of Donne, Blake, Dickinson, and Hopkins are frequently polyrhythmic, and substitutions of one metrical foot for another are common in both classical and romance verse forms. We know that perfectly regular rhythm is a sure sedative to the ear. It follows that the variations rather than the regularities of metered verse give the work of its great practitioners a signature charm. On the other hand, vers libre frequently contains an underlying beat that comes close to regular measure. Richard D. Cureton, writing on the prosody of free verse, observes: "If we are interested in the rhythmic structure of a poetic text, the appropriate question is not *Is this text rhythmic?* but *At what level and to what degree is this text rhythmic?"*

Regular meter is pleasing because we can readily anticipate the rhythm of the lines to come. The pleasure lies in having our expectations fulfilled. Irregular meter, on the other hand, pleases because it delivers something unforeseen, though, in retrospect, well-prepared for. Free verse is most compelling when most rhythmic: the poet must shape the irregular rhythms of language to underscore, contradict, or in some way reinforce the poem's content. Occasional lapses into regular meter frame the more jagged lines and help the reader appreciate their unpredictable music. For example, when a long iambic line is followed by a spondee or two, the rhythms are thrown into high relief. It's a little like placing a swatch of red next to a swatch of green: when juxtaposed these complements increase each other's vibrancy.

Prosody provides a comprehensive means of discussing traditional metered verse. But free verse is seldom subjected to any such systematic analysis in our literary magazines. There is, however, an insightful and growing body of literature by scholars of prosody, linguistics, and musicology on the rhythms of free verse. I think of Stephen Cushman's new book *Williams and the Meaning of Measure* (which in advancing our understanding of Williams' prosody advances our understanding of free verse); Charles O. Hartman's *Free Verse, An Essay on Prosody;* Cooper and Meyer's work on musical rhythm; linguist Ray Jackendoff's model of hierarchical structure in language as applied to music; David Stein and David Gil's linguistic insights concerning prosodic structures; phonologist Elizabeth Selkirk's study of the relationship between sound and structure; Donald Westling's syntactic theory of enjambment, which he calls "grammetric scissoring"; and Richard D. Cureton's analysis of the "myths and muddles" of traditional scansion. However, to judge from their opinions, many of the critics, essayists, and poets holding forth in our literary journals are unaware of such studies and, consequently, of any of the newer theories of prosody. As reviewers, they are content to describe the content of the poems and praise the poet's skillful use of blank verse. If the poet does not write in blank verse or in any of the more obvious metrical forms, the poems simply are not scanned. It's as if the reader, upon scanning two lines and finding dissimilar rhythms, gives up the search and regards the poem as a formless mass of words. I'd argue, however, that all poems have shape—whether it's pleasing or perceptible to the reader is something else. It's time that we, as poets, readers, and critics, begin to discern and analyze the subtle, governing structures of free verse and to talk more about its operative tropes.

Rather than placing the emphasis upon the formal devices of regular rhythm and meter, why not consider the whole panoply of design and pattern? As J. V. Cunningham noted, "A poem is a convergency of forms. It is the coincidence of forms that locks in the poem." Prosody is too specific an instrument to describe all the pattern-making possibilities of verse. To devote our analytical energy and aesthetic passion solely to metrical form is to deny the existence (and importance) of the myriad structural options available. At the very least, responsible formal analysis must define the details it chooses to disregard.

What are some of the formal schemes awaiting our investigation? As a beginning, we might look at the smaller linguistic units that influence or enlarge a text, such as allusions, puns, apostrophe, and pronouns with their function of insinuating gender. Or we could dissect the poem's larger governing organization: its rhetorical questions, conceits, virtuoso listings, registers of diction, and lineations. Cushman effectively argues that Williams wrote a prosody of enjambment, a counterpointing of visual line and syntactic unit. We might analyze the poem's enjambment within a syntactic-grammatical context or consider its use of resistant or resolved line-breaks. As Cureton notes, enjambments alone can dramatize the "curve of emotion" in the text, from relaxation to tension to resolution. It's also important to consider the poem's visual form on the page, which changes the way we hear words. Is the use of white space mimetic, abstract, or temporal; do such effects serve to emphasize or to defamiliarize the line? We also should be attentive to the poem's use of reiterative devices such as epanalepsis (ending a sentence with its own opening words—*Leaves of Grass* has many examples), refrain, chorus, or repetend (a repetition that occurs irregularly or partially, as in Delmore Schwartz's poem "Do the Others Speak of Me, Mockingly, Maliciously"). And, as Jonathan Holden has pointed out, we can regard many contemporary poems as analogues that borrow their form from letters, horoscopes, television listings, fugues, etc. The deep logic of a poem may be based upon such concepts as the microcosm moving toward macrocosm; the linkage of opposites (oxymoron); stasis; dynamism; and equilibrium. Because English, unlike the Romance languages, does not contain a multitude of rhymes, we need to appreciate and make use of aural difference rather than similitude. French and Spanish poetry can afford to value endings, which contribute so much to the irregular texture and attendant richness of our language. With this in mind, we might consider the orchestration of verse through echo (assonance, consonance, irregular rhyme, front rhyme, half-rhyme, accords, and so on). It's also interesting to analyze the operative rhetorical strategies, such as paralipsis (a passing over with brief mention in order to emphasize the suggestiveness of what was omitted) and parataxis (placing words or phrases next to one another without coordinating connections). In rhythm, we could turn our attention to the use of accentual or syllabic verse, to irregular meter that enforces content (i.e., the tension of strong-stress rhythms or the relaxation of pyrrhic, atonic lines). If we wish to be more ambitious, Cureton's theory of hierarchical scansion provides a formal mechanism for representing comparable rhythmic shapes at different linguistic levels. (The major levels are narrative, syntactic, and phonological.) We also could consider the formal devices of asyndeton (omission of conjunctions, common in the work of Ammons or Swenson, for example) and its opposite, polysyndeton (repetition of conjunctions).

The last two devices, though opposite in principle, both have the effect of making the content more vivacious and emphatic. In fact, I hope that discussion of form will lead to considerations of content. Without this obligation, formalism becomes a comfortable means of avoiding responsibility for what is being said. It's safer to speak of metrical finesse or blunders than to appraise the subjects poets choose. In too many reviews, I find lengthy *descriptions* of content, which do little more than paraphrase. Descriptive criticism is fine as a place to begin, but few critics go on to question why particular subjects continue to be chosen (while other topics suffer poetic banishment). Brave criticism might ask what is this subject's value to me, as reader? And, what world views, values, or secular mythologies are implicit in the poet's stance? Surely we must consider the cultural assumptions questioned or supported by the text, as well as the style in which these concerns are voiced.

Quantum physics teaches us that the act of measuring changes what is being measured. It follows that the act of measuring language (by putting it into regular meter) must change what is being said. Part of the resistance toward metered verse is coupled with a belief that passion or sincerity evaporates when the poet takes to counting stresses and feet. I'd contend that the content of metered poems can, at times, take on a greater urgency by means of a regular rhythm. The exigencies of form foster such careful choices that each word can become a palimpsest of implication. In fact, I value the qualities of rhythm and multidimensional language in all poetry, whether the meter is regular or not. If it is true (and I'm not sure it is) that the poetry of social commitment is often written in irregular meters, perhaps this is because the poets write from a tradition other than that of English prosody. We should respect the richness of such cultural contexts. It is ethnocentric to regard traditional English prosody as the one sure means of writing poetry. Such a stance also fails to consider the changes our language underwent in becoming American.

Several critics have lamented the repose of free verse into stylistic plainness. Mary Kinzie has even coined a new literary term, "the rhapsodic fallacy," which speaks to the problem. Kinzie's position is too complex to summarize here, but the rhapsodic fallacy describes, in part, the equation of a prosaic style with authenticity of engagement. The observation is an important one. Have we forgotten that the plain-style represents a conscious aesthetic choice, rather than a simple outpouring of pure feeling? The word "style" itself points to language as a selective construct. As such, flat style poetry is no more "sincere" or "engaged" than are the constructs of metered verse. And when the majority of poets choose to write in a given style, one suspects it is becoming a convention, as well as an artful device. (However, free verse is not to be equated with plain style or any other calcified aesthetic. If it were, there would be nothing free about it.) Perhaps readers are bored by the plethora of poems in simple language; perhaps they feel manipulated by the poet's guileless pose. As solution to the monotony of flat style poetry, Mary Kinzie calls for a return to "those forms associated with the eighteenth century: formal satire, familiar epistle, georgic, pastoral." Lamenting the blurring of high and low styles into "the low lyrical shrub" that is contemporary poetry, she would have poets write in clearly delineated genres. This stance supposes that by segregating high style from low and by restricting subject one may write "heart-piercing" poetry, to borrow Kinzie's adjective. But hearts are subjective entities, steadfast only in their refusal to be reliably pierced by aesthetic programs—that's the great thing about them! They remain willful little blobs, despite our best efforts at persuasion.

Robert Hillyer's *In Pursuit of Poetry* classifies the language of verse into two styles: "the rhetorical, heightened and dignified, and the conversational, informal and familiar. . . . Each has its dangers as well as its virtues; the first may become bombastic, the second prosaic." I don't agree that the language of verse falls neatly into binary registers of diction. If so, where would Chaucer or Shakespeare land in the aesthetic shakedown, combining as they do, the dignified with the familiar, the high with the low? To my mind, great work is large enough to include a multiplicity of styles, tones, and subjects. However, our attention for the moment is on the two styles Hillyer describes, rather than the wide diversity of work he excludes. I think his description of the dangers common to high and low style holds true. Poets are just as likely to write rhapsodic epics that ring false as they are to write fallacious, plain-style lyrics. If Mary Kinzie's programme should catch on, we'd undoubtedly see vast numbers of insufferable "genre" poems, written to fit the bill. Isn't this what happened in the eighteenth century?

Perhaps the impulse for simplicity began as a corrective when the formal post–World War II poem was felt to have degenerated (through imitation and overuse) into a polished veneer of language. The veneer might have been gold plate or marble, but everyone suddenly felt a yen for solid oak—or formica. And since the early 1960s the majority of poets have forsaken the primrose path for the plain one, which now begins, in its turn, to feel like an aesthetic shortcut.

In the largest terms, the search for a style is a search for a language that does justice to our knowledge of how the world works. According to one ordering of the canon, poetry has consistently reflected the world views of its age. Thus, in the Middle Ages, when everyone believed the world was created and run by a divine being, and earthquakes were viewed as a result of God's intervention (rather than of shifting plates), poetry mirrored the religious hierarchy. Dante's conception of the world as a series of spheres—the enormous heavens, the crystalline planets, the earth's elements, and the seven circles of hell—gave everyone a proper place, from king to serf. Newtonian physics replaced the hierarchical model with a physics of ordinary matter ruled by mathematical laws. And the literary climate of the early eighteenth century mirrored the harmony of a universe seen as a great, logical clock. The lawful and orderly cosmos was taken for proof of God's presence and goodness. Christian Wolff evolved the first sytem of German Rationalism from aspects of Newton's *Principia.* And the idea of Nature as order (prominent in *Principia*) also influenced such representative eighteenth-century literature as Pope's "Essay on Man." Later in the century, the rise of democracy, which posits an equality between parts of the social machinery, found expression in an enthusiasm for the simpler modes of folk poetry. And by the early nineteenth century, Wordsworth's "Preface to Lyrical Ballads" argued for the democratic readmission of "rustic" speech and subjects into English poetry.

Just as Newton shattered the medieval hierarchical conception of the world, modern physics has smashed Newton's mechanistic clockwork. Modernism may indeed have been a true reflection of Einstein's physics. He, after all, never accepted quantum theory and held to the old-fashioned hope that a realistic vision of the world could be congruent with the quantum facts. In his autobiography he states, "I still believe in the possibility of a model of reality—that is, of a theory which represents things themselves and not merely the probability of their occurrence." If we substitute "ideas" for "probability," we have a restatement of Williams' famous "No ideas but in things."

However, Niels Bohr's claims that there is no deep reality represents the prevailing view of contemporary quantum physics. Bohr insisted "There is no quantum world. There is only an abstract quantum description." Physicist N. David Mermin summed up Bohr's antirealist position by stating, "We now know that the moon is demonstrably not there when nobody looks." Perhaps popular literature and culture have made people aware of this and other quantum theories, such as the view that reality consists of a steadily increasing number of parallel universes; that consciousness creates reality; or that the world is twofold, consisting of potentials and actualities. Heisenberg's uncertainty principle, which forbids accurate knowledge of a quantum particle's position and momentum, is certainly well known. A truly engaged and contemporary poetry must reflect this knowledge. As a body of literature it might synthesize such disparate theories into a comprehensive metaphor for the way the world appears to us today. Or it may be that synthesis and unity are fundamentally premodern concepts. In this case, a fragmentary, diffuse literature is the perfect expression of our world knowledge. In a sense, our search for a language mirrors science's search for a quantum reality. As Nobel laureate Richard Feynman remarked, "I think it is safe to say no one understands quantum mechanics. Do not keep saying to yourself, if you can possibly avoid it, 'but how can it be like that?' Nobody knows how it can be like that." This reluctance to attempt meaning is clearly reflected in postmodernist literature and deconstructionism, where "meaning" is no longer the issue.

Perhaps it shouldn't surprise us, then, that the term *free verse* has lost its meaning and become a convenient catch-all whereby any piece of writing with wide margins may be defended as poetry. Pound's advice was to "compose in the sequence of the musical phrase, not in sequence of a metronome." He didn't say poetry should have no music at all. And founding mother Amy Lowell preferred the term "cadenced verse" to vers libre, noting that "to depart satisfactorily from a rhythm it is first necessary to have it." Frost, of course, thought that writing free verse was like playing tennis without a net. But surely the Net-Nabbing Freeform Tennis Club would waste no time in inventing another restriction. They might move the game indoors, use the walls as obstacles, and call their new sport "raquetball." In the same way, when free verse absconded with the net, it created other means of limitation. The best poets of free verse work long and hard to structure their poems. But as readers and critics, we have been slow in finding ways to discern and discuss the orders of their irregular form. But form *is* regularity, you might protest. If so, how much regularity constitutes pattern and structure?

Perfect Euclidean forms occur rather rarely in nature. Instead we find a dynamic world made up of quantities constantly changing in time, a wealth of fluctuations—such as variations in sunspots and the wobbling of the earth's axis. In 1977, the mathematician Benoit Mandelbrot observed that "twenty-five or thirty years ago, science looked at things that were regular and smooth." In contrast, he became intrigued by what are called chaotic phenomena: the occurrence of earthquakes; the way our neurons fire when we search our memories; patterns of vegetation in a swamp; price jumps in the stock market; turbulence in the weather; the distribution of galaxies; and the flooding of the Nile. Mandelbrot saw similarities in shapes so strange that fin de siècle mathematicians termed them "pathological" and "monsters." These earlier scientists never supposed that such "monstrous" shapes bore any relation to reality. Mandelbrot, on the contrary, believed they described nature much better than ideal forms. He found that certain chaotic structures (including the preceding list) contained a deep logic or pattern. In 1975, he coined the word *fractals* (from the Latin *fractus,* meaning "broken or fragmented") to describe such configurations. (Pound's injunction to "break the pentameter" is nicely implicit in the term.)

To put it simply, each part of a fractal form replicates the form of the entire structure. Increasing detail is revealed with increasing magnification, and each smaller part looks like the entire structure, turned around or tilted a bit. This isn't true of the classical Euclidean forms of lines, planes, and spheres. For example, when a segment of a circle is subjected to increasing magnification it looks increasingly like a straight line rather than a series of circles. But a fractal form has a substructure (we might say a subtext) that goes on indefinitely, without reposing into ordinary curves. The bark patterns on oak, mud cracks in a dry riverbed, a broccoli spear—these are examples of fractal forms: irregular structures containing just enough regularity so that they can be described. Such forms are, at least to my perception, quite pleasing. Like free verse, they zig and zag, spurt and dawdle, while retaining an infinite complexity of detail. (In contrast, formal verse travels at a regular pace and is less dynamic, less potentially volatile.) The fascination of these intricate forms ("the fascination of what's difficult," you might say) indicates that we don't need an obvious or regular pattern to satisfy our aesthetic or psychological needs. Nonobjective art, which often reflects the fractal patterns of nature, makes the same point. In fact, asymmetrical or turbulent composition may be the essence of twentieth-century aesthetics.

There are two kinds of fractals: geometric and random. The geometric type repeats an identical pattern at various scales. As a corollary, imagine a poem structured on the concept of the oxymoron. The linkage of opposites on the smallest scale might appear in antonymic word usage, on a larger scale in one stanza's ability to oppose or reverse the form and content of another, and at the grandest scale in the poem's overall form becoming a paradoxical or self-reflexive contradiction of content. Thus far, the poem could be a sonnet or an ode. After all, ordered forms about chaos were rather popular in the eighteenth century. But let's suppose that the poem's rhythm is also oxymoronic: that a smooth, regular line is purposefully followed by a rambunctious or jagged utterance. If repeated throughout, this juxtaposition would constitute the poem's metrical form. Random fractals, to consider another possibility, introduce some elements of chance. In the composition of poetry, this could be as simple a factor as opening a book at random and using the metrical pattern happened upon as a contributing factor in your verse.

In his essay "How Long Is the Coast of Britain?" Mandelbrot showed that a coastline, being infinitely long with all of its microscopic points and inlets, is best treated as a random fractal rather than as an approximation of a straight line. While complication is characteristic of coastlines, there is also a great degree of order in their structures, which are self-similar. A self-similar mechanism is, formally speaking, a kind of cascade, with each stage creating details smaller than those of the preceding stages. As Mandelbrot writes, "Each self-similar fractal has a very specific kind of unsmoothness, which makes it more complicated than anything in Euclid." Fractal form, then, is composed of constant digressions and interruptions in rhythm.

Scientists are just beginning to uncover all the events, things, and processes that can be described through fractals. Clouds follow fractal patterns. (Incidentally, you'll notice that the previous sentence is composed of three trochaic feet, with one extra stressed syllable at the beginning, How regular! And irregular.) Since fractals can be illustrated by means of computer graphics, it's possible to *see* the basic fractal properties in all their intricacy and beauty.

Mandelbrot's discoveries could change the way we look at the world and, by extension, the way we look at poetry. Certainly the discovery of order within the turbulent forms of nature should encourage us to search for patterns within the turbulent forms of art. Fractal form may allow a more precise measure of those poetic shapes that aren't governed by the strategies of prosody. Though it's been around for over one hundred years (if one counts Whitman), in regard to free verse we're a little like primitive people who've never seen a two-dimensional image and can't, at first, ascertain that the shapes in photographs from faces or bodies. We must develop our ability to recognize subtle, hidden, and original patterns as the time-honored (and more obvious) metrical orders of prosody. And we might pay more attention to the irregularities of traditional formal verse, the freedoms and deviations within a context of similitude and correctness. (After all, deviance can't exist without an orderly context from which to differ.)

Since "free verse" has become a misnomer, perhaps we could use the irregular yet beautifully structured forms of nature as analogue and call the poetry of irregular form *fractal verse*. Its aesthetic might derive from the structural limitations of self-similar fractal form. I offer the following as a tentative exploration of fractal precepts: any line when examined closely (or magnified) will reveal itself to be as richly detailed as was the larger poem from which it was taken; the poem will contain an infinite regression of details, a nesting of pattern within pattern (an endless imbedding of the shape into itself, recalling Tennyson's idea of the inner infinity); digression, interruption, fragmentation, and lack of continuity will be regarded as formal functions rather than lapses into formlessness; all directions of motion and rhythm will be equally probable (isotropy); the past positions of motion, or the preceding metrical pattern, will not necessarily affect the poem's future evolution (independence).

Poems are linguistic models of the world's working. Now our knowledge of form includes the new concept of manageable chaos, along with the ancient categories of order and chaos. If order is represented by the simple Euclidean shapes of nature and by metered verse, chaos might be analogous to failed free verse and gibberish. (It's somehow reassuring that chaos is still with us, evident in natural forms that show no underlying pattern.) And manageable chaos or fractal form might find its corollary in fractal poetry. One thing seems certain: our verse should be free to sing the wildly harmonious stuctures that surround and delight us, the body eclectic, where geography ends and pebbles begin.

REFERENCES

Abrams, M. H., ed. *The Norton Anthology of English Literature,* Volume 1. New York: W. W. Norton, 1979.

Breslin, Paul, Alan Shapiro, Stephen Yenser, Marjorie Perloff, Julia Randall, and Bonnie Costello. "Responses to Mary Kinzie's 'The Rhapsodic Fallacy.' *Salmagundi,* no. 67 (1985):135–153.

Cooper, Grosvenor, and Leonard Meyer. *The Rhythmic Structure of Music.* Chicago: University of Chicago Press, 1960.

Cunningham, J. V. "The Problem of Form." *Shenandoah* 35:113–116.

Cureton, Richard D. "The 'Measures' of 'Free Verse." *William Carlos Williams Review,* forthcoming.

———. "Traditional Scansions: Myths and Muddles." *Journal of Literary Semantics,* Vol. 15, no. 3 (1986):171–208.

———. "Rhythm: A Multilevel Analysis." *Style* 19(2) pp. 242–57.

Diggory, Terence. "Two Responses to Mary Kinzie: I: Dr. Johnson on the Arid Steppe." *Salmagundi,* no. 65 (1984):80–85.

Gardner, Martin. "Mathematical Games." *Scientific American,* December 1976, p. 124, and April 1978, p. 16.

Hartman, Charles O. *Free Verse, An Essay on Prosody.* Princeton: Princeton University Press, 1986.

Herbert, Nick. *Quantum Reality.* Garden City, N.Y.: Anchor Press/Doubleday, 1985.

Hillyer, Robert Silliman. *In Pursuit of Poetry.* New York: McGraw-Hill, 1960.

Hofstadter, Douglas R. "Metamagical Themas." *Scientific American,* November 1981, p. 22.

Holden, Jonathan. "Postmodern Poetic Form: A Theory." In *Poetics: Essays on the Art of Poetry,* ed. P. Mariani and G. Murphy, pp. 13–34. Green Harbor, Mass.: Tendril, 1984.

Jackendoff, Ray, and Fred Lerdahl. *A Deep Parallel Between Music and Language.* Bloomington: Indiana University Linguistics Club, 1980.

Kinzie, Mary. "The Rhapsodic Fallacy." *Salmagundi,* no. 65 (1984):63–79.

———. "Learning to Speak." *Salmagundi,* no. 67 (1985):154–162.

Leithauser, Brad. "Metrical Illiteracy." *The New Criterion,* January 1983, pp. 41–46.

Lerdahl, Ray, and Fred Jackendoff. *A Generative Theory of Tonal Music.* Cambridge, Mass.: MIT Press, 1983.

Mandelbrot, Benoit. *Fractals: Form, Chance, and Dimension.* San Francosco: W. H. Freeman, 1977.

———. *The Fractual Geometry of Nature.* San Francisco: W. H. Freeman, 1982.

———. "Fractals and the Geometry of Nature." In *1981 Yearbook of Science and the Future,* Encyclopaedia Britannica.

McDermott, Jeanne. "Geometric Forms Known as Fractals Find Sense in Chaos." *Smithsonian,* December 1983, p. 110.

Molesworth, Charles. "Two Responses to Mary Kinzie: II: Sleeping Beside the Muse: Formalism and the Conditions of Contemporary Poetry." *Salmagundi,* no. 65 (1984):86–96.

Preminger, Alex, ed. *Princeton Encyclopedia of Poetry.* Princeton: Princeton University Press, 1974.

Selkirk, Elizabeth O. *Phonology and Syntax: The Relations Between Sound and Structure.* Cambridge, Mass.: MIT Press, 1984.

Stahl, E. L., and W. E. Yuill. *German Literature of the Eighteenth and Nineteenth Centuries.* London: Cresset Press, 1970.

Stein, David, and Davil Gil. "Prosodic Structures and Prosodic Markers." *Theoretical Linguistics* 7:173–240.

Westling, Donald. *The New Poetries: Poetic Form Since Coleridge and Wordsworth.* London and Toronto: Associated University Presses, 1985.

SOUND AND SENTIMENT,
SOUND AND SYMBOL

NATHANIEL MACKEY

1

Senses of music in a number of texts is what I'd like to address—ways of regarding and responding to music in a few intances of writings which bear on the subject. This essay owes its title to two such texts, Steven Feld's *Sound and Sentiment: Birds, Weeping, Poetics and Song in Kaluli Expression* and Victor Zuckerkandl's *Sound and Symbol: Music and the External World.* These two contribute to the paradigm I bring to my reading of the reading of music in the literary works I wish to address.

Steven Feld is a musician as well as an anthropologist, and he dedicates *Sound and Sentiment* to the memory of Charlie Parker, John Coltrane, and Charles Mingus. His book, as the subtitle tells us, discusses the way in which the Kaluli of Papua New Guinea conceptualize music and poetic language. These the Kaluli associate with birds and weeping. They arise from a breach in human solidarity, a violation of kinship, community, connection. *Gisalo,* the quintessential Kaluli song form (the only one of the five varieties they sing that they claim to have invented rather than borrowed from a neighboring people), provokes and crosses over into weeping—weeping which has to do with some such breach, usually death. *Gisalo* songs, sung at funerals and during spirit-medium seances, have the melodic contour of the cry of a kind of fruitdove, the *muni* bird.[1] This reflects and is founded on the myth regarding the origin of music, the myth of the boy who became a *muni* bird. The myth tells of a boy who goes to catch crayfish with his older sister. He catches none and repeatedly begs for those caught by his sister, who again and again refuses his request. Finally he catches a shrimp and puts it over his nose, causing it to turn a bright purple red, the color of a *muni* bird's beak. His hands turn into wings and when he opens his mouth to speak the falsetto cry of a *muni* bird comes out. As he flies away his sister begs him to come back and have some of the crayfish but his cries continue and become a song, semi-wept, semisung: "Your crayfish you didn't give me. I have no sister. I'm hungry. . . ." For the Kaluli, then, the quintessential source of music is the orphan's ordeal—an orphan being anyone denied kinship, social sustenance, anyone who suffers, to use Orlando Patterson's phrase, "social death,"[2] the prototype for which is the boy who becomes a *muni* bird. Song is both a complaint and a consolation dialectically tied to that ordeal, where in back of "orphan" one hears echoes of "orphic," a music which turns on abandonment, absence, loss. Think of the black spiritual "Motherless Child." Music is wounded kinship's last resort.

In *Sound and Symbol,* whose title Feld alludes to and echoes, Victor Zuckerkandl offers "a musical concept of the external world," something he also calls "a critique of our concept of reality from the point of view of music." He goes to great lengths to assert that music bears witness to what's left out of that concept of reality, or, if not exactly what, to the fact that something *is* left out. The world, music reminds us, inhabits while extending beyond what meets the eye, resides in but rises above what's apprehensible to the senses. This co-inherence of immanence and transcendence the Kaluli attribute to and symbolize through birds, which for them are both the spirits of the dead and the major source of the everyday sounds they listen to as indicators of time, location, and distance in their physical environment. In Zuckerkandl's analysis, immanence and transcendence meet in what he terms "the dynamic quality of tones," the relational valence or vectorial give-and-take bestowed on tones by their musical context. He takes great pains to show that "no material process can be co-ordinated with it," which allows him to conclude:

> Certainly, music transcends the physical; but it does not therefore transcend tones. Music rather helps the thing "tone" to transcend its own physical con-stituent, to break through into a nonphysical mode of being, and there to de-velop in a life of unexpected fullness. Nothing but tones! As if tone were not the point where the world that our senses encounter becomes transparent to the action of nonphysical forces, where we as perceivers find ourselves eye to eye, as it were, with a purely dynamic reality—the point where the external world gives up its secret and manifests itself, immediately, *as symbol.* To be sure, tones say, signify, point to—what? Not to something lying "beyond tones." Nor would it suffice to say that tones point to other tones—as if we had first tones, and then pointing as their attribute. No—in musical tones, being, existence, is indistinguishable from, *is,* pointing-beyond-itself, meaning, saying.[3]

One easily sees the compatibility of this musical concept of the world, this asser-tion of the intrinsic symbolicity of the world, with poetry. Yeats' view that the artist "belongs to the invisible life" or Rilke's notion of poets as "bees of the invisible" sits agreeably beside Zuckerkandl's assertion that "because music exists, the tangible and visible cannot be the whole of the given world. The intangible and invisible is itself a part of this world, something we encounter, something to which we respond" (71). His analysis lends itself to more recent formulations as well. His explanation of dynamic tonal events in terms of a "field concept," to give an example, isn't far from Charles Olson's "composition by field." And one commentator, to give another, has brought *Sound and Symbol* to bear on Jack Spicer's work.[4]

The analogy between tone-pointing and word-pointing isn't lost on Zuckerkandl, who, having observed that "in musical tones, being, existence, is indistinguishable from, *is,* pointing-beyond-itself, meaning, saying," immediately adds: "Certainly, the being of words could be characterized the same way." He goes on to distinguish tone-pointing from word-pointing on the basis of the conventionally agreed-upon referen-tiality of the latter, a referentiality writers have repeatedly called into question, frequently doing so by way of "aspiring to the condition of music." "Thus poetry," Louis Zukofsky notes, "may be defined as an order of words that as movement and tone (rhythm and pitch) approaches in varying degrees the wordless art of music as a kind of mathematical limit."[5] Music encourages us to see that the symbolic is the orphic, that the symbolic realm is the realm of the orphan. Music is prod and precedent for a recognition that the linguistic realm is also the realm of the orphan, as in Octavio Paz's characterization of language as an orphan severed from the presence to which it refers and which presumably gave it birth. This recognition troubles, complicates, and contends with the unequivocal referentiality taken for granted in ordinary language:

> Each time we are served by words, we mutilate them. But the poet is not served by words. He is their servant. In serving them, he returns them to the plenitude of their nature, makes them recover their being. Thanks to poetry, language reconquers its original state. First, its plastic and sonorous values, generally disdained by thought; next, the affective values; and, finally, the expressive ones. To purify language, the poet's task, means to give it back its original nature. And here we come to one of the central themes of this reflection. The word, in itself, is a plurality of meanings.[6]

Paz is only one of many who have noted the ascendancy of musicality and multivocal meaning in poetic language. (Julia Kristeva: "The poet . . . wants to turn rhythm into a dominant element . . . wants to make language perceive what it doesn't want to say, provide it with its matter independently of the sign, and free it from denotation."[7])

Poetic language is language owning up to being an orphan, to its tenuous kinship with the things it ostensibly refers to. This is why in the Kaluli myth the origin of music is also the origin of poetic language. The words of the song the boy who becomes a *muni* bird resorts to are different from those of ordinary speech. Song language "amplifies, multiplies, or intensifies the relationship of the word to its referent," as Feld explains:

> In song, text is not primarily a proxy for a denoted subject but self-consciously multiplies the intent of the word.
>
> . . . Song poetry goes beyond pragmatic referential communication because it is explicitly organized by canons of reflexiveness and self-consciousness that are not found in ordinary talk.
>
> The uniqueness of poetic language is unveiled in the story of "the boy who became a *muni* bird." Once the boy has exhausted the speech codes for begging, he must resort to another communication frame. Conversational talk, what the Kaluli call *to halaido,* "hard words," is useless once the boy has become a bird; now he resorts to talk from a bird's point of view. . . . Poetic language is bird language.[8]

It bears emphasizing that this break with conventional language is brought about by a breach of expected behavior. In saying no to her brother's request for food the older sister violates kinship etiquette.

What I wish to do is work *Sound and Sentiment* together with *Sound and Symbol* in such a way that the latter's metaphysical accent aids and is in turn abetted by the former's emphasis on the social meaning of sound. What I'm after is a range of implication which will stretch, to quote Stanley Crouch, "from the cottonfields to the cosmos." You notice again that it's black music I'm talking about, a music whose "critique of our concept of reality" is notoriously a critique of social reality, a critique of social arrangements in which, because of racism, one finds oneself deprived of community and kinship, cut off. The two modes of this critique which I'll be emphasizing Robert Farris Thompson notes among the "ancient African organizing principles of song and dance":

> *suspended accentuation patterning* (offbeat phrasing of melodic and choreographic accents); and, at a slightly different but equally recurrent level of exposition, *songs and dances of social allusion* (music which, however danceable and "swinging," remorselessly contrasts social imperfections against implied criteria for perfect living).[9]

Still, the social isn't all of it. One needs to hear, alongside Amiri Baraka listening to Jay McNeely, that "the horn spat enraged sociologies,"[10] but not without noting a simultaneous mystic thrust. Immanence and transcendence meet, making the music social as well as cosmic, political and metaphysical as well. The composer of "Fables of Faubus" asks Fats Navarro, "What's *outside* the universe?"[11]

This meeting of transcendence and immanence I evoke, in my own work, through the figure of the phantom limb. In the letter which opens *From A Broken Bottle Traces of Perfume Still Emanate* N. begins:

> You should've heard me in the dream last night. I found myself walking down a sidewalk and came upon an open manhole off to the right out of which came (or strewn around which lay) the disassembled parts of a bass clarinet. Only the funny thing was that, except for the bell of the horn, all the parts looked more like plumbing fixtures than like parts of a bass clarinet. Anyway, I picked up a particularly long piece of "pipe" and proceeded to play. I don't recall seeing anyone around but somehow I knew the "crowd" wanted to hear "Naima." I decided I'd give it a try. In any event, I blew into heaven knows what but instead of "Naima" what came out was Shepp's solo on his version of "Cousin Mary" on the *Four for Trane* album—only infinitely more gruffly resonant and varied and warm. (I even threw in a few licks of my own.) The last thing I remember is coming to the realization that what I was playing already existed on a record. I could hear scratches coming from somewhere in back and to the left of me. This realization turned out, of course, to be what woke me up.
>
> Perhaps Wilson Harris is right. There are musics which haunt us like a phantom limb. Thus the abrupt breaking off. Therefore the "of course." No more than the ache of some such would-be extension.[12]

I'll say more about Wilson Harris later. For now, let me simply say that the phantom limb is a felt recovery, a felt advance beyond severance and limitation which contends with and questions conventional reality, that it's a feeling for what's not there which reaches beyond as it calls into question what is. Music as phantom limb arises from a capacity for feeling which holds itself apart from numb contingency. The phantom limb haunts or critiques a condition in which feeling, consciousness itself, would seem to have been cut off. It's this condition, the nonobjective character of reality, to which Michael Taussig applies the expression "phantom objectivity," by which he means the veil by way of which a social order renders its role in the construction of reality invisible: "a commodity-based society produces such phantom objectivity, and in so doing it obscures its roots—the relations between people. This amounts to a socially instituted paradox with bewildering manifestations, the chief of which is the denial by the society's members of the social construction of reality."[13] "Phantom," then, is a relative, relativizing term which cuts both ways, occasioning a shift in perspective between real and unreal, an exchange of attributes between the two. So the narrator in Josef Skvorecky's *The Bass Saxophone* says of the band he's inducted into: "They were no longer a vision, a fantasy, it was rather the sticky-sweet panorama of the town square that was unreal."[14] The phantom limb reveals the illusory rule of the world it haunts.

2

Turning now to a few pieces of writing which allude to or seek to ally themselves with music, one sense I'm advancing is that they do so as a way of reaching toward an alternate reality, that music is the would-be limb whereby that reaching is done or which alerts us to the need for its being done. The first work I'd like to look at is Jean Toomer's *Cane*. Though *Cane* is not as announcedly about music as John A. Williams' *Night Song*, Thomas Mann's *Doctor Faustus*, or any number of other works one could name, in its "quieter" way it's no less worth looking at in this regard. First of all, of course, there's the lyricism which pervades the writing, an intrinsic music which is not unrelated to a theme of wounded kinship of which we get whispers in the title. Commentators have noted the biblical echo, and Toomer himself, in notebooks and correspondence, referred to the book as *Cain* on occasion. His acknowledged indebtedness to black folk tradition may well have included a knowledge of stories in that tradition which depict Cain as the prototypical white, a mutation among the earlier people, all of whom were up to that point black: "Cain he kill his brudder Abel wid a great big club . . . and he turn white as bleech cambric in de face, and de whole race ob Cain dey bin white ebber since."[15] The backdrop of white assault which comes to the fore in "Portrait in Georgia," "Blood-Burning Moon," and "Kabnis" plays upon the fratricidal note struck by the book's title.

Indebted as it is to black folk tradition, *Cane* can't help but have to do with music. That "Deep River," "Go Down, Moses," and other songs are alluded to comes as no surprise. Toomer's catalytic stay in Georgia is well-known. It was there that he first encountered the black "folk-spirit" he sought to capture in the book. Worth repeating is the emphasis he put on the music he heard:

> The setting was crude in a way, but strangely rich and beautiful. I began feeling its effects despite my state, or, perhaps, just because of it. There was a valley, the valley of "Cane," with smoke-wreaths during the day and mist at night. A family of back-country Negroes had only recently moved into a shack not too far away. They sang. And this was the first time I'd ever heard the folk-songs and spirituals. They were very rich and sad and joyous and beautiful.[16]

He insisted, though, that the spirit of that music was doomed, that "the folk-spirit was walking in to die on the modern desert" and that *Cane* was "a swan-song," "a song of an end." The elegaic weariness and weight which characterize the book come of a lament for the passing of that spirit. In this it's like the music which inspired it, as Toomer pointd out in a letter to Waldo Frank:

> . . . the Negro of the folk-song has all but passed away: the Negro of the emotional church is fading. . . . In my own . . . pieces that come nearest to the old Negro, to the spirit saturate with folk-song . . . the dominant emotion is a sadness derived from a sense of fading. . . . The folk-songs themselves are of the same order: the deepest of them, "I aint got long to stay here."[17]

So, "Song of the Son":

> *Pour O pour that parting soul in song,*
> *O pour it in the sawdust glow of night,*
> *Into the velvet pine-smoke air to-night,*
> *And let the valley carry it along.*
> *And let the valley carry it along.*
>
> *O land and soil, red soil and sweet-gum tree,*
> *So scant of grass, so profligate of pines,*
> *Now just before an epoch's sun declines*
> *Thy son, in time, I have returned to thee,*
> *Thy son, I have in time returned to thee.*
>
> *In time, for though the sun is setting on*
> *A song-lit race of slaves, it has not set;*
> *Though late, O soil, it is not too late yet*
> *To catch thy plaintive soul, leaving, soon gone,*
> *Leaving, to catch thy plaintive soul soon gone.*
>
> *O Negro slaves, dark purple ripened plums,*
> *Squeezed, and bursting in the pine-wood air,*
> *Passing, before they stripped the old tree bare*
> *One plum was saved for me, one seed becomes*
>
> *An everlasting song, a singing tree,*
> *Caroling softly souls of slavery,*
> *What they were, and what they are to me,*
> *Caroling softly souls of slavery.*[18]

Cane is fueled by an oppositional nostalgia. A precarious vessel possessed of an eloquence coincident with loss, it wants to reach or to keep in touch with an alternate reality as that reality fades. It was Toomer's dread of the ascending urban-industrial order which opened his ears to the corrective—potentially corrective—counterpoint he heard in Georgia. In the middle section of the book, set in northern cities, houses epitomize a reign of hard, sharp edges, rectilinear pattern, fixity, regimentation, a staid, white order: "Houses, and dorm sitting-rooms are places where white faces se-

clude themselves at night" (73). The house embodies, again and again, suffocating
structure: "Rhobert wears a house, like a monstrous diver's helmet, on his head. . . .
He is sinking. His house is a dead thing that weights him down" (40). Or: "Dan's eyes
sting. Sinking into a soft couch, he closes them. The house contracts about him. It is
a sharp-edged, massed, metallic house. Bolted" (57). Compare this with Kabnis' fis-
sured, rickety cabin in the South, through the cracks in whose walls and ceiling a
ventilating music blows:

> The walls, unpainted, are seasoned a rosin yellow. And cracks between the
> boards are black. These cracks are the lips the night winds use for whispering.
> Night winds in Georgia are vagrant poets, whispering. . . . Night winds whisper
> in the eaves. Sing weirdly in the ceiling cracks. (81, 104)

Ventilating song is what Dan invokes against the row of houses, the reign of suffocating structure, at the beginning of "Box Seat":

> Houses are shy girls whose eyes shine reticently upon the dusk body of the
> street. Upon the gleaming limbs and asphalt torso of a dreaming nigger. Shake
> your curled wool-blossoms, nigger. Open your liver lips to lean, white spring.
> Stir the root-life of a withered people. Call them from their houses, and teach
> them to dream.
>
> Dark swaying forms of Negroes are street songs that woo virginal houses. (56)

Thirty years before the more celebrated Beats, Toomer calls out against an airtight
domesticity, a reign of "square" houses, and the domestication of spirit that goes with
it, his call, as theirs would be, fueled and inflected by the countering thrust of black
music.

Not that the beauty of the music wasn't bought at a deadly price. Its otherwordly
reach was fostered and fed by seeming to have no home in this one ("I aint got long
to stay here"). What the night winds whisper is this:

> *White-man's land.*
> *Niggers, sing.*
> *Burn, bear black children*
> *Till poor rivers bring*
> *Rest, and sweet glory*
> *In Camp Ground.*

The singing, preaching, and shouting coming from the church near Kabnis' cabin
build as Layman tells of a lynching, reaching a peak as a stone crashes in through one
of the windows:

> A shriek pierces the room. The bronze pieces on the mantel hum. The sister
> cries frantically: "Jesus, Jesus, I've found Jesus. O Lord, glory t God, one mo
> sinner is acomin home." At the height of this, a stone, wrapped round with
> paper, crashes through the window. Kabnis springs to his feet, terror-stricken.
> Layman is worried. Halsey picks up the stone. Takes off the wrapper, smooths it
> out, and reads: "You nothern nigger, its time fer y t leave. Git along now." (90)

Toomer put much of himself into Kabnis, from whom we get an apprehension of music as a carrier of conflicted portent, bearer of both good and bad news. "Dear Jesus," he prays, "do not chain me to myself and set these hills and valleys, heaving with folksongs, so close to me that I cannot reach them. There is a radiant beauty in the night that touches and . . . tortures me" (83).

Cane's take on music is part and parcel of Toomer's insistence on the tragic fate of beauty, the soul's transit through an unsoulful world. This note gets hit by the first piece in the book, the story of "Karintha carrying beauty," her soul "a growing thing ripened too soon." The writing is haunted throughout by a ghost of aborted splendor, a specter written into its much-noted lament for the condition of the women it portrays—woman as anima, problematic "parting soul." These women are frequently portrayed, not insignificantly, singing. The mark of blackness and the mark of femininity meet the mark of oppression invested in music. Toomer celebrates and incorporates song but not without looking at the grim conditions which give it birth, not without acknowledging its outcast, compensatory character. "Cotton Song," one of the poems in the book, takes the work song as its model: "Come, brother, come. Lets lift it; / Come now, hewit! roll away!" (9). Like Sterling Brown's "Southern Road," Nat Adderley's "Work Song," and Sam Cooke's "Chain Gang," all of which it anticipates, the poem excavates the music's roots in forced labor. Music here is inseparable from the stigma attached to those who make it.

This goes farther in fact. Music itself is looked at askance and stigmatized in a philistine, prosaic social order: "Bolted to the endless rows of metal houses. . . . No wonder he couldn't sing to them" (57). Toomer's formal innovations in *Cane* boldly ventilate the novel, a traditional support for prosaic order, by acknowledging fissures and allowing them in, bringing in verse and dramatic dialogue, putting poetry before reportage. This will to song, though, is accompanied by an awareness of song's outlaw lot which could have been a forecast of the book's commercial failure. (Only five hundred copies of the first printing were sold.) *Cane* portrays its own predicament. It shows that music or poetry, if not exactly a loser's art, is fed by an intimacy with loss and may in fact feed it. This comes out in two instances of a version of wounded kinship which recurs throughout the book, the thwarted communion of would-be lovers. Paul, Orpheus to Bona's Eurydice, turns back to deliver an exquisitely out-of-place poetic address to the doorman and then returns to find Bona gone. Likewise, the narrator holds forth poetically as he sits beside Avey in the story which takes her name, only to find that she's fallen asleep. A play of parallel estrangements emerges. His alienation from the phantom reign of prosaic power—the Capitol dome is "a gray ghost ship"—meets her detachment from and immunity to prepossessing eloquence:

> I talked, beautifully I thought, about an art that would be born, an art that would open the way for women the likes of her. I asked her to hope, and build up an inner life against the coming of that day. I recited some of my own things to her. I sang, with a strange quiver in my voice, a promise-song. And then I began to wonder why her hand had not once returned a single pressure. . . . I sat beside her through the night. I saw the dawn steal over Washington. The Capitol dome looked like a gray ghost ship drifting in from sea. Avey's face was pale, and her eyes were heavy. She did not have the gray crimson-splashed beauty of the dawn. I hated to wake her. Orphan-woman . . . (46–47)

3

Beauty apprised of its abnormality both is and isn't beauty. (Baraka on Coltrane's "Afro-Blue": "Beautiful has nothing to do with it, but it is."[19]) An agitation complicates would-be equanimity, would-be poise. "Th form thats burned int my soul," Kabnis cries, "is some twisted awful thing that crept in from a dream, a godam nightmare, an wont stay unless I feed it. An it lives on words. Not beautiful words. God Almighty no. Misshapen, split-gut, tortured, twisted words" (110). The tormenting lure of anomalous beauty and the answering dance of deformation—form imitatively "tortured, twisted"—also concern the writer I'd like to move on to, William Carlos Williams. The harassed/harassing irritability which comes into the "Beautiful Thing" section of *Paterson* recalls Kabnis' "Whats beauty anyway but ugliness if it hurts you?" (83). In black music Williams heard the "defiance of authority" he declares beauty to be, a "vulgarity" which "surpasses all perfections."[20]

Williams' engagement with black music was greatly influenced by his sense of himself as cut off from the literary mainstream. At the time the two pieces I'd like to look at were written Williams had not yet been admitted into the canon, as can be seen in the omission of his work from the *Modern Library Anthology of American Poetry* in 1945, at whose editor, Conrad Aiken, he accordingly takes a shot in *Man Orchid*, the second of the two pieces I'll discuss. His quarrel with T. S. Eliot's dominance and influence doesn't need pointing out, except that it also comes up in *Man Orchid*. Seeing himself as a victimized poet, Williams celebrated the music of a victimized people. In a gesture which has since been overdone ("the white negro," "the student as nigger," analogies between "women and blacks"), he saw parallels between their lot and his own. This can also be seen, though in a slightly more subtle way, in the first of the two pieces I'd like to turn to, "Ol' Bunk's Band."

Both pieces grew out of Williams' going to hear New Orleans trumpeter Bunk Johnson in New York in 1945. A revival of interest in Johnson's music was then going on and Williams caught him during a 3½-month gig at the Stuyvesant Casino on the lower east side. He soon after wrote "Ol' Bunk's Band," a poem whose repeated insistence "These are men!" diverges from the dominant culture's denial of human stature to black people. He goes against the grain of accepted grammar in such things as the conscious "vulgarity" of the triple negative "and / not never / need no more," emulating a disregard for convention he heard in the music. The poem in full:

> These are men! the gaunt, unfore-
>   sold, the vocal,
> blatant, Stand up, stand up! the
>   slap of a bass-string.
> Pick, ping! The horn, the
>   hollow horn
> long drawn out, a hound deep
>   tone—
> Choking, choking! while the
>   treble reed
> races—alone, ripples, screams
>   slow to fast—
> to second to first! These are men!

> *Drum, drum, drum, drum, drum,*
>> *drum, drum! the*
> *ancient cry, escaping crapulence*
>> *eats through*
> *transcendent—torn, tears, term*
>> *town, tense,*
> *turns and back off whole, leaps*
>> *up, stomps down,*
> *rips through! These are men*
>> *beneath*
> *whose force the melody limps—*
>> *to*
> *proclaim, proclaims—Run and*
>> *lie down,*
> *in slow measures, to rest and*
>> *not never*
> *need no more! These are men!*
>> *Men!* [21]

The "hound deep / tone," reminding us that Johnson played in a band known as the Yelping Hound Band in 1930, also conjures a sense of underdog status which brings the orphaned or outcast poet into solidarity with an outcast people. The repeated assertion "These are men!" plays against an implied but unstated "treated like dogs."

Threaded into this implicit counterpoint are the lines "These are men / beneath / whose force the melody limps," where "limps" reflects critically on a crippling social order. The musicians do to the melody what's done to them, the social handicap on which this limping reports having been translated and, in that sense, transcended, triumphed over. Williams anticipates Baraka's more explicit reading of black music as revenge, sublimated murder. Looking at *Paterson*, which hadn't been underway long when "Ol' Bunk's Band" was written, one finds the same complex of figures: dogs, lameness, limping. In the preface to Book 1 the image conveyed is that of a pariah, out of step with the pack:

> *Sniffing the trees,*
> *just another dog*
> *among a lot of dogs. What*
> *else is there? And to do?*
> *The rest have run out—*
> *after the rabbits.*
> *Only the lame stands—on*
> *three legs. . . . (11)*

This leads eventually to the quote from John Addington Symonds' *Studies of the Greek Poets* which ends Book 1, a passage in which Symonds comments on Hipponax's choliambi, "lame or limping iambics":

> Hipponax ended his iambics with a spondee or a trochee instead of an iambus, doing thus the utmost violence to the rhythmical structure. . . . The choliambi are in poetry what the dwarf or cripple is in human nature. Here again, by their

acceptance of this halting meter, the Greeks displayed their acute aesthetic sense of propriety, recognizing the harmony which subsists between crabbed verses and the distorted subjects with which they dealt—the vices and perversions of humanity—as well as their agreement with the snarling spirit of the satirist. Deformed verse was suited to deformed morality. (53)

That Williams heard a similar gesture in the syncopated rhythms of black music is obvious by Book 5, where, after quoting a passage on Bessie Smith from Mezz Mezzrow's *Really the Blues,* he makes his well-known equation of "satiric" with "satyric":

> *a satyric play!*
> *All plays*
> *were satyric when they were most devout.*
> *Ribald as a Satyr!*
>
> *Satyrs dance!*
> *all the deformities take wing. (258)*

This would also be a way of talking about the "variable foot," less an aid to scansion than a trope—the travestied, fractured foot.

Williams here stumbles upon, without naming and, most likely, without knowing, the Fon-Yoruba orisha of the crossroads, the lame dancer Legba. Legba walks with a limp because his legs are of unequal lengths, one of them anchored in the world of humans and the other in that of the gods. His roles are numerous, the common denominator being that he acts as an intermediary, a mediator, much like Hermes, of whom Hipponax was a follower. (Norman O. Brown: "Hipponax, significantly enough, found Hermes the most congenial god; he is in fact the only personality in Greek literature of whom it may be said that he walked with Hermes all the days of his life."[22]) Like Hermes' winged feet, Legba's limp—"deformities take wing"—bridges high and low. Legba presides over gateways, intersections, thresholds, wherever different realms or regions come into contact. His limp a play of difference, he's the master linguist and has much to do with signification, divination, and translation. His limp the offbeat or eccentric accent, the "suspended accentuation" of which Thompson writes, he's the master musician and dancer, declared first among the orishas because only he could simultaneously play a gong, a bell, a drum, and a flute while dancing. The master of polyrhythmicity and heterogeneity, he suffers not from deformity but multiformity, a "defective" capacity in a homogeneous order given over to uniform rule. Legba's limp is an emblem of heterogeneous wholeness, the image and outcome of a peculiar remediation. "Lame" or "limping," that is, like "phantom," cuts with a relativizing edge to unveil impairment's power, as though the syncopated accent were an unsuspected blessing offering anomalous, unpredictable support. Impairment taken to higher ground, remediated, translates damage and disarray into a dance. Legba's limp, compensating the difference in leg lengths, functions like a phantom limb. Robert Pelton writes that Legba "tranforms . . . absence into transparent presence,"[23] deficit leg into invisible supplement.

Legba's authority over mix and transition made him especially relevant to the experience of transplantation brought about by the slave trade. The need to accommodate geographic and cultural difference placed a high premium on his mediatory skills. He's thus the most tenaciously retained of the orishas among New World Africans, the first to be invoked in vodoun ceremonies, be they in Haiti, Cuba, Brazil, or elsewhere. There's little wonder why Williams' work, concerned as it is with the New World as a ground for syncretistic innovation, would be paid a visit by the African bridge between old and new. What he heard in Bunk Johnson's music was a rhythmic digestion of dislocation, the African genius for enigmatic melding or mending, a mystery of resilient survival no image puts more succinctly than that of Legba's limping dance.

Legba has made more straightforward appearances in certain works written since Williams' time, showing up, for example, as Papa LaBas (the name he goes by in New Orleans) in Ishmael Reed's novels. Or as Lebert Joseph in Paule Marshall's *Praisesong for the Widow*, a novel whose third section is introduced by a line from the Haitain invocation to Legba and in which one comes upon such passages as: "Out of his stooped and winnowed body had come the illusion of height, femininity and power. Even his foreshortened left leg had appeared to straighten itself out and grow longer as he danced."[24] One of his most telling appearances in the literature of this country, though, is one in which, as in Williams' work, he enters unannounced. In Ralph Ellison's *Invisible Man* one finds adumbrations of Legba which, bearing as they do on the concerns addressed here, deserve more than passing mention.

Invisible Man, like *Cane*, is a work which draws on black folk resources. While collecting folklore in Harlem in 1939 for the Federal Writers' Project, Ellison was told a tale which had to do with a black man in South Carolina who because he could make himself invisible at will was able to harass and give white people hell with impunity.[25] This would seem to have contributed to the relativizing thrust of the novel's title and its long meditation on the two-way cut of invisibility. On the other side of invisibility as exclusion, social death, we find it as revenge, millenarian reversal. The prominence of Louis Armstrong in the novel's prologue brings to mind Zuckerkandl's discussion of the case music makes for the invisible, as invisibility is here both social and metaphysical. The ability to "see around corners" defies the reign of strict rectilinear structure lamented in *Cane* by going outside ordinary time and space constraints. Louis' horn, apocalyptic, alters times (and, with it, space):

> Invisibility, let me explain, gives one a slightly different sense of time, you're never quite on the beat. Sometimes you're ahead and sometimes behind. Instead of the swift and imperceptible flowing of time, you are aware of its nodes, those points where time stands still or from which it leaps ahead. And you slip into the breaks and look around. That's what you hear vaguely in Louis' music.[26]

This different sense of time one recognizes as Legba's limp. It leads to and is echoed by a later adumbration of Legba, one in which Ellison hints at a similarly "offbeat" sense of history, one which diverges from the Brotherhood's doctrine of history as monolithic advance. Early on, Jack describes the old evicted couple as "already dead, defunct," people whom "history has passed . . . by," "dead limbs that must be pruned away" (284). Later "dead limbs" play contrapuntally upon Tarp's contestatory limp, a limp which, as he explains, has social rather than physiological roots. It was caused by nineteen years on a chain gang:

> You notice this limp I got? . . . Well, I wasn't always lame, and I'm not really now 'cause the doctors can't find anything wrong with that leg. They say it's sound as a piece of steel. What I mean is I got this limp from dragging a chain. . . . Nobody knows that about me, they just think I got rheumatism. But it was that chain and after nineteen years I haven't been able to stop dragging my leg. (377–78).

Phantom limb, phantom limp. Tarp goes on, in a gesture recalling the protective root Sandy gives Frederick Douglass in the latter's *Narrative,* to give Invisible Man the broken link from the leg chain he dragged for nineteen years. Phantom limb, phantom limp, phantom link: "I think it's got a heap of signifying wrapped up in it and it might help you remember what we're really fighting against" (379). This it does, serving to concentrate a memory of injustice and traumatic survival, a remembered wound resorted to as a weapon of self-defense. During his final confrontation with the Brotherhood, Invisible Man wears it like a set of brass knuckles: "My hand was in my pockets now, Brother Tarp's leg chain around my knuckles" (462).

4

"The trouble has been," Olson writes, "that a man stays so astonished he can triumph over his own incoherence, he settles for that, crows over it, and goes at a day again happy he at least makes a little sense."[27] Ellison says much the same thing toward the end of *Invisible Man* when he cautions that "the mind that has conceived a plan of living must never lose sight of the chaos against which that pattern was conceived" (567). This goes for both societies and individuals, he points out. Legba's limp, like Tarp's leg chain, is a reminder of dues paid, damage done, of the limbs which have been "pruned away." It's a reminder of the Pyrrhic features every triumph over chaos or incoherence turns out to possess. The specter of illusory victory and its corollary, the riddle of deceptive disability or enabling defeat, sit prominently among the mysteries to which it witnesses. "No defeat is made up entirely of defeat," Williams writes in *Paterson* (96).

In *Man Orchid,* the second piece which grew out of Williams' going to hear Johnson's band, the stutter plays a significant role. What better qualification of what can only be a partial victory over incoherence? What limping, staggering, and stumbling are to walking, stuttering and stammering are to speech. "To *stammer* and to *stumble,* original *stumelen,* are twin words," Theodore Thass-Thienemann points out. "The use of the one and the same phonemic pattern for denoting these two different meanings is found in other languages too. Stammering and stuttering are perceived as speech *im-pedi-ments.*"[28] The stutter enters *Man Orchid* largely because of Bucklin Moon, the author of a novel called *The Darker Brother.* Moon was at the Stuyvesant Casino on the night of 23 November 1945, the second time Williams went to hear Johnson's band. He ended up joining Williams and his friends at their table, among whom was Fred

Miller, editor of the 1930s proletarian magazine *Blast* and one of the coauthors of *Man Orchid*. Because of his novel and his knowledge of black music, Moon was incorrectly taken by them to be black, though Miller asked Williams in a letter two days later: "Would you ever think that Bucklin Moon was a Negro, if you passed him—as a stranger—in the street? He looks whiter than a lot of whites."[29] Moon evidently spoke with a stutter whenever he became nervous and unsure of himself, which was the case that night at the Stuyvesant Casino. Miller goes on to offer this as a further peculiarity: "a stuttering or stammering Negro is a pretty rare bird indeed: your darker brother is articulate enough, when he isn't too frightened to talk." Like Legba's limp, Moon's stutter would come to symbolize a meeting of worlds, a problematic, insecure mix of black and white.

At the Stuyvesant Williams suggested that he and Miller publish an interracial literary magazine. Miller was enthusiastic at the time but soon lost interest. He suggested within a couple of weeks, however, that he and William collaborate on an improvisatory novel which was to be written as though they were musicians trading fours: "You write chap. I, send it to me, I do the 2d Chap., send mess back to you, you do 3—and so on." Williams liked the idea, and *Man Orchid* was launched. They spent the next year working on it, off and on, bringing in a third collaborator, Lydia Carlin, in March. The work was never completed, and what there is of it, forty pages, remained unpublished until 1973. It's going too far to call it a novel and outright ludicrous to call it, as Paul Mariani does, "Williams' black novel," but the piece is interesting for a number of reasons, not the least of them being its anticipation of the bop-inspired attempts at collaborative, improvisatory writing which became popular among the Beats a decade later.[30]

Wray Douglas, *Man Orchid*'s black-white protagonist, is based in part on Bucklin Moon and intended to embody America's yet-to-be-resolved identity. As Williams writes: "To resolve such a person would be to create a new world" (77). But other than his presumed black-white mix and his stutter not much of Moon went into the figure. Wray Douglas is clearly his creators' alter ego, the narrated "he" and the narrator's "I" in most cases the same. Want of resolution and the stubborn problematics of heterogeneity are what *Man Orchid* most effectively expresses, the latter symptomized by the solipsistic quality of the work and the former a would-be flight from the resolute self (false resolution) which the solipsism indulges even as it eschews. Two white writers sit down to create a black protagonist whose model is another white writer. The ironies and contradictions needn't be belabored.

The stutter thus becomes the most appropriate, self-reflexive feature of an articultion which would appear to be blocked in advance. Williams' and Miller's prose in *Man Orchid* both stutters and refers to stuttering. Here, for example, is how Williams begins Chapter 1:

> Is it perchance a crime—a time, a chore, a bore, a job? He wasn't a musician—but he wished he had been born a musician instead of a writer. Musicians do not stutter. But he ate music, music wrinkled his belly—if you can wrinkle an inflated football. Anyhow it felt like that so that's what he wrote (without changing a word—that was his creed and always after midnight, you couldn't be earlier in the morning than that). All good writing is written in the morning.

Is *what* perchance a crime? (One) (or rather two) He ate and drank beer. That is, he ate, he also drank beer. A crime to be so full, so—so (the thing the philosophers hate) poly. So p-p-poly. Polypoid. Huh? (77)

Thinking, perhaps, of the use of singing in the treatment of stuttering. Williams identifies writing with the latter while looking longingly at music as the embodiment of a heterogeneous wholeness to which his writing will aspire, an unimpeded, unproblematic wholeness beyond its reach. Miller's contribution to *Man Orchid* is likewise touched by a sense of writing's inferiority to music. Early on, referring to Bessie Smith's singing, he asks: "What were the little words chasing each other like black bits of burnt leaves across the pages he held—[compared] to that vast voice?" (79). Two pages later he answers:

> More printed words like black bits of burnt leaves. They had the right keyhole, those guys, but the wrong key. The only words that could blast like Bunk's horn or smash like John Henry's hammer were the poet's, the maker's, personal, ripped out of his guts: And no stuttering allowed. (81)

Throughout *Man Orchid,* however, the writer's emulation of the musician causes rather than cures the stutter. Imitating the spontaneity of improvisatory music, Williams and Miller approach the typewriter as a musical keyboard on which they extemporize "without changing a word." Wrong "notes" are left as they are rather than erased, though the right ones do eventually get "played" in most cases. This results in a repetitiveness and a halting, staccato gesture reminiscent of a stutterer's effort to get out what he wants to say. Thus Williams: "American poetry was on its way to great distinction—when the blight of Eliot's popular verse fell pon—upon the gasping universities—who hadN8t hadn8T hadn't tasted Thames water for nearly a hundred years" (82). By disrupting the fluency and coherence available to them Williams and Miller attempt to get in touch with what that coherence excludes, "the chaos against which that pattern was conceived." This friendly relationship with incoherence, however, constitutes a gesture toward but not an attainment of the otherness to which it aspires, an otherness to which access can only be analogically gotten. *Man Orchid,* to give the obvious example, is a piece of writing, not a piece of music. Nor, as I've already noted, is the color line crossed. The stutter is a two-way witness which on one hand symbolizes a need to go beyond the confines of an exclusionary order while on the other confessing to its at best only limited success at doing so. The impediments to the passage it seeks are acknowledged if not annulled, attested to by exactly the gesture which would overcome them if it could.

One measure of *Man Orchid*'s flawed embrace of otherness is the prominence in it of Williams' all too familiar feud with Eliot, a feud into which he pulls Bank Johnson. Johnson's music is put forth as an example of an authentic American idiom, "the autochthonous strain" (85) whose dilution or displacement by "sweet music" paralleled and anticipated that of a genuine "American poetry [which] was on its way to great distinction" by *The Waste Land:*

> Eliot would not have been such a success if he hadn't hit a soft spot. They were scared and rushed in where he hit like water into the side of a ship. It was ready

for it a long time. Isn't a weak spot always ready to give way? That was the seccret of his success. Great man Eliot. They were aching for him, Aiken for him. He hit the jackpot with his popular shot.

But long before that, twenty years earlier ol' Bunk Johnson was all washed up. Sweet music was coming in and jazz was through. But I mean THROUGH! And when I say through, I mean through. Go ahead, quit. See if I care. Take your band and go frig a kite. Go on back to the rice swamps. See if I care. Sell your ol'd horn. See if I care. Nobody wants that kind of music any more: this is a waste land for you, Buddy, this IS a waste land! I said Waste Land and when I sez Waste land I mean waste *land.*

. . . Thus American poetry, which disappeared about that time you might say, followed the same course New Orleans music had taken when sweet music displaced it about in 1906 or so. (83–84)

Fraternity with Johnson is less the issue than sibling rivalry with Eliot, a literary quarrel in which Johnson has no voice but the one Williams gives him. What it says is simple: "Black music is on Williams' side." (The Barbadian poet Edward Kamau Brathwaite provides interesting counterpoint, picturing Eliot and black music as allies when he notes the influence of Eliot's recorded readings in the Caribbean: "In that dry deadpan delivery, the riddims of St. Louis . . . were stark and clear for those of us who at the same time were listening to the dislocations of Bird, Dizzy and Klook. And it is interesting that on the whole, the Establishment couldn't stand Eliot's voice—far less jazz!"[31])

The possibility that otherness was being appropriated rather than engaged was recognized by Miller and for him it became an obstacle to going on. When he began to voice his misgivings Williams brought in Lydia Carlin, who not only added sexual otherness to the project but a new form of ethnic otherness as well, in that, though she herself was English, one of the two chapters she contributed was about a Polish couple, the Czajas. Her two chapters are much more conventional, much less improvisatory than Williams' and Miller's and tend to stand apart from rather than interact with theirs. Her taking part in the project did nothing to solve the problem and as late as Chapter 7 Miller is asking:

Now returning to this novel, Man Orchid. Why the orchid?—to begin with. There's the old, tiresome and at bottom snobbish literary assumption that the Negro in America is an exotic bloom. Negro equals jungle. Despite the fact that he has been here longer than the second, third, even ninth generation Eurp European—Negro equals jungle. Then why doesn't the ofay bank president of German descent equal Black Forest? The Rutherford doctor of Welsh descent equal the cromlechs? or Welsh rarebit? (111)

As bad if not worse is the fact that the choice of that particular orchid because of its phallic appearance plays upon a stereotypic black male sexuality. The distance from this to Norman Mailer's "Jazz is orgasm" isn't very great, which is only one of a handful of ways in which *The White Negro* bears upon this predecessor text.

Miller, though he could agonize as above, was no more free than Williams was of stereotypic equations. To him Johnson and his music represent a black essence which is unselfconscious and nonreflective: "Only the Bunks're satisfied to be Bunks, he told himself enviously. Their brain don't question their art. Nor their left hand their RIGHT. Their right to be Bunk, themself" (79). The vitiation of "black" nonreflective being by "white" intellectuality is largely the point of his evocation of Wray Douglas and the trumpeter Cholly Oldham. The latter he describes as having "too much brain for a musician." Oldham stutters when he plays and wants to be a painter:

> There was between Cholly and Bunk—what? a difference of thirty, thirty-five years in age, no more. But the difference otherwise! Hamlet son of Till Eulenspiegel. Showing you what the dry rot of intellectuality could do to the orchid in one generation. Progress (! Up from Slavery. That night-colored Hamlet, he wants to paint pictures now. (82)

Black is nonreflective, white cerebral. So entrenched are such polarizations as to make the notion of a black intellectual oxymoronic. In May, Miller wrote to Williams that it had been a mistake to model their protagonist on Bucklin Moon: "I don't know enough about him and his special type, the colored intellectual (although I've been acquainted with and 've liked lots of ordinary Negro folk, laborers, musicians et al)" (73). Small wonder he questioned the idea of an interracial magazine by writing to Williams:

> Is there sufficient Negro writing talent—of the kind we wd. have no doubts about, AS talent, on hand to balance the white talent? I don't believe any more than you that publishing second-rate work with first-rate intentions would serve any cause but that of bad writing. (68)

To what extent was being looked upon as black—as, even worse, that "rare bird," a black intellectual—the cause of Moon's nervousness that night at the Stuyvesant? Could a sense of distance in Williams' and Miller's manner have caused him to stutter? Miller's wife recalls in a letter to Paul Mariani:

> Moon began with easy speech and there was talk at first of the interracial magazine but Moon soon took to stammering. To me Williams was always a warm congenial person, but he would become the coldly analytical surgeon at times and the effect it had on those around him at such a time was quite devastating. (67)

That "coldly analytical" scrutiny would seem to have been disconcerting, making Williams and Miller the agents of the disarray about which they would then go on to write—as good an example as any of "phantom objectivity," the social construction of Moon's "mulatto" selfconsciousness.

What I find most interesting about *Man Orchid* is that it inadvertently underscores a feature which was then coming into greater prominence in black improvised music. With the advent of bebop, with which neither Williams, Miller, nor Carlin seem to have been much engaged, black musicians began to assume a more explicit sense of themselves as artists, conscious creators, thinkers. Dizzy Gillespie would don a beret and a goatee, as would, among others, Yusef Lateef, who would record an album called *Jazz for the Thinker.* Anthony Braxton's pipe, wire-rim glasses, cardigan sweater, and diagrammatic titles are among the present-day descendants of such gestures. The aural equivalent of this more explicit reflexivity would come at times to resemble a stutter, conveying senses of apprehension and self-conscious duress by way of dislocated phrasings in which virtuosity mimes its opposite. Thelonious Monk's mock-awkward hesitancies evoke an experience of impediment or impairment, as do Sonny Rollins' even more stutterlike teasings of a tune, a quality Paul Blackburn imitates in "Listening to Sonny Rollins at the Five Spot":

> *There will be many other nights like*
> *me standing here with someone, some*
> *one*
> *someone*
> *some-one*
> *some*
> *some*
> *some*
> *some*
> *some*
> *some*
> *one*
> *there will be other songs*
> *a-nother fall, another* _____*spring, but*
> *there will never be a-noth, noth*
> *anoth*
> *noth*
> *anoth-er*
> *noth-er*
> *noth-er*
>   *other lips that I may kiss,*
> *but they won't thrill me like*
>   *thrill me like*
>   *like yours*
> *used to*
>   *dream a million dreams*
> *but how can they come*
> *when there*   *never be*
> *a-noth* _____[32]

Though Williams and Miller insist that Bunk Johnson doesn't stammer, the limp he inflicts on the melody is ancestral to the stutter of Monk, Rollins, and others.

As among the Kaluli, for whom music and poetry are "specifically marked for reflection," the black musician's stutter is an introspective gesture which arises from and reflects critically upon an experience of isolation or exclusion, the orphan's or the outsider's ordeal; the rare bird's ordeal. Like Tarp's leg chain, it symbolizes a refusal to forget damage done, a critique and a partial rejection of an available but biased coherence. Part of the genius of black music is the room it allows for a telling "inarticulacy," a feature consistent with its critique of a predatory coherence, the cannibalistic "plan of living" and the articulacy which upholds it. *Man Orchid,* where it comes closest to the spirit of black music, does so by way of a similar frustration with and questioning of given articulacies, permissible ways of making sense. In Chapter 6 Williams attempts to make racial distinctions meaningless, the result of which is part gibberish, part scat, part wisdom of the idiots ("the most foolishest thing you can say . . . has the most meaning"). His inability to make sense implicitly indicts a white-dominated social order and the discourse of racial difference by which it explains or makes sense of itself:

> Not that black is white. I do not pretend that. Nor white black. That there is not the least difference is apparent to the mind at a glance. Thus, to the mind, the eye is forever deceived. And philosophers imagine they can have opinions about art? God are they dumb, meaning stupid, meaning philosophers, meaning schools, meaning—learning. The limits of learning are the same as an egg to the yolk. The shell. Knowledge to a learned man is precisely the sane—that's good: sane for same—the same as the egg to the hen. No possibility of inter-change. Reason, the shell.

> No matter how I try to rearrange the parts, to show them interchangeable, the result is always the same. White is white and black is the United States Senate. No mixing. Even if it was all black it would be the same: white. How could it be different? (100–101)

The very effort to talk down the difference underscores the tenacity of the racial po-larization *Man Orchid*'s liberal mission seeks, to some degree, to overcome—a tenac-ity which is attested to, as we've seen, in other ways as well, not the least of them being the authors' preconceptions.

5

The play of sense and nonsense in Wilson Harris' *The Angel at the Gate* is more immediately one of sensation and nonsensation, a complex mingling of endowments and deprivations, anesthetic and synesthetic in-tuitions. One reads, for example, late in the novel:

> Mary recalled how deaf she had been to the voice of the blackbird that morning on her way to Angel Inn and yet it returned to her now in the depths of the mirror that stood beside her. Half-reflected voice, shaded sound, silent echo. Was this the source of musical composition? Did music issue from reflections that converted themselves into silent, echoing bodies in a mirror? Did the marriage of *reflection* and *sound* arise from deaf appearance within silent muse (or was it deaf muse in silent appearance) from which a stream of unheard music rippled into consciousness?[33]

In dialogue with and relevant to such a passage is a discussion in Harris' most recent critical book, *The Womb of Space,* a discussion which touches upon Legba as "numi-nous shadow." Harris writes of "metaphoric imagery that intricately conveys music as the shadow of vanished but visualised presences": "Shadow or shade is alive with voices so real, yet strangely beyond material hearing, that they are peculiarly *visual-*

ised or 'seen' in the intricate passages of a poem. *Visualised presence* acquires therefore a *shadow and a voice* that belongs to the mind's ear and eye."[34] Music described in terms pertaining to sight is consistent with inklings of synesthetic identity which run through *The Angel at the Gate.* It's also part and parcel of Harris' long preoccupation, from work to work, with an uncapturable, ineffable wholeness, a heterogeneous inclusiveness evoked in terms of nonavailability ("silent echo," "unheard music") and by polysemous fullness and fluency ("a stream . . . rippled").

The Angel at the Gate's anesthetic-synesthetic evocations recapitulate, in microcosm, the translation between media—aural and visual, music and writing—it claims to be. The intermedia impulse owns up to as it attempts to advance beyond the limits of a particular medium and is a version of what Harris elsewhere calls "a confession of weakness."[35] The novel acknowledges that its particular strength can only be partial and seeks to "echo" if not enlist the also partial strength of another art form. Wholeness admitted to be beyond reach, the best to be attained is a concomitance of partial weaknesses, partial strengths, a conjunction of partial endowments. This conjunction is facilitated by Legba, upon whom *The Womb of Space* touches as a "numinous frailty" and a "transitional chord." In *Da Silva da Silva's Cultivated Wilderness,* an earlier novel which likewise leans upon an extraliterary medium, the painter da Silva's advertisement for a model is answered by one Legba Cuffey, whose arrival infuses paint with sound: "The front door bell pealed it seemed in the middle of his painting as he brooded on past and future. The sound of a catch grown sharp as a child's cry he thought in a line of stroked paint."[36] In this case painting, like music in *The Angel at the Gate,* is an alternate artistic arm with which the novel extends or attempts to extend its reach. "So the arts," Williams writes in *Man Orchid,* "take part for each other" (85).

Music figures prominently at the end of Harris' first novel, *Palace of the Peacock,* where Legba's limp, the incongruity between heaven and earth, is marked by the refractive obliquity and bend of a passage from one medium to another. The annunciation of paradise takes the form of a music which issues through the lips of Carroll, the black namesake singer whose father is unknown but whose mother "knew and understood . . . [that his] name involved . . . the music of her undying sacrifice to make and save the world."[37] The narrator notes a discrepancy between the sound Carroll's lips appear to be making and the sound he hears: "Carroll was whistling. A solemn and beautiful cry—unlike a whistle I reflected—deeper and mature. Nevertheless his lips were framed to whistle and I could only explain the difference by assuming the sound from his lips was changed when it struck the window and issued into the world" (147). The deflection from apparent sound reveals not only the insufficiency of the visual image but that of any image, visual, acoustic, or otherwise. Heaven is wholeness, meaning that any image which takes up the task of evoking it can only fail. Legba's limp is the obliquity of a religious aspiration which admits its failure to measure up to heaven, the bend legs make in prayer. As in the *Paradiso,* where Dante laments the poem's inability to do heaven justice by calling it lame, the narrator's evocation of Carroll's music is marked by a hesitant, faltering geture which whenever it asserts immediately qualifies itself. It mimes the music's crippling, self-correcting attempts to register as well as redeem defects. The music repeatedly breaks and mends itself—mends itself as a phantom limb mends an amputation:

It was an organ cry almost and yet quite different I reflected again. It seemed to break and mend itself always—tremulous, forlorn, distant, triumphant, the echo of sound so pure and outlined in space it broke again into a mass of music. It was the cry of the peacock and yet I reflected far different. I stared at the whistling lips and wondered if the change was in me or in them. I had never witnessed and heard such sad and such glorious music. (147)

This is the ongoingness of an attempt which fails but is repeatedly undertaken to insist that what it fails to capture nonetheless exists. Legba's limp is the obliquity of a utopian aspiration, the bend legs make preparing to spring.

Inability to capture wholeness notwithstanding, *Palace of the Peacock* initiates Harris' divergence, now into its third decade, from the novel's realist-mimetic tradition. The accent which falls upon the insufficiency of the visual image is consistent with the novel's earlier suggestions of an anesthetic-synesthetic enablement which displaces the privileged eye:[38] "I dreamt I awoke with one dead seeing eye and one living closed eye" (13–14). And again: "I had been blinded by the sun, and saw inwardly in the haze of my blind eye a watching muse and phantom whose breath was on my lips" (16). That accent encapsulates Harris' quarrel with the cinematic pretense and the ocular conceit of the realist novel, a documentary stasis against which he poses an anesthetic-synesthetic obliquity and rush. This obliquity (seeing and/or hearing around corners, in Ellison's terms) is called "an angled intercourse with history" in *The Angel at the Gate* (113), the medium for which is the Angel Inn mirror, described at points as "spiritual" and "supernatural." Mary Stella is said to perceive the world "from a meaningfully distorted angle in the mirror" (113), a pointed subversion of the mirror's conventional association with mimesis. Angularity cuts with a relativizing edge: "How unreal, yet real, one was when one saw oneself with one's own eyes from angles in a mirror so curiously unfamiliar that one's eyes became a stranger's eyes. As at the hairdresser when she invites one to inspect the back of one's head" (21).

Late in the novel Mary Stella's "automatic codes" are said to have "propelled her pencil across the page of a mirror" (122)—clear enough indication that the novel sees itself in the Angel Inn mirror, that reflection and refraction are there the same. Angled perception is a particular way of writing—writing bent or inflected by music. *The Angel at the Gate* is said to be based on Mary Stella's automatic writings and on notes taken by her therapist Joseph Marsden during conversations with her, some of which were conducted while she was under hypnosis. In the note which introduces the novel mention is made of "the musical compositions by which Mary it seems was haunted from early childhood," as well as of "a series of underlying rhythms in the automatic narratives" (7). Like the boy who became a *muni* bird, Mary Stella, an orphan from the age of seven, resorts to music in the face of broken familial ties—those with her parents in the past and in the present her troubled marriage with Sebastian, for whom she's "the same woman broken into wife and sister" (13). Louis Armstrong's rendition of "Mack the Knife," the song her mother frequently sang during her early childhood, animates a host of recollections and associations:

> . . . the music returned once again coming this time from an old gramophone her mother possessed. It was "Mack the Knife" sung and played by Louis Arm-

strong. The absurdity and tall story lyric, oceanic city, were sustained by Armstrong's height of trumpet and by his instrumental voice, hoarse and meditative in contrast to the trumpet he played, ecstatic cradle, ecstatic childhood, ecstatic coffin, ecstatic grieving surf or sea.

. . . Stella was shivering. The fascination of the song for her mother was something that she grew up with. Mack was also the name that her father bore. Mack was her mother's god. And her mother's name? *Guess,* Stella whispered to Sebastian in the darkened studio. Jenny! It was a random hit, bull's eye. It struck home. Jenny heard. She was weeping. It came with the faintest whisper of the sea, the faintest whisper of a flute, in the studio. Mack's women were the Sukey Tawdreys, the sweet Lucy Browns, of the world. Between the ages of four and seven Stella thought that the postman was her father. Until she realized that he was but the middleman between her real father and Jenny her mother. He brought the letters from foreign ports with foreign stamps over which Jenny wept. On her seventh birthday the last letter arrived. Her father was dead, his ship sunk. It was a lie. It drove her mother into an asylum where she contemplated Mack clinging for dear life to sarcophagus-globe even as she vanished into the arms of god, bride of god.

Stella was taken into care by a Social Welfare Body and placed in an orphanage in East Anglia. (44–45)

Mary Stella's automatic narratives, prompted by her thirst for connection and by "her longing to change the world" (46), instigate patterns of asymmetric equation into which characters named Sukey Tawdrey, Mother Diver, Lucy Brown, and so forth enter. The song, it seems, populates a world, an alternate world. Her music-prompted hand and its inscription of far-flung relations obey intimations of unacknowledged wholeness against a backdrop of social and psychic division. "To be whole," we're told at the end, "was to endure . . . the traffic of many souls" (126).

The novel's concern with heterogeneous wholeness invokes Legba repeatedly—though, significantly, not by that name. As if to more greatly emphasize Legba's association with multiplicity, Harris merges him with his trickster counterpart among the Ashanti, the spider Anancy, tales of whose exploits are a prominent part of Caribbean folklore. An asymmetric equation which relates deficit leg to surplus legs, lack to multiplicity, brings "a metaphysic of curative doubt" (78) to bear on appearances. Apparent deficiency and apparent endowment are two sides of an insufficient image. When Sebastian discovers Mary Stella's attempt at suicide "his legs multiplied" (14), but later "there was no visible bandage around his ankle but he seemed nevertheless as lame as Anancy" (33). Other such intimations occur: Marsden described as a cane on which "something, some invisible presence, did lean" (29), Sebastian asking of the jockey who exposed himself to Mary Stella, "Did he, for instance, possess a walking stick?" (50), and Jackson, Mary Stella's "authentic messenger" (125), falling from a ladder and breaking his leg. The most sustained appearance occurs when Mary Stella happens upon the black youth Anancy in Marsden's study. The "funny title" of a book has brought him there:

. . . He turned his eyes to the desk. "The door was open and I saw the funny title of that book." He pointed to the desk.

"Sir Thomas More's *Utopia*," said Mary, smiling against her fear and finding her tongue at last. "I put it there myself this week." His eyes were upon hers now. "I put it . . ." she began again, then stopped. "I brought you here," she thought silently. "*Utopia was the bait I used.*" The thought came of its own volition. It seemed irrational, yet true. There was a ticking silence between them, a deeper pull than she could gauge, a deeper call than she knew, that had sounded long, long ago, even before the time when her father's great-great-grandmother had been hooked by an Englishman to bear him children of mixed blood. (26–27)

Mary Stella's pursuit of heterogeneous relations carried her out as well as in. She discovers an eighteenth-century black ancestor on her father's side. That discovery, along with her perusal, in Marsden's library, of seventeenth- and eighteenth-century parish accounts of money spent to expel children and pregnant women, several of them black, arouses her desire for a utopian inclusiveness, the "longing to change the world" which "baits" Anancy. The world's failure to comply with that desire leads her to distance herself from it, to practice a kind of cosmic displacement. Her schizophrenia involves an aspect of astral projection, as she cultivates the "capacity to burn elsewhere" (85) suggested by her middle name: "Ah yes, said Stella, I am a mask Mary wears, a way of coping with truth. We are each other's little deaths, little births. We cling to sarcophagus-globe and to universal cradle" (44).

Displacement and relativizing distance account for the resonances and agitations at work in the text, an animated incompleteness whose components tend toward as well as recede from one another, support as well as destabilize one another. The pull between Mary Stella and Anancy is said to arise from "a compulsion or infectious Cupid's arrow . . . related to the target of unfinished being" (26). Some such pull, together with its other side, aversion, advances the accent on relationality which pervades the novel and has much to do with Harris' distinctive style. The sought-after sense of dispersed identity makes for staggered equational upsets and elisions in which words, concepts, and images, like the characters, are related through a mix of contrast and contagion. The musicality of Harris' writing resides in its cadences, imaginal concatenations, and poetic assurance, but also in something else. *The Angel at the Gate* offers a musical conception of the world whose emphasis on animate incompleteness, "unfinished being," recalls Zuckerlandl's analysis of tonal motion:

> A series of tones is heard as motion not because the successive tones are of different pitches but because they have different dynamic qualities. The dynamic quality of a tone, we said, is a statement of its incompleteness, its will to completion. To hear a tone as dynamic quality, as a direction, a pointing, means hearing at the same time beyond it, beyond it in the direction of its will, and going toward the expected next tone. Listening to music, then, we are not first *in* one tone, then in the next, and so forth. We are, rather, always *between* the tones, *on the way* from tone to tone; our hearing does not remain with the tone, it reaches through it and beyond it. . . . pure betweenness, pure passing over. (136–37)

A mixed, middle ground which privileges betweenness would seem to be the realm in which Harris works. He alludes to himself as a "no-man's land writer" at one point (23) and later has Jackson say, "I must learn to paint or sculpt what lies stranded between earth and heaven" (124). An "attunement to a gulf or divide between sky and earth" (123) probes an estrangement and a stranded play in which limbs have to do with limbo, liminality, lift:

> The women were dressed in white. They carried covered trays of food and other materials on their head. There was a statuesque deliberation to each movement they made, a hard-edged beauty akin to young Lucy's that seemed to bind their limbs into the soil even as it lifted them very subtly an inch or two into space.

> That lift was so nebulous, so uncertain, it may not have occurred at all. Yet it was there; it gave a gentle wave or groundswell to the static root or the vertical dance of each processional body. (122)

What remains to be said is that to take that lift a bit farther is to view the outsider's lot as cosmic, stellar. Social estrangement is gnostic estrangement and the step from Satchmo's "height of trumpet" to Sun Ra's "intergalactic music" is neither a long nor an illogical one. In this respect, the film *Brother from Another Planet* is worth —in what will serve as a closing note—mentioning briefly, That it shares with *The Angel at the Gate* a theme of cosmic dislocation is obvious enough. That the Brother's limp is the limp of a misfit—the shoes he finds and puts on don't suit his feet—is also easy to see. An intermedia thread is also present and bears on this discussion, especially the allusions to Dante (the Rasta guide named Virgil) and *Invisible Man* (the Brother's detachable eye), where it would seem the film were admitting a need to reach beyond its limits. What stronger suggestion of anesthetic-synesthetic displacement could one want than when the Brother places his eye in the drug dealer's hand? Or than the fact that the movie ends on a seen but unsounded musical note as the Brother gets aboard an "A" train?

NOTES

1. Examples of *gisalo* and other varieties of Kaluli song can be heard on the album *The Kaluli of Papua Niugini: Weeping and Song* (Musicaphon BM 30 SL 2702).

2. *Slavery and Social Death: A Comparative Study* (Cambridge, Mass.: Harvard University Press, 1982).

3. *Sound and Symbol: Music and the External World* (Princeton, N.J.: Bollingen Foundation/Princeton University Press, 1956), 371. Subsequent citations are incorporated into the text.

4. Stephanie A. Judy, " 'The Grand Concord of What': Preliminary Thoughts on Musical Composition and Poetry," *Boundary 2* 6, no. 1 (Fall 1977):267–85.

5. *Prepositions* (Berkeley: University of California Press, 1981), 19.

6. *The Bow and the Lyre* (New York: McGraw-Hill, 1973), 37.

7. *Desire in Language: A Semiotic Approach to Literature and Art* (New York: Columbia University Press, 1980), 31.

8. *Sound and Sentiment: Birds, Weeping, Poetics and Song in Kaluli Expression* (Philadelphia: University of Pennsylvania Press 1982), 34.

9. *Flash of the Spirit: African and Afro-American Art and Philosophy* (New York: Vintage Books, 1984), xiii.

10. *Tales* (New York: Grove Press, 1967), 77.

11. Charles Mingus, *Beneath the Underdog* (New York: Penguin Books, 1980), 262.

12. *Bedouin Hornbook* (Charlottesville: Callaloo Fiction Series/University Press of Virginia, 1986), 1.

13. *The Devil and Commodity Fetishism in South America* (Chapel Hill: University of North Carolina Press, 1980), 4.

14. *The Bass Saxophone* (London: Picador, 1980), 109.

15. Quoted by Lawrence W. Levine in *Black Culture and Black Consciousness: Afro-American Folk Thought from Slavery to Freedom* (New York: Oxford University Press, 1977), 85.

16. *The Wayward and the Seeking* (Washington, D.C.: Howard University Press, 1980), 123.

17. Quoted by Charles W. Scruggs in "The Mark of Cain and the Redemption of Art," *American Literature* 44 (1972):290–91.

18. *Cane* (New York: Liveright, 1975), 12. Subsequent citations are incorporated into the text.

19. *Black Music* (New York: Morrow, 1967), 66.

20. *Paterson* (New York: New Directions, 1963), 144–45. Subsequent citations are incorporated into the text.

21. *Selected Poems* (New York: New Directions, 1969), 115.

22. *Hermes the Thief: The Evolution of a Myth* (New York: Vintage Books, 1969), 82.

23. *The Trickster in West Africa: A Study of Mythic Irony and Sacred Delight* (Berkeley: University of California Press, 1980), 80.

24. *Praisesong for the Widow* (New York: Dutton, 1984), 243.

25. Levine, 405–6.

26. *Invisible Man* (New York: Vintage Books, 1972), 8. Subsequent citations are incorporated into the text.

27. *Human Universe and Other Essays* (New York: Grove Press, 1967), 3.

28. *The Subconscious Language* (New York: Washington Square Press, 1967), 96 n.

29. Quoted by Paul L. Mariani in "Williams's Black Novel," *The Massachusettes Review* 14, 1 (Winter 1973):68. This article is part of "A Williams Garland: Petals from the Falls, 1945–1950," edited by Mariani, which includes *Man Orchid,* 77–117. Subsequent ciations of Mariani's article and of *Man Orchid* are incorporated into the text.

30. See, for example, "This is what it's called" by Albert Saijo, Lew Welch, and Jack Kerouac in *The Beat Scene,* ed. Elias Wilentz (New York: Corinth, 1960), 163–70.

31. *History of the Voice: The Development of Nation Language in Anglophone Caribbean Poetry* (London and Port of Spain: New Beacon Books, 1984), 31.

32. *New Jazz Poets* (Broadside Records BR 461).

33. *The Angel at the Gate* (London: Faber and Faber, 1982), 109. Subsequent citations are incorporated into the text.

34. *The Womb of Space: The Cross-Cultural Imagination* (Westport: Greenwood Press, 1983), 130–31.

35. "The Phenomenal Legacy," *The Literary Half-Yearly* 11 (1970):1–6.

36. *Da Silva da Silva's Cultivated Wilderness and Genesis of the Clowns* (London: Faber and Faber, 1977), 8–9.

37. *Palace of the Peacock* (London: Faber and Faber, 1960), 83. Subsequent citations are incorporated into the text.

38. "The eye and its 'gaze' . . . has had a lockhold on Western thought," notes, as have others, Paul Stoller in "Sound in Songhay Cultural Experience," *American Ethnologist* 2, no. 3 (1984):559–70.

PART THREE

READINGS

THE "TECHNIQUE" OF RE-READING

MARVIN BELL

God knows, there exist more techniques for writing than are usually acknowledged. Probably, each of us uses a hundred or more all at the same time. Some of them may occur before a word is put to paper. For example, you go for a walk because you have noticed that afterward you feel like writing. Or you stay up extra late at night because you have noticed that after midnight you somehow elude the more banal levels of rationality. Or you begin to get up earlier than the rest of the family because you have noticed that, by afternoon, the poetry you might have written has gone into caring for the children. Or you sharpen twelve pencils because a better first line seems to emerge after a little stalling. Or you use a fountain pen, or a typewriter, or examination bluebooks or yellow paper or lined pads, or a quill pen. You smoke or drink coffee. You don't smoke or drink coffee. Like Hart Crane, you drink cheap wine and play Ravel's "Bolero" on the phonograph. You walk about. You pull your hair. You eat your beard. You sit in the corner of the cafeteria during lunch hours. You sit at the kitchen table after breakfast. You hide in a studio out back in which you scheme to build a trap door and a tunnel to the sewers of Paris. These are "Writing Techniques." If you are lucky and talented, you may not need much else. You will be able to do your best work by following the method suggested for writers by W. M. Pirsig in *Zen and the Art of Motorcycle Maintenance:* "Make yourself perfect and then write naturally."

Certainly, that seems a worthy goal: gradually to replace labor with inspiration, to achieve in maturity that condition in which poetry arrives as easily, as Keats would have it, as leaves to trees.

In the meantime, which is where most of us find ourselves, we need among our stores of writing techniques a method for noticing the little things in language, and for seeing how others did, consciously or unconsciously, all that we hope to do later by nature.

That method is re-reading. Not reading by *re*-reading. We all know readers who have looked their way through great libraries of books without absorbing any. On first reading, such readers may experience a poem as fully as any of us, but their experience of the poem is perforce limited to the least experience of reading and to the associations a text may stir as one's thoughts wander.

Reading as a writer is another matter. Language is a reflexive medium, even for the most unconscious of poets. In addition, writing usually assumes a strong linear base—one word at a time. Self-reflexive and linear, a poem read once has not been fully read. To learn from language itself and from poetry, we think about *how* it says what it says, as well as *what* it says. You must know and, knowing, you must be able to say. If you cannot say it, you probably don't know it.

There is another side to this. Learning to re-read your own work and others' is an absolute necessity because it is crucial to those of you who intend to go on writing that you learn how to continue to educate yourselves in the absence of teachers. Everyone knows that conferee in search of answers which would at once kick his or her writing up a level. In applications to the program in which I teach, we sometimes note that an applicant has studied with A through M in school, and also N through Z for periods of a week or two during summers. Teaching *can* make a difference, but only for the essentially self-reliant.

Sometimes a student brings me poems that have already been discussed by another teacher. In such cases, the poet must be taking votes, right? "The other guy said this poem was bad but you like it, so it must be a good poem after all." Or, "The other guy liked it, so what does it matter if you don't? I was just checking your taste."

I get questions about revising poems that are based on there being a "correct" way to say a thing, or to lineate a free verse poem, or to begin or conclude or . . . But you know the questions. Not one of them has an answer. The plain truth is that, except for mistakes that can be checked in the dictionary, almost nothing is right or wrong. Writing poems out of the desire to find a way to be right, not wrong, is the garden path to dullness.

You have to learn to learn, if you're serious about writing. It's not that hard. First, you should realize that no teacher is ever going to tell you all that he or she knows. Second, however much he or she tells, you will only hear as much of what is said as you are able at the moment. You can take from a given teacher a few tricks, perhaps one or two ways of writing, but what you might better seek beyond that, for the long haul, is an attitude toward writing and an attitude toward how to read as a writer.

Reading as a writer is not the same as reading as a nonwriter. The writer is looking for what he or she can use. The writer reads on the edge of his or her chair. The writer goes slowly and doubles back.

Teachers were my teachers when I went to school, but poems have been my teachers since. I don't say *books,* but poems—one by one. Reading, or perhaps just scanning, entire books of poems is what the critic does when he or she discusses style and theme. In an ideal world, I sometimes think, we would not review books at all—as if individual poems did not have content. We would write reviews of single poems. Come to think of it, sometimes students do that. Is it possible that students are smarter than reviewers?

Nor need you wait to be "tempted," like they say, to reread poems. Poems are not movies; one doesn't lie back in the dark and demand stimulation. You go forward. At least, you lean a little. In part, that's what poetry is: a quality you experience because you pay it a special attention.

Richard Wilbur's poem, "The Writer," is an accomplishment of sanity and intelligence. It is also a fine example of how one small move in the language can lead to others and how poetic showmanship can lead to serious concern.

In her room at the prow of the house
Where light breaks, and the windows are tossed with linden,
My daughter is writing a story.

I pause in the stairwell, hearing
From her shut door a commotion of typewriter-keys
Like a chain hauled over a gunwale.

Young as she is, the stuff
Of her life is a great cargo, and some of it heavy:
I wish her a lucky passage.

But now it is she who pauses,
As if to reject my thought and its easy figure.
A stillness greatens, in which

The whole house seems to be thinking,
And then she is at it again with a bunched clamor
Of strokes, and again is silent.

I remember the dazed starling
Which was trapped in that very room, two years ago;
How we stole in, lifted a sash

And retreated, not to affright it;
And how for a helpless hour, through the crack of the door,
We watched the sleek, wild, dark

And iridescent creature
Batter against the brilliance, drop like a glove
To the hard floor, or the desk-top,

And wait then, humped and bloody,
For the wits to try it again; and how our spirits
Rose when, suddenly sure,

It lifted off from a chair-back
Beating a smooth course for the right window
And clearing the sill of the world.

It is always a matter, my darling,
Of life or death, as I had forgotten, I wish
What I wished you before, but harder.

Wilbur's poem is accentual—three stresses apiece in the first and third lines of each stanza, and five apiece in the middle lines—but I haven't chosen it to discuss meter. Rather, I'd like to look at how it begins, continues, and ends.

That's a simple enough first line, isn't it? We can write that, can't we? Imagine yourself writing it out: "In her room at the front of the house . . ." No, not "front," but "prow." One word has been changed in a phrase any of us might utter over coffee or on the telephone. Instead of "her room at the front of the house," Wilbur says, "at the *prow* of the house."

Why? Well, any reason will do, and it's possible that the poet simply thought to jazz it up a bit, to be figurative because poetry derives at times from figurative language and because this poet has a talent for making figures. It's even possible that the poet's house vaguely resembles a boat in its shape. My own suspicion is that this is simply one more example of a poet using what comes to mind. Wilbur is a sailor; he served in the Navy; he vacations in Key West on the Atlantic. To him it's natural to identify the front of a house with the prow of a boat.

Lines two and three announce the place and the plot. What could be more straightforward? "My daughter is writing a story," And what could be more natural but that the proud father, a writer himself, pause in the stairwell to listen? He stands outside her door and hears the typewriter going, and how does he describe it. First, as "a commotion of typewriter-keys." That's more figure-making, at first blush an elementary sort, the kind of prepositional phrase figure-making we were asked to list on the blackboard in grade school—an "enigma of elephants," and so forth—except that this one contains nothing made-up. What he hears is, in fact, a noisy commotion, in which the clamor of the keys additionally seems to express the commotion of the creative turmoil going on inside her room.

Here Wilbur decides to extend the figure with a simile. Well, the poem must continue to listen to itself and to give visible indications of listening to itself. Hence, having likened the front of the house to the prow of a boat, he chooses another nautical item to which to liken the sound of the typewriter: the sound of a chain being hauled over a gunwale. Is she, then, pulling up anchor?

Stanza three, likewise, is witty and showy. If the house is a ship, why then her life in it carries cargo, some of it heavy, and one may wish her a lucky passage—both in her story and on the seas of life. That's easy: serious but easy.

The poem is still listening—re-reading—itself. And what has it heard so far? It has heard a proud father saying the usual things, albeit with grace and flair. And so we come to the second part of this poem, in which the father will realize how casually one may say good luck. Please notice, by the way, that he didn't write, "But now it is she who pauses, to reject my thought and its easy figure." No, that would have been mere fancy. He can't know what the silence means, and so he writes, "*as if* to reject my thought and its easy figure." His simile was an easy figure for her typing; his metaphor was an easy figure for her writing and her life; *he* is, likewise, an easy figure pausing for a moment outside her door, calm against the clamor of her keys.

At this point in the poem, it might seem that there is nothing further to say, at least not if one is able to resist the siren call of one's abstract ideas and bald statements of feeling. It is time to look elsewhere, and the poet looks, as poets will, into memory. For when the poem listens to itself, the poet has been listening to *himself,* and listening to oneself is itself an act of listening to the past. Language can eat the future, but it lives off the past.

He remembers a trapped bird, in that very room it happens, who had to try and try. When it fell, he tells us, it fell "like a glove," sometimes to the"desk-top," and one thinks of the writer's hand slumping from the keys to the desk in between sentences. But there is more to the parallel. The bird grew humped and bloody in its effort. Its success is getting out of that room depended on its wits, or brains, and it had to learn the hard way on its own.

Finally, it makes it, "clearing the sill of the . . . window." No, the "sill of the *world*." If we didn't get it, we do now: his daughter's writing a story is part of her growing up and away. She too will someday clear the sill of their world: the world of the family and of her room at the prow of the house.

Guess what? This is serious business after all. The triumph of this poem, the big thing which depends on all the little things along the way, lies in the speaker, the father, taking his daughter more and more seriously. Finally, he says it: "It is always a matter, my darling, / of life or death, as I had forgotten. I wish / what I wished you before, but harder." One thing that poems do is to give a phrase or sentence or thought more meaning. Or to find out how much more it meant all along. "I wish what I wished you before, but harder."

When I reread this poem, I see many reassuring things for a writer. I see that simple details can have meaning beyond furnishing a world or telling a story. I see that the past may relate to the present and vice-versa. I see that what begins in word-play may end in honor. I see again how the very essence of a poem may be to arrive at that spot at which the speaker may call his daughter his darling.

Ok, that's groundwork. How is my reading of it affected by my being a writer? Primarily, in this way: that, having read it and first been taken by the reality and clarity of its feelings, I go back to see how the poem might have been written. I try to imagine myself freely arriving at the same words, images, associations, thoughts, in the same order.

You know, it's a truism that one learns to write by reading. But not necessarily by *wide* reading. Rather, by *deep* reading. One might read a few things over and over, perhaps over a period of years, and so be more lastingly influenced than by a slighter acquaintance with more.

Of course one may read and reread happily without thinking about it, hoping to learn by intuition, and certainly some poems are less discussable than others. I have a theory—just one of many theories that come and go, depending on the context— that the great achievements of American poetry have been essentially rhetorical, those of rhetoric rather than of image and metaphor, or of imagination, structure, and vision. In American poetry, as you all know, great emphasis has been placed on an individual tone of voice. The great Mommas and Daddies of modern poetry in English are enormously distinctive, one from the other. The great generation of American poets now in its fifties and sixties contains individuality of style and tone of voice in profusion. From the late 1950s until the late 1960s, it seemed as if no two books dared to have anything of method in common. Method, mind you, and language, not content, which I dare to say retrospective analysis will find far less individuated than styles among the poets in question. Nonetheless, the Imagists had said that a new cadence meant a new idea, essentially a defense of formalism, whether in traditional forms, variants of them or so-called free verse. Not a new imagination, mind you, a new *idea*. The emphasis on ideas, baldly stated or only insinuated, in American poetry, has meant an emphasis on those aspects of a poem which are essentially rhetorical. The secrets of tone are, for the most part, those of syntax and words without meaning, so-called "function words" which indicate relationships: subordination, coordination, conjunction, opposition, etc. Syntax is logic, or the appearance of it, and new logic inevitably produces a new tone of voice.

In the classroom, we tend to marvel at rhetoric, and to discuss most freely poems held together by rhetoric, poems in which, however frontal the narrative, however rich in objects, images, or metaphors, however insistent in vision, the poem is primarily a set of rhetorical maneuvers.

It is harder, much much harder, to learn from poems which skip that rhetorical level and which present themselves as associational texts in which the reasoning is in between the lines while the lines themselves present only the emblems of experience and, sometimes, of epiphany.

TO THE SAGUARO CACTUS TREE IN THE DESERT RAIN

> I had no idea the elf owl
> Crept into you in the secret
> Of night.
>
> I have torn myself out of many bitter places
> In America, that seemed
> Tall and green-rooted in mid-noon.
> I wish I were the spare shadow
> Of the roadrunner, I wish I were
> The honest lover of the diamondback
> And the tear the tarantula weeps.
>
> I had no idea you were so tall
> And blond in moonlight.
>
> I got thirsty in the factories,
> And I hated the brutal dry suns there,
> So I quit.
>
> You were the shadow
> Of the hallway
> In me.
>
> I have never gone through that door,
> But the elf owl's face
> Is inside me.
>
> Saguaro,
> You are not one of the gods.
> Your green arms lower and gather me.
> I am an elf owl's shadow, a secret
> Member of your family.
>   —*James Wright*

James Wright's poem may seem "farther out" than Wilbur's "The Writer." Its images seem to lie on the page as if disconnected, each from each. If by rhetoric the poem establishes its tone of voice and hints at connections, nowhere do we come on anything so bald as, "It is always a matter, my darling, of life or death, as I had forgotten." Instead we get, "I have never gone through that door, but the elf owl's face is inside me."

Look back at the first three lines. From the writer's point of view—that is, from the point of view of a thief—what's to notice? The basic sentence is a simple statement of fact: the elf owl creeps into the saguaro at night. But Wright says "secret" of night. "Secret" is one of James Wright's words. It shows up often in his last three books. From its recurrent use we can see that it holds symbolic and visionary overtones for Wright, much like certain words in the poems of Emily Dickinson: such words as "grace," "noon," "seal," "purple," and "circumference." From the canon of Wright's poetry we might see that his use of the word "secret" arises from a fierce belief that a man's life is something inside, out of view of others, not one's public life at all—something private, personal and intimate. But of course you don't have to know any of that. The phrase here, "secret of night," makes perfect sense all by itself. Night is the great cover. The elf owl *creeps* secretively into the tree.

The other tiny "extra" in what would otherwise be a plain sentence of desert lore is the rhetorical maneuver at the start: "I had no idea." That's immediate involvement: the voice of the poem is at once strong and engaged. A stance has been taken. While such small maneuvers may come to be second nature to any one of us, using them is quite as much a matter of technique as is calling a part of one's house by the name for a part of a boat.

From here on, the poem will be an expression of increasing identification with the elf owl. Wright says that he has had to tear himself away from many places that seemed to be, like the cactus tree that is home to the elf owl, tall and green-rooted. But they were not. Like Whitman, he thinks he could turn and live with the animals; he wishes he were something of nature without the self-consciousness of man. But, being a man, he wasn't able to live in a cactus tree. His desert was that of the factories where he worked and quit.

Still, there is in each of us a secret life. A life in which we identify with the elf owl and in which we see ourselves living at night in a cactus tree in the welcome desert rain. And so he says, addressing the tree, "You were the shadow / Of a hallway / In me." And while, being a man, he has never gone through that door, he can say of himself that he carries the elf owl's face inside.

The poem listens to itself. That is how it arrives at tall and green-rooted places in mid-noon, to echo and parallel a cactus tree in the desert. That is how it finds its way to factories which are themselves scorched deserts.

But the poem does not merely repeat itself. Try out the last stanza without its second line. Without "You are not one of the gods," it would merely be more of the same. What is added? For one thing, in case you were wondering, no he is not according the tree divinity. Moreover, it contains a certain insistence on facts and this world, the sort of insistence we saw four lines earlier when he said, "I have never gone through that door." Without such moves, a poem turns into mere fancy: a story, say, about a man who could live inside a cactus and talk to elf owls. No; it is not a story at all, but an expression of a secret identification and a longing to be naturally at home.

From the first time I came upon this poem, it held my interest as a writer. Wright, as you probably know, began writing as a formalist, indebted to the poems of Edwin

Arlington Robinson. With the book *The Branch Will Not Break,* his writing underwent a sea-change, apparently influenced by his reading and translating of Spanish poets and the German expressionist poet, Georg Trakl. Thereafter, Wright was always said to be a surrealistic image-maker. In later books, he put back the open rhetoric he had forsaken in *The Branch Will Not Break* but continued also to write great flourishes of surrealistic imagery. In this poem to the saguaro, the landscape is made surreal—it helps to be in the desert among The Friends of Salvador Dali—but it is not fanciful. Everything here is real.

We should all, I would think, want to be able to write such lines as "You were the shadow / Of a hallway / In me," and I am an elf owl's shadow, a secret / Member of your family." It may help, therefore, to notice how Wright gets to such lines and fills them with meaning. You don't get to "You were the *shadow* of a hallway in me" unless you first see in the cactus tree a hallway for an elf owl. One of the things poems do is add meaning to what has already been said: "I wish what I wished you before, but harder."

Now pause a moment over the last two lines of the poem. There are the words "shadow" and "secret" again. Are the images in these lines just vague emotional equivalents to the speaker's feelings, or do they make sense based on what "shadow" and "secret" meant when he used them earlier? I'll put it in terms of simple logic: if the cactus tree was a hallway to the elf owl in the desert, and was therefore the shadow of a hallway to the worker in the hot factories, then the worker could become the shadow of the elf owl. Each is a part of the other. The elf owl doesn't live exclusively in the cool tree but also in the burning desert. Indeed, he "creeps" into the tree, a secret act in the night. Nor does the worker's entire life take place in the brutal light of factories. He has his naturally cool places, his secret life. The living elf owl and the living man are one, more so than the speaker realized, perhaps, when he wished openly to be the shadow of the roadrunner, the lover of the diamondback, and the tear wept by the tarantula. He is, in a sense, all of those things—the more so if he knows it. If the green arms of the saguaro do not lower and gather him *in fact,* in his mind he is able to rise to embrace them and to affirm his identification with all the world and with all its forms of life.

Sometimes, at the end of a poem, the world is larger, and the speaker is less alone.

After awhile, James Wright started to write pieces of short prose. He explained that he "wanted to learn to write prose." Are they prose, or prose-poetry, or are they poems that happen to have been set down in paragraphs? I would say that it is a sign of the times—some would say a bad sign, others would say a good sign—that we need not linger on the question. Our various technical definitions and technical standards for poetry have been greatly added to by a larger, untechnical standard and definition based on the quality of imagination in poetry, and on what we might call "poetic structure": how the writer moves from one thing to another and how meaning is apprehended, enlarged or diminished.

Our American poetry, and the ways in which we speak about it, have been changed since the mid-1960s, not as much by the examples of our own best poets or by those who have been brought to our shores from other English-speaking countries aboard barrages of East Coast publicity as much as by poetry in translation. Not just the finest, most considered, and most accurate translations (for example, Mark Strand's translations of Alberti and Andrade, or Charles Simic's versions of Vasko Popa, or Alistair Reid's of Pablo Neruda, or translations of Zbigniew Herbert by Czeslaw Milosz and Peter Dale Scott, or Edmund Keeley and George Savidis' versions of Cavafy)—not just the finest and also most accurate, but also those which, like Ezra Pound's translations of Li Po, take liberties with literal accuracy to render, perhaps even exaggerate, the spirit of the poem (for example, Robert Bly's versions of Neruda, Lorca, Jimenez, Rumi, Rilke, Martinson, Ekelof, Tranströmer and so many others, and W. S. Merwin's translations from both eastern and western languages)—and not just the very best of the anthologies of poetry in translation (of which I will mention Mark Strand and Charles Simic's *Another Republic*, Czeslaw Milosz's *Postwar Polish Poetry*, Hardie St. Martin's *Roots and Wings: Poetry from Spain, 1900–1975*, and that hoary old favorite, perhaps now forgotten, Robert Payne's anthology of Chinese poetry, *The White Pony*, first published in 1947 and seemingly added to on republication in 1960)—not only the finest, the most accurate, the most conscious of spirit and imagination, nor the best gathered books of translations have influenced us to think more broadly about poetry but so also have translations by poets who have done merely a little of this or that, using a "pony" and a dictionary to translate a few Persian ghazals or one or two poems by the Spanish poet, Unamuno, say. In every translation, there comes to us a new wave of permission, an increased sense of freedom. Is it because we are forced to abandon our prejudices and personal likes and dislikes if we are to enjoy travel? Is it because other cultures do not share our overwhelmingly technical view of things? Is it because the pressures of empire, even a crumbling empire involved in a desperate holding action, affect our point of view? No doubt it is all these things and others. One thing is certain: every literature has grown fresh, and every great writer been made greater, by writers looking to other cultures and languages for new words and renewed permission.

So, if we look at a short poem by Tomas Tranströmer, translated from the Swedish by Robert Bly, we have to adjust our way of learning. Let's read it.

AFTER A DEATH

Once there was a shock
that left behind a long, shimmering comet tail.
It keeps us inside. It makes the TV pictures snowy.
It settles in cold drops on the telephone wires.

One can still go slowly on skis in the winter sun
through brush where a few leaves hang on.
They resemble pages torn from old telephone directories.
Names swallowed by the cold.

It is still beautiful to feel the heart beat
but often the shadow seems more real than the body.
The samurai looks insignificant
beside his armor of black dragon scales.

—Tomas Tranströmer
trans. by Robert Bly

The poem is titled "After a Death." One could easily misremember it as "After a Shock," for that is what it is about. It is not an elegy. We are told nothing about the person who has died nor even his name. We read that the death was a shock. There is a mention of television. Perhaps it was someone famous. Perhaps it was an assassination. Perhaps it was the killing of John F. Kennedy. In fact, it was. Tranströmer says so. But I have taken note again and again that he does not say so in the poem nor even offer a dedication or an epigraph *in memoriam.* The poem is more general than that. Indeed, Tranströmer says that an uncle died around the same time and that the deaths combine in the poem. In my mind I contrast it with the American rush to dedicate poems, to mention the names of famous friends and to publish elegies for poets before the ink has dried on their obits.

Of course, our rush to identify and dedicate is not born of bad intentions. We want everything to be particular. We love particulars. We have faith in particulars. We honestly believe that, if we can get the particulars correct and in the right order, our job will be done and the poem complete.

Perhaps we favor particulars in part because our choice has long seemed to lie exclusively between particulars and rhetorical explanation. We therefore, and for important reasons, favor the concrete over the abstract, the particular over the general, presentation over explanation, showing over telling.

Yet so much poetry from other cultures exhibits both the tensile strength of the particular and the active force of the general. How does this happen?

I can notice elements in this Tranströmer poem that line up with the question. Conventionally, we can say that a long, shimmering comet tail is a fine metaphor for the sudden, fiery grief that exploded in front of us when Kennedy was assassinated and then streaked into darkness. Or for any death that comes as a shock. But I notice also the first thing, which is simply the poet's leap into the heavens and then his sudden drop back to earth and the domestic: "It keeps us inside," a wonderful detail; "It makes the tv pictures snowy." Do these things make sense emotionally? Obviously. Do they make sense physically, in the world of current physical theory? Yes, for a comet tail might be thought to affect electronic reception. If it's exaggeration, it only imitates in hyperbole the extreme emotions of shock and grief. And the fourth line—"It settles in cold drops on the telephone wires"—continues the images of difficult communication, messages, all in the air. If the telephone lines themselves sweat cold beads, what effect must the news have on human beings?

Some kind of thinking must have taken place between stanzas one and two. I can imagine it. While the poet was asking himself, unconsciously, "What next?" for his poem, he came to the same question about his subject. For there is nothing notable to say about the anatomy and biology of death which would advance this poem. The rest of the event is only news.

This is another way in which a poem can listen to itself. The poem does not merely listen to itself so that it can gain applause by showing that it did. No, it listens for clues. "What next?" Imagine this. You are sitting at your kitchen table, writing. You have written four lines. You read those four lines as if you were someone else, someone who asks a question or expresses disagreement. Now you know what to say next.

After a shocking death, one can still go out into the same world, on skis if you are in the right country for them, but the world will seem changed. The few leaves hanging on winter brush will resemble pages. And here we notice something perhaps having no basis in the original language of the poem: that the English plural of "leaf" is "leaves." But pages of what? The poem is still paying attention to itself. Remember those telephone wires in line four? "Pages torn from old telephone directories"; hence, "names swallowed by the cold." Cold drops on the wires, names swallowed by the cold, a lump in the throat—as separate as the images may seem when we first come upon them, they live in one neighborhood.

When I look at how the final stanza of this poem begins, I am reminded of the distance between our poets and many of our critics. Few of our critics would care for a line like, "It is still beautiful to feel the heart beat." Half of our poets and most of our critics write as if they believe that, since life ends in death, we are essentially dead. Hence, they believe, sometimes without knowing it, that *any* uncomplicated emotion about life is excessive: therefore, sentimental. Let me give you this one idea to chew on: Poetry, because it is written by the living to be read by the living, is a way of *life*. It is always about *living*, even in the shadow of death. The samurai's armor of black dragon scales, which Tranströmer saw in the Stockholm Museum, overshadows the swordsman, and the shadow often "seems more real than the body," but it is "still beautiful to feel the heart beat." Without line nine, the poem would be different. Without line nine, it would not be wisdom but complaint.

Now this Tranströmer poem, in translation, does not show a certain vibrancy of language I myself favor, nor a fiercely idiomatic character, nor a sharply etched individual tone. It comes to us in a neutral tone, an impersonal voice, yet I find in it a certain intimacy regardless—perhaps because of the very objects in the poem (tv, telephone, brush, and leaves), and perhaps because it asks the question most of *us* would ask, "What next" And perhaps in part simply because it actually employs the word "us."

And it accomplishes extra meaning in its last sentence, just as the Wilbur and Wright poems did. That the suit of armor dwarfs the samurai might be merely a museum fact, something which moves us to say, "Look at that!" Put where it is in the poem, however, we are more likely to say, "*Think* about that!" Thus the writer has given a detail from a showcase an emotional weight it always possessed but which had to be released by those acts of imagination which preceded it in the poem. I find this quality in poetry from other countries more often than in American poems: the quality, that is, of releasing from objects the emotional force they hold in quiet.

Now I'd like to strengthen or weaken my case, and add a dimension to it, by confessing that I sometimes read, in private, my own poems. And that I read them, after awhile, the same way—to see, as much as is possible, what occurred in the process of writing them.

You might think I ought to have known all that at the time, but what we first do consciously later becomes second nature, and, in any case, I believe in inspiration, spontaneity, association, accident, and temporary insanity. During the interminable time of a writing block, I employ a rubber stamp which reads, "Temporarily Deceased."

I'll read through "To an Adolescent Weeping Willow."

TO AN ADOLESCENT WEEPING WILLOW

I don't know what you think you're doing,
sweeping the ground. You
do it so easily, backhanded, forehanded.
You hardly bend. Really, you sway.
What can it mean
when a thing is so easy?

I threw dirt on my father's floor.
Not dirt, but a chopped green
dirt which picked up dirt.

I pushed the pushbroom.
I oiled the wooden floor of the store.

He bent over and lifted the coal
into the coalstove. With the back of the shovel
he came down on the rat just topping the bin
and into the fire.

What do you think?—Did he sway?
Did he kiss a rock for luck?
Did he soak up water
and climb into light and turn and turn?

Did he weep and weep in the yard?

Yes, I think he did. Yes,
now I think he did.

So, Willow, you come sweep my floor.
I have no store.
I have a yard. A big yard.

I have a song to weep.
I have a cry.

You who rose up from the dirt,
because I put you there
and like to walk my head in under
your earliest feathery branches—
what can it mean
when a thing is so easy?

It means you are a boy.

—Marvin Bell

Right away, I notice things. It seems to me that this poet did something sincere but also tricky to start the poem. He challenged the tree. Even before he told us one thing about it, he got worked up. Immediate emotion. Condition *Now.* A rhetorical maneuver, in the idiomatic language of common people, similar to the beginning lines of certain favorite poems by James Wright: "The Old WPA Swimming Pool in Martins Ferry, Ohio," for example, which begins, "I am almost afraid / To write down / This thing." Or "To the Saguaro Cactus Tree in the Desert Rain," which begins, "I had no *idea.* . . ." Influence? More likely, something of experience and language held in common but not always welcomed into one's writing unless, sometimes, one first notices it elsewhere.

I can hear the poem listening to itself, using the rest of the first stanza to explain the challenge of the first line. And I can see, now, that the poet simply turned his back on the question he had posed: "What can it mean when a thing is so easy?"

For this poet, poems are not about what one already knows so much as they are about what one didn't know one knew. To find out what one doesn't know one knows, one must sometimes look elsewhere. It's a process similar to going to bed to sleep on a problem and waking with the answer. Physicists do it all the time. Freud did it. Will it matter *where* one looks while looking away? It probably does, but another question occurs to me to undermine that one: Could one possibly look away *without* intuitive reference to what has been on one's conscious mind and surely still lingers beneath it at the moment one turns away? I think not. The self has a coherence, and the poet, good or lucky or both, can retrace those connections later on.

Looking back, it all seems patently obvious. The willow stands swaying easily in dirt. The speaker in the poem, the poet as it happens, once did something with dirt that might have been easy to do but which seems, at first glance, to contain the seeds of unease—so much so that the poet immediately retreats to explain. He wasn't bad, he didn't make trouble for his father; he was good, he helped.

In fact, he did more. He swept up and oiled the floor.

"Yes," says that invisible reader, lurking behind the writer's shoulder but never in the direction in which the writer looks for him, "Yes, but what did *he* do while you were handling your childhood chores? Didn't he do the harder things? Let's name a couple to remind you."

And that's enough of *that.* Is this a poem about running a five-and-ten? No, we don't know what it's going to be about, mostly, finally, but it won't be that. "Don't forget," says the second self, "you're talking to a tree. You asked it a question, so far unanswered. Can you answer it or not? No, not yet? Then why not ask the tree some more questions?" *Hotshot tree, doing everything so easily . . . Do you think my father was like you? Did he sway, kiss a rock, soak up water and climb into light?* And now comes a lucky moment in the language. It's not just any old tree; it's a willow, a *weeping* willow. "Did he weep and weep in the yard?" That means one thing for the tree and another for one's father. Asked about a tree, it's a light piece of wit, but it's damn serious when asked about the father.

Suddenly, the poet is forced to answer his own seemingly rhetorical questions. When he began his questions directed toward the tree, they were questions to suggest differences. One expected them to be answered with "No's" but it turns out the answer was "Yes" all along, particularly to the first and the last question.

So now the weeping willow—at the beginning bothersome, even offensive, in its ease—can be accepted. The poet has asked his challenging question and, though he has yet to answer it, has bled the confusion and confrontation from it. The willow and his father have something in common.

The differences, however, are still at issue. *Willow, come sweep my floor. I have no store, but I have a yard. I do the father's singing and crying now. Not only that, I planted you there.*

So what, then, of the question posed in lines five and six: "What can it mean when a thing is so easy?" Looking back at this poem, trying to imagine myself at the time of writing it, it seems to me that by writing the poem I found the answer to what I meant by the question—to what *I* meant, not to what the same question might mean when asked by one of you. The question itself had to be given more meaning by the poem, meaning that lurked underneath when the poem began.

It takes the poem to answer the question. Then it takes only one sentence of six monosyllabic words to deliver the answer. The willow is an adolescent. That is why some things are easy for it. Moreover, the seeming ease of youth is characteristic of the distance in time between any father and any son, not the distance of not getting along but the distance of cold fact: the son knows little of the consciousness of the father. The son hangs around, sweeps the floor. He thinks it's more or less the same for his father, who fires the coalstove and kills rats in the basement. He doesn't know, like they say, shit. Not because he is stupid or unsympathetic. It means only that he is not a man but a boy. He will know the difference when he is a man.

I am reassured when I look again at this poem. It says to me that I can pose a question and not answer it while the poem goes on, confident that an answer will arrive. It says to me that I can talk to one person (or tree) about another. I see, as I have always suspected, that I feel a heightened and immediate engagement when I address someone or some thing directly—that, in that sense, I want the poem to matter because someone is listening. I see that, when I ask a question, I want it to be answered. I suspect that I could derive from this poem a method by which to write others. The method would require a challenging remark, some description of what is being addressed, a question to be answered at the end, and a set of memories set down one after the other until a connection is achieved between memories and one thing being addressed, a welcome in place of the initial challenge, and the answer. I'm not interested in applying such a method myself, if it is one, but I see that it might be done, and that something similar might be done with any poem one admires sufficiently. I know one poet who writes her poems primarily by extrapolating requirements from other people's poems. After all, your own obsessions and language will surface regardless.

In conclusion, I'd like to talk about what it takes besides talent and perseverance to make the big leagues. Everyone knows that, no matter how good you are in your home town, at some point you have got to play with and against the best. If your kid is really that talented with the violin, he needs a world-class teacher. It's no accident that a large share of the best basketball players in the country come from a few well-known schools and playgrounds, or that hotshot high school baseball players and tennis players head for those particular warm climates where the other hotshots have gone. Louis Armstrong and Miles Davis didn't get to play that way by stepping on the football field with the high school band to play simple marches. You want to be a carpenter, you've got to apprentice yourself to a good one. You want to be a tailor, it helps to know at least one person who can make a suit.

Well, one can't always give up everything and go off to hang around the right playground or teacher. But, in literature, it's different: one *can* hang out with the best. It's all right there in the library.

Still, the books are not the process. What's in the books is the end result. It's as if one saw the ball going through the basket again and again, without ever seeing the moves that made the shot possible. Consequently, if you are to learn from what is given you, the poem itself, you must put yourself into it again and again, imaging the process—nay, *inventing* the process by which the poem may have come to be. More often than not, what you invent will be sort of what the poet did.

From rereading, you will grow up and go free. Then, getting your poems written will depend on need, luck, and perseverance. The rest is genius.

NOTES

This essay began as an informal talk presented at the 1982 Bread Loaf Writers' Conference.

DICKINSON'S PARADOXICAL LOSSES

ALFRED CORN

The issue of sexuality never stands far off from instances of loss, partly because one of the first (and therefore powerfully imprinted) losses undergone by the child is the discovery that it cannot be the same sex as both its parents; its anatomy is irrevocably different from one of the powerful, loved figures that preside over the early human universe. This loss is experienced as a psychological-somatic mutilation; and if we look for the root meaning of loss, we discover that it suggests division, or separation from something formerly attached to us. Among the most potent myths are those that tell of mutilations, severings, dismemberments—Oedipus' eyes, Samson's hair, Procne's tongue. For females in patriarchal societies, the sense of loss is compounded when experience makes it clear that power and authority have been assigned to the anatomy that is not theirs. This may begin to explain why so many of the best writings about loss are by women. But of course both sexes are always interested in the problem of loss because both inevitably experience loss in the course of a normal life. The recurrent question is whether the loss is irredeemable.

Loss is not always separation from something that belonged to us. It can also be the abandoning of a claim to something we have desired but never actually possessed. In this case, we separate ourselves from one of our hopes, often with a sharp sense of psychological harm. This is the kind of loss described by the Dickinson poem numbered 67 in standard editions:

> *Success is counted sweetest*
> *By those who ne'er succeed.*
> *To comprehend a nectar*
> *Requires sorest need.*
>
> *Not one of all the purple Host*
> *Who took the Flag today*
> *Can tell the definition*
> *So clear of Victory*
>
> *As he defeated—dying—*
> *On whose forbidden ear*
> *the distant strains of triumph*
> *Burst agonized and clear!*

Dickinson announces the topic, Success, with the first word of the poem. Among possible terms, this one is the most general word she could choose. From its etymology it suggests a following in the footsteps of an eminent predecessor. A prince succeeds to the throne of his parent; one president succeeds another, and so on. By keeping the kind of eminence or triumph envisioned general, Dickinson allows it to cover more cases.

Her view of this general category is paradoxical and therefore contentious. The paradox is constructed very intently along the lines of Emerson's theory of compensation, which sees reality as a great balance sheet where every gain involves a corresponding loss, and every loss a corresponding gain. Many of Dickinson's poems explore variations of this theory, and if they do the cause can be found in a psyche that was sharply focused on things that seemed out of reach or denied to it. The mind of a great artist doesn't simply rest content with dejection or deprivation; somehow a way will be found to valorize adverse circumstance, to transmute lead into gold. Dickinson, confronted with insufficient understanding from her family, with the failure of a life companion to appear and to remain, with the lack of public recognition of her special gifts, and the limitation imposed on women by nineteenth-century society, sought nevertheless to discover—actually, to create—value even under such conditions. To this list of adversities, we must also add the great limitation imposed on life by death, a problem that concerns so many of Dickinson's best poems. She was able to write about death from many standpoints because she saw it variously, not as one thing only, certainly not always and throughout as an evil.

Death and success, then, are equally various and multifaceted. But what, in poem 67, are the facets of success being explored? The words "sweetest" and "nectar" introduce a notion of success as something tasted and consumed. Success is like a precious liquor, delectably sweet, that satisfies an extreme need. But the assertion is clear: enjoyment immediately satisfies but is inferior to deprivation for the reason that satisfaction offers less comprehension of the thing consumed. The human truth here is plausible enough. Just to observe a child at a pastry shop window is a lesson in Dickinsonian compensation. None of the customers buying the pastries will have as acute an understanding as the one who buys nothing, the one who gazes intently at the pastries and imagines what it would be to taste them. Satisfaction will be theirs; comprehension is the child's.

Stanza two introduces without transition a second metaphoric system, one based on military conflict and victory, and the rest of the poem follows out the argument within that framework. (The change between stanza one and two could be seen, in traditional terms, as a shifting of ground from a "feminine" to a "masculine" example: an instance of sweetness and nourishment, and then one of violent struggle.) Formally, the last two stanzas are a single sentence that completes the whole, so stanza one could be thought of as an introduction, announcing the theme at its most easily graspable and then going on to develop a more complex illustration of it. Whereas satisfaction and need are contrasted in stanza one, stanza two contrasts victory and defeat. The paradoxical assertion made in this second metaphoric passage is that the defeated understand what victory is better than the victors. Dickinson portrays one of the defeated—defeated and even dying—with special vividness and pathos, the soldier "On whose forbidden ear / The distant strains of triumph / Burst agonized and clear!" The last word is "clear," which is the only word (apart from connective words) repeated in the poem. Clarity of perception and understanding is a kind of "success," but it is purchased at the price of agony and defeat.

Since Dickinson was neither a soldier nor ever killed in battle, the emotional conviction of these lines must arise from some other experience of hers for which this part of the poem is only a figuration. What, then? First, we must return to the earlier observation that loss is connected with sexuality. In this light, the phrase "forbidden ear" will yield more than its surface meaning. Even the surface meaning of "forbidden" is strange in the present context: why is the soldier "forbidden"? At the level of fact, a defeated soldier is simply defeated, not banned or excluded. To attach notions of exclusion to a part of the anatomy associated with receptivity, is to touch on the male-female contrast implicit in losses of many kinds; but we need to see how it functions with other figurations in the poem. Experienced readers of Dickinson will know to prefer a multiple to a single interpretation. The terms of the metaphor can direct us to all sorts of triumphs and limitations, including sexual bliss that is merely overheard by one deprived of it, or, on quite another plane, recognition as a poet. The reference to the soldier's "ear" and to the music of triumph rather than to, for example, the soldier's arm or his weapons, should lead us in that direction.

This poem was one of the half dozen actually published during Dickinson's lifetime, and the only one that appeared in a book. The anthology that presented it was titled *A Masque for Poets,* published in a venture called the No Name series, in which poems were published anonymously. It was only after Helen Fiske Jackson, a literary friend of Dickinson's, urged her to let the poem be included that Dickinson gave her reluctant consent. And of course whatever recognition might have come her way for this one poem was effectively sabotaged by the anonymity and implicitly inferior rank that went with the No Name series. For all real purposes, Dickinson remained an unpublished poet. Invoking the axiom of compensation, however, one could say that publication and fame bring disadvantages, just as remaining unpublished brings advantages. Dickinson wrote a well-known poem *against* publication (numbered 709), calling it "the Auction of the Mind of Man."

> *Publication—is the Auction*
> *Of the Mind of Man—*
> *Poverty—be justifying*
> *For so foul a thing*
>
> *Possibly—but We—would rather*
> *From Our Garret go*
> *White—Unto the White Creator—*
> *Than invest—Our Snow—*
>
> *Thought belong to Him who gave it—*
> *Then—to Him Who bear*
> *Its Corporeal illustration—Sell*
> *The Royal Air—*

In the Parcel—Be the Merchant
Of the Heavenly Grace—
But reduce no Human Spirit
To Disgrace of Price—

It's interesting to see that Dickinson connects the wearing of white with *not* being published, as though publication were a kind of besmirching, a loss of purity or virginity. Yet Dickinson wanted readers and not just the immediate audience of those to whom poems were vouchsafed during her lifetime along with a present of bread or fruit preserves. Otherwise she would not have taken the trouble to store away her work so carefully in little bound fascicles to be discovered after her death. I believe she also wanted the consummation of a complete human love but, since that was not to be, devoted her poetic powers to discovering compensation for the circumstance. To go a step farther and say that she wanted the powers and perquisites that custom and law allowed only to men is not quite the same as saying she wanted to *be* a man. But by the axiom of compensation, she would have certainly understood what those powers and perquisites really were better than those who exercised them.

One of these of course is publication. Despite the exceptions of writers like Mrs. Hemans, the Brontës, Elizabeth Barrett Browning, and the American popular writer who published under the name of Fanny Fern, literature was considered an activity really only suitable for men, and the notion of the woman writer was as strange as the woman soldier. And yet Dickinson's protagonist in poem 67 is a soldier, and she is willing to take the risk of considering herself a poet here and in more than a thousand other works. One of the painful things to note about Dickinson's poems, however, is that the poems almost never refer to their author with a feminine pronoun. Either they are written in the genderless first-person singular or plural, or, when written in the third-person typological mode, use male protagonists and masculine pronouns. "She" is used to designate other people or things, friends or imaginary characters, or personified natural creatures, but not the poet herself. The great exception is the poem "The Soul selects her own Society," and no doubt one of the reasons for the poem's special power is the complex of feeling released for Dickinson in the use of the feminine pronoun in connection with one of her representative types.

In poem 67, though, the representative figure is a soldier, a man referred to as "he," even though representing the emotions of a woman author. Allowing for the possibility that the "success" described in the poem covers literary success, and defeat, the failure to win recognition, can we look for other possibilities as well? I can think of one that should be proposed, partly because it has never been suggested before and partly because it harmonizes the two distinct metaphoric systems of the poem. The kind of "success" suggested is the triumph of achieving religious faith. We know that Dickinson never counted herself among the faithful, or rather that she refused to join the Congregational church she attended, along with her family, from childhood until her thirtieth year. In Congregational practice of the time, one did not actually join the church until compelled to do so by inner prompting. And those who were not members were considered as not having attained salvation. Since the Great Awakening of the eighteenth century, there had been many waves of revivalism in New England, and some half dozen of these waves swept over Amherst during the 1840s and 1850s. Eventually all the Dickinsons except Emily joined the church, but she herself never marched to the front of the congregation to proclaim her acceptance of salvation and church membership. In her letters there is ample evidence that she regretted her inability to attach herself to a faith so many others around her managed with no difficulty, and her abstention must have puzzled everyone who knew her—all the more given that she so clearly possessed a fervent and meditative cast of mind. But she never joined the church and in 1860 stopped attending services altogether.

Poem 67 was probably written in 1859, at a time when America had just emerged from the Mexican War and was moving toward the Civil War. To say that the temper of the time was militaristic is easy enough, and so much is this the case that there's no surprise in noting that even styles of religious behavior were affected. The second half of the nineteenth century was to see the founding of the Salvation Army and the popularity of "The Battle Hymn of the Republic" and "Onward Christian Soldiers." Religious discourse and hymnody both used metaphors of battle, defeat, and victory to convey the urgency of individual salvation. In fact, this is the discourse that Dickinson adopts in the poem, very possibly as a way of describing her relationship to the problem of faith.

Beginning with stanza one and the discourse of consumption, we should pause at the word "nectar," which means more simply "a sweet drink." In classical mythology, nectar was the drink of the gods, able, along with ambrosia, to confer immortality on whoever partook of it. In Christian rite, the elements of the eucharist correspond to this divine food and drink and promise an analogous immortality. To be deprived of this food is to be utterly lost to eternal life.

With stanza two, the pouring out of grace and faith is rendered as a military victory. Apart from signifying the soldiers of an army, the word "Host" reminds us again of the eucharist as well as the phrase "the Heavenly Host," the collectivity of holy angels. Dickinson's military "Host" is taking the flag, a sign of victory that stands for individual proclamation of faith. If these new faithful wear purple, that is because purple is the liturgical color associated with penitence, as it is more generally associated with royalty. To win this victory, to take one's stand for a new spiritual condition, brings the reward of a crown of eternal life.

Dickinson's method of implying several meanings within one framework is very impressive here. Consider the concept of "immortality," which figures not only in religious discourse but also in secular contexts. Since classical times poets have seen their works as winning for them a kind of "immortality" that outlives the body and even whole historical epochs. This sort of immortality, however, depends on having readers, so poets who do not publish lose their chance for it. What they do not lose, according to the theory of compensation, is a deeper understanding of what literary immortality is.

By the same argument, the religious temperament who still cannot believe nevertheless attains a better understanding of faith than those who take it for granted. He or she is like the defeated, dying soldier who gains special insight into the nature of victory and public honor. He or she also understands immortality precisely because it has been denied. A further inference we could make is that Dickinson understood God all the better for never having attained the certainty of faith and dogma. Christianity is a religion centered on paradox ("He who humbles himself will be exalted"; "He who would save his life will lose it, while he who loses his life for my sake will have eternal life"; and so forth). Even these paradoxes hardly prepare us for the moment in the passion story when the Son of God himself, the second person of the Trinity, says, "My God, my God, why hast thou forsaken me?" But Dickinson would have understood these words very well indeed, to judge by the number of poems that deal with forsakenness. In that condition of forsakenness she stands very close to the Christ figure, closer no doubt than she might had she been willing to march with the victors down to the altar rail of the Amherst Congregational Church, where the patriarchal minister waited to receive them. The last line of the poem reminds us that agony brings its own kind of clarity, and surely this is the clarity that characterizes both the great artist and the true believer.

That, however, may not have been the general opinion in the Amherst of Dickinson's time. Dickinson may have felt that the exemplary writer, if she was to be heard, should be orthodoxly Christian. Male writers such as Emerson might be allowed his skepticism and transcendental mysteries. But the unorthodox female faced a great deal of opprobrium. Apart from the metaphysical dilemma of disbelief, there was also the practical problem that it left her with few subjects allowed as appropriate for a woman to write about. Dickinson wrote her "forbidden" poems but saw soon enough that there was little point in attempting to publish them in the climate of her day. To have imagined that there was a reason to save them, that another era would understand their worth, was part of her own idiosyncratic faith, which the century following her death has justified.

MARIANNE MOORE AND E. McKNIGHT KAUFFER: THEIR FRIENDSHIP, THEIR CONCERNS

GRACE SCHULMAN

In 1951, Marianne Moore observed that "a few real artists are alive today—Casals, Soledad, E. McKnight Kauffer, Hans Mardersteig, Alec Guinness, the Lippizan horsemen" (*Prose*).[1] The third artist, E[dward] McKnight Kauffer, was a trusted friend whose thematic concerns were remarkably similar to the poet's. Apart from the question of influence, which tends to be mysterious in aesthetic matters, their friendship is of interest in considering the poet's life and art.

Born in the Middle West within three years of one another (Kauffer in Great Falls, Montana, in 1890, and Moore in Kirkwood, Missouri, in 1887), the two artists grew to maturity in an America whose culture was overlayered with foreign influences. While Marianne Moore remained at home, Kauffer left America for Paris in 1913 and settled in England in 1914, where he remained until the outbreak of World War II. He returned to America and lived in New York until his death in 1954.

In New York in the 1940s he and Marianne Moore became close friends, meeting and corresponding frequently, finding stimulation in each other's thoughts about books, events, and mutual acquaintances. When the need arose, they supported one another in times of acute personal difficulties that were also times of spiritual renewal. Although both were stoic American Protestants who sought, in their art, to transform suffering, Kauffer experienced occasional waves of acute sadness that sapped his strength and halted his work. In a letter dated "Easter Day, 1954," Marianne Moore wrote to Kauffer of her belief, despite affliction and suffering, in "ana-stasis—the going forward."[2] Referring, as she frequently did, to Dr. Alvin E. Magary, pastor of her Lafayette Avenue Presbyterian Church in Brooklyn, she wrote:

> Dr. Magary reminded us that as these mortal bodies are wasting away, the inner spirit is renewed day by day; therefore we do not lose heart. Though afflicted, persecuted and struck down, there are some things that do not pass away. (Like John Fiske,) "we believe as a supreme act of faith in the reasonableness of God's work;" falteringly even doubtingly believe that this corruptible shall put on the in corruptible. So let not your heart be troubled, neither let it be afraid.

Earlier, in a letter dated November 23, 1952, she wrote to her friend of a sermon given by Dr. Magary and then reflected:

People's chief concern today is to be comfortable; whereas one can't live in these days, at ease and live a life that is right. Do you not feel that this is true? More than innocence is demanded of us. I feel very strongly that when we submit, accept hardship and don't insist on a triumph, life flowers—in some sense at least. As Dr. M. said sometime ago: spiritual triumphs are not attended by acclamation.

Well—there is no proof that one is right. We have the conviction, however, that one can live at peace in turmoil—like a certain pond fed by springs only seen in winter in the hard season. I hope I do not burden you by insisting on the anomaly of promise, in Hopelessness. Do think about it, Edward.

Both artists affirmed the wisdom of persistence despite obstacles; they believed that freedom is gained in the face of limitation, spiritual happiness found through material deprivation. "What is there / like fortitude!" is the exclamation in "Nevertheless," and "The Jerboa" is a small rat that "lives without water, has / happiness." In "What are Years?" we find one who, in his imprisonment rises

> *upon himself as*
> *the sea in a chasm, struggling to be*
> *free and unable to be,*
>   *in its surrendering*
> *finds its continuing.*
>   *(Poems,* 125, 13, 95)[3]

In 1949, she wrote about Kauffer's drawings for *Checkmate,* which had been commissioned by England's Royal Ballet Company, and about his illustrations for an edition of Edgar Allen Poe. She wrote: "E. McKnight Kauffer is a very great artist. Instinctiveness, imagination, and 'the sense of artistic difficulty' with him have interacted till we have an objectified logic of sensibility as inescapable as the colors refracted from a prism." In his work, she said

> Shadows are as arresting as objects; numerals and letters are so rare in themselves that opposing angles, contrasting sizes, and basic parallels, are of consummate elegance—the only kind of eloquence not intrusive. This language of blacks and grays is color in the sense that Chinese brush masterpieces are color. Literal color, moreover, rivals the acetylene blues of the cotinga and the tones in the beak of a toucan. We have here a poetry of synonyms like "the immediate meaning and possible meaning" of poetry, as where a Mexican hat has the form of a plane, the heroism of helplessness is symbolized by a Greek child, and "the medieval tower is half castle and half castle in the air." (*Prose,* 427)

Her comment shows her to be in the act of discovering a bridge between criteria for poetry and for the visual arts: "the language of blacks and grays," "a poetry of synonyms." Indeed, as we know from her *Collected Prose,* Moore was attracted to other visual artists of her time, such as Marsden Hartley, Georgia O'Keefe, and Alfeo Faggi, as well as to masters such as da Vinci, El Greco, Dürer, and Gargallo. And in her letter to Ezra Pound of January 9, 1919 (she in New York, he in London), she wrote of the importance of current art in America: "Over here it strikes me that there is more evidence of power among painters and sculptors than among writers."[4]

Her regard for the visual arts is evident throughout her poems, in which she finds creative work arising from a true response to nature and, conversely, nature assuming artistic forms. She depicts the observer recalling the perfection of cherished art masterpieces when he beholds creatures of the physical world. For example, she says of the plumet basilisk:

> *As by a Chinese brush, eight green*
> *bands are painted on*
> > *the tail—as piano keys are barred*
> > *by five black stripes across the white.*

And, in the climactic section of "The Paper Nautilus," classic sculpture is invoked. Just before we learn that the relationship between the sea animal and her young demonstrates that love "is the only fortress / strong enough to trust to," the eggs coming from the shell are seen

> *leaving its wasp-nest flaws*
> *of white on white, and close-*
>
> *laid Ionic chiton-folds*
> *like the lines in the mane of*
> *a Parthenon horse ...*
> > *(Poems, 22, 122)*

In her poetry, animals are exemplary beings, their nobility and heroism models for humankind, and the similes for art objects or processes are exalted in like manner: the Chinese brush design (one of many tributes to Chinese art in her poems)[5] is likened to the basilisk's intricate pattern; the eggs of the nautilus, which are admired for their beauty and strength, recall the Parthenon horse.

In their works, Moore and Kauffer shared traits fundamental to their primary effects. Creating art of common lives and of knowledge, both were eclectics of subject matter, insisting on the artist's freedom to contemplate any information without diminished energy. The two craftsmen extended the range of art by transmuting material that is, essentially, banal: "here if nowhere else in the world, 'street art' is art," Moore wrote in her note on Kauffer's drawings, and the observation applies to his images of umbrellas, winter coats, telephones, and traffic signals as well as to her "American menagerie of styles" and "glass that will bend" ("An Octopus"), her "workless clocks" ("Four Quartz Crystal Clocks"), her icosasphere.

Both artists depicted living things with exactitude, building their effects on a foundation of precise, factual information. In Moore's poetry, both the subject—a desert rat, an Indian Buffalo, a sparrow-camel—and its perceiver are seen from all sides. In Kauffer's drawings and posters the concrete detail evokes a living world. For example, the human hand is shown, splayed, to create comedy, in a poster for a production of Leonid Andreyev's "He Who Gets Slapped." Elsewhere, the hand is used to indicate strength, as in a poster of seamen's hands grasping rope; authority, as in the display of a hand arresting traffic, its movement captured by the use of three colors; and a meeting between humanity and technology, as in the depiction of a hand holding a telephone receiver.

If precision was their common aim, however, it was counterbalanced by their faith in the imagination's power to transform reality, for they distilled their art from the interaction of the mind with commonplace objects. One book Moore borrowed from Kauffer and discussed with him was the New Directions edition of Paul Valéry's *Selected Writings,* containing an essay that Kauffer had marked: "Fragments from 'Introduction to the Method of Leonardo da Vinci.'" In this piece, Valéry wrote that the mind of the artist, seeking exactitude, groups perceptions around an object and projects a structure of multiple properties. This kind of transmutation is at the heart of the work of both Kauffer and Moore. "What is more precise than precision? Illusion," the poet wrote (*Poems,* 151), and the paradox illuminates their common tendency to depict real things under the changing, enchanted gaze of the mind's eye. In two of Kauffer's posters, "The Tower of London" is presented as a structure, half real and half allegorical; his country family in "Whitsuntide Holiday" are solid common people and angels.

So, too, Marianne Moore's concrete details are transformed under inquisitive scrutiny. As she wrote of Kauffer's art, she knows well "the immediate meaning and the possible meaning of poetry." In "An Octopus," the forms of elements change under inquisitive scrutiny: as the eye moves over it, the mountain transforms its animals and vegetation and is transformed by them. The mountain changes its foliage to the extent that trees, hardly recognizable, resemble "dustbrushes," their branches shrinking in trying to escape "from the hard mountain 'planed by ice and polished by the wind.'" Bears are "inspecting unexpectedly / ant-hills and berry bushes" while their den is "concealed in the confusion / of 'blue-forests thrown together with marble and jasper and agate'" and a goat's eye is "fixed on the waterfall which never seems to fall." Human visitors, eager to see everything, see nothing: the mountains unchangeable in the face of change and remote from conventional perception (*Poems,* 71, 72, 75).

Moore's note on Kauffer's drawings incorporates the rhythms and some language of her poems: "'What is to be feared more than death,' the man asked; the sage replied 'Disillusion.' Here, actually, we have a product in which unfalsified impulse safeguards illusion" (*Prose,* 427). For both, illusion was the life-apprehending quality of art; both believed in the power of the artist to effect transformation—image into symbol, image into another image—paradoxically by the ruse of exactitude. Thus, we have "The Pangolin," Moore's poem in which the anteater of the title, which is created in minute detail, affords the means by which the poet works through to a new definition of man.

For both artists, the employment of technical means to transform the raw material is a result of their simultaneous awareness and control of life's terrors. Both concentrated on the mathematic regularities in man-made enterprises as well as in nature. Geometric shapes were organizing principles of Kauffer's perception, as one of his notebook observations indicates: "Designing is order—the cube—the circle—the triangle all parts of equipment—and symbols of order."[6] In a 1933 poster that advertises Shell Oil, he conveys the certainty of the product by presenting an unbreakable chain of elongated links. His use of the triangle and the circle serve the precision and naturalness of his famous poster, "The Early Bird," which appeared in London's *Daily*

Herald in 1919 (see Fig. 1). Drafts of the painting are in the Museum of Modern Art in New York and in the Victoria and Albert Museum in London. The painting's central image is an explosion of birds in flight, their unruliness restrained by the orderly geometric pattern they assume.

Mathematic regularity was compelling to Marianne Moore, as well. At the outset of "The Icosasphere," a tribute to a twenty-faced structure built by an engineer, she quotes Kauffer's observation about geometry in nature:

> *"In Buckinghamshire hedgerows*
> *the birds nesting in the merged green density*
> *weave little bits of string and moths and*
> *feathers and thistledown*
> *in parabolic curves."*

In contrast to the birds' accomplishment in precision is the icosasphere's gift of "steel-cutting at its summit of economy, / since twenty triangles conjoined, can wrap one / ball or double-rounded shell . . ." (*Poems*, 143).

Apart from the poet's fascination with geometric order, as expressed in poems such as this and "Four Quartz Crystal Clocks," there is an affinity for symmetry, pattern, and form throughout her work. We find it in her imagery, as of the pangolin's "scale / lapping scale with spruce-cone regularity" (*Poems*, 117), in her repeated stanza forms, and, more importantly, in the balanced images, sonic concurrences, and grammatical tensions the poet uses as scaffolding for her verse.[7] For example, in the three-part sequence originally titled "Part of a Novel, Part of a Poem, Part of a Play" and appearing in *Complete Poems* as "The Steeple-Jack," "The Student," and "The Hero," recurrent words such as "danger," "hope," "see," "hero," bind the parts together. Further, recurrent *ee* and *o* sounds in the first and last poems point up the key words of "The Hero," hero and see. Her patterning emphasizes the importance of perception, directing the reader to the lines "study is beset with / dangers" (*Poems*, 101–102).

Related to their interest in mathematic accuracy was their curiosity about machines and their mutual desire to know how things were made. However intrigued they were about technology, though, their delight in machines had the converse expression of suspicion and even fear. Kauffer indicated his attraction to machines in designs such as "El Progreso," a bale label illustration, in which he approximates the speed and power of a railway train. His "Metropolis" (1926), now lodged at the Museum of Modern Art, is a painting that embodies a "waste land" of skyscrapers and industrial wheels. Partially obscured by the wheels, pitifully subjugated men walk like robots, their heads bowed. The theme is common to the visual arts and to poetry of the 1920s. Kauffer's bowed citizens resemble Eliot's wretched crowds in *The Waste Land* and Williams' human automatons in *Paterson*.

Moore responded to that theme, writing in "People's Surroundings" of "the vast indestructible necropolis / of composite Yawman-Erbe separable units," and of "New York / the savage's romance, / accreted where we need the space for commerce" (*Poems*, 55, 54). In her later poems that deal with modern technology, such as "The Icosasphere," "Four Quartz Crystal Clocks," "The Staff of Aesculapius," the prevailing tone combines wonder with a persistent inquisitive investigation into how structures

Figure 1. E. McKnight Kauffer. *The Early Bird,* 1919. Lithograph.

are built and how scientific experiments are carried out. The same tone characterizes "A Carriage from Sweden," which concerns no modern device but rather "this country cart / that inner happiness made art" (*Poems,* 131).

To be sure, the great range of emotion in her work includes fear, but it is fear of a modern reality so murky as to resist investigation. In "The Steeple-Jack," for example, life's disorders overwhelm the notion of a placid landscape as an orderly scene changes to disorder and the speaker finds himself in spontaneous disarray. The sudden shift from calm to storm is accompanied by images of "seeing," which are emphasized by assonance. The speaker is a perceiver, attempting to understand the nature of the disorder and to impose the familiar on the hazardous unknown. And in "Marriage," the poet uses language that captures an irrational current of the mind in passages conveying the destruction of reason by passion.

These contrasts of harmony and chaos are found in Kauffer's greatest work. In "Route 160, Reigate," Kauffer presents a row of black gnarled trees backed by straight trees in a brilliant unearthly red color. The gnarled and the straight, the black and the red, combine to give an effect that is all the more strange for its partial adherence to naturalness.[8] In his book-jacket illustration for *Winds,* by St.-John Perse, Kauffer employs geometrically neat lettering, but places near the title a jagged line that extends off the page. It is the precision and, conversely, the deceptively unruly view of life, coexistent in the mind, that the two artists confronted in their major achievements. Theirs was a combined adventurousness and control that brought curiosity to staggering dangers and risks.

NOTES

All previously unpublished material by Marianne Moore is printed with the permission of Clive E. Driver, literary executor of the estate of Marianne C. Moore.

1. *The Complete Prose of Marianne Moore,* ed. by Patricia C. Willis (New York: Viking, 1986), p. 648. This volume is abbreviated *Prose.*

2. The originals of the letters quoted here are in my possession; copies are in the Rosenbach Museum and Library.

3. *The Complete Poems of Marianne Moore* (New York: Macmillan and Viking, 1981). This volume is abbreviated *Poems.*

4. Charles Tomlinson, ed., *Marianne Moore: A Collection of Critical Essays,* Twentieth Century Views (Englewood Cliffs, N.J.: Prentice-Hall, 1969), p. 17.

5. Bonnie Costello devotes a chapter to Moore and the visual arts in *Marianne Moore: Imaginary Possessions* (Cambridge, Mass.: Harvard University Press, 1981).

6. The quotation is from the late E. McKnight Kauffer's notebooks, in my possession. They were given to me by the artist.

7. A fuller discussion of the poet's rhythmic patterning is found in "The Spoken Art of Marianne Moore" chapter in my book, *Marianne Moore: The Poetry of Engagement* (Urbana: University of Illinois Press, 1986).

8. E. McKnight Kauffer's "Reigate" (1915) can be found at the Victoria and Albert Museum, London.

A HYMN OF NON-ATTAINMENT:
DINO CAMPANA

JONATHAN GALASSI

Anyone who drives from Faenza to Florence—through the rich, flat farms of Romagna up into the wooded foothills of the Apennines which form a natural barrier with Tuscany, then across the stony yellow pastureland atop the old mountains themselves and down on into the valley of the Arno—will experience an essential component of Dino Campana's poetry. He was born in Marradi, a small town wedged into the narrow valley of the Lamone River on the Faenza side of the divide (though the town belongs legally to the province of Florence). An incessant wanderer all his adult life, he made long walking trips in the historic and holy territory of the Casentino, the shell of mountains stretching north and west of Arezzo where the Arno begins. These places, along with the ancient cities of northern Italy—Florence, Bologna, Faenza, Genoa—are evoked with great sensual immediacy in the "musical, colored poetry" that constitutes one of the most radical and pure moments in modern Italian literature. In Campana's work, the primal elements of his world—rock, wind, water, sky, sun, heat, night and its lights, as well as women, song, and the greatest element of all, the immense Mediterranean in which everything else is formed and bathed—endlessly combine, dissolve, and reunite in the stream of patterns formed by his restless inspiration.

Campana is a unique case in Italian poetry, comparable in some ways to what Rimbaud is for the French or Hart Crane for our own tradition. As the critic Emilio Cecchi wrote, he "passed like a comet" across the firmament of Italian letters, leaving it astonished, though finally more or less unchanged, so idiosyncratic and eccentric was his contribution. Campana appeared in the midst of the great political, social, and cultural turmoil that the turn of the century was in Italy and throughout Europe, and in his own peculiar way he absorbed and expressed the multifarious influences of that moment, including symbolism, the Italian Twilight, and futurism, as well as Walt Whitman, Edgar Allan Poe, and Nietzsche. Out of all this, and from his own personal turbulence, he forged a powerful obsessive song, a violent pure poetry of undirected and thus unsatisfiable desire and need, which has a visionary, even hallucinatory intensity. The continuous, almost undifferentiated paean-lament that runs through the *Canti orfici* and much of the rest of his work, is certainly the harshest and most relentless lyric utterance in the history of a highly rationalized and convention-bound tradition. Eugenio Montale, the greatest twentieth-century continuator and interpreter of this tradition, whose own radicalism was much more internal and rationalized, liked to repeat the dictum of the baroque Jesuit poet Tommaso Ceva that poetry is "a dream dreamed in the presence of reason." But this balance, so strongly adhered to in Italian letters, is wildly off in Campana. For him the dream, the nightmare is virtually everything.

Campana's poems are not really conventionally finished lyrics at all. At their most concise they are more like lyric fragments; more often, they are prose meditations or journal entries. They can be repetitive, obscure, contradictory, sometimes virtually inarticulate. Yet their very failure to communicate is tremendously effective in conveying the erotic and emotional blockage, the non-attainment, that is the true burden of Campana's work. Campana's failure to express is in a way the most expressive, the most universal thing about him. His poetry seems almost involuntary, and this may explain why his work has left so few obvious traces. Writing of this urgency is impossible to imitate.

The futurists, too, had experimented, more willfully and manipulatively, with obscurity and the irrational, and Campana clearly learned from their work, but he took pains to dissociate himself from them. To him the futurists were "empty," and their poetry was lacking in genuineness. As he wrote to Bino Binazzi, who was preparing the second edition of the *Canti orfici* in 1928: "Every now and then I wrote bizarre poems but I was not a futurist. Futurist free verse is false, it is not harmonic. It is an improvisation without color or harmony. I was making a little art."

Campana's personal history is tragic. He was born in Marradi on August 20, 1885. His father was the principal of the local elementary school. His mother, who came from a well-to-do family, was, according to I. L. Salomon,[1] "an eccentric" who "used to wander up into the hills fingering her rosary, frequently forgetting to prepare dinner for her husband and children." Campana's emotional difficulties first became apparent in 1900, when, as his father later told one of his doctors, the adolescent demonstrated "a brutal, unhealthy impulsivity in the family, especially toward his mother."[2] It was at this point, too, that his wandering began. "I travelled a great deal," he wrote to Binazzi. "I was urged on by a kind of mania for wandering. A sort of instability forced me to change continually. . . . From the age of fifteen, a powerful nervousness took hold of me, and I couldn't live anywhere." In 1902, after studying intermittently in Turin and Carmagnola, he returned to Marradi where he wrote his first poems, heavily influenced by the nineteenth-century classical master Carducci. In 1904, at the suggestion of a family friend who was the pharmacist in Marradi, he enrolled as a chemistry student at the University of Bologna. ("I studied chemistry by mistake and understood nothing about it. . . . I should have studied literature. If I had studied literature, I could have lived. Literature was a more balanced thing, the subject pleased me, I could have earned a living and straightened myself out. I didn't understand chemistry at all, and so I gave myself up to the void.")

Campana's restlessness sent him from school to school. In 1905 he was studying pharmaceutical chemistry in Florence. The next year, he took up the same subject in Bologna and was also confined for the first time in an asylum, at Imola. The following year he traveled to Argentina, where he tried working at an incredible array of jobs: "I played the triangle in the Argentine Navy. I was a porter in Buenos Aires." He was also a "gaucho, a collier, a miner, a policeman, a gypsy, . . . a juggler, the manager of a rifle range, an accordian player . . . a stoker on commercial ships." In 1910, after returning to Marradi via Odessa, where he sold pinwheels in a fair, and Belgium, where he was jailed in Brussels and confined in a sanatorium at Tournai, he embarked on a pilgrimage to the ancient Franciscan monastery at La Verna, the subject of the journal that makes up a major part of the *Canti orfici*. He published a few poems in student magazines in Bologna in 1912 and, under the influence of futurism and Rimbaud, began to write the *Canti orfici* in Marradi.

The manuscript was finished in the fall of 1913, and in December Campana walked the forty miles to Florence, where he delivered his work to Giovanni Papini and Ardengo Soffici, editors of the influential futurist-oriented literary review *Lacerba*. Soffici lost the manuscript, however, and Campana was forced to reconstruct it from memory. He and a printer friend published it together in Marradi in 1914, with subtitle (in German) "The Tragedy of the Last German in Italy," and a dedication to "Wilhelm II, emperor of the Germans," which Campana told Soffici was aimed at the mindless patriotism of "those idiots in Marradi." He sold the book himself in the literary cafés, at the Paszkowski and the Giubbe Rosse in Florence, and the San Pietro in Bologna. It was reported that he picked fights with other writers and tore out those pages of his book which he felt the purchaser was not worthy to receive, but Campana denied this to Binazzi: "A journalist's invention. If I sold the book it was because I was poor."

In 1915, after publishing his poem "Toscanità" in the famous review *Riviera ligure,* he went to work in Geneva but was eventually returned home, and when he tried to enlist in the military he was committed to a sanatorium. The pattern of alternating wandering and confinement continued, intensified. In the summer of 1916, he met and fell in love with the writer Sibilla Aleramo, author of the renowned feminist novel *Una donna* (*A Woman*), but their relationship lasted only a few months. Its demise seems to mark the end of Campana's attempt to live in the world.

Early in 1918, he was permanently admitted to the psychiatric hospital of Castel Pulci near Badia a Settimo, just west of Florence. Here, he wrote Binazzi ten years later, "I am very well off and I hope not to leave. . . . Who can say which among us all is crazy? But I am crazy! I have days of lucidity and days I cannot remember. I had a nervousness that was terribly profound and I couldn't live in any way. I was ill, certainly, exhausted in such a way that I was useless to society. . . . I live quietly. . . . I had some art but no longer do."

Campana died of septicemia at Castel Pulci on March 1, 1932. He was forty-six. He is buried in the church at Badia a Settimo.

Campana's critical fate in Italy, both during his lifetime and afterward, is discussed in Montale's 1942 essay about him. My concern here is to try to say something about why this poetry is of interest today to readers from a very different tradition. What is there in Campana that comes across successfully into English?

To a reader who comes to Campana's work fresh it seems to me that what stands out above all is its helpless obsessiveness, its evasive centering on the sexual act and on the strangeness, the irreducible otherness of woman, seen not as another kind of human but as an almost monolithic fact of nature. There are no characters other than the perceiving "I" in Campana, only apparitions, figures, chimaeras, all of them female. "The Night" is the only poem which comes close to describing an actual encounter, with an "older woman" or "serving girl." Elsewhere, woman becomes a generalized metaphor for the dazzlingly enigmatic world: "the strong-smelling streets where women sang in the hot weather." The heat, the smell, the street, the women, their song—all are part of the otherness that Campana's poem is constantly trying to embrace and encompass (and perhaps extinguish) in a hymn of endlessly unfulfilled attraction:

> O woman I've dreamed over, woman adored, strong-minded woman, your profile ennobled by a memory of Byzantine stillness, noble and mythic head in strong, smooth lines gilded by the enigma of sphinxes: twilit eyes in a landscape of towers dreamed there on the banks of the war-torn plain, on the banks of rivers drunk down by the savage earth there where Francesca's cry is lost forever: from my childhood a liturgical voice over and over intoned in prayer slowly and movingly: and you from that rhythm sacred to me and much moved arose already restless with vast plains, with distant miraculous destinies: my hope reawakens on the endlessness of the plain or the sea when I feel a breath of grace flutter: nobility incarnate and golden, golden depth of your eyes: huntress, lover, mystic, benign in human nobility ancient Romagna
> —"La Verna" translated by Charles Wright

Campana's is an atmosphere of heat and fire, of ancient primordialness. Aspects of symbolist painting come to mind—the eerie visionary stillness of Redon, the sexual rapacity of Khnopff, the atmospheric luminescence and sense of enclosure of Moreau. Yet there is also a sense of Mediterranean openness and nature, a feeling of location which is missing in these northern artists. Much as the world is Other, Campana's native place in it is very strongly felt. As with so many poets and artists of his culture, Campana's landscape is so much a part of his understanding of his character that it comes to represent his own state of mind.

This deep rootedness, in a congenitally restless temperament like Campana's, may be one of the things that it is hardest for Americans to understand. Certainly his given vocabulary, the fund of imagery and experience on which he draws, is not familiar to us. The mythic, ancient, blood-ridden Mediterranean culture to which his title refers; the ascetic, penitential Catholicism of Andrea del Castagno and La Verna; the classic *toscanità* or Tuscanness that is Campana's ground and heritage, "bare and elegant, simple and austere"—all of this we can at best appreciate rationally, not feel. Campana's understanding of the ancientness of his place and culture is something no non-European can fathom about Europe. Yet the strangeness at the heart of this strangeness, the sense of personal isolation, of sexual need, of physical and metaphysical displacement, are deeply familiar. They have affinities with what we can feel in different, perhaps less desperate form in the work of Rimbaud and Eliot, Kafka and Montale, Celan and Artaud.

Campana's portrayal of himself as a lone traveler in a land of eerie Leonardine lakes and caves and De Chirican squares, his "mystic nightmare of chaos," his sense of himself as both Orphic Priest-perpetrator and Orphic/Christian victim[3]—is a distilled, intensified version of modern existential anxiousness. And his artfully raw and eerily beautiful presentation of his dislocation answers to our psychologically overeducated, even prurient hunger for "real" data, for the pure, unadulterated, uncleaned-up expression of feeling.

Campana's vision is extreme in a way that we have come to identify as authentic. The ecstatic pressure of his language, its relentless, manic lyricism, its violent beauty, its verging on incoherence, are the essence of its attraction for a readership that has only really begun to absorb the "de-civilizing" displacement that European modernism, and surrealism in particular, has wreaked on the empirical Anglo-American tradition. Yet unlike so much in this new tradition (including the futurism he rejected) Campana's work has the force of necessity behind it. Its strangeness is truly, irreducibly strange.

Campana's obscurity, when he is obscure, is in homage to his own peculiar perception of what surrounds him. It is impossible for him to "understand" and thus codify and denature the Other. Instead, naked and alone, he confronts the irreducible difference, the final unknowability, of what is out there. And we, from within the thin protective shell of our constructed culture, respond with amazement to his courage in facing and identifying what seems, on closer inspection, to be some previously hidden part of ourselves.

NOTES

1. In the introduction to his translation of Campana, *Orphic Songs* (New York: October House, 1968).

2. This remark and all quotations from Campana himself are drawn from the biographical note by Enrico Falqui in the 1966 edition of the *Canti orfici e altri scritti* (Firenze: Vallecchi).

3. The *Canti orfici* end with this misquotation from Whitman's *Song of Myself:* "They were all torn and cover'd with the boy's blood."

ON BONNEFOY

RACHEL HADAS

The poetry of Yves Bonnefoy offers both the pared-down exclusiveness of lyric and the reassuring rhythms of what feels like narrative. Bonnefoy condenses his world to a few elements—stone, tree, sill, shoulder— and then works artful variations on those essences. His poems are thus both generous and stingy, repetitious and spare. They recall the hushed rhapsodies of Stevens and— strongly at times—the mythical voyages and Mediterranean aridity of Seferis. Finally, though, Bonnefoy—simultaneously somber, lush, and disembodied—is a law unto himself.

> *Your leg, deepest night,*
> *Your breasts, bound,*
> *So black, have I lost my eyes,*
> *My nerves of agonized seeing*
> *In this darkness harsher than stone,*
> *O my love?*
> *("A Stone," 25)*

What follows is not an attempt to analyze frequently hermetic work that has already been artfully anatomized by students of Bonnefoy. Rather, this is a series of brief appreciations of, and meditations on, elements in Bonnefoy's work that have struck one reader. The translations quoted are all from Richard Pevear's excellent volume, *Yves Bonnefoy: Poems 1959–1975* (New York: Vintage, 1985).

HIS COLORS

Poets often spend quantities of words trying to fix what they see, striving to find the right adjective or simile to capture a gesture or a scene. Bonnefoy works the other way, from inside out. Starting from a kind of eternity (an infinite series of moments; a gesture indefinitely suspended or repeated), he proceeds to give us selected details. What Bonnefoy refuses to do is painstakingly to depict a bush, lizard, or pebble. He is drawn to intermediate conditions and places, as the title of his 1975 collection *The Lure of the Threshold* indicates: thresholds between night and dawn, or sleep and waking, as well as between indoors and outdoors.

> *When the wide winds cross*
> *The threshold where nothing sings or shows.*
>
> *It is John and Joan and the plaster of day*
> *Falls from their gray faces and I see again*
> *The window of long past summers. Do you remember?*
> *Brightest in the distance, the arch, child of shadows.*
> *("John and Joan," 25)*

Is it a coincidence that phenomenological criticism like Gaston Bachelard's *The Poetics of Space* might almost have been written with Bonnefoy in mind?

Bonnefoy doesn't care about capturing the precise hue of a dawn sky, a moonlit field. Like certain painters, he seems to see in color rather than identifying and assigning colors to the appropriate object. We might say that his vision has a palette, and that palette has access to language; but the actual vocabulary of Bonnefoy's color terms is obsessively limited. What we perceive or imagine as we read is as vivid, yet as abstract, as the word paintings of another Mediterranean poet, Homer, whose *xanthos*, *oinops*, and *glaukos* do not convey the universal primary colors.

If there is such a thing. What is a universal color, anyway? Pevear translates Bonnefoy's ubiquitous *rouge* as red, but the word is repeated so often that it seems a leitmotif, then a nonsense syllable, and finally a covering, a layer that conceals rather than reveals. Perhaps for this last reason, "red" is often used in connection with a wrapping, a cloth.

> *The ship of one summer, and you*
> *As if at the bow, in the fullness of time,*
> *Unfolding painted cloths, talking softly.*
> *("The Summer's Night," 3)*
>
> *In its chests the dream has folded*
> *Its painted cloths away,*
> *And the shadow of this face stained*
> *With the red clay of the dead.*
> *("The Garden," 11)*
>
> *Further than the star*
> *In what is,*
> *The child who bears the world*
> *Bathes simply.*
> *It is night still, but he*
> *Is of two colors,*
> *A blue, beginning to mix*
> *With the green of the treetops,*
> *As a fire grows lighter*
> *Among fruits*
>
> *And a red like the heavy*
> *Painted cloths*

> The Egyptian girl, the unawakened,
> Had washed at night in the river . . .
> ("Two Colors," 93)

> O dreams, fine children
> In the light
> Of torn dresses,
> Of painted shoulders.

> "Since life has no meaning,"
> Breathes the voice,
> It's enough if we paint
> Our bodies with red clouds . . .
> ("The Clouds," 141)

No matter how often I read Bonnefoy, the separate poems blur and merge into one another. The oeuvre can be read, not for memorable individual poems, but as one looks at certain large paintings, following shapes and tracing motifs, pleased to encounter familiar patterns but never coming to depend upon a particular action, a recognizable feature, a human scene. Bonnefoy manages to avoid the trap into which poets often fall when they attempt to depict a scene meticulously using the hopelessly inadequate medium of language, so that the reader may think in frustration that the old saw about one picture's being worth a thousand words is only too true.[1] Sticking close to the poetic equivalent of nonrepresentational painting (though with plenty of recognizable motifs), Bonnefoy doesn't arouse expectations he fails to fulfill; plot, incident, portraiture. One reads him in a spirit of alert serenity.

HIS ESSENCES

The archetypal character of Bonnefoy's poetry is hard to convey except through quotation; but it cannot be too strongly stressed. Writing of biblical imagery in literature, Northrop Frye has declared that every tree (for example) in Western poetry is a version of *the* tree, the ancestor of all other trees, from which Adam and Eve picked the apple. Thus in some sense, according to Frye, all poetic trees are the same, or "of many one," in the phrase Wordsworth applies to a memorable tree in the immortality ode. Indeed, this tree, and the accompanying "field that I have looked upon," are emblematic of lost paradises, for "both of them speak of something that is gone." Nevertheless, Frye's claim that *all* poetic trees are "of many one" seems too broad to be very meaningful.

But the "of many one" resonance does seem remarkably appropriate to Bonnefoy's imagery—to those few repeated elements that gain power from recurrence and are not tied to a camera's-eye view. Bonnefoy isn't concerned with the appearance or species of a tree, with what his favorite poet, Shakespeare, has called "a local habitation and a name." What Bonnefoy most urgently conveys, instead, is the universal, mythical quality of tree, ship, or sky—a quality harder to communicate than color or girth.

> *We no longer need*
> *Harrowing images in order to love.*
> *That tree over there is enough for us, loosed*
> *From itself by light, knowing nothing*
> *But the almost uttered name of an almost incarnate god.*
>
> *And this high land burnt by the One in its nearness,*
>
> *And this white-washed wall that simple time*
> *Touches with its hands that know no sadness*
> *And have made their measure.*
> *("The Dialogue of Anguish and Desire," 53)*

How does such communication work, then? Partly the grave simplicity of Bonnefoy's diction, the repetitious cadences of his verses, create a gravity approximating the feel of biblical poetry, with its emphasis on essences rather than appearances.

> *Yes, I the stones of evening, light-struck,*
> *Consent.*
>
> *Yes, I the pool*
> *Wider than the sky, the child*
> *Stirring up its mud, the iris*
> *In the restless, unmemoried reflections*
> *Of the water, consent.*
>
> *And I the fire,*
> *The pupil of the fire's eye, in the smoke*
> *Of grass and centuries, consent.*
> *("The Earth," 125)*

And partly the sense of archetype is a reflection and expression of Bonnefoy's "of many one" vision—a vision in which each earthly phenomenon functions as a Platonic reflection of an eternal and ideal reality. For this reason the voice of Bonnefoy's poems, at once impersonal and authoritative, seems to be reaching the reader's listening ear from an immense distance. It's a matter, that is, of not just imagery but also tone. Rimbaud's apparently archetypal lines "Si j'ai du goût, ce n'est guères / Que pour la terre et les pierres" sound positively confessional, even sensational, by comparison.

For some of Bonnefoy's readers—possibly English-speaking ones in particular—the vatic voice will sound inflated; the distance will be too great. There exists these days an unformulated but strong aesthetic of the poem as either anecdote or photograph. Pace and punchline in the former, extreme precision in the latter—these were, and are, the technical effects often successfully striven for by poets as diverse, skilled, and original as the late Elizabeth Bishop and Philip Larkin, not to mention a swarm of lesser writers following what began to be felt as the fashion. Judged by such poetic standards, Bonnefoy seems fuzzy, vague, and ponderous—as indeed he can occasionally be. But it must be remembered that he is working in a tradition of prophecy. His poetry is impersonal because Bonnefoy has no use for the persona. He is a listening ear, a writing hand (this may account for his lack of interest in the exact look of the things of this earth, no matter how beloved); his task is to record the speech of the elements, speech which sometimes takes the form of dialogue and at other times sounds like dream murmurings.

> *O fragile country,*
> *Like the flame of a lamp carried out-of-doors,*
> *Sleep being close in the world's sap,*
> *Simple the beating of the shared soul.*
>
> *You too love the moment when the light of lamps*
> *Fades and dreams into daylight.*
> *You know it's the darkness of your own heart healing,*
> *The boat that reaches shore and falls.*
> ("The Tree, The Lamp," 35)

The notion of the poet listening to rather than gazing at his world is beautifully exemplified in Leopardi's "The Infinite," where "this lonely hill, this hedge"—sights of the phenomenal world—give way as the poem gathers force to the perceptions of the "inward mind." These perceptions finally take the form not of visions seen but of language heard:

> *and I recall the eternal seasons dead*
> *and all the living seasons of our time*
> *whose speech is at my ear.*
> *(translated by Irma Brandeis)*

In Bonnefoy, too, the world is often distilled to a voice (or sometimes, as we'll see, a text). Hence rather than arriving at clearly framed visual closures, Bonnefoy's poems frequently seem to die out like a receding voice. Often the reader, not the poem, actually withdraws. Bonnefoy's poems are lavish with elliptical interludes (. . . . . . .), and these remind me of cicadas shrilling away on a sunbaked, otherwise silent southern hillside. The hypnotic sound seems to fill both time and space; but when one finally, reluctantly gets up and dizzily walks into the shade, the chorus of shrill clicking dies away.

HIS STORY

Bonnefoy's effects are abstract, yet he almost always writes about things we *think* we can visualize. Partly as a result of his stubbornly concrete language, the story one is tempted to extract from Bonnefoy's work is—in words reminiscent of the "of many one" idea—"one story and one story only" (this phrase is the opening of Robert Graves' poem "To Juan at the Winter Solstice"). This story seems almost hieroglyphic in its reliance on substantives—ideogrammatic, perhaps, in a truer sense than Pound's reticulation of images and incidents. Verbs, striking though they can be in Bonnefoy's lexicon, are relatively unimportant in his poems, often weakened into participles and sometimes missing entirely. There's little direct action.

(The horn of plenty with its red fruit
In the turning sun. And the bee-like humming
Of a sweet, impure eternity over
The meadow, so near and still so burning.)
                ("The Bee, Color," 39)

Streaks of blue and black.
Furrows swerving toward the foot of the sky.
The bed, wide and broken like a flooded river.
  ("Evening," 39)

         Hour
Cut off from the sum, now.
Presence
Undeceived by death. Bulb
That kneels in silence
And burns
Deflected, shaken
By the summitless night.
        ("The Lure of the Threshold," 85)

    What are the constituents of this story? Without much confidence, I think I discern a quest, a landscape with a couple of houses, a dialogue, a love affair, a hymnlike incantation to a transcendent presence. There are beds, trees, stars, bodies, hours of the day or evening. There is even a markedly Proustian line (especially in French, where the opening word is *longtemps*), which turns out, if I'm not mistaken, to be the utterance of a stone. Looking at the entire lyric in question, we see how oddly scaled Bonnefoy's work can be: are these thirteen lines a miniature narrative or (Combray emerging from the tea cup) a fantasy, an improvised flourish or lyric loop that actually takes us nowhere?

Childhood was long by the grim wall and I was
The mind of winter, bending
Sadly, stubbornly, over an image,
Bitterly, over the reflection of another day.

Having desired nothing
So much as to help in the blending of two lights,
O memory, I was
Diurnal oil in its glass vessel
Crying its red soul to the long veins of the sky.

What will I have loved? The sea's foam
Above Trieste, when the gray
Of the sea of Trieste dazzled
The eyes of the erodible sphinx of the shores.
        ("A Stone," 27)

It might be rewarding to compare this mind of winter with a verbally identical creation in Stevens' "The Snow Man." Both poems (spoken by inhuman entities?) move from this winter mind into vacancy, Bonnefoy's "having desired nothing" and Stevens' "listener," who "nothing himself, beholds / Nothing that is not there and the nothing that is." Both poems seem to give by taking; denying incident or even substance beyond the ghostly "nothing that is" or the sea's foam, they still retain not only interest but tension and poignancy, tightening the screws of our metaphysical attention.

I've said that Bonnefoy's individual poems blur in the memory. More than that: one can read his work either backward or forward, dipping and skipping, and still get the same inimitable impression. This must mean that his story actually goes nowhere; that his work operates spatially like a painting and not in time like music or speech. Yet we get the feeling of an extended order, not what the analogy with painting might suggest—a snapshot or vignette. One of the greatest puzzles is how Bonnefoy manages to void the imagistic self-regard of much non-narrative poetry—the narcissism of pure looking. There's always an impatient pressure to transcend mere appearances.

> Unrevealed,
> Too vast, too mysterious for our steps,
> Let us only brush her dark shoulder
> And not disturb her who draws with calm breath
> From the earth's reserves of dream. Night come,
> Let us set down, simply, these stones
> Where we read the sign, by her barren side.
> ("The Scattered, The Indivisible," 163)

Part of what enables Bonnefoy to transcend the visible is his lavish use of apostrophe on a sublime scale. Few poets writing now make more effortless or appropriate use of what has been called the essential trope of lyric.[2]

> Waters of the sleeper, tree of absence, shoreless hours,
> In your eternity a night is ending.
> How shall we name this new day, my soul,
> This gentle glowing mixed with blacker sand?
> ("The Summer's Night," 9)

> O with your wing of earth and darkness wake us,
> Angel wide as the earth, and bring us
> Here, to the same spot on the mortal earth,
> For a beginning. . . .

> Open, speak to us, burst,
> Burnt crown, bright pulse,
> Amber of a solar heart.
> ("The Dialogue of Anguish and Desire," 55–57)

HIS TEXT

Even more crucial than apostrophe in Bonnefoy's strenuous stretch toward transcendence is the poet's concern for the essential meaning, rather than the outward appearance, of what he sees—meaning troped not as a symbol but as a sign—some kind of spoken or, more likely, written message (see "these stones where we read the sign," quoted above from "The Scattered, The Indivisible").

Thus the elements of Bonnefoy's world are not limited to a romantic landscape of tree, ocean, and sky—a Rousseau-like world of unspoiled illiteracy. Bonnefoy's utopia is akin to *Walden:* far from escaping into some simple natural retreat, Thoreau brings the best of civilization with him, devoting a whole chapter explicitly and much more space implicitly to "Reading and Writing."

If *The Lure of the Threshold* gives a clue to the liminal nature of Bonnefoy's imagination, his other collections title, *Written Stone* (1965) is equally crucial, indicating as it does the poet's sense of nature as inscribed. But that inscription is not always monumental or enduring or *aere perennius;* it can be fugitive.

> *Words like the sky*
> *Today,*
> *Something that gathers, and scatters.*

> *Words like the sky,*
> *Infinite*
> *But all here suddenly in the brief pool.*
>   *("The Scattered, The Indivisble," 177)*

Sometimes words rise to the surface with the enigmatic evocativeness of a dream.

> *Knock,*
> *Knock forever.*

> *In the lure of the threshold.*

> *At the sealed door,*
> *At the empty phrase.*
> *In iron, awakening*
> *Only the word, iron.*

> *In speech, blackness.*

> *In he who sits*
> *By night, motionless*
> *At his table, laden*
> *With signs, glimmers. And is called*

> *Three times, but does not get up.*
> . . . .
> *In the gathering, that failed*
> *Of celebration.*

> *In the deformed wheat,*
> *The parching wine.*

> *In the hand that holds on*
> *To an absent hand.*
>
> *In the uselessness*
> *Of recollection.*
>
> *In writing, hastily*
> *Garnered at night*
>
> *And in words that die out*
> *Before dawn.*
> *("The Lure of the Threshold," 69–71)*

This remarkable passage is a good example of Bonnefoy's miniature narratives. The few but eloquent words lightly evoke both St. Peter's denial and the fairy tale motif of threes; yet paradoxically the poem explicitly utters the failure of celebration (or communion), of recollection, of communication. Both the wheat and wine (deformed and parched) and the "table, laden / with signs" suggest a festivity gone wrong; the elements are there, but (as in dreams) cannot be grasped ("words that die out / Before dawn"). Later in the same poem we find the note of frustration once again: "All the wavering visible / Unwrites itself . . ." (85).

But for every such moment of effacement, there are passages of authority and what sounds like confidence that, however indistinct the message, however muffled and frustrating, still the world is offering us a book to read. The very word "book" seems to coincide with Bonnefoy's most triumphant peaks, so rich is the very idea of its possession.

> *You will grow old*
> *And, fading amid the color of the trees,*
> *Casting a slower shadow on the wall,*
> *Being at last, in your soul, the threatened earth,*
> *You will take the book up where you had left it,*
> *You will say, These were the last obscure words.*
> *("The Book, for Growing Old" p. 49)*

I'll end by quoting a longer passage that shows beautifully how Bonnefoy's poetry both offers and withholds luminosities of meaning. Never easy, it is still somehow a poetry of generosity.

> *"Though you come for this closed book,*
> *I will not allow you to open it.*
> *Though you come to break the seal,*
> *Burning, pitted with night, bent, leaves*
> *Under the prowling threat of a storm,*
> *I will not let you touch the wax.*
> *Though you come 'only in order to' glimpse,*
> *As in a dream, how speech can be*
> *Metamorphosed in the dawn of meaning*

(And I know that a ploughshare has worked
A long time in that hope and, fallen back
Into the earthly phrase, shines there
Devastated at the edge of my light), listen,
I am silent in your dreaming voice ...
Though you come to lay waste the writing
(All writing, all hope), in order to recover
The unclouded surface that reflects the star,
To drink of the passing water and to bathe
Under the vault where fruit, not meaning, ripens,
I have not allowed you to forget the book."
                    ("The Clouds," pp. 139–141)

And it's true: we have not been allowed to forget the book, and, even if we're not to open it, somehow it will nourish us anyway.

NOTES

1. See Jonathan Holden, "Landscape Poems," *Denver Quarterly* 20/21, nos. 4/1 (Spring/Summer 1986); 159–76.

2. Jonathan Culler, in his essay on apostrophe, "Changes in the Study of the Lyrics" in *Lyric Poetry: Beyond New Criticism*, ed. Patricia Parker and Chaviva Hosek (Ithaca, NY: Cornell University Press, 1985), pp. 38–54.

WHAT COMES UP OUT OF THE GROUND:
ON BUDENZ, HEANEY, ASHBERY, AND OTHERS

AMY CLAMPITT

Since about 1970, Julia Budenz has been at work on a long poem. Excerpts from it have appeared in a few literary journals, and in 1984 Wesleyan University Press brought out a volume entitled *From the Gardens of Flora Baum*, constituting no more than two sections of Book Two, Part Five. The completed work is to consist of five books; at the time I last inquired, Julia Budenz was at work on Part Three of the third book, and there were already 555 typewritten pages—which would mean that for sheer length such things as *Kaddish* or *The Auroras of Autumn* have been left behind in favor of, say, *The Faerie Queene.* A first encounter with such a work in progress is likely to be baffling. But with each installment, and still more with rereading, I have found newly thrilling a poem whose design is not entirely revealed, but whose execution thus far is wonderfully various, beguiling, and funny.

Critics thus far have not, however, had much to say of Julia Budenz—for the reason, I suppose, that since she does not write short poems, it is hard to compare her with anyone. The often extended cadence of her lines, for example, suggests not that she has been influenced by Whitman but rather that like him she has long been at home with the English Bible. An occasional bit of word play ("And you—/ Do you write / English / ? . . . / Sicker I do") might suggest Joyce; but not the reference to Calypso:

> She was kind to me.
> But she wanted me to forget
> The fires burning blue above
> My Ithaca. Her soft
> Words, her soft . . .

Or to Circe:

> The schoolroom was restless
> Like a pen of navy-blue-white-collared calves,
> With big bronze eyes turned outward. Groping
> Along the bronze passages, I imparted the thread
> Which I could hardly claim to descry.
> How to fast, how to feast, how to speak, and how
> To shut up. Around us we heard
> The endless rooting and grunting.

These tell us only of a like immersion in the *Odyssey*. And perhaps it is no more than the copious botanical exactitude of a work that is, in its own mysteriously spacious and leisurely way, concerned with horticulture, which invites comparison with *Remembrance of Things Past* and its hawthorns, its chrysanthemums and cattleyas: in tone there is hardly any resemblance. Memory is evoked, certainly; but it is memory of a less idiosyncratic kind, more steadily resonant and strange. In *The Gardens of Flora Baum*, the long common memory of the classical world opens as a habitable place, along with (among others) Florida, the coast of Scotland, and the freezing thoroughfares of Cambridge, Massachusetts. It is part of a vision of how everything connects, of how it is possible at any moment to step from the everyday into the sacred, and back again.

In this, if in nothing else, it is natural to connect Julia Budenz with Seamus Heaney. They have both done some moving about, as poets tend to these days. "We're all nomads," as I heard one say not long ago. In Cambridge itself, I believe Heaney is regarded not as a nomad but as a seasonal phenomenon, a kind of mythological recurrence. One colleague, anyhow, refers to his Persephone-like reappearances when spring is on the way. And the notion does make sense when one considers that the first poem in his first book has to do with what comes up out of the ground. It's about digging potatoes, about his grandfather.

> *Heaving sods over his shoulder, going down and down*
> *For the good turf. Digging.*
>
> *The cold smell of potato mould, the squelch and slap*
> *Of soggy peat.*

It concludes with a poet's declaration:

> *Between my finger and my thumb*
> *The squat pen rests.*
> *I'll dig with it.*

And that is what he has been doing ever since. I think it can be said that with each new book Seamus Heaney has gone deeper into the soil of his native Ireland. As one who likes to think of herself as a poet of place, I'm a mere once-over-lightly, a butterfly, by comparison with the intense, muscular, down-to-earth, if not actually subterranean imagery of poem after poem. There are also, of course, the more delicate effects, such as the flowers of the elderberry "like saucers brimmed with meal": I knew them in my own childhood, but what I didn't know until I read the "Glanmore Sonnets" is that in Ireland the elderberry is the boortree, the *bower* tree in other words; and the thought of that adds a whole dimension to what I myself remember, which of course is what poetry is all about. There are the long views, of shorelines and estuaries, the scenes still darkened by the tragic stain of past events. There are the excavated remains which become the subject of *North:* the hoard of past existence embedded in the contours of the landscape. Even when he purports to be writing about California— in "Westering" or "Remembering Malibu"—Heaney is still writing about Ireland. There are the aerial views:

> *the patchwork earth, dark hems of hedge,*
> *The long gray tapes of road that bind and loose*
> *Villages and fields in casual marriage.*

And there is the literal bird's-eye view of *Sweeney Astray*—a kind of winged nomad of the treetops, who knows every one of those trees down there more intimately than some of us ever know our human neighbors. Just how deeply and totally his poetry is embedded in the particular and the local may be gathered from what Seamus Heaney has to say about Sweeney, the mad king of Dal-Arie who for his obstreperous behavior—out where I come from they would call it orneriness—was transformed into a bird. His kingdom, we are told, "lay in what is now south County Antrim and north County Down, and for over thirty years I lived on the verges of that territory, in sight of some of Sweeney's places and in earshot of others—Slemish, Rasharkin. . . ." When he began work on the translation of the medieval tale of Sweeney from the Irish, the poet says further,

> I had just moved to Wicklow, not all that far from Sweeney's final resting ground at St. Mullins. I was in a country of woods and hills and remembered that the green spirit of the hedges embodied in Sweeney had first been embodied for me in the persons of a family of tinkers, also called Sweeney, who used to camp in the ditchbanks along the road to the first school I attended. One way or another, he has been with me from the start.

But this lifelong identification with the Irish landscape is not the whole story. In an early essay, Heaney recalls the pump at the back door of his childhood home, from which five households drew water and which for him "centered and staked the imagination, made its foundation of the omphalos itself." To this, the ultimate in classical associations, may be connected a statement from another essay: "If you like, I began as a poet when my roots were crossed with my reading"—which is another way of saying how deeply we are all of us, those who care for poetry, embedded in the literature of the past. What stirs me most, at any rate, is so often a borrowing, a digging, a recovery, and thus a continuation, that it becomes possible to define poetry itself as what comes up out of the ground.

In Seamus Heaney's own "Requiem for the Croppies," those Irish rebels who in 1798 supported the attempted invasion by the French and who carried grain in the pockets of their greatcoats ("No kitchens on the run, no striking camp") are commemorated:

> *Terraced thousand died, shaking scythes at cannon.*
> *The hillside blushed, soaked in our broken wave.*
> *They buried us without shroud or coffin*
> *And in August the barley grew up out of the grave.*

Quite aside from the unmistakable echo of Emily Brontë's "Remembrance," I don't know how much this may owe to the "Merlin" of Geoffrey Hill; but it must owe something, and the more the debt is considered, the richer the experience of reading both poems:

I will consider the outnumbering dead:
For they are the husks of what was rich seed.
Now, should they come together to be fed,
They would outstrip the locusts' covering tide.

Arthur, Elaine, Mordred; they are all gone
Among the raftered galleries of bone.
By the long barrows of Logres they are made one,
And over their city stands the pinnacled corn.

Things that come up out of the ground and are scattered: Wallace Stevens gave thought, as so many before him had done, to their presence and their recurrences:

whirlings in the gutters, whirlings
Around and away, resembling the presence of thought,
Resembling the presences of thoughts, as if,

In the end, the whole psychology, the self,
The town, the weather, in a casual litter,
Together, said words of the world are the life of the world.

Which takes us back to Shelley's leaf-dispersing west wind, and from that to Milton's metaphor of the leaves at Vallombrosa, back to the third canto of the *Inferno,* to the sixth book of the *Aeneid,* and to the eleventh book of the *Odyssey:* the Underworld, the fluttering multitudes whose resemblance to fallen leaves was, in the original Greek, only implicit, not yet a metaphor.

There is a kind of thinking that regards all this as a misfortune, at least for us latecomers. But I find it hard to see how such thinking can be taken far, or very seriously. If it were, all poets would end up in the condition of one I remember hearing publicly declare, "I want to die of my own poison"—and who since then, so far as I know, has ceased to be heard from at all. At a polar remove from such a fate are the likes of Julia Budenz, at home in Cambridge, Massachusetts, but also with that long common memory:

To sing of presidents and revolutions,
Apollo chided, tapping the other shoulder,
Crouch in your cave another twenty years,
Piling the volumes high above your head,
Tunneling through big books until you see
The culmination of your drawn-out song.

Thalia, the Blossoming One, is present; the cave is hers. Or it is Plato's. Others make their appearance there from time to time. Diotima is one of them:

She had a question:
What do we think would happen if it happened
To one to see the beautiful itself . . . ?
It was Socrates again, it was Plato, it seemed for a moment like Jove,
I almost let go, it was a bull, bold and resolute,

> *Huge, horned, garlanded, white, wide-eyed but not innocent, foxy, flighty,*
> *mighty, muscular, determined, that seemed to have run up from the*
> *fens*
> *And was carrying me, back across the Charles, through Roxbury, into*
> *Dorchester Bay, across the ocean, to Europe, to Old Europe, where*
> *Jove was at home . . .*

Though the classical learning behind this may be exceptional, the nature of the presence is not. Such recurrences, if we are to believe Harold Bloom—who calls them misreadings, and after some resistance I now find that fair enough—are what makes the world go round. Rereading the title poem of *A Wave*, and admiring it more with each rereading, I have come to think of it as a twentieth-century equivalent of *The Prelude*. John Ashbery rewriting Wordsworth? Admittedly,

> *To be always articulating these preludes, there seems to be no*
> *Sense in it, if it is going to be perpetually five o'clock*

would appear to connect with Eliot's plural preludes rather than Wordsworth's in the singular. But there are enough references to such things as gibbets and waterfalls, along with so many recurrences of the word *love* as to constitute an excess—as one tends to find an excess of them in *The Prelude*—that when I came to

> *Moving on we approached the top*
> *Of the thing, only it was dark and no one could see,*

I thought Aha!—the ascent of Mount Snowdon. The hunch seemed confirmed, half a page later, by

> *But behind what looks like heaps of slag the peril*
> *Consists in explaining everything too evenly. Those*
> *Suffering from the blahs are unlikely to notice that the topic*
> *Of today's lecture doesn't exist yet . . .*

There can be little doubt, in any event, that what Ashbery in "A Wave" is wrestling with is the problem of poetic form, the very thing that gave Wordsworth, an innovator himself, such endless trouble. "One idea," Ashbery continues,

> *is enough to organize a life and project it*
> *Into unusual but viable forms, but many ideas merely*
> *Lead one thither into a morass of their own good intentions . . .*

More Wordsworthian still is the reference to

> *a moan that did not issue from me*
> *And is pulling me back toward old forms of address*
> *I know I have already lived through . . .*

Recurrences, old forms of address already lived through: innovator that he was, Wordsworth lived with them too. I came to an interest in him by way of his sister

Dorothy—a marvelous writer, though with so little aptitude for poetic form that when she tried to write verse, the life pretty much went out of what she had to say. Her journals are unmatched for the sense of *living*, of being one with the act of observing the qualities of the light and the weather, along with those minutely faithful notations of living beings, including human ones, that so often went into what her brother wrote. Dorothy Wordsworth was interested above all in experience, and I believe the same can be said of her brother. It is true that he offered some theories in defense of his use of language, and certainly that use was experimental at times. (Can it be, in fact, that "The Idiot Boy" and "Peter Bell" are so experimental that we still haven't caught up with them?) Passionately absorbing as I now find *The Prelude*, I do so at least partly as a record of struggle and failure: all those fragments spliced and moved about and spliced again, over and over. No, what Wordsworth cared about most wasn't language, it was experience, his own experience—and how something with the proportions of a classical epic could be made of it.

Rereading the later books of *The Prelude*, I find it not so much a history of the poet's mind as what T. S. Eliot called a fever chart, a day-to-day chronicle of ups and downs, to be read the way one reads Dorothy's journals. There is that moment when the poet says—and the frankness of it is shocking—"I am lost." One thinks of Rilke's "Who, if I cried out, would hear among the angelic orders?" Such admissions of bewilderment must account for an assertion that used to puzzle me, that Wordsworth is the first modern poet. The multiple crises of those later books—the loss of confidence, loss of his bearings as an individual—may be modern; but their antecedents are classical. Looking about for guidance, as Dante had done, Wordsworth found no Virgil; but he did find Coleridge, and when one thinks of their friendship Dorothy becomes a kind of Beatrice. Having made that connection, one has to conclude that Wordsworth, this innovator, this prototypically modern poet, is nevertheless the author of a classical epic, whose central episode goes underground—becomes yet another version of the descent into hell.

Why did I find this discovered connection so thrilling? One might as well ask Julia Budenz the same about Thalia's cave. Or Seamus Heaney, who says he began as a poet when his roots were crossed with his reading, about the *terza rima* in which so much of "Station Island" is written. Or Wallace Stevens about the tercets of "An Ordinary Evening in New Haven." The answer is so fundamental as almost to go without saying: there is no avoiding what comes up out of the ground.

REVOLUTIONARY LOVE: DENISE LEVERTOV AND THE POETICS OF POLITICS

SANDRA M. GILBERT

In an age of psychic anxiety and metaphysical *angst,* Denise Levertov's most revolutionary gesture is probably her persistent articulation of joy—joy in self, delight in life, sheer pleasure in pure *being.* In different poems, her frequently mystical self-definitions achieve varying degrees of intensity: in "Stepping Westward," for instance, she is "realistic," scrupulously celebrating "what, woman / and who, myself / I am," while in "Song to Ishtar" she is more "fantastic," exulting that "the moon is a sow . . . and I a pig and a poet." Yet at her best Levertov has always expressed an exuberant self-knowledge, the mysterious self-contact of what in "The Son" she called "the rapt, imperious, sea-going river," along with an appreciation of otherness that continually leads her to seek new ways of affirming "Joy, the, 'well . . . *joyfulness* of / joy.'"

Especially in her early collections, from *Overland to the Islands* through *Relearning the Alphabet,* Levertov produces a succinct yet detailed record of experience in which the perceiving mind, confronting the apparent ordinariness of the world, is continually surprised by joy. A section of "Matins," from *The Jacob's Ladder* (1961), reveals the paradoxically insouciant reverence with which this poet of the particular can celebrate the visionary pleasures of daily reality:

> *The authentic! I said*
> *rising from the toilet seat.*
> *The radiator in rhythmic knockings*
> *spoke of the rising steam.*
> *The authentic, I said*
> *breaking the handle of my hairbrush as I*
> *brushed my hair in*
> *rhythmic strokes: That's it,*
> *that's joy, it's always*
> *a recognition, the known*
> *appearing fully itself, and*
> *more itself than one knew.*

Later in this suite of ceremonial praise "the real, the new laid / egg" and "the holy grains" of a child's breakfast are added to the poet's hairbrush, her "steaming bathroo[m]" and kitchen "full of / things to be done" as *loci* of "Marvelous Truth," of the "terrible joy"—the awesome, eternal delight—which is always, in some sense, waiting to illuminate and transfigure the facade of the ordinary.

That the *lares* and *penates* of the household seem to Levertov to contain such symbolic potential is surely significant. Though she is not an aggressively feminist poet, she is very much a woman poet, or perhaps, more accurately, a poet conscious that the materiality of her life as a woman is not matter to be transcended; it is material in which poetry is immanent. Like "the worm artist" in *The Sorrow Dance* who "is homage to / earth [and] aerates / the ground of his living" (*Poems*, 176), this writer consciously inhabits a domestic world whose grounds her words record, revere, transform. Indeed, throughout Levertov's career, the house itself becomes an emblem of not only physical but spiritual shelter, its mysteries the secrets not just of habit but of in-habitation.

The comparatively early "Overhead," from *O Taste and See* (1964) suggests the literal resonance Levertov attributes to her dwelling place:

> *A deep wooden note*
> *when the wind blows,*
> *the west wind.*
> *The rock maple is it,*
> *close to the house?*
> *Or a beam, voice*
> *of the house itself?*
> *A groan, but not*
> *gloomy, rather*
> *an escaped note of*
> *almost unbearable*
> *satisfaction, a great*
> *bough or beam*
> *unaware*
> *it had*
> *spoken.*
> (Poems, *106*)

Suavely cadenced, with pauses whose careful timing emphasizes this artist's consistent attention to "where the silence is" as well as to the flow of her verse's "inner song" (*The Poet in the World*, 22, 24), this piece clearly represents Levertov's commitment to the skillful deployment of "organic form," an aesthetic strategy for which she has often been praised. But the very technique of "organic form," as Levertov defines it, cannot be separated from attention to, and celebration of, indwelling mysteries. "For me," she has written, "back of the idea of organic form is the concept that there is a form in all things (and in our experience) which the poet can discover and reveal" (*The Poet*, 7). Thus, with comparable fluency, a number of her other poems also explore both the personal and the poetic meanings of inhabitation.

"From the Roof," for instance (*Poems*, 51), begins with the poet in a wild wind, "gathering the washing as if it were flowers," meditating on a move "to our new living-place" and asking "who can say / the crippled broom-vendor yesterday, who passed / just as we needed a new broom, was not / one of the Hidden Ones?" The piece's final answer—"by design / we are to live now in a new place"—suggests the significance of place, of house, of "indwelling" to this artist. Similarly, "Invocation," which concludes *Relearning the Alphabet* (1972), dramatizes a family's preparation for moving with a prayer:

> O Lares,
> *don't leave.*
> *The house yawns like a bear.*
> *Guards its profound dreams for us,*
> *that it return to us when we return.*

More playfully, "What My House Would Be Like if It Were a Person," in *Life in the Forest* (1978), incarnates the house itself as a mysterious, even mystical, creature:

> *Its intelligence*
> *would be of a high order,*
> *neither human nor animal, elvish.*
> *And it would purr, though of course,*
> *it being a house, you would sit in its lap,*
> *not it in yours.*

At the same time, though, such a Levertovian vision of the house-as-personality is luminously complemented by a vision of the person-as-house. The beautiful "Psalm Concerning the Castle" (*Poems*, 217) almost seems to follow Gaston Bachelard's *Poetics of Space* in its scrupulously elaborated analysis of "the place of the castle . . . within me":

> *Let the young queen sit above, in the cool air, her child in*
> *her arms, let her look with joy at the great circle,*
> *the pilgrim shadows, the work of the sun and the play of*
> *the wind. Let her walk to and fro. Let the columns*
> *uphold the roof, let the storeys uphold the columns,*
> *let there be dark space below the lowest floor, let the*
> *castle rise foursquare out of the moat, let the moat be a*
> *ring and the water deep, let the guardians guard it, let*
> *there be wide lands around it, let that country where it*
> *stands be within me, let me be where it is.*

But if the figure of the house itself is cherished by this woman poet, the activities associated with it are equally important to her. For Levertov, the ancient female tasks of keeping and cleaning, sewing and baking, loving and rearing, often become jobs as sacred as the apparently humdrum task of spinning the prayer wheel in the archaic temple—which is not to say that she is the "Dear Heloise" of poetry but rather that she is a sort of Rilke of domesticity, turning her talent for what the German poet called *einsehen* ("inseeing") toward those supposedly mundane but really central occupations which bring order out of the chaos of dailiness. Whether gathering rebellious laundry or stirring holy grains, she means to invest her housework (and her spouse's) with meaning, and she is often awestruck by its implications. As early as *Here and Now* (1957) she celebrates the dull job of "Laying the Dust"—"What a sweet smell rises / when you lay the dust" (*Collected*, 48)—and a year later, in *Overland to the*

Islands (1958), she develops a metaphor of sewing to which she returns in her recent collection, *Oblique Prayers* (1984). "I would like," she says in the earlier verse, "to make . . . poems . . . mysterious as the silence when the tailor / would pause with his needle in the air," (*Collected,* 78), and in the later she notes that "a day of spring" is "a needle's eye / space and time are passing through like a swathe of silk" (*Oblique,* 87). With the same intensity, moreover, "The Acolyte," in *Candles in Babylon* (1982), enters a large, dark, enigmatic kitchen to explore a woman's sense of the magical ambitions inspired by bread-baking:

> *She wants to put*
> *a silver rose or a bell of diamonds*
> *into each loaf;*
> *she wants*
>
> *to bake a curse into one loaf,*
> *into another, the words that break*
> *evil spells and release*
> *transformed heroes into their selves;*
> *she wants to make*
> *bread that is more than bread.*
>> (Candles, *69)*

But of course, as the proverb would have it, the loaf that rises in the oven is often really (that is to say, symbolically) the child, and it is the child—her son Nikolai—for whom Levertov most often finds herself stirring the holy grains. From "The Son," in *The Sorrow Dance* (1967), to "He-Who-Came-Forth," in *Relearning the Alphabet,* a poem whose title works off the first line of "The Son," she exults in the miraculous separateness of the life to which she has given birth: "He-who-came-forth was / it turned out / a man," exclaims the first text, while the second marvels that his "subtle mind and quick heart . . . now stand beyond me, out in the world / beyond my skin / beautiful and strange as if / I had given birth to a tree."

Perhaps even more than in her poems about and to her son, however, Levertov elaborates her sense of the strangeness, as well as the joy, of *relationship* in a number of erotic poems about married love. Though her work has often been discussed in terms of stylistic innovations associated with the Black Mountain School, though she is generally classified as a "neo-Romantic," and though she is frequently seen as a determinedly political poet, Levertov is not often defined as what used to be called a "love poet." Yet, especially in *The Jacob's Ladder* (1961), *O Taste and See* (1964), and *The Sorrow Dance* (1967), she has produced a set of remarkable verses, poems which, like Christina Rossetti's sonnet-sequence *Monna Innominata,* dramatize the female side of the story of desire. These poems are sometimes lushly sensuous, as in "Song for a Dark Voice"—

> *Your skin*
> *tastes of the salt of Marmora,*
> *the hair of your body casts*
> *its net over me"*
>> (Poems, *25)*

—or "Our Bodies"—

> *Your long back,*
> *the sand color and*
> *how the bones show, say*
>
> *what sky after sunset*
> *almost white*
> *over a deep woods to which*
>
> *rooks are homing, says.*
> (Poems, 145)

Thus, mythologizing male beauty the way male poets have traditionally celebrated and sanctified female beauty, they suggest the Song of Songs in which an Eve, untaught silence and submissiveness, might have given voice to her erotic love for Adam. More, melodiously articulated and passionately phrased, they imply the essential connection between "the authentic" miracles of the physical house and the inescapable authenticity of the body, whose "terrible joy" the house holds and reveals. "A Psalm Praising the Hair of Man's Body," for instance, hints at the theology of Eros which Levertov more openly expresses in "Eros at Temple Stream" or "Hymn to Eros":

> *Husband thy fleece of silk is black,*
> *a black adornment;*
> *lies so close to the turns of the flesh,*
> *burns my palm-stroke....*
> *. . . . .*
> *Hair of man, man-hair, hair of*
> *breast and groin, marking contour as*
> *silverpoint marks in cross-*
> *hatching, as river-*
> *grass on the woven current*
> *indicates ripple,*
> *praise.*
> (Poems, 154)

In other love poems, however, Levertov explores the tension between the desire for merging with the beloved that is manifested in her erotic verses and the inexorable separateness of lovers. "Bedtime" begins with near-fusion—"We are a meadow where the bees hum / mind and body are almost one"—but moves to an acknowledgment of what Whitman called the "solitary self": "by day we are singular and often lonely" (*Poems,* 167). Similarly, "The Ache of Marriage," which deserves to be quoted in its entirety, dramatizes the paradoxes of separateness-in-togetherness, unity and duality:

> *The ache of marriage:*
>
> *thigh and tongue, beloved,*
> *are heavy with it,*
> *it throbs in the teeth*

We look for communion
and are turned away, beloved,
each and each

It is leviathan and we
in its belly
looking for joy, some joy
not to be known outside it

two by two in the ark of
the ache of it.
                              (Poems, 77)

"*It is leviathan*": though, as I have already noted, Levertov is not an aggressively feminist writer, her rigorous attentiveness to the realities of her own life as a woman has inevitably forced her to confront the contradictions implicit in that condition. Desire entraps lovers in an ark—a covenant as well as a Noah's ark steering toward survival—that is also an ache, an institution in which the married pair are buried as in the belly of the whale. "Don't lock me in wedlock, I want / marriage, an / encounter—" (*Poems*, 140) the poet exclaims in "About Marriage," yet, despite her reverence for those details of desire and domesticity which manifest "the authentic," she often implies that the wife-mother who is an artist, a woman who *sees* and says what she sees, can never be wholly one with her life, for to see is to be set apart by the imperatives of perception and expression. Where the clean and comely homemaker wears "a utopian smock or shift" (*Poems*, 143) and, "smelling of / apples or grass," merges with the nature of her life and life of nature, the artist-wife, "dressed in opals and rags," separates herself from the kindly routines of the household.

In a number of poems, therefore, Levertov characterizes herself as *two* women— the one who lives, loves, nurtures, and the one who observes, sings, casts spells. Such a strategy of doubling is of course a traditional one for women artists: as Susan Gubar and I have argued elsewhere, nineteenth-century writers from Charlotte Brontë to Emily Dickinson frequently imagined themselves as split between a decorous lady and a fiercely rebellious madwoman. Interestingly, however, where her precursors experienced such splits as painful if liberating, Levertov usually describes them as purely liberating, further sources of "the, 'well . . . *joyfulness* of / joy.'" The early "The Earthwoman and the Waterwoman," from *Here and Now* (1957), dramatizes polarities of female experience that appear throughout most of the poet's subsequent volumes. The wholesome, nurturing "earthwoman" has children "full of blood and milk," while her opposite, the prophetic "waterwoman / sings gay songs in a sad voice / with her moonshine children"' (*Collected*, 31); at night, while the earthwoman drowses in "a dark fruitcake sleep," her waterwoman self "goes dancing in the misty lit-up town / in dragonfly dresses and blue shoes." Yet despite the opposition between these two, both are exuberant, both celebrate "the authentic" in its different manifestations.

The speaker of the later "In Mind," from *O Taste and See* (1964), is more frankly confessional about her own relationship to these antithetical selves, and franker, too, about the pain that at least one of them, the mystically self-absorbed waterwoman, may cause to others. "There's in my mind a woman / of innocence," the poet explains, a woman who "is kind and very clean . . . but she has no imagination" (*Poems,* 143). But the double of this woman, she adds, is a "turbulent moon-ridden girl // or old woman . . . who knows strange songs"—and *she* "is not kind." Unkind though she may be, however, the visionary singer inexorably exists, and significantly Levertov does not apologize for her existence. On the contrary, even while in "The Woman" (*The Freeing of the Dust,* 1975) she concedes the problems that the female split self poses for a "bridegroom"—

> It is the one in homespun
> you hunger for
> when you are lonesome;
>
> the one in crazy feathers
> dragging opal chains in dust
> wearies you . . .

—she is adamant about this complex psychic reality: "Alas, / they are not two but one," she declares, and her groom must "endure / life with two brides. . . ." (*Freeing,* 53).

In fact, it is particularly when she undertakes to analyze and justify female complexity that Levertov makes her most overtly "feminist" political statements. "Hypocrite Women," from *O Taste and See,* simultaneously expresses contempt for "a white sweating bull of a poet" who declared that "cunts are ugly" and rebukes women for refusing to admit their own strangeness, their own capacity for prophetic dreaming. Cunts "are dark and wrinkled and hairy, / caves of the Moon," yet

>   *when a*
> *dark humming fills us, a*
>
> *coldness towards life,*
> *we are too much women to*
> *own to such unwomanliness.*
>
> *Whorishly with the psychopomp*
> *we play and plead . . .*
>   (Poems, *142*)

Similarly, "Abel's Bride," in *The Sorrow Dance* (1967), urges acquiescence in the female mystery that is associated with the confrontation of earthwoman and waterwoman, a confrontation enacted in the interior household where vision and domesticity coexist. Though "Woman fears for man [because] he goes / out alone to his labors" (and by implication, his death), she must recognize her own complex fate: "her being / is a cave, there are bones at the hearth" (*Poems,* 163). In fact, those—both male and female—who do not acknowledge the "dark humming" of the spirit that imbues the flesh with meaning are like "The Mutes" (also in *The Sorrow Dance*), inarticulate men whose "groans . . . passing a woman on the street" are meant to tell her "she is a female / and their flesh knows it" but say, instead,

> 'Life after life after life goes by
> without poetry,
> without seemliness,
> without love.'
>
> *(Poems, 197)*

Finally, indeed, Levertov declares that it is precisely in her womanhood—in its tangible flesh of earthwoman as well as in its fluent spirit of waterwoman—that her artistic power lies:

> When I am a woman—O, when I am
> a woman,
> my wells of salt brim and brim,
> poems force the lock of my throat.
>
> *(Freeing, 49)*

Given such a visionary and mystically (if not polemically) feminist commitment to female power, it is not surprising that some of Levertov's strongest and best-known poems offer homage to the muse-goddess whom she sees as patroness of her poetry. Among her earlier verses, the piece called "Girlhood of Jane Harrison," in *With Eyes at the Back of Our Heads* (1960), suggests one of the forces that shaped her thought on this matter, for in her monumental *Prolegomena to the Study of Greek Religion* (1903) the British feminist-classicist had sought to document the dominance of the Great Mother in ancient Greek culture. Levertov's famous poem "The Goddess," also in *With Eyes at the Back of Our Heads,* plainly develops Harrison's theories as its praises the deity "without whom nothing / flowers, fruits, sleeps in season, / without whom nothing / speaks in its own tongue, but returns / lie for lie!"—the goddess who empowers not only the flowering grounds on which the earthwoman lives but also the strange songs of the waterwoman. Similarly, "The Well," in *The Jacob's Ladder,* as well as "Song for Ishtar" and "To the Muse," in *O Taste and See,* celebrate "The Muse / in her dark habit" and with her multiple manifestations. Finally, that this divinity inspires and presides over the essential solitude in which the woman poet inscribes her tales of earth and water is made clear in "She and the Muse," from the recent *Candles in Babylon,* a poem which shows how, after "the hour's delightful hero" has said "*arri-vederci,*" the "heroine . . . eagerly" returns to the secret room of art, where "She picks a quill, / dips it, begins to write. But not of him" (*Candles,* 67). In the last analysis, the joyfulness of this woman's life and love is *made* authentic through the joy of language, the pleasure of musing words in which "the known" appears "more itself than one knew."

Although Levertov's joy is sometimes playful ("The authentic! I said / rising from the toilet seat"), it is rarely ironic or skeptical. Neither the relieved exstasis of the sufferer momentarily released from pain (the kind of exhilaration sometimes enacted by, say, Sylvia Plath) nor the brief tentative reconciliation to things-as-they-are of what we might call the *eiron maudit* (the kind of affirmation sometimes dramatized by Robert Lowell), Levertov's delight in existence depends, rather, on the steady celebratory patience of the believer who trusts that if you wait long enough, if you abide despite forebodings, the confirming moment of epiphany will arrive. Thus she assimilates those metaphysical anxieties which Wordsworth in a very different context defined as "fallings from us, vanishings" into a larger pattern based on faith in the inevitability of joy renewed.

Even some of her verses about absence—the actual or imminent absence of self, body, spirit—suggest confidence in the restoration of presence. "Gone Away," in *O Taste and See*, confesses that "When my body leaves me / I'm lonesome for it," but depends on a knowledge that the physical self will return, while two mirror poems, "Looking-Glass" (also in *O Taste and See*) and "Keeping Track" (in *Relearning the Alphabet*), trace the "shadow-me" in the glass "to see if I'm there" and, by implication, to verify an expected sense of authenticity. Even more dramatically—and more characteristically—"To the Muse," in *O Taste and See*, maintains that though the poet, the "host" of the house of art, fears that his aesthetic patroness is hiding,

> all the while
>
> *you are indwelling,*
> *a gold ring lost in the house.*
> A gold ring lost in the house.
> *You are in the house!*

And the mystery of creativity is precisely that the muse's "presence / will be restored" (*Poems*, 99).

Inevitably, perhaps, for a poet of Levertov's bent, a poet who trusts that a thread of potential joy is woven into every inch of the fabric that constitutes daily reality, any ripping or clipping of that secret, sacred thread threatens cataclysm. Thus, like such other poets of affirmation as Blake, Shelley, Whitman, or in our own age Bly, she is a deeply political writer—and I am using the word "politics" in its most ordinary sense, to mean public matters having to do with "the policies, goals, or affairs of a government" (*American Heritage Dictionary*). For in the "real" world, it is political action—the burning of villages, the decapitation of villagers, the building of bombs—that most threatens the authority of daily joy. Yet, paradoxically enough, despite their often revolutionary intensity, Levertov's most artistically problematic poems are precisely those no doubt overdetermined verses in which she explicitly articulates her political principles.

Comparatively early in her career, Levertov began to try to find a way of confronting and analyzing the horrors of a history—especially a twentieth-century history—which denies the luminous integrity of flesh-and-spirit. But even one of her better poems in this mode, "Crystal Night" (in *The Jacob's Ladder*), now seems rhetorically hollow, with its generalized description of "The scream! The awaited scream" which "rises," and "the shattering / of glass and the cracking / of bone" (*Poems*, 68). The better-known "Life at War," in *The Sorrow Dance*, is more hectic still, in its insistence that

> *We have breathed the grits of it [war] in, all our lives,*
> *our lungs are pocked with it,*
> *the mucous membrane of our dreams*
> *coated with it, the imagination*
> *filmed over with the gray filth of it*

and in its editorial revulsion from the complicity of "delicate Man, whose flesh / responds to a caress, whose eyes / are flowers that perceive the stars" (*Poems*, 229).

In a splendid essay on verse in this mode ("On the Edge of Darkness: What is Political Poetry?" in *Light up the Cave*, 1981), Levertov herself observes, about the "assumption by partisan poets and their constituencies that the subject matter carries so strong an emotive charge in itself that it is unnecessary to remember poetry's roots in song, magic, and . . . high craft," that such a belief is "dangerous to poetry" (*Light*, 126). Yet in most of her political verse she seems herself to have disregarded her own astute warning. Because she has little taste or talent for irony, her comments on social catastrophe lack, on the one hand, the sardonic ferocity that animates, say, Bly's "The Teeth Mother Naked at Last" (e.g., "It's because we have new packaging for smoked oysters that bomb holes appear in the rice paddies"), and, on the other hand, the details of disillusionment that give plausibility to, say, Lowell's "For the Union Dead" (e.g., "When I crouch to my television set, / the drained faces of negro school-children rise like balloons"). At the same time, despite the impressive sincerity of her political commitment, her exhortations fail to attain (as perhaps postmodernist exhortations inevitably must) the exaltation of, for instance, Shelley's "Men of England, wherefore plough / For the lords who lay ye low?"

Still, as Levertov's personal commitment to the antinuclear movement and to support for revolutionary regimes in Central America has intensified, the proportion of politicized work included in her published collections has risen drastically. *Oblique Prayers* (1984) contains a section of ten manifestos, most of which, sadly, dissolve into mere cries of rage and defiance. The tellingly titled "Perhaps No Poem But All I Can Say And I Cannot Be Silent," for instance, protests against "those foul / dollops of History / each day thrusts at us, pushing them / into our gullets" (*Oblique*, 35) while "Rocky Flats" depicts "rank buds of death" in "nuclear mushroom sheds," and "Watching *Dark Circle*" describes the experimental "roasting of live pigs" in "a simulation of certain conditions" as leading to "a foul miasma irremovable from the nostrils" (*Oblique*, 38, 39). Though I (along with, I suspect, the majority of her readers and admirers) share most of Levertov's political convictions, I must confess that besides being less moved by these poems that I have been by the more artful verses of Bly, Lowell, and Shelley, I am rather less moved than I would be by eloquent journalism, and considerably less affected than I would be by a circumstantially detailed documentary account of the events that are the subjects of Levertov's verses, for certainly there is little song, magic, or high craft in some of their phrases. The muse is still, I trust, "indwelling" in this poet's house, but she has not presided over some of the writer's recent work.

To be sure, the muse *has* inspired several of Levertov's political verses. "Thinking about El Salvador," in *Oblique Prayers* opens with the poet's confession that "Because every day they chop heads off / I'm silent . . . for each tongue they silence / a word in my mouth / unsays itself," and concludes with a poignant vision

> *of all whose heads every day*
> *float down the river*
> *and rot*
> *and sink,*

> *not Orpheus heads*
> *still singing, bound for the sea,*
> *but mute.*
>
> *(Oblique, 34)*

And the much earlier "A Note to Olga (1966)" dramatizes the poet's sudden vision of her dead sister at a political rally:

> *It seems*
> *you that is lifted*
>
> *limp and ardent*
> *off the dark snow*
> *and shoved in, and driven away.*
>
> *(Poems, 239)*

But what moves these poems, as opposed to Levertov's less successful polemics, seems to be not ferocious revulsion but revolutionary love—not the hate that is blind to all detail except its own rhetoric ("foul dollops") but the love that sees and says with scrupulous exactitude the terror of the severed heads that are "not Orpheus heads" and the passion of the ghostly Olga, "limp and ardent." And as these works show, such rebellious *caritas,* perhaps as surely as Bly's ironic inventiveness, Lowell's meticulous weariness, or (even) Shelley's hortatory energy, can impel the poetics of politics.

In fact, the phrase "revolutionary love" itself is from Levertov's fine essay on Pablo Neruda: "Poetry and Revolution: Neruda is Dead—Neruda Lives" (in *Light up the Cave*), a piece that beautifully complements and supplements her meditation on political poetry. "Neruda's revolutionary politics," she declares here, "is founded in revolutionary love—the same love Che Guevara spoke of. Revolutionary love subsumes a bitter anger against oppression and oppressors. . . . But revolutionary love is not merely anthropocentric; it reaches out to the rest of creation." For, she adds, Neruda's celebrations of animals and vegetables, of the earth and sky and sea, "are not irrelevant, dispensable, coincidental to his revolutionary convictions, but an integral part of them" (*Light,* 133–34).

About Levertov's own revolutionary love, with its often brilliantly precise elaborations of the joyfulness of joy, the same statement could be made. Yet it is instructive to compare her expressions of "bitter anger" with those of her Chilean precursor. Neruda's classic "The United Fruit Co.," for instance, begins with scathingly sardonic, surrealistic detail:

> *When the trumpet sounded, it was*
>
> *all prepared on the earth,*
> *and Jehovah parceled out the earth*
> *to Coca-Cola, Inc., Anaconda,*
> *Ford Motors, and other entities:*
> *The Fruit Company, Inc.*

> *reserved for itself the most succulent,*
> *the central coast of my own land,*
> *the delicate waist of America.*
> *(translated by Robert Bly, Neruda,*
> *and Vallejo:* Selected Poems, *85)*

And even more strikingly than Levertov's "Thinking about El Salvador," Neruda's poem ends with a terrifying image:

> *Indians are falling*
> *into the sugared chasms*
> *of the harbors, wrapped*
> *for burial in the mist of the dawn:*
> *a body rolls, a thing*
> *that has no name, a fallen cipher,*
> *a cluster of dead fruit*
> *thrown down on the dump.*

Though of course it is intellectually coherent with the poem's theme ("sugared chasms," "a cluster of dead fruit"), this brilliant detail, in which we recognize "the known / appearing fully itself," is an image shaped by revolutionary love, by the love that yields itself not so much to editorial convictions as to the muse's telling, the goddess' indwelling.

When Levertov is at her best, such love underlies both her celebrations and her cerebrations; indeed, precisely because she is not an artist of irony or disillusionment but a poet of revolutionary love, she succeeds at recountings of the authentic in daily experience and fails at what Swift called *saeva indignatio.* Clearly, moreover, she knows this in some part of herself. One of the best poems in *Candles in Babylon* is "The Dragonfly-Mother," a piece in which Levertov reexamines the split between earth-woman and waterwoman specifically in terms of her own split commitment to, on the one hand, political activism, and, on the other hand, poetry.

> *I was setting out from my house*
> *to keep my promise*
>
> *but the Dragonfly-Mother stopped me.*
>
> *I was to speak to a multitude*
> *for a good cause, but at home*
>
> *the Dragonfly-Mother was listening*
> *not to a speech but to the creak of*
>   *stretching tissue,*
> *tense hum of leaves unfurling.*

"Who is the Dragonfly-Mother?" the poem asks, then goes on to answer that she is the muse, "the one who hovers / on stairways of air," the one—by implication—who sees and says the authentic in the ordinary, the revolutionary love continually surprised, and inspired, by joy. Her imperatives are inescapable: "When she tells / her stories she listens; when she listens / she tells you the story you utter."

It is to such imperatives that, one hopes, this poet will continue to be loyal, for what the Dragonfly-Mother declares, over and over again, is that the political is—or must be made—the poetical: the fabric of joy should not be ripped or clipped, yet the activist artist must struggle to praise and preserve every unique thread of that fabric, against the onslaughts of those who would reduce all reality to "foul dollops." Toward the end of this poem, Levertov seems to me to express the central truth of her own aesthetic, the truth of the joy *and* the pain born from revolutionary love:

> *Dragonfly-Mother's*
> *a messenger,*
> *if I don't trust her*
> *I can't keep faith.*
>   (Candles, *13–15*)

CAVE OF RESEMBLANCES,
CAVE OF RIMES:
TRADITION AND REPETITION IN
ROBERT DUNCAN

MICHAEL DAVIDSON

In attempting to characterize the tone of Bay Area poetry during the 1940s, Kenneth Rexroth used the term "elegiac" to refer to its brooding, somewhat nostalgic quality.[1] The elegiac mood was a response to the War's devastation, to be sure, but it was also a reaction to the literary climate of the time. The heroic innovations of the Modernists had been reified into more palatable substitutes by a new generation and as Delmore Schwartz observed, "what was once a battlefield (had) become a peaceful public park on a pleasant summer Sunday afternoon."[2] Presiding over the expanding New Critical hegemony in literary periodicals and university classrooms was the example of Eliot, both as poet and as cultural critic. His literary essays could be (and were) read as directives for a new sensibility, one in which thought and action, art and culture, individual talent and tradition could, after an interregnum of two centuries, be once again reconciled. The latter pair provided, of course, an aesthetic that extended far beyond Eliot's 1919 essay, "Tradition and the Individual Talent" and perhaps a good deal beyond his original concerns. Any rapprochement between tradition and innovation could be had only at the expense of personality. The introduction of the "really new" work of art to the canon was seen to alter the "existing monuments," not by any contingent relationships to the author's biography or historical moment but by art's universal appeal. In order to write and write well, one had to keep "the whole of the literature of Europe from Homer" in one's bones at the same time one fought to "extinguish" the private ego—an intimidating task for any young poet.

For those young poets who gathered around Rexroth in the 1940s, the critical problem was not Eliot's version of tradition—an organic totality in which the values among the canon are altered by the noncanonical—but, rather, the prescriptive application of certain aspects of Eliot's criticism in order to delimit "a" tradition, presumably one circumscribed by western, Judaeo-Christian culture. Certainly the methodological imperative behind an aesthetics of "impersonality" was anathema to the kind of testamentary and expressive poetry being written not only in San Francisco but in other avant-garde circles during the late 1940s. Robert Duncan, looking back to this period from the vantage of the later 1950s, remembered "powers of love"

> *and of poetry,*
> *the Berkeley we believed*
> *grove of Arcady—*
>
> *that there might be*
> *potencies in common things,*
> *"princely manipulations of the real"*[3]

The cult of romance in which he, Jack Spicer and Robin Blaser participated during the "Berkeley Renaissance" is the most obvious contrast to the New Critical version of Eliot's tradition with its strong valorization of the seventeenth-century metaphysical poets, its antiromantic stance, its neo-Kantian aesthetics. It is not that Duncan and his peers substituted the romantic tradition for some neoclassical fashion of the times—a replacement of one canon with another—but that he so radically transformed the notion of tradition altogether. This transformation was made possible partly through the terms of romanticism itself, but only by means of a rather idiosyncratic and expansive definition.

For Robert Duncan, the romantic tradition represents more than a historical period or canonic body of texts. It represents an ancient quest for knowledge about the nature of life forms—knowledge which, for a variety of reasons, cannot be summoned or articulated according to the usual channels. In cultural terms, this quest is most vital when informed by a diversity of sources. The Hellenistic period is the most obvious example of such diffusion and interpenetration, and Duncan often refers to the theological and philosophical writings from this era as exempla of a fruitful admixture of Eastern and Western, classical and modern, pagan and Christian influences. In literary terms, this quest is reflected through those works in which a mythopoeic strain is dominant. Mythopoeia occurs in two forms, "the lordly and humble, . . . mythological vision and folklorish phantasy."[4] Thus, the quest romance is as much a dimension of *The Odyssey* as it is of "The Owl and the Pussycat" or "Wynken, Blynken and Nod." For Duncan, romanticism involves "powers of love" that are primordial, locked in the forms of biological and psychological life. Because of their potency, these ideas cannot appear except in veiled or occult forms. What Duncan calls "permission" refers to the poet's ability to participate in these "potencies in common things" and release them, beyond all reference to literature, to a swirling, changing universe.

This participatory stance toward the "lordly and humble" aspects of tradition has little to do with what we characteristically designate as "originality," the creation of new or unique artistic artifacts. In a paradox central to his poetics, Duncan often speaks of his originality in terms of an ability to resuscitate origins. In an unpublished preface to *The Opening of the Field,* he defines his own relationship of originality or individual talent to tradition:

> In this sense, in that I am concerned with forms and not with conventions, with an art and not with a literature, I may be a modernist. But I do not care particularly about the brand-newness of a form, I am not a futurist, I work toward immediacy; and I do not aim at originality. The meanings in language are not original, any more than the sounds; they accrue from all the generations of human use from the mists of the *schwa* and first objects to the many vowels

and common universe of things of today; they are radical, sending roots back along our own roots. I am a traditionalist, a seeker after origins, not an original.[5]

The poet's individual talent may be expressed not in his originality—his transformation of the tradition as Eliot had defined it—but in his ability to respond to the demands of immediacy. Implicit in this idea is the notion of repetition, or what Duncan prefers to call "rime," by which original moments, events, ideas are interrelated in a dense weave. The structure of rime or repetition is the dynamic rendering of original moments that, in order to be such moments, can only be responded to, not invented out of whole cloth. To put it in other terms, the structure of rime refers to the poem's ability to resonate with the world without either destroying or representing it. Where "tradition," to the hegemonous New Critical aesthetic, implied artisanal mastery within a specifically literary history, for Duncan and others of his generation it meant cooperation with and response to the open field of creative life.

Duncan's radical "traditionalism" marks him as one of the most paradoxical of contemporary poets. He resolutely refuses to accept the designation "Modernist" or (more vehemently) "Post-Modernist." As he says in an interview, "I'm not a Modernist. . . . I read Modernism as Romanticism; and I finally begin to feel myself pretty much a 19th century mind."[6] This idiosyncratic stance produces a series of seeming contradictions: he is a poet of "open" forms who continues to write, as well, in classical modes like the sonnet and the ballad; he is a firm believer in verbal immediacy and testimony who, nevertheless, uses a heightened rhetoric more appropriate to the Victorian age; he is an avowedly romantic poet who has written masques in the Augustan manner worthy of Swift or Dryden; he is a political poet who, while attacking American imperialism in Southeast Asia, is still capable of celebrating war. The list of artists whom he is ambitious to "emulate, imitate, reconstruct, approximate, duplicate" would confuse even the most subtle genealogist of literary influence. It includes

> Ezra Pound, Gertrude Stein, Joyce, Virginia Woolf, Dorothy Richardson, Wallace Stevens, D. H. Lawrence, Edith Sitwell, Cocteau, Mallarmé, Marlowe, St. John of the Cross, Yeats, Jonathan Swift, Jack Spicer, Céline, Charles Henri Ford, Rilke, Lorca, Kafka, Arp, Max Ernst, St.-John Perse, Prévert, Laura Riding, Apollinaire, Brecht, Shakespeare, Ibsen, Strindberg, Joyce Cary, Mary Butts, Freud, Dali, Spenser, Stravinsky, William Carlos Williams and John Gay.

> Higglety-pigglety: Euripides and Gilbert. The Strawhat Reviewers, Goethe (of the *Autobiography*—I have never read *Faust*) and H. D.[7]

Such paradoxes are very much a part of Duncan's aesthetic, "a poetics not of paradigms and models but of individual variations and survivals."[8] He cares little for "good and bad works" but of "seminal and germinal works cast abroad in the seas of the world."[9] What offends some critics is Duncan's refusal to stay put, to obey some paradigmatic version of what the poet must be. A poet of this order seems irresponsible, unable to synthesize a strong literary ethos or heritage into his own work. But responsibility, as Duncan points out, means "the ability to respond,"[10] the ability to read the fluctuating pattern of reality as a meaningful text and to read all texts as versions of the "Grand Collage" of man's representations.

Perhaps the most important negatively critical assessment of Duncan's view of tradition came not from a conservative critic but from his peer and mentor, Charles Olson. In "Against Wisdom as Such," Olson admonishes Duncan for what he takes to be a sectarian fetish of wisdom, extricable from its sources and processes. Wisdom, Olson feels, "like style, is the man." It is not

> extricable in any sort of a statement of itself; even though—and here is the catch—there be "wisdom," that it must be sought, and that "truths" can be come on (they are so overwhelming and so simple there does exist the temptation to see them as "universal"). But they are, in no wise, or at the gravest loss, verbally separated. They stay the man. As his skin is. As his life. And to be parted with only as that is.[11]

Reading between the lines of Olson's cryptic prose we may see a Coleridgean faith in the organic synthesis of ideas and form. Duncan is accused of trafficking in knowledge for its own sake without reference to its immediate applicability to the individual's life and projects Wisdom, for the creator of Maximus, is the product of the self-reliant individual, wresting time out of a continuum in order to create rhythm rather than witness its effects.

Duncan's response to Olson exhibits a Freudian bias in favor of surfaces: wisdom regarded as story rather than as symbol:

> In a sense (Olson) is so keen upon the *virtu* of reality that he rejects my "wisdom" not as it might seem at first glance because "wisdom" is a vice; but because my wisdom is not real wisdom. He suspects, and rightly, that I indulge myself in pretentious fictions. I, however, at this point take enuf delight in the available glamor that I do not stop to trouble the cheapness of such stuff. I like rigor and even clarity as a quality of a work—that is, as I like muddle and floaty vagaries. It is the intensity of conception that moves me.[12]

The argument between the two men (an enormously generative one, as Don Byrd points out[13]) is an argument over two notions of tradition: one as the archaeological (and archetypal) structure of certain dynamic ideas realized throughout history by a few capable imaginations, the other as the open-ended series of variations on a corrupt and corruptible text. Olson's theory of tradition is recuperative; Duncan's is interpretative. For Olson, a writer like Melville transforms not only literature but physical space as well; he exists as a nodal point in the nineteenth-century imagination, along with Keats, Rimbaud, the geometers, Bolyai and Lobatschewsky, and the mathematician Riemann, within which constellation an entirely new conception of space was developed.[14] For Duncan, on the other hand, Dante and Shakespeare represent spirit guides in the poet's attempt to reanimate a core myth of creation. But as Michael Bernstein says, this treatment of past masters involves a reciprocal recognition on the part of both master and ephebe:

> But if . . . a poet's "permission" to enter into his poethood depends upon a reciprocal selection—his being "called" by a certain constellation of "masters"

requires, of course, that he himself also be ready to heed just those voices, be ready, that is, to constitute himself as their successor—then one of the surest indices of a potentially new voice is the enrichment/subversion he can bring to the established heritage of his own mentors, his capacity significantly to add to the horizon of "pre-texts" already marked out as canonic by the prior selection of his teachers.[15]

As verification of Bernstein's remarks, one has only to look into Duncan's encyclopedic meditation on the Modernists, *The H. D. Book*, in which the poet's own personal history is fused with a reading of certain modern masters so that, ultimately, the distance between private and literary life is broken down. The poet H. D. is the subject of the book, but not simply as an "influence" on Duncan's own work. Rather she projects and anticipates Duncan's life and art. By reading through her works (and the works of her generation), Duncan is permitted to reenter the world of his own personal identity in which fictions, stories, poems, and tales were formative influences. In fact, a substantial portion of the early chapters of *The H. D. Book* are devoted to the very earliest hearings of certain poems (H. D.'s "Heat," Basho's frog-pond-plash poem, Joyce's "I Hear an Army Charging Upon the Land") and to the circumstances of their encounters. He wants to record the luminous aura surrounding his own inaugural entry into story so that he may suggest how this moment "rhymes" with his later vocation as a poet. The great reading of Modernism (and ultimately of tradition in general) becomes a reading of origins as well.

For Duncan, the task of reading is never passive. It implies a readiness to receive and grapple with a story larger than himself, beyond the immediate event of reading. Jacob's wrestling with the angel is as much an allegory of reading as it is of Christian salvation, and Duncan often makes use of the story in exactly this double sense. Instead of hermeneutically recovering the text in an act that leaves it essentially unchanged, the poet actively translates its terms into a new text:

> Our work is to arouse in a contemporary consciousness reverberations of old myth, to prepare the ground so that when we return to read we will see our modern texts charged with a plot that had already begun before the first signs and signatures we have found worked upon the walls of Altamira or Pech-Merle.[16]

This charged, participatory act of reading has its origins in another kind of tradition: the hermetic, theosophical tradition inherited from his adopted parents and from his grandmother, the latter of whom had been an elder in an hermetic brotherhood.[17] For his parents,

> the truth of things was esoteric (locked inside) or occult (masked by) the apparent, and one needed a "lost" key in order to piece out the cryptogram of who wrote Shakespeare or who created the universe and what his real message was.[18]

In his childhood environment every event was significant as an element in a larger, cosmological scheme. Although Duncan never practiced within any theosophical religion, he easily translated its terms into Freud's dreamwork, which proposes a similar sort of interpretation. Within both theosophical and Freudian hermeneutics, story is not simply a diversion or fiction but an "everlasting omen of what is." The dream becomes a model for how that omen is received as a cryptic condensation and displacement of a "sentence":

> *I ask the unyielding Sentence that shows Itself forth*
> *in the language as I make it,*
>
> > *Speak! For I name myself your master, who come to serve.*
> > *Writing is first a search in obedience.*[19]

These "sentences" from the first of his "Structure of Rime" series reflect the basic double-bind in Duncan's version of romanticism. The poet must become both subject and object of his creation, open to a language he does not invent and yet, by the agency of this language, a maker. The Sentence is both an imperative (an "unyielding Sentence") and a grammatical construct just as the dream text is both *beyond* yet *of* the dreamer:

> It is in the dream itself that we seem entirely creatures, without imagination, as if moved by a plot or myth told by a story-teller who is not ourselves. Wandering and wondering in a foreign land or struggling in the meshes of a nightmare, we cannot escape the compelling terms of the dream unless we wake, anymore than we can escape the terms of our living reality unless we die.[20]

The consequences of this collapsing of subject and object is a poetry deeply self-conscious of its textual nature without, at the same time, reducing itself to an endless series of footnotes on its own operations. Many of Duncan's finest poems are "readings" of other texts, his own poem serving as meditation and transformation. *Medieval Scenes* (1947) originated around a series of epigraphs that led directly into the individual poems; "A Poem Beginning With A Line By Pindar" reads the story of Eros and Psyche into a line by the Greek poet; *Passages* begins with two texts from the Emperor Julian's "Hymn to the Mother of the Gods," and includes many other texts within its separate poems; *A Seventeenth-Century Suite* consists of variations on poems by Raleigh, Southwell, Herbert and others; *Dante Etudes,* similarly, involves poetic reflections on passages from Dante's prose; and poems often begin in the margins or blank pages of the poet's own books (*Poems From the Margins of Thom Gunn's MOLY, The Five Songs*). The point is that texts appear within Duncan's poems not as privileged signs of cultural order (as they often do in Pound and Eliot) nor as allusions but as generative elements in the composing process.

Duncan's mythopoeic hermeneutics derives, as I have said, from his family's theosophy as well as from Freudian dream-analysis and romanticism. All of these traditions propose a search for "first things," but for Duncan this search is not some sort of constitutive recollection of innocence. Returning to a "place of first permission" is to see it for the first time since, to adapt Williams, "the spaces it opens are new places / inhabited by hordes / heretofore unrealized." That is, the poetic descent into origins occurs in time, the present thus contributing to and changing how those early stories and traumas are reexperienced. A naive reading of Duncan's poetic statements on the subject of origins might see him yearning toward some totalized scheme of corre-spondences whereby time, in a Proustian or Joycean epiphany, is at last stilled or transcended. As Joseph Frank has observed, Modernist texts like *A la Recherche du Temps Perdu, Ulysses,* or *The Waste Land* rely for their unity on epiphanic moments that transcend temporal flux, allowing for a spatialized time that the text recovers.[21] Duncan's moments of "permission" are not recuperative; although they serve to link him to the past, they do so only to more fully engage the present. On the one hand he desires a kind of Emersonian participation in the world; on the other, he recognizes that the temporal apprehension of the world structures how that involvement might occur:

> Working in words I am an escapist; as if I could step out of my clothes and move naked as the wind in a world of words. But I want every part of the actual world involved in my escape. I bring the laws that bound me into an aerial structure in which they are unbound as outlines of a prison unfolding.[22]

Duncan's structure of repetition is similar to that described by Kierkegaard in his essay "Repetition." Here, Kierkegaard makes a distinction between "recollection," the attempt at reconstituting that which has been, and "repetition," the adumbration of what has been in a new formation. Recollection, he says, is what the Greeks called knowledge: the realization of eternal forms. Repetition continually generates life out of that which was once partially glimpsed but never fully realized. "The dialectic of repetition is easy," Kierkegaard says, "for that which is repeated has been—otherwise it could not be repeated—but the very fact that it has been makes the repetition into something new."[23] For Duncan, poetry is the structure of repetition in exactly these terms: a return to "roots of first feeling" and yet a projection forward based on terms discovered in that return.

> The morphology of forms, in evolving, does not destroy their historicity but reveals that each event has its origin in the origin of all events; yes, but in turn, we are but the more aware that the first version is revised in our very turning to it, seeing it with new eyes.[24]

A useful place to explore Duncan's ideas on repetition as well as his inheritance from the romantic tradition is his open-ended series, *The Structure of Rime.* Origi-nally conceived as imitations (readings) of Rimbaud's prose poems in *Illuminations, Structure of Rime* has become the poet's ongoing study of the role of rhyme, measure, and correspondence. These categories are experienced, by the poet, as "persons of the poem," dramatic voices that speak from various aspects of language: from the vocalic resources of the voice to syntax and, ultimately, to the informing matrix of myth and story.

> I started a series without end called *Structures of Rime* in which the poem could talk to me, a poetic seance, and, invoked so, persons of the poem appeared as I wrote to speak. I had only to keep the music of the invocation going and to take down what actually came to me happening in the course of the poem.[25]

"Persons of the poem" are not fictive, in the sense of dramatic personae, nor is their apprehension, to extend our Kierkegaardian terms, "recalled." They are encountered as "rhymes" with the creative order of life and are translated into the poet's creative order. The various mythic and daemonic figures who appear (Black King Glélé, The Woman Who Resembles the Sentence, The Master of Rime, The Beloved, etc.) appear in various guises throughout the series, but their participation in a basic configuration of powers and dominions remains. They are elemental forces in a cosmic drama, played out upon the stage of language.[26]

Like Duncan's other open-ended series, *Passages, The Structure of Rime* is an ongoing project that appears throughout the poet's *oeuvre*, occasionally intersecting with other sequences (as in "Apprehensions" and *The Five Songs*) and at least once with *Passages*.[27]) More recently, Duncan has dropped ordination (as he has with *Passages*), presumably to eliminate any notion of sequence or chronology.

Presiding over the series is "The Master of Rime" who acts as a daemonic muse on the order of Nietzsche's Zarathustra or Blake's Orc:

> The master of Rime, time after time, came down the arranged ladders of vision or ascended the smoke and flame towers of the opposite of vision, into or out of the language of daily life, husband to one word, wife to the other, breath that leaps forward upon the edge of dying.[28]

The Master of Rime represents poetry's ability to penetrate into the larger text of the world by creating "an absolute scale of resemblance and disresemblance." He enters through the "language of daily life," a language unheard until engaged by the poem. Within the poem, rhymes and resonances occur that the poet, aided by the visionary faculty of the Rime Master, is able to translate. The individual "Structure of Rime," as the passage above should illustrate, does not replicate this daily language, but provides a rhetorical mise en scène in which the process of visionary translation occurs. Rimbaud and Blake are not far behind the Master of Rime for their own entry into Duncan's language.

As the theory and practice of rime, it is perhaps all the more appropriate that the series is, for the most part, written not in lined verse but in prose. *The Structure of Rime* is not an *ars poetica* on the order of Pope's "Essay on Criticism" or Shapiro's "Essay on Rime," versified discussions of poetics. It is, instead, a dramatization of poetics, acted out by Duncan's heightened rhetoric and convoluted syntax:

> You too are a flame then and my soul quickening in your gaze a draft upward carrying the flame of you. From this bed of a language in compression, life now is fuel, anthracite from whose hardness the years spring. In flame
>
> beings strive in the Sun's chemistry as we strive in our meat to realize images of manhood immanent we have not reacht, but leave, as if they fell from us, bright fell and fane momentary attendants . . . [29]

Duncan is here describing the power of the Beloved, but the force of syntactic subordination, suspension, and combination works to destroy linguistic boundaries. To adapt the imagery of the passage, the language has taken fire from a "language in compression." The passage enacts what it describes; qualifying phrases and subordinate clauses suspend the syntactic term while predicates are further and further separated from their subjects. The fullest use of acoustic values (assonance, alliteration, rhyme, and near-rhyme) are exploited to give the passage the same sense of excitement and wonder inspired by the gaze of the lover. Language does not simply describe the erotic; words, by their sensual interplay, are eroticized.

If the Master of this ordering and disordering of language is Master of Rime, the Muse of the series is the "woman who resembles the sentence." At one level, she represents Duncan's own mother, lost at the time of his birth and thus the lost link to his own biological past:

> She has a place in memory that moves language. Her voice comes across the waters from a shore I don't know to a shore I know, and is translated into words belonging to the poem . . . [30]

On another level, she is syntax itself, the scale of resemblances and disresemblances upon which the poet plays his individual variations. Biological life (genetic coding) and creative life (linguistic coding) are thus fused under one common law:

> *Have heart*, the text reads,
>   *you that were heartless.*
> *Suffering joy or despair*
> *you will suffer the sentence*
> *a law of words moving*
> *seeking their right period.*

I saw a snake-like beauty in the living changes of syntax.

> *Wake up*, she cried
> *Jacob wrestled with Sleep—you who fall into Nothingness*
>   *and dread sleep.*
> *He wrestled with Sleep like a man reading a strong*
>   *sentence.*[31]

What appears to be going on in the interchange between the "I" and the "woman who resembles the sentence" is a retelling of the fall of man. The poet seeks to return to that "place in memory" before which language had become plural, a prelapsarian state in which words and things are not separate, in which discourse and poetry are one and the same. But he may only return via the language as he has inherited it, the original speech having been lost through an obsession with a "snake-like beauty in the living changes of syntax." His punishment, if indeed this is how we must characterize it, is to "suffer the sentence" of that first mother of language, to struggle, like Jacob, with the Angel of syntax. Thus, as the end of this opening Structure of Rime indicates, the poet will remain an adept in the service of language, creating "sentence after sentence" in her image:

> In the feet that measure the dance of my pages I hear cosmic intoxications of the man I will be.[32]

We have heard versions of this allegory of creative life throughout romantic literature (notably in Blake, Emerson, Shelley, Whitman, Stevens), and in one sense, *The Structure of Rime* is a homage to that tradition, without naming it as such.[33] What differentiates Duncan's version of the Adamic mythos from that of Emerson or Stevens, for example, is his dramatic rendering of voice and presence. His method is often dialogical, voices entering into the poem to cajole, warn, debate, and invoke while being responded to by the poet himself:

> The actual world speaks to me, and when it comes to that pitch, the words I speak with but imitate the way the mountain speaks. I create in *return*. In the structures of rime, not "I" but words themselves speak to you.[34]

In order to create "in return," Duncan must empty out what Olson called the "lyrical interference of the ego" and allow the complexities of image and syntax free reign. Here, for example, he invokes the Muse who commands:

> *Return your intelligence into the threshold of the real from the chamberd brain to the seeing fingers of the eye that feels, to the equilibrations of the inner ear to dwell in the light and dark of the rainbow from which color streams towards the music sound imitates; in the heavy and light in which desire arrives, burrow deep if you would reach that Grand Burial of the Mind where it may rest.*[35]

The complex image presented here is of a body extended into the world it senses so that there is, finally, no boundary of Mind and no objective world. The accumulation of phrases and their seeming lack of closure accomplish on a linguistic level the very dissolution described. This and others of the series thus become a reading of the romantic tradition through the agency that it bequeaths to poets.

Structure of Rime, as a continuing poetic series, is informed by a doctrine of linguistic and mythological correspondences. The history of our language, from our entry into it at childhood to its most complicated manifestations in poetry, is also the history of fictions by which we mutually cohere. To differentiate phonemes or recognize similar sounds is to become engaged with the realm of story—and of tradition—at its most basic level. As a conceptual field, *Structure of Rime* is informed by a cellular model in which all parts contribute to the whole and yet whose boundaries are continually evolving. Darwin's picture of evolution is, for Duncan, a visionary proposition of our heritage that claims, for man, relationships with the species beyond the historical moment. At the same time, it is in the immediacy of the moment, in its specific and time-bound nature, that our sense of commonality is discovered: "We must begin where we are. Our own configuration entering and belonging to a configuration being born of what 'we' means."[36] And the real "we," as Duncan points out, is "the company of the living."

In attempting to differentiate Duncan's theory of tradition from that of Eliot and his New Critical followers, I have perhaps glossed over what might be seen as a shared organicism. Duncan would probably not argue with Eliot's sense that innovation affects the past as much as it affects the present or that the poet must work with the "historical sense" in his bones. Works like *Structure of Rime* and *Passages* illustrate, however, the breadth and range of materials thus incorporated into the dynamics of literary change. And at the same time, these highly speculative, processual works involve immediacy and passional statement where Eliot would encourage discretion.[37] In making this contrast I have availed myself of a model of repetition, derived from contemporary hermeneutics, that introduces into Duncan's doctrine of rime and correspondence what I hope is a more dialectical movement. Thus the phrase from which my title derives, "Cave of Resemblances, Cave of Rimes," should not only evoke the cave of Plato but that of Freud as well.

NOTES

1. See Duncan's letter to Rexroth printed in Robert Duncan and Jack Spicer, *An Ode and Arcadia* (Berkeley, Calif.: Ark Press, 1974), n.p.

2. Delmore Schwartz, "The Present State of Poetry," in *Selected Essays of Delmore Schwartz*, ed. Donald A. Dike and David H. Zucker (Chicago, 1970), p. 44.

3. Robert Duncan, *The Opening of the Field* (New York: Grove Press, 1960), p. 14.

4. Robert Duncan, *The Truth and Life of Myth: An Essay in Essential Autobiography* (Fremont, Mich.: The Sumac Press, 1968), p. 38.

5. Robert Duncan, "Notebook A," in the papers of Robert Duncan at the Bancroft Library, University of California, Berkeley, p. 99.

6. "Interview with Robert Duncan," in *Towards a New American Poetics: Essays and Interviews*, ed. Ekbert Faas (Santa Barbara, Calif.: Black Sparrow Press, 1978), p. 82.

7. Robert Duncan, "Pages from a Notebook," in *The New American Poetry*, ed. Donald M. Allen (New York: Grove Press, 1960), p. 407.

8. Robert Duncan, "Notes on Grossinger's *Solar Journal: Oecological Sections* (Santa Barbara, Calif.: Black Sparrow Press, n.d.), n.p.

9. "Notes on Grossinger's *Solar Journal*," n.p.

10. *The Opening of the Field*, p. 10.

11. Charles Olson, "Against Wisdom as Such," in *Human Universe and Other Essays*, ed. Donald Allen (New York: Grove Press, 1967), p. 68.

12. Robert Duncan, "From a Notebook," in *The Poetics of the New American Poetry*, ed. Donald Allen and Warren Tallman (New York: Grove Press, 1973), p. 185.

13. Don Byrd provides an excellent account of Olson and Duncan's relationship in his essay, "The Question of Wisdom as Such," in *Robert Duncan: Scales of the Marvelous*, ed. Robert J. Bertholf and Ian W. Reid (New York: New Directions, 1979), pp. 38–55.

14. See Olson's essay, "Equal, That Is, to the Real Itself" in *Human Universe and Other Essays*, pp. 117–22.

15. Michael A. Bernstein, "Bringing It All Back Home: Derivations and Quotations in Robert Duncan and the Poundian Tradition," *Sagetrieb* 1, 2 (Fall 1982):184.

16. Robert Duncan, "Two Chapters from *H. D.*" *Tri-Quarterly* (Spring 1968):67.

17. See Duncan's discussion of the occult tradition in part I, chapter 5 of the *H. D. Book*, printed as "Occult Matters" (Stony Brook, 1/2), pp. 4–19.

18. *The Truth and Life of Myth*, p. 8.

19. *The Opening of the Field*, p. 12.

20. "Occult Matters," p. 18.

21. Joseph Frank, "Spatial Form In Modern Literature," in *The Widening Gyre* (Bloomington: Indiana University Press, 1963), pp. 3–62.

22. Robert Duncan, *Bending the Bow* (New York: New Directions, 1968), p. v.

23. Søren Kierkegaard, *Repetition,* ed. and trans. Howard V. Hong and Edna Hong (Princeton, N.J.: Princeton University Press, 1983), p. 149.

24. *The Truth and Life of Myth,* p. 51.

25. Robert Duncan, "Man's Fulfillment in Order and Strife," *Caterpillar* 8/9 (Oct. 1969), p. 239.

26. Duncan discusses the role of "persons of the poem" in *Structure of Rime* in an interview with Kevin Power, "A Conversation with Robert Duncan," *Revista Canaria de Estudios Ingleses* 4 (April 1982):100–103.

27. Robert Duncan, "Apprehensions," in *Roots and Branches* (New York: Scribners, 1964), pp. 30–42; "Structure of Rime *Of the Five Songs*" in *The Five Songs* (La Jolla, Calif.: The Friends of the UCSD Library, 1981); "Passages 20 (Structure of Rime XXVI)" in *Bending the Bow,* p. 68.

28. *The Opening of the Field,* p. 17.

29. *Bending the Bow,* 37.

30. *The Opening of the Field,* p. 12.

31. Ibid.

32. Ibid.

33. Duncan provides an extensive discussion of the romantic roots of *Structure of Rime* in *Maps 6,* pp. 42–52.

34. "Man's Fulfillment in Order and Strife," p. 238.

35. Robert Duncan, "The Shadow of the Muse," in *Ground Work* Vol. I (privately published), p. 38.

36. *Bending the Bow,* p. ii.

37. Duncan has, on numerous occasions, pointed out the discrepancies between Eliot's theory and practice when it comes to personal confession. I am speaking less about Eliot's actual practice in the poems than I am of the canonization of his theory of "impersonality" by a later generation of critics.

THE ASSEMBLING VISION OF RITA DOVE

ROBERT McDOWELL

Rita Dove has always possessed a storyteller's instinct. In *The Yellow House on the Corner* (1980), *Museum* (1983), and *Thomas and Beulah* (1985), this instinct has found expression in a synthesis of striking imagery, myth, magic, fable, wit, humor, political comment, and a sure knowledge of history. Many contemporaries share Dove's mastery of some of these, but few succeed in bringing them together to create a point of view that, by its breadth and force, stands apart. She has not worked her way into this enviable position among poets without fierce commitment.

Passing through a graduate writing program (Iowa) in the mid-1970s, Dove and her peers were schooled in the importance of sensation and its representation through manipulation of The Image. The standard lesson plan, devised to reflect the ascendancy of Wallace Stevens and a corrupt revision of T. S. Eliot's objective correlative, instructed young writers to renounce realistic depiction and offer it up to the province of prose; it promoted subjectivity and imagination-as-image; it has strangled a generation of poems.

How and why this came to pass is less important, really, than admitting that it is so. Literary magazines are gorged with poems devoid of shapeliness and scope. Imagistic, cramped, and confessional, they exist for the predictably surprising, climactic phrase. A historically conscious reader, aware of literary tradition, might understandably perceive an enormous cultural amnesia as the dubiously distinguishing feature of such poems. Such a reader will rue the fact that the writing and interpretation of poetry has diminished to a trivial pursuit, a pronouncement of personal instinct. If this is the dominant direction of a discouraging Moment, then Rita Dove distinguishes herself by resolutely heading the other way.

Unlike the dissembling spirit indicted above, Dove is an assembler who gathers the various facts of this life and presents them in ways that jar our lazy assumptions. She gives voice to many positions and many characters. Like the speaker/writer of classic argumentation, she shows again and again that she understands the opposing sides of conflicts she deals with. She tells all sides of the story. Consider the titles of her books, their symbolic weight. The personal turning point *House on the Corner* evolves, becoming the public Museum (symbol of preserved chronology); that, in turn, gives way to the names of two characters whose lives combine and illustrate the implicit meanings of the personal House and the public Museum.

The Yellow House on the Corner, first of all, is a showcase for Dove's control of the language. This is our first encounter with the powerful images we have come to associate with her work:

> *The texture of twilight made me think of*
> *Lengths of dotted Swiss.*
>
> *(p. 50)*

> *As the sun broke the water into a thousand needles*
> *tipped with the blood from someone's finger . . .*
>
> *(p. 40)*

> *This nutmeg stick of a boy in loose trousers!*
> *(p. 60)*

These are the observations of original sight.

There is also the rich and heavily symbolic use of color—red, orange, blue, yellow, and black and white. They usually appear as adjectives, but her adjectival preoccupation comes across with a difference. For example, while repeatedly employing *black* as an adjective ("black place," "black table," "prune-black water," "horses black," "black tongues," "my black bear"), she never settles for quick agreement based on obvious connotations. Instead, she injects the adjectives with tantalizing ambiguity and new meanings based on their relationships to other words. She redefines our connotative relationship to them. She outdistances most poets simply because she understands that adjectives enhance nouns by better defining them; they are part of the equations we are born to cope with, not substitutes for weak noun counterparts.

The Yellow House also introduces the poet's devotion to myth, her determination to reveal what is magical in our contemporary lives.

THIS LIFE

> *The green lamp flares on the table.*
> *You tell me the same thing*
> *as that one,*
> *asleep, upstairs.*
> *Now I see: the possibilities*
> *are golden dresses in a nutshell.*
>
> *As a child, I fell in love*
> *with a Japanese woodcut*
> *of a girl gazing at the moon.*
> *I waited with her for her lover.*
> *He came in white breeches and sandals.*
> *He had a goatee—he had*
>
> *your face, though I didn't know it.*
> *Our lives will be the same—*
> *your lips, swollen from whistling*
> *at danger,*

> *and I a stranger*
> *in this desert,*
> *nursing the tough skins of figs.*

In this poem, "The Bird Frau," "The Snow King," "Beauty and the Beast," and others, she echoes, distorts, and revises ancient myths; in "Upon Meeting Don L. Lee in a Dream" and "Robert Schumann, Or: Musical Genius Begins with Affliction," she focuses on characters whose actual lives have been the stuff of myths.

These and a number of short love poems comprise one side of Dove's Grand Equation. Travelogue poems (consistent throughout her work) erect a transitional bridge between her myth-making component and the historical, public side of the equation: poems examining race relations in America. At their best, poems from the myth-making category are lyrical and mysterious; poems from the latter category are heartbreakingly honest and inescapable. Though these last poems are placed throughout the volume, the third section is made up entirely of them, a fact which makes it the most relentless and coherent segment of the book.

In these poems, Dove makes the reader aware of the relationship between private and public events. "The Transport of Slaves from Maryland to Mississippi" (p. 37), for example, is based on an incident of 1839 in which a slave woman thwarts the escape of a wagonload of slaves by helping the driver regain his horse. The narrative point of view shifts three times, revealing the complexity of the incident and of the characters involved in it. No prescriptive strategy limits expression, as the woman's opening monologue makes clear. Describing the driver she says, "his eyes were my eyes in a yellower face. . . . He might have been a son of mine." The justification of her act is poignant even though its consequences are disastrous for her fellows.

This section of *The Yellow House* is bold and beautifully elegiac, presenting the motives and gestures of all of the dramatic players. The poet's wise utterance peels back the rhetorically thick skin of injustice and exposes Man's inhumanity for what it is: unbearable, shameful, unforgettable.

> *Well,*
> *that was too much for the doctor.*
> *Strip 'em! he ordered. And they*
> *were slicked down with bacon fat and*
> *superstition strapped from them*
> *to the beat of the tam-tam. Those strong enough*
> *rose up too, and wailed as they leapt.*
> *It was a dance of unusual ferocity.*
>
> *("Cholera")*

That final grim understatement intensifies the reader's outrage.

Dove's synthesis of a historical consciousness, devotion to myth, and virtuoso manipulation of parts of speech convey us into the world of her major thematic preoccupation. In one poem she writes "My heart, shy mulatto" (p. 29), which informs the closing lines of a later poem like "Adolescence—III."

> *. . . I dreamed how it would happen:*
> *He would meet me by the blue spruce,*

> *A carnation over his heart, saying,*
> *"I have come for you, Madam;*
> *I have loved you in my dreams."*
> *At his touch, the scabs would fall away.*
> *Over his shoulder, I see my father coming toward us:*
> *He carries his tears in a bowl,*
> *And blood hangs in the pine-soaked air.*

This poem, and this volume's cumulative thrust, redefines the poet's need to reconcile the conventional, Romantic American wish (that life be a fairy tale) with the cruel facts of Black America's heritage.

Museum begins with travelogues, which prepare the reader for travel poems that eclipse the personal by introducing overlooked historical detail. "Nestor's Bathtub," a pivotal poem in this respect, begins with the lines "As usual, legend got it all wrong." This announces a dissatisfaction with the conventional ordering of events and an intention to rejuvenate history by coming up with new ways of telling it. In successive poems ("Tou Wan Speaks to Her Husband, Lu sheng," "Catherine of Alexandria," "Catherine of Siena," "Boccaccio: The Plague Years," and its companion piece, "Fiammetta Breaks Her Peace"), Dove adopts a variety of personae that bear witness to the struggles of victimized women in societies in which men are dubiously perceived as gods.

This strategy continues into the book's second section, though the subjects and personae are primarily male ("Shakespeare Say," "Banneker," "Ike"). Here is the narrator in "Reading Holderlin on the Patio with the Aid of a Dictionary":

> *The meaning that surfaces*
> *comes to me aslant and*
> *I go to meet it, stepping*
> *out of my body*
> > *word for word, until I am*
> *everything at once.*

As in *The Yellow House,* in *Museum* Dove focuses on characters, and chooses characters to speak through, from the historical rosters of those whose lives have been the stuff of fable. Toward the end of this section, her identification with historical and mysterious male-female consciousness is most complete in "Agosta the Winged Man and Rasha the Black Dove." In this poem she tells the story of a pair of German circus performers, an inscrutable deformed man and an equally inscrutable black woman who dances with snakes. These characters are performers, who like the poet, look at the world in unique ways.

> > *Agosta in*
> > *classical drapery, then,*
> *and Rasha at his feet.*
> *Without passion. Not*
> *the canvas*
> > > *but their gaze,*
> > > *so calm,*
> *was merciless.*

The poem that follows, "At the German Writers Conference in Munich," examines and exploits this preoccupation from another angle. In the poem another art—another way of performing—is described. The calm, stiff characters of a tapestry are not outwardly grotesque as they are the characters in the preceding poem. Nevertheless, they appear to be out of step with their woven environment, existing as they do in a world of flowers. The two poems, together, illustrate a brilliant shifting of focus, a looking out of the eyes of characters, then a merciless looking into them.

The third section of *Museum* contains a focusing down of this strategy in a tight group of family poems in which the father is the dominant character. He is perceived by the innocent narrator as the teacher, the bearer of all that is magical in the world.

> *I've been trying*
> *to remember the taste,*
> *but it doesn't exist.*
> *Now I see why*
> *you bothered,*
> *father.*
> ("Grape Sherbet")

Whether he is making palpable an impalpable taste or miraculously rescuing roses from beetles ("Roses") or deftly retrieving what is magical from a mistake ("My Father's Telescope") he is clearly the narrator's mentor, inspiring a different way of meeting the world:

> *this*
> *magician's skew of scarves*
> *issuing from an opaque heart.*
> ("A Father Out Walking On the Lawn")

But even in this tender, celebratory section, Dove includes one poem, "Anti-Father," which satisfies her self-imposed demand that she tell all sides of the story.

> *Just between*
>
> *me and you,*
> *woman to man,*
>
> *outer space is*
> *inconceivably*
>
> *intimate.*

The innocent narrator, now a knowledgeable woman, reverses roles here, contradicting the father but offering magical insight in doing so.

The closing section of Rita Dove's second volume summarizes all that has preceded it, and in two remarkable poems anticipates *Thomas and Beulah*. The narrator of "A Sailor in Africa" spins off from a Viennese card game (circa 1910) and unravels the adventures of the characters in the game. A black slave, who is actually a sea captain, outwits his captors and takes over their ship. He is shipwrecked later, only to discover great wealth in his isolation. This effortless storytelling combines Dove's great strengths—memorable images, wit, travelogue, fable, complex representation of motive and gesture, historical awareness—in a groundbreaking poem.

It is balanced and rivaled by "Parsley," the book's concluding poem, which tells the story of a dictator who orders the annihilation of 20,000 blacks because they cannot pronounce the letter "r." The poem is constructed in two parts. The first, a villanelle, presents the entire drama; it is all the more terrifying because the facts smash against the stark and beautiful container of the form itself. In the second part of the poem, a third-person narrator examines the dictator's relationship to his mother, who can "roll her 'r's' like a queen."

> *As he paces he wonders*
> *who can I kill today . . .*
>
>   *Someone*
> *calls out his name in a voice*
> *so like his mother's, a startled tear*
> *splashes the tip of his right boot.*
> My mother, my love in death.

As she often does, Dove unerringly combines private and public political history in this and in many other poems in *Museum*. It is a direction that flourishes on a book-length scale in *Thomas and Beulah*.

"These poems tell two sides of a story and are meant to be read in sequence." So begins *Thomas and Beulah*. Their story is told twice: from Thomas's point of view in the twenty-three poems of "Mandolin," and from Beulah's point of view in the twenty-one poems of "Canary in Bloom." The time, according to an extensive Chronology at book's end, covers the years from 1919 to 1968. Most of the story takes place in Akron, Ohio, a city, which the Chronology also tells us, had a Negro population of 11,000 (out of a total population of 243,000) in 1940.

The chief narrative method employed, the story twice-told, does not rely so much on action; it relies on reactions of characters to events and circumstances that affect them even though they are wholly beyond them. The questions generated by this approach are chilling and clear: if two characters, deeply involved with one another, interpret events (inner and outer, private and public) so differently, what does this suggest about our manipulation of history; what does it say about our reliability as witnesses, as teachers of successive generations; what is true?

Truth in *Thomas and Beulah* is found in the characters themselves. In "The Event," the first poem in the section entitled "Mandolin," Thomas leaves Tennessee for the riverboat life. He travels with a good friend, Lem, and a magical symbol, a talisman which gathers pain and wards it off—his mandolin. In a turn that explodes the deliberate echo of Mark Twain's *Huck Finn*, Lem dives overboard to collect chestnuts on a passing island and drowns. This tragedy, at the outset of his journey, will haunt Thomas for the rest of his life. We observe his arrival in Akron in 1921, deftly and desperately playing his mandolin for pay. He is a driven figure, confronting his guilt and his second-class citizenship in a racially divided country. His half-hearted attempts to sell himself in such a country will drive the more sheltered Beulah to find fault in him. It is a key element of his tragedy that he faults himself for it, too:

> *He used to sleep like a glass of water*
> *held up in the hand of a very young girl.*

and later,

> *To him work is a narrow grief*
> *and the music afterwards*
> *like a woman*
> *reaching into his chest*
> *to spread it around.*
> *("Straw Hat")*

After their marriage, the promise of equality and upward mobility is profoundly betrayed. The world is threatening, malicious after all. In "Nothing Down," they buy a new car for a trip to Tennessee, but the symbol and the dream it represents are destroyed when they're passed by a carload of jeering whites; in "The Zeppelin Factory," Thomas lands construction work, laboring on the largest building in the world without interior supports (another appropriate, unforgettable symbol for the world we make) and hates it; Thomas ponders the impending birth of a third daughter against the backdrop of union violence ("Under the Viaduct"); Thomas walks out of a movie house to witness a splendid natural phenomenon ("Aurora Borealis"), but even this double-barreled symbolic magic is overpowered by the grim facts of the world around him. Finally, he finds even his oldest companion, his mandolin, estranged:

> *How long has it been . . . ?*
> *Too long. Each note slips*
> *into querulous rebuke, fingerpads*
> *scarred with pain, shallow ditches*
> *to rut in like a runaway slave*
> *with a barking heart. Days afterwards*
> *blisters to hide from the children.*
> *Hanging by a thread. Some day,*
> *he threatens, I'll just*
> *let go.*
> *("Definition in the Face of Unnamed Fury")*

Only in his own good heart is Thomas vindicated, and the physical manifestation of his goodness is his family. In "Roast Opossum," he spins two tales for his grandchildren: hunting opossum for Malcolm, a tale of horses for the girls. This tender poem makes a case for salvation implicit in one generation's nurturing another by gathering and making palpable history and myth, fact and fiction. In such ritual we discover our one defense against the inhuman things we do to one another.

The section concludes with three elegiac poems covering the events of Thomas's declining health and eventual death. "The Stroke" contains a lovely memory of Beulah during pregnancy and his certainty that the pain he feels is Lem knocking on his chest. In the end, Thomas appropriately suffers his final heart attack behind the wheel of his car ("Thomas at the Wheel").

Whereas Thomas's life is a perpetual scramble toward definition, Beulah's, as presented in "Canary in Bloom," is preordained. She will marry; she will bear children.

These restrictions force her to develop an inward, private life. For example, her fear and distrust of male figures is established early in "Taking in Wash." Her father comes home drunk:

> *Tonight*
>
> > *every light hums, the kitchen arctic*
> > *with sheets, Papa is making the hankies*
> > *sail. Her foot upon a silk*
> > *stitched rose, she waits*
> > *until he turns, his smile sliding all over.*

This is the seed of her reaction to her suitor and future husband. She would prefer a pianola to his mandolin; she hates his yellow scarf. When they marry, "rice drumming / the both of them blind," she sees Thomas as "a hulk, awkward in blue serge." Her father places her fingertips in Thomas's hand, and men in collusion have delivered her up to her fate.

From this point on, Beulah's story seeks the form, the shape, of meditation. In "Dusting" she fondly remembers a boy at a fair, comparing that magical location and meeting with the hard news of her life. In "Weathering Out" she daydreams through her seventh month of pregnancy, glad to be rid of Thomas as he daily hunts for work. In the sad "Daystar" she reclines in the backyard while the children nap and dreams of a place where she is nothing. In "The Great Palace of Versailles" she works in a dress shop, frequents the library, and temporarily loses the facts of her own life in the magic of lords and ladies.

Beulah's development of a rich inner life is the result of meditation with an outward eye. Throughout her long battle with the prescribed role she was born to play, she continues to cope admirably and compassionately with the world outside. She manages her family; she feeds transients during the Depression; she shows kindness to the daughter of a prejudiced neighbor. As the poems progress her wisdom deepens. Her attitude toward Thomas softens, too. While sweeping she recalls the drive to Tennessee, how

> *Even then*
> *he was forever off in the woods somewhere in search*
> *of a magic creek.*
> > *("Pomade")*

And later, addressing him in "Company":

> *Listen: we were good,*
> *though we never believed it.*

If she does not change her life, Beulah through wisdom comes to understand it. She also comprehends the lives of her daughters. At their husbands' company picnic—a segregated picnic—Beulah remembers the march on Washington and its effects on the lives of her children. Her meditative impulse blossoms. Her preferred inner life squares off against the world of iniquity, and the succeeding generation is better off for it.

When I consider the discouraging Moment I mentioned at the beginning of this article, when I despair of it, I turn to only a few poets of my generation and am revitalized. Rita Dove's development through three volumes reminds us of the necessity for scope in poetry. A wide range of talent in service to an assembling vision is the tonic we need for discouragement.

A GENEROUS SALVATION:
THE POETRY OF NORMAN DUBIE

DAVID ST. JOHN

One of the most intriguing—and perhaps profound—shifts in recent American poetry between the years 1965 and 1985 has been the renewed interest in history and the increased prominence of historical considerations in the work of younger American poets. As an escape from the solipsism of the available styles often in vogue, and as a way to establish the self in a broader, more generous context, some poets have moved toward a greater historicity in their work, and history itself has begun to serve as both a force and a backdrop in the poetry of some of our most adventurous poets.

In my view, the most influential and accomplished of these historically attentive younger poets has been Norman Dubie, whose *Selected and New Poems* (Norton, 1983) remains one of the most radical and compelling collections of recent years. Perhaps this is because Dubie's reckonings with history are never simply reiterations of past events; instead, his poems constitute a fierce investigation into the history of consciousness itself.

Most often, Norman Dubie's poems exist at the place of juncture of several "realities," sometimes historical and sometimes personal. For Dubie, "reality" is a condition of perception; that is, it is a complex of perceptions in constant flux. In each poem, a "sensibility" works to define the nature of the poem's "reality" as details of history (or of "objective" reality) begin to intrude upon and intersect with the speaker's own meditation and perceptions, his own sequence of realities. In this way, multiple correspondences arise out of Dubie's poetry even as their constant narrative impulses drive them on. With the very first poem in *Selected and New Poems*, "For Randall Jarrell, 1914–1965," we are introduced to the condition common to many of Dubie's poems—we are caught at the juncture of two worlds. Here, in a realm touched by both the world of the living and the world of the dead, is the poem:

FOR RANDALL JARRELL, 1914–1965

What the wish wants to see, it sees.

All the dead are eating little yellow peas
Off knives under the wing of an owl
While the living run around, not aimlessly, but
Like two women in white dresses gathering

Hymnbooks out on a lawn with the first
Drops of rain already falling on them.

Once, I wrote a sudden and enormous sentence
At the bottom of a page in a notebook
Next to a sketch of a frog. The sentence
Described the gills of a sunfish
As being the color of cut rhubarb, or
Of basil if it is dried in a bundle
In a red kitchen with the last winter light
Showing it off, almost purple.

Anything approaching us we try to understand, say,
Like a lamp being carried up a lane at midnight.

Jeremy Taylor knew it watching an orange leaf
Go down a stream.
Self-taught, it came to us, I believe,
As old age to a panther who's about to
Spring from one branch to another but suddenly
Thinks better of it.
She says to us from her tree:
"Please, one world at a time!" and leaps—

Making it, which could mean,
Into this world or some other. And between.

In the leap which ends this poem, all possibilities are true; we are given the suspended emblem of the panther, invoking the twinned quality of the living world with that of the dead, and of the interpenetration of those worlds. The transgression of one world by another remains a constant preoccupation in Dubie's work; often, the transgression of reality by illusion or imagination—the objective by the subjective—is a poem's true occasion. For Dubie it is this multiplicity of worlds which creates whatever universal harmonies exist.

Norman Dubie's poems look out into our world and find the replication and repetition of image and emblem, of the figure and the figurative, of the shifting perspective and the broken tableau—he finds these all in movement, in the world's shifting mutations of context. His poems consider the nature of experience as influenced by the multiplicity of our perceptions and by the multiplicity of correspondences available in those perceptions. Often, in a Dubie poem, we find the natural, the violent, and the intimate all conjoined in a single poetic whole. There is a melancholy of detail, often painterly in ambition and scope, and through the disruption of those details (sometimes a syntactic disruption; Dubie is one of the most complex and yet absolute lyricists of the moment) the reader finds the vision both in and of the poem being dramatically transformed. The fine, delicate confusions of mind and eye are transfigured for us into the speech and voices of poetry. Dubie's narratives work on the principle of *release*—detail, nuance, gesture—and this allows an accretion of understandings to coalesce as his landscapes quietly reveal themselves. Every story turns visual in Dubie's meditations, just as all of his landscapes imply latent narratives. Dubie is always positing the congruent possibilities of an experience and, in spite of their overwhelming elegiac tenor, his is a poetry of celebratory illustration and illumination. Here is one such illustration detailing Dubie's concern with repetition and replication, coupled with his persistent visual richness:

FEBRUARY: THE BOY BREUGHEL

The birches stand in their beggar's row:
Each poor tree
Has had its wrists nearly
Torn from the clear sleeves of bone,
These icy trees
Are hanging by their thumbs
Under a sun
That will begin to heal them soon,
Each will climb out
Of its own blue, oval mouth;
The river groans,
Two birds call out from the woods

And a fox crosses through snow
Down a hill; then, he runs,
He has overcome something white
Beside a white bush, he shakes
It twice, and as he turns
For the woods, the blood in the snow

Looks like the red fox,
At a distance, running down the hill:
A white rabbit in his mouth killed
By the fox in snow
Is killed over and over as just
Two colors, now, on a winter hill:

Two colors! Red and white. A barber's bowl!
Two colors like the peppers
In the windows
Of the town below the hill. Smoke comes
From the chimneys. Everything is still.

Ice in the river begins to move,
And a boy in a red shirt who woke
A moment ago
Watches from his window
The street where an ox
Who's broken out of his hut
Stands in the fresh snow
Staring cross-eyed at the boy
Who smiles and looks out

Across the roof to the hill;
And the sun is reaching down
Into the woods

Where the smoky red fox still
Eats his kill. Two colors.
Just two colors!
A sunrise. The snow.

It is not often enough said that Dubie's poems are quite commonly concerned with situations of dailiness. Even in those poems, often monologues, in which conspicuously "famous" artists, writers, scientists, or musicians appear, these figures are always dealt with in basic and human terms. The poems that employ these presences are never contingent upon the speaker's or subject's renown for their power as much as upon the richness and surprise of their perceptions. For Dubie, the intuitive and intimate response is consistently the most primary concern, not the literary, well-read response. There has always been, it seems to me, a basic misunderstanding of Dubie's use of renowned personages as speakers and subjects. For Dubie, they hold no special attraction simply because of that renown; instead, he sees them as crucial historical exemplars of new and radical ways of thinking and perceiving from throughout our past. These speakers are the very voices of those historical junctures in the arts and sciences, in music and philosophy, that have changed the ways in which we think about ourselves as human beings. Dubie's poems about or spoken by artists and scientists are not simply considerations of art and science, they are more basically meditations on thought itself and the nature of perception, on the process of *seeing* and *thinking* that is common to us all but which, in some, seems raised to a higher power.

Dubie's regard for the past is one which finds itself manifested repeatedly in elegiac homages to those sensibilities (those "perceivers") he admires and finds most instructive, most honorable. It is the dignity of the radical pursuits and perceptions of these figures that Dubie wishes to champion and preserve. Invariably, Dubie's great "perceivers" are minds at work against the odds of convention. Yet he allows us to see them in their most ordinary and human moments; sometimes, in fact, we see them exposed in some element of ugliness or cruelty. Dubie finds it crucial to allow his speakers to find as their backdrops the ordinary, *lived* world.

Dubie's poems exemplify a world view which posits the congruence and simultaneity of all acts and temporalities, all artistic and daily endeavors. Necessarily, this interaction and interdependence of memory and experience, of one's perceptions and hopes, includes the interweaving of the worlds of the living and the dead. In his *APR* interview, Dubie said in regard to his own work, "in any tradition of talents, the new artist is completed by the dead artist." Dubie's monologues can sometimes suggest a collaborative effort between the poet and the past "perceiver"; yet, even when the poems convey a serious and weighty historicity their speakers continue to wear their destinies calmly, usually with great grace and even humor. The list of renowned figures in Dubie's work is long, including Chekhov, Klee, Jacob Boehme, Ovid, Gide, Virginia Woolf, Mayakofsky, Ibsen, Beethoven, Rodin, Melville, and Coleridge. Yet one of the most powerful and moving of all of Dubie's speakers is a failure on many counts and not a terribly illuminating thinker at all—he is the prideful, captive, and soon to be executed Czar Nicholas of Russia:

THE CZAR'S LAST CHRISTMAS LETTER:
A BARN IN THE URALS

You were never told, Mother, how old Illya was drunk
That last holiday, for five days and nights

He stumbled through Petersburg forming
A choir of mutes, he dressed them in pink ascension gowns

And, then, sold Father's Tirietz stallion so to rent
A hall for his Christmas recital: the audience

Was rowdy but Illya in his black robes turned on them
And gave them that look of his; the hall fell silent

And violently he threw his hair to the side and up
Went the baton, the recital ended exactly one hour

Later when Illya suddenly turned and bowed
And his mutes bowed, and what applause and hollering

Followed.
All of his cronies were there!

Illya told us later that he thought the voices
Of mutes combine in a sound

Like wind passing through big, winter pines.
Mother, if for no other reason I regret the war

With Japan for, you must now be told,
It took the servant, Illya, from us. It was confirmed.

He would sit on the rocks by the water and with his stiletto
Open clams and pop the raw meats into his mouth

And drool and laugh at us children.
We hear guns often, now, down near the village.

Don't think me a coward, Mother, but it is comfortable
Now that I am no longer Czar. I can take pleasure

From just a cup of clear water. I hear Illya's choir often.
I teach the children about decreasing fractions, that is

A lesson best taught by the father.
Alexandra conducts the French and singing lessons.

Mother, we are again a physical couple.
I brush out her hair for her at night.

She thinks that we'll be rowing outside Geneva
By the spring. I hope she won't be disappointed.

Yesterday morning while bread was frying
In one corner, she in another washed all of her legs

Right in front of the children. I think
We became sad at her beauty. She has a purple bruise

On an ankle.
Like Illya I made her chew on mint.

Our Christmas will be in this excellent barn.
The guards flirt with your granddaughters and I see . . .

I see nothing wrong with it. Your little one, who is
Now a woman, made one soldier pose for her, she did

Him in charcoal, but as a bold nude. He was
Such an obvious virgin about it; he was wonderful!

Today, that same young man found us an enormous azure
And pearl samovar. Once, he called me Great Father

And got confused.
He refused to let me touch him.

I know they keep your letters from us. But, Mother,
The day they finally put them in my hands

I'll know that possessing them I am condemned
And possibly even my wife, and my children.

We will drink mint tea this evening.
Will each of us be increased by death?

With fractions as the bottom integer gets bigger, Mother, it
Represents less. That's the feeling I have about

This letter. I am at your request. The Czar.
And I am Nicholas.

This is a poem of tremendous tenderness, generosity, and beauty. In the extremity of these historical circumstances, we find a voice which transfigures our understanding of a person and a period. Dubie is a master of the impassioned, elliptical story. In his monologues (Dubie once called the dramatic monologue "a chosen profession"), Dubie asks: What is it that grants this speaker a unique place along the continuum of history? What, in each figure, is *like us;* what, in fact, is universal and human? Dubie doesn't so much recall history as recast histories; we constantly find his speakers redefining their relationships to their world, to their own observations and experiences. History is what time has left us in its wake; history is the story, the compilation of stories, we tell about time. Time has only one story it wishes to tell us: we are heading toward our deaths. Dubie, in his rescue of the dead and their visions, is able to forestall that sense of passage. Like Scheherazade, each poem, each story keeps him alive against time. It is in part this that makes Dubie so unafraid to champion ennobling acts, just as he is equally unafraid to champion the idiosyncratic, the momentary, and the domestic.

The object of Dubie's poetry is twin: natural sympathy and psychic renewal, or if you prefer, psychic sympathy and natural renewal. It is perhaps because of his capacity for sympathy with his speakers that Dubie has written the finest monologues in the voices of women (that is, of those written by a man) of anyone since Randall Jarrell; in my view, Dubie's monologues in the voices of women surpass Jarrell's because they avoid the pathos so many of Jarrell's poems enjoy. What a pleasure it is to reread these poems: "The Pennacesse Leper Colony For Women, Cape Cod: 1922," "Monologue of Two Moons, Nudes With Crests: 1938," "Nineteen Forty" (spoken by Virginia Woolf), the stunning "Aubade of the Singer and Saboteur, Marie Triste," and a new poem, "Penelope." In "The Pennacesse Leper Colony For Women, Cape Cod: 1922," a young woman writes to her faher about her life as a leper on the island. What she describes is the living and physical replication of the body's disintegration after death; what we as readers discover is that the poem's true subject is the transcendence and issuance of the spirit. As she says in her letter, "We are not kept / In; even by our skin."

Many of Dubie's poems want to ask of history: What is primitive? What is civilized? How does *this* world supersede *that* world, if not by a more open and humane understanding of itself? The poems ask: What is the place of the will in the natural world? Is this the source of our constant struggles? Yet Dubie's poems are often also tinged with a light that is almost mystical; they invite into themselves a spirituality that itself transcends any conventional sense of spirituality because it is contingent upon the mind's simultaneous intersection with and recognition of many worlds beyond the natural world. In one of his new poems, "Revelations," we find this visionary side of Dubie, just as it exists perhaps in its most finely orchestrated state in the superb poem, "Elegies for the Ochre Deer on the Walls at Lascaux," a masterfully conceived meditation on will and being, on death and regeneration.

In reviewing the book *The City of the Olesha Fruit,* Peter Stitt noted that Dubie's poems "are not, no matter how obliquely, written in honor of the personality. They are written to celebrate the power of the imagination. The stance of the poet is objective, curious, interested in the known wonders of the world and in its possibilities." Indeed, the power, resiliency, and scope of the imagination often figure as subjects in many of Dubie's best poems, including the title poem of the volume above. In "The City of the Olesha Fruit" we find one of Dubie's most marvelous figures, Rumen, "an old man without legs," who, unable to go out into the real city, "has / invented the city outside the window." Rumen (whose "favorite writer is the great Russian / Yuri Olesha") not only gives his city its people and its stories, he provides and changes the weather as well. Rumen is the author of his own city, filling it with his memories and his imagination. Rumen shares his stories, the stories of his city, with Yuri Olesha—that is, with the Olesha of his imagination, the "companion" Olesha he addresses in his mind. In the second section of the poem, the narrator of the story of Rumen and his city *himself* addresses Olesha with stories of his own life and experiences. Quietly, the poem has turned toward a meditation on the indelibility of memory (and on the perpetual constructions of the imagination as well). As readers, we're presented with three fictive levels—Rumen's, the narrator's, and the poet's; and all of these are drawn against the background of Yuri Olesha's own fictions. Yet it is not the sophisticated leveling of narrative which so moves us in "The City of the Olesha Fruit"; it is the sympathy we feel with both Rumen and the narrator, and the desire we feel to join them in their imaginative constructions and creations of cities, people, and grand stories. We can understand the great nourishing power of memory and the imagination, the healing it holds available to us. Rumen's novelistic inventions help us to understand that, for the self to survive, in Dubie's work as well as in all others, the imagination must make a profound investment in the real.

To say that Dubie's poems are not autobiographical and not, as Stitt puts it, written "in honor of the personality" is not to say they are not personal. To the contrary, there is always the freedom of great intimacy and the privilege of the highly personal at work—and always vulnerable—in Dubie's poems. Even when his poems clothe autobiographical urges and urgencies in the voices of history and in the concept of the "other," Dubie still treats every voice and every speaker as if it were himself; he speaks with the urgency of *that* self and so makes each narrative monologue in some part autobiographical. And of course there are the deeply personal poems such as "Comes Winter, the Sea Hunting," a poem about his daughter's birth, and love poems like the marvelous new poem, "At Midsummer." Because so many readers are first struck by the persistent verbal imagination in Dubie's work, the deeply natural and simple voices in his poetry are rarely given their due. Let me suggest, as an antidote to this, the poem "A Grandfather's Last Letter," with its wisdom and understated tenderness. It is a moving and memorable poem.

Though what I consider to be the more operatic of the long poems are absent from his *Selected and New Poems,* Dubie has included many of his better-known longer poems, including the aforementioned "Elegies for the Ochre Deer on the Walls at Lascaux" and "The City of the Olesha Fruit," as well as "The Composer's Winter Dream," "The Parallax Monograph for Rodin," "The Scrivener's Roses," and a powerful new poem (about artistic responsibility and personal urgency), "Pictures at an Exhibition." In these longer poems, Dubie's architectures are simultaneously delicate and complex. He loves to employ disguised technical apparatuses and his phrasings seem as proper to a cinematic grammar as to a linguistic grammar. The impulse in Dubie's narratives is almost always compositional, in painterly and musical terms, and it is also theatrical in that he often invokes a dramatic staging for his poems. And over and over, in delivery and syntax, we find the cinematic textures of the poems coloring and disturbing the expected order of perception. There is, as Lorrie Goldensohn saw in her comprehensive review of Dubie's work, "that cross-cut, frame-cancelling gesture which is very nearly a Dubie signature."

Goldensohn also noted "a slow, prosaic specificity of utterance peculiarly Dubie's own." Dubie manages to write a poetry that exhibits those virtues seen (by, for example, poet and critic Robert Pinsky) in a highly discursive poetry while losing none of the activated surface, none of the muscular and energetic rhythms, none of the complexities of syntax sometimes absent in a more discursive poetry.

Dubie's poems show a quality of poetic thought capable of absorbing a rhetoric of discourse without suffering its constraints. Perhaps, in part, this is due to the fact that Dubie sees the function of language as providing a fluent body of possibility; that is, he constantly wants to ask: What is the sustaining character of poetry? What is its capacity for generosity, hope, and tolerance? With Dubie's speakers we are faced with a testimony of history, yet the conjunctions of moral questions appear without any judgmental impositions. As such, the poems force us to consider the potentiality of each voice, and the lines build as a sequence of permissions. Dubie's poems are important because structures of language and structures of thought are our only models for self-consideration (aside from visionary or hallucinatory models). In this regard, Dubie has sought a style which both subtly instructs us about and consequently frees us from the ordinary structures of poetic investigation. And we ourselves must ask, reading Dubie, what constitutes "hope" at any time in history except the possibility of alternative structures of thought and language and consciousness, structures that will allow us to understand ourselves in new ways and free us from our repetitive and constraining despairs. It seems to me the responsibility of poetry, and of all of the arts, is to rehearse eternally these possible alternatives for us.

For Dubie, and for other poets as well, a sense of unity can be found through the acceptance and inclusion of the world's great variance, its multiplicity of realities. Like Kepler attempting to show the "harmony" of the cosmos, Dubie's response to the fragmentary nature of experience is to gather and balance it, showing its echoes and refractive or reflective qualities. Still, however philosophical, artistic, or spiritual the concerns of Dubie's poems, the stories and tableaus illustrating those concerns remain resolutely human. More than ever, Dubie's new poems show the powerful intimacy active in all of his work. It therefore seems to me proper that his *Selected and New Poems* ends with an elegy for two of American poetry's most personal and intimate poets, James Wright and Richard Hugo. The poem, a parable about Saint Jerome, is another of Dubie's gifts to his readers. In calling his poem simply "Elegy For Wright & Hugo" Dubie allows his story of Jerome's wisdom and saintliness to reflect upon our own understanding of the compassion and sympathy of the two poets. Obliquely, yet inevitably, we feel in the poem the way in which poetry is the repeated story of human understanding and misunderstanding—of each other, of ourselves, of all other sentient creatures, and of nature itself. For a man or a woman who lives, at whatever expense, the life of those stories (Dubie seems to be saying), that realm of what we call "poetry" allows us the most generous salvation we have any right to expect.

ANATOMIES OF MELANCHOLY

J. D. McCLATCHY

Then praise was for a kind of art
Whereof there is no school;
There the unlettered instinct rides
In all its bodily skill.
                    "Speech," Anthony Hecht

At one point in a poem about his childhood, Anthony Hecht takes a small inventory. It is a poet's inventory, whereby gift is symbol, image conjures image, and a present predicts the future.

> *Here is the microscope one had as a child,*
> *The Christmas gift of some forgotten uncle.*
> *Here is the slide with a drop of cider vinegar*
> *As clear as gin, clear as your early mind.*
> *Look down, being most careful not to see*
> *Your own eye in the mirror underneath,*
> *Which will appear, unless your view is right,*
> *As a darkness on the face of the first waters.*
> *When all is silvery and brilliant, look:*
> *The long, thin, darting shapes, the flagellates,*
> *Rat-tailed, ambitious, lash themselves along—*
> *Those humble, floating ones, those simple cells*
> *Content to be borne on whatever tide,*
> *Trustful, the very image of consent—*
> *These are the frail, unlikely origins,*
> *Scarcely perceived, of all you shall become.*

The kind of research that goes on here is twofold. The poem these lines are part of, the astonishing "Green: An Epistle," is itself a *recherche*, a finely detailed Proustian recovery of lost time, both a historical project and a personal obsession. And the passage also describes a literal research that peers into a world that makes itself manifest in the shapes and colors and rhythms of words. In fact, these lines comprise a miniature allegory of origins—of any lyric poet's "unlikely origins." But it is how this allegory is fractioned, into a darkness and two impulses, that most intrigues me, because it goes to the heart of Hecht's work. That primal darkness, first of all. That it is the very image of the poet's own eye echoes Emerson: "The blank we see in Nature is in our own eye." And it is crucial to remember how often Hecht takes this darkness as his subject. Few contemporary poets have so persistently and so strikingly come to terms with evil and violence in history, or what we literally call *human nature*. And throughout his four collections are occasions of madness, paranoia, catatonia, hallucination, and dream; there are exile, plague, miscarriage, murder, genocide. Indeed, the intricate trelliswork of his stanzas—some of them feats of engineering not seen since the seventeenth century—and the grandiloquent diction that are the hallmarks of Hecht's style seem at odds with such subjects: too composed.

"In each art," Richard Wilbur once wrote (Hecht quotes the sentence in his 1966 essay "On the Methods and Ambitions of Poetry"), "the difficulty of the form is a substitute for the difficulty of direct apprehension and expression of the object." Elaborate schemes, then, substitute for painstaking analysis. And in general that is true of Hecht. It is true as well that he seeks to dramatize both the difficulty and the apprehension by means of his style. Sharply contrasting tones of voice—lambent figures and Latinate turns suddenly giving way to slang—are used not just to color his poems, but to structure them. His poems continually favor such sorts of doubleness—paired perspectives, sentiment cut with cynicism, moral standards undercut by doubt. Some poems depend on abruptly juxtaposed points of view. Others work with the dynamics of motion and stasis. "The Cost" is one: a young Italian couple race on their Vespa around Trajan's Column. Theirs is a world—or a moment in the world—of "weight and speed," "risks and tilts," "the spin / And dazzled rinse of air," "their headlong lurch and flatulent racket." What they circle is, in a sense, the image in stone of themselves: the spiraling bas-relief of the emperor's troops, long since motes of dust like those the latter-day motorcycle kicks up. The couple's very motion depends on their *not* thinking of the difference. Self-consciousness, or what Hecht here calls "unbodied thought," is entropy.

Or, to return to the terms in the allegory I began with, we have two shapes, two forms of stylistic life, two modes of being—the flagellates and the simple cells. I want in this essay to look through the other end of the microscope: to look back at Hecht's work through these contrasting impulses and to find the eye of the poet in the darkness visible . And, though I will want to make connections with other poems of his, I want to take one poem as my "slide"—one of Hecht's most familiar and successful poems, "A Hill," first published in the *New Yorker* in February 1964 and collected in *The Hard Hours*.

> In Italy, where this sort of thing can occur,
> I had a vision once—though you understand
> It was nothing at all like Dante's, or the visions of saints,
> And perhaps not a vision at all. I was with some friends,
> Picking my way through a warm sunlit piazza
> In the early morning. A clear fretwork of shadows
> From huge umbrellas littered the pavement and made
> A sort of lucent shallows in which was moored
> A small navy of carts. Books, coins, old maps,
> Cheap landscapes and ugly religious prints
> Were all on sale. The colors and noise
> Like the flying hands were gestures of exultation,
> So that even the bargaining

Rose to the ear like a voluble godliness.
And then, when it happened, the noises suddenly stopped,
And it got darker; pushcarts and people dissolved
And even the great Farnese Palace itself
Was gone, for all its marble; in its place
Was a hill, mole-colored and bare. It was very cold,
Close to freezing, with a promise of snow.
The trees were like old ironwork gathered for scrap
Outside a factory wall. There was no wind,
And the only sound for a while was the little click
Of ice as it broke in the mud under my feet.
I saw a piece of ribbon snagged on a hedge,
But no other sign of life. And then I heard
What seemed the crack of a rifle. A hunter, I guessed;
At least I was not alone. But just after that
Came the soft and papery crash
Of a great branch somewhere unseen falling to earth.

And that was all, except for the cold and silence
That promised to last forever, like the hill.
Then prices came through, and fingers, and I was restored
To the sunlight and my friends. But for more than a week
I was scared by the plain bitterness of what I had seen.
All this happened about ten years ago,
And it hasn't troubled me since, but at last, today,
I remembered that hill; it lies just to the left
Of the road north of Poughkeepsie; and as a boy
I stood before it for hours in wintertime.

The poem is animated—urged, structured, and colored—by all of the contrasts I have mentioned and by the "painful doubleness" its displacements enact. It stands with a group of poems central to Hecht's achievement—among them "Coming Home," "Apprehensions," "The Grapes," "The Short End," and "The Venetian Vespers"—that are essentially anatomies of melancholy. They are poems richer in incident and memory than others. They seem to cast a wider net and into deeper waters. But their purpose is peculiar. That purpose can be seen all the more clearly when a poem with the opposite motive—"Peripeteia" would be my example—is placed beside this group. *Peripeteia* is Aristotle's term for the reversal of fortune or intention on which the action in a drama turns, and in Hecht's poem it is an extraordinary turn of events. The poet is alone—that is, he feels a "mild relief that no one there knows me"—in a theater that is filling with people before a play. He is, he says, "a connoisseur of loneliness," and his "cool, drawn-out anticipation" this night is less for the play to be performed than for a long-running "stillness" before the curtain rises. Even without knowing that the play is to be *The Tempest*, we might have guessed this poet to be a sort of Prospero (or Shakespeare) in contented exile (or retirement), enisled in loneliness, his island (or "isolation") his work, his muse a miraculous daughter:

Each of us is miraculously alone
In calm, invulnerable isolation,

> *Neither a neighbor nor a fellow but,*
> *As at the beginning and end, a single soul,*
> *With all the sweet and sour of loneliness.*
> *I, as a connoisseur of loneliness,*
> *Savor it richly, and set it down*
> *In an endless umber landscape, a stubble field*
> *Under a lilac, electric, storm-flushed sky,*
> *Where, in companionship with worthless stones,*
> *Mica-flecked, or at best some rusty quartz,*
> *I stood in childhood, waiting for things to mend.*
> *A useful discipline, perhaps. One that might lead*
> *To solitary, self-denying work*
> *That issues in something harmless, like a poem,*
> *Governed by laws that stand for other laws.*
> *Both of which aim, through kindred disciplines,*
> *At the soul's knowledge and habiliment.*

The image of the child standing, waiting, alone in an empty field—as the man he became is waiting in the theater—will bring at once to mind the child in "A Hill." But whereas the latter poem ends with the forlorn child, "Peripeteia" starts there, with some complacency, and then with an astonishing turn of the poem's fortunes moves on to quite another stage of "self-granted freedom." The play begins, unfolds its plot. By a sly and implicit irony, Hecht may mean for us to understand that his speaker has gradually fallen asleep, and that the play resumes in his dream. But no matter. The see-through magic of theater or dreams or desire itself comes to the same thing, as suddenly

> *Leaving a stunned and gap-mouthed Ferdinand,*
> *Father and faery pageant, she, even she,*
> *Miraculous Miranda, steps from the stage,*
> *Moves up the aisle to my seat, where she stops,*
> *Smiles gently, seriously, and takes my hand*
> *And leads me out of the theater, into a night*
> *As luminous as noon, more deeply real,*
> *Simply because of her hand, than any dream*
> *Shakespeare or I or anyone ever dreamed.*

The eyes widen. The lush rhetoric, the sweetness at once improbable and inevitable, the whole panoply of redemption and enchantment have a truly Shakespearean resonance in Hecht's redaction. But, as I say, this is an unusual gesture. The group of poems of which I take "A Hill" to be representative does the work of disenchantment.

I want to start at the most literal level of reading; the biographical. All of these anatomies of melancholy seem the most autobiographical of Hecht's poems, even when they include the added displacement of characterized voices and plots. That might just make them the more identifiable as dreams. Like "Peripeteia," "A Hill" calls itself a vision or a dream. And it seems more of a private poem than a personal one. Its juxtaposition of images—piazza and hill—is evidently charged with private associations and meant to operate both within the poem and on the reader as dream-work will. The images are not superimposed but displaced, the one by the other, the later by the earlier—and both recalled, as if by an analysand, a decade later. The poem cannot be read as any simple alternation of manifest and latent meanings. The action here is the emergence of a suppressed memory. The poem itself does not offer any elaboration or explanation. But the reader who remembers a bit of Hecht's biography may have some clues. The Roman setting, for instance. During the Second World War, Hecht served in the Army, in both Europe and Japan, and returned home to a slow and difficult period of readjustment. "Like most others who saw any combat at all," he writes, "I experienced a very pronounced and fully conscious sense of guilt at surviving when others, including friends, had not." Then, in 1951, he was awarded the first Prix de Rome writing fellowship ever granted by the American Academy in Rome, and he returned to Europe. Rome, then, carried for the poet a sense of triumph and guilt. And it is not just the burden of history or of artistic tradition (mention of the Farnese Palace focuses that) that presses on the poet until, like Dante, he faints at the intensity of his own imagining, but the fact that Rome is where he has been *sent*, as if in luxurious exile, that makes it appropriate as a scene of instruction.

And what of the hill, the infernal landscape? Poughkeepsie? Perhaps. A state of soul? More likely. And with its factory wall and hunter, it is a landscape out of Auden as well. Let us say it is actual *and* literary, psychological *and* metaphysical. And with only slightly altered topography it recurs in several other poems. It serves an overtly symbolic function in such poems as "Exile," which is dedicated to Joseph Brodsky:

> *Vacant parade grounds swept by the winter wind,*
> *A pile of worn-out tires crowning a knoll,*
> *The purplish clinkers near the cinder blocks*
> *That support the steps of an abandoned church*
> *Still moored to a telephone pole, this sullen place*
> *Is* terra deserta, *Joseph, this is Egypt.*

Or, in his nasty, brutal, long poem "The Short End," when Shirley turns away from the Live Entombment and faces another kind of death-in-life:

> *A grizzled landscape, burdock and thistle-choked,*
> *A snarled, barbed-wire barricade of brambles,*
> *All thorn and needle-sharp hostility,*
> *The dead weeds wicker-brittle, raffia-pale,*
> *The curled oak leaves a deep tobacco brown,*
> *The sad rouge of old bricks, chips of cement*
> *From broken masonry, a stubble field*
> *Like a mangy lion's pelt of withered grass.*
> *Off in the distance a thoroughly dead tree,*
> *Peeled of its bark, sapless, an armature*
> *Of well-groomed, military, silver-gray.*
> *And other leafless trees, their smallest twigs*
> *Incising a sky the color of a bruise.*

It is the same bleakness, out of Kafka or Beckett, and its props grow familiar: the ruined building, the tree, the military echo. The apparent sound of a rifle-shot (what he first *thinks* he hears is more important than what it turns out to be—a dead and no golden bough) in "A Hill" brings to mind other allusions to the Second World War. The execution in "'More Light! More Light'" The soldier-orphan in Part III of "The Venetian Vespers." Or in "Still Life," where the exquisitely rendered natural detail of a misted landscape before dawn gives way to light—and to a sudden memory:

> *As in a water-surface I behold*
> *The first, soft, peach decree*
> *Of light, its pale, inaudible commands.*
> *I stand beneath a pine-tree in the cold,*
> *Just before dawn, somewhere in Germany,*
> *A cold, wet, Garand rifle in my hands.*

Such memories hover over the landscape of "A Hill." But for Hecht himself, though he rigorously excluded them from the poem, there are specific personal associations. In a letter to me, he once explained:

> As for "A Hill," it is the nearest I was able to come in that early book to what Eliot somewhere describes as an obsessive image or symbol—something from deep in our psychic life that carries a special burden of meaning and feeling for us. In my poem I am really writing about a pronounced feeling of loneliness and abandonment in childhood, which I associate with a cold and unpeopled landscape. My childhood was doubtless much better than that of many, but my brother was born epileptic when I was just over two, and from then on all attention was, very properly, focused on him. I have always felt that desolation, that hell itself, is most powerfully expressed in an uninhabited natural landscape at its bleakest.

The most direct poetic version of these same events is "Apprehensions." (The title alone indicates the poem's mix of fear and guilt, understanding and arrest, and a dreaded anticipation of the future.) The poem recounts his brother's "grave and secret malady," its effect and that of the stockmarket crash on his family, and his father's attempted suicide (a double failure which is linked, by a stolen barbiturate, with the brother's illness). But those events, convulsive in themselves, seem the background to the primary relationship in the poem, that between the young Hecht and his Fräulein, "a Teutonic governess / Replete with the curious thumb-print of her race, / That special relish for inflicted pain." The world of this childhood, this poem, is one "made of violent oppositions" which the child could placate only by "mute docility." The pain inflicted is linked, finally, to the Holocaust and the war; even more eerily, during the dream reunion at the poem's end, Hecht associates himself with this figure, a witch out of Grimm, a foster mother. In fact, through the whole poem is some strange way this menacing Fräulein stands in for the child's mother, who is barely mentioned. The sense of abandonment, loneliness, and cruelty in the child's home life is balanced— or compensated for—in the poem by two gifts, two modes of apprehension, a book and a vision, both of them associated with the creative imagination and thereby with the poet's later vocation. The *Book of Knowledge* gave him encyclopedic access to the treasury of the world's stories; a minutely detailed vision out the apartment window—whereby a taxicab, and then the street, and the city, and then the continent are held and transfigured in the transfiguring eye of the artist—gave him a sense of some other available power. In a young life marked by what he calls "elisions," these experiences are fulfilling. But they *are* compensatory: fugitive, fragmentary, the stuff of romance, in every sense imaginary. To put this poem side by side with "A Hill" is to be struck with the similarity between the *Book of Knowledge* and the Farnese Palace, the Manhattan avenue and the Roman piazza—a world of figures apprehended there. The child standing alone in front of the open window is a type of the solipsist, the artist; he is "superbly happy" because he is alone. (Freud defined melancholia as regressive narcissism.) But this is a rare indulgence of Hecht's, and not altogether to be trusted. It is most likely a screen memory. The child standing alone in front of the hill is perhaps a screen memory, too. A hill, a mound or barrow, may be a tomb, and this poem's genre is less the dream-vision than the elegy, perhaps an elegy for the self. A hill is also traditionally a symbol of the mother. It is where the dead abide, and entrance to the otherworld, the matrix. My guess is that the mother is the unspoken, unacknowledged but looming presence in "A Hill," or at least in the second part of the poem—its landscape the mother's body—where a primal world supplants the busy, bright masculine Roman scene. And I suspect the figure of the mother is the focus of those feelings of fear and guilt, abandonment and loneliness in so many of Hecht's poems. His own account substitutes his brother, but he is the occasion, not the cause. The opening of "The Venetian Vespers"—a poem set in a water-borne city—connects "the stale water and glass / In the upstairs room when somebody had died" (the somebody, it soon emerges, is the child's mother) with

> *those first precocious hints of hell*
> *Those intuitions of living desolation*
> *That last a lifetime. They were never, for me,*
> *Some desert place that humans had avoided*
> *In which I could get lost, to which I might*
> *In dreams condemn myself—a wilderness*
> *Natural but alien and unpitying.*
> *They were instead those derelict waste places*
> *Abandoned by mankind as of no worth,*
> *Frequented, if at all, by the dispossessed,*
> *Nocturnal shapes, the crippled and the shamed.*

In fact, some lines later, the speaker associates his mother's death with the image of "underwater globes, / Mercury seedpearls"—Mercury the hermetic psychopomp to the dead. Another poem, "The Grapes," makes a similar association. The speaker now is a no-longer-young chambermaid, an antitype to the Fräulein. (In this poem, has Hecht cast himself, under the name of Marc-Antoine, as her neglected lover?) Her experience of the vision-of-the-hill is a daydream, an image generated by a magazine article, the image of a sole survivor of a crash, adrift in a rubber boat in mid-Pacific, "that blank / Untroubled waste." And her disenchantment comes when she happens to be gazing,

> *Gazing down at a crystal bowl of grapes*
> *In ice-water. They were green grapes, or, rather,*
> *They were a sort of pure, unblemished jade,*

> *Like turbulent ocean water, with misted skins,*
> *Their own pale, smoky sweat, or tiny frost.*

Again, the underwater globes; something—a whole world—drowned and distant. The maid in "The Grapes" is mourning her own life, but the pattern persists, poem to poem. The most frightening appearance of the mother in all of Hecht's books comes in "Behold the Lilies of the Field," where, from the couch in a psychiatrist's office, the speaker relates a vivid fantasy of having attended at the flaying of a Roman emperor by his barbarian captors:

> *When they were done, hours later,*
> *The skin was turned over to one of their saddle-makers*
> *To be tanned and stuffed and sewn. And for what?*
> *A hideous life-sized doll, filled out with straw,*
> *In the skin of the Roman Emperor, Valerian,*
> *With blanks of mother-of-pearl under the eyelids,*
> *And painted shells that had been prepared beforehand*
> *For the fingernails and toenails,*
> *Roughly cross-stitched on the inseam of the legs*
> *And up the back to the center of the head,*
> *Swung in the wind on a rope from the palace flag-pole;*
> *And young girls were brought there by their mothers*
> *To be told about the male anatomy.*
> *His death had taken hours.*
> *They were very patient.*
> *And with him passed away the honor of Rome.*

> *In the end, I was ransomed. Mother paid for me.*

This nasty little oedipal fantasy and its erotic violence—an impulse that fascinates and horrifies this poet—stand at one extreme of the group of poems I am discussing. "A Hill" stands at the other. Neither poem, nor any of those between, can be reduced to a textbook formula. I do not mean to *solve* the poem, to pluck the heart out of its mystery, but only to suggest that its mysterious force derives in part from such pressures. Besides, when I invoke the word "mother," I mean it to stand in for the source of light and love, as well as the Queen of the Night. She is the preconscious. She is memory. She is the muse. The sense of abandonment makes the poet invert her sustaining warmth into a lifeless cold, the pit of hell. In other poems it is a grave for Jews. In "The Short End," whose remote, admonitory parent-figures are George Rose and Miss McIntosh, it is a coffin for George Rose whose "other-worldliness" leads to a lesson that *love* and *bitterness* are the same. None of these anatomies of melancholy offers the reader—as distinct from their protagonists—an easy lesson. Indeed, I want to suggest the probing complex of emotions—the controlled disorder, painful doubleness—that drives the poem and is pursued through an intertexture of images that touches, obscurely or overtly, most of the major poems in Hecht's work.

Melancholy is Hecht's keynote, especially in *The Hard Hours,* whose first poem is "A Hill" and whose epigraph is "*Al that joye is went away.*" Darkness and suffering suffuse the book. Its ironies curdle into cynicism; its wrenching horrors are dwelt upon. I wonder if the book's many victims aren't projections of the poet himself; if the sufferings of wartime Europe don't find their subjective correlative in the poet's own. There are also references in the book that puzzle. "Adam," for instance, is a poem addressed to one of his sons by his first marriage. It is a poem with the book's title in it ("Adam, there will be / Many hard hours, / As an old poem says, / Hours of loneliness."). Its concluding stanza is peculiar, except in the usual metaphoric way:

> *Think of the summer rain*
> *Or seedpearls of the mist;*
> *Seeing the beaded leaf,*
> *Try to remember me.*
> *From far away*
> *I send my blessing out*
> *To circle the great globe.*
> *It shall reach you yet.*

(Watery seedpearls, globe . . . already the central cluster of images has been invoked.) Likewise, "A Letter" ends ominously:

> *There is not much else to tell.*
> *One tries one's best to continue as before*
> *Doing some little good.*
> *But I would have you know that all is not well*
> *With a man dead set to ignore*
> *The endless repetitions of his own murmurous blood.*

I have asked the poet what lay behind such lines—behind the entire book, really—and he answered in a letter that I quote now with his permission:

At the termination of five-and-a-half years of a painfully unhappy and unsuccessful marriage, a separation settlement was made, followed by a divorce, which required of my ex-wife that she live within 150 miles of New York City, so that I should be able to see the children on a regular basis. I must add that, while the marriage had been an unhappy one virtually from the start, its failure was a terrible blow to my self-esteem, and it was not I who sought to terminate it. When it was over I invested all my frustrated familial feelings on the two boys whom I saw, like most divorced fathers, on weekends, making those days unhealthily emotional, and completely without any ease or naturalness. In a way, I resented this arrangement: I had a job to perform during the week (teaching at Bard in those years) and such spare time as I had was devoted entirely to the children, who were pretty young in those days, the younger one still in diapers when all this began. So I had no private life of my own, and consequently invested too much emotional capital in the children. I was the more inclined to do so because I knew their mother to be completely irresponsible with regard to them. Then one day she told me, as I was delivering the children to her at the end of a weekend, that she had fallen in love with a Belgian, and that while I could legally prevent her from moving to Europe, as this man wished her to do, if she were forced to stay in this country she would be very unhappy, and if she were very unhappy, the children would be very unhappy. There was, of course, no argument to counter this. I had asked my lawyer, before the separation papers were drawn up, whether it would be possible for me to obtain custody of the children. He told me that it was virtually impossible, and in those days he was right. So she took the children off to Belgium, and I sank into a very deep depression. I felt no incentive even to get out of bed in the morning. I don't believe I thought in terms of suicide, but neither did life seem to hold out any attractions whatever. My doctor was worried about me, and suggested that I commit myself to a hospital, chiefly, he said, for the administration of medication. It was thorazine, and some other drug the name of which I no longer recall. I was there for three months, toward the end of which time I was allowed to go out during the days. Lowell was particularly kind to me during this period. The hospital was called Gracie Square Hospital, and there were some public pay phones on my floor, on which incoming calls to patients would be carried. Anyone could pick up a phone when it rang, and then page in a loud shout whoever the call was for. It was the custom of the patients to announce, in a loud and cheerful voice, on picking up the phone: "Crazy Square." Many of the patients were on electric shock; it had been agreed before I went in that I would be treated solely with medication, and this was observed. And the medication did indeed control the depression. What would have been a grim three months was, while by no means cheerful, yet remarkably endurable. The only thing I remember complaining about—it was pointless, of course, to complain about the food or routine—was the pictures. The plain bare walls were occasionally "enlivened" by framed pieces of cloth with arbitrary patterns on them, things that might have been drapes or upholstery. The chief point about them was that they were non-representational, and would not remind any patient of anything that carried an emotional burden.

This memoir is all the more moving for its dispassionate and at times even witty tone. The "frustrated familial feelings" should by now be familiar ones. Hecht's own childhood feelings of abandonment are first recklessly overcompensated for and then sadly reinforced when his own children are taken away. The subsequent breakdown is as marked a contrast to his frenetic life before the children left as is the contrast of moods in "A Hill." And the symptoms of his resulting depression have also made their way into later poems. But there are just two details in this letter that I want to draw particular attention to. One is that pun, "Crazy Square." Even when drugged and confined, the poet's ear is attuned to the incongruous, to the play of words—as if, even when sliding around, language could still hold its meanings together. The other is his complaint about the hospital "art." The very words he uses here recall phrases in "A Hill"—"the plain bare walls" echoing "a hill, mole-colored and bare." and "I was scared by the plain bitterness of what I had seen." I will suggest that what he is looking at has a great deal to do with "A Hill," and ask a reader to keep in mind this letter's memory of Hecht's complaint about those nonpicturing pictures. Ironically, their "function"—not to stir any old emotional burdens in a patient—had the effect of rousing Hecht. The burden they may have carried to him is a factor of their resemblance to the hill in his poem.

In his essay "On the Methods and Ambitions of Poetry," Hecht talks about the homage a poem pays to "the natural world, from which it derives and which it strives to imitate.

And there is in nature a superfluity, an excess of texture which plays no necessary part in the natural economy." *Excess of texture* neatly defines that aspect of Hecht's own style we register as baroque. I say an aspect because he turns to it—turns it on, even—usually as a deliberate thematic maneuver. There are swags of it in "The Venetian Vespers," for instance. The poem's speaker, like the child in "Apprehensions," is looking out his window:

> *Here is a sky determined to maintain*
> *The reputation of Tiepolo,*
> *A moving vision of a shapely mist,*
> *Full of the splendor of the insubstantial.*
> *Against a diorama of palest blue*
> *Cloud-curds, cloud-stacks, cloud-bushes sun themselves.*
> *Giant confections, impossible meringues,*
> *Soft coral reefs and powdery tumuli*
> *Pass in august processions and calm herds.*
> *Great stadiums, grandstands and amphitheaters,*
> *The tufted, opulent litters of the gods*
> *They seem; or laundered bunting, well-dressed wigs,*
> *Harvests of milk-white, Chinese peonies*
> *That visibly rebuke our stinginess.*
> *For all their ghostly presences, they take on*
> *A colorful nobility at evening.*
> *Off to the east the sky begins to turn*
> *Lilac so pale it seems a mood of gray,*
> *Gradually, like the death of virtuous men.*
> *Streaks of electrum richly underline*
> *The slow, flat-bottomed hulls, those floated lobes*
> *Between which quills and spokes of light fan out*
> *Into carnelian reds and nectarines,*
> *Nearing a citron brilliance at the center,*
> *The searing furnace of the glory hole*
> *That fires and fuses clouds of muscatel*
> *With pencilings of gold. I look and look,*
> *As though I could be saved simply by looking. . . .*

And of course he cannot be saved: the grandeur is a delusion and its excess a measure of his own inabilities. Everywhere is *seems* and *like.* Left behind, but behind it all, is thin air. The empurpled passage stands as both tribute to and accusation of the imagination. Trope is a contrivance, a twisting, a turning aside.

Readers in the past have missed Hecht's canny relationship to such gold pencilings. "Somebody's Life," a pair of unrhymed sonnets, is a sly satire on this impulse of art. A poet sits atop a cliff, overlooking the sea and rocks. In an attitude of sublimity he "Felt himself claimed by such rash opulence: / There were the lofty figures of his soul." The poem then goes on to ask a more serious question, "Was this the secret / Gaudery of self-love, or a blood-bidden, / Involuntary homage to the world?" (That last phrase an involuntary allusion to the essay published eleven years earlier?) In any case, the poem avoids a direct answer, as if thereby to acknowledge there is none, and instead juxtaposes the actual and the figurative:

> *As it happens, he was doomed never to know.*
> *At times in darkened rooms he thought he heard*
> *The soft ruckus of patiently torn paper,*
> *The sea's own noise, the elderly slop and suck*
> *Of hopeless glottals. Once, in a bad dream,*
> *He saw himself stranded on the wet flats,*
> *As limp as kelp, among putrescent crabs.*
> *But to the very finish he remembered*
> *The flash and force, the crests, the heraldry,*
> *Those casual epergnes towering up*
> *Like Easter trinkets of the tzarevitch.*

Again the notion of salvation; "epergne," or glass serving dish, is from a French word meaning "to save," and the mention of "Easter trinkets" hints at resurrection, though the tsarevitch, like the poet in his own dream, is doomed.

The extravagance of the high style in a Hecht poem should signal some unknowing desperation, some pride before a fall. It often verges toward a Latinate diction, and the added syllables give a kind of tumbling motion to the rhythm. Or appositional phrases and clauses are heaped up for momentum's sake. There is a brilliantly colored blur, a manic rush. One hears it, sees it, at the beginning of "A Hill":

> *A clear fretwork of shadows*
> *From hugh umbrellas littered the pavement and made*
> *A sort of lucent shallows in which was moored*
> *A small navy of carts. Books, coins, old maps,*
> *Cheap landscapes and ugly religious prints*
> *Were all on sale. The colors and noise*
> *Like the flying hands were gestures of exultation,*
> *So that even the bargaining*
> *Rose to the ear like a voluble godliness.*

The language here is loaded with emptiness: "shallows," "gestures," the bogus art. At this pitch of exultation, the vision occurs. It is, first of all, a transformation scene, the world's flapping backdrops revealed as *teatrum mundi*. When Hecht says the "pushcarts and people dissolved / And even the great Farnese Palace itself / Was gone, for all its marble," certainly we are meant to hear the echo of Prospero's lines:

> *And, like the baseless fabric of this vision,*
> *The cloud-capp'd towers, the gorgeous palaces,*
> *The solemn temples, the great globe itself,*
> *Yea, all which it inherit, shall dissolve*
> *And, like this insubstantial pageant faded,*
> *Leave not a rack behind. We are such stuff*
> *As dreams are made on, and our little life*
> *Is rounded with a sleep. Sir, I am vex'd.—*
> *Bear with my weakness—my old brain is troubled.*

What at the start is proposed as "real," the Italian setting, is described in language charged with metaphor, color, allusion, artifice. The "vision" that intrudes is described as starkly, as naturalistically as possible. A shred of ribbon, a distant crack . . . these are all that remain. And a whole series of contrasts is stressed: palace and hill, Rome and Poughkeepsie, commotion and stillness, warmth and cold, adult and child, lucent shallows and dark depths, sensual consciousness and numbed instinctual memory. The plain style of the poem's second half befits the stillness, the "cold and silence." And what is crucial to understand is that this deflation or disenchantment that works to mock the high style and reveal the insubstantiality of metaphor in fact accords with Hecht's own sense of the true art of poetry. In the essay I've already quoted from, he begins by asserting that "art serves to arrest action rather than promote it, and to invite instead a state of aesthetic contemplation." Twice in this poem its action is arrested, first by the scarifying vision and a decade later by a sudden memory. And the poem then ends abruptly, even melodramatically, as if further to arrest the action of interpretation. The speaker reverts to childhood, and stands—as, in a sense, the reader does too—before the hill in winter, blank as a page. The clarification and connections we might expect to follow are omitted. But the point of the poem, what the reader is invited to contemplate, is not really the explication of personal experience, but an understanding of the competing forces of experience itself—forces that are embodied in the poem's contrasting styles. The poem ends with an image, not a moral. The tense of the last line could as well have been changed from the historical past to the present indicative—"It is winter. I am standing, for hours, before it."—to underscore the fact he is describing a condition rather than an occurrence. Hecht's essay on poetic methods concludes with what may as well be the final word on "A Hill": "in allowing us to contemplate, even within a single poem, such diversity of experience, both the good and the bad, brought into tenuous balance through all the manifold devices of art, the spirit is set at ease by a kind of katharsis, in which we are brought to acknowledge that this is the way things are."

That last catch phrase, by which Rolfe Humphries called his translation of Lucretius's *De Rerum Natura,* brings me to a final observation about Hecht's anatomies of melancholy. Though his imposing rhetoric often belies it, Hecht is by temperament closer to Frost than to Stevens and like Frost a poet in the line of Lucretius, who wrote, as he says at the head of Book IV of his epic, "clear verse about dark things." Lucretius was a poet of violence and profound melancholy, of intellectual rigor and imaginative grandeur. He searched in his poem the ground and limits of human life, its instability and monotony, and celebrated its mechanism—those principles of Strife and Love by which nature decays and regenerates, unraveling by night what was woven by day, and out of which we make our ideas (like Death Wish and Life Force), and gods (like Mars and Venus Genetrix), our fantasies and our metaphors. In *Three Philosophical Poets,* from which Hecht drew the epigraph and orphic title of his first book *A Summoning of Stones,* George Santayana summarizes Lucretius' philosophical perspective and his poetic method:

> Naturalism is a philosophy of observation, and of an imagination that extends the observable; all the sights and sounds of nature enter into it, and lend it their directness, pungency, and coercive stress. At the same time, naturalism is an intellectual philosophy; it divines substance behind appearance, continuity behind change, law behind fortune. It therefore attaches all those sights

and sounds to a hidden background that connects and explains them. So understood, nature has a depth as well as surface, force and necessity as well as sensuous variety. . . . Unapproachably vivid, relentless, direct in detail, he is unflinchingly grand and serious in his grouping of the facts. It is the truth that absorbs him and carries him along. He wishes us to be convinced and sobered by the fact, by the overwhelming evidence of thing after thing, raining down upon us, all bearing witness with one voice to the nature of the world.

That description comes as close to Hecht's purposes too as any critic can. He is a contemplative rather than a lyrical poet. A steady contemplation of things in their order and worth—the facts of his own life, the course of history, the archive of myth and belief—is his goal. And it is, in Santayana's phrase, the truth that absorbs him and carries him along: a wary, circumscribed but certain knowledge on which one erected love's monuments, and hope's ideal cities, and all the bright, revolving orders of the imagination. But he indulges their excesses precisely in order to test and often to undermine them. They are his rough magic, and he will abjure them.

PART
FOUR

TRACING THE PERSONAL

THE TREES WIN EVERY TIME:
READING JULIA RANDALL

MARILYN HACKER

In April 1982, I was at Yaddo. It was unseasonably cold and wet: most days the weather precluded the two-mile walk to Saratoga Springs' three bookshops and bakery-cafe whose English-style cream teas would have been my reward for working all morning. I was translating part of the autobiography of a black Brazilian rural worker born in 1910, whose life could not have been more different from mine except for our both being women and both having the stubborn habit of putting words on paper. I was avoiding poetry as I was avoiding thinking about vacancies, uncertainties, in the city life to which I'd be returning. It snowed past midmonth, a good eight inches. The ten people who gathered in the library for the early, somewhat institutional dinners were increasingly able to predict each other's conversations. Shipboard nerves.

It was in the midst of this cabin fever that I—probably looking or Rich, Roethke, or Rukeyser—fingered *The Puritan Carpenter* by Julia Randall out of the shelves of books by Yaddo alumni that lined the off-season dining room and opened it to "To William Wordsworth From Virginia":

> *I think, old bone, the world's not with us much.*
> *I think it is too difficult to see,*
> *But easy to discuss. Behold the bush.*
> *His seasons out-maneuver Proteus.*
> *This year, because of the drought, the barberry*
> *Is all goldflakes in August, but I'll still say*
> *To the First Grade next month, "Now it is Fall.*
> *You see the leaves go bright, and then go small.*
> *You see October's greatcoat. It is gold.*
> *It will lie on the earth to keep the seed's foot warm.*
> *Then, Andrew Obenchain, what happens in June?"*
> *And Andrew, being mountain-bred, will know*
> *Catawba runs too deep for the bus to get*
> *Across the ford—at least it did last May,*
> *And school was out, and the laundry wouldn't dry.*

Most of what I wanted from a poem at that moment was in those opening lines. There was a firm, unabashed connection with the mental nation of poets and poetry, its history, customs, and concerns. There was an equally firm mooring in a present moment, offered and realized (August, Virginia, the barberry bush, a year when there'd be both flood and drought) and an imagined future that fixed the speaker in a profession as well as a habitation, contrasting, in a homely example, things as they should be with things as they are. I was engaged by a speaker who addressed both Wordsworth and farm-bred six-year-olds in her interior dialogue. And I liked the deceptively effortless iambic pentameter that carried its reader from interior monologue to imagined dialogue, from summer to fall, from Wordsworth to the first-graders, hardly calling attention to its own suppleness, rhymes cast off like leaves, lush language.

Was it complacent, all this lushness? It was not. A dialogue with language, with poetry, especially as personified by Wordsworth, does not mean that the poet avoids confronting the prerequisites—and the limitations—of language's magical potential:

> *What do they tell the First Grade in Peru,*
> *I wonder? All the story: God is good,*
> *He counts the children, and the sparrow's wing.*
> *God loved William Wordsworth in the spring.*
> *William Wordsworth had enough to eat.*
> *Wye was his broth, Helvellyn was his meat,*
> *And English was his cookstove. And where did words*
> *Come from, Carlyle Rucker? . . .*

"William Wordsworth had enough to eat." The line may be followed and embellished by a metaphor, but it stands, too, a simple declarative sentence in midpoem. Just as the speaker addresses the future (next season, another generation) along with the past, her colloquy with plenitude does not erase her consciousness of privation, implied since the opening lines, picked up at the closing:

> *But sir, I am tired of living in a lake*
> *Among the watery weeds and weedy blue*
> *Shadows of flowers that Hancock never knew . . .*
> *There is not a god left underneath the sun*
> *To balk, to ride, to suffer, to obey.*
> *Here is the unseasonable barberry.*
> *Here is the black face of a child in need.*
> *Here is the bloody figure of a man.*
> *Run, Great Excursioner. Run if you can.*

Because of what has come before, "the black face of a child in need" is not a poster image eliciting liberal guilt; it is one more piece of descriptive information about Andrew Obenchain or Carlyle Rucker, who have told what they know about the changing of the seasons. This is a poem whose created world includes Wordsworth and hungry black schoolchildren and will not minimize its commitment to either.

I had the book in my room by then, had reread that poem, and gone on to others. I mention Yaddo, the cold spring, the library, the year, because I had never heard of Julia Randall before then. And yet I read poetry, poetry criticism, and book reviews constantly; I had just assumed editorship of a literary journal devoted to women writers, had researched to teach a course on twentieth-century American women poets. I was excited by my "discovery" at the same time as I regretted the communications gap or lag that had made it somehow difficult for this reader and this writer to find each other as it would have been had Randall only been published in Australia.

In fact, *Adam's Dream*, the book that followed *The Puritan Carpenter*, was published in 1969 in New York by Knopf (who would become "my" publisher in 1976—but Randall's book was out of print by then). And, now that I was looking, I found two of Randall's poems in the ground-breaking women's poetry anthology *No More Masks* (edited by Florence Howe, published by Doubleday-Anchor in 1974). Between Denise Levertov and Jane Cooper, according to birth dates, are the poem I've already discussed and "For A Homecoming", also from *The Puritan Carpenter*. This (it could be a companion piece to Mona Van Duyn's "The Fear of Flying") is spoken in loose iambic pentameter couplets and triplets, by a woman awaiting her husband's return by air, and affirms, most uncharacteristically (for Randall), albeit ironically, that "Man does, woman is":

> *Oh, I know*
> *I'd be content in a cave, and I know that some*
> *Incredibly curious germ of evolution*
> *Lets you conceive a rafter and a beam*
> *And a plastic tablecloth. A single name*
> *Is all my woe, whatever was first on the tongue*
> *In the beginning . . .*

But who is, in fact, affirming what? Modern American readers are overaccustomed to assuming that the speaker of a poem is, *de facto*, "the poet," transforming autobiographical material, unless the poem is entitled "Antinous: The Diaries" (by Adrienne Rich) or "The Talking Back of Miss Valentine Jones" (by June Jordan). As far as I know, from discreet biographical notes, Julia Randall has neither married nor taught in an elementary school. Other poems posit children, celibacy, friendships, violence, travel, but this reader soon learned to take each text on its own terms and merit, not to attempt the scrying of one story from their progression. Randall's dramatic voices are less varied than Randall Jarrell's, Pamela White Hadas' or Norman Dubie's: there are no carnival performers, Russian nobles, GIs, or twelve-year-olds. Nonetheless, the locus or perception shifts, and fixing it is a reward for the reader, appreciating another facet of the maker's skill. The schoolteacher in colloquy with Wordsworth and rural six-year-olds is more fully realized because we are *not* asked to conflate her with "the poet," however much of the poet's information and conviction have confirmed her interior speech.

When reading Randall's dramatic monologues, which are not always immediately distinguishable from her lyrics, I am challenged to flesh out the speaker and the speaker's story from the poem's clues: language, diction, choice of metaphor. The speaker of "Falling Asleep in Chapel" (from *The Farewells*) is, I think, a man, a father, possibly a clergyman, meditating alone in church at the dawn of Easter:

> *It is morning by the clock. Under the dark*
> *where the loose hound bays night*
> *on Dead Man, and the cooped cock*

sleeps starring
the field-bones crack with spring.
Palm, plume, blade, and tongue
swell in the valley's skin; waters awake
for Christ's sake, fools of light
rising, come in a night,
come in a night and gone,
temple and vine,
child after child, and man,
after his swollen stem
has seeded up the sky,
man gone. And I
come to this empty house,
glad of an iron sun
falling on sterile stones,
to listen to what I am.
　. . . . .
The dream dies, and I wake
Adam, in Christ's name's sake,
Adam newly begun,
ribbed with creation. See,
my knees pray, my lungs move
mounds of tall air. I stare
into the iron sun. I warm. I walk
into the nightfall spring . . .

Another poem in the same volume, "Outliving," is the reflection of a woman near seventy on her mother's death, long past, at a younger age. "A Farewell to History" happens in the wake of a violent lovers' quarrel and separation:

Broke, bloody, bitter, and bereaved, we departed
the last stand—you to the station (I suppose)
and I to the Emergency Room, where the intern
snickered as he needled my lip and nose.

What I most resented, I didn't understand
then: you broke my glasses. Dark ones on,
I cursed you down the passes, across the wide
apple and cow valley, by the North Fork,
the Maury, Buffalo Creek—all the way to work.

Much more domestic female personae are created in "Recipes" and "A Dream of Reunion," both from *Moving in Memory*, two poems which rise from quotidian language and concerns to wider speculations, presenting traditionally female preoccupations as springboards to the metaphysical:

Of course I give my recipes away.
Last night I gave Esterlee
the zucchini casserole, and she'll give it to Jessie,
and so it goes. No keeping a secret. I may revert

> to Maryland chicken and angel cake. The fit survive
> and the raw materials
> don't change much in a lifetime, but they change:
> there was no tea at Stonehenge.
> . . . .
> I poach the flounder in my mother's dish.
> The scholars say my mother was a fish.
> The strict constructionists say man
> strutted around on two legs of his own
> all around Eden. Maybe he did,
> sharing his recipe with only God, and his spare rib
> with woman.
>
> She found apples
> good eating. Naturally she shared.
> She discovered blood,
> guts, seasonings; how to make stock; how best to grow
> salads and sesames; and how to raise
> bread. One son discovered how to raise the dead
> but he never told.

These monologues are united, despite their disparate voices, by the sense of place. Most of the poems are very specifically located in Maryland or Virginia, by place-names, descriptions of landscape, foliage and seasonal change, reference to local history. Other places and times are evoked, but whatever personae Randall creates evoke them from a realized, localized present. Like those of Robert Frost, although Randall's speakers ought not to be confused with the auctorial presence, they are mostly citizens of the same county, neighbors: the landscape itself becomes an agent in the poems.

Randall's personae differ too strongly from one another to make of her Mid-Atlantic states a *paysage moralisé,* corresponding to or inducing human behavior and attitudes. (The speakers quoted might disagree on everything from foreign policy to breakfast food.) But landscape is more than backdrop to Randall, no more interchangeable than people are, or ideas. The opening poem of *Moving in Memory* states:

> I am Piedmont born and bred
> between far hills and sea,
> great hardwoods overhead,
> and waters gently
> falling down to the Bay.
>   (*"Middle Age, Middle East"*)

In the same volume, a concert commentator's remark invites the speculation:

> the lake and the mountains will do
> as well as anything. The mere suggestion
> conjures Whiteface and Winnisquam
> and all things Appalachian. Equally well
> it conjures Buttermere and Furness Fell.

> But not Naivasha. It's a bracken hill,
> snowy in season; pine is sentinel. The level
> lake may ship a hero or a gull; . . .
> ("Translation")

Julia Randall is currently the author of four book-length collections: *The Puritan Carpenter* (University of North Carolina Press, 1965); *Adam's Dream* (Knopf, 1969); *The Farewells* (Elpenor Press, 1981); and, most recently, *Moving in Memory* (Louisiana State University Press, 1987). The assortment of presses may partially explain why I hadn't known of her work earlier. Because most books of poetry disappear from circulation so quickly, it seems barely reasonable to discuss a collection published a dozen years ago, while fiction of that vintage is regularly assigned reading in seminars and secondary schools. A poet's latest book does not erase or supersede previous ones; it stands beside them, *ought* to bring new readers to them as surely as (say) Toni Morrison's *Beloved* renews interest in—and sales of—*The Bluest Eye; might* do so if they were easily available to be read.

Randall's books lend themselves to a unified discussion because her work is of a piece: it has evolved and changed stylistically, but without rupture, and its concerns remain constant. Some of those concerns have already been discussed or touched upon here: the sense of place and its influence on lives lived in that place; the nature of memory and the memory of nature; the more than seven types of solitude; the conscient individual's relationship to what s/he defines as God; the sense of the past, of human history (and literature) as it influences or is severed from, the future. She does not write, by and large, about: romantic thralldom; class, race, ethnic, or gender identity; family relationships; national or international politics; yet her poems are often as illuminating or illuminated on these subjects than more confrontational texts:

> The Curriculum Committee
> is meeting in the Board Room of the Library
> deciding whether a familiarity
> with Xenophon is essential
> to the educated man.
> .   .   .   .
> I usually put
> History on the kitchen floor, against dog tracks,
> boot tracks, sink splashes, and spilled beer.
> The tortured children stare
> up, and remind me of the dead
> no-name of suffering unsuffered
> messy creation. I have had
> my world as in my time; beer in hotel bed-
> room, publication and promotion.
> I have had property and found it good,
> oiling the knee-hole desk and the upright knees.
> I have dressed for faculty teas.
> I have taught how the poet felt
> in Cumberland, the hills about his head,

> *flat France a memory, and the unwed*
> *partner of his child*
> *paid off. "The weather was mild*
> *on Sunday, we walked to Gowbarrow." I walked to Carvin's Cove*
> *with the dogs. My cousin Xenophon*
> *broke camp, and marched*
> *out of the parched basin*
> *toward the redeeming sea that smacked of home.*
> ("A Meditation In Time of War," Adam's Dream)

"And yes, I think / I will vote for Xenophon" the poem concludes: not a foregone conclusion, in the 1960s, among poets thus conscious of man's inhumanity to man, and woman. But Randall's world view is a conservative one, in the word's radical sense: Xenophon is her cousin, Wordsworth (as elsewhere Emily Dickinson and Virginia Woolf) her correspondent: flawed, yes; limited, perhaps, but vital participants in the human conversation.

From the vantage point of her chosen local habitation, Randall has written of being, as well, a mental inhabitant of Grasmere and Amherst. Yeatsian cadences echoed in her earlier music too. They sounded clear in the title poem of *The Puritan Carpenter*:

> *Come, build a cage for the mind.*
> *Set it water and meat.*
> *That else would rage through the night*
> *With honey and gall to eat,*
> *And bruise its travelling feet*
> *On the mountain-tracks of desire.*

But, in each succeeding volume, Randall's language and rhythms become more individual. *The Farewells* is an elegiac book; *Moving In Memory* is, of the four, the most immediate. With undiminished linguistic precision and formal elegance, the poet creates, in this newest collection, deceptively transparent and demotic voices, evoking homely things and familiar landscapes that become numinous precisely through their ordinariness. I've already cited the collector of recipes; in "Thunder," dogs indoors in a storm lead to an exploration of the nature of trust and of fear: *timor mortis* that is (perhaps) uniquely human and the *terror mundi* that we share with other creatures.

A poem entitled "Video Games" can begin:

> *In Claude Lorrain, the trees win every time*
> *The violent spots of color are a game.*

and move from the painter's bright, incidental foreground figures to:

> *Sue's ship's in bits and Bill has all the castles.*
> *But Brother Dragon wings the upper air . . .*
> *Space-fox! Sue yawns into her coke,*
> *and Sally's boyfriend, bored, begins to stroke*
> *Sally, but Bill is dead-set now to win.*
> *Dad, blasted, ambles toward another gin . . .*

then back to "Claude's careless creatures," coming to resolution with the speaker, hitherto absent:

> *I exist from the beltway, overviewed*
> *by Channel 13's copter, where right lane*
> *must turn right . . .*

finding in the "poor three-times cut-over woodlot" where she walks her dogs, the diminished image of the trees that triumphed over the tohu-bohu of events in Claude Lorrain's paintings.

The newer poems extend and develop Randall's synthetic ability. As the first-graders followed Wordsworth and the burning bush, the title poem, "Moving In Memory," goes from a local exasperation:

> *Moving within memory, I can count*
> *Virginia, Maine, Vermont,*
> *and to a wild extent*
> *Wyoming. I am sick*
> *of my blasted county: Albert Lacey's truck*
> *ten times a day; beltway; industrial park; high density*
> *housing; and Hartline's oak*
> *sickened, that might have seen*
> *Calvert's lieutenants dickering with red men.*

to an argument with (this time) Descartes:

> *If you'd been born in Cody, say,*
> *you'd think, but you'd think differently,*
> *and if you'd been born*
> *no place (which is a contradiction*
> *in terms)—say issued straight*
> *from the Thinker into thin air—*
> *what would you think about?*

and ends with a paean to language as means to "body out / pure loveless thought," praising, as it goes, Dylan Thomas and Keats, who also cared for trees:

> *In words, no doubt, those words*
> *coaxed from our cradle in some foreign tree. We see*
> *by leaflight, and we name the leaf*
> *rock maple, sassafras,*
> *laurel, or blue-eyed grass.*

I have read a few contemporary poets whose love and attention for the natural world so clearly integrated and included the thinking human creature and human artifact, especially language, with that world. For Randall, there is no dichotomy between Descartes and dogwood, Channel 13, Claude Lorrain and tulip poplar, Maryland chicken and resurrection.

Randall's ideal reader is participating, I believe, in the same conversation, between nature and namer, between knowledge received and solace sought, between Wordsworth and Carlyle Rucker; s/he shares the supposition that origins and effects bear observation, that poetry is both a kind of, and spur to, interior examination and an ongoing exchange with the past and with the future. Randall does not propagandize, even for poetry; she does not manipulate readers' appetites or emotions; neither does she seem to hold that a structure of words is an object of *virtu* in its own right, to be revered because we are told it is Art. Her poems please in their verbal beauty and balance, but always, also, incite speculation. They do not plead "Weep!" or exhort "Arise!"; they say, plainly and in all complexity, "Think."

LESSONS IN FORM

LAURA JENSEN

FIRST LESSONS

I do not remember being born. Books tell us it is after our births that we begin to discover ourselves. This self is a human being's prior knowledge. The human lives within the skin of that human self, it senses itself:

> *We think by feeling. What is there to know?*
> *I hear my being dance from ear to ear.*
> *I wake to sleep, and take my waking slow.*
>
> *Of those so close beside me, which are you?*
> *God bless the Ground! I shall walk softly there,*
> *And learn by going where I have to go.*
> *Theodore Roethke, "The Waking"*

To this prior self we must return for identity's sake. Selfish senses are there to declare us ourselves. In sleep we return. We return when we find a corner chair and eat or read an old children's book—we return to our prior self, to that one self within the skin of a human being.

We must return because it is from within that skin that we look outward to attend to human myths. We learn the pattern around us; we learn how we fit in. We do not know these are our lessons in form. We know it as knowledge of the real world. When I first made words with a pencil the word *form* to me was only the way I misspelled *from* on my earliest envelopes of notes to my family. The patterns of letters were the real way words were done. But it was really a lesson in form, only one pattern of the many human patterns, only one language.

When I was a child my mother and uncles performed in their Gord Family Orchestra, a dance band for Scandinavian music. I watched my uncles on accordian and banjo and drums and my mother on piano, heard the feet of the dancers stamp on the floor at the end of the schottische. A holiday dance for the Scandinavian brotherhood they belonged to, or one of their songfests, or a family wedding—there was always a holiday. There was always a holiday at my grandmother's house where the kitchen window looked down at the bay—Thanksgiving. Christmas. Or Sunday. Or weekday afternoons when cranes moved among the piles of boards at Dickman's Mill below us, the boards like sugar wafers on Grandmother's cookie plate. Machinery noises, then the whistle as the train passed. These high holidays structured a calendar of expectation for me. There were always other children. My sister, my cousins.

The calendar's most important holiday was the day school began. Those first days were very warm and the sky brilliant blue outside the panes crossed by cream-colored framework. One day a new boy came to meet our kindergarten class as we sat in the large window seat filled with sun. He met us by feeling our faces because he could not see. He would be in our school in the fall, and when I sat near him that fall I saw technology—his Braille typewriter and cream-colored Braille sheets. At six I learned he could use technology to transcend, that technology was wonderful. But more than that, this meeting told me that I could see.

The holidays always to come—those were my first lessons in form.

TEACHING FORM

Grown up, we continue good lessons. One lesson we learn is meeting ourselves again in other new children. The poet Daniel Halpern looks from a window to the beach and wants to advise the child there:

> *When you think too much about all there is*
> *You begin to lose what you have.*
> *Daniel Halpern, "Child Running"*

The child cannot hear him and is listening to something Halpern cannot hear.

Children approach us, we do not approach them. In 1985 it snowed for two weeks, and the house where I lived was covered with icicles—icicles like the teeth of a monster or Scheherezade's swords hanging from the tin roof outside the kitchen door. I asked some children who were marching through the neighborhood with a shovel to clear the back steps—after I paid them the oldest boy seized one icicle sword and brandished it away with him, flourishing it happily, as I stood diminished and surprised. Lessons from meeting children's creativity give us back the pattern of ourselves as children then and the pattern of the new children now.

TRANSFORMATION

We feel we must form as poets:

> *And I can't get rid of the tempting tic of pentameter,*
> *Of the urge to impose a form on what I don't understand,*
> *Of that which I have to transform because it's too grim*
>   *as it is.*
> *Carolyn Kizer, "Singing Aloud"*

One day I came out of the rain while waiting for a bus to spend a couple of minutes inside the dry drugstore. "Are the kids bothering you?" asked the clerk. "I don't have any kids," I answered. I knew she meant the mental patients waiting for the bus. These are not kids; to call them kids is to refuse to acknowledge them, to call back an image of the Bethlehem Hospital that brought the word "bedlam" to our language. The image does not acknowledge that the purpose of care is improvement. These are not children but adults whose mental hell and traumatic real experiences could happen to anyone. According to Richard Warner in *Psychology Today,* many symptoms of schizophrenia may be the common psychological effects of long-term unemployment. The schizophrenic rate rises and falls as the job market falls and rises; the schizophrenic who recovers is the one who finds a job. By working, the person transforms the life. In a way the word "kids" comes close to being correct—like children, all adults need to form and transform.

One day I rode home from Seattle from visiting a friend and listened to a rider with a small child talking to a rider who was going home to her child from work. The ride was not dismal, but her words transposed the ride, took it up a few notes into another key. Her face had a scrubbed look. Her child must have contained within himself a certain moment in his age because he looked like an angel. It was not as though she needed to be understood but as though her life were beautiful. But what was the beauty about? Housework for her sister once a month? The Bumbershoot Arts Festival crowd and her boyfriend's band there? Or about her kind of intonation of *helicopter* for her son, his hands on the bus window? The helicopter rose heavy above a smoky industry. She had transformed the rock band, the housecleaning, the ride on the bus on a gray day.

In spring we see black branches transformed to a flowering fruit tree. It seems like magic. But most transformations are subtler, are transpositions or variations, just enough to entertain the senses, not so much that form is completely altered.

TO FORGET FORM

Last year I saw the world take on new form—that form was a kind of formlessness. The world was delayed, then sudden—unpredictable, filled with barricades and messages left for others that I could not ignore; these confused me. Much information bore no resemblance to the truth; much true information was not about the topic that interested me. The old world was unfamiliar and inappropriate. The world was too loud, too dangerous, too heavy—it weighed a ton and a half. Noise screamed past ignoring me. The news was of hard times, violence. Sirens, alarms alerting me that once again dreadful things had happened I could never know the truth about. No word for it.

I may be describing a world turned incoherent as an essay for Composition is incoherent when all the information is old information. For coherence Composition recommends a mixture of the old and new.

I may be describing grief. For at the time my god-mother had died. My mother was ill. I worried but worked hard because I was of a mind to work hard.

I may be describing a world of mixed feelings. While this formless world repelled so, it still had my attention.

I may be describing a world without enough money, a world of financial insecurity, for I was using food stamps, not for the first time, and its uncertainties alarmed me.

I may be describing the world Benjamin Péret views as a world of unthinking activity. He believes unthinking activity is the established view of reality. His alternative is to dream; and to meditate. To never separate day and night.

But I think I am describing a feeling expressed in a poem of mine in *Ploughshares*. The poem is called "Possessions," and we enter the poem half-way in, at the park, waiting for the runner with the torch:

> *I say it is like*
> *a cover from an old*
> *Saturday Evening Post by*
> *Norman Rockwell—the blue*
> *sky roped by stars and stripes,*
> *the old brick restaurant,*
> *the green canopy over us,*
> *the old people in hats and mesh*
> *chairs. After some serious*
> *waiting, a number*
> *of false here they ares,*
> *the children release*
> *their balloons as rehearsed,*
> *and from back of the crowd*
> *I see the runner dimly,*
> *and clearly above him the torch.*
> *He tells me each*
> *keeps the torch he ran with.*
> *And we walk and wheel*
> *back to the ducks.*
> *Where the shadows of a willow*
> *reflect, he tells me*
> *I'd be an alcoholic*
> *if I had a glass like that*
> *to drink from.*

A traditional scene and an ambiguous comment on it. The words mean the little scene will not be enough. The words sound disillusioned. I think I am describing disillusion—in which we forget form.

FALSE FORM

There is a first source on form to which we may turn—Platonic idealism. For Plato, the false was a group of philosophers called the Sophists. They created illusions and led Greek youths into false beliefs. Should we believe a false thing, to be disillusioned is a great Truth. The world, the formless world of disillusion is not false if it replaces a false belief. The Sophists could be recognized in three ways—they treated the student as prey, they used a method of argument that was contentious, and they performed their teachings strictly on a monetary basis.

My mother had a money box with a coin till under the lid. She counted bills and coins at the kitchen table, did addition and subtraction. The money had to last. But there was a savings account for college, so there was hope. The first time I bought clothing for myself, a sweater, when I was young, I knew I could buy the sale sweater and bring home something from the larger bill my mother had given me. In high school I worked at the public library twenty hours a week for two years and had the privilege of saving every check for college. I learned that everything costs money. But there was a savings account for college, so there was hope.

A world where there must be a money box is wrong only if our thoughts dwell only on the money box. We need to always consider the hopes behind the money box. We do not deal with a world of false illusions as long as we define our will toward who we are and toward our work.

FORMULATION

The poet has always the act of writing in mind, an act a critic might name formulation. That mind forming has an accuracy in view. Accuracy is a word with mundane connotations—typing class, measuring cups in kitchens. But our accuracy is not an accuracy to a model or a recipe; our accuracy is a future accuracy, an accuracy of what has not yet been. It is an accuracy of vision, an account of now, an account of a memory or a vision, an account of a dream, of a fiction totally imagined, described, accurately and exactly to our best ability beyond misstatement, beyond misshaping any shape in our Idea. In our practice as poets, to be Inaccurate becomes a real Lie. All our attention is on the page. We cannot account for the hours spent—we have only the page. A radar screen watcher works a high vigilance profession. Our attention is so intense that it is a vigilance, too.

Some of us find what we hear must be in accord with our vision. We can become very critical of life. Matthew Arnold wrote that poetry is a criticism of life. Then to refrain from turning to the page can be a real Lie. I think many poets also become critics because to allow misunderstanding about that important matter at hand, a poem, would be a real Lie.

But we know it is a lie to browbeat with truths beyond our listeners' endurance. A lie to betray their willingness to attend. To be unceasingly accurate until their illusions vanish is a lie, for cruelty is a lie about mercy. Hence the minimalist less is more. Hence is a merciful several stanzas often more memorable than a cruel several hundred pages. Hence our devotion to poetry as the truest language art of all.

To the writer the word *form* has mostly to do with the verb *to form*. And that has to do with the hand and page and eye.

PLATO'S THEORY OF FORMS

In daily life people deal with things, imperfect realizations of the Idea. Plato and philosophers contemplate the Idea. Amazing that the human mind sees beyond particulars to universals. Political change happens because the mind can look beyond what exists in this world to what really exists in the world of the imagination. Shelley, mourning the death of Keats, writes:

> *The One remains, the many change and pass;*
> *Heaven's light forever shines, Earth's shadows fly;*

Life, like a dome of many-coloured glass,
Stains the white radiance of Eternity,
Until Death tramples it to fragments.—Die,
If thou wouldst be with that which thou dost seek!
Follow where all is fled.—Rome's azure sky,
Flowers, ruins, statues, music, words, are weak
The glory they transfuse with fitting truth to speak.
Percy Bysshe Shelley, "Adonais"

In the autumn I read Francis Cornford's translation of Plato and found the words from Shelley chosen for illustration. Artists are also concerned with the Idea. Artists make things appear to represent Ideas that do not exist in the particular room.

One evening I happened to talk to a friend, Dan Blachly. Over the phone he told me he was waiting for his trial. Others had pleaded guilty and been excused, but he and another had not hesitated to plead not guilty to jumping the fence at Fort Lewis when they came to distribute their fliers. Because of their plea they could state their political case in court and did state their case. They were fined five hundred dollars, not a small amount for someone who plays the piano and also does moving and hauling with a battered truck.

In responding to events, we do not hesitate, a life as an activist is created. If in responding to the empty page, we do not hesitate, a life as a writer is created. The words *free verse* first meant to be that I need not hesitate. In what we do not hesitate to do, so is a pattern of our lives created.

The activists stayed on my mind. I looked up and saw an extra sky. I saw Shelley's domed sky singing the theory of forms, the theory of ideas. What I saw surprised me. I saw a panel of sky that is total disarmament. It showed the nuclear complex as an illusion waved before us by Sophists. Meaningless activity exhausts us into acceptance of what exists as the truth. But is not something that can destroy us not true, but false? I was born in 1948. For the first time in my life I looked up at sky and saw total disarmament. I had never seen that before.

WHAT THE MOCKINGBIRD SAID

MOLLY PEACOCK

When I first began to write, I often felt amazed by what I had accomplished. After being told by others just what that accomplishment was, I was further startled, feeling both proud that I'd done something at last and fearful because I was so ignorant of what that something was. I felt an innocent power, like that of the bat poet over his natural gift, yet I also felt vaguely shamed by the mockingbirds in my life, though I hated how distant their erudition was from what I felt.

"Why, I like it," said the mockingbird. "Technically it's quite accomplished. The way you change the rhyme-scheme's particularly effective."

The bat said, "It is?"

"Oh yes," said the mockingbird.

"And it was clever of you to have that last line two feet short."

The bat said blankly: "Two feet short?"

"It's two feet short," said the mockingbird a little impatiently. "The next-to-the last line's iambic pentameter, and the last line's iambic trimeter."

The bat looked so bewildered that the mockingbird said in a kind voice: "An iambic foot has one weak syllable and one strong syllable; the weak one comes first. That last line of yours has six syllables and the one before it has ten: when you shorten the last line like that it gets the effect of night holding its breath."

"I didn't know that," the bat said. "I just made it like holding your breath."
(Randall Jarrell, *The Bat-Poet*, p. 14)

I wanted very much to know what the mockingbirds knew, both so I no longer would be overpowered by them *and* so that I might acquire a new power: a mastery of language that would enable me to write what I saw so clearly in my mind. During my twenties, when I began to write seriously, things so often turned out to be not what I'd felt or saw at all, but something else, something only approximating my vision. It was like feeling I could draw but not knowing how to hold a pencil. Although I didn't want to become supercilious, like those knowing mockingbirds, I did not want to remain as blind as the little bat.

A dreadful dualism in me said: either be a bat, powerful because quickened by true emotion, *or* be a mockingbird, all technique and no guts. Slowly I learned that technique could give me an entrance to my emotions and a way to express them with clarity. I learned this because I valued clarity above all else in writing and was so often disappointed by my obscureness. This obscuring was going on in my emotional life, as well as in my linguistic one. As I became more and more conscious of how I felt, I became more and more aware of the need to find ways to convey these varieties of feelings. Just as discovering hidden aspects of my life helped me to take hold of my life, discovering poetic devices, especially rhyme, helped me to take hold of my poems.

Rhyme has become a kind of organizer of my poetic world. Just as recognition of the patterns of my experience helps me to understand my life, so recognition of the patterns of sound helps me to structure my experiences into art. All this is in the service of clarity, provided clarity includes rich design, for patterns "play" into one another, forming the texture of our experiences, and this playfulness forms the basis of many poetic gestures. "Merely By Wilderness" and "Dilation, Termination, and Curettage" were painful, but relieving, to write. Together they tell part of the story of an abortion. How to express private, *completely* private, emotions with order and care was my dilemma, as it often is.

In "Merely by Wilderness" rhyme was practically a wheelchair, for I was almost disabled by the weight of so much feeling and unable to express it except in the smallest possible units. The rhyme in this poem is completely internal: the end word rhymes with a word found somewhere inside its own line. I see now that each line is pregnant with itself although, at the time, what I wrote was so painful to express that all I could do was to get to the next rhyme, four or five words at a time:

> *The breasts enlarge, and a sweet white discharge*
> *coats the vaginal lips. The nipples itch.*
> *A five-week foetus in the uterus,*
> *as the larger share of a large soft pear,*
> *soaks quietly there. Should I run directly*
> *and insist that he marry me? Resist*
> *is what we do. It is this: I'm in what*
> *I never thought I could be caught in,*
> *and it's a strong net, a roomy deluxe net,*
> *the size of civilization. To shun*
> *this little baby—how can I? Maybe*
> *I could go it alone, fix up a home*
> *for us, never ask why inside the lie*
> *we'd not look beyond, so not ask beyond:*
> *a poor scratch-castle with a beat-in door.*
> *I can't do this alone, yet I am so alone*
> *no one, not even this child inside me, even*
> *the me I was, can feel the wild cold buzz*
> *that presses me into this place, bleakness*

> that will break me, except I cannot be
> broken merely by wilderness, I can only
> be lost.
>
> ("Merely By Wilderness")

The first four lines, the hardest for me, set up the stringent expectations: "enlarge/discharge," "lips/itch," "foetus/uterus," "share/pear." Later on, the rhymes are either repeated works, "what/what, net/net, beyond/beyond, even/even." or very unobtrusive, "alone/home, presses/bleakness, thought/caught in." These occur when the story gathers momentum, when meaning is of utmost importance, when pure description is abandoned, when play gives way to conclusions and when I am less afraid.

Fear has often played into the process of making a poem for me. One of my fears of "technique" was that it had to be "perfect." My own demands for perfection so permeated my life that the thought of such a demand in my poetic world (where I was "really" alive) seemed unbearable. My fears had led me to misunderstand "form" as an act on high wire without a net: if you fall off, you're dead. I did not want to die in my poems because they were a way for me to be truly alive.

But Paul Fussel in his book *Poetic Meter and Poetic Form* relieved me very much when he discussed how the "form" of a poem is set in the first few lines. He explains how the prosody of the opening lines sets up the expectations for the remainder of the poem. Well, I thought, if this is true (and I knew of course that it was) then a "mistake" or a missed beat of some kind (a hanging line, an inappropriate rhyme) would be caught in the net of the poem. This is a much different way to understand poetic acrobatics because the prosodic scheme becomes a net over which to perform, in safety, on the high wire of poetry. The wire no longer is a rigid code to follow under penalty of "death." The safety net *is* the formal structure. The wire is the truth we step out on!

This idea of "form," made for daring, is what allows me to make "imperfect" poems; and to try to write an "imperfect" poem allows me to write more fearlessly. By imperfection I don't mean an easy way out of formal structures; I mean instead a way out of the *formulaic* nature of the structures. Allowing for risks, and therefore mistakes, for "falling off the wire," leads to a greater tolerance for incongruity and thus to a greater adherence to the truth. I hope that the willingness to risk linguistic imperfection allows my poems incongruities which, by falling into the net of tradition, become a kind of innovation.

The couplets of "Dilation, Termination, and Curettage" are an example of a safety net employed for risk.

> A curette has the shape of a grapefruit spoon.
> They dilate the cervix, then clean out the womb
> with jagged prow, just like separating
> the grapefruit from its skin, although the softening
> yellow rind won't bear another fruit and
> . . . and this womb will? Well, this womb can,
> if two will. Oh, I am sick of will and all
> unconscious life! I am sick of the Fall
> and the history of human emotion!

Who knows the need of our commotion except
God, the novelist? Once my heart leapt straight
from its socket, say-beating Change Your Fate,
yet I found in order to live my heart
had to beat back in its own pocket: the start
of change ending by continuing living
with wet possibility lingering
like a light rain glazing our separate
apartment buildings now where, unpregnant,
unmarried, and with no one to worry over
us in our old age as we were sure this never-
born child would, we don our raincoats and goofily
smile under our umbrellas, unceasingly
happy to see one another as we meet,
on the street.

("Dilation, Termination, and Curettage")

Some couplets are perfect and specific, establishing the net, for example: "all/Fall," "straight/Fate," "heart/start," and "meet/street." Other couplets use the net that these establish. For example: the short end line "on the street" couples rather spastically with the line before, and "living" and "lingering" *try* to rhyme, as do "separate" and "unpregnant." One conscious gaffe is two middle lines that are rhymed to the ear but softened by an unrhymed ending that, I hope takes away the clang of too much closure: "and the history of human *emotions!* / Who knows the end of our *commotion except*" [italics not in poem]. The way I hope to use near rhymes in the middles of the poems is for general linkage, letting thoughts run down the lines unimpeded by the stop-and-hear nature of exact rhyme.

I think of these two poems as houses. "Dilation, Termination, and Curettage" has its door safely shut by a couplet: "happy to see one another as we meet, / on the street." But in "Merely By Wilderness" the door is left open so that the storm rushes in: "except I cannot be / broken merely by wilderness, I can only / be lost." At these endings I hope to use rhyme, or its shocking absence (in view of the expectation set up by so many previous rhymes) either to close the experience completely, or to leave the experience frighteningly unresolved. There is fear again.

The mockingbird calls the bat-poet clever for ending a poem with only half a line and the bat-poet is astonished to discover that the half line is how he achieved his effect. The half-line that almost trips a reader (and writer, too) can provide a startling ending (the ending that is not really an ending for it has no graceful closure) with a pressure of meaning that carries the poem out to meet larger possibilities. That is what I hope I've done in both the poems.

Once I heard a doctor say that "in the description is the prescription" and pricked up my ears because of the satisfying rhyme. I've remembered this saying because it has great meaning for me. I do believe that if I describe the world clearly, then I will find the order in the world, the reasons for things, or, if not the reasons, then a pattern of experience. It is this search for order that in my poems becomes an orderly search. Somehow, if I order *the expression*, I shall find order in the world it expresses. I shall find the pattern, and from the pattern, I will be able to discover meaning. Also, if I have a large and worldly structure, I shall be able to say small and private things without sentimentality. The grandness of the pattern will make anything allowable, even the blasphemy of sectioning a womb like a grapefruit, or the blasphemy of calling God a novelist, or the giddy meeting of the post-father and post-mother on the street, or, ultimately, the fact of the abortion itself.

One thing, at least, that I don't fear as much is that my work will lose power by my acknowledged love of language. It's clear to me that my love of language is also a love of the texture of feeling and meaning. If the idea of formality does not polarize "language" and "life," then the poem can burst with vital incongruity as it emerges from its formal system. So, while delighting in the power of the bat-poet, I relish the mockingbird's high-mindedness, and have sympathy both for his impatience with the novice bat and for his acceptance of the bat's bewilderment. I respect the bird's irascible willingness to listen and to teach, for technique can teach feeling how to make its way. The mockingbird is knowledgeable, and knowledge dissipates my fear.

NOTES ON IMPROVISATION,
WILLIAM CARLOS WILLIAMS, AND JAZZ

JAMES McKEAN

In 1972 my friend and I drove his Volkswa-
gen bus with California plates from Pasco, Washington, to Guadalajara, Mexico, via
Illinois. We knew what lay ahead when we completed our 12,000 mile circle, returning
to where we had started—jobs, the routine, the kind of thinking that prepares for the
future—but we had only a general idea of what lay in between on "the crooked road
of genius." We took our blues music and books—Gary Snyder's *Six Sections from
Mountains and Rivers Without End* and *Earth House Hold,* Kenneth Patchen's *Journal
of Albion Moonlight,* Robert Duncan's *Roots and Branches,* and Williams' *Pictures
from Brueghel*—and our own hard-bound blank books into which we could compose
as we drove, just as Williams composed as he drove the country road to his house
calls:

> How smoothly the car runs. And these rows of celery, how they bitter the air—
> winter's authentic foretaste. Here among these farms how the year has aged,
> yet here's last year and the year before and all years. One might rest her time
> without end, watch out his stretch and see no other bending than spring to
> autumn, winter to summer and earth turning into leaves into earth . . .

or

> How smoothly the car runs. This must be the road. Queer how a road juts in.
> How the dark catches among those trees! How the light clings to the canals!
> Yes, there's one table taken, we'll not be alone. This place has possibilities.[1]

Driving the road is the ground beat, and Williams improvises, circling into his own
subjectivity in the first passage so that he loses track of time or direction, eventually
to find at the end of his journey only an empty house, "It's dark here. Scratch a hurried
note. Slip it over the sill. Well, some other time." In the second passage there is no
transcendence, no lyrical and timeless landscape of the mind, but rather tension of
light and dark, the nervousness of real possibility and the incomplete sentence, the
road still to be traveled to its end.

My journal says that my friend and I drove south on Highway 55 through Memphis
and Mississippi heading for New Orleans. We were looking for a bayou because of the
Creedence Clearwater song, and we found one. But we discovered much more. One
journal entry: mile after mile sit shack houses up on brick pillars at the corners as if
ready for the Mississippi to flood. Most seem to have tin roofs and clapboards. All face

the road. All have a front porch and one or more rockers. I'm thinking now of the narrator in Toomer's story "Fern": "From the train window I saw her as I crossed her road. Saw her on the porch, head tilted a little forward where the nail was, eyes vaguely focused on the sunset. Saw her face flow into them, the countryside and something that I call God, flowing into them."[2] And from our car window we see a road sign announcing a mansion in so many miles and tours and times, and then brilliantly white on the horizon appeared the two-story replica of neoclassic perfectibility—doric columns, circular drives, a monument to past times and present attitudes, an ornate and heavy bookend that holds up all the hard-worked and dog-eared lives, even the country itself in between.

Or maybe this building is like the traditional melody in a jazz piece from which the improvisation breaks away into an individual and momentary voice. In fifty miles we see another. A journal entry two days later: how beautiful the woman is in Mandeville, Louisiana, a little town on the north side of Lake Pontchartrain. About fifty with blond-silver hair, she looks cool in the warm June afternoon. She sells us food from her small store, and it is no surprise that she wonders a moment about us, bearded and obviously from somewhere else, before she greets us in the drawl we expect, slow and rhythmic like sorghum, like the humid day we will camp in next to the Tchefuntca River. What does seem surprising, however, is that she is interested in talking to us at all and does so, but not in a drawl that could be anybody's drawl in the South, but in her own voice, clear and softened, faster but still rhythmic so that the last words in her sentences fall on the last beat in the song in her voice. Her sentences seem just long enough. She wouldn't have sounded better if she'd practiced. Where were we from, and where were we going? New Orleans, we said. We wanted to write. We wanted to listen to jazz.

In the winter of 1945 Robert Creeley was attempting to write short stories and lyrics that rose out of his listening to jazz and reading the poetry of William Carlos Williams, undoubtedly finding in the syncopation of jazz and in the lyric style of Williams, in his "line breaks and words breaks, his qualifiers and pronomial indeterminacies, his shifts from a rising to a falling measure," a shelter to see him through the winter of the "Eliotic and academic tradition which dominated the literary scene in the half-decade following World War II."[3] Like all wars, I presume, this war left a residue of confusion and dilemmas and a need to return to a personal life that resembled the old, naive life of memory. Something was lost, and impatience remained. Creeley says, "So we had that reason to move upon something—upon a clarity that could confront these dilemmas more adequately than the generalities we had been given," and a "very specific example" of that clarity was "Williams, who, in 1945, I don't think was even regarded as a minor poet. It's curious to remember that."[4]

In 1922 T. S. Eliot's *The Waste Land* was published, and Williams watched Eliot's rise in literary fame and power while his own hopes seemed to be limited to small private editions. In his *Autobiography* (1951) Williams remembers the shock and disappointment, how *The Waste Land* "struck like a sardonic bullet":

> Eliot had turned his back on the possibility of reviving my world. And being an accomplished craftsman, better skilled in some ways than I could ever hope to be, I had to watch him carry my world off with him, the fool, to the enemy.[5]

The "enemy" we can suppose is many things: the iambic pentameter line, Milton, the English and English, and the past, all those "generalities" that Creeley found so unsatisfactory twenty-three odd years later as he sat on his farm in the woods where he could "raise a family and poultry and prize pigeons, play jazz, think, think . . . and write."[6]

Perhaps the dilemmas, the false generalities, and the need for clarity that confronted Robert Creeley in 1945 were similar to the problems facing the literary community in the years immediately following World War I. There seemed to be a crisis at hand, and, as Geoffrey Perrett explains, "large numbers of educated people were now ready to accept what only a handful of advanced thinkers had formally countenanced—that all belief is rooted in a desire to believe, not in nature; that all ethical systems are based on custom and imagination, not on divine sanction. Man turned out to be the measure of all things after all. Following the slaughter of the Western Front, that was a thought to chill the blood."[7] Suddenly, the individual was set adrift from the "repression" of the old moral orders so that he might discover, given good tides and favorable winds, a version or versions of himself. The winds were as substantial as Freud or fickle as Ouija boards. Such a voyage with all its confusions and unknowns was surely a test of one's intellectual and artistic mettle. Williams must have thought so and began his "Improvisations" to see what lay on the horizons of his own mind: "The virtue of it all is in the opening of the doors, though some rooms of course will be empty, a break with banality, the continual hardening which habit enforces. There is nothing left in me but the virtue of curiosity, Demuth puts in. The poet should be forever at the ship's prow."[8] Others, however, faced with a discarded past and an ambiguous future, simply took flight. Perrett concludes that "disgusted with what they were or what their country had become, they sought escape in bohemia, in sex, in psychoanalysis, in yoga, in Couéism, in death, in art, in nudism, in spiritualism. It was an obsession with self which we now take for granted as being typically modern."[9]

But for Williams the problem seemed larger than merely an obsession with a given self. He saw the times as presenting him a choice—between the old or the new, between an English or an American idiom, between a language given to him by tradition or a language he could develop out of American speech—a choice by which the self might be created. In an interview entitled "Speaking Straight Ahead" Williams speaks in favor of poetry that

> . . . is in a chaotic stage. We have to reject the standard forms of English verse and put ourselves into chaos on purpose, in order to rediscover new constellations of the elements of verse in our time. We have to break down poetry into its elements just as the chemists and physicists are doing. In order to realize ourselves. In order to reform the elements.[10]

It is not surprising that Williams found Eliot's choosing the old almost disloyal. And it is not surprising that Williams was angry and perhaps not a little jealous, stating in the same interview that Eliot was a conformist and looking backward and someone who had rejected America and thus Williams himself. "Prufrock" represented to Williams a step in the wrong direction, away from the future and toward the dry lessons of the classroom.

From Louisiana we took the long hot drive around the edge of the gulf of Mexico—Baton Rouge to Galveston to Corpus Christi to Brownsville where we stopped to rest and to prepare ourselves for the crossing. We were going to Mexico to learn Spanish better than we had ever learned it before because across the border we would lose our English. *Desnudos* repeats Cabeza de Vaca over and over. *Desnudos* both literally and metaphorically for de Vaca, perhaps just metaphorically for us in that we would leave behind the clothes of the familiar both in our language or our customs and we would be forced by our new context to learn and to grow into the language of another culture.

Was this what it was like for my grandmother who by herself at nineteen rode the train from Boston to Seattle in 1909, looking for work? She had seamstress skills, money enough for a room, and a .32 derringer to accompany her home at night after work. Although she had moved West for good, she never lost the "r" from behind "idea," and I would repeat it out loud to myself when I was very young, "idear, idear," and be scolded by my mother. For what? I can't remember. Irreverence maybe.

Or did it have something to do with the need to leave the past in the past, to look forward into the community, the future, America here and now. Was it the same reason why my wife's mother was never taught Norwegian on cold nights in North Dakota winters, although her parents spoke fluently and would argue in their secret language about what remained their secret past? The future was their children and their children, born between 1909 and 1915, were American and would speak English.

As we crossed the border into Matamoros, all we knew about the future was that our visas allowed us to be there fifty days. We were looking for a way to speak and to understand ourselves, perhaps by contrast, by driving far enough away from our own language that we might see and hear from a distance, that we might learn to speak on our own. Although we may have been silent to begin with and all the pages in our journals started blank, we did not have, as Hayden Carruth suggests in his *Sitting In: Writings on Jazz, Blues and Related Topics* "a commitment to disaffirmation . . . to silence," a silence that results from a loss of faith in the imagination especially in the face of "threatened extinction, and its related terrors."[11] Carruth accuses the generation born after 1945 of defeat. No. Extinction is terror enough. I remember the bomb drills in grade school when the bell rang and we all crouched beneath our desks. I remember watching the film of the effects of an atomic blast on a two-story house—the smoldering, then the flames, then the shock wave blowing the fire and the house completely away. I gave my desk in the Navy-barracks-turned-grade-school in Seattle little chance. Maybe the generation born after 1945 is not so much silent as stunned, taking a long time to recover its breath after a variety of shocks: a stupid tragic war, the loss of illusions, critical theories which further subvert motions of certainty, and the continual wash of all those words selling everything from perfume to body counts. I remember the cry was "Why can't Johnny read?" Maybe nobody wanted him to. Maybe Johnny began to suspect that there was a difference between a symbol and the thing it stands for. Maybe language itself grew suspect. *Caveat emptor.* Too many lies.

On the other hand, Hayden Carruth suggests over and over again in his book that jazz improvisation "is paradigmatic of the evolution of all the arts in the twentieth century" and suggests that the jam session—and the poetry workshop he adds parenthetically—can be a sort of sanctuary in which the individual imagination itself might discover what it has to say, that is under the right conditions. Carruth concludes, "Like a town, a nation, a world, the jam session coheres only in love." Despite Carruth's disappointment, a great many born after 1945 understand these conditions and work diligently to find their own voice. We knew this long before our fifty-day visas expired and our notebooks were full, and we could return over long miles to the set melody of English.

In 1921 Albert Einstein received the Nobel prize "for his contributions to mathematical physics and especially for his discovery of the law of the photoelectric effect." Such an understatement. The scientific community, as well as the American public at this time, was much more excited about another Einstein discovery and its ramifications, particularly after a polar expedition in 1919. One purpose of the expedition was to observe an eclipse and to test several of Einstein's theories. In the *New York Times* of November 9, 1919, a three-column article was headed "Eclipse Showed Gravity Variation: Hailed as Epochmaking."[12] A headline on November 10, 1919, read "Lights All Askew in the Heavens" and below that "Men of Science More or Less Agog Over Results of Eclipse Observations," and beneath that, "Einstein Theory Triumphs." In part the article quotes Sir Joseph Thompson, President of the Royal Society, who states,

> The results of the eclipse expedition demonstrating that the rays of light from the stars are bent or deflected from their normal course by other aeriel bodies acting upon them and consequently the inference that light has weight form a most important contribution to the laws of gravity given to us since Newton laid down his principles. (p. 17)

The subsequent responses to Einstein's discoveries were, needless to say, mixed, ranging from the incredulous and dismissive to the lighthearted and joking to the serious.

For the man on the street or the artist in the studio, the mathematics of Einstein's theory of relativity may have remained scientifically incomprehensible, but from the time of the expedition's verification in 1919 to Einstein's first visit to the United States in 1921, the theory and the man himself grew to represent the new possibilities that lay in all forms of human thought. Suddenly, here was liberation from the old, fixed, preconceived, Newtonian world, and here was liberation that applied equally well to the artist, writer, and scientist. An article in *The New Republic* (July 6, 1921) celebrates the liberation possible with a truly new idea:

> Despite the insistence of intellectual mediocrity that the proper study of mankind is mankind, nothing is of such truly human interest as the nature of the physical world in which we live. Moreover, to gain a genuinely new fundamental idea such as involved in the theory of relativity is an experience akin to that which comes in the highest creative art or religion—a liberation from the dead complacency of the accepted views and an enlargement of our being by an enlarged vision of new possibilities.[13]

The analogy of science and the arts seemed more fruitful than ever. A concurrent article from the May 1921 issue of *The Dial*, "Art and Relativity," discusses "an aesthetic analogue which has hitherto received no critical attention" as well as points out how the new idea of relativity forces us to see the limitation of Newtonian systems and laws:

> In his special theory of relativity Professor Einstein has demonstrated with brilliant finality that Newton's laws of inertia are true only for a Newtonian system of co-ordinates. . . .
>
> The fixed co-ordinates upon which the Newtonian measurements were erected have their parallel in more than one aesthetic manifestation. It is no consequence that these manifestations have differed in tendency—there has always existed a common bond of interest, a rigid system of judgments corresponding to an immovable reference-body, and it is this abstract quality which establishes the analogy between the old art and classical mechanics. Professor Einstein's general theory of relativity has shaken the whole physical structure; similarly has the modern painter broken with classical traditions. . . .
>
> The artist of to-day is not seeking the impossible, the overthrow of the past; he asks that the relativity of truths being acknowledged; he is convinced that the real meaning of art lies beyond precise lines of definition, and is searching for a new point of departure, a system of co-ordinates that allows him to achieve coherence without falling back on the laws of visual experience, knowing that these laws invariably become static. . . . It is undeniable that the great man of former periods has broken the laws of his age, has revolted against the aesthetic dogma handed down to him.[14]

The idea that what is true for the art of painting is true for the art of poetry surely crossed Williams' mind, how poetry need no longer be tied to a fixed system of coordinates, need no longer be subject to an "aesthetic dogma handed down," need no longer reflect the "classical mechanics" of meter and form, and might at last depart from the "dead complacency of accepted views." Given the opportunity for growth and change with Einstein's marvelous paradigm to lead the way, no wonder Williams was perturbed with Eliot because "He (Eliot) was a conformist. He wanted to go back to the iambic pentameter." Williams says "It's all linked up in my mind with Eliot's walkout on the liberal feelings of America, which I believe in. And in walking out he left modern poetry behind."[15]

To honor Einstein's first visit to the United States and perhaps to celebrate the "liberation" suggested by the new theories, Williams wrote an occasional poem called "St. Francis Einstein of the Daffodils," which was published in the Summer 1921 issue of *Contact.* A few stanzas should illustrate Williams' obvious pleasure at Einstein's arrival:

> *In March's black boat*
> *Einstein and April*
> *Have come at the time in fashion*
> *up out of the sea*
> *through the rippling daffodils*
> *in the foryard of*
> *the dead Statue of Liberty*
> *whose stonearms*
> *are powerless against them*
> *the Venusremembering wavelets*
> *breaking with laughter—*

Sweet Land of Liberty,
at last, in the end of time,
Einstein has come by force of
complicated mathematics
among the tormented fruit trees
to buy freedom
for the daffodils
till the unchained orchards
shake their tufted flowers—
. . . .
Einstein has remembered us
Saviour of the daffodils!

April Einstein
through the blossomy waters
rebellious, laughing
under liberty's dead arm
has come among the daffodils
shouting
that flowers and men
were created
relatively equal.
Oldfashioned knowledge is
dead under the blossoming peachtrees.

Einstein, tall as a violet
in the latticearbor corner
is tall as a blossomy
peartree! The shell
of the world is split
and from under the sea
Einstein has emerged
triumphant, St. Francis
of the daffodils.[16]

It seems to be the case with many occasional poems that the occasion draws more of the author's attention that does the language of the poem, and the original version of "St. Francis Einstein of the Daffodils" seems no different. Although it is full of jubilation and celebration, the language of the poem and the many references to Einstein seem forced. The central theme of the poem is the rejoicing at the liberation Einstein brings: "Einstein has come / bring April in his head" which brings "springtime of the mind." Thus the natural world is liberated: "freedom / for the daffodils," and so are we in our relative equality with a natural world where "Oldfashioned knowledge is / dead under the blossoming peachtrees." In terms of the actual concept of relativity, Williams seems to understand first that what may be true for one observer may not be true for another so that "Einstein, tall as violet" can also be "tall as a blossomy / peachtree" and second that the standard three dimensional world may have more dimensions in time and space, as Williams implies in the penultimate stanza: "O spring days, swift / and mutable, wind blowing / four ways, hot and cold."[17] Williams must have realized later what he had done as the real poem in "St. Francis Einstein of the Daffodils" rose to the surface. His *Selected Poems* offers a much different version of the poem which contains only one internal reference to Einstein: "Einstein, tall as a violet." It's as if Williams took the occasion out of the poem and put it into a dedication just below the title: "*On the first visit of Professor Einstein to the United States in the spring of 1921.*" The result is shorter, more concise, and a better crafted poem.

A journal entry: driving south from Ciudad Victoria we climb slowly the switch-back, two-lane road into the Sierra Madres. Back and forth in second gear, a day of twists and turns, of the rising and falling engine, of the sheer rock face at our left and clear air to our right. All morning we climb. We have guide books and grammars and dictionaries. I feel as if we are climbing out of our old language. The new signs say *Curva Peligrosa*. And then, just before the summit, we turn once more and find a dead horse on the shoulder, and the vulture we surprise steps off the horse and unfolds its wings and glides in circles far over the thread of road we have left behind. "How smoothly the car runs. This must be the road," Williams says.

Although caught up in the excitement of the certification of Einstein's theories and his subsequent visit to the United States, Williams in 1921 had not fully realized the importance of the relativity of measurements. But he would. The idea of relativity was to lead him to formal poetic changes and to serve as an analogy in justification of his "variable foot."[18] It might be worthwhile to note here that the idea of locality also interested Williams. In the first issue of *Contact* in January of 1921, for which he was the editor, Williams includes two blurbs, one by John Dewey which reads "We are discovering that the locality is the only universal," and the other by Maurice Vlaminck which reads "Intelligence is international, stupidity is national, art is local." Thus, rather than an observation about a general and perhaps abstracted "Waste Land," we have from Williams *Paterson*, in which he locates specifically his desire to discard the old form and to search for the new:

> *Without invention, nothing is well spaced,*
> *unless the mind change, unless*
> *the stars are new measured, according*
> *to their relative positions, the*
> *line will not change, the necessity*
> *will not matriculate; unless there is*
> *a new mind there cannot be a new*
> *line, the old will go on*
> *repeating itself with recurring*
> *deadlines; without intervention*
> *nothing lies under the witch-hazel*
> *bush, the alder does not grow from among*
> *the hummocks margining the all*
> *but spent channel of the old swale,*
> *the small foot-prints*
> *of the mice under the overhanging*
> *tufts of the bunch-grass will not*
> *appear; without invention the line*

will never again take on its ancient
divisions when the word, a supple word,
lived in it, crumbled now to chalk.[19]

Williams is again appealing for a new measure and warning that unless there is a new "line," both a new way of thinking and a new metric, then the "old" will continue in its "deadlines." What is needed is invention, relative position, and "a supple word." What is needed is Paterson, New Jersey, and a new form Williams calls the American idiom and the variable foot.

I would like for a moment to circle back to 1919. A week after the startling headlines such as "Einstein's Theory Triumphs," another article appeared in the *New York Times* in which Professor Charles Lane Poor reassures his readers by deflating this Einsteinian balloon. Convinced that science has been invaded by a spirit of unrest not unlike the unrest of the war, the strikes, and the Bolshevist uprising, Professor Poor speculates that worldwide mental disturbances underlie the "psychological speculations and fantastic dreams about the universe." He suggests that the displacement of the stars in the recent eclipse was the result of defraction not gravity and concludes by stating,

> I have read various articles on the fourth dimension, the relativity theory of Einstein and other psychological speculation on the constitution of the universe: and after reading them I feel as Senator Brandegue felt after a celebrated dinner in Washington. "I feel," he said, "as if I had been wandering with Alice in Wonderland and had tea with the Mad Hatter." (Nov. 16, 1919, sec. B, p. 8)

In retrospect Professor Poor's science seems an easy mark, and, although he probably would rather have been remembered as an astute scientist, he remains more interesting as a social observer and as an example of a type of attitude. He accurately points out the conflicts of the times—the social, scientific, political, and artistic need for change or growth or movement, throwing in his timeless anecdote of the politician who thinks, I assume, that the executives of Washington are dreamers or mad. And as an example of an attitude he represents the very thing artists and revolutionaries were fighting against: the established, conservative norm, the given theories, the tried and true, "the well-tested theories upon which have been built . . . "; and we may fill in the rest. It is all that Williams was working against.

There is something else of interest in this article. In all caps the head of this article reads "JAZZ IN SCIENTIFIC WORLD."

What does it mean? Had an anonymous headline editor at the *New York Times* been to Harlem and listened to jazz? (Who was Creeley listening to in 1945? Duke Ellington? Cootie Williams? Charlie Parker? Dizzy Gillespie?) Did the headline editor imply that there was now some "liveliness" in science or in Professor Poor's argument, or was he suggesting that Einstein's theory was like jazz music, "sophisticated, pervaded by the jazz spirit, lively, unconventional" and perhaps a little suspect as the August 1917 *Literary Digest* suggests, "Jazz music is the delirium tremens of syncopation."[20]

In 1919 the word "jazz" was relatively new in print. The music had been around at least since the birth of Storyville but to a limited audience, and it was not until 1917 that jazz became a national sensation when five white New Orleans musicians went to New York City and cut the first jazz record. They called themselves the Original Dixieland Jass Band and recorded songs such as "Livery Stable Blues" and "Dixieland Jass Band One-Step," and within weeks "jazz" was a national phenomenon.[21] The spelling "Jass" was soon dropped in favor of "Jazz," a term that Jelly Roll Morton had been using since 1902 to explain that he was not playing ragtime. Jazz was not what you played but how you played it. He felt that ragtime was a particular type of music, a particular type of syncopation, and a "blind alley." Jazz, however, was an expression of style in which the individual musician could liberate himself from structure and the dictates of a set line. The musician could improvise, could compose and play at the same time, and could create a music that in spirit was born out of the "protest against injustice, a music of a spirit that flaunts its joy in the face of scorn and oppression."[22]

Jazz seems made for the early 1920s. Perhaps the anonymous editor at the *Times* had listened to early recordings of jazz or had been fortunate enough to witness some of the Harlem Renaissance firsthand. It seems likely that William Carlos Williams would have had the chance to hear the jazz explosion firsthand. In the period from 1912 to 1922, Williams made frequent trips to New York City, both for medical conferences and for literary parties or gatherings, and given his contact with writers and painters, it seems as if references to jazz would be commonplace in Williams' writing. But they are not. The few times Williams mentions jazz he seems to dismiss it. For example, in a letter to Kay Boyle, Williams points out the limitations of jazz as an analogy to what he is trying to accomplish in his new verse:

> One more positive thing though—or minimal requisite. It seems to be that the "foot" being at the bottom of all prosody, the time has come when that must be recognized to have changed in nature. And it must be seen to have changed in it rhythmical powers of inclusion. It cannot be used any longer in its old-time rigidities. Speech for poetry is nothing but time—I mean time in the musical sense. That is where the real battle has been going on.
>
> The new verse is a new time—"rag-time" is only a penny sample: "jazz" is excessively limited when looked at thoroughly. Its rigidities are exactly like that of all we have outgrown. Take away its aphrodisiac qualities and it is stale. But time is the root of the matter.[23]

I still wonder, though, why Creeley listened to jazz as he read Williams, and why Williams himself, in mentioning the American idiom, saw fit to say that "It has as much originality as jazz."[24] And even though Williams may have wanted us to think beyond the aphrodisiac and staleness of jazz, perhaps there are still helpful analogies we can draw—what is Williams trying to do in language in time? What does jazz show us? There is, of course, their historical proximity and parallel developments. In addition, both Williams and jazz experiment in improvisation, Williams most evidently in his *Kora in Hell: Improvisations*. And perhaps too because both can be described by the words *American idiom*—jazz as the truly American music and the verse of William Carlos Williams as the poetic representation of truly American speech.

Each day we kept time by the odometer, one small Mexican town after another and then the long desert after the Sierras. And while one of us drove, the other would note the passing towns or play music or write or lie face up in the back, looking through the open sun roof at a stationary sky where vultures circled—over us, certainly, far beneath them. Keep moving.

We kept moving through the landscape, through the books we brought, through *Pictures from Brueghel* and its "Asphodel, That Greeny Flower" where Williams proclaims the voyage of the *Pinta,* the *Niña,* and the *Santa Maria,* saying "how the world opened its eyes." It is the voyage of discovery that Williams so admires, like Darwin's voyage of the *Beagle* and all the minds that "had been kindled" and set "dancing / to a measure, / a new measure." And it is the "exploding bomb" that Williams so despises, the bomb's speaking by which "we come to our deaths / in silence." The bomb. It is Carruth's "commitment to disaffirmation." It is Williams' witch trials and book burnings. It is the vultures circling over us, all the more reason to keep driving mile after mile through Mexico, to move on toward a new measure, and to keep writing so that we might "open our eyes / to the gardens of the world."[25]

Jazz also suggests a way to understand a little better what Williams may have meant by a "new line" or by something as "new measured," or in particular, by his invention of the variable foot. It has to do with "time in the musical sense" as Williams says to Kay Boyle, and James Collier's descriptions of the early jazz technique of Louis Armstrong helps:

> Another important characteristic of Armstrong's playing was the extent to which he escaped from the ground beat. This characteristic was something that grew steadily from his earliest recordings on. . . . As we have seen, he was, in those first records with Oliver, like "Riverside Blues," pulling his notes a considerable distance from the ground beat. Anyone who doubts that the practice was deliberate can examine "Skid-Dat-De-Dat," made in 1926. There is a passage, consisting of four whole notes, that appears four times early in the record. Armstrong regularly plays the first of the four whole notes slightly behind the beat, the second farther behind the beat, and the last two much closer to the beat, although we cannot always be sure about the fourth because he precedes it with a pickup note the last two times through. By 1927 and 1928, when he was making the greatest of the Hot Five and Hot Seven records, he was taking greater liberties with time, habitually extending his phrases, as a drawing on a sheet of rubber can be extended if one stretches the rubber. In these figures, where, say, five or six notes appear where we might expect eight, the relationship between the ground beat and melodic line is tenuous indeed.[26]

Collier further points out that by 1927 "Armstrong was not merely setting notes ahead or behind the beat; he was setting whole phrases in time schemes irrelevant to the beat, or in no time schemes at all." It is interesting to note that the vernacular of music uses the word "phrases," and Williams found it useful to refer to his words as "notes." The analogy to jazz, or at least to Armstrong's version of jazz, may be clear if we examine part of a letter in which Williams attempts to explain his prosody to Richard Eberhart:

> *(approximate example)*
> *(1)The smell of the heat is boxwood*

> (2)*when rousing us*
> (3)*a movement of the air*
> (4)*stirs our thoughts*
> (5)*that had no life in them*
> (6)*to a life in which*

(or)

> (1)*Mother of God!Our Lady!*
> (2)*the heart*
> (3)*is an unruly master:*
> (4)*Forgive our sins*
> (5)*as we*
> (6)*forgive*
> (7)*those who have sinned against*

Count a single beat to each numeral. You may not agree with my ear, but that is the way I count the line. Over a whole poem it gives a pattern to the meter that can be felt as a new measure.[27]

The analogy is to Armstrong's playing a variable number of notes per beat, just as Williams offers a variable number of words per line, and each line, as Denise Levertov suggests, has the same *duration* as the next line.[28] Just as Armstrong lengthens or shortens his phases and notes in terms of his ground beat so Williams varies the numbers of words (notes) in each of his feet, with the duration remaining nearly the same for each foot. In each case we have a unique voice creating a sense of cadence, personality, and each is "telling his story." Williams probably wouldn't agree with this.

If we were brazen enough to suggest to the lady in the store in Mandeville that she dropped her accent the minute she relaxed and spoke to us in her own voice, she probably wouldn't agree with us either. It's as if her heavily drawled phrases of greeting set the cadence, the tempo, the rhythm of her expression, and she was free after that to improvise in her own voice which rang beautifully of ease and song, each word trained in the rhythms of Louisiana but still uniquely hers. We bought more food than we needed and hung around until we were conspicuous, and, after three days of camping on the Tchefuncta river, we told her we were heading south to listen to jazz in New Orleans and then we said goodbye and she gave us "you'll come back now y'hear," slowly, the drawl returning with her farewell, as if we had recrossed a border, as if we had come full circle.

NOTES

1. William Carlos Williams, *Imaginations*, ed. Webster Schott (New York: New Directions, 1970), pp. 36–37. The excerpts are taken from the *Kora in Hell: Improvisations* section.

2. Jean Toomer, *Cane* (New York: Liveright, 1975), p. 17.

3. Paul Mariani, *A Usable Past: Essays on Modern & Contemporary Poetry* (Amherst; University of Mass. Press, 1984), p. 185.

4. Ibid., p. 186.

5. William Carlos Williams, *The Autobiography of William Carlos Williams* (New York: New Directions, 1951), p. 174.

6. Mariani, p. 186.

7. Geoffrey Perrett, *America in the Twenties: A History* (New York: Simon & Schuster, 1982), p. 147.

8. Williams, *Imaginations*, p. 28.

9. Perrett, *America*, p. 150.

10. Quoted from *Interviews with William Carlos Williams: "Speaking Straight Ahead,"* ed. Linda Welshimer Wagner (New York: New Directions, 1976), p. 60.

11. Hayden Carruth, *Sitting In: Selected Writings on Jazz, Blues, and Related Topics* (Iowa City: University of Iowa Press, 1986), p. 86.

12. *New York Times,* November 9, 1919, p. 17. All additional references to the *New York Times* are contained in the text.

13. Quoted from " 'A little touch of / Einstein in the night—'; Williams' Early exposure to the Theories of Relativity" by Carol C. Donley in *The William Carlos Williams Newsletter.* 4, no. 1 (Spring 1978): 11.

14. Thomas Jewell Craven, "Art and Relativity," *The Dial* 70 (May 1921): 535–537.

15. Wagner, *Interviews*, p. 64.

16. William Carlos Williams, "St. Frances Einstein of the Daffodils," in *Contact,* ed. William Carlos Williams, No. 4 (Summer 1921): 2–4. *Contact* contains the earliest version of "St. Francis Einstein of the Daffodils." Revised versions are contained in *Adam & Eve & the City* and in his *Selected Poems.*

17. For these and additional conclusions about how Williams may have understood relativity, see Donley, "Williams' Early Exposure to Relativity," pp. 12–13.

18. Ibid., p. 13.

19. William Carlos Williams, *Paterson* (New York: New Directions, 1963), p. 50. See also Joel Conarroe, *William Carlos Williams'* Paterson: *Language and Landscape* (Philadelphia: University of Pennsylvania Press, 1970), p. 34.

20. Definitions are from Mitford M. Mathews, ed., *A Dictionary of Americanisms on Historical Principles* (Chicago: University of Chicago Press, 1951), Vol. 1, pp. 900–901.

21. James Lincoln Collier, *The Making of Jazz: A Comprehensive History* (New York: Dell, 1978), p. 72.

22. Perrett, *America*, pp. 231–233.

23. William Carlos Williams, *Selected Letters*, ed. John C. Thirwall (New York: McDowell, Obolensky, 1951), p. 136.

24. Wagner, p. 74. See also Paul Mariani's *William Carlos Williams: A New World Naked* (New York: McGraw-Hill, 1981), especially pages 512–515. Mariani explains that in 1945 Williams listened to jazz records at home and to live jazz in New York (Buck Johnson and his New Orleans band) and responded by writing a short jazz-like poem called "Ol' Bunk's Band." At that time, in addition, Williams began a jazz improvisation—called, tentatively, *Man Orchid*—in collaboration with Fred Miller.

25. William Carlos Williams, *Pictures from Brueghel and other Poems* (New York: New Directions, 1962). The excerpted lines are from "Asphodel, That Greeny Flower," pp. 165–167.

26. Collier, *Making of Jazz*, p. 151.

27. Williams, *Selected Letters*, pp. 326–327.

28. Denise Levertov, "On Williams' Triadic Line; or How to Dance on Variable Feet," *Ironwood* 24 (1984): 97.

LAVENDER

MARY SWANDER

The bell tingled over the door as I entered the florist shop on Main Street, and a woman wearing a yellow smock, glasses, and tightly permed hair offered to help me. I had made this same entry many times as a child with my grandmother, then with my mother, and, although I couldn't call her by name, the woman behind the counter looked familiar, but in a town where the weekly newspaper often heralds such nuptials as "Grube marries Grube," most people look familiar.

It was a hot, humid August day, and the blast of air conditioning felt good as I stepped toward the counter. I had been driving across the state, blouse sticking to the plastic car seat, and had stopped in the small Iowa town where I was born to buy a bouquet to take out to the family cemetery. Because all my relatives in Manning were either dead or designing computer programs in Silicon Valley, I hadn't been in town for a good seven years. I knew I should be staying here a couple of days and visiting with the old neighbors and friends who still sent me Christmas cards every year: "Drive over for a visit one of these days." But I just didn't have time this trip to do more than say a few prayers at the Sacred Heart plot and make certain that the marble cross was still stationed atop the 1860s family marker, and the prairie grass hadn't swallowed the other plain limestone slabs that poked up out of the ground at a slant and announced nothing more than "Mother" or "Father."

"I'd like a bouquet of cut flowers," I told the florist. Her eyes surveyed me—from my straw hat all the way down to my Birkenstock sandals. Uh-oh, I'd hoped to just make this one stop, then be off to the cemetery and out of town. I didn't want anyone even to know I'd been through because this kind of visit was one you either had to really do or not. If you dropped in to see just one friend, then others would know before that afternoon's coffee klatch and would feel slighted. But, if everyone in town knew that you'd driven right through and hadn't even seen a single person, you'd be lumped with the old banker's daughter who still owned a quarter of the farms in the county and came through every summer from Chicago to administer the "estate" and stay at a *motel* in Carroll, the county seat twenty miles north of Manning. So, I was trying to make this trip anonymously. Then, I remembered how the presence of just one stranger in town created excitement. Manning is near no major highway, neither the train nor the bus stop anymore, and each year the population steadily drops as stores board up on Main Street. People want to know about strangers. But even twenty years before in the town's better days, I remember my grandmother walking two blocks down the street to the Virginia Cafe to ask the waitress who the strange man was sitting on the bench in front of the volunteer fire station.

I was trying to make this trip anonymously, but you can't be anonymous in western Iowa in Birkenstock sandals. The florist stared at my feet.

"What kind of flowers would you like? What colors?" She glanced up at my face and studied my features.

"Oh, whatever you have on hand." I saw several people I knew saunter by the plate glass window and didn't want to get involved in a long conversation.

"Well, we have some nice daisies. Let's see, and carnations."

"Whatever you think would make a nice selection."

"But these carnations are all pink. I don't know if you want that much pink." The florist stopped and studied me again. "Why don't you just tell me what this bouquet is for."

"I'll be taking it out to the cemetery."

"Catholic or Protestant?"

"Catholic."

"Oh, the Sacred Heart." The florist said and gathered up more daisies. "That helps." She arranged the flowers one way, then tried them again with the daisies more toward the center of the bouquet. She took out several pink carnations and put in some purple coneflowers. Then she hovered over the spools of ribbon. She tried a green ribbon against the bouquet but decided against it. She tried a brown ribbon but replaced it on the spool.

"If I just knew who these flowers were for, I'd have a better idea of what to do." The florist glared up at me.

I said nothing. Finally, the florist wrapped the flowers in a yellow ribbon and handed them across the counter. She rang up the cost on an old cash register, the little red numbers popping into the glass cage on top as she pressed down the keys. I gave her a ten-dollar bill, and she counted out my change. "If I just knew who these flowers were for," the florist repeated; then she lost all subtlety. "Whose grave are these going to go on?"

"My grandmother's." I evaded. My grandmother had been dead for twenty years, and I hoped that, even if the florist would force my grandmother's name out of me, nothing would connect.

"What's her name?" the florist nearly shouted.

"Lynch."

"Lynch?" She took a step toward me. "You're Nellie Lynch's granddaughter?"

I nodded.

"Why, of course!" The woman smiled. "Now, if I'd have known this bouquet were for Nell, I would have put more lavender in it. She just loved lavender! Oh, yes, how she loved lavender!"

This scene interests me not so much for what it says about the fabric of small town life but for what it says about storytelling and how it relates to story poems. Most good stories pull us through their characters. We are fascinated or repelled by, sympathetic for, or angry at the people involved, and we want to keep reading, on the most basic level, to "find out what happens" to these people. Yet, the only genre that has time to fully develop a character with all his or her complexities is the novel. The novel has the advantage of length. We see the character taking part in more scenes, more different kinds of situations. We hear the character say more; we hear more about what other characters say about him or her. We get right inside that character's head and feel the same emotions and are privy to his or her thoughts. After two to three hundred pages of prose, we have a rounded sense of the character.

The short story gives us another chance to experience rounded characters, yet, because the short story is simply fewer pages than the novel, its characters are more compressed, less complete, less round than the novel. The characters in short stories are usually involved in just one situation, or with one problem, or one strong emotion. A short story doesn't usually have time to develop more than two characters—the antagonist and the protagonist—and get those two people in a realized conflict.

Then what about a poem? In practical terms, even in a long narrative poem, this genre is reduced down in length from several hundred novel pages to maybe fifty pages. The old ballads usually pared down to a couple of printed pages, and at least the first and last stanzas were refrains. Not much time to develop characters or draw the reader into the piece through them. The characters in most ballads are static, "flat," made of cardboard. Then why were these poems sung over and over and passed down through generations, taken by immigrants to new continents and sung again, amended and reshaped to fit a new culture and geography? Is it only because the situation of "Sir Patrick Spens" is so baldly grotesque that we love the story? Do we relish the tale because we, as common folk, feel some sinister delight in a ship full of lords drowning at sea to "fetch the king's daughter of o'Noroway hame"? Like most tragic stories, we already know the outcome of Sir Patrick Spens. If we haven't heard the familiar tale before, the sailor's outcry should be enough to forewarn us that the voyage isn't going to be pretty:

> *O who is this has done this deed*
> *This ill deed unto me,*
> *To send us out, at this time o' year,*
> *To sail upon the sea?*

So, if we're not reading for plot, we're reading for irony? Sure. We shiver; we smile; we weep at the reversal, the pun of the last lines:

> *Half-owre, half owre to Aberdour,*
> *'Tis fifty fathoms deep;*
> *And there lies gude Sir Patrick Spens.*
> *Wi' the Scots lords at his feet.*

But what about Patrick Spens? Do we have any involvement with this old boy, with the other Scots lords and their ladies, or are their characterizations only a vehicle for the poem's irony, the dramatization of another gory incident? The old ballads had no one author. They were a communal experience written by and in the language of the common folk of the British Isles. One singer might start the song, often to accompany group dancing; then another singer could take up the basic story and improvise additional verses. Then the song poems spread across the country and to the United States like a game of telephone, each group of singers shaping the narrative to their purposes, adding new details to the same basic story. For example, it's difficult to find two identical written versions of "Barbara Allen." And it's those precise details in a ballad that allow the characters, even in their cardboard natures, to become alive, to push us on to care about their stories, to cement that final irony of the poem.

In the florist shop, the florist would have remained just a florist, and the story would have remained just an insignificant small town event without the addition of the exchange about lavender:

"Oh? You're Nellie Lynch's granddaughter? Well, what do you know."

But through the addition of the "lavender" detail, we discover valuable information about the florist's character that makes the incident a "story," not just an occurrence. We discover that the florist was so intimately linked to my grandmother that she knew my grandmother's favorite color and *still* remembered it, even after twenty years. Through that dimension of the florist's character, we profoundly feel the tightness of the community. We feel the continuity of the generations. Without the "lavender" detail, we would have felt that tightness, that continuity in a much looser way.

The florist remains a flat character in the story, but she takes on a greater resonance with the lavender detail. Lavender is a color, a sensual visual image with its own unique connotations. In our culture, lavender is used both as an image of grief, self-denial, renewal, and spirituality. (I think of the Lent and Easter seasons.) The lavender detail becomes symbolic and within a short amount of space gives the story the necessary punch to lift it from the ordinary to the memorable. And at the same time that the florist takes on more character so does the grandmother. Because we know that the grandmother's favorite color was purple, we gain some knowledge of what she may have been like as a person. Certainly, a person who favors lavender is very different in personality from one who loves kelly green or even yellow. Think what a different image of both women we would have if the color were brown. Or pink. So, both women become more focused with that single word. The lavender detail gives the florist soul and the grandmother flesh and blood. The detail, by providing a deeper portrait of the florist, allows us to have an emotional response toward her, allows us to step into the town, and for an instant, experience its human web.

The cork-heeled shoes and hats of Sir Patrick Spens and his crew are the resonant details in that ballad. Again, in a short amount of space, we, listeners and readers, must be given some symbolic item to hang our emotions on, to bring the story of the poem to its fullest. At the end of the ballad, nothing is left of the shipwreck but the cork-heeled shoes and hats of Spens and his crew floating on top of the water. Pure synecdoche. But these clothing details give us an eerie link to Spens himself by more fully sketching in his portrait or "characterizing" him. We visualize Spens in this clothing and imagine a clearer physical portrait of him. The shoes and hats create an image of sight as well as texture. Spens becomes more human, more like us with a hat on his head, shoes on his feet. And as we did with the florist, we then are allowed in this ballad to step into a world we hadn't experienced until this time.

The cork-heeled shoes and hats bobbing on top of the waves create a macabre counterpoint to the image of Spens in the final stanza. Here, Spens is on the bottom of the sea, drowned, holding "court" with his drowned lords "at his feet." Spens' feet become literal as his final glory is found in loss, his final rule over the dead.

A contemporary storyteller like Jim Heynen knows how a piece and its characters can click into place with the use of the correct sensual detail. In the prose-poems of his wonderful book *The Man Who Kept Cigars in His Hat*, we encounter the collective character of "the boys"—a gang of "neighborhood" farm kids who, in a fablelike way, experience the matter-of-fact cruelty, the comic curiosity, and the wonder of adolescent rural life. In "Strange Smells in the Night," we see now the detail of dust characterizes both the boys and the "other" of the poem.

One night as the boys were getting ready for bed, the smallest smelled a girl. The older boys pointed out that there was no girl in the room, just the curtain moving. The boys went to bed in the dark, but the smell grew stronger. After a while, one boy decided the smell wasn't a girl but a grown lady. They turned on the light and found no one, but then again in the dark the smell grew stronger. Another boy decided the smell was a grown lady. Again, finding no one, they settled down, and the smell grew stronger. Another boy decided the smell wasn't a girl, not a lady, but an old, old woman:

> *Again, the boys turned on the lights. The curtain*
> *was still moving. This time they saw something. It*
> *was dust, blowing in through the window. So they closed*
> *the window and went back to bed.*
> *After that, they fell asleep.*

Here, through the one image of dust, Heynen creates a character out of nothing. In this poem, the significant detail is olfactory and sets up the poem's antagonist, a spooky presence that moves from the raw energy of an adolescent girl, to the erotic stature of "a grown lady," to the death-mask of an "old, old woman." The smell caries us from youth to old age, from curiosity to acceptance of our own mortality. At the end of the poem, when the boys discover that the smell is dust, they confront it in a straightforward, anticlimactic manner. They close the window and go back to bed. After that, and only after that, can they fall asleep, entering their own mini-deaths.

This small moment of mortality makes the "boys" broader, rounder, with more depth. Like Sir Patrick Spens, the "boys" are set up as folk heroes without much dimension. The boys don't even have individual names. Like Spens, we are familiar with the boy's characters before the poem begins, and we know that characterization isn't the focal point of the poem but more of a vehicle for the poem's irony. Yet, again, we, as readers, need some way to identify with the characters, to nudge closer to them emotionally. In "Strange Smells in the Night" the boys sniff death and close the window on it. And only after that, can they sleep. That night, when the dust blows in, the boys grow up a little. We do too.

After the florist, I decided to go by the bank and clean out an old safety deposit box that still held unimportant papers. I hadn't closed it out before because I could never find a key for it. I envisioned the bank clerk lighting up the blow-torch. I imagined myself receiving the bill: $100—for blasting the door right off its hinges.

"I'd like to close out my box, but I'm afraid I've lost the key," I said to the teller, a young woman, her eyes brushed with blue shadow, lips smeared with red.

"What number is it?" she asked.

"I'm sorry. I can't really remember." I stared at the floor.

"Well," she cracked her gum. "What's your name?"

"S-W-A-N-D-E-R." I spelled, and she jotted it down on the back of a deposit slip, then disappeared into the dark backroom.

A few minutes later, the bank president, "Red" Arp, tottered up to the window. "Oh, Mary," he said. "We don't have a key for that box."

"I was afraid of that. Well, go ahead with whatever you have to do to open it."

"Well, now. Wait." Red bit his lip. "I believe Erwin Hansen's law office has a copy of that key. Yes, your grandmother left the extra one down there. You walk down the street and ask Karen. Tell her Erwin put it in the store room. Behind the door. On the hook. Above the coffee pot."

MY GRANDFATHER'S POEMS

EDWARD HIRSCH

1

My grandfather died when I was eight years old. He was sixty-four. I remember him as tall and thin, slightly stooped and round-shouldered, gentle, unobtrusive, and formal in his manner—a man, as Isaac Babel wrote, with spectacles on his nose and autumn in his heart. For as long as I can remember, everyone in my family said that I resembled him; photographs show that we have the same long face: dark, stubborn, hawklike. My grandmother used to throw up her arms in mock dismay at our apparent similarities. It was rotten luck that both her husband and her grandson were willful and impractical, a hopeless combination, two typically male Ginsburg traits. Thank heavens she had shown the good sense to deliver two daughters.

My *zaydee* always wore a plain dark suit and a slightly faded gray hat. We never saw him dressed informally; he wore a stiff white shirt and a dark tie even on those rare occasions when he accompanied our family to the beach, even when he came to babysit for my sister and me on Saturday evenings. We loved when he visited. He brought us small pleasurable gifts—a sky-blue dreidle, an elaborate puzzle with thick Hebrew letters, a pocketful of Hershey kisses—and allowed us to stay up nearly as late as we wanted. He never scolded us, no matter what we did. Sometimes he read us stories or sang Yiddish songs in a low, tearing whisper. He taught us word games. He hugged us. Always he kissed me on each arm before he sent me to bed for the night.

After my grandfather had a heart attack, my mother used to bring my sister and me to the hospital to see him. We weren't taken to his room—we were apparently too young to visit—but to the parking lot across the street from the hospital. He would walk to the window and wave to us from the seventh floor. We stood on the hood of the car and waved back—wildly, fervently. It was a kind of game; we'd continue waving until he'd finally get too tired and return to bed. The last time we saw him, he leaned over and pressed his lips against the window. The next day he was dead.

My mother idolized her father—as he must have adored her; after he died my grandfather was very much kept alive in our house. He was an affectionate memory, a constant human model, an old-world idea. In local family terms, he became his admirers, as Auden said of Yeats: in this case, my mother and my aunt. He was soft-spoken, loving, intellectual; he was passionate about politics (a devotee of Franklin

Roosevelt, a fervent Zionist) and loved books, especially history books. My father called these memories "a portrait of my grandfather," recognizable but softened around the edges.

For the last decade of his life, grandpa earned his living, such as it was, by selling clothes on Maxwell Street. He despised his job. He was as poorly suited to being a salesman as one could imagine. The family consensus was that the great professional mistake of his life had been to drop out of dental school after his father had died. His largest personal mistake may have been to marry my grandmother, his opposite in every way. Grandpa was soft-hearted, impractical, nostalgic, and European; grandma was hard-headed, pragmatic, forward-looking, American. He liked reading; she preferred playing cards.

It took my grandmother five years to agree to marry my grandfather. She liked the way that he courted her—with chocolate and books, with fine old-fashioned manners—but there was something unworldly about him that bothered her. She was well into her thirties before she finally consented. My grandfather was working for *The Book of Knowledge* at the time and had tucked away a little money. But the market for encyclopedias plunged along with the stock market, and so my grandfather moved his wife and daughter to Rochester to take over what had once been his father's dry goods business. It failed within months. He invested in a new kosher delicatessen, but lost all his money within the year (he refused to make illegal payments to the local rabbis—the source of his boundless contempt for the clergy—and was too shy to ask his partner to stop cheating him). Eventually, he moved his wife and two daughters to Chicago. For years after that he traveled through the Midwest as a stringer for the Yiddish newspaper, *The Day (Der Yidishe Tog)*. He traveled eleven months of every year, writing small unsigned pieces for what the masthead called "the newspaper of the Yiddish intelligentsia." I have often wondered what it was like for him to track down stories of "Jewish" interest in cities like Ottumwa and Cedar Falls. He liked the job, but after he suffered his first heart attack, he could no longer travel and was forced to work in the city. That's when he went to work on Maxwell Street. Despite his exemplary character, those last years were often held up to me as a negative model: don't be like your grandpa, become a professional, succeed.

2

Sometime during my childhood I discovered that my grandfather was a poet—or, at least, that he was always scribbling poems on the backs of envelopes or on small white pieces of paper. I'm not sure how I gleaned this information since I was never actually told about it. I don't think I ever read or saw one of his poems either. But the idea must have struck deep bottom and anchored—something half-remembered, half-forgotten out of the distant past. The first adult poem I remember consciously reading was "The Lady of Shalott." I found it in a worn anthology on a moldy shelf in the basement. For some reason I vaguely assumed my grandfather had written it. I never mentioned this to anyone, but I was proud of the beautiful high-sounding language the poem commanded. It sent me into sweet reverie.

It wasn't until I began to write my first poems years later that I began to think about my grandfather's poems again. Where were they? What were they like? What happened to them? I pestered my grandmother; I questioned my mother and my aunt. No one knew; no one seemed to know anything about those poems, except that they were written in Yiddish. Or were they written in Hebrew? Oh yes, he composed them all right, but never actually read them to anyone. He used to fold them and tuck them away between the pages of his books. Sometimes he wrote them directly on the inside covers of his Hebrew books. Where were his books then? My grandmother had given them away to a local charity after his death. Which charity? She couldn't remember; she couldn't understand why I cared so much. They were scattered by now. What did it matter? I couldn't believe she had given his books away, his books! What was she supposed to do, she asked with sudden contempt, keep them forever? Yes!, I shouted back. You're crazy, she said shaking her head with disapproval: you're as crazy as your grandfather. The conversation was over. My grandfather's poems had vanished forever.

No one ever thought to keep any of my grandfather's writing. No one missed his poems, or even wondered what they were about. Everyone in the family was aware that he wrote poetry—at least that's what they thought he was doing—but writing was considered something quirky that he liked to do, his particular form of amusement, like playing solitaire on long winter nights. It was also a sign of his estrangement from the mercantile world, from the realm of business—from success. That's one of the reasons my parents were so concerned when I began writing poems. My larger family treated the whole idea of poetry with faint distaste, as if I had contracted something unpleasant which I would hopefully outgrow, like acne. Even then I knew they associated writing poems with poverty, sadness, and failure, with the realities of my grandfather's life. I also recognized that my mother was just the tiniest bit pleased; I was, indeed, her father's grandson.

3

I have imagined my grandfather's poems many years now. They are always before me, an unnamed presence, a spiritual ideal. I recognize now that the voice I have discovered in other Eastern European poets is my grandfather's: by turns wry, tender, passionate, playful, modest, heartfelt; the voice of a quiet intellectual who understands that he lives inside history, who tries to speak with true feeling. Whenever I see a photograph of a Czech or a Hungarian Jewish poet, a Jiří Orten or a Miklós Radnóti, I think about my grandfather again. I wonder if his poems approached the strata of theirs: personal, outspoken, learned, heartbreaking. I imagine my grandfather's voice when Orten addresses God as "a bully who took away so much," or when Radnóti cries out in tender desperation "Oh you who love me, love me bravely!" I consider my grandfather's life again when Marina Tsvetaeva claims that in a gentile world "all poets are Jews." I think about him, too, when I read Yehuda Amichai's affirmation that we are all "festive weepers, etching names on every stone, touched by hope, hostages of governments and history, blown by wind and gathering holy dust."

FORGING A WOMAN'S LINK IN
DI GOLDENE KEYT:
SOME POSSIBILITIES FOR
JEWISH AMERICAN POETRY

IRENA KLEPFISZ

I began writing seriously in my teens. This was in the mid- and late 1950s. I don't remember the content, but I do remember writing poems in the voices of old men. I thought poetry should be wise, and wisdom resided only in old men who walked down long roads. In the eighth grade, I'd been forced to memorize the first ten stanzas of "The Ancient Mariner" so perhaps I was imitating Coleridge.

This period is vague. I wrote a lot but never showed it to anyone, although I did tell people I wanted to be a writer. Against all school counselors' advice and the prognoses of aptitude scores, I chose to be an English major in college. Everyone wanted me to be a science major, to study engineering like my father who'd been killed during the war. But I was drawn to literature, loved to read, loved to write and persisted, despite undistinguished, sometimes poor, grades. I did eventually make it into the honors English program at City College and won third prize in a short story contest. My image of a poet was Dylan Thomas dead drunk in a bar on the Upper West Side talking about being "a windy boy."

I decided to go on to graduate school and ultimately received my M.A. and Ph.D. from the University of Chicago. This was during the 1960s, a difficult period for me. Right after graduating from college, a close friend, another child survivor, four years my senior, committed suicide. Elza was in many ways my role model. She was brilliant in languages, translated Latin poetry, wrote her own poetry and fiction, had gone to Cornell and then graduate school. Partly because of Elza I wanted to write and distinguish myself. She too had admired Dylan Thomas and for my eighteenth birthday had given me a record of him reading his own work. When Elza died, I was left with a lot of questions and fears.

More than anything I wondered if our similar backgrounds, similar interests, and the very nature of being a poet indicated that I too would be a suicide. Was it a question of time? I wrote a great deal during those six years—almost exclusively about the Holocaust, about Elza. I wrote out of pain and terror. I abandoned the old man's voice and instead frequently wrote in Elza's voice—the dead poet, the child survivor, the woman incapable of being rescued. I wrote from within what I imagined to be her madness. It was an easy voice to take on. I reworked much of this poetry but never had it completely under control. It just poured out—one depressing poem after another, one atrocity after another, death always the central motif. I suspect that it was solid therapy, that it saved me.

I am not sure how or why this changed. Either I was through with it or I learned something or both. I came to New York to teach and, in the early 1970s, had contact for the first time with a young poet—and he was neither obsessed with death nor planning an early demise. It suddenly occurred to me that writing poetry could actually be a way of living. At the same time, I was teaching in a department with a number of poets and they, too, though all male, gave me a glimpse of possibilities, a way of being a poet in the world. I began rewriting in a different way. The act was no longer therapy—it was less concerned with releasing pain and more concerned with shaping poetry. I developed a way of laying words out on a page and surrounding them with empty space—the poems were sparse, the words far from each other. They were as much about speaking as about silence. I was not aware of this, but silence had become and remains a central theme in my writing.

During this period when I was beginning to develop what I now recognize as an identifiable voice, I worried that the sole significant topic of my poetry was the Holocaust. I felt that my strongest poems were "death camp," "herr captain," and "about my father." I wondered how long I could keep writing about this and if I wanted to. I was very determined not to play into the commercialism with which the Holocaust was becoming increasingly surrounded. I wanted true poems but was also drawn to write about other things. And during this period I first became conscious of feminism and gay issues.

I had, of course, written poems about the present—responses to places and events, to people and lovers. I always felt, however, these were dwarfed by my Holocaust poetry, and had little significance. But when I came out, I suddenly found myself confronted with unacceptable and taboo material. Feminist ideas, women's lives, lesbian love poetry, the whole gay world—all were subjects that had few outlets. With this consciousness I self-published in a cooperative venture with four other lesbian poets my first book of poetry, *periods of stress* (Out & Out Books). The book reflected the strict divisions between my Jewish and my lesbian lives. Right after in 1976, I helped cofound *Conditions* magazine. Open to all women and committed to women usually silenced and kept out of the mainstream, *Conditions* emphasized writing by lesbians. Helping to start a feminist press and a magazine made me begin to view writing and my present life in a more complex political and historical context.

But this sudden expansion had a surprisingly restrictive effect on me. As a lesbian, I felt alienated from the community of my roots. The original Jewish impulse behind my early poetry was still there, but it suddenly seemed out of place. I did not feel right in presenting my Holocaust poems in the lesbian community, and I felt to some degree unwelcome in the Jewish community. (Both communities have undergone significant changes in attitude since then.) It was a confusing time. The confusion and economic pressures and work on the magazine were not very conducive to creativity, and I wrote little in this period. What I did write, like the "Monkey House and Other Cages" was very Jewish—a direct outgrowth of my Holocaust poetry—but now the primary focus was women. My feminism led me also to write about office work. In 1973

I lost my teaching job as a result of economic circumstances that were to affect thousands of Ph.D.s in this country. I was frequently forced to do office work to support myself. This work experience was predominantly female, a subject that I realized could be explored further in poetry. No doubt, my Jewish socialist background helped in my ability to understand this—so did feminist writers like Tillie Olsen and lesbian poets like Judy Grahn. So I wrote "Work Sonnets." Again the material was *informed* by my Jewish upbringing but did not overtly deal with Jewish themes.

With "The Monkey House" and "Work Sonnets" I was also pushing boundaries of form and language. In the first I tried to deal with nonverbal beings expressing feelings through gestures—I pared down the language as much as possible. I did the opposite in "Work Sonnets" where I alternated between prose poems and lyrics. I stretched the sonnet to fifteen lines and explained that in an epigraph I ultimately discarded: "Under these conditions don't expect the perfect form." I forced more prose into the poem by adding two sections after the sonnets themselves: "Notes" by the writer doing office work; and "A Monologue about a Dialogue" in which the "career" secretary reveals her perceptions of the feminist she works with. I knew the sections were not poetry, yet they clearly belonged with the sonnets. These experiments taught me that new content frequently demands new genres, definitions, and boundaries.

It seemed, for a while anyway, that I had abandoned explicitly Jewish subjects. Ironically, activism within the lesbian and feminist movements pushed me back to earlier themes. The publication of *Nice Jewish Girls: A Lesbian Anthology* (Crossing Press), Israel's invasion of Lebanon, a more palpable anti-Semitism emerging outside and inside the women's movement—all contributed to my turning again directly to Jewish themes and the subject of the Holocaust. But this time the approach was not exclusively private or experiential. Now I tried to untangle both past and present issues as faced by a contemporary Jew in America. In addition, the Jewish content was *informed* by my feminism.

Three long poems—"Glimpses from the Outside," "*Bashert,*" and "Solitary Acts" focused on women in my family and other women in my life. I was using everything I had learned in the feminist movement and applying it to the Jewish experience. Thus, all the figures in the last section of *Keeper of Accounts,* "Inhospitable Soil," are women who struggled to survive in Europe, women who struggle to survive here. Without realizing it, I was beginning to think from a Jewish feminist perspective, helping make visible a woman's link in the chain of Jewish history.

For these poems I chose a variety of formats—prose poems, plain prose, ritual repetitions. I wanted to push the prose limits of poetry as far as possible. I did it to such a degree that I became afraid I would never be able to return to more rhythmical free verse. The result was "Solitary Acts," which by contrast is quite lyrical and formal. I also began to include, more deliberately, non-English words. The central poem of that last section, "*Bashert,*" uses some Yiddish (the word *bashert* means predestined or inevitable). I used the Yiddish word as the title because I realized there was no English equivalent to express a certain quality of Jewish experience.

Unlike my first book, *Keeper of Accounts* (Sinister Wisdom Books) laid itself out almost chronologically and felt completely integrated. It seemed an accurate reflection of my expanding consciousness and is highly autobiographical of my internal development as a poet, a feminist, and a Jew. It solidified for me certain aspects of writing, of the use of words in isolation and in large unwieldy clumps. I felt I had gained greater technical control over my material. With the completion of that book, I experienced a sense of closure, particularly with *"Bashert"* and "Solitary Acts."

I began looking around for new territory. Again my political activism pointed the way. Together with Melanie Kaye/Kantrowitz, I had been giving a lot of workshops on Jewish identity and for a number of years had worked with her on a Jewish women's anthology which would ultimately appear as *The Tribe of Dina* (Sinister Wisdom Books). I was thinking a great deal about assimilation, about the *effect* of the Holocaust (rather than the historical events themselves), on current and future generations. I was drawn to examine my own development and consciousness and began to realize the importance of *yidish-kayt,* Yiddish culture, in my life. It had always been there. I'd been raised with it and had internalized it to such a degree that I was barely conscious of its great influence. Certainly I had never thought I had any active role to play in its preservation. But now I began to think more about Yiddish itself and how I might use it in my own writing. I began to think of how the Holocaust had robbed my generation of the language and culture which should have been our natural legacy. More than sixty years ago, Kadia Molodowsky in the first poem of her series *"Froyen lider"* (Women poems) had lamented that *"mayn lebn* [iz] *an oysgeflikt blat fun a seyfer / un di shure di ershte farisn,"* her life as a woman was a torn page from a sacred book and that the page's first line was illegible. I realized that for me and many of my generation—as Jews and especially as Jewish women—*di sforim un di bikher,* the sacred and secular books, were lost altogether.

I was struck that as a poet, someone intensely involved in language who believes that the kind of language used should reflect what is being expressed, I had never thought about the discrepancy between *di yidishe iber-leybungen,* the Jewish experiences I was trying to write about and the language I was using. (The use of *"bashert"* was the beginning of that realization.) I was also struck by that fact that I had been intimately tied to Yiddish (I had attended Yiddish schools, studied it in college, had even taught it), and yet I had never considered incorporating Yiddish into my work. I began to try to conceive of ways of doing that. Chicana writer Gloria Anzaldúa, who mixes Spanish and English in her writing, was very influential in this area. And so I began experimenting with bilingual Yiddish/English poetry. *"Di rayze aheym /* The journey home" was one result, a poem in which I try to duplicate in language and form the thematic conflict in the poem itself—the loss of language and voice, the efforts to regain them. *"Etlekhe verter oyf mame-loshn /* A few words in the mother tongue" is an attempt at total integration—to merge feminism, lesbianism, and Yiddish language into one piece.

But I realized that being the only poet using Yiddish was not particularly gratifying since such isolation defeats what I want the very use of Yiddish to represent. I wanted a context within which this poetry would grow *tsuzamen mit di lider fun andere froyen,* together with the poetry of other women, a context incorporating the present and the past. I wanted to search for *di bikher un sforim* from which Molodowsky's page might have been torn. I naturally felt a need to know more about Yiddish women writers, particularly immigrants who faced some of the same issues I faced when I first came to the States. I was interested in their dealings with assimilation and the language issue and their consciousness of feminism. But the Yiddish cultural legacy, *di goldene keyt* which had been passed on to me was strictly male. As much as I loved such Yiddish writers as Morris Rosenfeld, Avrom Reisen, I. L. Peretz, H. Leivik, Sholem Aleichem, Chaim Grade, I was aware they were presenting male perspectives on Jewish life. I wanted to find out *vos di froyen hobn getrakht un geshribn,* what the women had thought and written. I was looking for a link to *yidishkayt* and to *yidishe froyen.* This could be in part done by establishing a dialogue *mit der yidisher fargangenhayt,* with the Yiddish/Jewish past, a dialogue that would have to include women. It would be presumptuous of any us to act as if nothing came before us. And I also realized that I had to find the women myself—much as I did Fradel Schtok—pick them up through references in my readings, in planned searches.

I knew that there were many women writers, but aside from a handful of poems (and these mostly by Kadia Molodowsky), no women prose writers have been translated or are known to American Jews. So I began to look through the literature and the *Leksikon* as well as articles and anthologies. The work of Norma Fain Pratt was of particular use. Having become better acquainted with some—Rokhl Luria, Kadia Molodowsky, Fradel Schtok—I became committed to translating their work and making them available to American Jewish women. (A couple of these translations appear in *The Tribe of Dina.*) One poem which resulted from my reading was "Fradel Schtok," a dramatic monologue in which I take on the voice of the writer as she expresses her confusion about adopting English and abandoning Yiddish. I hope to do more writing in this vein.

Not completely satisfied with how I have used Yiddish in some of my poetry, I remain unclear how Yiddish will manifest itself in my future writing. I sense that the bilingual mode is too artificial to maintain. I expect a strong Yiddish element will remain, however, because I feel deeply connected to that literary tradition and culture, and this must inevitably find expression in my work. With all the talk about Yiddish being a dead language, I feel it is important to use whatever Yiddish is available to me—even if at times it is fragmentary. As of now, I am using simple phrases in what are almost virtually exclusively English poems. Context usually explains the Yiddish, and the Yiddish, I hope, seems appropriate because of what is being referred to. For example, in the poem "Warsaw, 1983: *Umschlagplatz*" about my trip to Poland and what I experienced there, it seemed natural to use Yiddish when referring to a plaque written partly in Yiddish. In addition, I used an epigraph from a poem by the Yiddish poet H. Leivik. The desire to use the epigraph—a phrase I had heard all my life—"*In Treblinke bin ikh nisht geven*" (I was never in Treblinka) was but one small attempt to begin dialoguing.

Purists might ask: *Farvos shraybstu nisht bloyz oyf yidish?* But why not write only in Yiddish? I don't feel as in control of the language as I do of English. But there are other considerations. I want to remain accessible to as many people as possible, and by using Yiddish exclusively I would bypass the very audience that has appreciated and responded strongly to the presence of Yiddish in my work. The intensity and emotionalism of that response still takes me aback. Just a few Yiddish words, the very sounds of the language evoke very strong feelings and memories. So I am determined that Yiddish will never be a barrier, as it has been for many Jews whose parents spoke it only *az di kinder zoln nit farshteyn* (so the children won't understand). I realize I need to find ways in which I can use Yiddish, intertwine it with the English so that it is not directly translated but intelligible. This can be done by repetition, inference, paraphrasing, and so on. I'm beginning to consider more formal poems, such as the pantoum, whose forced repetitions would make integrating the two languages easier. I am still experimenting.

So the impulse for my writing at this stage is very different than it was when I wrote in my early twenties. I am more deliberate about choosing subjects, and I find myself needing to read, research, and internalize what I learn. I frequently start with an idea as in the case of the pantoum. Here the form is the idea. Often the content—a desire to create something about a certain subject—is the idea, as in "Fradel Schtok." So language, form, and content are new struggles for me at this stage.

My perception of Jewish content has, I believe, broadened. I no longer view the Holocaust as dwarfing my new themes. The present and the more distant past seem significant subjects for poetry. And this includes everything in the present—whether cultural issues such as Yiddish and Yiddish literature, forms of secular identity, relationship to the past, assimilation, Israel and the Palestinian struggle for self-determination—all are fitting subjects for contemporary American Jewish poets. By turning to these, by framing them in the present context, by presenting them from a feminist perspective, we can create a viable American Jewish poetry and poetics—one linked to the past and containing a legacy for the future.

I often ask myself who I am writing for and who is interested in Jewish poetry and poetics with a feminist or lesbian perspective. I feel some confusion at this point about the different audiences for my work. I am deeply committed to the lesbian and feminist movements, to Yiddish and *yidishkayt*, to the Jewish community, to radical politics. How to reach all these audiences through which journals and magazines are questions I have not answered. I am working on them in the same way I am working on my poetry.

What I am certain of is that my political work—consciousness raising on feminist, gay, and Jewish issues, building Jewish awareness of *yidishkayt*, teaching Yiddish, translating significant material, working toward a peaceful solution in the Middle East—has become as important to me as my writing. And this surprises me given how I began writing in such complete isolation. But my commitment to these political causes has become very deep, and I could never again think of poetry writing as the sole and central preoccupation of my life. I, of course, don't want to abandon entirely the personal, private inner life which was often the impulse behind my early work. But I have a keen sense of the present as historical, a turning point—Jews are shaping their future now. How we preserve and recast Yiddish culture and sensibility on American soil are questions I feel compelled to address in both my political activism and my poetry.

CAVES

GERALD STERN

I try to think of my favorite cave. There was one in the ancient cellar of a house I lived in in Philadelphia that you reached by walking through three other cellars and which felt as if you were in the dead center of this glorious existence. And there was one seven flights up in the abominable heaven they call "maids' rooms" in the City of Lights. I moved from that maid's room, that *chambre à femme*, with its little porthole and its tiny sink to a very old hotel on the *rue de la Boucherie*. It was only one flight up—a kind of miracle among those I knew and loved—and it had huge shutters that completely kept out the light and two giant pillows on the bed and a small carved writing table. It was a cave, though, partly because it was practically surrounded by a large courtyard and partly because, of all the languages spoken up and down those worn stone steps, Romanian, Polish, Arabic, Greek, French, none of them was English. One of my caves was an old lawyers' office in Indiana, Pennsylvania. I treasured it because of its seediness and its former use and its view out the alley and because my landlord, a young millionaire and a patron of the arts, who charged me only seven dollars a month rent, came himself in his blue suit and his camel-hair overcoat to bleed the pipes or do whatever other magic he had to to generate heat out of the inefficient furnace, his mouth open and breathing hard, his eyes half worried, half laughing, his hand searching around down there for some knob or other to turn or pull, one way or the other. One of my caves was above an Army-Navy store with a window full of dusty amazingly-cheap jackets and shirts and shoes, which I loved to study. That cave was ruined forever during one long Christmas vacation when the hideous sounds of "Rudolph the Red-nosed Reindeer" came surging through the cardboard walls, without letup, day and night. One cave, in New Brunswick, New Jersey, was so large I was able to play full-court handball with a friend from Connecticut in one of the three rooms. I loved that place because of the tree in the backyard and because of the fruit market downstairs. There was an electrical fire in the basement one freezing winter night, and I arrived with my eyes bulging and my heart pounding to see my books and papers scattered on the steps and on every inch of available floor space, my poor thoughts and fantasies exposed to the triple Hell of smoke and water and ice. I had to fight with the firemen to get in; I had to climb over those frozen hoses and struggle through that black air. I think the building was made over after that into small cheap apartments and that it lasted for another six years or so before Johnson & Johnson tore it down to make room for a large bush or an Italian ice cream parlor for its crazed employees across the way in that glass outhouse designed by Philip Johnson, one of the relatives, I guess. I think it's actually a children's garden, built out of railroad ties and garishly painted pipes. A corner of one of my poems is forcing its way between two bucolicly laid bricks on one of the walkways. It takes the place of dandelion or milkweed and is there for the picking. Some hungry child will eat it; or some clean mother will drop it in a wire basket in a sudden lurid fit of citizenship.

Wherever I wander, whether in Pennsylvania or Ohio or Mexico or Greece, I dream about the caves I might have lived in or worked in and compare them to the ones I did. I own a small house now in Easton, Pennsylvania, with a garret on the third floor and a small back room on the second floor overlooking a patch of garden and a church in the slight distance whose small bell rings on the hour, and both of these rooms move me to tears, as does the kitchen, a square room with a pine floor and an old cupboard and windows all around. For fifteen years I owned a house on the Delaware River in Raubsville, Pennsylvania, with walls two feet thick and a walk-in fireplace and wide plank floors. That house was *filled* with caves, and it was itself a kind of cave. I loved it most the day I bought it, before we converted it. It seemed gigantic then, and primitive, and open. I remember sitting on a cement step on the side porch, with bees attacking me and ivy getting ready to strangle me. I was half joyous because of the thick lilac trunks and the dark cool interior and the near-silence, and half in despair because of the rotting roofs and the rusty cisterns. I had another cave across the road overlooking the great river. I constructed it myself from a broken down three-car garage. I put vertical spruce on the outside and plaster on the inside and raised the roof to accommodate some large windows I had bought for a few dollars from a friend, a penniless painter from Kintnersville, who found them, I think, in a junk pile on the side of the road. It was a sharp climb down to the river on a hill covered mostly with maple and black locust. I loved the view best from the river's edge; then it seemed I was looking up into an Arizona or New Mexico apartment complex built a thousand or so years ago. For not only was there the hill itself, but a two-story cement retaining wall on which the low wooden building rode. I stood by the lapping water amazed at the beauty of that building and struck by my handiwork and my skill as a contractor. My truest of all caves, though, was the New York apartment on Vandam Street. I climbed up five stories to get there, but once I was inside I was overwhelmed by the silence and the remoteness. I adored sitting in the small living room studying the old plaster moldings and the light fixture. I could see the Empire State Building from my chair, beyond the rows of colonial houses in Soho and the darker taller buildings on Fourteenth and Twenty-Third streets. My bed looked onto one of those vertical shafts, and in the spring and summer the wind poured over me, caught in some mad and one-of-a-kind crosscurrent of shaft and window. I lay on my bed face-down, almost dizzy from the slight roar, and happy—if there ever was happiness—from those cold walls rising over me and from the peace and secrecy. My first cave in Iowa City was at the corner of Van Buren and Ronalds. It was brick and low and completely dutch in design, standing apart from the rows of white clapboard Victorian houses. It could have been the oldest house in Iowa City, and it was once, I'm told, a nunnery. Dutch, I'm sure. There was a large oven in the cellar, and three crumbling rooms on the first floor, and a cross between a step-ladder and a staircase going up to the second floor, which was one large garret, lying under the roof. My music system was on the second floor; I wrote either there—in bed—or downstairs in the kitchen, at a white wooden table. In fact, I had two rooms too many. I didn't need the living room or the extra bedroom, except perhaps to house my occasional guest or provide floor space for my plants.

I will never be done with caves. They certainly connect with a history not hundreds but thousands of years old, and they are loving reminders of our most delicate and perhaps our happiest time on earth. It is not only out of poverty and melodrama and disgraceful nostalgia that we live our real lives out in caves; we do so because only that way can we decipher the words assigned to us, and stray as we have to. For those who don't, or can't, there is no shame; there is merely no sacred life, and no language. I feel like saying it's the poet's job to remember, (and not only the poet's)—that is, to keep the past—but that's not saying it accurately. It's more to the point to say that he can't but help doing that, even if he struggles a little against it. It is in the cave that he remembers. Remembering is the art of the cave-dweller. And remembering is itself an act of living in the cave. I remember now unashamedly. I even reminisce. I will interrupt myself, or anyone, with a story from my childhood, or, for that matter, from theirs. I am amazed at the joy it brings me, as I am saddened by the ridicule. I am shocked at what is forgotten, or never known. Thirty-two years ago—the summer of 1955—I rented a bed on the Amalfi coast from a shrewd old Italian, who had found a way to get listed in the Youth Hostel Directory, albeit it was not, by a long shot, a hostel he and his wife Carolina ran. They merely lived there, on the second floor of their house, and let any foreigners who wanted—of whatever age—scramble for themselves in three or four crowded rooms on the first floor. He called himself "Papa Luigi," in that half-grand, half-derisory manner of the poor old. Carolina provided meals from her garden for anyone who wanted, and there was good talk and good drinking in the tiny dining room we assembled in at night. One day the afternoon peace was shattered by the sudden appearance of two American photographers who had stopped their car on the narrow highway that ran through Luigi's half-hectare. They quickly assembled their equipment—tripods, cameras, meters—and were just starting their assault on the rocky coast and the blue water when Luigi appeared, smiling. He told them his name was Papa Luigi, that he owned this land and was pleased to have them there, that it was the most beautiful spot on the coast and they were welcome to take pictures, that they should please wait while he went up to this house to get a photograph of himself taken the first year he was in America, in 1919, I think. He was in his late sixties or early seventies. He had short white hair, brown skin, and wore a pair of blue trousers held up by a rope, and simple cork sandals. He spoke broken English and couldn't read or write—in Italian *or* English. It took him at least five minutes to come back with the photo. The photographers waited, but they were terribly impatient. One of them—I remember he had very hairy arms—kept looking at his watch. The photo showed Luigi, a young man, standing stiffly with some others in front of a fruit store in Brooklyn. I think it was owned by his uncle. He made enough money his few years in America to buy his house and land and get his son (by a first marriage) started in a profession. That son was an *avocat* in the neighboring city of Positano. The two photographers looked at the old photograph, expressed their approval—half-patronizingly, half-embarrassed—and drove off. I think it was a 1954 Buick Roadmaster. One time I had to go upstairs to Luigi's apartment to get some towels or soap, and I surprised him and Carolina eating their spaghetti from a single dish. Normally he lorded it over her and scolded her in front of the guests, three or four Welshmen, a German or two. But I would never be fooled again. I had stayed there ten days, nursing a blistered foot, eating sun-drenched tomatoes and mortadello sandwiches, singing Neopolitan songs with Luigi. When I left he held my arms in his powerful hands and half shook me. "Don'ta forget Papa Luigi," he said. I never have. I don't know what the liberated shadow that Plato held so dearly actually saw when he emerged into the light. Or what he said to the others when he returned to the cave. What the intensity of their vision was on that sheet of wall in front of the flickering fire, what stories they told and dances they did, that Plato doesn't tell us. They must have lived in such ignorance and superstition. Surely they exchanged bones and grunted. And Plato, where had he wandered in Egypt and Sicily? What caves had he seen? I don't for a minute accept the parable as a metaphor for illumination and redemption. That was a cave the philosopher was talking about, and it was a cave he rejected, just as he rejected its poetry. I would have loved to have seen him with one foot out of his own cave, starting his long walk, maybe with his sandals over his shoulder, like Loyola, or Mao-Tse Tung. What a dream of light! Innocent and brutal.

Zeus himself was born in a cave. His mother had him there to keep him away from his greedy father—that is the official version—but it may also be a subtle reminder that the god of overwhelming power, represented by terrible lightning itself, had his first sensations—his first thoughts—in the secret dark. It wasn't the brilliant light that was under attack in Greece, as it would be hundreds of years later in western Europe and America, it was, as we all learned and taught, human arrogance and self-confidence. After all, they had more or less invented that light. The dialogue between Dionysus and Pentheus that takes place in *The Bacchic Women* is the best example I know for summing up the conflict between simple wisdom grounded in great complexity and prejudice grounded in neurotic repression and fear. It is amazing how lucid and light-footed Euripedes makes Dionysus, our god of madness. Pentheus, the grandson of Cadmus and ruler of Thebes, actually the cousin of Dionysus, is arrogant and self-important. He refuses to respect, or even recognize, the god; he has enormous faith in his own power; he is a blasphemer; he doesn't listen to counsel. For this, he is finally ridiculed and torn to pieces. There are many like him among the Greeks. Oedipus, before he is blind. Creon. They are famous. Odysseus, on the other hand, listened carefully to the gods, but there is a pedantry and a prudishness about his orthodoxy. Both he and Theseus fought against the cave, and they did so with recklessness and lack of reverence, although the stories that come down to us are only of the overcoming of the monstrous, the crude bull, the one-eyed giant, both of them ignorant and trusting, easy enough to outwit. That Calypso lived in a cave, but she was soft and loving. I don't think she ate human flesh, but the Minotaur did and Polyphemus did and Scylla, with her six dogs' heads. Not to mention the Maenads. Dionysis' cave—it was the right thigh of Zeus, where he was sewn up and nurtured; from which he was finally born; which he always remembered.

It may be that the large number of actual caves in the area of Greek hegemony led to the obsession, among Greek philosophers, with the great states of light and dark or—what is the same—the passion for opposites, including the defining of a thing by its other, or its nought; or it may be just that caves are perfect locations—metaphors—for our instinctive, and extreme, philosophical and poetic states. For me, Plotinus, that wounded Egyptian, is the best example of this. It may, in fact, have been his only obsession—light and dark—and all his ethical and metaphysical concerns have to be considered from that point of view. "The mind gives radiance out of its own store," he said, in the *Enneads* (IV, 6). It was, at once, the supreme answer to darkness and the only explanation for transcendence. Sitting there on some shadowy rock, or staring wistfully into some hole in the ground, he may not have been that different from St. Jerome in his dim grotto or Don Quixote waiting to be lowered into Montesino's cave. "Call it not Hell," Don Quixote said, "for it deserves a better name." It was a dream place he visited, "a royal and sumptuous palace of which the walls and battlements seemed all of clear and transparent crystal," an "enchanted solitude"; but he arrived there by committing himself to the "black and dreadful abyss," by letting himself down with a rope. One thing produced the other.

I sit in my chair reading Plotinus and longing to be in Ethiopia, in one of the remote churches carved out of solid rock, or in southern France studying an ochre antler in some hidden recess. It is my lower faculty, my nature-loving and generative faculty, that is doing this to me; although Plotinus would say that the material universe, where the lovely caverns lie, is modeled upon the Ideas laid up within the Divine Mind. I warn myself that it is all right to read Plotinus, but very dangerous to talk about him. He is such a bad writer, Porphyry tells us, because he not only didn't rewrite but didn't even read what he had written down. His handwriting was slovenly; he misjoined his words; he cared nothing about spelling. His one concern was for the idea. If one does nothing else the rest of the 1980s, he should read Porphyry's biography of Plotinus, at least the first few pages, to see what a great soul did in the third century of our era to escape the pain of existence, besides crawling like a worm across some bloody stone floor and mumbling in lost tongues like a wounded hyena or a stinking fox. "Plotinus, the philosopher our contemporary," Porphyry tells us, "seemed ashamed of being in the body. So deeply rooted was this feeling that he could never be induced to tell of his ancestry, his parentage, or his birthplace." His whole life—from the time he was twenty-eight on—was committed to the understanding of things—i.e., nonthings—so he could live, at the end, in the world—i.e., outside it—in wisdom and purity. At his death, according to Porphyry, he said that he was striving to give back the Divine in himself to the Divine in the All; very Emersonian. It was a philosopher's death pure and simple, concocted or not. Porphyry says a snake crept under the bed in which he lay and slipped into a hole in the wall at the very moment he died. He is from both worlds, isn't he, that snake? We know him well by now.

It's hard to know what Plotinus actually thought of caves. It depended on whether—at one moment or another—he was thinking of them as places of confinement or places of liberation—Plato or Pythagorus. In the extraordinary section of the *Enneads,* where he discusses the descent of the soul into the body, he refers specifically to Empedocles' grotto and Plato's cave, and he says that the function of the soul is to break its chains and rise to the place of intellection. (The intelligible world.) But at the same time he praises the descent and says—after Timaeus—that the Large Soul was sent into the world and small souls into each of us to make it a rational universe and to make the sense world complete by assuring that it contained as many kinds of organisms as in that, revered, intelligible world. (Place of Intellection.) Although no soul, he says, not even ours (he says), enters into the body completely. By her higher part the soul always remains united to the upper world—even if the lower part is turned toward the body (. . . every soul has something of the lower on the body side . . .). It is such familiar doctrine after all these centuries, after so many Christians and Humanists and Cabbalists have gotten hold of it. My own guess is that Plotinus, more than anybody else, much more than his own beloved Plato, even more than our own Jesus, has given us the modern version of the soul.

Prison poets in particular, they are the cavemen among us, the true Neoplatonists. It is as if they received two sentences—as if they were buried twice. I think of the long and shameful list, and I think of the crude and desperate systems of survival. I close my eyes and try to remember a whole poem by Nazim Hikmet. I know twelve lines of the cucumber poem but that was written after he had escaped from prison and exiled himself from Turkey. I read it aloud all the time, and I lecture my bewildered friends and students on the special function of the cucumber in eastern Europe and western Asia. I talk about its digestive qualities and its mystical history and its glorious associations with different creams and cheeses. He is a classical poet, Hikmet. He spares us the pure horror and lets us concentrate on some joy or some sadness.

> *One night of knee-deep snow*
> *my adventure started—*
> *pulled from the supper table,*
> *thrown into a police car,*
> *packed off on a train,*
> *and locked up in a room.*
> *Its ninth year ended three days ago. . . .*
> *("One Night of Knee-Deep Snow")*

> *The poverty of Istanbul—they say—defies description,*
> *hunger—they say—has ravaged the people,*
> *TB—they say—is everywhere.*
> *Little girls this high—they say—*
> *in burned-out buildings, movie theaters. . . .*
> *("13 November 1945")*

> *To talk to anyone besides myself*
> *is forbidden.*
> *So I talk to myself.*
> *But I find my conversation so boring,*
> *my dear wife, that I sing songs.*
> *And what do you know,*
> *that awful, always off-key voice of mine*
> *touches me so*
> *that my heart breaks.*
> *("Letters from a Man in Solitary")*

Hernandes is a little more bitter. He came from the bitter side of Europe. It is his last few letters that deal with the actual horror, the rat shit in his hair, the pus in his mouth. In his final poems he reflects, he embodies, the outright battle between light and dark, in which the prison—at Madrid, at Orthuela—is not only the poetic ground for metaphor but the living stage of his vision. The rage and weeping, the cruelty and isolation and boredom, the tenderness and hope, were expressed that way. He came finally to inhabit the same cave as St. John of the Cross; perhaps to fight the very same battle.

> *I go on in the dark, lit from within; does day exist?*
> *Is this my grave, or the womb of my mother?*
> ("*I Go On in the Dark, Lit from Within*")

> *I who was sure the light was mine*
> *see myself thrown down into darkness.*
> . . . .
> *But fighting there is one ray of sunlight*
> *always that leaves the darkness beaten.*
> ("*Eternal Darkness*")

I wish I could talk to Etheridge about this. I want to ask him if he began writing before he ended up in the joint. And I want to know if he felt guilty or ashamed because the spirit descended on him and left the others miserable and alone. If he felt more entrapped, or more liberated because he was writing. Who his critics were. I myself lay once under a bare light bulb on a terribly uncomfortable army cot, the mattress removed, with forty or so others lined up on either side of me. And I marched to an early breakfast with a number on my back and guards with loaded guns in front and back of me. And I fought with a pig of a provost-sergeant and was threatened with the hole. It feels odd—and alien—to talk about it now, and I feel foolish listing myself this way with the holy ones, for my time there was short, and my cause was absurdly small—compared to theirs. It was a guardhouse in Aberdeen Proving Grounds, in Maryland, and my job was to dump large garbage cans of dead animals—cats, squirrels, dogs, pigeons, rats—into an underground incinerator. Later, as punishment, I was assigned to a rock-breaking detail. I broke fieldstone ten to twelve hours a day with a twelve-pound sledgehammer while a guard with a carbine stood over me. My workplace was at such an odd angle—on the side of a little hill—that the provost-sergeant could surprise us in his jeep at any time without any warning. After two of my guards received summary court martials for talking with me instead of enforcing my work, I decided to just pound the rocks steadily the whole day and let it go at that. At night, when I was driven back to the guardhouse by my fat enemy, my fellow prisoners had food for me—and comic books and cigarettes. I think all forty of them were black. I was twenty years old at the time. I didn't know it then, but my soul had descended into that place for the sake of making the universe more complete, and I had lost my way, and I was expiating for my own, or someone else's, wrong. I began writing poetry there, weak and humid poetry, and I started to think a little like a poet. That helped me, and the physical labor helped me, and the love of my fellow prisoners. I read the New Testament there for the first time, and I talked to my friends about their terrors. They thought I was a preacher—because of my reading, I suppose—and I couldn't disenchant them. That provost-sergeant was shot dead one day a few years later in a court room by an angry prisoner—or his brother. I know I plotted his death for years and even remembered his name for a month or two. I will not recognize him when he comes on his smoking knees asking for forgiveness. Odd soul. Radnóti, the Hungarian poet, died sometime after October 31, 1944. Miklós Radnóti. He was shot in the head and buried in a mass grave at Abda, a small village in western Hungary. He had been an inmate, a slave, in a forced labor camp and was executed either by a German or a Hungarian guard. The grave was exhumed on June 23, 1946, and though the corpses were partially decomposed and there were only shreds of clothing, Radnóti's body was discovered there. In the back pocket of his trousers a small notebook was found, soaked in the juices of his body. The notebook was cleaned and dried in the sun. It contained his last poems. It is ironic that his final cave wasn't even a freezing barracks but a hole in the ground, a pit, which he shared with a few hundred other Jews and a few unlucky Christians. Although I don't know if it was a true cave since there was no way out—no light. His last poem was written for a fellow-slave, a violinist named Miklós Lorsi, who died a day or two before him. Here it is:

> *I fell beside him, his body rolling over,*
> *already taut, a string about to snap.*
> *Shot in the neck. You'll be finished like this—*
> *I muttered to myself—just lie still.*
> *Patience flowers into death now.*
> Der springt noch auf, *a voice said over me.*
> *Mud and blood both drying on my ear.*
> *("Szentkirályszabadja, 31 October 1944")*

The string about to snap was a violin string, the heart's blood of that musician. Think of him after a forced march, or after a day in the mines or on the roads, trying to remember a note.

The good institutions have been very busy with jailed poets and novelists from all the continents. There is a standard plot. The poet is whisked away in the middle of the night. It might be the only time in his whole life he is given such attention. His trial is held in secret, and his lawyer is either not permitted in court or is a spy for the police. The illegal action may have consisted of printing a poem or having a lucid opinion. If there is a charge, it is treason; murder is not quite appropriate. He is put in prison. As much as possible he is isolated and confronted with ambiguity. Sometimes he is abused—frozen, starved, tortured. That is almost for nostalgia's sake, for it is not needed. It is to remind the brutes they are brutes. The reason he is put in prison is simply to eliminate or reduce his effectiveness, his presence. The prisoner, the poet, understands this and is determined *not* to permit it to happen. He responds specifically through his poetry. His greatest act of rebellion is to find a medium to express himself in: toilet paper, soap, skin. His great victory is to commit his poems to memory or to communicate them to the world outside the prison. He stays alive by writing. I am reading the poems of a young Russian poet who has come to America. She was arrested in 1983 for "oral agitation and propaganda" (writing poetry). Her lawyer was not allowed to attend her trial. Her family and friends were barred. She was sentenced to seven years of hard labor, deported to a corrective labor camp in the swamplands three hundred miles southeast of Moscow and subjected to physical abuse, harassment, and humiliation. She went on a hunger strike to protest the harsh treatment of two other women and was brutally force-fed. She was sent to an isolation cell (the hole) for insulting officials. She edited a communal diary, which was smuggled out to the West. She wrote her poems with a matchstick on slices of soap. She managed to keep her poems alive by reciting and memorizing a certain percentage of them every day. She stored them in her brain. She was able to sneak some of them out. She was told by the officials that she was forgotten, that no one remembered her, that nobody wanted to help her. Her cause was taken up by poets living in the West. She was adopted by Amnesty International. PEN International lobbied for her. Her case was brought to the Soviet Writers' Union. She was freed by Gorbachev on the eve of the Iceland summit meeting, and she and her husband flew to America, to Chicago. Her name is Irena Ratushinskaya. I wish her joy and success.

The cynical and mean-spirited among us insist on pointing out that our writers in the West are not imprisoned because their words are not taken seriously; or they are ignored or drowned out in the general noise; or that writing, as such, cannot be a rallying point against the government. I think our state has demonstrated with great clarity that when writing is taken seriously—in the case of the blacklisted Hollywood writers, for example—it can move with great speed and ruthlessness, constitutional rights and humane traditions notwithstanding. There is no hole, but that's not necessary. Our poets have got to actually step on the White House lawn or damage a nose cone to get attention. Their poems are not enough. And this is as true of Ezra Pound as it is of the others. There is a certain tolerance and freedom of expression and movement in the institutional arrangements that the poet can take advantage of, even if they were not designed in any way for his benefit. Poets know this. They profit from the arrangement, even as they are overcome with guilt and anger. Sometimes they want to know what they would actually have to write down to make the state take offense. In the meantime they are permitted to type and to weep more or less in peace; they are even given a table and a little glass of water and a check. They all end up singing, one way or another. For them it is the notes that count, for they are true troglodytes, those poets. It is a way of outwitting the guards. I think we are specialists in imprisonment, even if we know very little of liberation and redemption. It is like going from cell to cell. Poe, Melville, Dostoevsky, Dickens, Kafka, Beckett, Rhys, Coetzee. If someone is spending his life staring stubbornly at a brick wall, he is one of us. If someone is being led hopelessly from room to room and building to building, he is too. He who lives in the light has to learn, above all things, he is living in darkness. Someone is finally being visited by his keeper; he asks the questions he has been rehearsing for weeks; he begs for his stub of a pencil back. Someone is bleeding to death from a hole in his stomach; he is covered with flies. Someone is so self-conscious and alone that he is almost bursting with regret and sadness.

There are caves where the light comes in on a single brilliant beam for one minute a day, and there are those where it enters only once a year. There are the cistern where Jeremiah ranted and the hole where David cut a corner from Saul's coat. There is the cavity in God's brain where the Virgin lay, and there is the grotto where Alexander Pope chanted. There are the Collective Unconscious of Jung and the electric corridors of Ludwig II. I open my Virgil to the World Below and find myself in sudden full belief, as Aeneas was. I had a Sibyl of my own, although I had no doves to guide me and no ghost to tell my fate and future. She lived in the great black stones of the Carnegie

Library, and it was through those books she spoke to me, as she spoke to the Greeks and Italians through bark and leaves. It was a honey-combed cave she lived in, Virgil tells us, and her voice bounded and drummed and hissed as it moved from room to room. Apollo rode her to make her sing. He goaded her as she stormed about her cave, trying to shake his influence from her breast. He tired her mad jaws. In the end the cavern's hundred mouths all of themselves unclosed to let her verses through. It is not easy to go into the underground. I remember how I listened to organ music on Sunday afternoons in the upper reaches of that building. I remember going from shelf to shelf in the poorly lit stacks and sitting cross-legged on the cold floor turning my pages. There was a huge dinosaur there in the great reptile room in the next wing, and there were dozens of marble reproductions in the corridors and recesses on the way over and back. I believed then in dinosaurs, in their pin heads and grinning mouths and giant tails. I believed that the very large ones were vegetarians the smaller more agile meaner ones were carnivores. And I believed that Greek men were like their statues, with long thick legs and short muscular torsos, and that Greek women were large and graceful, and always a little bent over so that you could catch sight of their stone breasts. The guards who were stationed throughout the enormous building were all old, with white hair and blue eyes and freckled skin. They were thin-lipped and short-tempered, and they all wore black uniforms—suits with gold buttons—and stiff white shirts. In Virgil, the way down was through a wide-mouthed cavern guarded by a dark pool and a gloomy forest, and deathly exhalations rose through the air. Aeneas offered up a fleeced lamb and a sterile cow and entire carcasses of bulls, pouring rich oil over the blazing viscera, and with the golden bough held stiffly in his outstretched hand he followed the Sibyl down through all the smells and noises of hell. That I did too, but I had no golden bough, and my path was different. I think, if anything, I went down and back daily since I had my own map. After a while it became easy. The stinking pools and the writhing hands bothered me very little. It is thirty and forty years later, and I look back on that time with love. If I had to, I could find that path again, and sacrifice, and walk through the darkness.

I have been searching all morning for a leaf to read my future by. It is the end of March, and there is not much left that is not already dry and broken or still wet and soggy. I could wait for a few weeks and find some new green leaves—there is a little fuzz already here and there—but that might be too much like looking for lines of inspiration in a baby's palm. One of the leaves I've picked up has other tiny leaves of a different hue sticking to its sides, and one of them has small glistening shells that remind me of half-grown ladybugs embedded in straw and stuck in the hollows. Worlds within worlds. One has to make a decision so I have reduced it all to five leaves, each one a different shape and a different color. I have put them on a Victorian end table and have turned on the lamp. I want to dry them a little, but I don't want the juices to leave them completely. I'm sure I will count the tiny threads to see how many more dozen years I will live and how many poems I will write and what love has in store for me. Maybe one leaf will be happiness, and one will be misery. I know I will get out my tree book and study the silhouettes and stare through the tissue paper. I know that after ten minutes I will be reading Babylonian once again and finally learning the signs of early Egypt that have eluded me decade after decade in this century. When the leaf is brown with a reddish hue and it has five lobes and the edges are a little curled and the veins are pronounced there is joy and cunning in the information. There is, believe it or not, a miniature tree in this leaf, and it is on one side only. It is as if it were stamped on, and though the leaf is an oak leaf, and it grows from Canada down to Missouri and thrives best in a dry gravelly soil, that miniature tree is not only tropical but seems to come from some humid swamp that, not so many eons ago, stretched into the north here, just a few hours away from Minnesota and its steaming lakes. As I look at it again, it seems almost fernlike, and that's what it is, I think, an ancient fern imprinted, in the heart of this prairie, on the leaf of a tree imported from some gentle ridge overlooking the Mississippi. I have my work cut out for me the next few days. I have to study the markings of four more leaves and set my life on course; it has so veered to the left and right; I have so moaned and twitched for week after week in my sculpted bed. One of these leaves is pitted—it may be mold, or some uncoded message. One of them is dancing; it has the head of a deer, the legs and tail of a fox, the folded arms of a cat. After a while I will stop reading and begin writing. I will follow the leaf's contour and move up and down the stems, though I don't know yet if I will use script or print. I dream that in some pocket or other I will find an old vision crumbled up as if it were tobacco, and I will drop it in a river and watch it slowly sink. I don't mean to say that all things come to naught. I mean to say that I will begin again with empty pockets, as I always do. I mean to say that in the archways and the moss-grown tufa rocks, on the railroad tracks and the rusted cars, in the wall-hangings and the torn rugs and the multicolored books, I will look again for wisdom.

PART
FIVE

HISTORIES

THE POET AND HISTORY

C. K. WILLIAMS

We too had many pretty toys when young:
A law indifferent to blame or praise,
To bribe or threat; habits that made old wrong
Melt down, as it were wax in the sun's rays. . . .

1

For a long time I have envied very deeply the great poems of Yeats' middle period, the long poems of *The Tower,* in particular, "Nineteen Hundred and Nineteen," "Meditations in Time of Civil War," and "The Tower," and recently I've come to realize that my feelings go beyond the poet's normal admiration of excellence and genius. What I have been jealous of is the way that Yeats' poetic prime and the moment during his life of the most intense historical necessity had coincided so sharply. Never mind that the poems are works of great sadness, nearly cries of anguish, for the Europe that was devouring itself in the nationalism of the Great War, and for his adored Ireland tearing itself to pieces for ideals as ill-grounded and as misbegotten, and for which Yeats felt, and may even have borne, some responsibility: "And I myself created Hanrahan / And drove him drunk or sober through the dawn / From somewhere in the neighboring cottages." Yeats was fifty-four in 1919, at the peak of his poetic power. The rest of his poetic life would be wonderfully fertile, in some ways he would become an even more interesting poet later on, but never would there be works which had such a broad resonance, such a brilliant fusing of the personal and public, the individual and the general, the autobiographical and the historical. The person who Yeats was and the poet he had made of himself as an actor in history came together in a poetry whose very music arose out of the conflicts of his awareness of that history and whose very beauty was soaked in horror, like the mother in "Nineteen Hundred and Nineteen," who must "crawl in her own blood."

It is quite feasible and not at all aesthetically immoral to define poetry in such a way that one has to feel neither a particular responsibility toward history nor any squeamishness about apparently omitting such concerns from one's work. The traditions of poetry are rooted as much in pure song, "life's own self-delight," to quote Yeats again, as they are in any sort of "meaning," whether historical, political, philosophical, or otherwise. A poem is grounded in its time, whether it articulates its consciousness of this or not, and it does not have to manifest a direct awareness of its historical situation in order to be significant and to fulfill a rich definition of poetry.

At the same time, once one does decide to try for whatever personal reasons to commit one's poetry as intentionally as possible to questions of direct historical and social significance, issues are raised which are not easily evaded, the central one of which seems to me to be this: how am I to reconcile my sense of limitation, even of inadequacy, in terms of my own actual position in history, with the apparently heroic self which these sorts of meditation seem to call for? If, as Wittgenstein could say, "The World is the case," how is one, as it were, really to take oneself as the lyric case?

2

The most extreme, and the most heroic, example we have in literature of the poet indeed taking himself as the case is Dante. As we know, Dante's entire comedy was as profoundly immersed in his vision of history as it was in his vision of the divine, and much of his greatness is in his fusion of realms, his bringing human history and divine history into congruence: the moral and the pragmatic, the metaphysical and the autobiographical.

Dante's technique for enacting these unifications was to designate himself as humanity's visionary, as the sole living human being who would be allowed, through the power of the inspiration of his mortal love for Beatrice, to explore the realms of the dead and of the eternal afterlife. Dante was to be the spiritual hero of the entire human adventure: it was he, and we only through him, who would actually experience how humans in history find their ultimate rewards and punishment in divine judgment. Dante is historically very specific: there are those he wishes to praise, and those he will blame—indeed, damn. There are popes whose actions he will find reprehensible, and kings like Charles Martel he will consider as lost saviors of the divine-human potential. Dante set the time of his travel through afterlife a dozen or so years before he was actually working on his poem so that he would be not only a moral mediator but an accurate prophet of what he found the limiting and destructive tendencies of his contemporaries. The history about which Dante was writing, and which fired so many of his deepest feelings, was a history that begins and ends in eternity but is enacted in an absolute present as banal and immediate as our own relentless quotidian. Those who carry out Dante's dramas of redemption are his acquaintances— indeed, his neighbors—as well as the princes and petty kings of Italy. Dante was to be the hero of the human attempt, but he was to be at the same time the flesh-and-blood Dante who was insecure enough in his human condition to need a mentor, a guide, a hero of his own, to take him through the more dire portions of his journey.

The reality of Dante's character, and the feelings of self-worthlessness which he experiences, is one of the recurring themes of the work. Dante is continually breaking down, swooning, swearing that he can no longer go on: first Virgil, then Beatrice have to hearten him, reassure him, sometimes chastise him for his timorousness and uncertainty. In the *Purgatorio* and *Paradiso*, this fear gradually becomes interwoven with the virtue of humility, so absolutely essential to the Christian soul, and in the glorious redemptive vision which Dante experiences in paradise, even this self-doubt is accounted for.

In the *Inferno*, though, where the non-Christian Virgil is Dante's teacher, the issue is quite different. Again, our casual response to Virgil's function in the *Commedia* has to do with his direct knowledge of limbo and of hell and purgatory: he is to instruct Dante, to encourage him past the frightful examples of human fallibility and evil before which Dante will quail. I believe, though, that Virgil's actual function is more elemental and much more basic: it is to enable Dante to make that leap by which he will in fact take himself as the case, in which he will dare to assume for himself the poet, and for poetry, tasks which were hitherto only incidentally conceived of as a part of their definitions. What Dante needed from Virgil was the model of someone who had dared himself to try to recapitulate various modes of history, however much Virgil's experience was limited from a Christian point of view.

The unification of apparently contradictory historical systems is actually one of the oldest gestures of significant literature: it begins for us with Homer's warriors who inhabit a half-myth world of gods and absolute passions, and Aeschylus' Orestes who flees from mythic history to the symbolic reality of Athens. When we participate in literature as readers, we are so accustomed to this movement that we hardly remark it, so deftly does Milton, as another example, poeticize his metaphysic and embody his historical-ethical imperatives in the divine history he is reincarnating. But when we, as poets, consider that movement, that attempt, that task, it is a forbidding undertaking. There are presumptions, about the self, about the social, about the metaphysical, so gigantic that one does not, literally, know how to begin. The sheer *will*, the intensity of the overcoming of one's vision of self that is called for, is so daunting.

Naturally we don't believe that we can will ourselves to be Dantes or Miltons, and neither do we—or most of us, anyway—have such a clear vision of the varieties of divine and human history: even if we are deeply religious, there has been in the conceptual mind of the West an apparently quite irrevocable split between the workings-out of the secular and the holy.

At the same time, though, history, past and future, remains for us the necessary matrix in which our most profound ideas and ideals will be enacted. Our metaphysics and our ethic evolve in a dialectic with whatever spiritual structure we happen to be born into or to construct for ourselves; but without the connection to a concrete historical reality with its necessities and its responsibilities and demands, we cannot even refer to an ethic as such: it will be simply a sort of Boy Scout handbook to good deeds.

It is here that our presumption isn't so audacious in defining ourselves by a spiritual gesture similar to the heroic Dante's, for we, too, when we dare to try to conceive of ourselves as active agents, active participants in the larger social and political histories around us, experience an acute and painful sense of insignificance and uncertainty. The actual history Dante participated in, the ebb and flow of those human events which he could quite clearly visualize as beginning at least as far back as the early Roman Empire and culminating in the Guelph-Ghibelline dispute, was quite accessible to him—perhaps in his exile he may even have thought it too much so. But where is our history now, how do we dare to think that we are actually participating in it in an ethically direct way, rather than being mere observers of it, passive recipients?

There is serious debate about whether the individuals' actual experience of self in history has really been heightened since the Age of Revolutions, since our rights as democratic agents have been elaborated for us, or whether many of us have not in fact become more separated from a real sense of a position in a history which is supposed to include us directly as a part of its purposes. Whether because of the difficult dis-junctions of industrialism, or the developments of bureaucratic governments which have in mind their own interests and perpetuation before anything else, it is really quite feasible for us to say that in many ways we are actually more estranged from a history which would be intimately available to us as individuals, than was the situation in the days when our situations were certainly more humble but more clearly defined.

I do not in any way mean to suggest here any sort of reaction or reversion to a condition which in nearly every other sense was intolerable: what I am indicating is that in some ways the courage which is demanded of us, the difficulties which face us in joining our intimate biographies to humanity's, are even greater, and possibly de-mand a heroism which is more rigorous, than Dante's or Milton's.

Frank O'Connor, in *The Lonely Voice,* defines the short story as different from the novel not so much by its length or for any technical reason but because, instead of having a hero, it has what he calls a "submerged population group" which may be, he points out, "Gogol's officials, Turgenev's serfs, Maupassant's prostitutes, Chekhov's doctors and teachers, Sherwood Anderson's provincials." O'Connor's arguments are compelling, but what is most interesting here is the term "submerged popula-tion" because I think that quite possibly it is not merely the short story that can be defined by the phrase but the consciousness of nearly all human beings in modern civi-lization.

How many American writers can one name, at least since 1850, who have *not* felt themselves to have risen out of some marginal group or submerged social class? How many of us can *assume* an involvement in history which has anything more than that observer status I alluded to? Among poets, there would be only Lowell, I think. Lowell was obsessed by history, and a good part of his obsession seemed to find its roots in his family genealogy, the power and status of the Boston Lowell's in American history. Lowell is aware of himself as at least potentially a patrician, the heir of a living body of events which were his by blood, as much as by concept. But when you go to his brilliant poems of history, they are in all but a few instances scholar's poems, the poems of the well-read dilettante. In the few poems in which Lowell does actually himself enter into the stream of living events, in his acquaintances with Robert Ken-nedy and Gene McCarthy, in his participation in the Pentagon March of the 1960s, his sense of being out of place, a usurper, a pretender, is as acute as that of Norman Mailer's, although Mailer could idealize Lowell as the living embodiment of various unattainable patrimonies and sureties which Mailer felt were forbidden to him.

The sense of being outside of things is not an American phenomenon of course: from Baudelaire to Vallejo, the poet's image of being at the margins of society, send-ing poems toward a center, has been almost the primary description of the poet's situation, or plight.

So there seems to be a double overcoming which is demanded of the modern poet who would take upon himself or herself the business of history, of being in history, or responsibility toward it and of conscious enactment in it. Not only is one presuming mightily to take oneself as the case, but even the larger group to which one belongs seems invariably to have a tangential relation to the direct realm of politics and social choice, to that world which one hopes is to be affected by the labors of the poet and the poem.

To observe, to comment, to pass notes back and forth to one another is not to participate in history as Dante or Yeats did. How are we to find our way, then, to a place near enough to the center so that our efforts to affect that center are not so feeble and futile that there is no point in even beginning, even putting pen to paper?

3

A year or so ago, in an undergraduate creative writing class, we were discussing nuclear war. It was the week of the showing of what turned out to be that lame film *The Day After,* and we had quite a lively discussion going. At one point, one of my more articulate students said something which at the time I more or less dismissed but which I've thought of often since. What he said in essence was: "Why worry so much about all of this? If there's going to be a nuclear war, there'll be one, it won't be for us to decide. Why pretend that we have anything to do with the choice? Why should we shorten our lives with worry?" (One of my other students chipped in that he'd heard the whole nuclear-freeze debate was a result of manipulation by the Russians, who were trying to shorten American life-expectancy by inducing stress in us.)

As I say, at first I didn't think much of what my good student had offered: I suppose I gave him some homilies about participatory democracy and the like, but, after I'd thought about it for a while, I came to realize that what he'd been making wasn't a polemic but a plea. Not to me, not to anyone in particular, but to things as they are, to reality itself. What he was asking, I think, was that he be allowed to live a while longer in his child's mind, that mind we begin with and which we carry with us all our lives which tells us that the adults are somehow, we don't know and we don't care how, going to take care of this, of anything and everything. The child broods and frets about ultimate issues much more than we give it credit for—anyone who has ever had a child recovering from even minor illness knows this—but those worries almost always subside into the conviction that those who are responsible for us will deal with what troubles us. And usually, of course, they do: most of us do have our bread on the table; we do have our beds to sleep in.

The hardest part about becoming adults is in giving up this conviction, in having to take responsibility for our own acts and actions, even, finally, for the well-being of our own children. But there is something in us which always longs to return to that past time of warmth and protectedness. Much of the working-out of our characters, we might even say, is a drama between those two tendencies in our psyches, and I think that we could also describe our societal life as well, as the conflict between the movement towards autonomy and the inertias of dependence which the child manifests.

Democratic government, for instance, in America at least, has come to almost rely on a general passivity and immobility on the part of the populace, except during elections, when presumably our affectedness is to be expressed and our general will enacted. Any sort of stirring of the waters between these carefully scheduled times, anything beyond letter-writing to congressmen and allowing one's pulse to be taken in polls, government tends to find subversive, and, if expressing deep disagreement, even dangerous: in the socialist world, such dissent is considered outright treason.

Government, then, would have us understand and accept that we are, in fact, children, that *it* is the adult, and that when we trouble it with our little wants—about nuclear war, for instance—all we're doing is intruding, impeding government from getting on with its business of taking care of us.

It isn't by chance that I use nuclear war as an instance here. I believe that the threat of nuclear war is much more central to our considerations of identity and of self than is usually given credence. I believe that the nuclear reality we all live in now has demanded of us a terrific act of repression of both the individual and collective psyche. I think that every morning when we awake and don't cry out in terror at the vile death that looms above us, we are reflexively defending ourselves with walls of psychic numbness as real and as debilitating as any neurosis. We can, and perhaps must, accept this mode of conscious life as necessary, as inescapable, and if we envisage nuclear holocaust as just so many individual deaths, then perhaps that is the case: we are all simply making the ancient gesture by which we protect ourselves against a too-vivid awareness of our mortality.

But I think the issues are more insidious than that. What we face in the nuclear age is not the death of so many individuals, but the death of the species itself, and this sort of total collective perishing is of a different quality entirely from individual death. The animal, and the human being, will under many circumstances sacrifice its individual life to the good of the species, to what we call the common good but which we might better understand as the historic good: the good by which the specie-body and the specie-identity will survive the individual. I think that when we are threatened by the death of all of us at once, of the species, there may very well be something in our genetic structure itself that makes our very organism cry out to us to act to avert this encompassing disaster. And perhaps we have another anguish: perhaps we know that what we fear comes from our realization that human existence is in some intimate connection to something greater than itself, and our deeper sadness might have as much to do with images of consciousness itself bringing itself to naught; it is the potential sadness of existence itself, or of God, which tears us so, with anguish, and perhaps with a pity that utterly transcends anything else we have ever felt.

But we don't *feel* all of these things, or only occasionally: we allow them to subside into those quieter portions of the psyche where they don't impinge on our everyday-ness, our wish to live, to experience, to possess lives as near to "normal" as we can. But what if the despair which we imagine awaits us with the annihilations of species and of consciousness in fact informs our souls as a much more constantly compelling fact that we take into account? Might we, in other words, be living in a state of despair right now, without quite even knowing it? And, further, as poets, might not this despair be unconsciously affecting our very definition of poetry, and even the ways in which we execute it?

In the course of my teaching, and of various other literary business—judging contests, editing, trying to keep up with and to encourage hopeful young poets—I get to read a really quite astounding number of poems. I'm not going to comment on the level of competence the poems might manifest—this has become a sort of whining hobby among the literati and shows little awareness of how literary culture actually operates—but I am struck by one thing, and that is the forbidding number of poems which deal with themes of childhood, which have to do with conflicts and memories about parents, grandparents, childhood traumas, schoolfriends, etc. As we know, since Wordsworth (although, interestingly, rarely before, excluding Traherne) the child, the child we were, is a necessary part of any serious meditation on self and society, and since Freud the tools and techniques of these introspections have become even richer. But I have the sense that such considerations are not really at the base of quite *this* much domestic obsessiveness. Neither does it arise from the unfortunate creative-writing class dictum of "writing what we know" (an instruction, by the way, which is harder than one might think either to surmount or really to make effective).

I wonder—and I'll only offer this as speculation because it might seem so far-fetched—I wonder if what might be behind all of this is in fact the despair we do feel before our dire potential fate and the impotence which overwhelms us when we consider how little say we actually have in possibly averting that fate? I wonder if our minds, despite our best will, might reel back to what I've called the child's mind, without consulting us at all about it, without even letting us know about it. Might we actually be living in a state of psychic emergency, something equivalent to the battle-field traumas that were a part of the inspiration for Freud's elaboration of the death-instinct? And might we, so traumatized, be responding with really quite paralyzing gestures of psychic self-defense?

As I say, this sounds rather farfetched, but I think it does bear consideration, especially in the terms of any consideration of the poet and history, and of the will that is clearly necessary if we are to insert ourselves into history.

There's another thing I've noticed about the younger poets I teach and have contact with, and that is how single-minded and passionate their dedication is to becoming accomplished poets. We usually consider such commitment to an art as an admirable end to be desired, and of course it is. But there's something I sometimes find troubling about how *exclusive* this dedication can seem. It sometimes seems to entail a sort of myopia, or even tunnel vision: the poet's world becomes so absolutely focused on poetry and poets that I can have the queasy feeling that I'm dealing with people who are partly illiterate in terms of any other system of knowledge and value. Another speculation: might this potential overdedication, this narrowing of interest and of competence, of system and of existence, be also a result of the despair I've been trying to articulate? That my students know little and care little about philosophy—about history, science, anthropology, art—is this a part of the ordinary poet's madness which we know is in our cultural heritage, or might this much intensity, an intensity which excludes so much, be rather something new? Might there not be a different sort of sacrifice implied than our traditional marriage to our art? Might there be a portion of our humanity which is at risk?

I speak of the younger poets, but I have to say that these are tendencies and direc-tions I've felt in myself as well, which is perhaps why I dare to offer such possible affront to so many I admire. I feel in myself a constant leaning toward a sort of limiting ambition, a tendency to become a poetic grind; I feel myself overwhelmed with a moral indolence about what certain tasks of my identity as human being, rather than as poet, entail.

What are those tasks? What does it mean to have an identity as a human being beyond that of the poet? We all, of course, define ourselves in many systems, and any of us would indeed be affronted to have only a single definition. Another observation, and another speculation: I have noticed also, and not only among my students now, that there is very little philosophizing these days about the nature of the human. Very rarely in our poems does one find the sorts of reflection on the basic attributes of the human soul, as, to use our examples again, are in Dante, Milton, or Yeats. Possibly there is nothing to fret about here because such reflection, such philosophical work, is assumed by any literary artifact. But might the question be deeper, might it be that something keeps us from reflecting on the nature of the human as the starting point of our mature considerations?

I am going to postulate another genre of despair now, possibly more available to our consciousness than the nuclear anguish we must live with but possibly just as much an obstacle to be overcome if we are to conceive of ourselves as participants and real agents of our history.

The process of defining our humanity is always a dialectic between our vision of what we see before us—the evidence—and of what we can conceive ideally for the human. What we call philosophical thinking is actually much more firmly grounded in the life we live, even the life philosophers live, than philosophy itself admits. Our image of philosophical thought is of an activity purified of the mucks and manias of human interchange and human emotion, but the dialectic by which one arrives at the most abstruse notions of consciousness and of ethical purpose should and must be embedded in the realities of history as fact and history as possibility. It is between these facts and these possibilities that the dialectic of our first definitions depends, and the task we must set ourselves in trying to make ourselves conscious of our philosophical and historical situation has very much to do with trying to clarify both the terms of that dialectic and what the facts of our history actually have been.

The facts of our recent history are nearly as depressing as our nuclear future. Wars, oppressions, colonialisms, concentration camps: the human animal hangs its head in shame, but our spirits have survived all of these; we have retained our hope, or so we like to think. But have we indeed kept a hope that is as real and as vibrant as that which poets have traditionally assumed? If defining the human reality also entails dreaming the human possibility, where are we in our history now? André Brink succinctly sums up the results of some centuries of human attempt by saying, "We are living amid the ruins of not one, but two, utopian visions of the world." The two empires Brink refers to are of course the Capitalist-Christian and the Socialist-Communist. Whatever one's political attitudes and ideals, it does not take a great deal of effort if not to agree with Brink then to entertain his point of view. Clearly capitalism as we know it is terribly flawed. The wealth and well-being it has undeniably brought to so many has also been forbidden to just as many, or more. Whether all the rich of the world are riding on the backs of the poor is a matter to be debated, but that those poor, whether in the Third World or in the slums of the industrial democracies, are not along on the rosy railroad of capitalist progress is certain. The failings of Soviet and Eastern communism are different but equally dismal. Societies in which the expression of the individual—whether artist, writer, or union member—is deemed to be a threat to the fabric of the society, can in no sense claim the mantle of idealism which Marx postulated for them. In some ways, then, the result of all our philosophizing, all the grand and good intent of all our houses, has been so disastrous that the attempt to define ourselves with any level of conviction seems to be nullified in advance, because we know by experience how such philosophical certainties will come to be enacted: in fanaticism, distortion, and hideous violence.

4

A friend of mine—a very good novelist—and I were recently discussing the Czech writer Milan Kundera. My friend said admiringly of him, "He writes about politics without you even knowing he's doing it." I agreed with my friend, but at the same time I was puzzled: why was it that we would find so virtuous such a mode of indirection? If one wishes to talk about politics in one's work, why shouldn't one? And, in fact, Kundera in his recent work does just that, but the point I was groping toward had more to do with my friend and me with whatever our system of valuation was that would make us think this. There are several ways to consider the question. First of all, one might say that literature by its very definition is not political, that it "transcends" politics and partisan political thinking. This is something one used to hear quite often in literature classes and literary journals, and it is to a great extent true that much literature works, to use the term again, by *assuming* the political and social reality as a background against which the rest of the work is enacted and presumably will illuminate that background for those who care to investigate it.

There's another wariness that we might feel beyond this, though, about this question, which has to do with wishing at all costs that our work not be considered as propaganda, in any sense of the term. To be too direct in one's expression of a political point of view is to lay one's self open to being "merely" a propagandist, a spokesman for that point of view. There is certainly enough in our recent history to make us suspicious of being front men for some party's ideological manipulations.

Both of these are feasible reasons for the indirection my friend was tacitly advocating. But might there be something else, something darker and more fearful in it? I've spoken of our nuclear despair, our philosophical despair: might there be another genre of despair, of near hopelessness that has to do with our effectiveness, our real sense of what the possibilities are for any individual, even the artist who has access to more than individual means, to do anything more than touch reality in the most oblique way? Dante wrote a treatise to advise rulers how they could operate their realms so as to best make matrices for a truly Christian empire on earth. He assumed his work would be read by the very princes he was addressing. A great part of the *Commedia,* too, is devoted to the embodiment of Dante's ideas on empire, good and bad rulers and the like, which, again, he presumed would come to the attention of those he wished to affect.

What poet among us would dare dream of such influence and such effect, of actually demanding a place in the living historical reality of our time? Would it not be the most outrageous *hubris* for us even to consider the possibility? But what if that hubris were not simply a condition of our existence, but rather something which arose out of a historical reality which defines our essential position for us? What if this hubris, this fear of pride, is really a fear of facing our own impotence, our lack of influence, or even our abdication from one of the rightful and primary functions of the poet and the poem?

What if, we might say, we have been *cheated* of history?

5

Poetry is power.

Perhaps it is a power that we are a little afraid of, that our situation in our social-political reality *not* as poets, but as people, has made us mistrust. We know that power in the modern world is the ability to change minds, to convince, often against the real interests of those whose desires are being manipulated, whether by advertising or by politicians who are geniuses of image and of shadow. That is propaganda: our best selves learn to distrust propaganda and perhaps we begin to consider our own work as potentially what we despise. We come to believe that what tries too hard to convince is not to be trusted. Therefore, we can actually mistrust our own work, its affective capabilities, its capacity for evoking in others what we passionately and painfully feel about the world ourselves.

And besides all of this, we don't even quite know who we're speaking to. We certainly wouldn't dream that a prince, in whatever disguise, would ever run across our work. We imagine a sort of literary bureaucracy, consisting of critics, scholars, and professors, who act as agents between the poem and its audience, a selection committee, a panel of judges: the world of poetry becomes a sort of Miss America contest.

And even if we did have a more direct access to our audience, what would that audience be, who would we be speaking to? Isn't our basic assumption about our audience that it would rather be watching television than, at best, reading a novel? But is this really the case, or is it another instance of how our perception of our function has been distorted? One of the cardinal sins of the poet is to undervalue our audience's capacities and our own efficacies.

Whitman noted: "I saw the profoundest service that poems or any other writings can do for their reader is not merely to satisfy the intellect, or supply something polished and interesting, nor even to depict great passions, or persons or events, but to fill him with vigorous and clean manliness, religiousness, and give him *good heart* as a radical possession and habit."

A good heart. If the power of propaganda is to change minds, perhaps the power of the poem is to change the soul because the poem is the most direct means of communication with the soul. What we call the soul is really a kind of song, a fugue of thoughts and emotions, perceptions, beliefs, ideals, hopes. It is what drives the philosophers crazy because they are trying to isolate an entity which could be spoken of precisely and defined precisely, but the soul is too complex, and too grand, for the mind, even the philosophical mind, to grasp. Poetry speaks incidentally *of* the soul, but it is the most articulate language we have for speaking directly *to* the soul.

But of what are we to speak?

In the song of the soul, everything is fused and balanced: all that we value, all that we conceive, is somehow elaborated into an order the harmonious working of which is the most profound delight of our existence. In that song, that hymn, our metaphysics marry with our morals, our ethics interweave with our notions of personal identity, our ideas of love are inextricably bound into our religious beliefs. Dante's work is the great expression of this song and of the unity which we possess, or might possess; but the world has changed since Dante, history has changed, what we conceive the greater world to be has changed, and even the function and use of poetry has changed.

In the modern world, the world since Baudelaire at least, and possibly the world since Blake, the peculiar function of poetry is that it is always the first element of our existence which expresses the disorder of our soul's song, which enacts the breaking down of modes of harmony between the private and the public, between the individual and the common. It is not infeasible for us to imagine ourselves as being as whole as anyone in Dante's age, but the preliminary labors toward that wholeness seem much more complex now. Which is what these reflections have really been about. Because the task of inserting ourselves as poets into history is not something that happens in the public world, in our lives as citizens, but in our monologues as selves. It is the most intimate activity for the poet; it is one of the most basic demands in the life of the poet.

We are in history, like it or not. The only question is how conscious we will be of how history is affecting us, and how we are possibly to affect it. Dante's history, too, afflicted him with despair and hopelessness. Yeats' "Nineteen Hundred and Nineteen" is a cry of anguish at the pass to which humanity seems to have brought itself. There must be a place within our poetry, too, for such naked cries of indignation and terror, of truth and of lost truth, even if the final truth seems—we hope it only seems—to be that we are helpless and that it would be terrifyingly easy to regard the human adventure as brutal and hideous.

The grounds for our despair are compelling, our sense of impotence and hopelessness insidious and debilitating. But what is asked of us then is a greater consciousness of our plight, for human history *is,* finally, consciousness; it is the ground for our experience and our despair, but it is also the recognition of our triumphs over that despair. What our poetry cannot allow itself is a perfunctory acceptance of experience as it is received, however elegantly that experience can be expressed, for this is to slight both history and ourselves, the selves we are and the selves we might become, both as individuals and as nations, peoples and humanity.

NOTES

This essay was first delivered as a talk on January 5, 1985, to the M.F.A. students at Warren Wilson College.

DANCING AT THE DEVIL'S PARTY:
SOME NOTES ON POLITICS AND POETRY

ALICIA OSTRIKER

> If you/I hesitate to speak, isn't it because we are afraid of
> not speaking well? But what is "well" or "badly?" With
> what are we conforming if we speak "well?" What hier-
> archy, what subordination lurks there, waiting to break
> our resistance? What claim to raise ourselves up in a wor-
> thier discourse? Erection is no business of ours: we are
> at home in the flatlands.
> —Luce Iragaray, "When Our Lips Speak Together"

My education in political poetry begins with William Blake's remark about John Milton in *The Marriage of Heaven and Hell.* "The reason Milton wrote in fetters when he wrote of Angels & God, and at liberty when of Devils & Hell, is because he was a true Poet and of the Devil's party without knowing it." The statement is usually taken as a charming misreading of Milton or as some sort of hyperbole. We find it lumped with other readings which supposedly view Satan as the hero of *Paradise Lost,* such as Percy Bysshe Shelley's in *A Defence of Poetry,* although neither Blake nor Shelley says anything of the kind.

I consider Blake's statement simply accurate. I think it the best single thing anybody has ever said about *Paradise Lost.* If not clear as a bell, then at least as compressed as diamonds. The insouciant opening gesture takes for granted what to Blake (and to me) is obvious: that the poetry qua poetry is better, more exciting, more energetic in the sections dominated by Satan, worse, duller, less poetic in the sections dominated by God. As a lover of poetry Blake has evidently struck a perplexity. Why (he asks himself) does Milton's Satan excite me and his God bore me even though he plainly intends me to adore God and scorn Satan? The answer could have been that Milton "wrote in fetters" where constrained by theology and the danger of lapsing into inadvertent sacrilege, but "at liberty" otherwise. Other critics have claimed that it is impossible to make God talk successfully in a poem, but the Book of Job is enough to refute that position. Why did Milton choose to make God talk at all? Dante cleverly avoided that difficulty.

The second half of Blake's sentence not only solves the *Paradise Lost* problem but proposes a radical view of all poetry which might be summarized as follows: All art depends on opposition between God and the devil, reason and energy. The true poet (the good poet) is necessarily the partisan of energy, rebellion, and desire, and is opposed to passivity, obedience, and the authority of reason, laws, and institutions.

To be a poet requires energy; energetic subjects make the best material for poems; the truer (better) the poetry, the more it will embody the truths of Desire. But the poet need not think so. He can be of the devil's party without knowing it.

The metaphoric train of Blake's sentence is as significant as its idea. "No ideas but in metaphors" might be a useful rule of thumb for poets and critics, especially when we engage in ideological discourse, where words so easily collapse into formulaic wallpaper. A metaphor gives us at least a fighting chance of saying something real. "Fetters . . . liberty . . . party" announces that the theological issue in *Paradise Lost* is inseparable from the political issue. "Are not Religion and Politics the Same Thing?" Blake asks elsewhere. "Prisons are built with stones of Law, Brothels with bricks of Religion," one of the pungently metaphorical Proverbs of Hell, draws the parallels neatly: in each case, an authoritarian system must create something to punish. Law creates Crime; Religion creates Sin. A century and a half later, Michel Foucault rediscovers this plain truth.

But to return to *Paradise Lost:* Milton's Supreme Being, at the apex of the cosmic hierarchy, is committed to maintaining his own "glory." At the opening of book three he himself explains it all. Created beings must have free will, or their adoration would be unsatisfying, mere puppet-love. Moreover, commands and prohibitions must be promulgated, or men and angels would have no opportunity to demonstrate their adoration through obedience. Foreseeing that Mankind will fall, God asks as querulously as any father whose son has totaled the car, "Whose fault? / Whose but his own? Ingrate, he had of me / All he could have." In making plans for man's redemption, the Father applauds himself for his own magnanimity, "so shall my glory excel" (*PL* 3:133). As William Empson long ago observed, Milton's God (which is really to say Christianity's God, in the moment of Milton's writing) is both tyrannical and dull, in addition to being disagreeably egocentric, legalistic, and self-justifying. Milton's Satan on the other hand is not at all a good fellow, but he is fascinating and complex—passionate, intelligent, eloquent, capable of introspection, responsive to experience and situation, sexually attractive (as in the scene where Eve is fascinated by the sinuous form of the serpent), and arousable. He can be haughty, humiliated, despairing, hopeful, awed, jealous, spiteful, self-deluding, generous, resolute, exhausted. He is one of us. He is interesting. Milton's God is at best a schoolmaster, at worst Blake's nasty Noboddaddy. And all this is conveyed quite magnificently by Milton's own poetry. At the same time, Milton unquestionably intended to justify God's ways to men, as a poet "enchanted" (C. S. Lewis' splendid term in the *Preface to Paradise Lost*) by the idea of hierarchy and the beauty of obedience. Most of his readers have unquestionably thought that he was doing so successfully. Only lately do we begin to learn that *Paradise Lost* contains two contradictory belief systems within one poem, and that herein dwells its genius.[1]

Milton's God-Satan opposition illustrates the way a repressive hierarchical structure must inevitably precipitate rebellion. When we look at Adam and Eve we see a parallel inevitability attending gender stratification. "He for God only, she for God in him." Adam is supposed to (benignly) lead and guide, as he has been created with the fuller measure of Reason. Eve is supposed to (voluntarily) follow, having been created with enough Reason to appreciate how wise and superior Adam is but not enough to be independently trustworthy, especially since she has been created with something of an overdose of Passion. What Milton's God has wrought, in other words, is an intrinsically unstable system. It has to break down and does break down as soon as Eve realizes that she does not like being the dominated and "inferior" half of the couple. Hierarchy, in the instant that it crosses the line from description to prescription, invites defiance. From the moment we meet Adam and Eve we see the crack in the crockery. It is going to break; it is going to—ah, it has broken. Again, Eve is more interesting poetically than Adam, a well-meaning fellow but a bit of a stiff.

If the true poet is of the devil's party without knowing it, what happens when the poet sets forth with malice aforethought as a devil's advocate? Well, Byron's self-conscious satanic heroes are almost as boring as Milton's God. De Sade, that half-conscious satanist, is not boring only because he is of God's party without knowing it, the hysterical Sadean railings against priests, nuns, virtue, motherhood, and so on, indicating the presence of a particularly virulent superego which he persisted in trying to crush. Blake himself, passionately heterodox as he was, harbored an unacknowledged seed of orthodoxy in the longing for certitude and transcendence which gradually revealed itself in his late prophecies. In Blake's work we see the energetic struggle to defeat these seductive cravings internally as well as externally; we see a man who insists that contraries are necessary to life and art; and we see an artist who, like Milton, contains within himself both sides of a monumental and age-old cultural and psychic quarrel.

But beyond good and evil? Beyond dominance and obedience? Beyond the dualities, however excitingly charged and contradictory? Of course: plurality. All trades: their gear and tackle and trim. The Whitman catalog, which delights by its scurry and randomness as we are delighted by the spectacle of a city street. The hundred unique characters of Shakespeare, trooping in their rings of alliance and conflict, each doubtless representing a vitally debatable political position but in bulk representing an infinite variety which ultimately dwarfs debate. What Dryden said of Chaucer: Here is God's plenty.

Dualities are human inventions which we impose on the world and on ourselves in the effort to tame and dominate whatever we conceive of as other. Meanwhile the world remains a continuum, infinite in all directions. The artist, then, defies (our, his, her) impulse to dominate by containing both halves of any argument and by the attempt to imitate the continuum. From *The Merchant of Venice* we can argue pro and con anti-Semitism, from *Lear* pro and con patriarchal absolutism, from *Antony and Cleopatra* the claims of the state against those of eros—but *The Complete Plays of Shakespeare* argues the smallness of argument. Exuberance, says Blake, is beauty. The man who imagined the Wife of Bath, with her gat-tooth, her debater's points against clerical misogyny, and her six or seven husbands—what's he but exuberant? And when we recall that he imagined as well the pious and priggish Prioress, the high-minded Knight, the low-minded Miller, the slimy Pardoner, the innocent Troilus, the experienced Cressida, and so forth, we cannot but wonder at readings which would reduce Chaucer to a Christian or a courtier. I believe, though I cannot prove, that the plenteousness of great writers is always their most radical quality, in that it implicitly defies category and authority. In whatever age, and whatever the writer's ostensible political positions, plenitude signals the democratizing/subversive impulse, the dance of the devil's party.

In *A Defence of Poetry,* Shelley says, "The great secret of morals is love; or a going out of our own nature. . . . A man, to be greatly good, must imagine intensely and comprehensively; he must put himself in the place of another and of many others." I take this to mean that we first crack the wall between ourselves and our enemy, discovering the foe within the self. Then we find that we and the world are neither single nor double but multiple.

"Trust thyself: every heart vibrates to that iron string." So urges Emerson. As the creation of the poem depends on this, so does the reading of it. I mean actual reading; what we do ourselves, for pleasure.

Suspicious as I am of theory, which is always prescribing to me what I should prefer and interfering with my personal responses, I want to stress the importance of a lively response to he political as to any other aspect of a poem. If a work fails to arouse me, how can I begin to understand it, much less judge it?

Yet there are different kinds of arousals. First of all, and let us be candid about this, we love what is on our side. Poems by Blake, Whitman, William Carlos Williams, Allen Ginsberg, for example, in my own case. The critic who attempts to disguise advocacy, pretending to possess literary standards without ideological implications, is not to be trusted—nor did any critic of major stature pretend to do so until the late nineteenth century. Yet we can also become excited in the presence of the enemy camp, if someone whose work runs contrary to our deep convictions is writing strongly enough to crystallize our differences. Eliot, for example, in my own case. A mild Albion's Angel, lost without the crutch of authority and orthodoxy, snob, anti-Semite, gynephobe—how beautifully he shows me the beauty of what I must struggle to oppose. Or, a more obvious and violent sort of foe, the Imamu Amiri Baraka (LeRoi Jones) of "Black Art" advocating "poems that kill" in the sleekest of jive rhythms, proving the attractiveness of hate. I like to think that I love in political poetry whatever I love in poetry anyway. Language being known and used by someone who delights in the lay of words together. Wit, grace, passion, eloquence, playfulness, compression, vitality, freshness. A voice that is at once the poet's voice and the voice of a time, a nation, a gender. The many, mysteriously funneled through the one: not I, not I, but the wind that blows through me. Only I hope to be aware that "whatever I love in poetry anyway" has, if I cut into it, a political dimension.

I like the word "love" better than the word "evaluate." Bring out number, weight, and measure in a year of dearth, says Blake. I find "love" more reliable than "evaluate." First, I see what I love; then I try to understand it. In this way it seems I can love one thing and another, each for different reasons, rather than the same thing over and over and smaller and smaller.

Take Elizabeth Bishop's "Brazil, January 1, 1502," with its brilliant description of a tropic landscape as if it were a tapestry or an embroidery, followed by a description of "the Christians, hard as nails, / tiny as nails, and glinting, / in a creaking armor," who arrive with a dream of "wealth . . . plus a brand-new pleasure":
Directly after Mass, humming perhaps

> L'Homme armé *or some such tune,*
> *they ripped away into the hanging fabric,*

> *each out to catch an Indian for himself—*
> *those maddening little women who kept calling,*
> *calling to each other (or had the birds waked up?)*
> *and retreating, always retreating, behind it.*[2]

The women are like the female lizard Bishop has earlier pictured, "her wicked tail straight up and over, / red as a red-hot wire." The poem delicately and ironically manipulates the parallel between women and land, alike subject to rippling/raping. In its resemblance to a just-finished embroidery, the landscape has already been feminized; the goddess who by implication has stitched it would naturally madden "the Christians." At the same time, the mediation of this embroidery conceit along with Bishop's casual half-amused tone, which throughout the poem negotiates slyly between the perspective of a twentieth-century viewer and that of a sixteenth-century conquistador, frames and distances our horror at the brutality to which the poem alludes. Finally, Bishop's conclusion implies, though in an equally bemused way, that the landscape and its natives may have been, may remain, mysteriously unconquerable.

Given the historical realities of conquest, rape, the slave trade, and genocide in Brazil and elsewhere, this conclusion is itself a bit maddening to me as reader. I instinctively look for more bitterness, more denunciation, some recognition that although Nature may be unconquerable, individual lives and cultures are not. Withholding these gratifications to my (perhaps correct) opinions, Bishop instead reminds me that a conqueror's rapacity may be insatiable precisely because it can never feel that it has truly possessed what it has conquered—and this is a still more distressing thought. As a consequence of Bishop's artistry, whenever I reread "Brazil, January 1, 1502," I am seduced anew by its fascinatingly elusive mix of calm and anger, disturbed anew by the sense of how profoundly rooted in the erotic and the sacred is the will toward empire.

Here is a part of another poem on the theme of conquest, using the same idea that the conquerors justify their acts by perceiving the conquered as animals. Untitled, it is by Lydia Yellowbird:

> *When you came*
> > *you found a people*
> > *with red skin*
> > *they were one*
> > > *with all living things*

> *But you did not see this*
> > *beauty*
> > *instead you saw them*
> > *as animals, primitive*
> > > *savage.*[3]

Compared to the Bishop poem, this is embarrassingly naive. It lacks irony and distance, its language is banal and abstract, it fails to imagine (as against stating) what the enemy "saw," and so it has no poetic interests beyond its message. Any poetry which is merely political—and nothing else—is shallow poetry, although it may serve a valuable temporary purpose. Or so I think. Yet if I heard this poem performed, let's say, in Santa Fe to the right audience, I might well be more stirred by it than by the Bishop poem. As Jerome Rothenberg and others have reminded us, Native American poetry is traditionally oral and functional, not literary, and one of its proper functions is to maintain a spirit of tribal community. Do I contradict myself? Very well then, I contradict myself. Another example: after a Ginsberg reading at Rutgers, I asked a graduate student of radical bent how she liked him. Well, he had been singing Blake's "Tiger," and she had been sitting there in the front row under his knees while he bounced his harmonium up and down and wagged his body around, for what seemed like forever. It was embarrassing. And had she not read Bakhtin, I asked; and did she not notice that Ginsberg's performance was *carnivalesque?* Oh, that's right, she said; it's so different when it's real life.

The poetry I know best, just now, is contemporary American women's poetry. When I began reading this body of work in the mid-1970s, it was speaking to me as woman and as poet in ways no other poetry ever had. Repeatedly I found myself lifted by some stroke of brilliant analysis or bold metaphor, frightened and spurred by acts of courage I could scarcely hope to duplicate in my life or my art. For "what oft was thought but ne'er so well expressed," in women's poetry, evidently meant what had long been locked under the censor's trapdoor and was now for the first time rushing forth into the light of consciousness and language. Gradually I became aware that I was living in the midst of a literary movement which I wanted not only to experience but to describe as a critic. The love, then, came first; the effort to comprehend followed.

What I had to work from, in writing *Stealing the Language,* was eventually something over two hundred individual volumes of poetry by women and a dozen or so anthologies. From these emerged a large but indistinct picture of the women's poetry movement in America since 1960, which slowly assumed focus. I was trying to define what was new, what was altering and expanding "poetry," "woman," those terms we so foolishly think we already know the meaning of. I needed to demonstrate how the advent of this writing was causing the past history of literature subtly, lightly, irretrievably to change. For as Eliot in "Tradition and the Individual Talent" so finely explains that the order of art rearranges itself whenever a genuinely original new work appears, so it must shift for larger scale literary movements as well. The women's poetry movement, it seemed to me, was destined to produce some substantial rearrangements. But of course one senses this in one's bones long before one can say precisely what has happened.

What then is important in contemporary women's poetry? Virtually all commentators agree that women's writing must be located in terms of its cultural marginality and its equivocal relation to what is usually called "the tradition" or the "great" tradition. The discovery that marginality may be a strength is a recent one.[4] Some linked motifs announce themselves: self-definition, the body, the eruption of anger, the equal and opposite eruption of eros, the need for revisionist myth making. What Adrienne Rich has called "the oppressor's language" comes into perpetual question in this poetry, along with the language's rooted dualisms: male vs. female, sacred vs. profane, mind vs. body, public vs. private, logos vs. eros, self vs. other, subject vs. object, art vs. life. Not surprisingly, the strongest women poets tend to oppose hierarchy; they like boundary-breaking, duality-dissolving, and authority-needling.

Formally and stylistically, too, there are interesting developments. I want here to sketch three of these, all of which derive from and relate to particular political issues and are, I feel, designed to subvert and transform the oppressor's language into something a little closer to the heart's desire. They are the exoskeletal style, Black English, and the feminist-communal ritual. I stress the matter of style because a new music in poetry always signals a new meaning. When the music changes, the walls of the city tremble, says Plato. It is by a tuned listening, prior to thought and reflection, that we instinctively locate the dance of the devil's party.

Presumably in response to our culture's identification of femininity with pliability, many of the best women poets use what I call an exoskeletal style: hard, steely, implacably ironic. This is a multipurpose device. It makes the condescending label "poetess" impossible, as it is conspicuously and exaggeratedly antisentimental. It is useful for satire and parody. It is a kind of formal shell like the armor on so many of Marianne Moore's beasts, a sign of the need for self-protection on the part of the vulnerable. Unlike Moore, however, these poets do not pretend to be charming eccentrics. Often this style is used to challenge the neutrality of the reader, addressing a "you" who is perceived as an antagonist or lover-antagonist and whose role the reader is forced to play. Usually at the same time the style implicates the poet in the oppressive scenarios she delineates. Among the finest deployers of this style are Diane Wakoski, Cynthia Macdonald, Margaret Atwood, and Sylvia Plath. In Plath's "Lady Lazarus," for example, the suicidal poet addresses the doctor who has restored her to life:

> *I am your opus,*
> *I am your valuable,*
> *The pure gold baby*
> *That melts to a shriek.*
> *I turn and burn.*
> *Do not think I underestimate your great concern.*[5]

Note the language-play by which "opus" mocks the world of art, "valuable" the world of commerce and commodity, and "pure gold baby" reduces both to the level of vulgar hype. Note too the rhyme, in the service of contempt and self-contempt. Plath is, as women are trained to be, a commodity, an act, an exhibitionist doing "the big strip tease." She is perhaps the female object in a male poem—perhaps one of those poems like *The Divine Comedy* or Wordsworth's Lucy poems in which she has to die first. She is perhaps Galatea in the shaping hands of Pygmalion. She is passive and compliant as someone who is truly feminine should be. The "you" of "Lady Lazarus" is in the first instance a kind of sleazy sideshow manager, then becomes "Herr Doktor . . . Herr Enemy," and finally that ultimate source and rationale for male cultural authority and control, "Herr God, Herr Lucifer." As Blake's Urizen compounded the qualities of Milton's rationality-obsessed God and Milton's heaven-exiled Satan, so Plath's supreme being is perfectly evil because he is perfectly good. Plath has begun "Lady Lazarus" by describing her skin as a Nazi lampshade and her face as a "featureless, fine / Jew linen." Critics who dismiss the holocaust imagery of this poem as childish self-aggrandizement or self-pity fail to notice its identification of a historical and political evil with ahistorical and cosmic masculine authority and the uncomfortable collapsing of good and evil into each other. Marjorie Perloff has argued that Plath "had really only one subject: her own anguish and longing for death. To a degree, she camouflaged this narrowness by introducing political and religious images. . . . But since the woman who speaks throughout *Ariel* hates all human beings just as she hates herself, her identification with the Jews who suffered at Auschwitz has a hollow ring."[6] The hatred and self-hatred in *Ariel* (certainly in "Lady Lazarus") is palpable enough. But far from concluding that this fact invalidates the poem's metaphor of self-as-Jew I would argue to the contrary that the combination of anger and self-hatred within victimized individuals and classes, including women, is probably a universal human pattern of precisely the sort we need poets to explore. Note, too that when a critic wishes to ignore the political dimension of a woman poet's work, the usual strategy is to assert that the work is "really" purely personal.

The "you" being hissed and snarled at in "Lady Lazarus" is also ourselves, her readers. Plath's portrait of the female artist as self-destroyer locks us inside a universe of concentric spheres of victimization in which we are invited if not compelled to recognize our complicity. To read is to occupy a position not unlike Milton's God. We are superior, remote, omniscient, judgmental, able to call the poet into life by picking up her book, able to "peel off" her disguises by critical examination. But of course Plath shares our complicity. For if this poem is a critique of control, who is more controlled than this artist? Plath's style, here and in much of her late work, brilliantly represents precisely what it despises; that is its genius, and it is the genius in a great deal of angry women's poetry.

Plath's status as representative feminist martyr invites a question: is such poetry politically useful? This is not a literary question, but it is still answerable. No, if we are looking for a correct position which cleanly distinguishes Us from Them, the good girls from the bad guys. Yes, if we are convinced that such distinctions are false and that accurate diagnosis must precede effective cure.

Women's poems are not of course necessarily written from within the dominant literary language. A powerful resource for poets lucky enough to have access to it is Black English, with its rich body of cadences and phrases lifted from field hollers, spirituals, gospel, and blues on its musical side, as well as the King James Bible, high-energy preaching, and verbal rituals like rapping and the dozens on its oratorical side. The artful mimesis of "uneducated" speech has been a strategy of social criticism since *Huckleberry Finn*, first because it lets us enjoy the pleasure of breaking school rules (and we all know in our hearts that rules are in the service of the rulers; to obey them is to accede to social structures for which grammatical structures are the gateway), second because it pits lively imagery against dry abstraction, humor against precept, the play of improvisation and the body's rhythms against the strictures of prior form.[7]

Compare, for example, both Elizabeth Bishop and Lydia Yellowbird with the dry wit of June Jordan in "Poem About My Rights." Jordan is angry that she can't "go out without changing my clothes my shoes / my body posture my gender my identity my age," recalls that in France "if the guy penetrates / but does not ejaculate then he did not rape me," and "if even after smashing / a hammer to his head if even after that if he / and his buddies fuck me after that / then I consented," and proceeds to elaborate the connection between rape and imperialism:

> *they fucked me over because I was wrong*
> *. . . . .*
> *which is exactly like South Africa*
> *penetrating into Namibia*
>
> *. . . . .*
> *and if*
> *after Namibia and if after Angola and if after Zimbabwe*
> *and if after all of my kinsmen and women resist even to*
> *self-immolation of the villages and if after that*
> *we lose nevertheless what will the big boys say will they*
> *claim my consent?*[8]

Without the unpunctuated rhythm, the combination of street-talk and authority-speak, without the legal-military "penetrate" next to the idiomatic "big boys," we would have a weaker poem. Again, in "The Rationale, or She Drove Me Crazy," Jordan composes a bravura piece with a surprise ending. The speaker in this poem is telling it to the judge:

> *"suddenly there she was*
> *alone*
> *by herself*
> *gleamin under the street lamp. I thought*
> *'Whoa. Check this out? Hey, Baby! What's*
> *happenin?' I said under my breath.*
> *And I tried to walk past but she was lookin*
> *so good and*
> *the gleam and the shine and*
> *the beautiful lines of her*
> *body sittin out there*
> *alone*
> *by herself*
> *made me wild. I went wild. But*
> *I looked all around to see where her*
> *owner/ where the man in her life could*
> *probably be. But no show. She was out.*
> *By herself. On the street:*
> *As fine, as ready to go as anythin you could*
> *ever possibly want to see so*
> *I checked out myself: what's this?*
> *Then I lost my control: I couldn't resist.*
> *What did she expect? She looked foreign*
> *besides and small and sexy*
> *and fast*
> *by the curb. So I lost my control and*
> *I forced her open and I entered*
> *her body and I poured myself*
> *into her*

> *pumpin for all I was worth*
> *wild as I was*
> *when you caught me*
> *third time apprehended*
> *for the theft of a Porsche."*[9]

Surprised? The obvious moral here is that a woman out alone is no more "asking for it" than a car asks to be stolen. A deeper point is that the poem's joke works as well as it does because our history leads us to think of women as property. As they used to say in the Gothics, he was burning to possess her, his dark-eyed beauty. But this point couldn't be made without Jordan's tuned ear for attractive jive talk. For the facts are that these are highly seductive rhythms and that the real secret of the poem is the poet's Shelleyan ability to put herself in the place of a bad black dude, in order to let us put ourselves there, hearing that voice of self-justification in our own heads.

And what else can it mean to be an outlaw, in language and ideology? For a less violent but no less incandescent effect, here is Lucille Clifton's "Admonitions," quoted in full:

> *boys*
> *i don't promise you nothing*
> *but this*
> *what you pawn*
> *i will redeem*
> *what you steal*
> *i will conceal*
> *my private silence to*
> *your public guilt*
> *is all i got*
>
> *girls*
> *first time a white man*
> *opens his fly*
> *like a good thing*
> *we'll just laugh*
> *laugh real loud my*
> *black women*
>
> *children*
> *when they ask you*
> *why is your mama so funny*
> *say*
> *she is a poet*
> *she don't have no sense*[10]

The radical quality of such a poem will not be fully apparent to readers for whom gender and race are political issues but maternity is not. But as feminist theory has for some time noticed, ours is a culture in which "mother" is object not speaking subject, for our psychology and literature alike represent maternity not from the maternal but from the child's perspective. Maternal autonomy, sexuality, and conflict are consequently suspect; mother is "good" insofar as she selflessly devotes herself to her offspring. A second consequence is that maturation of both male and female children in our culture is supposed to depend on rejection of the mother, identification with the father. A third, so pervasive that we scarcely recognize its absurdity, is the privatization of maternity: the mother's role in our culture is a domestic not a public one. She is a being whose love for her children must in no way impinge on society's power to dispose of these children as it chooses.

Contemporary women poets writing as mothers—including for example Alta, Susan Griffin, Adrienne Rich, Audre Lorde, Marilyn Krysl, Toi Derricotte, Sharon Olds, Marie Ponsot, Maxine Kumin, and me, to name a few—have come to challenge our social assumptions regarding maternity. Additionally, they tend in describing mother-child relationships to propose a profoundly antiheroical view of human power and need. What if we stopped assuming that to be powerful means to require worship and obedience? What if we imagined that it might mean the ability to participate in pain and joy? What if Milton's God, and the authorities modeled on his parental design, looked a bit more like Lucille Clifton? She tutors her children in defiance instead of obedience, is unafraid of her sons' lawlessness, her daughters' sexuality, and her own lack of conventional dignity. Her first two stanzas connect class war, gender war, and racism in the framing context of an opposed principle of maternal affection. Her final stanza connects maternity to poetry, and both to play, with a casual impropriety that suggests a contest already won. "Noble" has been changed to "no bull," as Williams promised; but the charm and unpretentiousness of such a poem increases its radicalism. Clifton's insouciance is of a similar order to Blake's, born of anger, love, and the confidence of ultimate victory. Or, as Ida Cox used to sing, "Wild women don't worry, / Wild women don't have the blues."

All these poems operate in a sense by being bilingual, negotiating between the dominant language and a marginal one, employing particularly provocative versions of what Nancy Miller calls "the irreducibly complicated relationship women have historically had to the language of the dominant culture" and what Rachel Blau DuPlessis calls the "both/and vision" of women's writing.

The poems I have cited (and feminist poems typically) have in common an "I" which readers will find intensely engaged and engaging, aligned with the feminist conviction that the personal is the political. The poems defy divisions between public and private life because they recognize that such divisions promote oppression; a corollary is that neither poet nor reader can occupy a neutral literary space like Bishop's in "Brazil, January 1, 1502" to render a centuries-old pattern of political violence with the clarity of a tapestry but without an appearance of personal engagement is one legitimate political strategy; to pursue transformation through the poetic implication of the self is another.

Some such logic lies behind the phenomenon of the ritual poem in feminist spiritual circles—that is to say, a poem intended to be performed, or to invoke an imagined performance, in a ceremonial setting. The primary intention of such poetry is to strengthen a sense of a group, communal, or collective identity and commitment; it may or may not simultaneously critique the dominant culture and its rituals. The poet in ritual poetry enacts a bardic, shamaness', or priestess' role; she may or may not also play the part of the self-examining individual we expect literary poets to be. For poet and reader-participant alike, ritual poetry implies the possibility of healing alternatives to dominance-submission scenarios. It suggests nonoppressive models of the conjunction between religion and politics, usually by reimaging the sacred as immanent rather than transcendent, by defining its audience as members of a potentially strong community rather than as hopelessly lonely individual victims, and by turning to nature (seen as sacred and female) as a source of power rather than passivity. The language of ritual poetry, as it approximates chant, foregrounds recurrent sounds and rhythms, the sensuous qualities of words, as against their referential qualities—or, as Julia Kristeva would have it, the semiotic above the symbolic. In this way too it withdraws from the logocentricity we associate with the oppressor's language and approaches the pleasurable condition of the mother tongue. "Transformation," observes Paula Gunn Allen, "is the oldest tribal ceremonial theme . . . common to ancient Europe, Britain, and America." As Deena Metzger writes in the collage-essay "Affiliations Toward the End of Dying of Silence," exemplifying the faith of many women poets for whom the notion of the isolated artist is a tired cliché, "breaking silence" for a woman writer "has the same meaning as breaking bread. / It is an act of community."[11]

At the present moment the writers of ritual poetry include black poets like Audre Lorde, Ntozake Shange, and Sonia Sanchez, Native American poets like Paula Gunn Allen, Wendy Rose, Carole Lee Sanchez, Joy Harjo, and Chrystos, Third World women like Sylvia Gonzalez and Jessica Hagedorn. African goddesses, voodoo, Spider Woman, and other emblematic spiritual beings already figure widely in these poems much as Zen eminences inhabit the writing of an earlier generation of white males who needed to find or invent a sacred space from which to critique both sacred and secular institutions of the dominant American majority. Unsurprisingly, ritual poetry has received little attention from feminist academic circles, which are not themselves exempt from either racism or logocentricity, although this neglect may diminish as the excellence of "minority" women's poetry in America makes itself increasingly felt.

The imagination of female sacredness coincides with the critique of language, and both are seen as necessary conditions for political change in Judy Grahn's "She Who," a poem sequence written in 1971–1972 which has subsequently become a lesbian-feminist classic. The opening section of "She Who" reads like glossolalia; a polyrhythmic set of repetitions imitates the noise of liturgical question and response, the noise of a congregation or the wind, and the naming of a goddess who might be anywoman:

> *She, she SHE, she SHE, she WHO?*
> *she-she WHO she-WHO she WHO-SHE?*
> *She, she who? she WHO? she, WHO SHE?*
> . . . .
> *She SHE who, She, she SHE*
> *she SHE, she SHE who.*
> SHEEE   WHOOOOOO[12]

If we compare this with, say, "Who is the king of glory? . . . The Lord of Hosts, he is the king of glory," at least one crucial distinction is Grahn's funniness. As in Blake's *Marriage*, fun is a method of resisting the culture's identification of the sacred with hierarchy and command. More important, the passage cannot be read solely with the eye. It requires the voice, the participation of the body, at which point we find that Grahn's sounds and rhythms (try it, reader) are both difficult and catchy. Succeeding sections of "She Who" cover much familiar (and some unfamiliar) feminist territory—the life cycle of a woman's body, her powerlessness as an object in society and culture, her potential for power and pleasure—in a succession of formal experiments full of word-play, teasingly disrupted syntax and narrative line, and, above all, hand-clapping and foot-tapping rhythms:

> *a fishwife a cunt a harlot a harlot a pussy*
> *a doxie a tail a fishwife a whore a hole a slit*
> *("SW," "The enemies of She Who call*
> *her various names")*

> *am I not crinkled cranky poison*
> *am I not glinty-eyed and frozen*
> . . . .
> *are you not shamed to treat me meanly*
> *when you discover you become me?*
> *("SW," "plainsong from an older*
> *woman to a younger woman")*

Most of "She Who," like most feminist writing, is preoccupied with struggle. Its final section, a catalog of sixty-one women, shifts from the defensively dual to the expansively plural as in Whitmanesque fashion it invites us to be large and contain multitudes:

> *the woman who carries laundry on her head*
> *the woman who is part horse*
> *the woman who asks so many questions*
> *the woman who cut somebody's throat*
> . . . .
> *the woman who eats cocaine*
> *the woman who thinks about everything*
> *the woman who has the tatoo of a bird*
> *the woman who puts things together*
> *the woman who squats on her haunches*
> *the woman whose children are all different   colors*
> . . . .
> *When She-Who-moves-the-earth will turn over*
> *When She Who moves, the earth will turn over.*

This move toward a litany—a chant of possible selves, a vision of multiplicity as revolutionary—at present remains a marginal gesture within a marginal literature. Women inclined toward mysticism tend to make such gestures more easily than women inclined toward social realism; those who write outside the literary and academic establishments more readily than those inside. Marginality perhaps helps to free the imagination; Grahn's "She Who" is sister to Blake's devil.

I like the gesture, the opening. My students enjoy performing "She Who" at the close of a semester. I believe that, as Luce Iragaray says in "When Our Lips Speak Together," to recognize the claims of plurality is to make hierarchy defunct: "You/I: we are always several at once. And how could one dominate the other?"[13] At its most radical, contemporary women's poetry begins to ask that question.

NOTES

1. Older writers, for example A. J. A. Waldock in *"Paradise Lost" and Its Critics,* have contended that if we find "a fundamental clash . . . between what the poem asserts, on the one hand, and what it compels us to feel, on the other," then it is an artistic failure. I have argued to the contrary, regarding the "duplicity" in many women writers as well as Milton, in *Stealing the Language: The Emergence of Women's Poetry in America.* Blake, Shelley, Empson, and—most persuasively and exhaustively to date—Jackie Di Salvo in *War of Titans: Blake's Critique of Milton and the Politics of Religion* contend that the contradictions within Milton constitute his aesthetic and intellectual value to us.

2. Elizabeth Bishop, "Brazil, January 1, 1502," *The Complete Poems* (New York, 1969), p. 106.

3. The quotation is from Lynda Koolish, *A Whole New Poetry Beginning Here: Contemporary American Women Poets,* 2 vols. (Ann Arbor, Mich., 1981), p. 179.

4. See my *Stealing the Language,* pp. 1–13, on the relation of women's poetry to tradition. Also see *Shakespeare's Sisters: Feminist Essays on Women Poets,* ed. Sandra M. Gilbert and Susan Gubar (Bloomington, Ind., 1979) and *Coming to Light: American Women Poets in the Twentieth Century,* ed. Diane Wood Middlebrook and Marilyn Yalom (Ann Arbor, Mich., 1985). For an excellent discussion of women poets writing on politics, history, and the self in the context of cultural patterns they hope to transform, see chapters 7 and 8 of Rachel Blau DuPlessis' *Writing Beyond the Ending: Narrative Strategies of Twentieth-Century Women Writers* (Bloomington, Ind., 1985), on H. D., Levertov, Rich, and Rukeyser. For a study of contemporary women's poetry which focuses on its political dimensions, see *A Whole New Poetry.* Volume 2 of this work is a collection of essays by women poets on their art; almost all perceive themselves as engaged in the radical transformation of self and society. Jan Clausen's *A Movement of Poets: Thoughts on Poetry and Feminism* (Brooklyn, N.Y., 1982) offers a thoughtful insider's account of the problems of politicization and the expectations of political correctness for poets within the feminist community. From these and other writers on women's poetry I have learned immeasurably.

5. Sylvia Plath, "Lady Lazarus," *The Collected Poems,* ed. Ted Hughes (New York, 1981), p. 246.

6. Marjorie Perloff, "Sylvia Plath's 'Sivvy' Poems: A Portrait of the Poet as Daughter," in *Sylvia Plath: New Views on the Poetry,* ed. Gary Lane (Baltimore, 1979), p. 173.

7. See Stephen Henderson, *Understanding the New Black Poetry: Black Speech and Black Music as Poetic References* (New York, 1973); June Jordan, "White English/Black English: The Politics of Translation," *Civil Wars* (Boston, 1981); and the discussions of gender, class, race, and language in *This Bridge Called My Back: Writings by Radical Women of Color,* ed. Cherríe Moraga and Gloria Anzaldúa (Watertown, Mass., 1981).

8. June Jordan, "Poem About My Rights," *Passion: New Poems, 1977–1980* (Boston, 1980), p. 87.

9. Jordan, "The Rationale," *Passion,* pp. 11–12.

10. Lucille Clifton, "Admonitions," *Good Times* (New York, 1969).

11. Paula Gunn Allen, "Answering the Deer: Genocide and Continuance in American Indian Women's Poetry," in *Coming to Light,* p. 230; Deena Metzger, "Affiliations Toward the End of Dying of Silence," in *A Whole New Poetry* 2:313.

12. Judy Grahn, "She Who," *The Work of a Common Woman: the Collected Poetry of Judy Grahn, 1964–1977* (New York, 1978), p. 77.

13. Luce Iragaray, *This Sex Which Is Not One,* trans. Catherine Porter with Carolyn Burke (Ithaca, N.Y., 1985), p. 209.

THE SEARCH FOR A PRIMAL POETICS

JEROME ROTHENBERG

When Charles Olson wrote "Projective Verse" in 1950, he was describing, like other artists before and since, both a method of composition and a stance toward reality. For Olson, the shift in the verse freed up mind and body, allowed the emergence of a work of projective size, larger than the single poet or on a par with the single poet pushed to his or her own limits, to the making of a newly maximal poem: an epic as a poem including history (E. Pound). Or, as Clayton Eshleman put it much more recently: "I am speaking of a poetry that attempts to be responsible for all an individual writer knows about himself and about his world." (And he added: "It is that simple and that awesome.")

In referring to all that, I only mean to say that I hope that anything I have ever said about the making of poetry has tried to show or to discover how that making might both reflect and influence the ways we live in this world or this world lives in us. This is the modernist—though possibly not the "post"-modernist—hope: that transformations in art and life are inextricably connected.

I mean here "modernist" in its avant-garde sense, not its academic one. The forerunners I cherish don't lead back to Lowell or Tate or Auden, but more significantly I think to Stein and Pound, Zukofsky and Williams, Tzara and Breton and Artaud, Khlebnikov and Mayakovsky, Huidobro and Vallejo. All of the above and more.

The history of twentieth-century poetry is as rich and varied as that of its painting and sculpture, its music and theater, but the academic strategy has been to cover up that richness. Imagine—now—in 1989—a history of modern art that left out abstract painting or collage or Cubism or Surrealism and Dada, and you have a sense of what the literary curricula (or the creative writing ones) look like to those of us who know that such things exist in poetry as well and that many of the earlier moves and movements (but Futurism, Dada, and Surrealism, in particular) were essentially the work of poets.

A characteristic of modern art (and poetry) so defined—but this carries into the postmodern as well—has been the questioning of art itself as a discrete and bounded category. Deconstruction, I used to think, was a decent enough word for this, but after a decade or two of abuse, says David Antin, "when I hear the word 'deconstruction.' I reach for my pillow." In an essay on Robert Wilson's earlier "theater of images," Robert Stearns writes: "The avant-garde might be characterized as those creators who do not take their environment and its traditions at face value. They separate and view its elements and realign them according to their own needs." The description, although devoid as yet of social purpose, is general enough to include the great range of strategies and stances in experimental art and poetry. Since nothing around us is (ideally) taken for granted and the conclusion or intention of the work (again ideally) arises or emerges from the work itself, the work by definition is experimental: its outcome unknown, its process crucial. Such experiments/redefinitions/reconstructions may work with structures, with ideologies (contexts and contents), with materials and technologies, or (in any instance) with combinations of all of the above. I will point here to examples in poetry and related language arts, rather than in those arts with which most of us are more likely to be familiar.

From my own point of view at least, I see the coming together of these possibilities as (still) the great opportunity for art and poetry in our time. On their structural/compositional side, the experimental moves have included developments in visual, typographic, and concrete poetry; in notably English language experiments with projective verse and composition by field; in systematic chance operations (Jackson MacLow and John Cage the chief practitioners); in variations of collage and montage from throughout the century. Ideological/ideational experiments permeated Dada and Surrealism during and after the First World War, Beat and Beat-related poetry in the 1950s and 1960s, and aspects of feminism and other consciousness movements during the 1970s and 1980s. Equally extreme but often less recognized experiments involved the materials and media of poetry—from the obvious return to poetry as an art of live performance to the creation of a new electronic poetry (soundtext, poésie sonore, etc.), the rudiments of a computer poetry, and the beginnings (toward the other end of the technological spectrum) of a poetry without sound in the culture of the deaf.

This is a larger field for experiment and change than has been brought forward in recent controversies about the "Language Poets" and so on, and it is characterized there and elsewhere by a sense that the old rules or what seemed to be the old rules— the basic definitions within each art or between the arts—are increasingly and deliberately set aside or reversed. The terms—as we may think of them now, at this latter end of the twentieth century—are thick, still thick, with paradox:

- imageless art and wordless poetry (or *soundless* poetry in the language of the deaf already mentioned);
- *musique concrete* in all its present versions—going back to Russolo's noise machines and art of noises;
- *free* verse (a paradox too, as William Carlos Williams taught us) and the *parole in libertá* (free words) of Marinetti;
- nonsyntactic or antisyntactic poetry from Stein to (again) the Language Poets (or "totally syntactic" in the words of one of them, Barrett Watten)—and a questioning, for them or me or most of us, of the nature and limits of meaning;
- a poetry of elementary forms—letters and numbers—that works with reduced alphabets (Otto Nebel) or extended ones (Isidore Isou) or that reads numbers as words (Kurt Schwitters) or words as numbers (neo-gematria and beyond).

None of these becomes dominant for long, though some may initially make a claim for dominance.

Similarly the boundaries between (and within) the arts dissolve, into an age of intermedia and hybrid forms of art. The distinction between poetry and prose breaks down, between word and picture. Definitions of high and low art fall away: the primitive chant, the pop song become part of the poet's arsenal: new instruments at our disposal. The language of everyday speech collides with or expels the exalted language of an older poetry—like the art that seeks to break the boundaries between itself and everyday life, to reenter the mundane world or "raise" the mundane into art. At the same time that some poets reclaim prophetic and visionary functions, they or their contemporaries are altering the physical nature and location of the poem: new shapes of books; new materials to print on (metal, acetate, and film; Karl Young's wood blocks; Emmett Williams' cuckoo clocks and fishes; poems on pens, on shirts, on bodies); poetry as sculpture in the works of Ian Hamilton Finlay or of Mathias Goeritz; the poetry reading and performance, moving off the page and into the lecture hall, the theater, the gallery, the coffee shop, the loft, the prison, and the street. Writes Michael Davidson of a postmodernism that extends one thrust of modernism: "The boundary to what is possible in writing is a fiction created by and within writing. Only when the boundary is recognized as movable can it become a generative element in art rather than an obstacle to its growth."

The old boundaries are now in question. Poetry is not the only language art (an art of words measured and arranged in time), but musicians like Cage and Berio and Stockhausen have also been composing with words. Artists have collaged words, painted words on canvases and walls. Dancers have danced to language, to words. It has been around a long time now, and it has made the ground of poetry a different thing from what it was before.

This century may be known by its push against the boundaries. Where once the definitions were apparent and the frame known, we have now come into the open; have taken up a stance outside the walls. The most interesting works of art—and poetry!— are those that question their own shapes and forms and by implication the shapes and forms of whatever preceded them.

Again some immediate—and fairly obvious—examples.

The prose poem (including, most interestingly, its recent extensions by language and other experimental poets) questions the boundary between poetry and prose.

The visual poem questions the boundary between poetry and painting.

The concrete—three-dimensional—poems in Ian Finlay's garden question the boundary between poetry and sculpture.

The poésie sonore of Henri Chopin questions the boundary between poetry and music.

But it is possible for one to become a master-of-poetry (or even a doctor-of-poetry) and still be ignorant of all this. (It may not even be possible to do so without that kind of ignorance.)

As the work is now one of reinterpretation/revisioning, the view of poetry reaches from the present into the past, from the (post)industrial first world to the remote corners of third and fourth worlds everywhere. Given that kind of thrust, a poetics becomes (or includes) an *ethno*poetics, as the work of the poet becomes in each instance *the search* ("in the excitedness of pure being," Gertrude Stein wrote) *for a primal poetry or art or theater or music.* The accompaniment to that search has been a century of countless inventions and reinventions in the art we make. In an art in which "the only failure," says Hugh Kenner, "is the failure to invent," each work becomes the model for some new possibility—not only each new work created but each work newly sighted in the worlds outside our own that open up to us.

The art created as a primal model may be minimal or maximal in nature, but the idea of the minimal (in both a traditional and modern context) is necessarily deceptive. What was called minimal art a few years ago is only a part of what I mean by it, for what I'm thinking of are all those experiments that explore the key reductive question of what it is that is absolutely essential to the art in question—like Jerzy Grotowski's *poor* (but not impoverished/empty) *theater* in which actor (and audience) provide sufficient means for the theatrical act; or Philip Corner's "Poor Man Music," restricting sound to the percussive possibilities of the human body. Allan Kaprow's "privacy pieces" (or the more poignant and political works of Milan Knizák in Czechoslovakia) imagine a performance without an audience. And something of the same sort enters the solitary autoperformances of the performance artist, and so on. It is a little like Emily Dickinson's poem on the minimal definition of a prairie: "It takes a clover and a bee / and reverie // The reverie alone will do / if bees are few."

But clover and bees proliferate; and alongside, or even within, the minimal works, maximal works emerge that explore the fullest and most extended range of human possibilities, all within the single work. The "poor theater" is coexistent with the epic theater or the utterly baroque theater of images (of Robert Wilson); intermedia (however renamed) remains a presence in the visual arts, where many works also seek maximal *scale*, whether for presentation of a simple form (Christo's running fence, say) or of a great melange of forms and images. And what Charles Olson called "projective size" brings poets into the area of the long poem, the multiphasic epic leading from Pound and Williams and Zukofsky into the immediate present.

Behind such visions there also lies the sense of a search for the primal that brings the present and the remote past together. (It is this kind of search that has engaged me for more than twenty-five years now.) A word often heard in discussions of intermedia and performance is Wagner's *gesamtkunstwerk*/total artwork—with its sense of *opera* (plural) superseding (opus) (singular)—as a reintegration of a unified primal art that had undergone division/*sparagmos*. For those like Wagner the primal source was most often Greek; for us it goes back to the more remote past or the (apparently) remote present with its surviving cultures and subcultures in which ritual, building on "existential situations" of "struggle and identity," creates a theater of multiple means and extremes, where "art and life converge." (The quoted terms are Stanley Diamond's.) Thus any given source work, if viewed as a whole, is complex—in much the way that Victor Turner described ritual, not as "an obsessional concern with repetitive acts (but) an immense orchestration of genres in all available sensory codes: speech, music, singing; the presentation of elaborately worked objects, such as masks, wall-paintings, body-paintings, sculptured forms; complex, many-tiered shrines; costumes; dance forms with complex grammars and vocabularies of bodily movements, gestures, and facial expressions."

"Primitive is complex," I said at the beginning of the Pre-face to *Technicians of the Sacred,* and something of this sort is what I had in mind.

But all of this is still too much from the side of art, too much as if the changes contemplated had only form in mind. Such redefinitions, limited to art-making or to poetry, are of course possible, and where modern art and "post"-modern art have been most easily accepted, it has probably been in this limited sense. (The easiest acceptance of a *new* poetry has, conversely, been largely on the side of content.) The bigger picture, among our own contemporaries and those who came before us, includes as well a redefinition of what it is to be human—by experiments on ourselves (our own works and thoughts) and observations of or interchange with others. The older paradigm—of humanity evolving hierarchically (vertically) from the "primitive" to the "civilized," from the nonwestern to the western, with European/"rational" *man* standing at the apex—developed with European imperialism and was its anthropological expression, while the new paradigm—of a common and diverse/multibranched humanity—arose first from within that same imperialism but started coming into sharper focus with its gradual disintegration.

The work now visible is enormous. As such it lets us see, as if for the first time, the many faces of poetry, whose range and variety make the idea of a single definition (in-our-own-image) seem obsolete, reductive. At the same time it shows the power of those singular traditions that have developed under particular historical conditions. Not surface only, but something like Williams' "primitive profundity" is at play here: the opening toward "mind" or "spirit" and the recognition that in either instance our experiments are both elemental and the culmination of all those cultural and psychological events that have come before us. The upshot of it all is this—that we now know, really know, that the source of poetry is in a truly human center: in ritual and work, in acts of speculation and imagination, in a shamanism whose proudest tool is language.

If we can say that now—and more!—we are not made shamans thereby—or priests or magicians—but our resemblances to and our differences from those others are the hidden theme of most of what we do. From my own perspective it is a work in common: a great collective work of synthesis. It is changing, always changing, because the ambition that propels it makes it volatile. At one point it seems to center on prophecy and vision, at another on the experiential moment that precedes the poem or, again, on the process of writing or composing or on the language of the poem become a focus in itself. In that last instance I have found the idea of a *language-centered* poetry not only among us but in the work of shamans and poets like the Mazatec Maria Sabina, who do not so much make poems describing an "experience" or even a "vision," but seek a language whose source is in the world beyond the merely experiential—more precisely for *her:* in language itself! It would be wonderful to touch all those bases on our own—and sometimes we do—but it is good too that there are others, as volatile as we are, doing what we fail to do.

The restlessness of our poetry is a reflection of a deeper restlessness—be it Diamond's "search" or, not that distant from it, what Robert Duncan called "this dark and doubtful presentiment [in which] . . . all things have been called into their comparisons . . . not in our identification in a hierarchy of higher forms but in our identification with the universe." It is—at the least—a comparison of all our possible humanities (and the works that arise therefrom) taken to its greatest (post)modern extreme. And yet the new paradigm, the model that this suggests, is still only partial, as the disintegration of the old imperialism/ethnocentrism is (we now know) also only partial.

TIME OUT OF MOTION:
LOOKING AHEAD TO SEE BACKWARD

CHARLES BERNSTEIN

It is only an auctioneer who should admire
all schools of art.
>—Oscar Wilde

Millennial Ballad
                    after Wilde
Each cent'ry kills the thing it loves
By each let this be heard
Some do it with a guillotine
Some with a genocide
Some do it with threshing machines
Some with atomic bombs

Yes, each period kills the thing it loves
But each century does not die

An enormous gulf separates us from the English-language poetry of the last decades of the nineteenth century. We do not speak or hear the same language: not just in the sense that all languages shift through time, but that American English, in the final decades of the last century, was invaded from without and, in the process of absorbing elements alien to it, irrevocably changed, cutting the umbilical cord to its putative English mother and seceding—in words a hundred years after the deed of 1776—from its Island-bound British father.

The immigrants of 1880 to 1900 radically subverted the language environment of the Northeast and Midwest as non-English speakers began to settle here at an almost geometrically escalating rate. By 1900, according to Peter Quartermain's assessment, about one-quarter of the white U.S. population either did not speak English or learned it as a second language—while in the mid-Atlantic states and New England perhaps only one person in four was a native speaker of English.[1] I take such facts to be important because I understand language not as an indifferent system for describing an independently external reality but as the perceptual and the conceptual unconscious of reality. Changes in language affect reality just as they reflect social and historical developments. For American poetry of the twentieth century, there is no more important fact than the fundamental alteration of the language base—who was speaking and how they spoke—that occurred in the 1880s and 1890s; indeed, it is perhaps that period's most lasting legacy for our literature.

The subversiveness of second-language speakers and writers is not necessarily great; it can be contained by tightly controlled conventions for correct diction, pronunciation, and syntax—aberrations actively repudiated and their perpetrators socially (and therefore economically) shunned. Having learned an immaculate French, one becomes (almost) a Frenchman. In America, the reverse has been the rule: far from colonizing the foreigners' consciousness, the foreigners colonized English. Island English—the language of the English people—was no longer the common yardstick but one of a number of inflected variants of a decentered confederacy.

In 1934, Gertrude Stein said much of what I am saying in her lecture "What Is English Literature?":

> . . . the poetry of England is so much what it is, it is the poetry of the things with which any of them are shut in in their daily completely daily island life. It makes very beautiful poetry because anything shut in with you can sing. . . . As I say description of the complete the entirely complete daily island life has been England's glory. Think of Chaucer, think of Jane Austen, think of Anthony Trollope, and the life of the things shut up with that daily life is the poetry, think of all the lyrical poets, think what they say and what they have.[2]

Of course, Stein did not cite demographics; but her personal history is the history of non-native English speaking. As Quartermain documents, Stein, Williams, and Zukofsky—three poets who created a ground for twentieth-century poetry—all learned English as a second language.[3] Zukofsky grew up in a Yiddish-speaking New York neighborhood, while Williams probably learned Spanish and English simultaneously. Stein's family moved to Vienna before she was one, where she had a Czech tutor and an Hungarian governess and probably spoke her first words in German; from four to six, she lived in Paris; the family then moved to Oakland. Stein spent her adult life listening to and speaking French while writing English.

To come to a language as a second tongue, to rethink and relearn the world in new and strange sounds, may inhibit a natural or unconscious acceptance of the relation of words to things. It may bring home the artificialness of *any* language—that, as Veronica Forrest-Thompson notes, language is both continuous and discontinuous with the world, a thing that for a poet can be as plastic as transparent; the translucency that illumines words when they are heard as sound as well as sense; the realization that we can shape, and are shaped by, the words we use.[4] Stein, Zukofsky, and Williams did not assume an Island English but invented their language word by word, phrase by phrase. In distinguishing the poetry of these three writers from more conventionally island-oriented practices, I would make a contrast between *etymologic* English and *associational* English. Etymologic writing is symbolic and connotative, while associational writing involves a lateral glissade into *mis*hearing, sound rather than "root" connections, dialect, "speech" in Williams' sense.[5] Extending this metaphorically to prosody, metered verse with regular rhyme schemes would be "etymologic," while free verse with irregular off-rhymes would be "associational."

What Stein, Williams, and Zukofsky created is sometimes called American English, but this is a nationalist misnomer for an English language writing for which Island English is no imperial sovereign but one of many tonguings, an English-language literature that does not evolve from Chaucer through other Island writers but has many roots in English and non-English; though the literature of the English people has a special fascination, it makes us feel a part of its daily island life succession like children looking at the painted ponies of a twirling carousel or going for a ride and later maybe building or buying a carousel concession.

When you look back a hundred years to the poetry that was being written in America you find an odd lacuna. Much of what is called nineteenth-century American literature was over. Poe and Hawthorne, Thoreau and Emerson were dead; Whitman and Melville were in their final years: those who had taken the Island out of English, secession upon secession, and found out what might be a new England or a Manhattan, still had not completely succeeded in seceding.

By the 1880s and 1890s there was little poetry being written in America that now attracts the interest of the work immediately preceding it and following it: the eye of a hurricane in which the language itself was tumbling and turning.[6]

In one sense, the most significant event for poetry in America's last *fin* of *siècle* was the posthumous, and *sense*ored, first publication of Dickinson's poems in 1890, a publication greeted with hostile reviews despite the editors' efforts to remove what might offend the ears of an Island-oriented audience. Dickinson achieved a greater textual eccentricity and self-sufficiency than any other nineteenth-century American writer; her work looked and sounded least like standard English, so it is altogether appropriate that it should emerge at a time of great transition for the language.[7]

If Dickinson can be said to have fashioned an idiolect, her work's publication in 1890 is then also consonant with the liveliest poetic practice of the period, one quite distinct from Island-oriented literature—dialect writing. While English was at this time absorbing the effects of the language of new European immigrants, it had had plenty of time to be transformed by the cultural traditions, as they manifested themselves in English, of blacks and native "Americans," as well as the unique speech and writing patterns of these groups and of rural whites. Jerome Rothenberg and George Quasha, in their anthology *America: A Prophecy,* document poems of two writers of the period who use a radically nonstandard syntax and vocabulary based, in part on regional dialect—Lafcadio Hearn's collage of New Orleans street cries that move from sound-associational English ("Cha-ah-ahr-coal!") to French ("Charbon! Du Charbon, Madame!) and Jacob Carpenter's North Carolina obituaries ("he wars farmer and made brandy / and never had Drunker in family"). Obviously, these examples only scratch the surface of such material.

Given this context, the black dialect poetry of Paul Dunbar seems all the more remarkable and speaks directly and significantly to a number of current preoccupations of English-language poetry. In Dunbar's dialect poetry, the sensuous pleasure in the sounds of the spoken language of a community is used to express the pleasures of the shared communions of a people poor in material possessions only. His local popularity among presumably nonliterary-minded audiences attests to this poetry's specific origins in time and place; the aesthetic failure of his nondialect poetry is an equal mark of the source of his work's power. Dunbar's dialect poems achieve a perfect symmetry of form and content, extolling the paradise in the daily—words' dominion not verbal tokens—over and above the postponed utopia of Redemption Day; as in "When De Co'n Pone's Hot" he compares the prayers, sermons, and songs of the church service unfavorably to the epiphany, not in a symbolic English hearth but in the particular, material smell of daily bread:

> *But dem wu'ds so sweetly murmured*
> *Seem to tech de softes' spot*
> *When my manny says de blessin'*
> *An' de co'n pone's hot.*[8]

"Wu'ds tech" in sound's ascent; Island succession is complete and the here (spelled ear) and now (spelled now) of this world (pronounced "worl"/whirl) begins:

> *Why won't folks gin up dey planin',*
> *An' jes' be content to know*
> *Dat dey's gitten' all dat's fu' dem*
> *In de days dat come an' go?*
> *Why won't folks quit movin' forward?*
> *Ain't hit bettah jes' to stan' . . .* [9]

Of course, one hundred years ago was also the time that the *first* of the *last* great American Island-oriented writers, Henry James, was in his bloom, transforming by that most exquisite of implosions all that Island English had meant or would ever mean again, so that the syntax of his work is an elegy for all that could no longer be, a plunging deep into an infinite regress of nuance, shades of gloss and glosses of shade, till in the last and greatest works all contact with that daily island life transubstantiated into crystallized reflections: the sublime artifice of infinite pains so like in excess, and unlike in temper, his contemporary Swinburne (the one so far inside Island English as to have bored a black hole in it, the other oscillating between that hole and the other side).

Historical periodicity is like a viper sucking up a living context into its dry, timeless air. What relations have we to fragments and segments of a past from which we are disconnected, without living root of transmission—foreign, lost? The violence of every generalization crushes the hopes for a democracy of thoughts: each paradigm excludes or forgets in disproportion to what it may elucidate. The nineteenth century never ended, or each day, as today, is its middle, end, beginning. A portion of the best is always lost, that which seems obscure or is obscured: those forgotten in their fleeting fame or total want of it; or that which never came into material existence. "In the case of painting, we pay for the failures," Viktor Shklovsky has written.[10] "A Rubens or a Rembrandt is so expensive, not because it took so long to paint but because its value covers the cost of the failures of many painters"—failures of recognition as well as art. There is no spirit of an age but incommensurable coexisting spirits; looking back, some may give us greater pause because they serve our purposes, because they tell something of where we are heading, more perhaps than where we have been: the mirror of 1886 is 2085. I wonder when I hear *fin de siècle* if it could mean the end of centuries not in an apocalypse but a slow dissolve of utilitarian ideas of sequence. Artists are not before their time, precursors, but their time is inadequately described by the soap opera of the causal narrative closure of both formalist and traditional historical literary criticism. The past is our living present: we breathe it with our ears and exhale it through our eyes. The trial and death of Oscar Wilde is not only an event of the final years of the last century but hangs over us now like Damocles' sword.

Wilde incited riot in the house of English literature. A gay Irish poet, he put on the manners of official English culture as a means of blasting away at its false pieties, its self-serving Enlightenment rationality, and its Victorian sexuality. "The first duty in life is to be as artificial as possible," he wrote.[11] For his transgressions, more spiritual and ideological than sexual in the narrowest sense, we witness like a recurring nightmare the imperial fist of English society smashing yet another in a succession of rebel poets. Certainly, he was not alone among poets of his time in his Mental Fight.—I have a vision of the Three Horsemen of England's 1880s and 1890s returning to lead a *fin de* millennium parade of "Nowhere" down Chicago's Lake Shore Drive: William Morris, brandishing a handcarved sword with swirls instead of edges; Oscar Wilde, bejewelled with a crown of gilded thorns; and Algernon Swinburne, reclining in a small horsecart and sipping pure spirits from a crystal flask. Lewis Carroll is writing the proclamation, and out of the shadows Gerard Hopkins intones an ecstatic benediction. Henry James covers the event for the BBC via a satellite video feed to his Boston suite.

The contemporaneity and relevance of Wilde, Swinburne, and Morris, as of Dunbar, increases as we head toward 2001. "What lies before me is my past," Wilde writes in *De Profundis:* the crucial word here is *lies*.[12] Wilde was a master antipositivist, and his *Decay of Lying* is a necessary and not outdated antidote to the emotional realism and ideologically repressed earnestness that makes up the bulk of today's magazine verse. Wilde's credo was that life imitates art, not the other way around. Swinburne, in his overdetermined assonance and alliteration, his dazzling and idle formal pyrotechnics, and Baudelairean sense of subject, literally brought Island English poetry to the end of the line. The artificiality that American poetry achieved, in part reactively, Swinburne's poetry realized by endogenous means, as an indwelling potential not in imperial Island English but in the traditions of the literature of the English people. Both Wilde and Swinburne spoke of the primacy of sound, a sound that overpowers and transforms sense. Their commitment to artifice—not easily understood by the motto "art for art's sake"—reflected the idea of a language that does not depict a separate external reality: art produces continually new Reals. Wilde said he wanted to create what is not rather than represent what is. For Swinburne, the flow and rhythm of words eclipsed any fixed picture, like waves rolling over a sandcastle, dissolving and absorbing all images in the ebb and flow of an oceanic language constantly devouring the present into its external pastness; the living presences of the past existing not as allusions but as mythos. It is no wonder that Swinburne champions Blake and Whitman in the same breath.

The utopian impulses in Wilde and Swinburne are more explicitly narrated by Morris, who took the transformation of art and poetry to be a central part of the struggle for socialism. All three made art that was not in the service of morality or religion but by its form realized the innate potentials of human beings. "We call ours a utilitarian age, and we do not know the uses of any single thing," said Wilde. And Swinburne: "The pure artist never asserts; he suggests, and therefore his meaning is totally lost upon moralists and sciolists—is indeed irreparably wasted upon the run of men who cannot work out suggestions."[13]

The pleasure of life *is* art, according to Morris; and the greatest enemy of art is the system of Commerce and Fashion that produces both unnecessary things and a slavish compulsion to possess them. *Work* for art's sake was his sense; the pleasure in daily work that he imagined was the experience of the artisans who collectively created Europe's medieval architectural legacy. These views lead Morris, variously, to the romantic medievalism of *The Earthly Paradise;* to his commitment to handcraft and his polemical critique of the deadly drabness of nineteenth-century English industrial design and architecture; to revolutionary socialism; and, significantly, to a militant environmentalism in many ways similar to our present-day ecology movement and the program of Germany's Greens. For Morris, leisure and idleness, as well as pleasure, were central components of any civilization worthy of the name. His insistence that there must always be *"waste* places and *wilds* in it"[14] suggests most acutely the originality of his position and his rejection of more utilitarian forms of social "progress." Morris' refrain in *The Earthly Paradise,* "the idle singer of an empty day," has been taken as oddly inappropriate for so prolific an artist. But idleness and emptiness are crucial notions for Morris, and his immensely popular early poetry was meant to serve as a respite from the toil of alienated labor; both the reading and the writing of poetry was to be an activity of pleasure ("joyance" is Morris' word, a Coleridgean term that would do nicely to translate Barthes' *jouissance*). Indeed, the poems become a means of transport to another world not inevitably correlated to this one: "a shadowy isle of bliss / Midmost the beating of the steely sea, / Where tossed about all hearts of men must be."[15]

Morris vowed early to conduct a "Crusade and Holy Warfare against the age"; for all their irreconcilable differences, Swinburne and Wilde joined in this crusade. Of the three, Morris surely was the deepest pragmatic political thinker; Wilde's strength was his aesthetics, although the political imagination of "Soul under Socialism" should not be underestimated; Swinburne had the most resonant ear for poetry, although his *Blake* is an important political and aesthetic tract.

The powerful antipositivist critique of these writers is still of urgent topicality: Swinburne's aestheticism and Wilde's artificiality, especially when considered in the light of Mallarméan "Symbolist" indefiniteness, prove a useful alternative both to Thomas Eliot's reassertion of an imperial Island English yardstick—the objective correlative as well as the "tradition"—and to the Imagist reductivism of Ezra Pound's "direct treatment of the 'thing'" and "use absolutely no word that does not contribute" (statements that dramatically contradict Pound's actual poetic practice and conceal his important debt to Swinburne). On the one hand, much of the most touted and least interesting verse of our century follows even more reductivist high antimodernist (also known as New Critical) precepts (following the most conservative doctrines, but not the more verbally adventurous practices of Pound, Eliot, or Williams). Compare Wilde's Nietzschean ambi*volence* (wanting multiple things) to the staid and staged irony of neoconventionalist parasymbolism from Lowell to Larkin; compare Swinburne's sonorous paradise of excess to the linguistically anemic contemporary plain style. On the other hand, much of the most formally adventurous, sonically sublime, and politically exemplary poetry of our century has rejected imperial measures and pursued the possibilities inherent in a non-Island-oriented English-language writing.

Writing within an Island context, Swinburne, a Northumbrian, used prosodically formal means to rupture his language from an imperial standard for clarity of message; "Only the great masters of style succeed in being obscure," as Wilde puts it.[16] When I say he brought Island English poetry to the end of the line, I mean that after Swinburne the realization of the wordness of language would be more radically achieved by abandoning the conventional use of meter. In its extreme self-containment through refraction of Island literature from Chaucer to the Rossettis and back further to the classical grounds of that literature, Swinburne's writing detonates the "shutinness" and "complete quality of completeness" that Stein describes:

> English literature then had a need to be what it had become. Browning Swinburne Meredith were no longer able to go on, they had come where they had come, because although island daily living was still island daily living every one could know that this was not what it was to be and if it was not to be this with all the outside belonging to it what was it to be. They Swinburne Browning and Meredith were giving the last extension. . . . And so, this is the thing to know, American literature was ready to go on, because where English literature had ceased to be because it had no further to go, American literature had always had it as the way to go.[17]

Now, as I've said, what Stein is calling American literature should, I think, be called English-language literature because there is New Zealand and Canada and Australia and because there are many different Americas. The Island English verse tradition is only one of many streams feeding non-Island English-language poetry, and for many contemporary poets it has little or no importance and need have none. But then even Island English is a misnomer since there is no one imperial standard for all the English-speaking people of England, with its dozens of dialects, much less for all of Britain and Ireland. (By *imperial* I mean a single, imposed standard for correctness of speaking or writing or thinking or knowing; I mean a unitary cultural canon: an artifice denying its artificiality.) "I do not want art for a few, any more than education for a few, or freedom for a few," Morris said.[18] He believed that for art not to perish utterly it must cross over "a river of fire," making a decisive break with imperialist politics as well as with imperial language. And this was not, he said, something only for *other* countries, quoting Goethe's response to a man who said he was going to America to begin life again: "Here is America, or nowhere."[19] So even in the so-called British Isles the most imaginative poetries of this century, to my vantage, have staged a series of secessions from imperial English. Think of Bunting's Northumbrian or MacDiarmid's Scots; think of the escalating series of Irish secessions from Yeats' founding of the Irish Literary Society in 1891 and publishing of *The Celtic Twilight* in 1893; think of Woolf's revealing of an inside of Island English's imaginary that previously had been mostly hidden. So that today the poetry of the most interesting English poets is Island poetry in the sense of being local and specific, decisively breaking from an English that is meant as an empire's Standard; and the variety and eccentricity and vitality in British poetry at this time is enormous—and the best of it is almost completely excluded from the official organs of Island literary culture.

For the present, I value eccentricity in poetry for its ability to rekindle writing and thinking, for the possibility of sounding an alternative to the drab conformist fashion-minded thinking that blights our mental landscape full as much as the nineteenth-century mills poxed the English countryside. Not eccentricity as opposed to centrism—there is no center, only the hegemony of homogenizing processes—but particularity and peculiarity of place and time and person acknowledged as such. The alternative to "art for a few" is not one art for all, which tends to degrade and level as it comes under the sway of commercial incentives—but many arts, many poetries. The possibly good intentions of "one art for all"—and the related agendas of clarity, plainness, accessibility—unfortunately tend to merge with the oligarchic marketing imperatives of modern telecommunications, "keep your message simple and repeat it many times"—a formula that dominates not only American commercial advertising but also political and aesthetic discourse. (The "simple message" is the visible effect of a series of hidden agendas—call them ideologies—that remain obscured.) The cultural segmentation, complexity, and communicative refractoriness of much contemporary poetry, which excludes it from "major media" dissemination, are in fact the kernels of its intertwined political and aesthetic value.

English is now one of the few global languages, in itself a lingua franca: this means that many different grammars and vocabularies are merged into constantly newly forming English tongues. In the face of this plethora, one centrist response has been to disparage a "poetry glut," while another has been to lament poetry's lack of significant social impact. Both these views are based on imperial standards that fail to comprehend that different English-language poetries are valuable to different groups or individuals; that the inability to evaluate overall poetic activity because of the amount of it or the diversity of it is a positive development; that more people read and write English language poetry than ever before, except that they don't read and write a common poetry. Morris' contribution, for example, is not as one of the Immortal English Poets but as a monumental model for this new situation. Indeed, he "never made great claims for his own poetry, treating it as 'a mere matter of craftmanship.' 'If a chap can't compose an epic poem while he is weaving a tapestry,' said Morris, 'he had better shut up; he'll never do any good at all.' "[20]

By emphasizing eccentricity, I want to acknowledge the significance of group-identified poetries (ethnic, racial, linguistic, social, class, sexual, regional) in shattering the neoconventionalist ideal of fashioning by *masterly* artifice a neutral standard English, a common voice for all to speak (or, getting in deeper, a common voice for all Mankind). All poetry is geographical and ethnic and sexual as much as historical, period-bound: these limits are any poetry's horizons. *A period is a sentence.* But groups are composed of subgroups, which are composed of fractionate *differences* that can be recombined into other formations incommensurable with the first. In principle, fashioning the common voice of a nation or language, which, in turn, is as precarious as fashioning the common voice of an individual. In practice, the poetic force of expressing what has been repressed or simply unexpressed—whether individual or collective—has been considerable. Yet there is also the necessity of going beyond the Romantic idea of self and the Romantic idea of the spirit of a nation or group (*Volksgeist*) or of a period (*Zeitgeist*), a necessity for a poetry that does not organize itself around a dominant subject, whether that be understood as a self or a collectivity or a theme—writing, that is, that pushes the limits of what can be identified, that not only reproduces difference but invents it, spawning nomadic syntaxes of desire and excess that defy genre (birth, race, class) in order to relocate it.[21]

All these multifoliate creations of language chime—some would say clang—at once, so that there *is* an acentric locus to English-language poetry: the negative totalization of many separate chords, the better heard the more distinct each strain. *Difference* is not isolating, but the material ground of exchange; though perhaps it is a dream to hope, in these times, that the pleasurable labor of producing and discerning difference can go beyond the double bind of group identification/individual expression and find idle respite in blooming contrariety—the sonic shift from *KA* to *BOOP* in which the infinite finitude of sound and sensation swells.

NOTES

This essay was first presented at a panel arranged by the Division of Comparative Studies in Twentieth-Century Literature on "Fin de Siècle: Theirs and Ours," MLA Annual Meeting, Chicago, December 28, 1985.

1. In 1882, only about one-fifth of new immigrants spoke English while about one-third spoke German. In 1900, 38 percent of the total U.S. population was foreign born or first generation (probably doubling the figures for 1850). By 1910, probably one-third of the U.S. population did not speak English or spoke it as a foreign language. If the South is left out of these statistics—significantly for white Southern writing, non-English immigrants played a minimal role in the South—the prevalence of non-English speakers in America is even more dramatic. Peter Quartermain, "Introduction," in *Dictionary of Literary Biography,* vol. 45: *American Poetry 1880 to 1945,* First Series, ed. Quartermain (Detroit: Gale Research, 1986). Quartermain has also provided me with additional compilations and observations based on Census Bureau reports and *Reports of the Immigration Commission* (1907–1910).

2. Gertrude Stein, *Look at Me Now Here I Am: Writing and Lectures 1909–1945.* ed. Patricia Meyerowitz (Baltimore: Penguin, 1971), 34–35.

3. Peter Quartermain, " 'Actual Word Stuff, Not Thoughts for Thoughts,' " in *Credences* 2,1 (1983):114.

4. Veronica Forrest-Thompson, *Poetic Artifice: A Theory of Twentieth-Century Poetry* (New York: St. Martin's press, 1978), 118. James Clifford discusses some of these issues in respect to both Conrad and Malinowski—"both Poles condemned by historical contingency to a cosmopolitan 'European' identity [and pursuing] ambitious writing careers in England"—in his essay "On Ethnographic Self-Fashioning: Conrad and Malinowski" in *Reconstructing Individualism* (Palo Alto, Calif.: Stanford University Press, 1985), which is reprinted in *The Predicament of Culture: Twentieth Century Ethnography, Literature, and Art* (Cambridge, Mass.: Harvard University Press, 1988). "Conrad accomplished the almost impossible feat of becoming a great writer (his model was Flaubert) in English—a third language he began to acquire at twenty years of age. It's not surprising to find his writing permeated by a sense of the simultaneous artifice and necessity of cultural, linguistic conventions. His life of writing, of constantly *becoming* an English writer, offers a paradigm for . . . ethnographic subjectivity" in Malinowski. Clifford goes on to read *Heart of Darkness* "as an allegory of writing and of grappling with 'language' and 'culture' in their emergent twentieth-century definitions"; it's worth noting that Conrad's experiences in the Congo, which form the basis for *Heart of Darkness,* occurred in the 1890s. Conrad was born in 1857; his first novel was published in 1896; *Heart of Darkness* was published in 1902.

5. I base this distinction on some remarks by Quartermain, in his *Credences* essay (111, 121): "Laura Riding acutely remarked in *Contemporaries and Snobs* that 'None of the words Miss Stein uses have ever had any experience. They are no older than her use of them. . . . None of these words has ever had any history.' I think that applies equally well to both Williams and Zukofsky. . . . Neither Williams nor Zukofsky play around with or rely on the connotations of words, so that there is a difference indeed between Eliot's 'multifoliate rose' in 'The Hollow Men' and Williams' 'rose.' Eliot . . . is close to the English tradition, playing for the connotations, moving towards the symbolic. Williams and Zukofsky are struggling to establish the American. 'I'm of this time,' Zukofsky wrote . . . 'my elders rather end off something European.'" Of course, no writing can ever be purely "associational" or "etymologic": these are *tendencies* reflected both in poetics and poems. Zukofsky, for example, plays both ends against the middle, and Stein's "rose" is both a punningly associational re-sounding of a literary symbol and a resurrection of it (a rose is arose). Another extension of this distinction would be the contrast in structural metaphor, if not textual practice, between *Finnegans Wake* and *Tender Buttons.* "Etymologic" and "associational" can as usefully be considered attitudes toward form as toward lexicon.

6. I'm thinking here of American poets born between the mid-1830s and the mid-1850s or poetry that emerged most fully in the eighties and nineties. An interesting exception is Stephen Crane (1871–1900), who wrote poetry that in its directness of image marks an important break with English verse. The most popular poet of this period was Eugene Field (1850–1895).

7. "She built a new poetic form from her fractured sense of being eternally on intellectual borders, where confident masculine voices buzzed an alluring and inaccessible discourse, backward through history into aboriginal anagogy. Pulling pieces of geometry, geology, alchemy, philosophy . . . and philology from alien territory, a "sheltered" woman audaciously invented a new grammar grounded in humility and hesitation. HESITATE from the Latin meaning to stick. Stammer. To hold back in doubt, have difficulty speaking. "*He* may pause but *he* must not hesitate"—*Ruskin.* Hesitation circled back and surrounded everyone in that confident age of aggressive industrial expansion and brutal Empire building. Hesitation and Separation. The Civil War split America in two. *He* might pause, *She* hesitated. Sexual, racial, and geographic separation are at the heart of Definition. Tragic and eternal dichotomy—if we concern ourselves with the deepest Reality. . . . The renunciation and to be (herself) without. Outside authority, eccentric and unique. . . . What is the communal vision of poetry if you are curved, odd, indefinite, irregular, feminine. I go in disguise. Soul under stress, thread of connection broken, fusion of love and knowledge broken, visionary energy lost, Dickinson means this to be an ugly verse. First I find myself a Slave, next I understand my slavery, finally I re-discover myself at liberty inside the confines of known necessity." Susan Howe, *My Emily Dickinson* (Berkeley: North Atlantic Books, 1985), 21–22, 28, 117–18. Howe's discussion of "sovereignty" (79ff.) is related to the discussion of imperial Island standards in this essay.

8. *The Complete Poems of Paul Laurence Dunbar* (New York: Dodd, Mead, 1913), 57. Dunbar was born in 1872; his poems began appearing in 1895; he died in 1906.

9. Dunbar, "Foolin Wid De Seasons," 139. The reference here is to the "almanac" farmer who is always thinking of the next season and never living in the present one. Read politically, this poem may seem profoundly conservative, but that would be to misread its pointedly political rejection of utilitarian displacement as ameliorative reconciliation.

10. Viktor Shklovsky, *Mayakovsky and His Circle,* trans. Lily Feller (New York: Dodd, Mead, 1972), 144.

11. "Phrases and Philosophies for the Uses of the Young" (1884), in *The Artist as Critic: Critical Writings of Oscar Wilde,* ed. Richard Ellmann (New York: Random House, 1969), 433. Wilde (1854–1900) was sentenced to two years hard labor in 1895 for "committing acts of gross indecency with other male persons"; he never recovered from the effects of the imprisonment and related public humiliations.

12. "De Profundis" (1897), in *The Portable Oscar Wilde*, ed. Richard Aldington (New York: Viking, 1946), 564. The quotation in subsequent text is from p. 564.

13. Algernon Charles Swinburne, *William Blake: A Critical Essay* (1868), ed. Hugh J. Luke (Lincoln: University of Nebraska Press, 1970). Swinburne: 1837–1909.

14. "Art and Socialism" (1884), in *Political Writings of William Morris*, ed. A. L. Morton (New York: International Publishers, 1973), 128; italics added. Morris: 1834–1896.

15. Both this citation, and the citation immediately preceding, are from the "Envoi" to *The Earthly Paradise* (1870).

16. *Critical Writings of Oscar Wilde*, 1969, 434.

17. Stein, *Look at Me Now Here I Am*, 56–57.

18. "The Lesser Arts" (1877), in *Political Writings of William Morris*, 54. "No, rather than art should live this poor thin life among a few exceptional men, despising those beneath them for an ignorance for which they themselves are responsible, for a brutality that they will not struggle with—rather than this, I would that the world should sweep away all art for awhile . . . ; rather than the wheat should rot in the miser's granary, I would that the earth had it, that it might yet have a chance to quicken in the dark." Morris hopes that life might become more simple; but, as Raymond Williams has observed, the sort of social transformation imagined by Morris would in fact result in *greater* complexity: this suggests the limits of Morris' thinking. "That art will make our streets as beautiful as the woods, as elevating as the mountain-sides: it will be a pleasure and a rest, and not a weight upon the spirits to come from the open country into a town; every man's house will be fair and decent, soothing to his mind and helpful to his work" (55).

19. *Political Writings of William Morris*, 131–32.

20. William Morris, *News from Nowhere* and *Selected Writings*, ed. Asa Briggs (New York: Penguin, 1984), 19.

21. Such a poetry of immanence is not waiting to be validated by a future that is, at best, inscrutable and, at worst, terminal. The loss of the certainty of the future quickens the moment, heightens the torsions and tensions, and firms the resolve that whatever is to be published needs to be published now, that today's readers, however few, are the only ones we can count on. However, negative millennialism quickly falls into cliché, despite the fact that ours is the product of sober empirical deduction, not religious projection. On the contrary, the religious fanaticism of our time is the belief in a future, the pervasive orderliness by which we continue, day by day, to cling to comforts and distractions, only occasionally peeking into the voids.

NOTES ON THE NEW FEMALE VOICE

MARGARET RANDALL

In 1981, June Jordan opened her essay "Many Rivers to Cross" with this sentence: "When my mother killed herself I was looking for a job."[1] Quickly she sets a picture of a young professional black mother, recently abandoned by a husband she has seen through school, and jobless. Then she zeroes in on the events surrounding her mother's suicide and her father's inability even to determine whether or not his wife is dead—his fear, ineptitude, and vindictive rage. This extraordinary piece concludes:

> And really it was to honor my mother that I did fight with my father, that man who could not tell the living from the dead. And really it is to honor . . . all the women I love, including myself that I am working for the courage to admit the truth that Bertolt Brecht has written . . . "It takes courage to say that the good were defeated not because they were good, but because they were weak." I cherish the mercy and the grace of women's work. But I know there is new work that we must undertake as well: that new work will make defeat detestable to us. That new women's work will mean we will not die trying to stand up: we will live that way: standing up. (p. 26)

Among this new women's work, is—I will argue—a new writing, a female voice. A body of literature in the United States that is *qualitatively* different as well as (obviously) written and published in quantitatively greater volume than writing by women ever has been written or published here before. Is there a "woman's—or female—voice"? As with related questions (is there a woman's eye, a woman's musical score or symphony conduction, a woman's art in general), we have an increasing body of work to which we may go in search of answers.

The Jordan quote exemplifies something important about the new female voice, about the work of women like June Jordan—and Jane Cooper, Maxine Hong Kingston, Toni Morrison, Adrienne Rich, Audre Lorde, Alice Walker, Marge Piercy, Leslie Marmon Silko, Joy Harjo, Sonia Sanchez, Susan Sherman, Cheryl Clark, Kate Rushin, Sandra Cisneros, Judith McDaniel: absurd to make lists that will forever be partial at best, at worst insulting in their omissions. What this writing exemplifies is centuries of silent honing, a courageous externalization of the inner map *truly connected to the world at large*, craft by any standard as good as the best (and often a good deal more *meaning-fully* experimental), and a real dialectical bonding: of women back through time, across current manmade barriers, and into the future.

On another level, real flesh and bone women are now among our literary protagonists. This may seem simplistic to some, glaringly evident to others. But I think it's important to stop and ask what it meant for women writing, and for people reading, that Meridel LeSueur's *The Girl* remained unpublishable for twenty years because, as one editor after another told its author, a book about a woman who is not a victim just won't sell.[2]

As a body of work the new female voice addresses the large social issues with a power only the most intimate vision can bring, showing that the personal is political and the political personal. We have never lived in ivory towers and so we reject ivory tower notions of art. Our writing involves the breakdown of formal genre divisions through the offering up of the ordinary—and now retrieved—female voice. We claim that voice as literature by pushing or choosing to disregard the traditionally male-imposed limits of essay, criticism, poetry, private journals, and letters; and our mixing of categories makes its way even into our medical texts. The female voice is a revelation of our human self calling forth a profound degree of risk (gay and lesbian narrative, work by women with disabilities, incest and abuse stories, etc.). And it teaches a willingness, indeed a need, in our commodity-oriented society, to place process before product.

I intentionally say female voice rather than (only) women's writing. On philosophical principle I do not believe these new frontiers can be explored *only* by women, and I do not believe only women are feminists (or that all women are feminists simply by virtue of our gender). Necessarily, however, women are the groundbreakers here, and we of course vastly outnumber men in our explorations of the territory. Many minority writers (or writers of color—both categorizations suffer from the erroneous vision that views only white men as "central," everyone else as "other") express themselves out of a similar if not identical consciousness. Clearly feminism, as philosophy and experience, has made possible the particular literary renovation I will here call the female voice. As school children most of us—girls and boys—were urged to "write about what you know." For the past two decades, with notable forerunners, women writers have come into their own doing just that.

> *. . . Rainer had written my requiem—*
> *a long, beautiful poem, and calling me his friend.*
> *I was your friend*
> *but in the dream you didn't say a word.*
> *In the dream his poem was like a letter*
> *to someone who has no right*
> *to be there but must be treated gently, like a guest*
> *who comes on the wrong day*
>   *Clara, why don't I dream of you? . . .*

This is from Adrienne Rich's compelling "Paula Becker to Clara Westhoff."[3] Many of the most powerful women writing in the United States today have looked to our foremothers for sustenance and voice; poets like Muriel Rukeyser, Jane Cooper, Audre Lorde, Adrienne Rich, and others have researched histories of those women who have gone before us (Mmanthatisi, Rosa Luxemburg, Sojourner Truth, Paula Modeson Becker, Willa Cather, Ethel Rosenberg). We have retrieved role models. And we have insisted on speaking doubly: with their voices stopped in time and with our own voices sharpened because they lived. Some of the best among us *assume* those women's voices, giving them back in rich and varied ways.[4] This actual "taking on" of another's memory, speaking in it, breathing it filtered through a fierce redemption enraged by centuries of denial, is undoubtedly one important component of the new female literature.

Important moments in this ongoing process, have been Magda Bogin's discovery that the female troubadours did in fact write differently from their better-known male counterparts,[5] Blanche Cook's gift of Crystal Eastman's writings[6] and her forthcoming biography of Eleanor Roosevelt,[7] Barbara Sicherman's use of Alice Hamilton's letters to weave a plausable and highly readable correspondence-biography of the latter's life,[8] Georgia O'Keeffe's letters,[9] Diane Arbus' personal journals,[10] Evelyn Fox Keller on Barbara McClintock,[11] and teacher/writers like Audre Lorde writing about themselves.[12]

Among the writers allowing us to look into their own lives, a new autobiographical work, *Assata* by Assata Shakur, is not only wrenchingly and beautifully written but also speaks from an experience held by many but rarely translated into literature.[13] It is a particularly female experience, that of a black woman in prison for a crime she has not committed, who preserved her self against terrifying odds, escapes, and makes a gift of its telling. This black woman is at once unique and all women of color. This prisoner is at once herself and the inhabitant of a hideously extreme, compressed, version of the prison our female condition has occupied for centuries. I want to quote at length from this book. What follows is the first paragraph:

> There were lights and sirens. Zayd was dead, My mind knew that Zayd was dead. The air was like cold glass. Huge bubbles rose and burst. Each one felt like an explosion in my chest. My mouth tasted like blood and dirt. The car spun around me and then something like sleep overtook me. In the background i could hear what sounded like gunfire. But i was fading and dreaming. Suddenly, the door flew open and i felt myself being dragged out onto the pavement. Pushed and punched, a foot upside my head, a kick in the stomach. Police were everywhere. One had a gun to my head. "Which way did they go?" he was shouting. "Bitch, you'd better open your goddamn mouth or I'll blow your goddamn head off!" (p.3)

Near the end of the book Assata chooses to give us this climactic moment, very much a woman's moment, very much a mother's:

> My mother brings my daughter to see me at the clinton correctional facility for Women in new jersey, where i had been sent from alderson. I am delirious. She looks so tall. I run up to kiss her. She barely responds. . . . I go over and try to hug her. In a hot second she is all over me. All i can feel are these little four-year-old fists banging away at me. Every bit of her force is in those punches, they really hurt. I let her hit me until she is tired. "It's all right," i tell her. "Let it all out." She is standing in front of me, her face contorted with anger, looking spent. She backs away and leans against the wall. "It's okay," i tell her. "Mommy understands." "You're not my mother," she screams, the tears rolling down her

face. "You're not my mother and I hate you." I feel like crying too. I know she is confused. . . . I try to pick her up. She knocks my hand away. "You can get out of here if you want to," she screams. "You just don't want to." "No i can't," i say, weakly. . . . I look helplessly at my mother. Her face is choked with pain. "Tell her to try to open the bars," she says in a whisper. "I can't open the door," i tell my daughter. "I can't get through the bars. You try and open the bars." My daughter goes over to the barred door that leads to the visiting room. She pulls and she punches. She yanks and she hits and she kicks the bars until she falls on the floor, a heap of exhaustion. I go over and pick her up. I hold and rock and kiss her. There is a look of resignation on her face that i can't stand. We spend the rest of the visit talking and playing quietly on the floor. When the guard says the visit is over, i cling to her for dear life. She holds her head high, and her back straight as she walks out of the prison. She waves good-bye to me, her face clouded and worried, looking like a little adult. I go back to my cage and cry until i vomit. I decide that it's time to leave. (pp. 257–258)

And, coming down now, this fragment very close to the book's end:

Freedom. I couldn't believe that it had really happened, that the nightmare was over, that finally the dream had come true. I was elated. Ecstatic. But i was completely disoriented. Everything was the same, yet everything was different. All of my reactions were super-intense. I submerged myself in patterns and textures, sucking in smells and sounds as if each day was my last. I felt like a voyeur. I forced myself not to stare at the people whose conversations i strained to overhear. Suddenly, I was flooded with the horrors of prison and every disgusting experience that somehow i had been able to minimize while inside. I had developed the ability to be patient, calculating, and completely self-controlled. For the most part, i had been incapable of crying. I felt rigid, as though chunks of steel and concrete had worked themselves into my body. I was cold. I strained to touch my softness. I was afraid that prison had made me ugly. (p. 266)

Along with the content of this narrative, we may note the literary devices—easily identifiable—adding texture to the writer's ideological fabric: her use of capital and lower-case letters, her particular use of tense.

At the same time, women writers, never as eurocentric as many of our male peers, have looked beyond the limits of the North American and/or Western literary scene in our exploration of a whole new genre: testimony. As women listening to women, the pioneering works of Latin Americans and others of the Third World have been important.[14] I'm talking about classics like *Let Me Speak!* and *I, Rigoberta Menchu.*[15] More recently we have read works by Filipino, African, Middle Eastern, Australian, and New Zealand women. These moving books encouraged us in the art of listening, and we have chosen to listen to our sisters' voices historically ignored, silenced, despised.

Some of us have learned to listen in a particularly useful way to the multiple parts of our own retrieved identity. Such is the case of Gloria Anzaldúa who explores her many-layered reality as Mexican/American/female/lesbian in an extraordinary rediscovery of language and meaning called *Borderlands/La frontera.*[16] Straightforward narrative, poetic prose, and poetry combine English, Spanish, and Nahuatl words to reveal a new sense of self, one which because of the existence of this book now belongs to all of us.

Finally, cognizant of the wealth of exciting material out there waiting to be gathered in, published, or read, we have repossessed pages of sheer beauty, forgotten while lesser works by men in the same period and/or place continue to receive endless acclaim; I'm thinking particularly of Hemingway's "great white hunter" vision of Africa compared with Beryl Markham's *West With the Night.* Both Hemingway and Markham were foreigners on African soil, although she lived and worked there while he made occasional visits. His books have become classics; it took the explosion propelled by the women's movement to bring her to the surface. "Did you read Beryl Markham's book, *West With the Night?* I knew her fairly well in Africa and never would have suspected that she could and would put pen to paper except to write in her flyer's log book[*sic*]. As it is, she has written so well, and marvelously well, that I was completely ashamed of myself as a writer." This is Hemingway himself, describing the prose of a woman all but lost to literature![17]

> *I have held hands*
> *with fear;*
> *We have gone steady*
> *together.*
> *Sorrow has been*
> *my mate;*
> *We have been bed-*
> *companions.*
>
> *The days of my night*
> *have been long.*
> *They have stretched*
> *to eternity.*
> *Yet have I outlived*
> *them. And so shall you.*

"I Have Held Hands with Fear" is a poem by Mitzi Kornetz. Out of a poetry anthology? No. I have taken this testimonial verse from the chapter called "Cancer" in *Ourselves, Growing Older,* the new self-help compendium from The Boston Women's Healthbook Collective.[18] We have taken our literature out of the academic texts and coffee-table artifacts and used it as well in books on health, exercise, dealing with cancer, addictions, incest, dying, and other difficult areas of life. And it has not seemed important to us to limit our field to "a chosen few." In our lives and in our publications we welcome the contributions of women who might not define themselves as writers but whose writing speaks to us.

> . . . He lets up the pressure for a second. "Mommy!" I scream. The door opens. She is here. The light from the hallway is bright; I am safe. In one thousand seven hundred and fifty seven days I will be sixteen years old. "What did you do that for?" he shouts. "This has nothing to do with her." "Mommy," I cry. Her arms are folded across her chest. All I can ask is that she rescue me. I cannot ask her for comfort. "Kate," she says. "You shouldn't upset your father. . . ."

These are a few lines from "Like the Hully-Gully But Not So Slow" by Anne Finger. It's only one of dozens of nearly uniformly excellent pieces of poetry and prose in *With the Power of Each Breath, A Disabled Women's Anthology.*[19] Testimonial writing by women with disabilities,[20] prostitutes,[21] addicts and codependents,[22] incest and abuse survivors,[23] lesbians and their mothers[24]—these comprise a body of *literature*, not simply a collection of first-person accounts, how-to manuals, or scientific theses.

The women's movement taught us how silenced and hidden from us our role models have been. We have founded and sustained women's presses and magazines[25] not simply to publish ourselves (an overriding concern of the largely male-dominated small press renaissance of the 1950s and 1960s) but to make available this heritage as well. And so we have retrieved our great classics, Zora Neal Hurston's *Their Eyes Were Watching God*[26] and Agnes Smedley's *Daughter of Earth*,[27] to mention only two of the most extraordinary. Classics by any standard, yet in most of our universities still considered neither "great books" nor even basic reading on contemporary American literature syllabi.

There is immense variety in this new women's literature. Fantasy is explored in books like Sally Miller Gearheart's *Wanderground.*[28] Ursula K. LeGuin is only one of a host of women who writes science fiction.[29] A female interpretation of the natural world can be found in writers like Susan Griffin.[30] Anne Cameron's books explore spirituality and traditional women's wisdom.[31] Spiritual *and* political connections are made in such classics as Marge Piercy's *Woman on the Edge of Time.*[32] Making connections is, in fact, a pervasive and defiant part of this writing.

> *"Why" is not "how"*
> *is not a recital of physical causes*
> *physical effects*
> *it is meaning*
>
> *The bullet pierced her flesh*
> *because a finger pressed a trigger*
> *& she was in the way*
> *is "how"*
>
> *Why that gun was there at all*
> *why she was in front of it*
> *why that policeman's finger pressed the trigger*
>
> *not muscles   but years are behind the answer*
> *not reflexes*
> *   people . . .*

This is from a poem by Susan Sherman. It's called "Facts,"[33] and it deals head-on with the mesmerizing media hype lulling us daily in an attempt to make us think that things are not what they seem so that *we* will not believe we are who we are. Women must engage in battle even to reclaim our history, our memory, ourselves. We are creating a literature that does that, that helps *us* do that.

> Home once again, I walked out alone
> nearly every day that first week. Or:
> still floating just above my body,
> I watched me walking out alone. The eighth day
> I met my mother, dead eight years.
> As she walked toward me I peered
> into her face. She was crying and smiling
> at the same time. I had questions
> to ask her but we did not speak.
> I wanted to know how I could go on
> living with so much shame:
>
>   I mean
> with the memory of the children sitting
> at their desks in the school that was only
> a roof. Those bright questioning eyes
> welcomed me, tested the cut of my blouse
> and hair, welcomed my foreignness. Last year
> they huddled in ditches as mortars
> shelled their village for twelve days.
> Seven died. I helped buy the bullets . . .

Judith McDaniel is dealing here with her roots, decision to take risks, and perception of her relationship to events in Central America. McDaniel has been speaking out of the new female voice for as long as she's been writing. Her novel *Winter Passage* is about relationships between women. *Metamorphosis* is a collection of poems written out of the experience of alcoholism recovery. The above fragment is from a poem called "Dangerous Memory," in her most recent book *Sanctuary, A Journey.*[34]

A finely woven tapestry of essay, interview, poetry, poetic prose, and journal-writing, *Sanctuary* not only crosses the boundaries of literary genre but those of "personal" and "political" concerns as well. A powerful message in this type of work is that the traditional genre divisions are arbitrary at best. The female voice has, I believe, spoken to the problem of form and content in particularly relevant ways. Tracing this to feminist explorations of emotion/reason (and other sexual stereotyping) isn't difficult.

So many of our writers are prolific in the ease with which they inhabit a variety of genre: we have an Alice Walker whose novel, short story, essay, and poetry are equally powerful, a Marge Piercy who is as fine a novelist as she is a poet, a June Jordan whose political essays sing right along with her verse. But we do not define the new female voice through "stars" alone. Indeed, our refusal to do so is itself an important part of our commentary upon it.

Our work is peopled by bodies; not the fragmented pieces of ourselves rearranged by those who have crafted a male literature (often resembling the world of advertising). Our bodies age and come in different shapes. They have "unsightly" hair, odors, and sagging flesh. And they are learning, painfully, to feel.

More precise definitions include a repossession of history/memory/self, an attention to and honoring of process, a gender- and race- and class-conscious ear. We are concerned with stories and the ordinary voice. We make connections and search for the multiple faces of a new creative vision: one that insists on a world with everyone in it.

Women have begun to produce, as well, knowledgeable compendiums of our own literature. A particularly fine anthology of new women's poetry is *Early Ripening: American Women's Poetry Now,* edited by Marge Piercy.[35] The following is from her introduction:

> women are writing immensely exciting, approachable, rich, funny and moving poetry that can speak to a wider readership than it usually gets. Women are writing much of the best poetry being written, way more than half of it I believe, but remain poorly represented in anthologies, textbooks, reading series, prize lists, awards, and every other institution controlled by white men who like the way things are presently run just fine. Women are still mostly read by women; men remain under the delusion that the poetry women write will not speak to them. I think that means that many men miss out on poetry that could get them far more involved than what they're inclined to read, or more likely, inclined to bow the head at and pass by: that's high culture, may it rest in peace. (p. 2)

While the proverbial male anthologies have almost always been homogeneous (read: white, middle-class, academic, safe), this volume of women's work is homogeneous only in its literary excellence—many black, Hispanic, Native American, and Asian American as well as white women poets represented; both unpublished and well-known names; lesbian as well as heterosexual women; poets who write out of a feminist perspective and others who simply write as women—all poets unafraid of anger, physicality, process. I would like to close by quoting in full one poem from this anthology. I might have chosen another. But this one, like much of the new female writing anthologized by Piercy, is strong in the language of our image. It has memory and vision; it takes risks. It is Joy Harjo's "The Woman Hanging from the Thirteenth Floor Window":

> *She is the woman hanging from the 13th floor*
> *window. Her hands are pressed white against the*
> *concrete moulding of the tenement building. She*
> *hangs from the 13th floor window in east Chicago,*
> *with a swirl of birds over her head. They could*
> *be a halo, or a storm of glass waiting to crush her.*
>
> *She thinks she will be set free.*
>
> *The woman hanging from the 13th floor window*
> *on the east side of Chicago is not alone.*
> *She is a woman of children, of the baby, Carlos,*
> *and of Margaret, and of Jimmy who is the oldest.*
> *She is her mother's daughter and her father's son.*
> *She is several pieces between the two husbands*
> *she has had. She is all the women of the apartment*
> *building who stand watching her, watching themselves.*

When she was young she ate wild rice on scraped down
plates in warm wood rooms. It was in the farther
north and she was the baby then. They rocked her.

She sees Lake Michigan lapping at the shores of
herself. It is a dizzy hole of water and the rich
live in tall glass houses at the edge of it. In some
places Lake Michigan speaks softly, here, it just sputters
and butts itself against the asphalt. She sees
other buildings just like hers. She sees other
women hanging from many-floored windows
counting their lives in the palms of their hands
and in the palms of their children's hands.

She is the woman hanging from the 13th floor window
on the Indian side of town. Her belly is soft from
her children's births, her worn levis swing down below
her waist, and then her feet, and then her heart.
She is dangling.

The woman hanging from the 13th floor window hears voices.
They come to her in the night when the lights have gone
dim. Sometimes they are little cats mewing and scratching
at the door, sometimes they are her grandmother's voice,
and sometimes they are gigantic men of light whispering
to her to get up, to get up, to get up. That's when she
wants to have another child to hold onto in the night, to
be able to fall back into dreams.

And the woman hanging from the 13th floor window
hears other voices. Some of them scream out from below
for her to jump, they would push her over. Others cry
softly from the sidewalks, pull their children up like
flowers and gather them into their arms. They would help
her, like themselves.

But she is the woman hanging from the 13th floor window,
and she knows she is hanging by her own fingers, her
own skin, her own thread of indecision.

She thinks of Carlos, of Margaret, of Jimmy.
She thinks of her father, and of her mother.
She thinks of all the women she has been, of all
the men. She thinks of the color of her skin, and
of Chicago streets, and of waterfalls and pines.
She thinks of moonlight nights, and of cool spring storms.
Her mind chatters like neon and northside bars.
She thinks of the 4 a.m. lonelinesses that have folded
her up like death, discordant, without logical and

beautiful conclusion. Her teeth break off at the edges.
She would speak.

The woman hangs from the 13th floor window crying for
the lost beauty of her own life. She sees the
sun falling west over the grey plane of Chicago.
She thinks she remembers listening to her own life
break loose, as she falls from the 13th floor
window on the east side of Chicago, or as she
climbs back up to claim herself again.[36]

NOTES

1. June Jordan, "Many Rivers to Cross," in *On Call, Political Essays* (Boston: South End Press, 1985).

2. Meridel LeSueur's work was in fact silenced almost in its entirety when she was subpoenaed by the House Unamerican Activities Committee in the early 1950s. HUAC, a by product of the McCarthy era, affected artistic freedom in this country in ways still being felt. Indeed, the censorship and self-censorship generated by that particularly dangerous phenomenon changed the course of our artistic expression. LeSueur's work began to be available again when in the early seventies she was rediscovered by the women's movement. West End Press reissued a number of her books; Feminist Press followed with what remains the most complete collection, *Ripening*. LeSueur, at 88, is still writing.

3. Adrienne Rich, "Paula Becker to Clara Westhoff," in *The Fact of a Doorframe, Poems Selected and New 1950–1984* (New York: Norton, 1981).

4. This assumption of women's voices from other historic moments has been a poetic practice exercised by North American poets Muriel Rukeyser, Jane Cooper, Adrienne Rich, and others. It has also influenced the way women have approached the research and writing of biographies of our foremothers.

5. Magda Bogin, *The Women Troubadors* (New York: Norton, 1980).

6. Blanche Wiesen Cook, ed., *Crystal Eastman on Women and Revolution* (New York: Oxford University Press, 1978).

7. Blanche Cook has been working for a number of years on a biography of Eleanor Roosevelt soon to appear. It promises to combine Cook's meticulous research with her profoundly revealing historical sense.

8. Barbara Sicherman, *Alice Hamilton, A Life in Letters* (Cambridge, Mass: Harvard University Press, 1984).

9. Most recently in the catalogue for the traveling show, *Georgia O'Keeffe, Art and Letters* (Washington, DC: National Gallery of Art, 1987).

10. In the 1972 *Aperture* collection of Diane Arbus' photographs, journal entries edited by Diane's daughter Doone. *Aperture* will be reissuing the collection in 1988.

11. Evelyn Fox Keller, *A Feeling for the Organism, The Life and Work of Barbara McClintock* (New York: W. H. Freeman, 1983).

12. Audre Lorde's early biomythography *Zami, A New Spelling of My Name*, was published by Crossing Press in 1982. More recent are *The Cancer Journals* and the forthcoming (from Firebrand) *A Burst of Light*. Among her books of poetry is *The Black Unicorn* and *Chosen Poems, Old and New*. *Sister Outsider* is an important book of essays. Most of Lorde's books are published by Norton; the essays appear under the Firebrand imprint.

13. Assata Shakur, *Assata, An Autobiography* (Westport, Conn.: Lawrence Hill, 1987).

14. Although I still tend to use the term "Third World" for more immediate reader comprehension, I would like to quote from a note with which June Jordan opens her book *On Call:* "Given that they were first to exist on the planet and currently make up the majority, the author will refer to that part of the population usually termed Third World as First World."

15. Domitila de Chungara, *Let Me Speak!* as told to Moema Viezzer (New York: Monthly Review Books, 1979); and Elisabeth Burgos-Debray, ed., *I, Rigoberta Menchu, An Indian Woman in Guatemala* (London: Verso Editions, 1984). There have been a number of other such books in recent years, including: Margaret Randall, *Sandino's Daughter, Testimonies of Nicaraguan Women in Struggle* (Vancouver and Toronto: New Star Books, 1981); Media Benjamin, ed., *Don't Be Afraid, Gringo—A Honduran Woman Speaks from the Heart* (San Francisco: Food First, 1987); and *Enough is Enough, Aboriginal Women Speak Out,* as told to Janet Silman (Toronto: The Women's Press, 1987).

16. Gloria Anzaldúa, *Borderlands/La Frontera* (San Francisco: Spinsters/Aunt Lute, 1987).

17. Beryl Markham, *West With the Night* (San Francisco: North Point Press, 1983).

18. Boston Women's Health Book Collective, *Ourselves, Growing Older* (New York: Simon & Schuster, 1987).

19. Susan E. Browne, Debra Connors, and Nanci Stern, eds., *With the Power of Each Breath, A Disabled Women's Anthology,* (Pittsburgh and San Francisco: Cleis Press, 1985).

20. I have used *disabled* and then *differently-abled* until I read E. J. Graff's important letter in the January 1988 issue of *Sojourner.* She writes: "I prefer to think of myself as a woman with a disability, not a disabled woman. The former recognizes my handicap. The latter seems to define my entire being" See also Marsha Saxton and Florence Howe, eds., *With Wings, An Anthology of Literature by and about Women with Disabilities* (New York: The Feminist Press, City University of New York, 1986).

21. See Frederique Delacoste and Priscilla Alexander, *Sex Work, Writings by Women in the Sex Industry* (Pittsburgh and San Francisco: Cleis Press, 1987), among others.

22. There are a great number of literary titles in this category, as well as many books by psychologists and others. A visit to a good woman's bookstore or library will provide a wealth of material.

23. Among the titles in this category, I would recommend Patricia A. Murphy, *Searching for Spring* (a novel from Naiad, 1987) and Margaret Randall, *This is About Incest* (Ithaca, N.Y.: Firebrand Books, 1987).

24. Lesbian literature—novels, short stories, poetry, essays—is too broad a category to even begin a comprehensive listing here. A look in any good woman's bookstore will reveal dozens of excellent books. In poetry I particularly recommend Cheryl Clarke's *Living As a Lesbian* (Firebrand, 1986). An excellent humorous novel is Georgia Cotrell's *Shoulders* (Firebrand, 1987).

25. Some of the important U.S. publishers of women's writing are Feminist Press, Firebrand, Naiad, Cleis, Spinsters/Aunt Lute, Seal and Crossing. Although West End is not a women-only publisher, its recent series of books by strong women of color is worth noting. Among the many good feminist literary magazines are: *IKON, Sinister Wisdom, Heresies, Calyx, Conditions,* and *Thirteenth Moon.*

26. Zora Neal Hurston, *Their Eyes Were Watching God* (Urbana: University of Illinois Press, 1978).

27. Agnes Smedley, *Daughter of Earth* (New York: Feminist Press, 1973).

28. Sally Miller Gearhart, *Wanderground* (Watertown, MA: Persephone Press, 1979).

29. Among Ursula K. LeGuin's many titles, the most important is probably *The Left Hand of Darkness* (New York: Ace Books).

30. Susan Griffin's *Woman and Nature: The Roaring Inside Her* was groundbreaking. *Made from this Earth, An Anthology of Writings* (1982) is a comprehensive introduction to her work. *Like the Iris of An Eye* is poetry. Griffin's books are published by Harper & Row.

31. Anne Cameron's books include *The Journey* (Spinsters/Aunt Lute), *Daughters of Copper Woman* (Press Gang) *How Raven Freed the Moon* (Harbour Publishing), all prose; and *Earth Witch* and *The Annie Poems* (Harbour), poetry.

32. *Woman on the Edge of Time* as well as most of Marge Piercy's other novels are available from Ballantine-Fawcett. *Circles on the Water* (Knopf, 1982) is an anthology of her poetry through *The Moon is Always Female. Available Light* (New York: Knopf, 1988) is her most recent.

33. "Facts" by Susan Sherman, first published in IKON Second Series 5/6, New York City, 1986. It will be part of her volume *We Stand Our Ground,* her most recent.

34. Books by Judith McDaniel. *Winter Passage* was published by Spinsters Ink in 1985. *November Woman* came out from Loft Press (no date), and *Metamorphosis, and Other Poems of Recovery* is from Long Haul Press, 1986. *Sanctuary, A Journey* came out under the Firebrand imprint in 1987.

35. Marge Piercy, ed., *Early Ripening, American Women's Poetry Now* (London: Pandora, 1987, Methuen, 1988).

36. Joy Harjo, *She Had Some Horses* (New York: Thunder's Mouth Press, 1983).

... SHE STILL WROTE OUT
THE WORD KOTEX ON A TORN PIECE OF PAPER
WRAPPED UP IN A DOLLAR BILL. ...

CHERYL CLARKE

In her critically responsible article, "Black Women Poets from Wheatley to Walker," in *Sturdy Black Bridges* (Bell, Parker, Guy-Sheftall 1979), Gloria T. Hull assesses, for the first time in our history, the literary undertakings of black women poets prior to the Black Arts Movement of the 1960s. While her task is not to examine expressions of sexuality in the poetry of these women, she does engage in a process of criticism that bears on my efforts here: care, thoroughness, respect for the work, identification of woman-orientation, challenging of sexist notions and proscriptions, placing the poets in an historical context, formal and analytical approaches to evaluating the works' literary effectiveness.

In "Interstices: A Small Drama of Words," a dense and variously humorous paper delivered at the 1982 Scholar and the Feminist IX Conference at Barnard and subsequently published in *Pleasure and Danger: Exploring Female Sexuality* (Vance 1984), black feminist critic Hortense Spillers makes this observation about the language of black women's sexuality:

> With the virtually sole exception of Calvin Hernton's *Sex and Racism in America* and less than a handful of very recent texts by black feminist and lesbian writers, black women are the beached whales of the sexual universe, unvoiced, misseen, not doing, awaiting *their* verb. (74)

Well, if not our verb, then at least more precise metaphors.

Through an examination of selected texts by black women poets since 1969, I will present an overview of various linguistic expressions of sexuality, sexual identity, and the erotic. I have chosen to focus on poetry published since 1969 because this juncture signifies a variety of expressions speaking to sexual experience, desire, identity, and gratification. I am defining "sexuality" as literal and metaphorical references to the sex act (with women, with men, with self), references to male and female genitals and body parts. By "sexual identity," I mean the language—coded and explicit—that defines the poetic persona's recognition of self as a sexual being whoever or whatever the object of her desire. And with respect to the "erotic," I will use a definition I find implicit in Audre Lorde's exploration in her published speech, "The Uses of the Erotic:

The Erotic as Power" (1978)—that is, any sensual connection of self to others, to work, to sex, to the here-and-now; a primordial energy, an enabling vision. And when I use the term "lesbian," in reference to the texts, as I will throughout, I am, like Barbara Christian (1985), limiting its definition to "women who find other women sexually attractive and gratifying" (189).

I hope my paper will raise questions about the role and function of black feminist criticism; will continue some of the dialogue opened by black feminist critics like Barbara Smith (1977), Barbara Christian (1980), Hortense Spillers (1979), Deborah McDowell (1980), Gloria Hull (1979), and others, on the subject of lesbian perspectives and lesbian criticism. (Here, I am using the term "lesbian" in the broader sense as a way of revisioning and envisioning emotional, sexual, political connections among women in explicitly lesbian as well as nonlesbian texts; and here also, the term "lesbian" implies "feminist."

Black women in the United States have constantly been in the position of proving or feeling we must prove our sexual morality due to racist, misogynist devaluation in the United States or in Western culture. Much like white women, who are either whores or virgins, black women are either passive-aggressive wet nurses or inarticulate belle sauvages. In Frances E. W. Harper's 1892 novel, *Iola Leroy*, the character Dr. Gresham, a white Yankee, in offering his hand in marriage, makes this presumptuous plea to the mulatto, exslave protagonist, Iola:

> "Iola. . . . You must not judge me by the worst of my race. Surely our country has produced a higher type of manhood than the men by whom you were tried and tempted." (115)

Iola responds, "as a deep flush overspread her face," in defense of her honor:

> "Tried but not tempted. . . . I was never tempted."

Because of presumptions like that of the character Dr. Gresham and the corresponding projection of images of black women's sexual depravity, black women poets have avoided references to explicit sexuality, to genitals, to sexual acts or sexual gratification in our poetry until the late 1960s. And not to mention, United States' culture did not and does not sanction open discussions of sexuality from anyone or any group. Spurred on by the new philosophy of black self-determination, the era of the so-called "sexual revolution," and the later women's liberation movement, black women poets began to evince an explicit consciousness of ourselves as sexual beings, primarily heterosexual sexual beings except in rare cases.

As Spillers also states in the previously cited article, black women's

> sexual experiences are depicted but not often by them and if and when by the subject herself, often in the guise of vocal music, often in the self-contained accent and sheer romance of the blues. (74)

The blues was not all "sheer romance," as we will discuss later.

In her discussion of black women singers in "Slave Codes and Liner Notes" (Hull, Scott, Smith 1982), Michele Russell says that Bessie Smith "humanized sex for black women" (131) and "articulated how fundamental sex was to survival." Of course, I am not going to push a comparison of black women singers and black women poets because many formalistic, audience-related, economic, class, and cultural issues differentiate the exponents of these two genres. But I do believe the blues *period*, as a form, is a great teacher for poets—in terms of its linguistic facility and directness.

In the songs of black women particularly those of the classic or city blues form, we find brazen admissions of sexual desire and need, feelings about the uses and uselessness of men, money, sex/love relationships. Women spoke on when, how, who with and how long, and what one must do to get "*it*" (sex) with humor, bravada, and aplomb. There are plenty of songs that express loneliness and rejection, but just as many express the heroic, the independent, the in-control, tit-for-tat, out-there-on-the-make-with one-or-more-men woman.

> *Now let me tell you, baby,*
> *your mind is too full of sin.*
> *Now let me tell you, baby,*
> *your mind is too full of sin.*
> *Don't forget pretty daddy,*
> *that this world is full of other men.*
> *("Wise Woman Blues," sung by Dinah Washington, 1943–1945)*

or

> *I'm crazy bout a good time*
> *like a dog is crazy bout his bone.*
> *So when you run out of money*
> *get a cab and send me home.*
> *("Good Time Mama," sung by Martha Copeland, 1927)*

or

> *I will not sell it.*
> *I will not give it away.*
> *I will sit on it the rest of my days.*
> *("No Voot, No Boot," sung by Dinah Washington, 1943–1945)*

Gloria Hull's (1979) historical, critical, and textual assessment of poet Angelina Weld Grimké's life, times, and work was an astonishing revelation as we learned of Grimké's "explicitly woman-identified poems" (17). Although we know and can imagine the constraints, isolation, and class imperative under which Grimké wrote about her lesbianism—much of it in secret—and the more public, bohemian, reputedly hedonistic lifestyle of her contemporary, Gertrude Malissa Pridgett, better known as Ma Rainey, we can compare the intents of Grimké's "A Mona Lisa," first published in Countee Cullen's *Caroling Dusk* (1927) and quoted by Hull in the context of Grimké's lesbianism and a few bars from Rainey's infamous "Prove it on Me," a bawdy and explicitly lesbian song recorded in 1928:

> Grimké: *I should like to creep*
> *Through the long brown grasses*
> *that are your lashes*
>
> Rainey: *I looked and to my surprise*
> *the gal I was with was gone.*
> *Where she went I don't know.*
> *I mean to follow her everywhere she go.*

Grimké's use of the pronoun "your" might still throw us off were it not for Hull's discovery of other lesbian poems—and I suppose it could still be argued that the object of the persona's desire might be other than female—whereas Rainey identifies for us which gender the object of her pursuit is with specific female references. She also says things in the song like, "Yes, it's true I wear a collar and tie . . . talk to the women like any ole man. . . ." And, of course, the famous refrain: "I went out last night with a crowd of my friends. Musta been women cause I don't like no men." And one does not get the impression that the persona of "Prove it on Me" will be creeping in pursuit.

In addition to the repression, in a misogynist culture, of women's acknowledgment of our sexual-erotic energies, for many black women that repression has also functioned in the black community. So black women receive no encouragement anywhere to address ourselves as sexual beings. In her essay, "Uses of the Erotic: The Erotic as Power," black lesbian feminist poet Audre Lorde charges that women have been made to suppress "the erotic as a considered source of power and information within our lives" (1). Lorde responds similarly in *Black Women Writers at Work* (Tate 1983), to interviewer Claudia Tate's self-observation about the jarring effect of realizing that the speaker in Lorde's poetry is a woman and that the "object of affection is likewise a woman" (110). Lorde says:

> Women have been taught . . . to suspect the erotic urge, the place that's uniquely female. . . . So just as we reject our blackness because it has been termed inferior as women we tend to reject our capacity for feeling, our ability to love, to touch the erotic because it has been devalued.

The 1970 anthology, *The Black Woman* (Cade, ed.) created a public forum for black women to address each other and to criticize our second-class citizenship within the black political community. I was particularly struck by Cade's stunning proposal in her essay, "On the Issue of Roles," for reconciling the gender politics therein:

> Perhaps we need to let go of manhood and femininity and concentrate on black-hood. . . . It perhaps takes less heart to pick up the gun than to face the task of creating a new identity, a new self, perhaps an androgynous self, via commitment to the struggle. (103)

Clearly Cade saw this "androgynous self" as a means of eradicating the unequal power relationships inherent in gender roles—at least in Western culture. But whenever androgyny is put forth, there is the implication of bisexuality and thus homosexuality. No wonder this staggering proposal was met with silence and resentment.

The issue of the erotic as power, as creative force arises again in *Black Women Writers At Work* from Tate's question to poet Sonia Sanchez, "How do you fit writing into your life?" Sanchez describes her process in a way that bears out her final analogy of the act of writing and the sex act:

> I work in two or three notebooks. . . . I do everything long hand. I hate to see first drafts. I read them out loud. They're terrible, and then I read successive drafts. . . . All of a sudden there is a poem. I sometimes literally jump up and down. I might go cover up the kids and kiss them because I want to share my joy. It's a joy that has never been duplicated, perhaps the closest comparison is sex. (142)

Now, does the interviewer respond to this revelation with a question that might allow further exploration of this analogy; for example, does the poet consciously use her erotic power to craft her verse? Or, failing such a question, does Tate join with the poet to acknowledge that she's taken a risk? No, she plows right on to the next question, "For whom do you write?" The interviewer seems to fall into the same pattern of denial Lorde discusses in the statement cited earlier from the same work.

Gloria Wade-Gayles in a recent book of black feminist criticism, *No Crystal Stair* (1985), charges that Gayl Jones' novel *Eva's Man*—a study of insanity—reads like "the script of an X-rated film" (175) because Jones uses graphic language and images to convey sexuality and sexual exploitation. Is the critic then relieved of evaluating the work? Would it were that the scripts of X-rated films were as well-written or written with as much truth! Though we can say that the previously cited critic's evaluation is symptomatic of the prudery, fear, and censoring of sexually explicit language—to say nothing of the acts themselves—it's also one of the ways black women are denied forums to discuss our sexuality, particularly if the discussion takes us outside the familiar realm of male-initiated sexual encounters, penile sex, or the cult of romance.

In an otherwise respectful and elucidatory article, entitled oddly, "In the Name of the Father: The Poetry of Audre Lorde" (Evans 1983), Jerome Brooks dismisses Lorde's claiming, in *Cancer Journals,* of her experience of breast cancer as "A Black Lesbian Experience." The perspective is only valid for Lorde, he says, postulating, "Her remarks are certainly of wider interest than the subtitle would indicate (275)." "Lesbian," like "sex" or the "erotic," is, in the words of Ntozake Shange's adolescent heroine Indigo, the word "Kotex" written "on a torn piece of paper wrapped up in a dollar bill" (1982) and sent to the drugstore via a child. Because Brooks does not wish to explore the meaning of Lorde's lesbian perspective, it's only valid for Lorde. And the rest of us can be left out here wondering about lesbianism like daughters are left wondering by their mothers what the meaning of menstrual blood is to the rest of life. So, I feel it is important to acknowledge that whenever black women express themselves sexually on paper or in the sack, we're taking the risk of being rejected, misunderstood, silenced. And the more non-male-oriented and women-centered, non-heterosexual and non-penile-oriented our expressions or acts, the greater the risk.

In my reading of the texts, I have noted four main types of sexual discourse in the poetry:

- *Wished-for sex,* which includes a variety of fantasy, wanting and not getting, and lack of gratification;
- *Hyperbolic expression,* which includes grand metaphors, conceits, and images of sex as something other than what it is; may include perverse, distorted, and violent images of sex;
- *Sexual loneliness,* which includes statements of unrequited love, fear of intimacy, betrayal, rejection, and lots of circumspection;
- *Sexual graphics and explicitness,* which includes concrete images of sexual encounters as sexual encounters; may also include perverse, distorted, sometimes violent images of sex.

Erotic language, images, and acts might appear in all four types. There is overlap. And admittedly, there are far fewer of the sexually graphic and explicit expressions than of the other three types. I am not using poems in which sex acts are vehicles for imagizing other events. (Jayne Cortez is an exponent of this type of poetry.) In the poems I've chosen, sex is the subject of the comparison, and the poets may use a range of images to convey their concepts of sex.

At the beginning of the 1960s Black Arts Movement, black women poets as well as black men tended to mythologize and deify black women as nation builders, custodians of the revolution, and monolithic forces of regeneration, typified in Mari Evans' poem, "I Am A Black Women," from her volume of poems of the same name:

> *. . . tall as a cypress*
> *strong*
> *beyond all definition still*
> *defying place*
> *and time*
> *and circumstance*
> > *assailed*
> > *impervious*
> > *indestructible*
>
> *Look*
> > *on me and be*
> *renewed.*

Nikki Giovanni's poem, "Ego Tripping," is another such example, with all its references to ancient African kingdoms. Hyperbole was needed, at that time, to create the larger-than-life archetype, the superwoman, the quintessential matriarch to offset the devaluing images of black women. However, since then we've discovered that queens like common women have physical needs that find us falling off the pedestals; consider, for example another poem by Evans, "I Who Would Encompass Millions," which expresses sexual loneliness in the image of the "single bed":

> *I*
> *who would encompass*
> *millions*

. . . she still wrote out the word

> *am adrift on*
> *this*
> *my single bed. (17)*

While we as poets have linguistic options aplenty and feel so deeply about so many things, our metaphors of sexuality, sexual desire, sexual need, sexual gratification are not often adventurous. We are usually tied to the values of heterosexual sex and sexual monogamy. Rarely are we as experimental in our pursuit of sex as the singers. We are not confident about and less direct in dealing in the here-and-now for conceit. We wish a lot for sex. In her poem, "Marrow of My Bone," Evans either wishes for or asks her lover to:

> *Fondle me*
> *caress*
> *me*
> *with your lips*
> *withdraw*
> *the nectar from*
> *me*
> *teach me there is someone.*

Nikki Giovanni, putative princess of the Black Arts Movement or, as Michele Wallace describes her, "a kind of nationalistic Rod McKuen" (1979, 166), gained popularity for her assertiveness in the sexual language of her poetry. In her poem, "Seduction" (1970), she boldly fantasizes about initiating sex with her black nationalist warrior:

> *. . . i'll be taking your dashiki off*
> *. . . i'll be licking your arm*
> *. . . unbucklin your pants*
> *. . . taking your shorts off. (38)*

Giovanni usually reserves her more graphic sexual images for expressing criticism as in "No-Dick" from her poem "Nixon" (1970) or bitterness as in "Woman Poem"—her first and probably only feminist statement, which brings together black women's ambivalence about sexuality, the needing but not getting, the fear of appearing vulnerable. In a tight series of graphic descriptives, the poet posits the sexual roles black women deny ourselves:

> *gameswoman, romantic woman*
> *love-needer*
> *man-seeker*
> *dick-eater sweat-getter*
> *fuck-needing love-seeking woman. (78)*

In a poem called "Gray," published in *Callaloo's* special issue on (black) women poets, Alice Walker treats the theme of fear of intimacy in a sequence of questions to and answers from a woman friend, whom she "adore(s)," who is, perhaps, turning gray from being "frantic and alone":

> 'How long does it take you to love someone?'
> . . . .
> 'A hot second' . . .
>
> 'And how long do you love them?'
> 'Oh, anywhere up to several months.'
> 'And how long does it take you to
> get over them?'
> 'Three weeks . . . tops.' (63)

This, I might add, could also be interpreted as a poem of latent lesbian affection.

The wished-for, fantasy sentiment and expressions of sexual loneliness appear in a poem by Sybil Dunbar, also in the *Callaloo* issue, called "Words for Solitude's Pen":

> wish i could light you candles
> at midnight
> and watch you glow
> in the deep blue haze
> of my wanting hours
> then i'd never again
> turn my shivering body
> beneath cold sheets
> or part my legs
> to dream figures
> who beat their songs
> on silent drums (110)

(Incidentally, there are no explicitly lesbian poems or poems by "out" lesbian poets in this issue of *Callaloo*.)

And Gayl Jones, in a poem called "Chance," also in this special issue on women poets, echoes the fear of intimacy, the danger of love and sexual relationships:

> He reaches for her.
> She kisses him with fear.
> She's afraid to be tender,
> afraid he'll think she wants something.

Sonia Sanchez has put forth a consistently sexual self in much of her poetry. Men (or a man) were and are the objects and subjects of her desire, lust, and her disappointment. She waits for black men ("To All Brothers," 1970); she extends her hand to them ("Poem at 30," 1970); they make her breathe ("Black Magic," 1970). A more recent poem, "I have Alked A Long Time"—also in *Callaloo*—makes one wonder if the persona has ever been gratified sexually. In a catalog of dense and exquisite images and metaphors, the persona's struggles and losses are tallied. She mourns the loss of sensuality, the erotic, and creativity:

> ah, i have not loved
> wid legs stretched like stalks
>   against sheets

. . . she still wrote out the word

> *wid stomachs drainen the piracy of*
> > *oceans*
> *wid mouth discarden the gelatin*
> *to shake the sharp self.*
> *. . . . .*
> *between the yellow rain*
> *and ash,*
> *I have heard the rattle*
> *of my seed.*
> *so time, like some pearl necklace*
> > *embracen*
> *a superior whore, converges*
> *and the swift spider binds my breast. (19–20)*

And, after this lush verse, the persona beseeches, characteristic of Sanchez:

> *You, man, will you remember*
> *me when I die? (20)*

In the poetry of many black women sex is fraught with danger, the threat of loss, fear of vulnerability, fear of objectification, and most of us have sworn at one time or another, like Silla Boyce in Marshall's *Brown Girl, Brownstones* (1959):

> *I wun let a Judas smile*
> *and Judas words in the night*
> *and* thing *turn me foolish.*
> > *(39, my emphasis)*

In our silence and denial is the fear of betrayal and also the guardedness that comes with the objective knowledge of male dominance. Toi Derricotte, in her first volume of poetry, *The Empress of the Death House* (1978) presents graphic and explicit language with grotesque and perverse images of sex. In the hyperbolic poem, "Sleeping with Mr. Death," she opens this volume:

> *you go down on him*
> *he bursts in yr mouth*
> *a thousand stars*
> *flicker then die*
>
> *chalk dry, mr death (13)*

On her graphic references to genitals and use of gory, visceral images of an aggressive, vengeful female sexuality in the poem, "divorcee," spoken as a warning to men:

> *she has been bit so often*
> *in the cunt*
> *she has sewn it closed.*
>
> *she is teaching them [her daughters] to buy*
> *genealogy on time:*
> *on cunt hair a month. . . .*

> *she is teaching them that eating eating eating*
> *causes a woman to grow a penis*
>
> *She blasphemes   teaches her daughter*
> *that the first man splintered off eve's pelvis*
> *& was born in a bag of pus*
>
> *she is teaching them to paint X's on the doors of*
> *churches*
> *in menstrual blood*

These images, as Audre Lorde says in her endorsement of *Empress,* are not easy. They make us uncomfortable.

Black lesbian poet, Audre Lorde, whose work is always at the edge of pain and alienation and at the center of anger and hope, evokes the danger implicit in sex, especially for lesbians. Lorde has spoken often of her ostracism by the black literary community because of her explicit lesbianism. In her love poetry, Lorde is in the here-and-now and sees always the potential of pain, rejection, or destruction. Her metaphors are awesome for their sometime hermetic inaccessibility. In "love poem," an explicitly lesbian poem first published in 1974 in her volume, *New York Head Shop and Museum,* and later reprinted in *Lesbian Poetry* (Bulkin and Larkin 1981) and *Chosen Poems: Old and New* (1982), earth is a conceit for the lover. The persona begins with an invocation to the earth that contains an hyperbole her hips:

> *make sky flow honey out of my hips*
> *rigid as mountains*
> *spread over a valley*
> *carved out by the mouth of rain.*

And then she comes down to earth in a long stanza with a series of metaphorical and literal images of digital penetration, cunnilingus, female genitals, body parts, secretions and erogenous zones. The voice is active and the tone reflects the awareness of risk:

> *And I knew when I entered her I was*
> *high wind in her forest hollow*
> *fingers whispering sound*
> *honey flowed*
> *from the split cup*
> *impaled on a lance of tongues*
> *on the tips of her breasts on her navel*
> *and my breath howling into her entrances*
> *through lungs of pain.*
>
> *(Lesbian Poetry,* 23)

Lorde is more than anything sensual and explicit, even when her metaphors are inaccessible. Even lesbians suspend their guardedness in Lorde's wished-for poem, "woman," from *Black Unicorn* (1978):

452

. . . she still wrote out the word

> *I dream of a place between your breasts*
> *to build my house like a haven*
> *where I plant crops*
> *in your body*
> . . . . . .
> *and your night comes down upon me*
> *like a nurturing rain. (82)*

In "Fog Report" (*Black Unicorn*) she raises the issue of loss of self in intimate relationships. The sensual imagery, as usual, is unequivocal as are the desperation and humor:

> *I am tempted*
> *to take you apart*
> *and reconstruct your orifices*
> *your tongue your truths your fleshy altars*
> *into my own forgotten image*
> *so when this fog lifts*
> *I could be sure to find you*
> *tethered like a goat*
> *in my heart's yard.*

And in the searingly beautiful, "Meet," again Lorde returns to the store of images of common and exalted people and places she used throughout *Black Unicorn*, to talk to this dangerous love, replete with ingenious hyperbole, well-placed allusions, and explicit references to physical intimacy:

> *You shall get young as I lick*
> *your stomach*
> *hot and at rest before*
> *we move off again*
> *you will be white heat in*
> *my navel*
> *I will be sweeping night*
> *Mauwulisa foretells our bodies*
> . . . .
> *Taste my milk in the ditches of*
> *Chile and Ouagadougou*
> . . . .
> *in the innermost rooms of moment*
> *we must taste of each other's fruit*
> *at least once*
> *before we shall both be slain (34)*

The inventive Ntozake Shange in *nappy edges* (1978) and *A Daughter's Geography* (1984) continues the style of love poetry which characterized the black poetry of the 1960s—replete with allusions to Africa, the South, black music and musicians, black historical figures, and metaphors of love and sex as natural wonders and ancient monuments and latter day revolutionary movements and third world landscapes. Shange is consistently male-identified in terms of her muses and sexual references in poetry, despite her flirtation with the theme of lesbianism in *Sassafrass, Cypress, and Indigo.* Her verse is not only free; it is wild. Her poetic diction is, what Alice Walker would call, a "black folk language" or what a friend of mine calls "Shange-ese."

> *i can't allow you to look*
>   *at me*
> *how you do so i am*
>   *naked and wantin*
> *to be explored like a*
>   *honeysuckle patch*
> *when you look at me how you do so*
> *i am all lips and thigh*
> *my cover is blown & the kisses*
> *run free/only to hover sulkin over*
> *yr cheek/while i pretend*
> *they are not mine*
> *cuz it's happenin/but you don't know*
> *abt it.*

The same whimsicality and coyness express themselves in "Where the Amazon meets the Mississippi":

> *you fill me up so much*
> *when you touch me*
> *i can't stay here*
> *i haveta go to my space. (28)*

She uses animal imagery to convey the feeling of sexual gratification as in "You are such a fool," from *A Daughter's Geography:*

> *you make me feel like a*
> *cheetah*
> *a gazelle*
> *something fast and beautiful. . . .*

While Shange is an effective exponent of the hyperbolic style of sex poetry, I also believe poets are obligated to liberate our sexual discourse as well as our sexuality from the flowers, collard greens and okra, from nights in Tamaris, from fierce animals, and some black male musician's tenor solo.

However, Shange is guarded about sex and can become quite graphic, like Giovanni, when she wishes to convey bitterness, fear, or anger. In "Improvisation," a nine-part poem with stanzas separated by treble and bass clefs and musical time notations, using choking as a metaphor, she is stifled by "this place"—a physical as well as emotional terrain. Not only are there "pollutants," drugs, desperate women, and decadence, but also:

. . . she still wrote out the word

> *some man/wants to kiss my thighs*
> *roll his tongue around my navel*
> *put his hands all up my ass*
> *& this place is in my throat (14)*

In an erotic poem, "Take the A Train," she transfers her sexual desire for men to a sensual connection with black people:

> *i could sleep with a man*
> *but i'll lay with the souls of black folks*
> *maybe i could grow me something*
> *some azure flower that would smell*
> *like life to me . . . (18)*

In the imagistic play, *No,* a political, erotic-romantic, woman-identified poetic statement of *negritude,* Alexis DeVeaux offers this spare, direct, and celebratory recipe called "Cuntery":

> *I will make a savannah of my*
> *dreads*
>
> *I will make an incense of my*
> *pussy*
>
> *I will make breadfruit of my*
> *hands*
>
> *I will make a fetish of your*
> *love.*
> *(also appearing in* Blue Heat, *a chapbook)*

DeVeaux effectively mixes, like Lorde, a literal and figurative erotic language, and like Shange she expresses her work in a black folk language. Like Shange and Lorde, her work is replete with allusions to ancient African kingdoms, queens, goddesses. Where Lorde is filled with the sense of danger implicit in women being with women, DeVeaux is filled with the sense of infinite possibility. Except for her story, "The Riddles of Egypt Brownstone," which also appeared in *Midnight Birds* (Washington 1980), *No* is rather other-worldly, seemingly set in some mythic zone. Sometimes one wonders where these women are. They may be in "The Land of Fa"; but wherever they are, the stuff of erotic dreams is happening amidst "Musk oil and lapis lazuli . . . nipples . . . tongue . . . and sassy blackness," "somewhere on the edge of Brooklyn." Though quite often DeVeaux's work reveals a black lesbian world, she does not choose to define her woman-centered poetics as "lesbian." In fact, in the poem, "Are there no more proph-ets," she argues that:

> *the problem is still whatcolor/*
> *whichgender*
> *if is not sex*

or if you are what sex you
　　sleep with
or when
or how many ways
　　a week
how many times an hour you can come.

Another instance of an attempt to silence expressions of female sexuality occurred during the production of *No* in New York City at the Henry Street Settlement House Theatre in 1981 in an article that appeared in the *Amsterdam News*, a black publication in New York City noted for its homophobic journalism. A black male reviewer published an attack on DeVeaux for what he defined as themes of "lesbianism" in the play, charging that homosexuality is not fit subject matter for black writers to be addressing. He admitted to leaving at the play's intermission.

Lastly, in a poem called, "The Diver," using diving to convey the idea or act of sex, DeVeaux is at her inventive, loving, humorous best:

dives into me/tongue first
into mouth suc culent
breath like ethiopia supple
Black girl
swing among my poems and flaws
swim diva: come, up for air
swim against my tide(s)
breast stroke the waves
I'm watching on the sidelines, baby
I'm rooting for you

SUMMATION

Sexually explicit language makes women uncomfortable, for it so often is the language of female sexual objectification, especially when used by men. As writers, particularly as feminists, we do not use language that depicts sex graphically for fear of being judged "politically incorrect" or irresponsible. When black women project our sexuality, we frequently use exalted language, or we're filled with ambivalence and circumspection, sometimes fatalism. This fatalism is consistent with the culture we live in that often likens sex to death or "sin"—for which the wages are death. But sex is dangerous for us—it has meant violation, vulnerability, loss of economic security, devaluation, loss of independence more than it has meant pleasure and gratification. While black women singers use material that is more direct and earthy about sexual need and desire, much of their material has been written by men—and white men at that—who are projecting a male view of women and a male view of black women. I believe the poets, when we do express sexual views, perhaps represent a more authentically female perspective of sex because we are the writers. Our visions have been repressed because of a coerced adherence to acceptable sexuality. Usually those models are heterosexual and monogamous. Recently, we've witnessed greater experimentation with themes of lesbian sexuality in our fiction and poetry, by lesbians and by women who aren't lesbians. And this is happening at a time of great pressure from the conservative and moral majority communities to censor sexually explicit and graphic language and images while at the same time they bombard us with television commercials, magazine ads, and billboards full of subliminal and not so subliminal and distorted images of male and female sexuality.

We have much to work against and for. We have to work against the custom of silence as well as our own fear of power as sexual beings.

The implications for feminist criticism are the responsibilities of both looking at the ways black women writers treat sexuality in their work, not glossing over its expression, and examining the language of sexuality, the absence of the language, and what the discourse means. Also more of us are beginning to break down the isolation of lesbians by looking at the work of lesbians, looking at what traditions lesbians have created within the literature, and beginning to adjust the heterosexist myopia through which we've viewed black women's sexuality (and literature).

I think black women writers—poets and fiction writers—could stand to lose some primness, some fatalism, and one-dimensional sexual perspective: one man (or woman), one body, one way, and fade out to flowers.

I say to throw away the Kotex, forget the tampon, and BLEED!

NOTES

This essay was first presented by Cheryl Clarke at the Black Women Writers in Diaspora Conference, East Lansing, Michigan, Oct. 27, 1985, as part of the panel, "The Politics of Romance and Sexuality in Twentieth-Century Literature by Black Women." The title of the essay is from the novel *Sassafrass, Cypress and Indigo* by Ntozake Shange (New York: St. Martin's Press, 1982).

REFERENCES

Brooks, Jerome. "In The Name of the Father: The Poetry of Audre Lorde" in Mari Evans, ed. *Black Women Writers 1950–80: A Critical Evaluation.* Anchor/Doubleday, Garden City, N.Y., 1984, pp. 269–276.

Cade, Toni, ed. *The Black Woman: An Anthology.* New American Library, New York, 1970, p. 103.

Christian, Barbara. *Black Feminist Criticism: Perspectives on Black Women Writers.* Pergamon Press, New York, p. 189.

Derricotte, Toi. *The Empress of the Death House.* Lotus Press, Detroit, 1978, pp. 13, 24–25.

Dunbar, Sybil. *Callaloo: A Black South Journal of Arts and Letters,* Vol. 2, Feb. 1979, p. 102.

Evans, Mari. *I Am A Black Woman.* William Morrow, New York, 1970, pp. 12, 17, 32.

Giovanni, Nikki. *Black Feeling Black Talk, Black Judgement.* William Morrow, New York, 1968, pp. 38, 78.

Grimké, Angelina W., in Countee Cullen, ed., *Caroling Dusk: An Anthology of Verse by Negro Poets.* Harper and Brothers, New York, 1927, p. 42.

Harper, Frances. *Iola Leory.* AMS Press, New York, 1971, p. 115.

Hull, Gloria T. "Black Women Poets from Wheatley to Walker" in Bell, Parker, Guy-Sheftall, eds. *Sturdy Black Bridges.* Anchor-Doubleday, New York, 1979, pp. 69–85.

———. "'Under the Days': The Buried Life of Angelina Weld Grimke" in *Conditions: Five, The Black Women's Issue,* 1979, pp. 17–25.

Lorde, Audre, in Bulkin and Larkin, eds. *Lesbian Poetry.* Persephone Press (reissued by Gay Press Association, 1985), 1981, p. 23.

———. *The Black Unicorn.* W. W. Norton, New York, 1978, pp. 33, 70, 82.

———. *Uses of the Erotic: The Erotic As Power.* Out & Out Books, Trumansburg, N.Y., 1978.

Marshall, Paule, *Brown Girl, Brownstones.* The Feminist Press, Old Westbury, N.Y., 1981, p. 121.

Russell, Michele. "Slave Codes and Liner Notes" in Hull, Scott, and Smith, eds. *All the Women Are White, All the Blacks Are Men, But Some of Us Are Brave: Black Women's Studies.* The Feminist Press, Old Westbury, N.Y., 1982.

Sanchez, Sonia, in Gwendolyn Brooks, ed. *A Broadside Treasury.* Broadside Press, Detroit, 1971, pp. 136, 137.

———. *Callaloo,* Vol. 2, Feb. 1979, pp. 19–20.

Shange, Ntozake. *Sassafrass, Cypress & Indigo.* St. Martin's Press, New York, 1982, p. 23.

———. *nappy edges.* St. Martin's Press, New York, 1978, pp. 26–28.

———. *A Daughter's Geography.* St. Martin's Press, N.Y., 1984, pp. 14, 18, 28.

Spillers, Hortense, "Interstices: A Small Drama of Words" in Carol Vance, ed. *Pleasure and Danger: Exploring Female Sexuality.* Routledge, Kegan-Paul, London, 1984, p. 74.

Tate, Claudia, ed. *Black Women Writers at Work.* Continuum, New York, 1983, pp. 109, 141–142.

Wade-Gayles, Gloria. *No Crystal Stair: Visions of Race and Sex in Black Women's Fiction.* Pilgrim Press, New York, 1985, p. 175.

Walker, Alice. *Callaloo,* Vol. 2, Feb. 1979, p. 63.

Wallace, Michele. *Black Macho and the Myth of the Superwoman.* The Dial Press, New York, 1979, p. 166.

RECORDS

Washington, Dinah. *Wise Woman Blues: Rare and Early, 1943–45 + 1.* Rosetta Records, 115 West 16th Street, New York, 10011, 1984.

Rainey, Ma. *Ma Rainey.* Milestone Records, 10th & Parker, Berkeley, Calif. 94710, 1974.

Copeland, et. al. *Mean Mothers: Independent Women's Blues, Vol. 1.* Rosetta Records, New York, 1980.

SHADOW WORK

SAM HAMILL

Plato, who despised and distrusted poets, believed that love (in its largest sense) was *gnosis,* the binding (*re-ligio*) which transforms opposites into a unity. For Plotinus, love was the result of "strenuous contemplation in the soul." Kenneth Rexroth, in his beautiful "Letter to William Carlos Williams," defines a poet as one "who creates sacramental relationships that last always." And in the *Timaeus,* Plato says, "It is impossible for the determination or arrangement of two of anything, so long as there are only two, to be beautiful without a third. There must come between them, in the middle, a bond which brings them into union."

"By right means, if possible, but by any means, make money,"—Horace. Dr. Johnson wrote, on April 5, 1776, working on his "own time" and without remuneration for his thinking, "No man but a blockhead ever wrote, except for money." And Nigel Dennis exclaimed, "One is always excited by descriptions of money changing hands—it's much more fundamental than sex!"

A poet's work was defined by Dr. Williams in *Spring and All:* "to refine, to clarify, to intensify that eternal moment in which we alone live." Williams sought a poetry which would not control energy, but would release it. A reinvigoration of the spirit.

A poet's work is shadow work. I borrow the term, altering it slightly, from Ivan Illich's 1981 book of that name (Marion Boyars), and it would be improper not to permit him the initial definition:

> I do not mean badly paid work, nor unemployment; I mean unpaid work. The unpaid work which is unique to the industrial economy is my theme. In most societies men and women together have maintained and regenerated the subsistence of their households by unpaid activities. The household itself created most of what it needed to exist. These so-called subsistence activities are not my subject. My interest is in that entirely different from of unpaid work which an industrial society demands as a necessary complement to the production of goods and services. This kind of unpaid servitude does not contribute to subsistence. I call this complement to wage labor "shadow work." It comprises most housework . . . shopping . . . the homework of students, the toil expended commuting to and from the job . . . compliance with bureaucrats, . . . and many of the activities usually labelled "family life."

A poet's work is shadow work; it is work performed without regard for remuneration of any kind, most often without consideration for even the possibility of remuneration.

The major difference between the shadow work of the poet and that of all of us lies in the fact that a poet's work contributes virtually nothing to the formal economy. Nor is the poet's work (except in certain "chairs" of certain universities) an unpaid condition of employment. Poetry has nothing to do with "employment" except in its most Latinate sense: *implicare*—to enfold or involve. The poets' involvement is most likely to be through the employment of contemplation, a sublime activity which is not an action.

The poet, contemplating the experience of love, creates an expression of the irrefutable unity of opposites, that is, the poet seeks to discover the third thing, the bond that binds, the "sacramental relationship" that can, through the poem, be rediscovered again and again. When Buson writes his poem,

> *By white chrysanthemums*
> *scissors hesitate*
> *only an instant*

his poem is not about scissors and chrysanthemums. It is an essay on birth and life and death and the rhythm of days and seasons, and it suggests profound unity. He balances action against perfect stillness, life against death, beauty against emptiness. But he excludes none of them. Against the death of chrysanthemums, he places the human hand with all its implications of beauty and life in flowers which the human mind holds dear. Against the cutting, he places the moment's hesitation, a perfect stillness. And in that perfect stillness, we glimpse the great void of which we are a part. Through the poem, we are invited into the reality of the "other" life.

Poetry is not commerce. It is not something which can be exchanged or traded. It is a gift to the poet, a gift for which the poet, eternally grateful, spends a lifetime in preparation, and which the poet, in turn, gives away and gives away again. The actual work of preparation is shadow work: it must be performed without thought of money, and it is "essential" work in that it enables the poet to recognize and accept the gift and, in giving the gift away, do so with a great accompanying energy. But that energy, that experience we name poem, cannot be traded on the marketplace because it cannot be subverted. It won't light a light bulb, run a heater or an airconditioner or a microwave oven. It is only a poem: necessary, and inviolable, an articulation of a world beyond the possibilities of money.

As the audience for poetry shrank, as social awareness even of the existence of poetry evaporated, poetry turned more and more toward the inner, other world. Poetic language has always been confused with religious language. Since World War II, poetry has spoken almost as a religion, but as a religion without a bureaucracy and with an almost complete absence of dogma. As Heidegger said,"We are too late for the gods, and too early for being, whose poem, already begun, is being."

"All the new thinking," Robert Hass writes, "is about loss. /In this it resembles all the old thinking."

Illich has some illuminating observations on the nature of what we call work: "Both 'work' and 'job' are key words today. Neither had its present prominence three hundred years ago. Both are still untranslatable from European languages into many others.

Most languages never had one single word to designate all activities that are considered useful. Some languages happen to have a word for activities demanding pay. This word usually connotes graft, bribery, tax or extortion of interest payments. None of these words would comprehend what we call 'work.'"

To the Greek mind, handwork was antiaristocratic and best left for servants. St. Paul's declaration that "who does not work does not eat" was generally ignored by the Christian hierarchy. The Rinzai Buddhists had their own version, "No work, no food," which they generally honored. Yet throughout these cultures, as throughout most others, there has been a consistent shadow work that provided, necessarily, for the health of the spirit or the soul. It is *gnosis,* the work of knowing. It is not the same as "scientific" work which is often more the exercise of technology than the labor after knowledge and which is subsidized. The poet's work cannot be subsidized except that subsidies can "purchase time" for a poet. And that "purchased time" is used almost in its entirety for shadow work.

But before examining the poet's shadow work, it might be helpful to understand just when and how the economic division of labor into productive and nonproductive types came about. Illich claims that it was "pioneered and first enforced through the domestic enclosure of women." And while its roots predate the Industrial Revolution, it was indeed our faith in technology combined with our insatiable lust for "goods" that divided the home and that removed the hearth from the center of production, transforming it into a center of consumption only. "An unprecedented economic division of the sexes," Illich says, "an unprecedented economic conception of the family, an unprecedented antagonism between domestic and public spheres made wage work into a necessary adjunct of life. All this was accomplished by making working men into the wardens of their domestic women, one by one, and making this guardianship into a burdensome duty."

While men were encouraged to pursue new vocations beyond the home (and beyond "mere" subsistence), women were being redefined through the lenses of biology and philosophy. This newly defined "nature of woman" has been amply explored in Susan Griffin's magnificent *Woman and Nature* (Harper & Row, 1978). Woman was thought to be the matrix of society, one for whom common economics should have no meaning, one for whom the keeping of the household and the overseeing of children would be reward enough. "This new conception of her 'nature' destined her," Illich says, "for activities in a kind of home which discriminated against her wage labor as effectively as it precluded any real contribution to the household's subsistence. In practice, the labor theory of value made man's work into the catalyst of gold, and degraded the homebody into a housewife economically dependent and, as never before, unproductive. She was now man's beautiful property and faithful support needing the shelter of home for her labor of love."

But in materialist culture, what is the "value" of "labors of love?" Man began to perceive himself as utterly dependent upon wage work, he began to perceive himself the sole arbiter of society's problems, and he began to see the "requirements" of women and wife and family as a kind of extortion. Suddenly, man and woman were completely estranged from subsistence work. The family cow disappeared. The family garden went fallow or turned into a small flower garden.

"Capital gains" replaced the family's customary reinvestment in the means of family production, and the family-as-means-of-production disappeared.

Womankind became mystified. "Woman's work" was born simultaneously with the devaluation of shadow work and subsistence labor. The sexes became increasingly divided, with man perceived as the "provider" and woman as the "consumer." We consoled woman, whose work was perceived as nonproductive, by further mystifying her reproductive capacities. In practical terms, sex became the paradigm for the economics of "women's work" at the direct expense of all notions of partnership and communion and true cohabitation.

The soap-making, weaving, sewing, broom-making, quilting, canning, planting and harvesting, rug-making, animal husbandry, and household repairs at which women excelled were taken over by technology. When women did begin to reemerge from the domicile and as they entered the marketplace, they found that, because their work was mystified and devalued, they would find employment only as menial assistants to production—at sewing machines, then at typewriters and telephones—for which they were paid second-class wages and at which they labored without union or insurance or retirement benefits—a position which was not in fact greatly different from that position now occupied by the poet or by the free-lance serious writer except that woman had little or no hope for advancement.

Shadow work was born with the invention of wage labor, and, as Illich says, both alienate equally. Both become forms of bondage—wage labor through the issuing of long-term credit, shadow work through its devalued nonproductive and noncapitalist characteristics. Industrial society produces victims as surely (and proportionately) as it produces wealth in the form of consumable goods. Just as South African apartheid supplies the white economy with "prosperity," Hitler expected his victims to "produce" while waiting for their inevitable extinction. It is the penultimate exclamation of the Work Ethic: *Arbeit macht frei.*

For the poet, whose work is a "labor of love," whose labor is to "refine, to clarify, to intensify that eternal moment," the real work becomes "feminized" and mystified in the eyes of the public. Poetry is perceived as something rarified, semiprecious, and nonproductive (to say nothing of counterproductive). Alienated from all forms of subsistence, from virtually all personal productivity, isolated on the assembly line of manufacturing or in the sterile executive suite in which no real product is actually produced, the contemporary male has relegated care of the culture, social work, family lay ministry, education, and all form of housework to the shadow economy. Divorced from the foundation of immaterial good, he struggles to make sense of his life, a life dictated to by forces entirely outside the self, outside partnership with spouse, and outside the domicile. He neither understands nor values gift labor.

To clarify the difference between "gift labor" (the work the poet invests in making the poem which will then be given away) and what I have termed "shadow work" (that work performed by the poet in preparation for the gift of inspiration), let me quote Lewis Hyde's remarkable study, *The Gift: Imagination and the Erotic Life of Property* (Random House, 1983)—"The costs and benefits of tasks whose procedures are adversarial and whose ends are easily quantified can be expressed through a market system. The costs and rewards of gift labors cannot. The cleric's larder will always be filled with gifts; artists will never 'make' money."

The poet's necessity to speak is bound to society's need for cultural, social, and spiritual livelihood. There is no "price" for a great painting or poem or musical composition. A true "bardic" tradition in which a poet is paid to sing the praises of the king produces less real poetry than does the shotgun granting we now see under the auspices of the National Endowment for the Arts. The poet can neither buy nor sell the poem just completed. There is no marketplace for poetry. But, to quote from Hyde again,

> There is a place for volunteer labor, for mutual aid, for in-house work, for healings that require sympathetic contact or a cohesive support group, for strengthening the bonds of kinship, for intellectual community, for creative idleness, for the slow maturation of talent, for the creation and preservation and dissemination of culture, and so on. To quit the confines of our current system of gender means not to introduce market value into these labors but to recognize that they are not "female" but human tasks. And to break the system that oppresses women, we need not convert all gift labor [and all shadow work] to cash work; we need, rather, to admit women to the "male" moneymaking jobs while at the same time including supposedly "female" tasks and forms of exchange in our sense of possible masculinity.

May Sarton has written that the greatest deprivation is that of being unable to give one's gift to those one loves. Then, she says, "the gift turned inward, unable to be given, becomes a heavy burden, even sometimes a kind of poison."

Without the shadow work, without the years of study and contemplation and self-searching, without the mastering of discipline from within, and without the years of trial and error, the years of work to know language and to gain a sense of craft in language, how can the abstract inspiration be transformed (through the appropriate infusion and release of human energy) into something worthy of being given? The "product" of love's labor. The quality of the economy in gift-economics is determined in part by quality of the shadow work which attends it.

A man I shall call X has a family. He is in his thirties. He has a dull office job in the city. Having been born and raised in the heart of the U.S.A., he rarely attends a church or a civic function, but has a deep abiding faith in God and Country. He loves his wife. He loves his three children. But his life is hard. He has very little vocabulary for his emotions. He often drinks too much in order to avoid his emotions, in order to obliterate them. He produces nothing with his own hands and knows of no one with whom he can comfortably and intimately confide. His closest friend is a man almost identical to himself. They work together, they play together, they drink to obliterate their feelings together and sometimes in order to gain courage to discuss what they cannot, when they are sober, comfortably discuss.

But X is afraid. He fears the blank gray future with its office dust and telephone and file drawers. He fears the twenty-three years left on his mortgage. He fears the two years left on his automobile loan and the loan he took last year to pay for the birth of his youngest.

He cannot give the quality of love to his family which he would like to give. He is overcome, almost daily, by a dreadful ennui. His nightly entertainment consists almost entirely of televised violence, and he often fantasizes himself as one who is physically inviolable, able to overcome all problems by sheer physical will.

It is one of the most common portraits in twentieth-century literature. From "The Hollow Men" to Willie Loman, from Tennessee Williams to Ernest Hemingway, modern man is with filled with existential dread which can be relieved only in shadow work and gift economics, those two "other" kinds of economics for which our families and schools leave us totally unprepared.

X needs and wants to give his family an enormous gift, but in order for that gift to be understood, it must be articulated in such a manner as to preclude any possibility of misunderstanding. X would also like to share his sense of frustration and, indeed, grief. The greatest gift he might receive from his family is the gift of understanding. His habitual drinking to escape reality may well turn to drunken expressions of rage that take the form of physical violence because he remains unable to articulate either his deepest love or his enormous frustration and his personal agony. Neither his home life nor his education have prepared him to meet the responsibilities that are concommitant with emotional health.

The poet's gift to X is the gift of articulation, the gift of good words. But the poet is also left to his or her own resources, for the shadow work of language has no place in public education, and even the language itself resists a poet's use. The actual working material of language, of poetics especially, was articulated by Paul Valéry in his essay "Pure Poetry" (*The Art of Poetry*, Bollingen, 1958):

> Before [the poet] is spread this ordinary language, this collection of means not adapted to his plan, not made for him. For him there was no physicist to determine the relations between these means; there was no constructor of scales; no tuning fork, no metronome; no certainty in that direction; all he has is the clumsy instrument of the dictionary and the grammar. Besides, he must address himself not a special and unique sense such as hearing—which the musician forces to undergo whatever he inflicts on it and which is moreover the supreme organ of expectation and attention—but to a general and diffused expectation, and he addresses it by means of language, which is an extremely odd mixture of incoherent stimuli. Nothing is more complex or more difficult to disentangle than the strange combination of qualities found in language. Everyone knows how rarely sound and sense are in accord; and moreover, everyone knows that a discourse may display very differing qualities: it may be logical and deprived of all harmony; it may be harmonious and insignificant; it may be clear and lacking in all beauty; it may be prose or poetry; and, to sum up all these independent modes, it is enough to mention all the sciences that have been created to exploit this diversity of language and to study it in its various aspects. Language falls successively under the jurisdiction of phonetics, metrics, and rhythmics; it has a logical and semantic aspect; it includes rhetoric and syntax. One knows that all these different disciplines study the same text in many different ways. . . . Here, then, is the poet at grips with this diverse and too rich collection of primal qualities—too rich, in fact, not to be confused; it is from this that he must draw his objet d'art, his machine for producing the poetic emotion, which means that he must compel the practical instrument,

the clumsy instrument created by everyone, the everyday instrument used for immediate needs and constantly modified by the living, to become—for the duration that his attention assigns to the poem—the substance of a chosen emotive state, quite distinct from all the accidental states of unforeseen duration which make up the ordinary sensitive or psychic life. One may say without exaggeration that common language is the fruit of the disorder of life in common, since beings of every nature, subjected to an innumerable quantity of conditions and needs, receive it and use it to further their desires and their interests, to set up communications among themselves; whereas the poet's language, although he necessarily uses the elements provided by this statistical disorder, constitutes, on the contrary, an effort by one man to create an artificial and ideal order by means of a material of vulgar origin.

In order for the poet to be in a position to give a gift that is useful, the poet must master the use of a material which is itself created and used everyday by people who have no conscious use for or faith in poetry. The poem exists in a condition of gift economics. But the work that precedes the poem, the years and years of preparation, come under the category of shadow work, just as the true poet continues to depend on shadow work in the form of reading, note-taking, researching, as well as furthering one's self-discipline, one's shamanistic practices, and one's spiritual life.

Poetry subverts materialistic economics because there is no "product" in the marketplace sense of the term and because poetry teaches us to participate in the economy of the gift and in the economy of shadow work. For X, who suffers as a result of his inability to articulate both his needs and his gifts of true emotion, life in the material economy alone is supremely dangerous—it leaves him "emotionally bankrupt"—and he is left with the fact of a television serving as a substitute for friendship, as a substitute for partnership, and, ultimately, with himself alone with his loneliness. The loves and hopes and fears that threaten to overcome X may well also overcome his family, taking domestic violence (which is, after all, an inarticulate expression of self-hatred) as their form. Not only does X require emergency help, but his family is similarly endangered. Unless the necessary shadow work is done, the exchange of true gifts (the gift of one's self, the gift of giving) cannot take place in any comprehensible way.

The quality of time and attention invested in the shadow work contributes directly to the quality of transformation of the gift (inspiration) in the hands of the maker (poet). The hunter says, "If you want to catch fish, think like a fish; if you want to catch bear, think like a bear." Wanting to speak for the voiceless, the poet must spend time with those for whom the articulation of complex ideas and emotions is an enormous (and, often, losing) struggle. Wanting to participate fully in the economy of gift-giving, in the economy of love and hope, the shadow work must be attended to, and attended to with all due care and commitment.

The blockhead who writes nothing except for remuneration remains isolated in the material economy alone. The holistic life, the life of health, requires finding a balance within the boundaries of all three separate but interlocking economies; all three are bound together in a sacramental relationship that lasts always.

EDEN AND MY GENERATION

LARRY LEVIS

THE CONNOISSEURS OF LOSS

At least since the Bible and Milton, much of English poetry has been preoccupied with the loss of Eden and the resulting knowledge which partially and paradoxically compensates for all solitary exile. But as myth became, in the artistic *and* general consciousness, more and more possible only in a radically *secular* way, poetry began to locate Eden, not in public myth, but in the privacy of personal experience, and to explore it in the lyric rather than the epic mode. Eden became a real *place;* it could be named, spoken of, lived in, and remembered. The Romantic poets understood Eden, not as an elsewhere, but as a place inside the poet's own life. Wordsworth's landscape becomes, in his recollection, his private, unauthorized, unorthodox Eden. Yet Wordsworth's decision to *make* such a landscape Edenic is a compromise in which he stands, warily but finally, at the center.

In just this fashion, the named, autobiographical, particular *place,* whether Paumanok or Paterson or Big Sur or Vermont, became a way to locate the theme—became, as place, the new and personally experienced Eden. The poetry of my own generation, however, has been turning away or aside from such named, secular but sanctified places. Instead, it generalizes self-consciously about the Edenic theme of loss and exile. And with that change has come a corresponding change in language. This resistance to a resolutely imagistic, autobiographical poetry, and a preference for a more abstract, meditative mode of thinking testifies not merely to private loss, exile, and knowledge, but to a *collective and generational* loss, exile, and knowledge. The very language used has become increasingly less innocent, or such innocence increasingly less possible. In a way my generation has had to invent a way of thinking and a language which could not only record its losses but could also question the motive behind every use of that language—especially its own. This need, however, is not only some necessary Oedipal and dialectal *agon* of one generation reproaching another. It is simply that for my generation there was no access *via* experience to the Eden of its parents. For to replace Eden in their own expressionist language is simply to mimic Eden or mock it. To find it is to find the words it needs in one's own time.

PLACE

Donald Hall begins an interesting essay on the nature of place in poetry with the following remarks:

> For some poets, poetry derives from a place. Poem after poem reaches back and touches this place, and rehearses experiences connected with the place: Words-worth's "Nature"; the Welsh farms of Dylan Thomas; T. S. Eliot's St. Louis and Dry Salvages; Wallace Stevens' Florida; Walt Whitman and Paumanok; architectural Italy for Ezra Pound; Gloucester for Charles Olson. . . . But I am not thinking only of poetry which is geographic or descriptive. I am thinking of places which to the poets embody or recall a spiritual state.[1]

But how do poems "embody or recall" these "spiritual" states? Hall's notions here have the flavor of truth, but perhaps it is wisest to realize these ideas specifically, as poems do. To begin with one personal example, the poet Gary Soto's San Joaquin Valley is the same geographical region I am from, and yet his experience of that place, both sacred and blasphemous, is that of a Mexican-American, and it is vastly different from my own experience of it as the son of a farmer, an "Anglo." In a way, we lived side by side, but in different worlds. Similarly, a few miles to the north in Fresno, David St. John was growing up, but into a place which even then considered itself a city. Against that more or less brutal and degenerating ambience, St. John refined his poetry, distilled it, into a bitter elegance. And ninety miles south, in Bakersfield, where *every* variety of vine refuses, finally, to grow, Frank Bidart must have been working. Talking once about his poems and speaking in defense of their lack of imagery, their brazen love of the abstract statement, I found myself saying that such an aesthetic as his could come only from Bakersfield, that the poems' lack of imagery resembled the impoverishment of their soil. I was naive, of course; it wasn't the poetry of Bakersfield; it was only the poetry of Bidart's *Golden State.* It is the geography of the psyche that matters, not the place.

And so a place in poetry, if it is good poetry, may be a spiritual state and not a geographic one. Compare, for example, T. S. Eliot's Gloucester with Charles Olson's. Similarly, my San Joaquin Valley is like no one else's, even though the same vineyards and towns may appear there. And obviously, a reader can't learn as much, factually, about a place from a poet as he can from a decent journalist. The place of a *poem*— Levine's Detroit; James Wright's Ohio; Lowell's Boston; the various Northwests of Gary Snyder, Carolyn Kizer, Richard Hugo, William Stafford, David Wagoner; Elizabeth Bishop's Nova Scotia—these are places we can never get to, and not simply because those places, every place, are subject to change and decay, or subject to that peculiarly ominous breeze at the end of Hugo's "Death of Kapowsin Tavern": "wind black enough to blow it all away." Rather, the poet has sealed those places away into the privacies of his or her work forever, so that, as William Gass observed, Joyce's Dublin is vastly superior to the *real* one. In a way, we can never get to those places because they don't exist—not really, anyway. But once, I tried to find such a place. I walked for days through Boston, wondering, idly, how it got there, and why. I did remember one line from Stevens: "The wise man avenges by building his city in snow." But mostly it was the grave, ruefully humorous poetry of Lowell's *Life Studies* that kept ringing quietly in my mind: "Boston's hardly passionate Marlborough Street" (which is actually a phrase Lowell borrows from William James) or "the trees with Latin labels" on Boston Common (they do have labels!). But then, to mimic Lowell, I was so out of things. At eighteen, I was so Californian I thought even Detroit was an "eastern" city, and to discover Boston through Lowell was like trying to discover Italy through Ezra Pound. I felt like a tourist with one of the most idiosyncratic and beautiful guidebooks ever written. But I did feel like a tourist. *Life Studies* gave me a way to *feel* a place which was not there anymore. It could never be there at all for me, really, for Lowell's Boston childhood and harrowing adult life consist primarily of what Bachelard would call "intimate" space—Lowell's poems usually occur in closed rooms, in privacies ("endurable and perfect") given up to him by his memory. It is not surprising that Lowell traces the inception of the first poem he wrote for *Life Studies* to the obsessive, recurring image of a "blue, china door-knob." And no doubt, by the time I arrived, someone else was living at 91 Revere Street. I don't know; I was too shy to go up and knock.

Place in poetry, then, or for that matter in much fiction, is often spiritual, and yet it is important to note that this spiritual location clarifies itself and becomes valuable only through one's absence from it. Eden becomes truly valuable only after a fall, after an exile that changes it, irrecoverably, from what it once was. When I returned to California in 1970 to teach, I returned to a withered Eden, and there was, all around me, even in the cool cynicism of stoned kids on Hollywood Boulevard, enough to confirm its demise. In one of his earlier poems, Robert Hass phrased that demise in strict couplets: "My God it is a test, / This riding out the dying of the West." Fallen, I returned to my home, and, if I did not have any real vision then, I did have eyesight. I could *see* the place—that is one of the consequences of falling.

It is no wonder, then, that Donald Hall, in his essay, goes on to ask:

> What kind of place must it be? It must be a place where we felt free. It must be a place associated not with school or with conventional endeavor or with competition or with busyness. It must be a place, therefore, in which we can rehearse feelings (and a type of thinking) which belong in evolutionary terms to an earlier condition of humanity. And it is this earlier mind that we wish to stimulate, in poetry. Sometimes we speak as if we wish to return to it; actually, we want it to return to us, and to live with us forever. Therefore the place which is golden is a place where we have loafed and invited the soul, and where the ego—not yet born—has made no demands on the soul.[2]

Perhaps all of this *is* true, even the earlier mind theory, if only in the substrata of the poet's memory. And yet the particular struggle, the *agon* and play which is a poem, usually records, laments, or testifies to our distance from this "golden place." That may be why, when Robert Hass writes a later and more analytical poem, "Meditation at Lagunitas," he begins by saying: "All the new thinking is about loss. / In this it resembles all the old thinking." It is almost as if, from "Tintern Abbey" to Lowell's "Grandparents," variations on the same theme were struck up, in different music, different chords. Even if we look at one of the most Edenic and pastoral of modern poems, Dylan Thomas' "Fern Hill," the poet's final agony is apparent when he concludes: "And wake to the farm forever fled from the childless land. / Oh as I was young and easy in the mercy of his means, / Time held me green and dying / Though I sang in my chains like the sea." It is only in his absence from such a farm that he can see its paradoxical meaning, that one is always in a state of becoming and that one is always, also, becoming nothing. If we endure our Edens, Thomas says, and that is what we must do, all easy jubilation ends.

But suppose a poet does not leave his home, his place, does not fall from his Eden, but in fact seems to stay there, as James Wright seems to stay, through memory and imagination, in his nature Ohio? But how can any Eden endure the Self? Much of the painful power and beauty in Wright's work comes from his witnessing the decay of his place:

> For a proud man,
> Lost between the turnpike near Cleveland
> And the chiropractors' signs looming among dead mulberry
>   trees,
> There is no place left to go
> But home.

He has almost said, or he may as well have said: "There is no home left to go to." When we fall, we begin to know, we begin to see. To stay in that special, spiritual place is, simply, to watch its dismemberment through time. As we mature, or just grow older, we are given *sight*, or rather our memories give us a particularly subjective (hence objective and objectifying) ability to remember what once was in distinction to what is, at each moment, around us. Such imagery, such memory and witnessing, affords the Ohio of James Wright much of its power. Even the place names, "Wheeling Steel," "Benwood," "Marion," participate in a past, not a present. The same is true of Lowell's *Life Studies*, Levine's *1933*, Gerald Stern's *Lucky Life*, Snyder's *Myths & Texts*, Bishop's *Geography III*, Robert Penn Warren's *Or Else*—the possible list is endless. Even if a poet chooses not to name his place, as Stanley Kunitz chooses in his poem, "Father and Son," the remembered place, the pond, becomes a radiance.

For many, of course, my idea of the Edenic will seem difficult to accept, or it will appear archaic, or merely silly. As a concept, it aligns itself so clearly to the Bible and to Milton that it seems permanently to recall its sources and to recall orthodox conceptions of sin, guilt, death, sex, or at least the knowledge of these. But I intend the term only in its loosest, and perhaps most relevant, sense: that is, I may not believe in the myth of The Fall, but it is still possible for me to feel *fallen*. Why? Because I can see and perhaps because the myth and the feeling is explainable as Freud explains it, in *Civilization and its Discontents*:

> Originally the ego includes everything, later it detaches from itself the outside world. The ego-feeling we are aware of now is thus only a shrunken vestige of a more extensive feeling—a feeling which embraced the universe and expressed an inseparable connection of the ego with the external world. If we may suppose that this primary ego-feeling has been preserved in the minds of many people—to a greater or lesser extent—it would co-exist like a sort of counterpart with the narrower and more sharply outlined ego-feeling of maturity, and the ideational content belonging to it would be precisely the notion of limitless

extension and oneness with the universe—the same feeling as that described by my friend as "oceanic."[3]

Later elaborations of this, perhaps even Lacan's "stade du miroir" theory, attest to similar separations. In his essay on the growth of landscape painting, Rilke phrases the idea with a simpler grandeur: "For men only began to understand Nature when they no longer understood it; when they felt that it was the Other, indifferent toward men, without senses by which to apprehend us, then for the first time they stepped outside of Nature, alone, out of a lonely world."

Poetry, the poetry of the spiritual place, can remind us, then, of the Edenic, even of the "oceanic." What seems to be a curious phenomenon of nineteenth- and twentieth-century poetry in particular is that the Edenic or "oceanic" is often retrievable only through a poem with a highly *specified* place: "Tintern Abbey"; Little Gidding"; "Brooklyn Bridge"; "Patterson"; "Paumanok"; "Gloucester"; "Dover Beach"; the New Englands of Dickinson and Frost; the South of Dickey, Penn Warren, Tate, Jarrell, Ransom; Jeffers' Big Sur; Bly's Minnesota. This involvement with place, from Romantic and Modernist poets to the present, has come about in part I think because a poet wants to locate himself or herself somewhere, to be "a man (or a woman) speaking to men (or women)"; it is also a way of testifying to the demands and limitations of lyrical experience, to say: "I was the man, I suffered, I was there." The lyric wishes to be antidogmatic, nondidactic, *honest.* Williams articulated the idea this way: "It is in the wide range of the local only that the general can be trusted for its one unique quality, its universality." And "the local" is that vestige of the"oceanic" which Freud says we carry within ourselves, withered, out of childhood. And it *is there,* in the place recalled by the poet, the sacred home. It can't be otherwise, the poems seem to tell us—the holy place *is* a few miles above Tintern Abbey; or is just under a particular cedar growing in the place of a vanished New England farm town in Frost's "Directive"; or it is in the burned-out remains of Hugo's Kapowsin Tavern; or in Levine's unburned Detroit in 1952; or on a mountain top in the Cascades where Gary Snyder pauses, "between heaven and earth" before going down "to stand in lines in Seattle, looking for work." It will be there, or nowhere, the poems *deceive us* into believing. Actually, reading such poems, we discovery, excavated by another's feeling, those places in ourselves.

However, I don't intend to suggest that poets write only about such places. They don't. And there are any number of strong poets whom I cannot associate with any particularized place, such as Creeley, Strand, Ashbery, Rich, and Merwin. And yet because of the predominance of place, especially in American poetry of recent decades, it is only to be expected that a turning away from a particular, named, autobiographical poetry of place might occur, and this is what I believe is happening in the work of some of the younger poets writing now. I should say that this poetry, abstract or meditative as it might be, is not new, however—see Rilke and Stevens. And I also want to say that even when this poetry is at its most meditative, the inhabiting or recalling of a spiritual place continues, and without serious impediments. But first I think it is important to speculate, at least for my own purposes here, on what sort of shift has occurred and to ask why it has occurred. For to turn away from one's own autobiographical, personal memory of a particular place is to appear, often enough, to have accomplished a dismissal of one tradition: that of the alienated, isolated artist.

And yet most younger poets still testify precisely to this alienation and isolation, this falling from Eden. Only they have changed it. It is as if the whole tradition has become, by now, shared, held in common, a *given*—or as if the poems confer the same sort of loss upon all of us, not only upon the privately suffering poet. And yet for a while, in the late 1960s and early 1970s in this country, it seemed to me that almost every American poem was going to locate itself within a more or less definite place, was going to be spoken usually in the first person singular, and would involve, often, the same kind of testimony to the poet's isolation. The problem of that poetic stance was, unfortunately, its real power—its irresistibly attractive, usually imagistic surface. So many young poets, responding honestly to the work of Bly, Wright, Snyder, Plath, Stafford, or Merwin, tended to write poems that looked stylistically imitative, even derivative, of those and of other poets. That imitative gesture began to feel faint, inauthentic, often simply insincere or naive. And finally, as if in despair of recreating the reality of prior visions, this poetry often took on a sarcastic or sardonic attitude toward experience (some of the dark humor of James Tate and Bill Knott might be read as a visionary reaction to older poets) and toward place itself, as in Cynthia MacDonald's funny satire of Bly's Midwest, in which an otherwise sensible young woman gives up her prior life, and, following Bly's advice, moves to South Dakota and spends the rest of her years working in a service station, far from anything except a randomly passing client. But many of the poems were not informed by any satirical purpose. They were *serious* and heartfelt. Even so, too many of the poems about Ohio or Illinois really began to merely anthologize a few clichés or commonplaces about the Midwest—clichés available to anyone who can read the cartoons in *The New Yorker,* or worse luck, *The Reader's Digest.* Often, the cartoons in *The New Yorker* at least were much more imaginative than some of the poems. The vast increase in small magazines, in the sheer number of them, seems in retrospect to have had nothing to do with authenticating American places: often the poets had no interest in becoming the mythographers of the place in which they happened to be, anyway, and so Gary Snyder's advice to this effect had little sway. What did this kind of poem typically look like? I will quote only one example, a poem called "Driving East,"—I am withholding the name of the poet, however, because this is, for him, a very early poem, and because his later and more mature work seems to me very beautiful and haunting:

> *For miles,*
> *the snow is on all sides of me,*
> *waiting.*
> *I feel like*
> *a lot of empty cattle yards,*
> *my hinges swing open to the wind.*

Pretty, yes, but as a whole it is just too easy. Besides, hinges don't swing open to the wind; gates do. Too often the poet could look like a tourist dressed in some other poet's style, and style itself, as is usually the case in America, became too important. More seriously, place meant nothing very important to these poets, and nothing very spiritual, and such a poetry wasn't even "regional." The larger problem, obvious by now, was that there simply wasn't much experience or craft in poems such as "Toledo, Ohio, As Seen from the Balcony of the Holiday-Inn." What had been a truly visionary prospect in the poetry of James Wright or Philip Levine became trivialized in the more immature imitations. But I am not maligning anyone, here, for being influenced. There probably isn't any other way to learn how to write poetry.

Still, so many of the poets of the 1960s and the 1970s had no place to go—and no home worth returning to.

Again, in some unspecifiably social sense, it may be that places themselves became, throughout much of America, so homogenized that they became less and less available as spiritual locations, shabbier and sadder. A friend from Alabama once lamented to me that he had, as a young fiction writer, no South left to write about, that the topless bars and MacDonald's in Birmingham were like topless bars and Mac-Donald's everywhere. He could only imagine a South that had disappeared, and this was a literary South. But to create such an imagined place in spite of the reality around him would eventually make him participate in a merely literary regionalism. And the problem with a poem, or a story, that is strictly regional is its vulnerability (like those too numerous photographs of collapsed barns) to time. For example, it is still possible for me to admire Sandburg's "Chicago," but much of my admiration for it must be mixed with indistinct feelings of nostalgia, distrust, even embarrassment. Yes, I say, Chicago is strong, and its ugliness is a variety of the Beautiful, and yet it is impossible not to know that what Sandburg celebrates is as corny as it is destructive. The poem has matured into a period piece. With shrewder art, this is not the case. For example, old brick buildings in New York can seem charming to me, even powerfully evocative, but then I remember that they are so evocative in this very precise way because I am remembering Edward Hopper's *Early Sunday Morning,* which is not, by the way, regional at all, but great. In a way, I don't, or can't, because of Hopper, see the place at all. Thus, sometimes, the world can turn comically into, and mimic, the art we thought was *about it.* But where the title of *regionalist* is conferred, isn't there a sense, too, of the anachronistic about the region, if not the artist? The regional dissolves almost too obediently into the picturesque. So *Spoon River Anthology,* in which Masters is often brilliant, remains *regional.* It survives, but it survives, like any truly regionalist poem, like those curious museum towns in New England, like the Maine town in "Skunk Hour" which Lowell satirizes—what once was vital and real comes down to a matter of a few old buildings, kept chronically on display, and housing a boutique, a restaurant, or antique shops. In a way, the *patina* used by the regionalist resembles the renovations of the decorator: it obscures the place. And yet, I am not advising anyone to move into the extreme alternative; besides, no one, knowing what he or she cannot possibly not know about American cities today, could justifiably celebrate Chicago as Sandburg once could celebrate it. But then, poets don't necessarily celebrate Chicago or Denver or Los Angeles, they celebrate loss, they celebrate Eden—the myth of the place in the psyche.

Now it would be easy, and too convenient, to divide older and younger poets into two groups: older poets who appear to have places, and homes, and younger poets who are writing a more abstract, contemplative, unlocalized poetry. Any distinction along these lines would be sophomoric and wrong, however. There are many younger poets who identify themselves with one or more places, and who do this, who claim a place, in methods that renew the tradition of older poets. Robert Hass, Dave Smith, Carolyn Forché, Greg Pape, David St. John, and Stanley Plumly are all poets whose work displays a strong attachment to place. Yet they are never limited *by* place and often write a poem which could happen anywhere.

And yet, so many younger poets today seem to have no home worth returning to, or worth specifying in the way that Hass specifies the Bay area of California, or Gary Soto specifies the San Joaquin Valley, or Smith specifies his particular region of the South. Jon Anderson, Thomas Lux, Laura Jensen, Michael Ryan, Tess Gallagher, Daniel Halpern, Marcia Southwick, and so many others appear to have experienced a kind of orphaning by and in America. It may be that this experience, this new homelessness, is what a number of these new poets have in common when they practice the "meditational" mode—for what they tend to hold in common is, at heart, a contradiction: an intimate, *shared* isolation. This isolation is a growth of all the older isolations, but the nature of it has been somewhat changed. Instead of the private loneliness of the first person point of view, there appears to be, even when unstated, a narrator who behaves as a "we" rather than an "I." Another distinction in this work is its reliance upon increasingly abstract statement and metaphors rather than upon image only. It is interesting to witness Robert Hass, a poet of place if there ever was one, in a sort of transition from one method to another. (I should note here, that many other poets are involved in the same kind of shift, and that it is dramatically obvious in David St. John's *Hush* and *The Shore*.)For what occurs in Hass' poem, "Meditation at Lagunitas," is memory, autobiography—but also the turning away of the poet from the place he confronts and from the poet he once was. It is as if the reader bears witness to a poet seeing through his own need for a place, for location. Truth is not at Lagunitas; it is within the meditation itself. And though this was always the case, Hass stresses it through the larger, abstract claims he makes in the poem.

MEDITATION AT LAGUNITAS

> All the new thinking is about loss.
> In this it resembles all the old thinking.
> The idea, for example, that each particular erases
> the luminous clarity of a general idea. That the clown-
> faced woodpecker probing the dead sculpted trunk
> of that black birch is, by his presence,
> some tragic falling off from a first world
> of undivided light. Or the other notion that,
> because there is in this world no one thing
> to which the bramble of blackberry corresponds,
> a word is elegy to what it signifies.
> We talked about it late last night and in the voice
> of my friend, there was a thin wire of grief, a tone
> almost querulous. After a while I understood that,
> talking this way, everything dissolves: justice,
> pine, hair, woman, you *and* I. *There was a woman
> I made love to and I remember how, holding
> her small shoulders in my hands sometimes,
> I felt a violent wonder at her presence

like a thirst for salt, for my childhood river
with its island willows, silly music from the pleasure
*   boat,*
muddy places where we caught the little orange-silver
*   fish*
called pumpkinseed. *It hardly had to do with her.*
Longing, we say, because desire is full
of endless distances. I must have been the same to her.
But I remember so much, the way her hands dismantled
*   bread,*
the thing her father said that hurt her, what
she dreamed. There are moments when the body is as
*   numinous*
as words, days that are the good flesh continuing.
Such tenderness, those afternoons and evenings,
saying blackberry, blackberry, blackberry.

The focus of the poem throughout is either directly or tangentially upon the problem of language itself—it uses, its illusions. In this sense the poem's vision is only partly personal, for Hass' speculations come as much from philosophical considerations, from Lacan or Derrida, as from his own experience. In fact, I think Hass would stress, *does* stress in the poem, that thinking itself amounts to experience, to a life, just as any other thing we do—play, work, sex, talking—amounts to life.

As *art* the poem is considerably calmer, seemingly more detached and reasonable in its phrasings than much of the poetry which flourished in the late 1960s or the early 1970s. There is nothing very surreal in Hass' methods, no concern over a deepening image, and in the poem's imagistic modesty there may be even a buried admonition (if only to the poet himself) that the impulse and gesture which can willfully create a wild imagery for its own sake is perhaps not worth the trouble, is perhaps even aesthetically disingenuous or dishonest. The gain of such a calm is real: the poet is free of what Stevens called "the pressure of reality," and he is at least allowed a place for meditation. The poem resists mere autobiography through a rapt, abstract energy or impulse. Hass has no sooner introduced the woman into his poem than she is, at least until his conclusion, dismissed. For a moment she even turns into a *law:* "Longing, we say, because desire is full / of endless distances. I must have been the same to her." But Hass is so conscious of what he is doing! He is conscious enough, even, to distrust the very method of thinking which has afforded his poem, and so, at poem's end, he returns to the truth of remembered, personal experience; then, characteristically, revealingly, he generalizes such experience: "Such tenderness, those afternoons and evenings, / saying *blackberry, blackberry, blackberry.*"

And yet how traditional Hass' poem is in its use of a spiritual place! Hass' river, the river of his childhood, provides the same Eden any other poem might. It is much more modest, of course, than Wordsworth's Wye, and it appears, as Hass mentions it so casually, even minimal, a random memory, though it is not. What is a little surprising, however, is the way in which Hass suppresses the name of that river, Feather or Sacramento, from his poem. Why? It is obvious that the name of the river does not figure importantly in his purposes here, and yet the fact that it does not is, to my way of thinking, full of implications. To name a place, in memory, is to singularize the Self, to individuate the Self, and to maintain belief in the power of the place *through* its name. But the intimation of this poem as a whole suggests that the New Intimacy of Hass or of other poets now working has gone or is going beyond the need for specified locations, and that naming itself, as a first human and poetic act, is what Hass is analyzing here into a sensuous mystery. For the entire, final burden of the poem depends on its success in reminding us that speech is pleasure, and that, paradoxically, the repetition of a word actually empties that word of meaning, of association—which is Hass' earlier fear in the poem. A place, any place, therefore, could be said only to exist *after* language itself, and to be anterior to language, or created by it. Hass' poem intends, like so many poems since the Romantics, to create the same spiritual place, but Hass is more aware of his traditions, of exactly what he is doing, and it is this which allows him to suggest that we are baptized, not into a location, not into any body of water, but into names, into a river of names. "A word is elegy to what it signifies" because the word is a reality as much as its referent. The new thinking about loss resembles the old thinking about loss exactly through the use of language, through poetry. The more we try to return to the Edenic place, the more our methods, our words, lock us out and turn the pain of our collective separation and exile into poetry. This is not exactly a victory, the poem reminds us, because you can't make love to a poem, and, in "Meditation at Lagunitas," it is sex that recalls Eden more honestly, more innocently and inarticulately, than art does.

And ultimately, a conscious attending to a collective loss is a little different from an attention to a private or confessional loss, even though the same sympathies may occur, finally, as a product of the poem. This poetry, as Stanley Plumly so rightly observed, is often haunted by an Idea more than an Image, a Mind more than a Life. There is a steadiness of control about it, and a poet like Jon Anderson is fond of collapsing private griefs and the singularity and isolation of the poet by stressing, in his own rather austere loneliness and alienation ("My grief is that I bear no grief / And so I bear myself"), how deeply such loss is intimately shared by others: "My friends and I have all come to the same things." In another poem, while passing houses at night, he says: "Each had a father. / He was telling a story so hopeless, / So starless, we all belonged." Below the "I" in Anderson's work there is often the abstract argument of a "we"—friends and loved ones. This "we" never lets us forget our participation in the poem, our inclusion by *it*.[4]

These distinctions can be clarified or thrown into higher relief more or less simply, I think. When Robert Lowell writes, in "Memories of West Street and Lepke":

> *Only teaching on Tuesdays, book-worming*
> *in pajamas fresh from the washer each morning,*
> *I hog a whole house on Boston's*
> *"hardly passionate Marlborough Street,"*

he is intimating, through the naming of a place a private, autobiographical experience. Its virtues are very much like those of Realism in fiction. He is saying, like Huck Finn, *this is what happened to me*. His narration will be, therefore, modest, insular, unpretentious, without a sermon for the reader. The reader can respond to the honestly or sincerity of that first-person pronoun, that "I." If a poet says, on the other hand, "Much that is beautiful must be discarded / So that we may resemble / A taller impression of ourselves," our whole experience of the poem will be dramatically different, and we will be much more aware that the poet (John Ashbery), in his choice of method, is both criticizing the alternative and more personal mode at the same time he is admonishing his audience, through his collaborative theme, against the choice, suicide, which the character in his poem has made. In a larger, historical sense, I am aware that both of these methods, in varying degrees of popularity and use, have always been at large in poetry. And of course as *methods* both are very much in use now, and neither one is superior, as an aesthetic choice, to the other. But they are different. Why have so many younger poets now working adopted the latter, the second method? It is often suggested that the influence of Ashbery has had something central to do with this, but I have my doubts that this is entirely true. I think that all of us, finally, live and have to live within a much larger and more various culture than the culture of poetry, and it is impossible for me to forget that most younger poets came of age in the late 1960s and the early 1970s, a time of real trouble in America. What I most remember, and what seems to me most valuable, even though it is now a subject of easy satire, is the sense of shared convictions and tenderness among my generation at that time. There was, for a while, a feeling of community, however frail or perishable, which mattered, and which is not apparent in the *chic* lame, New Left political rhetoric of the time—a frustrated rhetoric. So often what one felt as shared or communal could not quite be spoken or brought into speech, much less into poetry. Poets of an older generation, responding to that era and those pressures, wrote mostly out of singular agonies. If they were excessive at times in their use and dependence upon hyperbole and imagery, I think that the sheer ugliness of U.S. foreign policy might have had as much to do with that as the influence of Latin American translations. Often the insistence, in their work, on the beauty of the wild or surreal was a reflex of their anger. In retrospect, I think that what the poets of my generation experienced was not only a deep suspicion of any easy political rhetoric, but a suspicion of what began to seem to be poetical rhetoric as well, of a mannered imagistic poem which effectively kept the poet away from his or her experience. And if that generation felt an enormous disillusionment with the society itself, it felt, also and finally, an equally real disappointment with itself and with its inability to do the impossible task which it had promised itself to do, to reconstruct an Edenic place out of America. I have a clear memory of walking on a cold, winter day through the Haight-Ashbury district in 1970—a place that looked as if it was being evacuated before an approaching army. But there was no army coming. No one, anymore, was coming. There were only young men in pairs who would pass by on each side of me, asking if I wanted to buy acid or speed. The place looked, as someone said, like "a teen-age slum." And the subsequent phenomenon of hip boutiques in suburban shopping centers was not a solution to any problem; it was merely a betrayal of values, and a continuance (how could it be otherwise?) of capitalist culture. When Vietnam ended, my generation appeared, oddly enough, to be so much a part of the culture it had resisted. It was like America, or it was America. Without an enemy, it could not continue.

If the "we" of the younger poets is a plural pronoun, it is also obsessed with loss, but I think it is a loss more profound than the loss of political goals or partisan feelings. Part of what got lost is the possibility of wholly believing in the grand fiction of Romantic alienation and individuation. And yet the new poetry, the "meditative" poetry, appears to be an outgrowth of the more isolated imagistic thinking, and its subject, like that of its parents, is precisely that same testimony to alienation and loss. But it is a collective loss more than a private one. It would be comforting to think that even *collective*, as used here, might have some vestigial political significance, but the loss usually attested to has little to do with political solutions. In fact, the poems seem intensely wary of any political diction, seem to avoid it with great skill, for to locate one's loss in political terms is to locate it within time. But the loss and fall from the Edenic place is final, mythic, a thing that cannot be changed. To talk of it, to talk of some collective loss, means, quite possibly, to deflect one's attention from the subject which provokes the poem. In Marvin Bell's poem, "Stars Which See, Stars Which Do Not See" the *ut pictura poesis* of *La Grande Jatte* is both oblique and searingly personal.

> They sat by the water. The fine women
> had large breasts, tightly checked.
> At each point, at every moment,
> they seemed happy by the water.
> The women wore hats like umbrellas
> or carried umbrellas shaped like hats.
> The men wore no hats and the water,
> which wore no hats, had that well-known
> mirror finish which tempts sailors.
> Although the men and women seemed at rest
> they were looking toward the river
> and some way out into it but not beyond.
> The scene was one of hearts and flowers
> though this may be unfair. Nevertheless,
> it was probable that the Seine had hurt them,
> that they were "taken back" by its beauty
> to where a slight breeze broke the mirror
> and then its promise, but never the water.

Deflection? The name of a river. What matters is that the poem withholds its private sufferer, its poet, so that the place can be seen, and the common misery of the inhabitants can be seen: "it was probable that the Seine had hurt them," because the place is the location of their loss. The figures in the painting, the withheld figures they stand for, cannot quite understand the nature of their loss, and so blame it on the Seine, deflect what they can no longer articulate onto the river, the place itself which changes and does not change, but does not undergo the final change of the observers, those whose promise is broken by nothing outside themselves as they are reminded of it by something as ordinary as a "slight breeze."

What is it, then, that one loses? That everyone loses? Where I grew up, the specific place meant everything. As a child in California, I still thought of myself, almost, as living in the Bear Flag Republic, not in the United States. When I woke, the Sierras, I knew, were on my right; the Pacific was a two hour drive to my left, and everything between belonged to me, *was* me. I was astonishingly sheltered. It was only gradually that I learned the *ways* in which place meant everything, learned that it meant 200 acres of aging peach trees which we had to prop up, every summer, with sticks to keep the limbs from cracking under the weight of slowly ripening fruit. It meant a three-room schoolhouse with thirty students, and meant, also, the pig-headed, oppressive Catholic church which, as far as I could determine, wanted me to feel guilty for having been born at all. And it meant the gradual self-effacement and aging of my parents. Even in high school when I began to write, even when I hated the place most, and when I rejoiced when I read that Rimbaud (at fourteen!) called his home town of Charlesville a "shit-hole"—even when the desire to get away was strongest, I was dimly aware that my adolescent hatred of the place was transforming it, was slowly nurturing an Eden from which I was already exiling myself. After I had left for good, all I really needed to do was to describe the place exactly as it had been. That I could not do, for that was impossible. And that is where poetry might begin.

NOTES

This essay was first delivered as a lecture at the Aspen Writers' Conference in July 1980, Aspen, Colorado.

1. Hall, Donald, "The Poet's Place," in *Goatfoot Milktongue Twinbird,* pp. 205–7.
2. Hall, p. 207.
3. Freud, Sigmund, *Civilization and Its Discontents,* p. 15.
4. I notice that Ira Sadoff, in his article on meditative poetry (*APR,* September/October, 1980) uses the same examples of Hass and Anderson for his argument. I think it is curiously substantiating that both of us, two poets working unbeknownst to each other, should come up with the same examples.

REFERENCES

Freud, Sigmund. *Civilization and Its Discontents.* New York: W. W. Norton & Co., 1962.
Hall, Donald. *Goatfoot Milktongue Twinbird.* Ann Arbor: University of Michigan Press, 1978.

PART
SIX

SPECULATIONS

OTHERHOW

RACHEL BLAU DuPLESSIS

POETRY AND GENDER: some ideas

Possession of many of the elements that make poetry into poetry somehow depends on positioning women? Poetry gendered in a different way than fiction is? Sometimes it is possible to think so.[1] Love, Beauty, Nature, Seasonal Change, Beauty Raked by Time, Mediating Vision or Muse, the pastoral, the carpe diem motif, the satire—all these prime themes and genres from the history of poetry seem to have swirls of gender ideas and gender narrative blended like the marblized end papers of old books. It's so beautiful, so oily with color, who could want to pick it apart?

Knowing when to begin and end is knowing what to say between
poems being part

of the poem.

Helping them write a report, they need

silvery sky dusk lilac stars stars starry
bibelots rosy as a local coral
flouncing the poem is that the answer?

small folding arrangements?

Further, the centrality of the lyric voice (few characters in a poem little dialogue) means that one point of view is privileged. And the speaking subject is most often male.

> *'my female side' proudly*
> *'my anima'*
>
> *Overexposed post*
> *card of the 50's sans one bitty cloud to darken*
> *azure at the pectoral monument.*
> *By implication or odd window, houses'*

> *estranged effect*
> *boasting seedy pleasure withered or perspicacity*
> *deranged; what circle, what perimeter*
> *to draw around such interlinear spannings.*
> *While in a bourgeois novel, truth lies in between.*
> *The "bourgeois poem"?*

Now in the modern period, that lyric voice is ruptured, and poems can feature a controlled social array, as do novels. Even the masculine subject can be refused (interestingly, curiously, awkwardly by a male poet, as by fiat or assertion of Tiresias in Eliot's notes to *The Waste Land*). And women writers speaking in a female, or a neutral-yet-gendered voice are not necessarily confessional of their lives, though still they may be "confessing" their throwing themselves wildly against, careening into conventions of representation. Into the terrible inadmissable congruence of poetry and gender. So all in all, even with exceptions, the institution of gendered poetry and the male-gendered poetic voice are embedded in the history of poetry.

As a woman writing, my language space, my cultural space is active with a concatenation of constructs—prior poems, prior poetics—a lot of which implicate women. But not often as speaker. As ideal. As sought. As a mediator towards others' speech.

An "avant-garde" cannot discount this past, not only because it exists in poems, but because it exists in words.

A woman, while always a real, if muted or compromised, or bold and unheard, or admired but forgotten (etc.), speaker in her own work is most often a cultural artifact in the traditions of meaning on which she draws.

LANGUAGE AND GENDER

Writer? Becoming one on whom language plays and in whom language plays poetic convention, etymology, terrible puns, vernacular turns, ugly gobbets, professional jargon, mindless babble, baby syllables, dialect renderings, nursery rhymes, old pop music, precious adjectives, connectives, newspaper information, disinformation, conjunctions, pronouns playing with the social space evoked ("he" "she" "it" "we" "they"), words like *as* or *with*

"by" whom, beside whom and made by whom it may course or occur, declaring the destruction of uncontested rhetoric (but never the destruction of rhetoric).

Writer? A position to activate elements of language to join so that its activities enjoin the reader, you, (to hear a sound to know a space that "never" was before).

> *Comb the hairy*
> *language a vernac*
> *vert knack of saying what*
> *no one esp.*

desires
hearing—how much it's the same.

But always prior inscriptions. Incessant marking. A writing whose condition is over writing. Want "in fact" a description of our language situation? Neither language use nor language acquisition are gender neutral, but are "'imbued with our sex-inflected cultural values.'"[2] Talking. Eliding. Agreeing. Questioning. Completing. Insisting. Leaving no space for others to speak. Banality. Pause, "Utterance . . . is constructed between [at least] two socially organized persons" even in the absence of an actual addressee. Thus social status, hierarchical status, gender status all matter: "there is no such thing as an abstract addressee, a man unto himself, so to speak."[3]

Foregrounded, this statement suggests the multifarious gender allusions or gender situations that can be called up just by language and its shifting, its tones, the social resonances of idiom, of the colloquial. The dialogic creation of meaning, the subtle capacities for cueing, status, power, and the interconnection of social and verbal realms are facts that have barely been self-consciously accounted for in the understanding of poetry.

Still one could refind
a taste for this beauty.
Spillways of leaping
abyss to azure
extend thin ness ness ness
that rusts rustle rond soft spectacle.

If language is "overpopulated with the intentions of others," it is teeming with, inter alia, gender ideas.[4] I mean, I'm not talking of the signifier/signified, but of palimpsests of (saturations of) signifying. "Each word *tastes* of the context and contexts in which it has lived its socially charged life."[5] If each word has lived a socially charged life, each word has a "narrative" or two which it brings with it. What are the tactics which can either reaffirm the narrative(s) the word is telling or can try to break into it by distorting or deforming, opening the storied words?

Thinking about language in my poetry, I imagine a line below which is inarticulate speech, aphasia, stammer and above which is at least moderate, habitual fluency, certainly grammaticalness, and the potential for apt, witty images, perceptive, telling and therefore guaranteed "poetic." That is, readable (reasonable) within intentions we assume. Since "Medusa" (finished in 1979) and again since "Crowbar" (finished 1983) my poetry wanders, vagrant, seeking to cross and recross that line: mistaking singular for plural, proposing stressed, exposed moments of genuine ungrammaticalness, neologisms, non-standard dialect, and non-normative forms. I struggle to break into the sentences that of course I am capable of writing smoothly. I want to distance. To rupture. Why? In part because of the gender contexts in which these words have lived, of which they taste.

Otherhow

> *Shadowy the sombre emission of light tawnies.*
> *I read the paper naked*
> *government atop me*
> *sweet pea to myself.*
>
> *A sense of missing the*
> *important, redefining the minor the nothing the corner*
> *turned and missed it*
>
> *something mmmm say small*
> *that's not "the same."*

RUPTURE

To refuse the question as asked. To break through the languages of both question and answer. To activate all the elements of normal telling beyond normal telling.

Write the unwritten, paint the undepicted?

Must make a critical poetry, an analytic lyric, not a poetry that "decorates dominant culture" (to cite Michael Palmer) but one which questions the discourses. This situation makes of representation a site of struggle.

RECURRENT TERMS

delegitimate
deconstruct
decenter
destroy
dismantle
destabilize
displace
deform

explode

RUPTURING NARRATIVE SEQUENCE

An especially convincing part of the early feminist aesthetic of sincerity, authenticity, uncovering unmediated truth is the idea that many stories culturally produced and maintained did not include female(s)' experiences. The "images" projected on my screen were not constructed by me but only with a particular version of me in mind. I went to those movies and—look—there "I" was! All stories interpret experience, construct what we call experience. As a woman writing, I had to seize some power over story as a social institution. Seize the mask. Not carpe diem, the dominant injunction to me as delightful object in one poetic romance, but carpe personam, the female injunction to myself as critical subject in a politics of narrative. Seize the mask, the fictive, examine the instruments whereby writing "are" fabricated.

An intense play between subject and object(ified) is created in the invention of stories for the semisilenced, or unheard female, or other marginal characters in traditional tales (myths). This prevalent revisionary stance of female writers, happily now fore-grounded by feminist criticism, is incited when a writer receives, as Woolf said, "in imagination the pressure of dumbness, the accumulation of unrecorded life."[6] The silent faces of the others, the extras in the story, the ones to whom "it" is done, those who did not "get there" but always were there, without their tales of causes and effects, reasons and fates leave the impress of absence, gap, or void. This hoarse whispering silence is especially hard to bear and especially generative.

Curiously the simple idea of writing the woman's voice or "side" into a well-known tale (telling the same story from another side) creates an internal dynamic of critique out of simple reversal or an apparently contained point of view experiment. (I found this in writing "Eurydice" and "Medusa" in the 1970s.) It is not enough to tell another story, for such a story of the unreckoned is more than just one *more* tale; reckoned in, it wrecks the "in." Intellectual and political assumptions are ruptured, narrative sequence, causality, resolution, and possibly the meanings of words or apt language themselves are all brought into question.

RUPTURING ICONIZATION—text as object

Because of the way canonical texts are culturally used especially by literary criticism, as objects, as if final or fixed, with no sense of historical movement (no sense of the way texts are continually reused and transformed, remade in a social conjuncture with readers), I wanted to invent works that would protest or resist this process, not protect it.

(No more poems, no more lyrics. Do I find I cannot sustain the lyric; it is no longer. Propose somehow a work, the work, a work, the work, a work otherhow of enor-mous dailiness and crossing. All the 'tickets' and the writing. A work of entering into the social force of language, the daily work done everywhere with language, the little flyer fallen to the ground, the corner of a comic, a murder, burning cars, the pouring of realization like a squall green amber squall rain; kiss Schwitters and begin)

While modernism has gone far in eroding linear telos and syntactic direction, it still iconizes texts by proposing them as sacred objects, poets as priests, their status sub-lime. Certainly this position occurs because of political desperation—which it is only sensible to feel, but it replicates the power relations that we know, substituting "poet" for "legislator" but a secret one, an "unacknowledged" one, a hermetic one. A party (even the Poundian self-justified party of one) out of power, but waiting in the wings.

(Iconization seemed to be considerably abetted by text as one way street—ending in one place, repressing its drafts or choices, discounting in the poem events not-this-poem. The invitation to read once in one direction, start to finish, top to bottom, beginning to end seemed to symbolize iconization.

One way to disturb the "one way street" of the poem is to make a text run, like a musical piece, da capo al fine in a recursive structure that, by virtue of repeating the middle, drew attention to on-goingness, and impeded closure.

A second way, in a homage to Emily Dickinson, could draw upon her rhetorical strategy of indicating variants, to keep the poem open, perhaps; to indicate the enormous changes of meaning, even in a narrow compass, that could be achieved by a minute (in some cases) alteration of a word. I'd like to think that the variant words, lines, and more rarely, stanzas which she invented constituted her protest against the iconization of a text, against ending as statement, climax, moral thought. Against the stasis of poetry.

In "Crowbar," the whole argument comes to a poised end in the doubling of two words: *hungry* and *angry* which grasp towards the odd *-ngry* ending they hold in common. *Hungry* meant complicit with the psychic cultural construction of beautiful, seductive, and seduced women; *angry* meant critical of the same. The simultaneous overvoicing of the penultimate word in a very long poem means that ambivalence marks the end as it had the beginning. Explanation generates its own self-questioning.

Most recently, in a twenty-eight-section work called "Writing," I put words on the margin, try to break into the lyric center with many simultaneous writings occupying the same page space. I overwrite, or interleave lines of writing, sometimes in my own handwriting, not trying to obliterate, or to neutralize but to—to what? To erode some attitude toward reading and writing. I wanted simultaneous presence without authority. Wanted to make meanings that undid hierarchies of decidability. I wanted no right/correct sequences of feeling emblematic in right/correct sequences of reading. The desire to create something that is not a complete argument, or a poem with a climax, but where there are ends and beginnings all over the work. A working work.)

I was also rejecting that singular voice which "controls tone." The lyric voice. Controls tone? It hears the itch of, is in the center of languages. Voices are everywhere—the bureaucratic, the banal, the heightened, the friendly, the deadpan, the dreamy. Saturated with the multivocal, who can think of controlling tone? It is enough to collect them in one spot and call that spot a poem.

RUPTURING POETRY

Not incidentally, I am tired of "poetry"—that ready-made, that bike wheel mounted upside down thinking it is a real bike, forgetting it was undone by Duchamp. Tired of Hollywood poetry, like Hollywood cinema, endless discursive mimetic narration which only has different people in starring roles. And judging from their pictures in *APR*, the stars are pretty similar too.

There must be some way of reaching so deep into assumptions of and about poetry that this changes.

Write poetries. Write writings, write readings, write drafts. Write several selves to dissolve the bounded idea of the self

who is "I" who is "you"
who is "he" is "she"

fleeting shifts of position, social charges implying a
millenia of practice. To disturb the practice

by "itness" a floating referent, a bounding along the
multiplex borders of marginality. An avoidance of
transcendence everywhere, including in the idea of the artist—
—no genius. no god. no prophet. no priest.

RUPTURING THE HISTORY OF POETRY by *The "History of Poetry"*

To read something new, something different from the production of the figures of women and men that reproduce gender relations, I felt I had to write something different. What then could be more (or less) different than an/other version of poems that have already been produced, the "same" poems but respoken, written from the position of marginality. My desire has led me to construct counter poems—counterfactual poems—postulating that there are many women poets throughout history (some real, some imagined) who have written poems uncannily positioned as having views aslant of dominant views of themselves in whatever era is being reentered.

My aim is to refabricate—revamp, you might say—Western lyric tradition. So I call what I'm doing *The "History of Poetry."* This is because the very idea of a history of poetry is a fictional sequence formed by choices, exclusions, interests, silences—a whole and contingent politics of discourse. We are schooled to see the history of poetry as a museum of discrete, highlighted intact sequential objects; we may as well see them as an imperially assembled and classified but random set of fragments. Surrounded by the unwritten.

Within *The "History of Poetry"* the tactic of citation implies deep, wounding and even malicious dialogue with already-written poems. Instead of invention, at that point, there is (in Craig Owens' term) "confiscation" of the already done.[7] In writing, the supposed female writer uses that precise set of words that signals an intersection between her poem and very well-known texts. By putting known phrases from "great poems" (i.e., already written, disseminated, and absorbed poems) into a structure speaking differently, series of reverberating questions are set in motion that begin to dissolve or erode a former world view; or one has evoked in all the oscillating bliss, two opposite and alternative world views simultaneously. So at all times the critique and distancing are filled with yearning and complicity.

At the center of the poem "Crowbar" occur these lines about a gesture made by another woman poet, Karin Lessing, with whom I visited the Fontaine de Vaucluse, site famous for Petrarch and Laura.

> 'Tis poem
> that around
> its words
>
> it's Words.

> The silver ring she threw away
> ringed by the fountain's silver ring.

The whole *"History of Poetry"* could be seen like the gesture of a woman throwing a ring into the famous rock crevasse/fountain by which she is completely surrounded. Is it homage or marriage? that is, connection of the deepest kind. Or is it divorce, stripping oneself of any affiliation to the fountain image of woman. All our words are ringed by Words, all our rings are encircled by another powerful, fecund circle by whose flux and outpourings we are at times seduced. The doubled position of being outside and inside, critical and complicit marks the sequence.

FEMINIST POETICS, MODERNISM, THE AVANT-GARDE

The poetics this discusses of course draws on both modernism and the avant-garde. Both are powerful, richly developed practices, and consequently both may overshadow what I am saying, cause it to pale, turn, return invisible. I mean "Aren't you just talking about modernist practice?" "Aren't you just talking about the avant-garde?" "Haven't 'we' done this?"

Modernism is associated with an attempt to take various permutations of "new women" and return them, assimilate them to the classic western idea of woman as Other (angel or monster, Lady or Fresca). Otherness is a static, dichotomized, monolithic view of women. This view is necessitated by, interdependent upon the religious/spiritual transcendence also typical of modernist practice, its antisecular resolutions, even in texts midden-filled with the unsorted detritus of the dig into our culture. The eyes in the tent for Pound, the Lady in "Ash Wednesday," the Beautiful Thing in *Paterson*. And a female modernist like H. D., who of necessity has struggled with the idea of Woman? She projects the icon out from herself (liking being the icon); she plays fruitfully with the matrisexual coincidence of being the goddess and loving the goddess. She interests because in making a place for herself, she has to restudy and cut athwart the position she is, grossly, assigned in poetry.

Because of the suspicion of the center in avant-garde practice, the desire to "displace the distinction between margin and center," because of the invention of a cultural practice that "would allow us constructively to question privileged explanations even as explanations are generated," drawing on avant-garde practice seems more fruitful for me-the-woman.[8] Its idea of power and language seem more interesting: the resolute lack of synthesis, the nonorganic poetics, the secular lens.[9] But there are questions which the avant-garde must answer. (1) Does it secretly lovingly to itself hold the idea of poet as priest, poem as icon, poet as unacknowledged legislator? Then turn yr. back on it. Or, not to tell you what to do, My back. (2) Is its idea of language social; or does it claim, by language practices, to avoid (transcend), arc out of the limits posed by the social to its writing practices. Dialogic reading means dialogic writing. (3) Where is/are its women: where in the poems, serving what function? where in its social matrices, with what functions? where in its ideologies? How does it create itself by positioning its women and its women writers?

For all these questions, there are many emblematic moments. Try here the effective double sign: not only Pound cutting Eliot's *Waste Land,* but Eliot cutting Djuna Barnes' *Nightwood.*[10]

WHAT WRITES?

pigs as fingers, toes
hat tassel a "powder puff" tickle
tummy
doh doh doh doh

as transformation d-g d-g d-g,
long cadences ending maybe in yougurt.

pulling upon those wide winging blank labia
dat? dat?

Wandering stars and little mercies, space
so empty, notched each moment.

Tufted white nut rising who or which is
"I" is "yo" the parade feather tit
mouse, did she see her first real bird?

Made from hearing the deep insides of language, language inside the
language; made from pick-scabbing the odd natural wounds of language
outside, unspecial dump of language everywhere here.

"Paradoxically the only way to position oneself outside of
that hegemonic discourse is to displace oneself within it—to
refuse the question as formulated, or to answer deviously

(though in its words), even to quote (but against the
grain)."[11]
my father said my mother never had any talent
how to acknowledge altierity the marginality and speak from
its
historically, personally wounding presence without
so that she never did anything; implied, they had discussed
it
come to the conclusion, some people just have it some don't.
how to acknowledge anonymous (ourselves) but compel the
structures and tones, the social ocean of language to babble
burble, to speak
real talent, he said, would have found a way, this
conversation does not go on too long, shifts to "blacks"
of course.
The sung-half song.

If poems are posies what is this?
To whom?
And who am I, then, if it matters?

I am a GEN $\left\{ \begin{array}{l} \text{der} \\ \text{re} \end{array} \right.$ made by the writing; I am a GEN $\left\{ \begin{array}{l} \text{re} \\ \text{der} \end{array} \right.$ read in the writing.

Jan. 1985/June 1985/Aug. 1985
A note on the fabrication of
this piece: some was given at a
panel, New Langton Arts; some, the
bulk, as a talk at St. Mark's; it was
intended to speak about my own work in
"poetry" and hence the self-regard of
a few sections.

A poetics gives permission to
continue.

NOTES

1. Nancy Vickers, "Diana Described: Scattered Women and Scattered Rhyme" in *Writing and Sexual Difference*. ed. Elizabeth Abel. (Chicago: University of Chicago Press, 1982).

2. Annette Kolodny (citing Nelly Furman), "Dancing Through the Minefield: Some Observations on the Theory, Practice, and Politics of a Feminist Literary Criticism," in *The New Feminist Criticism: Essays on Women, Literature and Theory*. ed. Elaine Showalter. (New York: Pantheon Books, 1985).

3. Valentin Volosinov/ M. Bakhtin, *Marxism and the Philosophy of Language* (1930; rpt. New York Seminar Press, 1973), p. 85.

4. Mikhail Bakhtin, *The Dialogic Imagination* (Austin: University of Texas Press, 1981), p. 294.

5. Bakhtin, *Dialogic Imagination*, p. 293.

6. Virginia Woolf, *A Room of One's Own* (1929; rpt. New York: Harcourt, Brace and World, 1957), p. 93.

7. Craig Owens, "The Allegorical Impulse: Toward a Theory of Postmodernism," *October* 12 (Spring 1980):69.

8. Gayatri Spivak, "Explanation and Culture: Marginalia," *Humanities in Society* 2, no. 3 (Summer 1979):206.

9. Ideas from Adorno in Peter Burger, *Theory of the Avant-Garde* (Minneapolis: University of Minnesota Press, 1984), pp. 79–82.

10. Jane Marcus, unpublished monograph, "Laughing at Leviticus: *Nightwood* as Women's Circus Epic."

11. Teresa de Lauretis, *Alice Doesn't: Feminism, Semiotics, Cinema* (Bloomington: Indiana University Press, 1984), p. 7.

NON-EUCLIDEAN NARRATIVE COMBUSTION
(OR, WHAT THE SUBTITLES CAN'T SAY)

JOAN RETALLACK

Miss Phyllis Newcombe. On September 20, 1938, Miss
Newcombe, 22, combusted before a roomful of people
while waltzing in a dance hall in Chelmsford, England.
Blue flames erupted from her body and in a matter of
minutes she was reduced to a small pile of ash.[1]

1

The narrative momentum of nineteenth-
century novels, Hegelian dialectic, and empire-expanding locomotives seems, at least
in some intellectual landscapes, to have chugged around the bend into an absorbingly
unfocused vanishing point and fallen off the edge of an earth too mean or slippery or
sad for the ontological magnaminity of great story lines. To tell "well-made" stories
of any kind may be considered in some circles disturbingly naïve—as though subject
and object, signifier and signified, the familiar geography of beginnings, middles, and
ends had not been torn apart in the grammar of an aging and lethal century. The self-
conscious disorientation which many of us feel, and which is reflected in the odd
angles of our narrative forms, is perhaps the necessary curse of a culture telescoping
back on itself in amazement and horror. In the mushroom cloud, the concentration
camp, the terrorist's unwavering, small smile we confront the imperiled afterimage of
6,000 years of civilization—cannot erase it from our retinas, must stumble to the
dissonances of lost-waltz time half-blinded by it, our global innocence irrecoverable,
like Alice's in the more coherent afterimage of Looking Glass world.

There can be no more structuralist fantasies of undiscovered human possibility—
lost tribes in lost jungles on lost continents where the human spirit can be cleansed
and renewed. We are now in our "new worlds" as morally claustrophobic as Europe has
been since it lost its empires. This is the century in which our legacy of Enlightenment
optimism collided head-on with high-tech savagery, leaving us an archive of brilliantly
perverse fragments—the modernist canon, with its incalculable surprise . . . humor
. . . disappointment. History one way or another always manages to reduce things to
shards, usually for future generations to exhume and admire. It has not always happened so quickly. We can imagine the nineteenth-century train pulling into a station
somewhere near turn-of-the-century Vienna. One minute there is waltzing; the next
there is ash. Not peculiar, then, that the forms of our distinctly twentieth-century
narrative have affirmed the condition of fragmentation—Bohr's particle/wave discon-

tinuity, Heisenberg's uncertainty, Gödel's incompleteness . . . Beckett's breakdown in syntactic momentum, inviting the ruin in . . . Stein's gratuitous dislocation and repetition . . . the cultural and rhythmic dislocations of *The Waste Land* . . . Joyce's exploded semantics . . . Pound's collage . . . Woolf's dissolving frame . . . the indeterminacy of the Dadaists . . . the syntactic disjunctions of the Russian Futurists and our contemporary language poets . . . even the dissociated and local contingency of *The New Yorker* "slice of life."

Miss Newcombe's poignant moment of spontaneous combustion—no doubt the flash point in a too tidy life—will probably not earn her a place alongside Brünhilde or St. Joan, much less the martyrs of the triangle Shirtwaist Factory, Dresden, Hitler's crematoria, Hiroshima. The gratuitous circumstances of her immolation do not belong in our great narratives of cause and effect or ambition gone wrong. She has simply become, quite literally, somebody's old flame—explosively bland and reductive as any cliché or discredited metaphysical tale. The strain on the narrative digestive system to assimilate all our less than rational disarray—*Götterdämmerung* . . . world wars . . . Chelmsford . . . Beirut—has once again (it seems to happen every other era) taken its toll, and Miss Newcombe is in a way the deconstructionist sweetheart or decanonized saint. Her existence is not only gratuitous but entirely textual, glimpsed momentarily in the drugstore tabloid or questionable tract on "Some Curious Medical Anomalies." What is refreshing is that she is no more an embarrassment to the sophisticated intellect of the deconstructionist than is the high-minded systemist of metaphysical and moral philosophy/poetry/fiction. Why not propose her as patron saint of all wayward (violently humorous[2]) genres—a proper martyrdom at last; since in our fitfully grave culture, relying heavily on logics of justification, as certain non-Euclidean playfulness (in which no one cares about connecting the famous "two points") is often mistaken as trivial. If St. Jude, patron of lost causes in another denomination, could cure a thirty-year case of hiccups, no telling what Miss Newcombe's accomplishments might be.

2

Meanwhile, a less mindfully dubious genre, the textbook of composition, doggedly seeks to promote writing as the thoroughly wholesome Euclidean exercise it never was,[3] thrives on distinctions between subject and object; fact and inference; narrative and exposition; responsible and reckless assertions (into which categories does poor Miss Newcombe sift?); sound logic and the down-home world of the informal fallacy (*how many informal fallacies have you located in this sentence so far?*). It cannot treat the vagrant tangents of memories, dreams, licit and illicit desires which give words their odd force, without exploding its own snug genre or dangerously expanding the minds of the young while derailing the authors' tenure. So the indices are fallow with things unmentionable about what in writing is presupposed or left out—by design or psychic slip—and the vast spectrum of things uncontainable (Miss Newcombe again?) in the belated artifice of language.

Yet it is these unruly and highly combustible subtexts which make stories so vital to our humanity that children grow up strange without them and old people die when they feel they have no more to tell. If it weren't for early doses of nursery rhymes and fairy tales, fanning pyrotechnical and maniacal flames in impressionable minds, there'd be no one to write stories strange as life, much less poetry. Miss Newcombe would dance herself to ash in some other logically impossible world.

All this doesn't have much to do with Truth by any simple definition. It's easy (to a point) to live by the epistolary romance of Héloise and Abelard, forgetting how he became a late castrato in the violent revenge of her prim relations. As easy to think of Troy as the romantic scene of ingenious entry and heroism evoked in brand names for lovers' apparatus, overlooking the unfortunate association with Pyrrhic victories. Every family lives by lore as full of potent half-digested symbols, lies, and omissions as any sacred text. And there is the unconsciously planned amnesia of nostalgia and sentimentality, much like the planned communities to which many of us hope to repair in our declining years—worlds of infinite deprivation disguised as tidy fortresses against the disarray of death. Not without pockets of beauty, of course—flowering shrubs, duck ponds, autumnal hues—yet small in courage and intent. These "Wood Havens" and "Leisure Worlds" bring certain kinds of poetry to mind. Oh, that fearful tidiness! Blake might better have exclaimed, though symmetry can be bad enough. A question of many we might assay is how a poetry big enough to violate its own boundaries in the narration of our humanity; that is, big and wild enough to ignite and sustain life (requiring a fractal poetics) can be possible.

3

to rediscover in this history . . . the symbolic debt of
which his neurosis is the notice of nonpayment
—Jacques Lacan

Suppose we think of this life as a largely untranslatable foreign film and our glut of printed words the fanciful subtitles with which we reel through it. The film could be called *The Revenge of the Real,* in honor of Lacan, who warned that if we don't watch our psychic hygiene we can become the ill-conceived metaphors of our own making—Rat Man, Wolf Man, Spa Lady, Homecoming Queen, old flame . . . *À la* Godard, the screen might flash intermittent full-frame messages like "The word is redundant to what it symbolizes," "The Messiah is more than just fashionably late." Or, in another version—between scenes of tenderness, squalor, and classical ruin—we might read, "Let vs turne ageyne thys narracyon to thoes thynges the whyche we have lefte oute." Luxuriant and jerky pan shots of cities and jungles, native dancers, domestic quarrels, slow-mo sweethearts choreographing the benefits of incarnation are accompanied by a dubbed narrative drone full of morally piqued neutrality. The running recitation is of vanishing species, rising sea levels, the latest thing in plagues; holocausts accomplished and foreseen; medical, technological, and spiritual triumphs; new geometries of chaos.

Whatever images flash across the screen—Orange Bowl floats, wading Louisiana herons, alluring sea cows, prodigious lungfish, wailing children in landscapes of terror and desolation, dog-eared family snapshots, snapshots of family dogs, *Incendiis Cor-*

poris Humani Spontaneis—we are glued to the subtitles, transfixed by the voice-over, wanting them to make sense of what we're seeing, to translate this seductive confusion into a language that allows us to comfort, reassure, love, But the subtitles give the barest hint to what's going on. They are full of gaps and ludicrous errors: "*Darling, I relove you,*" "*I won't take this blackmale anymore!*"

The narrative voice, perversely following Gödel's law, provides no criteria by which its scope or reliability can be gauged. (We have achieved a moment of consciousness when all narrators are unreliable.) In the pandemonium on the screen (this must be an Epic Production) there is equally guilt and justification by association—a dense intimacy of thing and event in space/time where words seem almost alien. Without comic relief and other diversions; without religion, or psychoanalysis, or some other form of post-Enlightenment perspective (in which category does art fall or rise?); that is, without the consolation of narrative, whatever its shortcomings, we might fall into a steady state of dread.

The narrative voice—textual, oral (external and internal), Greek chorus, nagging conscience, warning, explaining, rationalizing—blow by blow, play by play, "At the scene of the Inferno this is Gail Jenkins for Channel 7 News"—accompanies our every move. Closer, perhaps to the piano player in the silent-movie house than we'd like to think, it imparts a certain brio but no hope of one-to-one correspondence between event and phrase. Even when it purports to be rigorously descriptive and explanatory, as in scientific texts and documentaries, it is operating in a medium as fundamentally different from the thing observed or undergone as Descartes' mind and body requiring the murky infiltrations of a pineal gland.

In the accretion of consciousness we call history, events are gone; words linger on, absurd, trivial, sublime, they become the complicating and incendiary subtext of everyday life in an event-thick present: Know thyself, *Sic transit gloria mundi, Esse est percipi, Delenda est Carthago,* Drink deep or not at all, *Liberté! Égalité! Fraternité!, Revenons à nos moutons,* Cretans lie, Oedipus wrecks, *Carpe Diem,* April is the cruelest month. Churchill's prose, taking up where Tallyrand's left off, narrates the knotty logic of the mega-courage of war: "Now this is not the end. It is not even the beginning of the end. But it is, perhaps, the end of the beginning." And we have the legacy of F. D. R.: The only thing to fear is the fear of fear of fear of fear of fffear itself. But is there such a thing as fear itself? (Sure, toots, don't you watch cartoons?) Perhaps it's another misnomer like "Wrong-way Corrigan" (who can say which way is right?) or a rhetorical device like Truman announcing the advent of atomic warfare with phrases like "God's grace" and "rule of reason." Granted, "what cannot be said, we must pass over in silence"; but, Hallelulia! "it's not over till the fat lady sings." Ah yes, just what is the fat lady, or anyone else, for that matter, singing these days, in the face of our characteristically human, chronically impending, not-always-so-grand finales?

"When I have least to narrate," says Richardson in *Clarissa,* "I am most diverting." Perhaps some higher form of diversion is all we really want. If not to evade, at least to postpone endings. Or to approach them from fresh angles, like Shakespeare with his three thousand splashy neologisms—pious, abruption, insisture, comply, courtship, academe, outpeer, perusal, bewitchment, bifold, predecease. . . . We should not be fooled by the etymology of "narrative"—*gnarus,* knowing. Narrative, particularly narrative poetry, is as importantly about what we do not want to, or cannot, know; what must be glimpsed most obliquely or passed over in silence (not only "facts," however defined, but also perceptions and sensations—our whole repertoire, as sensing, hypercerebral bipeds) as it is a "recounting" of events plain to any reasonable mind's eye. And the forms of narrative are in the most fundamental way—since they tend to invade and recompose our consciousness—about the experience of time.

I spent my adolescence staggering from one narrative time zone to the next: Hollywood soap-bubble time; school time (punctuality, punctuation, puncture, punk—me); stately and scintillating Bach time; the voluptuous leisure of the eighteenth-century landscape or the nineteenth-century novel; the eternal philosophical twilight; rollicking, Shakespearean free-verse time; the luminous moments of the metaphysicals; space-time folds of *The Waste Land*; frenetic, disjunctive TV time; anxious time of Zola and Dreiser; the manic simultaneity of Italian opera; *Wild Strawberries* stopped time . . .

And then there was Armageddon time in *Hiroshima Mon Amour*, and Holocaust time in Resnais's *Night and Fog*; time that was granular and slow and filled with dead space in which to hold our breath at the enormity of calculated horor: *A bomb goes off under five Ethiopian horsemen. "Look," says Vittorio Mussolini, "it's like a rose bursting into bloom."*

4

> Abba Kovner has asked how "a literary gesture could be enough to bear the depths of the suffering contained in the word 'ghetto.' "
>
> —Shirley Kaufman

> In order for a text to expect in any way to render the reality of the concrete world (or the spiritual one) it must first attain reality in its own world, the textual one.
>
> —Francis Ponge

Abba Kovner, an Israeli poet who died in kibbutz Ein Hahoresh in September 1987, was born in the Crimea in Russia in 1918, fought during World War II in the Resistance in the ghetto of Vilna, where over 40,000 Jews were killed, and later joined the Lithuanian partisans to fight the occupying German Army. What for the most of us is an infamous history, a haunting textual abstraction of sinister place names: Auschwitz, Treblinka, Bergen-Belsen . . . and unassimilable statistics: 40,000, 200,000, 6 million (a subtext of modernism) was for Kovner personal memory—the structure of his consciousness, the internal narrative which could engender, or cancel, a present, a future tense, a subjunctive, an indicative, a conditional: the grammar of a life capable of perspective, even joy. The reality of Kovner's world is incorporated into the textual one. It is the struggle between the need to remember and desire to forget (or vice versa). The long sequence which is the centerpiece of "My Little Sister" (and from which the book takes its name) is as much about what cannot be spoken or comprehended as it is about recollection:

41

enslaved
steal me out, take me
(door)
(door)
house of clay
undo me
(door)
(door)
my love a gazelle
who finds me who floods me
who sings when I
my love who speaks
(over)
(it's over)

sealed in a tomb
troops of scorpions rake me
voice of my love

house of life
renew me

who fills me
sorrow
near now

This section of the poem can, and should, be read in several ways: hearing the columns, each in their halting linearity; together, as voices grazing one another from a terrible remove (this is a poem of multiple, perhaps 6 million, narrators); from left to right, traversing (transgressing), like the mind of Zeno's stalled runner, the logical impossibility manifest in a waste of dead, almost impassable space/time: a wall of silence seemingly more substantial, less contingent that the search for *logos* in the words which hover at its fringes. At the intersection of these readings a mass begins to form which is itself unspeakable, but fully present, which, as Wittgenstein would say, shows itself. Kovner has begun his long poem, an accretion of fragments powerful in the undisguised inadequacy, with the words

> *They came up to a wall.*
> *On the seventh night until the dawn*
> *heard from the wall the drowning in the snow*
> *not seeing the marchers' faces*
> *in the white wind.*

That wall—"a cloister wall," "a wall of silence," "the wall," "the wall," "the wall . . ." "My sister is in the wall," "behind the wall," "And the wall keeps them from the world . . ." in Section 41 enters the semantic field of the poem as the unspeakable. It is not spoken again in the remaining sections except to refer specifically to the walls of the Bikur Holim Hospital. "The wall" has passed beyond symbolism into the form of the poetry itself.

What is always in question is not only the power of the language to bear witness but its capacity for great force short of choking on the burden of its own sentiment. This is, I think, accomplished most stunningly in the poem "Alte Zachen," twenty-three stanzas in its entirety and translated into English (on grounds that its original title is untranslatable) as "Potato Pie":

12
They loved the sea
because another country came close
reflected in its waters.

13
He dreamed he'd go back

14
. . . .
15
So he went back. The day he imagined
his father returned
he lost his voice. And more.

16
He stood on the threshold.

17
There was no witness to see
the father
still standing on the threshold

18
not remembering the time. How long
his mouth was wide open

19
                    and silent.
Until he moved his lips. Until his tongue
began to work, until his voice was back
and the echo
            the father

20
behind the muslin curtain and the boy,
a buzzing in his head.
. . . .
23
The pain passes as it comes.
Often
there's nothing in its place.

When we read this poem carefully observing the graphic cues—numbers, line breaks, space between words, ellipses—we enter into the psychological time of one who both savors and recoils from memory. The painstaking enumeration, 1–23, what can be remembered—the threshold, the father, the muslin curtain—things that can be said (with the exception of 14, which must be passed over in silence) but riddled with gaps, spatial and temporal dislocations, syntactic interruptions—all that cannot be said . . . this enumeration does not transgress the unspeakable, does not belie the fragility of memory stunned by horror. The tension between loss and recovery is palpable in the narrative structure. The numbers (which must be read as part of the poem) in their inviolable, relentless order, purity, necessity are both reassuring and grim. They are as persistent and unsentimental in their monodirectional march as time or final solutions. But mostly they contain with their desperate precision the terrifying asymmetry of the thinkable and unthinkable, the tension between a kind of absolute time and the fibrillating pulse of remembered time. The pause at 14 could go on forever, but somehow, amazingly, has not. And since it has not, since Kovner takes us through it, as far as 23, it seems, by some illusion of induction that numbers make possible, that the pulse is strong enough perhaps to go on.

What can be said undeniably to survive—the recipe for potato pie, the words *Alte Zachen,* a peddler's cry heard in Tel Aviv which "brought the image of my father back to me after many years of distance and forgetting,"[4] the flow of images released like branches of a dammed-up river to find their way in new terrain—all this is recoverable by a narrative structure which lets, as Beckett would say, the ruin in—the terrible distance and forgetting always threatening the fullness of the few treasured details (in earlier stanzas): "a narrow velvet collar," "the bank of the river."

What Kovner has done, in his most striking poems, is to shape the formal elements into a visual and oral recapitulation of the ontogeny of disaster, stretching the vitality of his language by means of strong graphic patterns and, in the original Hebrew, as his translator, Shirley Kaufman, tells us, "unusual syntax, dramatic shifts in diction . . . [which] can only be approximated in English." So the narrative is no longer just subtitle or picture, but is to some extent sensory analogue to the fragmentation of memories, dreams, desires by the turmoil of European history. We must as readers endure and savor the silences he writes into his poems (they are both chasms and respites, not the shortest distance between two points) in order to appreciate their strength fully. His work in this respect represents a bridge between the ancient fragment and the most contemporary avant-garde graphic disjunctions, the work of all three—ancient, European Jew, young avant-gardist—arriving on the page via diffractions of history.

"Eighth Gate," like Section 41 of "My Little Sister," is reminiscent of a Greek or an Egyptian text whose tables has been scarred, gouged, and cracked in the tumult of natural and unnatural cataclysm, whose midsection is irrecoverable, or of the Egyptian statue striding across centuries at the Metropolitan Museum of Art, with most of its torso, a thigh, and a forearm missing; the assortment of parts which have survived are held together with steel rods, wires, and the surface tension of our image of what constitutes a man.

EIGHTH GATE:
A PAUSE AT THE FOOT
OF THE MOUNTAIN

Mountain   *all that preceded*
the mountain   *all that preceded*
the mask   *that preceded*
the word
the barrier   *where*
did your footprints   *disappear?*

Proud. My desert is
too proud to answer.

Yes, it's true the center did not, does not hold. High culture with its carefully thought-out values and ethical principles lapses into barbarity; sometimes spectacularly, as with the Nazis, but certainly in little bits and pieces every day. Which is why the form of this poetry should not be unfamiliar to any of us. (Some of us call these events "lapses"; others, like Adorno, logical outcome. Wasn't it, after all, proof of the Nazis' degree of civilization that they troubled to disguise gas jets as shower heads, that they cared so deeply about the language of human transport in the precise records they felt obliged to keep?) What can we and our language do but hug the periphery when, as in the above text, the purported symmetry between word and thing breaks down? We are left with tormenting questions; but there is respite in silence, in a desert which is too proud to answer, in words which do not pretend to create a plenum where none can exist. Nature, it seems, only abhors a vacuum in a few of her many dimensions. "Eighth Gate" gives us, if not sub-, side titles in a great desert epic with two-thirds of its frames missing.

What makes this poetry more than the local account the editors of *Field* feared it might be when they published "Potato Pie" in 1984, with Abba Kovner's answers to their questions about its historical and cultural context, is the metanarrative of the Holocaust which reels through all of us as an unstoppable stream of titles and subtitles to empty and horror-filled screens; but also poetic forms which (not unlike Beckett's prose) lay out of the geometries of loss in the reader's mind—the arrangement of words in space and time that as reader/sayer/listener we must navigate, make contact with the coordinates and perimeters and infinite trajectories of irreversible destruction.

The inability to connect with "Potato Pie" occasionally experienced by my students comes of readings which ignore the numbers, run the lines together as though they were a string of near non sequiturs. This is the same kind of reading which can leave one impatient and frustrated with "language" poetry—one that overlooks its explicit grammatical cues. All poetry displays a set of instructions which when followed initiate the reader into a particular experience of linguistic space-time. When the graphic markers of "Potato Pie" (punctuation, line breaks, space between words, space between stanzas) are observed as the poem is read aloud, the room fills with silence and humor, grief, and dread. The notes on the historical context are strangely not necessary to this even when the student makes minimal connections with the historical metanarrative (metanarrative: a narrative which becomes engraved in our cultural consciousness as fundamental in defining our sense of reality—values, principles, truths). This seems to me to be a lesson, not in good old New Critical purity, but in the powerful consequences of form; in the possibility of *undergoing* a poem through the nature of one's reading rather than disposing of it in an act of superficial comprehension.

That Kovner is largely successful in avoiding sentimentality is extraordinary and has, I think, to do with his formal discipline. The poems are least successful when they are most "straightforward." The size and range and chaos of his experience is better suited to Fractal than Euclidean geometry. It is poems with less formal artifice than "Potato Pie" or "Eighth Gate" that are weak in the absence of contextual support. A poem like the first one in the volume, "They build Houses in Ein Hahoresh," despite (or perhaps because of) the poignancy of its title (and first line) cries out for deconstructing (e.g., his graphic and syntactic disruptions) in order to pass from heartfelt autobiography—"I'll call through the window / to you, my love"—to the dazzling, terrible public domain of the best art—that miracle play of words which both introduces us to and distracts us from the killing whine of emptiness.

To return to Kovner's concern about "bearing testimony": perhaps the most effective work of the poet is to move beyond testimony, which must convince us on the level of factual correspondence (the report) and logical coherence. There is a different possibility for the poet: to acknowledge the exhaustion of intellect in paradox (mind/body, good/evil) and register the intelligent interplay of the senses that blossoms in that moment of recognition; that is, to give it form. Abba Kovner's best work accomplishes this.

5

> Shakespeare knew, as we have forgotten, that feeling is as
> intellectual as thinking.
> —Germaine Greer

> Sorry, I can't make any metaphors. There is no
> talking horse. Billy the Kid did what he did, and
> he died. Death is no mid-wife birthing you to
> myth.
> —Marilyn Hacker, from "Geographer"

Marilyn Hacker's extraordinarily sensual intellect should delight Germain Greer. The narrative in "Geographer," a five-part sonnet sequence from *Separations,* Marilyn Hacker's second book (1976), takes place in a postmodern collision of contemporary, Death-as-Terrorist time with Petrarchan-Heroic-Shakespearean-Rag time. It *is* elegant and intelligent. It combines stately metrics, exquisite linguistic design, and pop vernacular in a style that hyphenates high culture, full of formal historical hindsight, and contemporary cultural critique:

> *I*
> *I have nothing to give you but these days,*
> *laying broken stones on your waste, your death.*
> *(The teeth behind kisses.) Nothing rhymes with death.*
> *Richter plays Bach. My baby daughter plays*
> *with a Gauloise pack. Once I learned pain and praise*
> *of that good body, that mouth you curved for death.*
> *Then your teeth clenched. Then you shivered. Seeing death.*
> *Another of those mediocre lays.*
>
> *Little brother, of all the wastes, the ways*
> *to live a bad movie, work a plot to death.*
> *You worked your myth to death: Your real death.*
> *I've put my child to bed. I cannot eat.*
> *This death is on my hands. This meat dead meat.*

And the end of part III of "Geographer":

> *Last night I heard*
> *of another poet dead, by her own hand*
> *it seems (oh how I wish there were more*
> *boozy women poets, aged sixty-seven:*
> *new book, new man, wit and kitchen noted for*
> *flavor). If there's a Rock-n-Roll Heaven*
> They sure have a Hell of a band.

The numbers that effect containment in these lines are not the Roman numerals which mark off the sections but those internal to speech rhythms—a musical notation which enables the word "death" to be played repeatedly as a discordant flat. The way in which this poem breaches its self- and conventionally defined boundaries is an example of how art can dissolve those sticky dichotomies, including art vs. life, edging toward life-death—as much as aesthetic continuum as space-time. The formal paradox here is that the scheme of the sonnet requires rhyme but "nothing rhymes with death," so what should rhyme, be resonant (living), can only repeat itself in a dull thud that cannot even approximate the literary grandeur of a "knell." It is invariable repetition (death) tacked onto a mind's process richly unfolding (life). Yes, death is tacky, "a bad movie," but so, a good deal of the time, is life. What more can be said? "Word, word, word: the cure / for hard nights."

Words and metrics and syllabics. It turns out they can constitute a narrative life with the spirited momentum. It is possible, for instance, to spend a vacation alone in Venice brimming with sage humor and visual acuity, and wit as sharp and mellow as a properly aged Gorgonzola (and as interested in the pleasure of cooking and eating as M. F. K. Fisher)—at least it's possible in the hendecasyllabic, extended (by one line) Sapphic stanza that draws "Letter from the Alpes-Maritimes" from playful salutation ("Carissima Joannissima, *ave*") are to sign-off twenty-seven stanzas later. Beginning with the fifth:

> *I watch the sky instead of television.*
> *Weather comes south over the mountains: that's news.*
> *Today the Col de Venice was crystalline. Blues*
> *stratospheric and Mediterranean*
> *in the direction*
>
> *of Nice. From Tourrettes, I could see Corsica.*
> *Sometimes I take myself out to dinner. I write*
> *between courses, in a garden, where twilight*
> *softens the traffic beyond the begonias,*
> *and my picher,* vin
>
> ordinaire, *but better than ordinary,*
> *loosens my pen instead of tongue; not my guard.*
> *I like eating alone; custom makes it hard*
> *to be perceived content though solitary.*
> *A woman alone*

> *must know how to be cautious when she gets drunk.*
> *I can't go rambling in night fields of horses,*
> *apostrophizing my wine to their apples,*
> *heaving an empty with a resounding thunk*
> *in someone's garden.*
>
> *(from* Assumptions*)*

Descriptions of local color are laced with humor, full of the kind of visual precisions a poet who was once a painter commands. One senses, in fact, a local burgeoning whenever Hacker travels with her nourishing, protean eye (*esse est percipi,* indeed):

> *The exotic novel Barnes could have written*
> *continues here: the old Countess and her child,*
> *further than ever from being reconciled,*
> *warily, formally, circle the old bone:*
> *an inheritance.*
> *. . . . . .*
> *I gave the mother a blood-red gloxinia.*
> *Hothouse perennial herself at ninety,*
>
> *terrible on the roads (Countess Báthory*
> *is rumored to be a direct ancestor),*
> *a war monument's*
>
> *long bones, selective eyes, a burnished ruin*
> *in white jeans, along the lines of Katherine*
> *Hepburn around the cheekbones and vulpine chin,*
> *her style half-diplomacy, half-flirtation:*
> *she gets what she wants*
>
> *(from* Assumptions*)*

Architecture may turn out to be the most fitting postmodern paradigm. In a world where something as fundamentally temporal as weather has become more a matter of place (e.g., the Bahamas) than time (local seasons); where casually disjunctive events are beamed via satellite into your study, bed, and rec room simultaneously; and where we all go around with a premature afterimage of Armageddon imprinted in our brains—the spatial may become again the predominant aesthetic dimension, as it was for the ancient Greeks, for whom destiny was a matter of place. The building that we call postmodern, with the complicated shadows—arch, Baroque pediment, Western boot, and cactus—bear structural resemblance to, say, Hacker's formal historical "quotations" and eclecticism, her sonnets, sestinas, and villanelles exploded cartoon-style into contemporary consciousness.

But perhaps more significantly, if the varieties of the postmodern can be seen as an evolving critique of the modern, then Hacker's work in its challenge to the white, male, heterosexual flavor of modernism, as well as to its avant-garde, purist stance, might be seen as one sort of prototype. With her linguistic straddling of high-low culture, and her transvaluation of values from implicitly masculine to explicitly, even randily feminine, a good deal of her work fits the image of the project outlined in

Andreas Huyssen's *After the Great Divide,* particularly in the chapter/essay called "Mass Culture as Woman," where he argues that

> . . . the gendering of an inferior mass culture as feminine goes hand in hand with the emergence of a male mystique in modernism (especially in painting), which has been documented thoroughly by feminist scholarship . . .

> Thus the nightmare of being devoured by mass culture through co-option, commodification, and the "wrong" kind of success is the constant fear of the modernist artist, who tries to stake out his territory by fortifying the boundaries between genuine art and inauthentic mass culture. Again, the problem is not the desire to differentiate between forms of high art and depraved forms of mass culture and its co-options. The problem is rather the persistent gendering as feminine of that which is devalued . . . It seems clear that the gendering of mass culture as feminine and inferior has its primary historical place in the late 19th century, even though the underlying dichotomy did not lose its power until quite recently. It also seems evident that the decline of this pattern of thought coincides historically with the decline of modernism itself.

Partly because of the fact that the heroes, with the strengths and weaknesses, feats and foibles, suddenly all became women; partly because of the readership—women looking for a nonarchaic self-image—Hacker's very personal narrative, a kind of continuing series of live studies, infiltrates the public metanarrative: those stories we tell ourselves about who we are, where we've been, what we've done, where we're going. "The Little Robber Girl Considers Some Options" is an example of something that (given our cultural assumptions) *surprisingly* isn't a story about a boy and derives its humor as well as its edge as critique from that gender shift:

> Who wouldn't love the bad old ladies? I'd rather not go gaga in a nursing home, or be preserved in plastic slipcovers with a sullen home attendant paid by a despicable son-in-law. If I can't grow sinewy on a hillside with my twenty years' mostly companion, selling books, pots or rocks in a ship and sitting to three healthy courses on the precise stroke of nine, then I could be captious in a crooked castle, more courted a ruin than ever I was a *rouée*. avid for gossip and close with my favor. The third choice, only granted as a reward, is to pack the gold hero's medal and the ornamental sword in a battered briefcase with one drip-dry shirt, and set out, on the very eve of your triumphal fireworks, to char in the ice dame's half-dismantled mansion, to bind the enemy's atlas with your last silk ball-gown, to tell bedtime stories to the torturer who brings you cream teas, and to the orphans for whom you butchered a horse with the ceremonial epée. Then your digestion will rival your memory, your breast will grow back while you learn Catalan, and your daughters slog across the icecap to get drunk with you.

Gossip and, in "Letter," shopping are not depicted as vices of soft-minded females but as wholesome activities. One thinks of Carol Gilligan's *In a Different Voice,* where the nonlinear "web" logic of narratives of relations—in our culture characteristically identified as feminine, "lower order" reasoning—is identified as a form of responsibility. Fairy-tale time in which you "set out" with minimal luggage and a few magical accessories to travel through dimensions of possibility, where you can conquer a world or two (Scheherazade or dragon slayer), has intersected with reality-principle time (twenty years selling books . . .) to suggest coordinates of a new logically possible world for women. That this happens for Hacker in a prose poem (evoking the form of the Hans Christian Andersen tale from which the little robber girl comes) matters, since she has seldom ventured outside the densely fortified poetic castle whose period wings are made of sonnets, sestinas, villanelles, etc.

As a formidably accomplished and still-young poet, Hacker's only significant weaknesses stem ironically from her unsurpassed facility with these forms. In her worst moments, she slips into a kind of virtuoso running commentary of a teaseful, or at least zestful, but rather superficial "life-style"—good wine, food, sex, travel . . . and not much else—as in the opening stanza of "Graffiti from the Gare Saint-Manque":

> *Outside the vineyard is a caravan*
> *of Germans taking pictures in the rain.*
> *The local cheese is Brillat-Savarin.*
> *The best white wine is Savigny-les-Beaune.*
> *We learn Burgundies while we have the chance*
> *and lie down under cabbage-rose wallpaper.*
> *It's too much wine and brandy, but I'll taper*
> *off later. Who is watering my plants?*
> *I may go home as wide as Gertrude Stein*
> *—another Jewish Lesbian in France.*
>   *(from* Assumptions*)*

There is, of course, great wit and a certain irony in the tenth-line refrain, "another Jewish Lesbian in France," evoking the image of Gertrude Stein throughout this poem, which follows the structure of the *Ballade Suprème.* But Stein's presence is as large lesbian, not poet, since as poet she stood for the antithesis of a form like the ballade. Gertrude Stein was, in fact the quite large robber woman on a lifelong adventure of formal innovation. When a few pages later the "Ballad [again "Suprème"] of Ladies Lost and Found" appears, whose refrain is inhabited by another, very different female ancestor: "and plain old Margaret Fuller died as well," I wonder whether Hacker is fully aware of the consequences of form in the reader's mind—that there is a kind of eradication of difference (the very thing Hacker must value greatly as a feminist poet) in uniform packaging. I want Hacker to claim Gertrude Stein as a genuine spiritual ancestor—to claim some of her lust as non-Euclidean poetic geometer. This is not to abandon discipline but to recognize the specific gravities and honors of formal choices.

In fact, there are formal departures in *Assumptions*[5] which expand the range of Hacker's and the reader's sensibilities by opening form to outside influences (as Kovner does to history). There can be loose ends which let possibilities proliferate and the reader take up some of the imaginative work (activity of the mind synonymous, according to Aristotle, with happiness) rather than being stuck always in the role of spectator at the Sun Queen's banquet—every detail a dazzling reflection of the will to create a poetic plenum in competition with the formally lapsed real world. Marilyn Hacker is too brilliant a poet to become impenetrably safe in her formal choices.

6

He would cook up these goulashes
Make everything shipshape
And then disappear, like Hamlet, in a blizzard
Of speculation that comes to occupy
The forefront for a time, until
Nothing but the forefront exists . . .
                    —*John Ashbery,* As We Know

Neither words nor the rigor of sentences, you said, could stem the steady acceleration of the past.

                              —Rosmarie Waldrop,
                              The Reproduction of Profiles

If one assumes the text must, as Ponge says, compete with reality via its own peculiar vitality, Hacker's means is to confabulate something as dense as any clot of friends enjoying dinner in a crowded café—to make *sense*—quite literally through speech rhythms and pungent detail—of *things*. There does not seem to be a mind-body problem in her work; the two are great buddies in a life where intellect is so palpably concrete in its apperceptions it is almost another of the senses. Abstractions hardly exist at all except as formal outlines which are filled in before we can notice any blank spots. There is robust faith in the equal weight and commensurability of word and object.

Rosmarie Waldrop, on the other hand, is dealing with a particular uneasiness about the relation of intellectual artifact to world inherent in a modernist aesthetic which has been historically self-conscious about, and investigative of, its own medium. She is, among other things, progeny of both Steins—Gertrude and Wittgen—and while raising many of the gender/genre questions which both Huyssen and Hacker address, unlike them she embodies the form of the question in her work. Her text is not so much in competition as in tentative dialogue with the world. This is, to use Wittgenstein's terminology, a different language game, with something else at stake, something like one's sense of mind-body integrity. The reader must enter into the line of investigation to experience fully the force of a text straddling philosophy and prose-poetry that creates an odd (fascinating, humorous) narrative disjunction of leisurely abstraction and sensual urgency:

> The proportion of accident in my picture of the world falls with the rain. Sometimes, at night, diluted air. You told me that the poorer houses down by the river still mark the level of the flood, but the world divides into facts like surprised wanderers disheveled by a sudden wind. When you stopped preparing quotes from the ancient misogynists it was clear that you would soon forget my street.

This is a keyhole glimpse of an acute mind barely grasping what is probably after all ungraspable—the slippery relation of "fact" to inference to person to other persons—the "I," "you," and "we" who exist in this work as purely linguistic protagonists. The unfinished nature of this line of inquiry, all that which "must be passed over in silence" (Wittgenstein again), shows itself graphically by pages conspicuously unconsumed—empty space which has more to do with the opening up of possibility, both delightful and frightening, than—as at times with Kovner and more often with Beckett—the catastrophe of its exhaustion.

Each prose-poetic section, all roughly the length of the above, is presented on a page a good two-thirds of which is left blank. In this book the blank space seems as crucial a part of the text as the numbers in Kovner's work. And though the sections of text superficially resemble the packaging of a sonnet sequence (some sections, e.g., 13 and 14, even scan into fourteen roughly iambic pentameter lines!—that template embedded in the mind of the poet writing in English), they differ radically in degree of density. The syntactic and semantic dislocations leave them all porous, "disheveled by a sudden wind" of cold intellectual terror, or emotional uncertainty, or unassimilable realization, as in the sudden eruption of narrative line toward a psychic vanishing point when it appears that the (male) "you" may have committed a rape:

> Then you came out with how you had jumped her and, trembling with courage, ridden up the hill into the interior, a landscape with something unfinished about it. I was tempted to register doubts as your description progressed, but the wind died down. Cold, at this hour. The moon sank down among the clouds as into a lake. A large bird, an owl perhaps . . . Regardless whether it was several owls or the same, you said, they could be arranged on the road and treated as outlaws of probability. But I hesitated, for fear of not encountering.

In this language game, perceptions cannot be trusted, and logic is so entangled with an obdurate world of irreducible things ("they could be arranged on the road," perhaps) and non sequitur emotions ("fear of not encountering") that it loses its impact. This is the sinister predicament of a world in which language, objects, and events are undeniably but mysteriously intertwined—where, because language is part of the human organism, a life could end

> as an abrupt, violent sentence, or be drawn out with economy into fall or winter, no less complicated than a set of open parentheses from a wrong turn to the shock of understanding our own desires.

The combination of uncertainty and intimacy is almost unbearable, but so is distance: the horns of the dilemma can make us horny, or threaten the violence of non-penetration, or abstract us from ourselves in what is certainly not a respite but a loss. Whatever the case, language is negotiating a precipitous edge:

> It is clear that distance devours the variables and leaves us with all propositions saying the same thing, but with such force that the desire takes us out of body. Tell me that she is beautiful, you demanded, even though you knew that I had always been pleased to lead you astray. A name, I said, cannot go from mouth to mouth, a clear mirror unclouded by breath. Remember that nightingales sing only in the upper pay scales. And we can't logically correlate a fact with a

soul, even if fiction sustains the tone of our muscles. Your lips trembled slightly as you said that logic could take care of itself.

Because sound and light take time to travel to ear and eye, we are always out of sync with one another. Usually we don't notice this, except in the fine-tuned abstractions of physics, since it is such a minute fraction of a split second that separates us, far less than a hairline crack. But this dissociation, displacement, fissure defines the foreground of Waldrop's book, permeated by Wittgenstein's idea of the language game as meaningful only insofar as it partakes of a form of life. When the form of life and the language game get confused or are too far apart, "I," "you," "we" are alienated, literally other, having dropped beyond the pale of the local grammars that constitute lives. The person proclaiming Zeno's proof against motion while striding across the stadium is a clown (or Beckett comedian) of sorts; one who gets struck halfway in another kind of predicament:

> But I get stuck. Single notes occupy my voice with their vertical shadows, luminous blue, so long, so stretched, so content to sink slowly back into. Or a flock of swallows, alarmed suddenly, sucked crazily in all directions. The light appropriates, even to the unsounded spasms of treble and flight, and the fields stretch into what, lacking male parameters, must be nowhere.

The narrative "I" is stuck in the blank space-time between incommensurable language games—those of sensuality and intellect, male and female, justification and relations. The situation is both humorous and dire. A sentence may begin in one language game and end in another: "I traced the law of sufficient reason down your spine"; "Waves can be resolved into a statement about unalterable form." Or an act of translation from mind to body, male to female, may be required, as though foreign languages were being spoken: "You said it might be different if we were able to stand outside logic. I knew by this you meant: barefoot." But—who knows why or how!—occasionally the two language games coalesce in a miracle of graceful choreography, partners no longer exiles from cultures unknown to one another:

> Waves can be resolved into a statement about unalterable form. It goes without saying they lap at your chin while you are still describing the dangers of dry land, after having loved it so long. The gulls stood still, though the light fell on their strained bodies. They could not be proved within the substance of the world, you said. So different their flight. I was happy to discover cause, the better to ignore effects. The clouds drowned silently in their reflection, pulling water down with them.

The second part of *The Reproduction of Profiles,* "Inserting the Mirror," ends with an acknowledgment of the inevitable futility of its own project as it takes the form of a rapidly self-destructing hypothetical: what if the conceptual violence of its necessary humor could be identified, with reassuring medical certainty, as "pain"—something that might have a cure? But pain, as Wittgenstein pointed out, is more elusive than is dreamed of in medical philosophies. We are in a dreadful sense alone with our pain, linguistically as well as physically, since the experience, in the terms in which we define it, is locked from the moment of our birth in irrevocably (despite fantasies and acts of fusion) separate bodies. It is, of course, as ludicrous as it is common to suppose that the pictures of exposed muscles and nerves in textbooks of anatomy will bring us any closer to what we have categorized in our dichotomy-ridden metaphysics as "inside." But if we could know at least that we were all talking about the "same thing"—have a sudden, inexplicable confluence of sense—would we be saved? Unfortunately, the question itself is nonsense, as Wittgenstein's *Philosophical Investigations* and Waldrop's wise humor make strangely clear:

> If everybody said, I know what pain is, could we not set clocks by the violent weather sweeping down from the north? Lesions of language. The strained conditions of colored ink. Or perhaps it is a misunderstanding to peel back the skin in order to bare the mechanics of mirage.

Wittgenstein's own assessment of his *Philosophical Investigations* comes to mind:

> The best that I could write would never be more than philosophical remarks; my thoughts were soon crippled if I tried to force them on in any single direction against their natural inclination. —And this was, of course, connected with the very nature of the investigation. For this compels us to travel over a wide field of thought criss-cross in every direction.—The philosophical remarks in this book are, as it were, a number of sketches of landscapes which were made in the course of these long and involved journeyings. . . . I should not like my writing to spare other people the trouble of thinking.

It's fitting—though "to fit" is a metaphor of coherence more suspect in our intellectual times than "to throw a fit"—that Wittgenstein's strain of deconstruction has found its poet, one who also negotiates the sensibilities of German and English.[6] Wittgenstein admired poets but recited the wrong one, one too full of narrative certainty (Tagore), to the positivist Vienna Circle[7] he wished to alarm. They were more alarmed at the young philosopher's behavior than the ideas of his poet. Wittgenstein was nonetheless right in his intuition that only a poetic language game could embody the collapse of metanarrative. (Derrida concurs with his poetic-prose style.) What Wittgenstein didn't realize was the importance of humor.

Bring on Rosmarie Waldrop, whose work embodies (so to speak) humor as conceptual shift.[8] Bring on St. Phyllis Newcombe, who gave herself to deconstruction without guile and represents the danger of dancing in nostalgic three-quarter time when the world is moving on to the Quantum Jump. There are volatile zones between incommensurable narratives in real space and time from literary biases to Gaza Strips. In fact, as space and time (with Einstein conducting at the Hollywood Bowl) continue to collapse into one another's arms, along with Fred and Ginger in big-screen ecstasy, promising romantic endings like grand unified theories, we might well wish to coax those more recalcitrant couples—open and closed form, particle and wave, mind and body, good and evil—onto the dance floor where they belong, yes/no? Not necessarily. Forced intimacy and narrative nostalgia are themselves doomed to self-destruct, like "sexual revolutions," Harlequin romances, and the Reagan era. What the subtitles can't say is what must always be in the process of invention right before our eyes: a future that is more than a thing of the past.

NOTES

1. This account is written variously, but always tersely, in lists of instances of Human Spontaneous Combustion.

2. Humor has, after all, to do with startling conceptual shifts; that is, with shiftiness in general.

3. Compare and contrast: two things equal/or not/to the same thing are equal/or not/to each other, etc.

4. From an interview with Abba Kovner in FIELD: *Contemporary Poetry and Poetics*, no. 30 (Spring 1984):26.

5. Though her most recent book, *Love Death, and the Changing of the Seasons*, a long narrative recounting of a year-long love affair is with few exceptions—mostly villanelles—entirely cast in well-made sonnets

6. Rosmarie Waldrop was born in Kitzingen/Main, Germany. But that's another essay.

7. Euclid's philosophical progeny.

8. I wonder if Thomas Kuhn realizes his "paradigm shifts" are instances of great humor in the history of science.

REFERENCES

Hacker, Marilyn. *Assumptions.* Alfred A. Knopf, 1985.

――――. *Separations.* Alfred A. Knopf, 1976.

Kovner, Abba. *My Little Sister.* Translated by Shirley Kaufman. FIELD Translation Series 11. 1986.

Waldrop, Rosmarie. *The Reproduction of Profiles.* New Directions, 1987.

POSTMODERN *BILDUNGSROMANS:*
THE DRAMA OF RECENT AUTOBIOGRAPHY

PAUL CHRISTENSEN

Occasionally in autobiography one gets the essence of a whole movement in literature, of an epoch of thought, a turn in the concept of the self. Within the broad movement known as postmodernism, there are two texts in particular where this occurs—in Charles Olson's *In Cold Hell, In Thicket,* published in 1953, and in Clayton Eshleman's *Indiana,* which appeared in 1969. Olson was a formidable thinker and arguer, among the two or three seminal minds that formulated postmodernism; it should be no surprise that he was capable of portraying the new self of postmodernism in his own autobiographical poetry, which he carefully sorted into a narrative scheme in his book, *In Cold Hell, In Thicket.* The title refers to the opening of Dante's *Inferno,* the "selva oscura," the dark wood Dante wanders into at the middle of his life, where he enters into the three spheres of the Christian universe. Olson's book is a similar excursion into visionary experience, where he struggles to wrest a new understanding from his own midlife and emerges in the third and final section of the book with a sense of himself as remade, a voice of his own times. It is his personal drama, using his own undisguised experience and conflict, calling himself by name. He means to direct the reader to Olson's personal reexamination in order to show the reader the wrenching process of deliverance, by turns grueling and funny, dramatic and trivial—a molting or rebirthing that is difficult, graceless, but necessary. He sheds old opinions, grudges, convictions as he struggles to adopt a new mind and perspective. The book was not considered all that remarkable at the time; it was lost among other, perhaps more colorful and dramatic poems by him and a wide circle of writers whom we now called postmodernists. Olson was better known for his essay "Projective Verse" (1950), where his key notions of a new poetry drew fire from traditional critics and aroused many young writers to try writing in the mode he suggested. But looking back these thirty years, it is clear that if one wants an essential text, autobiographical in substance, innovative in style, and central to an understanding of postmodernism, *In Cold Hell, In Thicket* is it.

Sixteen years later Clayton Eshleman's *Indiana* appeared, made up from previously published poems and arranged very carefully into a narrative sequence that again shows a poet sloughing off the influences of his past, his parents, his region, in order to acquire a new self fit for the times. There is much here that is plain, bluntly stated ideology—the principles forged out of twenty years of postmodernism. And the text is charged with all sorts of images of rebirth, delivery, transformation, metamorphosis—a particular motif is of the birth of a child, Eshleman's only son Matthew from a first marriage, whom he both greets and bids farewell to as he moves toward the culmination of his own rebirth. The caterpillar is also a frequent symbol—its chrysalis and pupation are compared to the poet's gestation of a new inner life. Eshleman called his first magazine, which he edited from the late 1960s to the early 1970s, *Caterpillar,* a journal of postmodernism in which many such self-remakings in poetry were featured in and discussed. It emphasized the work of Olson and those he influenced; Eshleman had fashioned *Indiana* under Olson's influence as well. I therefore make these two autobiographical works of poetry serve as book ends of the postmodernist age—they introduce and conclude a fertile era in American writing, where a new self is argued and portrayed in a rush of innovative portraits, whose elements converge to make a figure whose responsibilities and relations are calculated to address the present and to correct the previous notions of the self.

Postmodernism and the self of these texts constitute a new stage in the formulation of American character; the Transcendentalists were a first stage, followed by the self-analyses of the realists and naturalists, whose writings, which I broadly term the Midwest Theme, constitute a second stage. Each era of thought possesses its seminal theories and key autobiographical texts; each movement is predicated upon a discovery of a new self, which in turn aroused a vast outpouring of literature that sketched and fleshed in the rudiments of that new selfhood.

To understand the achievement of Olson and Eshleman, it is necessary to briefly review the earlier stages of self which they so forcefully rebutted and transformed. There is a paradigm of autobiography that is anterior to any of these stages, with long roots into the past. The remade self is an ancient preoccupation of art, but I will limit myself to those reconceptions of self that emerged at the early industrialization of Europe and England. The reconceived self is the pervasive issue of Blake's voluminous output—and indeed, no other Romantic writer is more often quoted or admired by the postmodernists than is Blake. His struggle to accommodate to the new times, to move from classic restraint to romantic protest, is the great force behind his sensuous visions. Industrialization was an imperative to artists to change all they knew—to summon forth a new sensibility that could survive the times and preserve the traditional notion of one's humanity. Wordsworth's 1805 *Prelude* gives us the paradigm in part, and so does Coleridge's *Biographia Literaria* (1817). But it is Carlyle's *Sartor Resartus,* first published in book form in Boston in 1836, that fully exploits the potential of the form. Here an old self is vigorously discarded, and a new self is borne out of the anguished thought and self-wrenchings of the writer. The reverse of the paradigm is the failure to find such a self from within, as in the 1852 preface to Arnold's *Collected Poems,* which spawned its own despairing tradition in twentieth-century poetry, beginning with Eliot's "Ash Wednesday" (1925) and running through the work of the Fugitives and into the midcentury's confessional poetry. Either one joins the times anew or concedes personal failure to fit in and writes of the loss of self under the crush of change. This is the essential polarity of autobiography in the Romantic Age. But to pick up the specific tradition of the postmodernists, we must turn to the transcendental writers first.

Emerson's essay on "Self-Reliance" transforms the God of the Puritans into a voice in the heart, a voice that draws on Puritan theology to form the conscience and on

Romantic theories of nature to form the instincts and urges of human nature. The individual who hears the voice in the heart will not err; its counsel is infallible in the making of heroes and leaders. Hence the reclusive personae of Whitman and Dickinson, who both retreat to hear the counsels of their voices. The person who ignores the voice will follow the many and live a life of emptiness and despair. Emerson scorns the crowd and incorporates the Puritan prejudice against the mass in his notion of conscience; the instincts are benevolent because nature is nothing less than the spirit in material form. The essay declared a new self whose store of grace was now in the form of a voice within. To heed it was to follow a path of righteousness which led ultimately to self-enrichment and to that goal of American selfhood—the discreet individual, the dream of the emigré whose past in Europe was of a millennium of bondage and anonymity. A galaxy of autonomous selves formed quickly around this text and gave us the basic permutations of self-reliance—Ahab, Hester Prynne, the Thoreau of *Walden Pond,* the intransigent Bartleby. Only Ahab discovers the limitations of that voice—the terrific isolation with which it burdens the self, which can only turn to greater and greater challenges to appease the aggressions of the voice, the core of self-reliance.

It has often been said that Emerson's idealism prompted migrations westward— settlers roamed the Western territories on the strength of that inner voice, following its infallible counsel in the midst of an untried, unexplored, but idealized nature. Ahab's demise in nature sounded the coming note of disillusion that fills the literature of what I call the Midwest Theme, which, in brief, proved false the high claims Emerson had made for self-reliance. The voice was there but its counsels were no defense against Indians, harsh weather, natural calamity, the viciousness of one's fellow man. In a brief span of years following the publication of "Self-Reliance," God was disputed by the geologists and nature was radically redefined by the biologists. The voice within collapsed under the accumulating weight of contradictions, but the settlers were nevertheless strewn across the desolate Middle Border in various stages of hardship and disaster, and by 1882 the literary evidence of disillusionment and contempt for New England idealism began pouring in. Emersonian idealism was held responsible for the sort of ruthless capitalism that now bullied the settlers out of their properties; once more the many, the crowd, had fallen prey to a managerial elite, and the realists and naturalists openly resented the source of this power in New England self-reliance.

Emerson stressed the separation between man and nature; he could encourage a relationship between them only at the level of contemplation. The various experiments in communal living in nature (Oneida, Brooks Farm) were impractical and short-lived, and bespoke the naivete of the idealists as to actual conditions of a life in nature. Muncie, Skokie, Terre Haute, the hard-pan prairie towns and squalid settlements of the upper north were the real thing, a far cry from the small protected enclaves thrown up for experiment in the New England woods. The Midwest experience showed the extent to which Emerson's vision was the unlived abstraction of man in nature—his faith had predicted the human supremacy over natural force. His rejection of the crowd was but another species of his general separation of man from the real world of tragedy and destruction.

The hermitic veil cast over man by Emerson's idealism is the very target of the naturalists. They reject at once the autonomy of the individual or the free will that is basic to Emerson's concept of the individual. Vernon Parrington's perception of the shift between New England to the Midwest is still useful: "The intellectual history of the generation born after the Civil War is the history of the transition from Emerson to Herbert Spencer, and from Spencer to Ernst Haeckle—from Transcendentalism to biology, and from biology to physics—from the doctrine of the innate Godhead to the doctrine of biological perfectibility through evolution, and thence to the doctrine of the mechanistic cosmos that makes no account of teleological ends." To sum up, he remarks that "In presence of such philosophical materialisms, the romantic optimism that suffused a genial glow over a egocentric universe, and the romantic freedom of the will that professed itself capable of shaping life to what ends it would, lost their sanctions and disintegrated, to be succeeded by a stark pessimism underlaid by a mechanistic determinism."

To the naturalists man was a creature too much with nature, too much its agent and victim. Farming might have staved off distrust of Emerson's idealization of nature, but it failed early in the Midwest settlements, leaving behind a great bitterness against nature that welcomed in the industrialization of the region. A wave of Central Europeans emigrated to the region late in the century, people who had known agricultural hardship in Poland and Germany, and who quickly turned to industry for livelihood, leaving behind a ghostly remnant of agrarian ways and a landscape of industry to remind its residents of the collapsed vision of the Transcendentalists. The self in the literature of the period was either the tragic foredoomed figure struggling against great forces in man and nature, or a lingering idealist still dreaming of Eden. Both figures fill the poems of Frost and Robinson. Jay Gatsby clings to self-reliance as late as 1925, but Yank in O'Neill's *The Hairy Ape* (1922) accepts his fate and dies brokenhearted and disillusioned. But Dreiser captures the self of naturalism best in his informal journal. *A Hoosier Holiday* (1916):

> But, oh these youngsters, the object of so much attention and solicitation, once they break away from these sheltering confines and precepts and enter the great world outside—then what? Do they fulfill any or all of the ideals here dreamed for them? I often think of them in the springtime going forth to the towns and cities, their eyes lit with the sheen of new life. Ninety nine per cent. of them, as you and I know, end in the most humdrum fashion—not desperately or dramatically—just humdrum and nothing at all. Death, disease, the doldrums, small jobs, smaller ideas claim the majority of them. They grow up thinking that to be a drug clerk or a dentist or a shoe dealer is a great thing. Well, maybe it is—I don't know. Spinoza was a watch repairer. But in youth all are so promising. They look so fine. And in a small town like this, they buzz about so ecstatically, dreaming and planning.
>
> . . . Oh bright young hopes! Oh visions! visions!—mirages of success that hang so alluringly in amethyst skies! (262–63)

At the bottom of the heart are the lingering vestiges of brute savagery, not the voice of God, as Emerson had claimed; the body was composed of the same cold, aimless molecules as was a stone, according to Ernst Haeckel. In a few more years, Freud would find the repository of savage nature in the bottom of the mind, the unconscious, which one listened to at one's peril and ignored at one's peril. Finally, with

Darwin, Haeckel, and Freud, one must add Herbert Spencer and Marx to the list of formulators of the self at the end of the nineteenth century, the ingredients that make up the selves of naturalism and modernist realism.

The modernists, curiously, had no new self to propose in their work: their movement built upon the complaints of the realists and stressed the objectivity necessary to escape the lures and enchantments of Emersonianism. Henry James' protagonists all seem to misconstrue the voice within or fail at the propitious moment to heed their own counsel and so head into the rest of life with dreary disappointment. Out of that projected disappointment arose the personae of Eliot; Prufrock and Tiresias are reincarnations of James' Winterbourn, Marcher, and Brydon, as are Pound's Mauberley and the protagonists of Fitzgerald. Modernism advances a new notion by neutering the concept of nature from what it had been to the naturalists. As a fragment of Emerson's natural benevolence, Pound stressed the need to perceive nature's own design, its self-forming powers which the artist, in Emersonian fashion, should emulate in his own compositions. Imagism was a curious paradox of purposes—an effort to escape Emersonian subjectivity by omitting to think or lyricize one's perceptions, while at the same time studying nature's own integrity through Emersonian contemplation. It was a have and have not poetic, rooted in the confusion of the times, when nature was at once of essential importance but a hazard to idealisms in art. One must return to the altars of nature but renounce one's egotism there. Pound's turn to economics in the 1930s will one day be connected with his overall esthetic—did he not try to undo the harm caused by capitalism, the philosophy of which had, curiously, unintentionally, nurtured itself on Emersonian self-reliance? Regardless of the impracticality of his reforms, Pound knew that the forces that were transforming Europe and the United States had been partly formulated from New England Transcendentalism, the roots of his own poetic tradition; at the same time, he could not ignore Emerson's insistent argument that in nature alone lay the terms and principles for beauty in human art. The split attention of Pound's modernism gave to his postmodernist heirs much to resolve; in Eliot, who retreated from the Jamesian line of failed heroes and from contemplation of nature as well, the postmodernists found nothing, and they avoided him. Selfhood had not advanced in conception among modernists; it had, in fact, disintegrated as the doctrines of idealism and naturalism collided in the early years of the century. There was no explicit autobiography in modernism; Henry Adams' self-study is called an *education,* which comes close to the paradigm of the remade self, but does so with great regret and reluctance—the future is bleak and embattled with alien powers. For the poets, autobiography was loosely distributed, in fragments, across one's own work, but the connectives and causality to link events was missing—the times were too much out of joint to make a full disclosure and apologia of one's experience.

Facing the postmodernists of 1945 were two dialectically opposed conceptions of the self. One saw the self as separate and unrelated to nature except in acts of contemplation, wherein it received the benevolence of a divinely ordained scheme of things, the "Wise Seer within me [that] never errs," as Emerson once put it. The other saw the self as the blighted figment of a blind, amoral determinism, a brute thing drifting through a maze. It was either the figure who had put a jar in Tennessee or an etiolated gent named Prufrock, choked in starched collar and tie, whose innards longed for a savagery which his mind had too successfully repressed—he was merely a tame bachelor with a few dirty thoughts, an uneasy truce of the two versions of self that had come down to him.

Postmodernism could only proceed by dismissing both versions of self as idealizations within a much larger misconception of nature attributable to Western civilization as a whole. Olson argued that the West had always tried to escape from nature. Beginning with Plato, one sees Western metaphysics longing for a realm of immaterial essence, safe from mutability and care. Plato's theory of forms is an early rejection of organic reality, for matter was at best an imperfect copy of a perfect essence, which was destined to be dirtied and to decay in the world. The West had built its citadels under the setting sun and longed for death and salvation in timelessness. Thus, nature had to be reconceived from a point of view outside Western habits of despair and rejection. In 1949, Olson published "The Kingfishers" in which he declared himself an heir to the Mayans and Aztecs, an inheritor of the sunny world of pre-Columbian metaphysics. Other postmodernists adopted the mythologies of American Indian culture; Snyder drew inspiration from early Japanese religion. Ginsberg took residence for a time in India and informally acquired a taste for Hinduism and Buddhism. Their collective efforts were designed to give poetry a new perception of nature untainted by Western abstraction and longings for unreal worlds. There was no systematic methodology to their research; the efforts represent the meanderings of a frustrated generation coming out of world war, worried over the might and authority of their nation, concerned that science and government had joined forces in a mad pursuit of global hegemony. To survive would require new beginnings, a self made from zero, pliable and sensuous, a mix of alien things heretofore avoided in Western art forms—indeed, it was in the great trash piles of Western philosophy that one might find the elements most needed to make up the new self.

To remake the self, postmodernists turned first to primitive, non-Western sources of belief; ancient civilizations had not drifted toward human isolation nor had they emphasized rationality in opposition to the irrational, as did the West. The dead of the Aztec burials were in repose, their remains heaped up with totems of human accord with nature; the mounds of dead at Buchenwald, glimpsed in the opening pages of *In Cold Hell,* show the ravages of Western humanism. Images of war, the atomic age, the American hegemony at 1945, these and other issues converge to delineate the adversarial reality which made a new self necessary. Sixteen years later, Eshleman's poems in *Indiana* shift focus to the tedious middle-class routines and artificiality of life in Indianapolis; that heartland city is viewed mordantly as a citadel of meek human values in an apocalyptic age. Eshleman opens *Indiana* with this line, "Tell her I can change my life," which echoes Olson's opening of "The Kingfishers," "What does not change / is the will to change." He too will fashion himself anew from primitive sources with the help of Reich (not Freud), and Jung, and with the constant motif of a wall in the mind to be broken down and penetrated, where other chambers, some of them connected to primitive layers of mind, open out and reveal the same primal sources Olson pursued. The goals of rebirth and delivery are given terrifying expression in the book's epigraph:

> *Today I have set my crowbar against all I know*
> *In a shower of soot & blood*
> *Breaking the backbone of my mother.*

The remaking of the self requires the renunciation of the will and its agent, the ego; Olson implies this throughout *In Cold Hell* but announces it blatantly in his essay "Projective Verse," where poetry should be made to avoid "the lyrical interference of the ego." Eshleman states it early in *Indiana* thus: "I feared my own energies had / become servants to will. . . ." Olson asks his reader, "Shall you uncover honey / where maggots are?"—meaning the West, whereas he will "hunt among stones," the Aztec past. Eshleman tells us that he "searched for that interval in the stone / by which I might enter" the will of the earth. "I must molt more than my face," writes Eshleman, "I must change more than the contour of my line." "Goodbye all I've ever known." Both poets desire to regain kinship knowledge of other animals, the Not Me of nature transformed beyond recognition as the enemy in Western thought. It was this destructive opposition that had led to the artificial civilization of America.

The key to self-renewal lay in the paradoxical phrase "human nature"—the terms were in opposition; the solution lay in rejoining them. Nature should have free play in the mind—in the deliberate release of mental content into the more sorted areas of human consciousness. One should let flow the content of one's animal self, the primitive part Jung had charted, and this should flow freely over the mechanism of human thought that seeks differentiation and isolation from nature. One should break down the abstracting part of mind, the conceptualizing organ, and charge it with mere physical data, overcharge it, and allow perception its willy-nilly course to make the sensual union of human and nature weld shut and exclude the ego and the will.

The consolidations of a new self emerge in the middle sections of both books. The second part of *In Cold Hell* opens with a poem called "La Chute," in which Olson demands the return of his lute and drum, fallen, he says, among the dead (the past), primal instruments for expressing a primal self. The title poem "In Cold Hell, In Thicket" dominates this section and poses as its opening question, "Who am I?" The answer is that union of opposites that had gone off in extremes in American culture. Emersonian idealism and Midwest pessimism must be composed in the new self:

> *. . . a man, men, are now their own wood*
> *and thus their own hell and paradise*
> *that they are, in hell or in happiness, merely*
> *something to be wrought, to be shaped, to be carved, for*
> *use, for others.*

In the middle section of *Indiana*, Eshleman writes a letter to the Peruvian writer Cesar Calvo, stating that "For the world to come through man must make himself transparent," that is, egoless, "that the 'mildness' is the seeing of oneself, one's organ, as part of a bank tangled with trees & flowers" (63). Both poets agree that man must be reunited with his nature and separated from an all-devouring ego and will. Both attempt to conquer their intellects, to accomplish what Eshleman describes as "resolving the body," bringing the body into balance with thought, mixing physical with mental awareness until the two are one. Out of this union will develop a new empathy with the world or what Robert Duncan called "participation mystique." Self-expression, both poets tell us, must issue from selflessness, from the instincts, the musculature, the central nervous system, the primordial ooze that still lines the skull and connects one with the Not Me of nature. Both call the poem of selflessness "open," that is, open toward nature, open to one's inner nature, and to one's human gift of perception as well. The poem must bridge mental and physical reality, linking self with nonself reality.

By such means, these poets attempt to go beyond the contrarieties of human identity, the polarities deeply laid within the phrase "human nature." In his tribute to the jazz musician Bud Powell, Eshleman claims that "Powell was snapped beyond the contraries I was prey to." Powell was "a person who began to unthaw you, to restore some of what you know is your humanity." The humanity was that Darwinian/Jungian tunnel leading down through consciousness and reason into the primal levels of natural evolution; the artist who could summon up the darkness of human origin without sorting or judging its murky content was the true artist of his age, one who had expanded and reshaped the materials of human selfhood and identity. Among the heroes of this new self were such progenitors as Jackson Pollock, D. H. Lawrence, Jung, Reich, the painter Soutine, whom Eshleman praises as "attached to nature." These are voices that draw from the deeps, who speak in disarrayed spontaneity, whose awareness and expression race ahead of conception or intention, spilling forth inner content like dredges in a deep canal.

Both poets emerge from the last section of their books as writers who have resolved the awful conflict of being two things in one: an animal and a human, a thing and a moralizer in an amoral universe. They have healed themselves by renouncing will, subjectivity, differentiation, all of which are present in the soul but only as fragments floating in the great centrifuge of human awareness. They have reasoned themselves out of reason, perceiving themselves as animals with ciphering powers, whose unity with nature is their strength and protean identity. For Olson, the demotion of intellect in the hierarchy of human powers frees him to chronicle life's great natural matrix; for Eshleman, it liberates him from masculine arrogance, from a sensibility that abused women and thrived on seduction, the reification of lovers; hence, the abandonment of his first marriage, based on such a seduction, and his entry into a new relation built up of parity and reciprocity.

Neither poet fully resolved the conflicts each labored to transcend in these *bildungsromans*—they end successfully enough, but neither poet can fully put on the new mind to explore the world. They have molted old skins and perhaps expressed the exhilaration of having achieved a new thoughtfulness, but each has gone on beyond these initial books to refine and further resolve the unities of the new self. Those unities open out into all venues of human activity, into history, culture, science, since the boundaries of the new persona are limitless, incorporating anything one cares to bring to this protean identity and attach to it. Its center is the truce of human and natural realms, to which may be fused anything from either side. The language that issues from this union is ideally a winding helical strain of feeling, sensation, perception, building up by small clusters and loose connections the image of a curious, all-eyed figure happily lost among natural things. The progenitors could only picture the struggle, however, and much of the work that followed *In Cold Hell, In Thicket*, and

Indiana remains combative, not edenic or satisfied. The effort to molt and transform is their own personal drama.

Meanwhile, in the sixteen years that span the appearance of these two books, the new persona emerged in fiction and poetry, easily detectable by their newly patterned narration and observation—a persona whose morality is suffused with natural sympathies, whose perception is altered to convey the rich, unsorted awareness of an animal's nature. The egoless observer, we might call him, surfaces in the novels of John Hawkes, Barth, Heller, Kesey, in the plays of Sam Shepard, in the endless serial and short lyrics of poets. The new persona has reached the canons of writing schools, and rays out into literary journals and small reviews, where young poets express renewed tenderness for nature, and dream of extending their identity to other species, even the inanimate things of earth.

The decay of postmodernism will come in the form of pastoralizing the version of this persona—of further idealizing the human embrace of nature, as occurs now in literary journals. A simpering quality of human sympathy now replaces the hard-edged language of Olson and Eshleman, of Duncan, Snyder and Creely—all of whom practiced the difficult art of diplomacy with the primitive and the alien, with the putative enmity with nature, inner and outer. The struggle of bright men and women to make truce with that which had grown to become the archenemy of man required that the language they used never fall victim to mere idealism or pastel blandishment. Nature must still be red in tooth and claw, mean, unpredictable, the savagely toothed mother of Bly's nightmare visions. It must remain the alien, intractable tyrant of man, and man must be seen as the arrogant, conquering villain of the earthly story; and these two, in their dark complexion, must be drawn into the ring for truce, not to be turned into a pampered, distilled version of themselves. Postmodernism arose on a sense of the meaner aspects of both parties, of the ill-suited nature of both of them for any sort of union or marriage in the human mind. It was the unlikely drama that made it all the more rich for art, stimulating any number of alienated artists to take up the challenge to thrust these warring, wrangling adversaries together. The collapse of postmodernism comes with facile vision, with ready-made truces of all sorts, with flimsy dreamscapes in which the Peaceable Kingdom is reimagined, the tigers declawed, the rams without horns, the human being wide-eyed and shepherdlike, a pastoralism already mined out and heaped in the trash of Western ideology. Satires of the West still abound, and Eshleman continues to plumb the depths of human origin in the cave art of Southern France. It is in that vein of things where postmodern art continues to survive; but its bold inception is to be found in those embattled *bildungsromans* at midcentury.

ON MEMORY

ANN LAUTERBACH

I don't really like the word *memory;* it makes a dull, muffled thudding sound, and the verb, *to remember,* strikes me as slightly grotesque, as if the process were one of sticking parts back on a broken sculpture. Although I know the word is rooted in the mental (the Latin *memoria* means mindful) it still has a vaguely sickly physicality for me; perhaps I am hearing the wrapped residue of *mummy.* In any case, I try to avoid using it in my poems, preferring the somewhat stiff *recollection,* Wordsworth's tranquilities notwithstanding. The reason is clear enough: I prefer the idea of a process of recollecting to one of remembering. Things collect in the present, or rather the present collects and then moves off into the past until it is recollected. This implies that in recollecting we also redistribute, that we get to arrange the collection differently from the way it was in the first place. I like the idea of this freedom. Memory is heavy. I picture it as a sack each of us must haul from place to place, getting heavier and fatter and more useless and cumbersome. In fact, I have a vivid image of just such a sack, made of gritty raw burlap, summoned from my childhood. *That* sack was pulled from floor to floor on the back stairs of the apartment house in New York by a young man collecting the garbage. His face and hands were always covered with soot and coal dust, and his blue eyes gazed out from behind this grim mask with a startling intensity, as if they were trying to escape. This young man was more interesting to me than the huge sack I could hear thudding behind him: *mem-or-y; mem-or-y; mem-or-y.* And yet, all I have to do is say the word "sack," and his image jumps forward. It is memory, then, that provides the literal from which we make metaphors, that allows us to feel correspondence between unlike things?

This morning I am thinking that the relationship between memory and writing is, for me, not unlike the one between dreaming and waking; language has something like the same facilitating effect of sleep. In dreams, fragments from "real life" combine with the psyche's inventions to make a new, compound event or story or image. Writing is a similar process, a reconstruction or revision of the real, if the real is what is already known or understood. What is already known or understood doesn't interest me when I write as much as what is not known, not understood. As E. M. Forster said, "How do I know what I think until I see what I say." (I think it was Forster, but I have a terrible memory for such things.) I like to say I write "into the unknown," which is, I suppose, another way of saying "I write into the future." But of course it is not possible to write into the unknown, the future, without the known, the past. The past is always there, the setting, the stance: it constitutes us, and we are its constituents.

> *Remembering to forgive. Remember to pass beyond you into the day*
> *On the wings of the secret you will never know.*
> *Taking me from myself, in the path*
> *Which the pastel girth of the day has assigned to me.*
>
> *I prefer "you" in the plural, I want "you,"*
> *You must come to me, all golden and pale*
> *Like the dew and the air.*
> *And then I start getting this feeling of exaltation.*
> *—John Ashbery, from "A Blessing in Disguise"*

From time to time in my dreams persons who have died show up, and I wake from these dreams with a melancholy pleasure, as if I had been, in fact, visited. Part of this pleasure is the illusion of life of course: these figures move around, say things, do things; sometimes they even acknowledge that they are dead. (My cousin Elisabeth paid such a visit not long after she died. "But Liz," I admonished, "You are dead!" "I know!" she exclaimed, and giggled with a rapturous, wicked glee.) Recently I had a dream in which my father, who died more than thirty years ago, returned from years of exile. In the dream he didn't look anything like pictures of him, nor did he have anything like the charismatic character people who knew him recall. In the dream he was feeble, defeated, sad. The disparity between the factual and the dream interested me, as if my father had slid all the way out of my memory of him, which at best is very vague, into one of complete fiction. The slide from the real to the fictive is one that memory, coupled with the imagination, guides, selecting, refuting, annotating, abridging. And, in that slide from real to fictive, names, words for things, for places, persons, become ghostly tropes. People die, but their names remain, like titles of books without books.

Does naming a thing make it exist? Is this our central *lie against time,* to use Harold Bloom's phrase? If we have a word, "soul," does that mean that there are such things as souls? Angels? Each name is simultaneously attached to its thing and free of it. The *tree* in this sentence is not the same as the *tree* in the line of Milosz's "circling a tree with your easels." That is one reason why some poets are so careful about naming things, so particular. Open Robert Hass' book *Praise,* and you will be hard pressed to find the generic word *tree:* you will find pines, maples, apples, red-woods, magnolias, and so forth. The effort to name becomes even more complex with things less tangible: colors, for instance. When I say "green," what is that, but five letters having no resemblance whatever to what we know to be green-ness. Which green? How could anyone name all the different ways in which green may be green? Even if I recall the exact color of the wall in the hotel in Italy that summer, there is no way I can put that color in my poem unless I paint it. Words, then, release things from the temporal and spatial settings in the real.

> Proust had a bad memory—as he had an inefficient habit, because he had an inefficient habit. The man with a good memory does not remember anything

because he does not forget anything. His memory is uniform, a creature of routine, at once a condition and function of his impeccable habit, an instrument of reference instead of an instrument of discovery.
—Samuel Beckett, *Proust*

I have what is usually called a terrible memory. It refuses to store particulars, and, even when it thinks it has, it gets them wrong, revises just enough to humiliate me. This impoverishment, *tabula rasa,* blank, is the main contributor to my incessant sense that I am always starting over. I seem to remember things only as they are reenacted: I do not remember the lines of the poem until I reread it; the film until I see it again; the painting, the title of the painting; forget about the names of characters in novels. It's an affliction worthy, I sometimes feel, of Job. And yet, something stays with me. I tell myself that my memory is of a different kind, that I remember conditions, aspects, effects, relationships between things, not the things themselves. I'm a woman of prepositions and conjunctions, not nouns. I have a store of responses to things, a repertoire of alignments. Writing is the unfurling of those effects, those relations, each word conveying a retrieval of sorts, but only the whole poem, with its internal fittings of line to line, the fully recovered discovery. Writing eases the panic of forgetting which reduces everything to a beginning, assuages the persistent desire, the yearning, for duration, continuity, development: whatever you call what comes after the beginning but before the end. Writing stretches out the *once* that is upon time. Each sentence or line enlarges the present, makes it contain more than itself as it fills with tenacity, forbearance, gratitude, as I watch my curiosity track its string of words before it is ransacked by closure.

The experience of writing is an intense encounter with the present, if the present is what we call how the future rides into the past. As I write, I *see* the present materialize out of the future, the not yet written, and into the past, the just written. The essential narrative characteristic of language, or writing, mimics this process, and poets like Frank O'Hara and Elizabeth Bishop are wonderfully adept at writing as if they were enacting:

> It is 12:20 in New York a Friday
> three days after Bastille day, yes
> it is 1959 and I go get a shoeshine
> —Frank O'Hara, from "The Day Lady Died"

in which the observer and the observed are made one. This is because the future is the fiction that the past creates, just as the past is the fiction that the future creates. As each word arrives, it claims *now* just before it rides off into *then. Now* is one of my favorite words. It elides know and hatches possession out of itself, shifting easily into own. Words are how we own our knowledge of now.

> Poetic language possesses—as does any language in general—its own particular dynamics, which impart to psychic movement an acceleration that takes the poet much farther than he imagined when he began the poem. . . . As a rule, a poet is considerably older when he finishes a poem than he was at the outset.
> —Joseph Brodsky, "Footnote to a Poem"

When I was growing up in New York the future seemed to me the most precarious of places. The city was a mine of dangerous incipiences waiting to explode. Nights, especially, were replete: sirens, footsteps, cats, planes, music, cries of love, rage, sorrow. I lay awake in a state of acute anticipation. My father, a foreign correspondent during World War Two, was often away, and my sense of vulnerability was greatly enhanced by his absence. He seemed to have taken the present away with him, leaving a gap, a void in which *was* and *will be* collided. When he returned from his trips, he brought with him *presents*, perhaps my first misheard misreading, the initial pun, the rhyme that healed broken time. When he left again, he carried with him a small Hermes typewriter, which I must have thought of as a magic tool, the agent of his adherence, his attachment to the world he traveled. Words would eventually become the agent of my Oedipal attachment to him and to the world he represented. Touching the keys of the typewriter, I resemble and imitate him, and I almost touch him: an intimate mimicry.

Years ago, I read something by Noam Chomsky to the effect that, although the number of phonemes and morphemes in the English language are finite, their potential combinations are infinite. This excited me. I thought: the finite parts are the past; the infinite part is the future. Language recasts the past into the future. Syntax is the privileged map of this excursion: a subject finds its object, the past finds its future: they couple in a pleasant annihilation. When I write, as I am writing, I lose all sense of clock-time. I feel as if I had entered another layer or strata, and I have the sensation that I am actually stealing time from itself. I am a thief, a liar. Ha! I say, Look what I stole! The world is going to hell in a handbasket while I am making another schedule of events, another script altogether: I am stealing and escaping simultaneously; I am elsewhere. As I write more and more poems, the primal script is eroded and replaced; time in my poems is reconstituted, renovated, released. As each event reemerges in a text it is given new life and is free from its first, original context. Sometimes a line will seem wholly "invented," made up; surreal, perhaps. I once wrote "We meet in a room called Rome, sleep in France." Rome of course is not a room, and so most people would think I was being figurative. But, in fact, I once visited a rather grand house in Ireland where the rooms were named for cities and countries. I met a nice woman named Deborah in her room, Rome. I slept in a beautiful room called France; Paris was its little antechamber.

People cannot be memorized. Our experience of them is internalized, not memorized. When our relationships are disbanded by the action of time upon them, by death in particular, we lose the conditions for relation; the dead take up residence within us. We cannot, for example, introduce them to our friends. Years ago, my mother began to appear in my poems not as herself at all but as a certain idea of the wild, of wilderness: a radiant but destructive force, alluring and frightful, beautiful and foul. She had disappeared, to be replaced by various linguistic tropes. Last year, when my sister Jennifer was dying, there suddenly started to appear in my poems a young girl. It was odd. This girl, this futurity, came into the map of the poems, and each time she appeared, each time she appears, I am consoled. She is the only consolation. She is not my sister, but she is the unfulfilled promise of my sister, the disembodied embodiment of her curtailed life. She is also, perhaps, a fragment of our childhood, although nothing she does in the poems refers directly to a specific time or place; also, perhaps, the daughter I do not have. Writing the girl does not fulfill broken promises or change the reality of loss, but it does, somehow, alleviate. She is not a symbol of something or someone else: not sister, not daughter, not death: she is a new thing in the world.

> From Christ to Freud we have believed that, if we know the truth, the truth will set us free: art is indispensable because so much of this truth can be learned through works of art and through works of art alone—for which of us could have learned for himself what Proust and Chekov, Hardy and Yeats and Rilke, Shakespeare and Homer, learned for us? and in what other way could they have made us see the truths that they themselves saw, those differing and contradictory truths which seem nevertheless, to the mind that contains them, in some sense a single truth?
> —Randall Jarrell, from "The Obscurity of the Poet"

When I was living in London I went to a lecture given by the remarkable doctor/theatrical director Jonathan Miller. The lecture was in a series that addressed the possible relationships between technology and art. Dr. Miller said (I remember this exactly): "Facts are not the things we pick up off the street like pearls or primroses; they are statements about things." It was a revelation. I saw that we do tend to think of facts as things, objects, material actualities. And that, because of this, we have managed to confound or collude ideas of the real with ideas of the true. But they are not the same. Truth, of course, is also a statement about things, sometimes a statement about reality. The twin agents of truth in art are memory and imagination. If we sever the imagined from the remembered, we are stuck with flat resemblances that merely report back to us the constraints of the real, and facts become things to pick up off the street like bottle-tops or pennies. Memory and imagination are the twinned agencies of truth.

> *I dwell in Possibility—*
> *A fairer house than Prose—*
> *More numerous of Windows—*
> *Superior—for Doors—*
> *—Emily Dickinson, from #657*

> *"It is possible, possible, possible."*
> *—Wallace Stevens, from "Notes Toward a Supreme Fiction"*

I locate my poems in the present tense, not to vacate the past but to provide a place for the possible. Language is its own experience, the fundamental way in which we get to choose and to change. We get to repeat things we love, destroy things we despise. We get to cheat destiny or fate by making another destiny or fate. We get to go places we have never been. How cheap! We get to sleep with persons we cannot sleep with, free of guilt or harm. We slay dragons, build temples, comfort the sick. Memory is a form of dream: it belongs to our single selves, alone. Telling you about something that happened does not, cannot, let you be there, not in the *as* but only in the *as if*.

The events of our lives are individual, unique. Our responses to them are shared. Writing, I want to make a primary event, one that will cause memory in you.

> *Loss of names is one kind of leakage*
> *But there is another: the actual scale*
> *Breezing along in daring episodes,*
> *Most of it escaping utterance, falling*
> *Back into the temple housing callow and amorphous*
> *As well as enchanted, and there waits*
> *To be spirited toward us, away from the unrecovered.*
> *—Ann Lauterbach, from "Graffiti"*

THREE MEDITATIONS
ON WALLACE STEVENS

DAVID LEHMAN

(I) DOMINANT X

the vital, arrogant, fatal, dominant X.
— *"The Motive for Metaphor"*

X. distrusts action; he has his is,
His was, *which shall be again, when*
The jangle of change is spent, the jingle
Of jargon clicks off, and peace in the jungle
Reigns in the tiger's snore, as before.

He has the exact change in his pocket.
He deposits it in the small glass booth
Of the bus he boards on his way to work.
He distrusts action; he has his window,
His view, and there is nothing he can do

To alter the ego of the age except now
And then to turn poplars into cypresses,
Poppies into irises, Monet to Van Gogh;
To turn, and then, turn back again.

(II) NEGATIVITY

After the final no there comes a yes
And on that yes the future world depends.
No was the night. Yes is the present sun.
*

It can never be satisfied, the mind, never.
— *"The Well Dressed Man with a Beard"*

Wallace Stevens seems nearly as fond of negative expressions, of nots and nevers and nuncles, as of jovial hullabaloos ("Such tink and tank and tunk-a-tunk-tunk"[1]) and state-of-being verbs. Three separate sentences in *Harmonium* negate the possibility of spring: "No spring can follow past meridian," the middle-aged lover sighs in "Le Monocle de Mon Oncle" (CP, 13), and the same sentiment concludes both "Indian River" ("Yet there is no spring in Florida, neither in boskage perdu, nor on the nunnery beaches," CP, 112) and "Depression

Before Spring" ("But no queen comes / In slipper green," CP, 63). It is easy to see the attractions this rhetorical device would have for the autumnal Mr. Stevens, whose speculations on the nature and function of the imagination take as their starting point a condition of absence, "An absence in reality, / Things as they are" (CP, 176). But in achieving their primary aim, that of indicating and specifying an absence, Stevens' negative expressions serve also as a means of inclusion, of making present in the text what is missing from the reality external to it, the reality defined as "things as they are." "There are no bears among the roses," Stevens writes in "The Virgin Carrying a Lantern" (CP, 71), thereby compelling the reader precisely to juxtapose the bears and the roses, just as Eliot's Prufrock invites us to compare him to Hamlet when he says "No, I am not Prince Hamlet, nor was meant to be." The negative in both cases creates an ambiguity; put either statement in positive form and you diminish, if not demolish, its poetic impact.

For Stevens, here as elsewhere, the *no* acts as a pivotal point in the encounter or exchange between reality and the imagination. As in Samuel Beckett's *Watt*, whose eponymous hero is employed by the elusive Mr. Knott, the relations, between *what* and *not* form a crucial subplot in Stevens' poetry, and we would do well to scrutinize some of his negative expressions for the light they may shed on his "motive for metaphor" and on the perpetual swinging of his poetic pendulum from absence to presence and back.

Stevens frequently uses *not* as a more accurate way of saying *like*—as a negative simile. A literalist of the imagination, he habitually dons his philosopher's hat in an effort to strip away from a "plain sense of things" those fictions that are merely falsehoods, that cheapen by sentimentalizing actuality. "The accuracy of accurate letters is an accuracy with respect to the structure of reality," he pronounces rather severely in *The Necessary Angel* (p. 71). It is this side of Stevens that insists, even as he exuberantly metamorphoses a pineapple, that the poet "must say nothing of the fruit that is / Not true, nor think it, less" (NA, 84). (One notes that the enjambment here compromises the face value of the injunction; the double negative makes a positive only after giving the misleading appearance of negative intent.) The "literalist" attitude is epitomized in the Williamsian title of Stevens' late poem "Not Ideas About the Thing But the Thing Itself" (CP, 534). It is as though, preparatory to the imagination's redemptive activity, the poet must take pains to behold life unadorned and man unaccommodated, to oppose an empty spirit to a vacant place. Relentlessly he must distinguish the naked *is* from the mythic and no longer credible *was*, as in the World War I poem, "The Death of a Soldier":

> *He does not become a three-days personage,*
> *Imposing his separation,*
> *Calling for pomp.*
>
> *(CP, 97)*

Heaven is empty; we live without a belief in nobility, let alone in miracles, and so the soldier's sacrifice is bereft of both the hope of resurrection and the power to impose itself upon the collective consciousness of humankind.

Nowhere does Stevens spell out with greater clarity the value of negativity as trope than in "Study of Two Pears," where, with Cézanne-like concentration, he affixes the beam of his gaze on an ordinary day's still life. The poem represents the turn to which "Someone Puts A Pineapple Together" provides the "tropically" sublime counterturn. Like the latter, it bills itself as an "academic piece"—its first words are "Opusculum paedagogum"—but there the resemblance ends. To use the categories set up in Stevens' essay "The Noble Rider and the Sound of Words," "Study of Two Pears" is emphatically "favorable to what is real" (NA, 12). "The pears are not seen / As the observer wills," the poem concludes; no, they must be seen "as in themselves they really are" (Matthew Arnold). Thus,

> *The pears are not viols,*
> *Nudes or bottles.*
> *They resemble nothing else.*
> *(CP, 196)*

The "not" skirts the borderline separating metaphor from simile or, more exactly, it defines the essential difference between the two figures. The double negative serves to differentiate *seems* from *is,* in the name of letting "be be finale of seem" (CP, 64). Two statements having equal validity are implied: "the pears resemble what they are not," and "the pears are not what they resemble." But in so distinguishing pears from "viols, / Nudes or bottles," has the poet not brought those very objects together? Has he not in fact shown us the pears "as in themselves they really are not" (Oscar Wilde)?[2] The "not," then, effectively turns the sentence into the antithesis of its own thesis. It furthers an accurate perception of reality, reminding us that the identity of a thing involves the subtraction of all its *semblables.* At the same time, however, it admits into the picture plane the possibility of a proliferation of resemblances. Stevens has it both ways. He makes us see the fruits as simultaneously distinct from, and like, the things of their shape and climate.

In poems that celebrate the mind's ability to abstract the real and place it in an enchanted realm, the metamorphoses forbidden in "Study of Two Pears" take place, whether despite or because of an intervening "not" or its equivalent. The heliotrope, in "Gubbinal," assumes the guise of

> *That strange flower, the sun,*
> . . . .
> *That tuft of jungle feathers,*
> *That animal eye,*
> . . . .
> *That savage of fire,*
> *that seed.*

Here the place of the *not* is taken by the imagined reply of the skeptic to whom the poem is addressed, who would presumably reject such primitive magic. "Have it your way," Stevens tells this straw man; and if you do,

> *The world is ugly,*
> *And the people are sad.*
> *(CP, 85)*

Such is the bleakness that comes from yielding without a struggle to "the pressure of reality." Nor does Stevens fail to let us know what kind of struggle he endorses. Among other things, it requires the assertion of an irrational mythy-mindedness, the will to dissolve distinctions and to lift, by disbelieving, "The weight of primary noon" (CP, 288). The nay-sayer in one must somehow be neutralized, the force of his negativity refocused, in order for things to break out of their confined limits, for them to conjugate and bring forth strange fruit, and for the tree they grow on to branch out in numerous metaphorical directions.

By its very title, "Study of Two Pears" has defined its project as an examination of what already exists. "Someone Puts a Pineapple Together," on the contrary, leaps from perception to construction and creation. In the course of the poem, "Someone" (the writer? the reader?) makes a mountain out of a pineapple; the poem charts

> *The momentary footings of a climb*
> *Up the pineapple, a table Alp and yet*
> *An Alp, a purple southern mountain bisqued*
>
> *With the molten mixings of related things,*
> *Cat's taste possibly or possibly Danish lore,*
> *The small luxuriations that portend*
>
> *Universal delusions of universal grandeurs,*
> *The slight incipiencies, of which the form,*
> *At last, is the pineapple on the table or else*
>
> *An object the sum of its complications, seen*
> *And unseen. This is everybody's world.*
> *Here the total artifice reveals itself*
>
> *As the total reality.*
>
> *(NA, 87)*

The pineapple has become an Alp, albeit "a table Alp"; the adjectival qualification has cushioned the force of negation sufficiently to permit the transformation to go on unimpeded. Whereas the "not" of "Study of Two Pears" warns the observer against seeing things as they might be, there is no such superego-interference in the pineapple poem. The charm of this invitation extended to the power of possibility is that, far from effecting an unreal product, it leads to "the total reality." The fruit is "more truly" seen as "more strange" (CP, 65). It is valuable precisely because it is "a fund" of images and because, in the words of another Stevens title, "Reality Is an Activity of the Most August Imagination" (OP, 110). Thanks to the fortuitous encounter of the pineapple and the imagination on the dining-room table, "The profusion of metaphor has been increased" (NA, 83). In the Florida of the mind the pineapple has, through the agency of metaphor, transcended itself.

Traveling the road to metaphor, which is the road to a supreme fiction, the poet has had to hurdle the high posts of negativity. He has had to say "no" to "no"; he must, he knows, "Divest reality / Of its propriety." How? By adding imagination, itself a part of reality; that is, by seeing the imagination as not incompatible with reality, which it means to complement not cancel. As a result of the process, "Casual exfoliations" in the form of twelve pineapple plots, each "Of the tropic of resemblances," each with the characteristic odor of the fruit, rise up into view, numbered for convenience's sake:

> 1. *The hut stands by itself beneath the palms.*
> 2. *Out of their bottle the green genii come.*
> 3. *A vine has climbed the other side of the wall.*
>
> 4. *The sea is spouting upward out of rocks.*
> 5. *The symbol of feasts and of oblivion . . .*
> 6. *White sky, pink sun, trees on a distant peak.*
>
> 7. *These lozenges are nailed-up lattices.*
> 8. *The owl sits humped. It has a hundred eyes.*
> 9. *The coconut and cockerel in one.*
>
> 10. *This is how yesterday's volcano looks.*
> 11. *There is an island Palahude by name—*
> 12. *An uncivil shape like a gigantic haw.*
>
> (NA, 86)

Each of the twelve is an aesthetic prerogative, a potential starting block for a purely imaginary race around the track of an "abstracted" reality. In each case, the fiction is left for the reader to complete so as virtually to ensure that he or she become an active participant in the proceedings. Whether the volcano erupts again, whether the genii grant our wishes or confound them, whether the distant peak is reached, is immaterial; it is the possibility that counts. The poem has at least this much in common with the OuLiPo, the French organization of experimental writers and mathematicians founded in 1960 by Raymond Queneau and François LeLionnais. (Its current membership includes Georges Perec, Italo Calvino, and Harry Mathews.) OuLiPo—an acronym of Ouvroir de Littéraire Potentielle, or "charity bazaar of potential literature"—seeks to arrive at new poetic forms and stratagems as ends in themselves; it honors pure possibility, as does Stevens in singing the pineapple's praises.[3]

In certain of Stevens' poems, the *not* cooperates quite amenably with the impulse toward divine, or at least exotic, potentiality. In "Disillusionment of Ten O'Clock," the negative expression permits the reader to behold something that is not there to compensate for the nothing that is. Only the first two lines of the poem concern themselves directly with inadequate actuality. The tone is sarcastic:

> *The houses are haunted*
> *By white night-gowns.*

The rest of the poem is given to lush alternatives to the drab and sterile suburban night:

> *None are green,*
> *Or purple with green rings,*
> *Or green with yellow rings,*
> *Or yellow with blue rings.*

None of them are strange,
With socks of lace
And beaded ceintures.
People are not going
To dream of baboons and periwinkles.
Only, here and there, an old sailor,
Drunk and asleep in his boots,
Catches tigers
In red weather.

(CP, 66)

We see, in effect, as on a split screen—things as they bleakly are, intimated by the reiterated negatives, off to one side, and things changed upon the blue guitar on the other side. The crucial words in the poem are *none* and *or* and *not,* for they make possible the multiplication of illusions. And by the poem's conclusion, no "no"—only an "only"—is needed to modify the figure of the poet as an old but virile sailor. What is absent from the real night has been made present in the poem, while what is present in the night becomes a shadowy "not," an absence, in the poem. We began with the disillusionment of the title and we end with fresh "illusionment" and the promise of more. This is entirely in line with Stevens' objections, made at several points in *The Necessary Angel,* to the "dis-illusory" enterprise of Freud's *The Future of an Illusion.* Such zealous rationalism, Stevens argues, is "inimical to poetry" (NA, 15).

"Things as they are," then, frequently amount to embodied nothingness. Seeing them that way becomes an exercise in negative capability and as such is an indispensable preliminary to the sleight-of-hand man's main act. "The Snow Man" is only the most devastating example of the equation of *what* and *not* in Stevens's poetry:

For the listener, who listens in the snow,
And, nothing himself, beholds
Nothing that is not there and the nothing that is.

(CP, 10)

The weight of the definite article, both here and at the end of "The Man on the Dump" (CP, 203) has occasioned much comment, but the double sense of "nothing" is equally worthy of consideration. The word is primal in the sense Freud intends in his essay "The Antithetical Sense of Primal Words": it means itself and its opposite.[4] All that is necessary to separate one "nothing" from another—the imagination's sweet nothings from the bitterly cold nothings of the day—is the *the.* Something and nothing reverse roles, and nothing is all. One thinks, in this connection, of the uses to which Henry Green put the word in his novel *Nothing.* One thinks too of the last line of A. R. Ammons' prefatory poem to *Sphere: The Form of a Motion.* "Nothing will ever be the same again," he writes, indicating either that a complete change has occurred or that, on the contrary, nothing stays itself, and "ever" shall.[5]

The "bodiless" serpent in the opening section of "The Auroras of Autumn" is, Harold Bloom argues, a symbol of Ananke, goddess of dread necessity, third in line after Eros and Dionysus for the Orphic poet to embrace.[6] It may also be read as a trope for poetry which, by relentlessly transforming its materials, sheds defunct versions of the self, as the snake discards successive skins. In Stevens' last poems, the discarding process advances to a final affirmation of the nothing that remains. To be sure, Stevens continues to rely on negative expressions for the old purpose of bridging the gap between absence and presence, mediating between reality and imagination. There is, for instance, the characteristic use of the negative simile in "Reality Is an Activity of the Most August Imagination":

> *It was not a night blown at a glassworks in Vienna*
> *Or Venice, motionless, gathering time and dust.*

But the end to which "The visible transformations of summer night" leads is

> *An argentine abstraction approaching form*
> *And suddenly denying itself away.*
>
> *There was an insolid billowing of the solid.*
> *Night's moonlight lake was neither water nor air.*
> *(OP, 110–11)*

As a way of first making distinctions and then transcending them, the negative expression has served as the perfect "dialectical" instrument. Now, having cleared the air of everything, it proposes itself as the one suitable linguistic forum for approaching the ultimate in "mere" being, "without human meaning. / Without human feeling" (OP, 117). The invisible is the negative of day's photograph, and it can be developed only on the darkroom of the imagination, the shadow of god. Here is the conclusion of "A Clear Day With No Memories":

> *Today the air is clear of everything.*
> *It has no knowledge except of nothingness*
> *And it flows over us without meanings,*
> *As if none of us had ever been here before*
> *And are not now: in this shallow spectacle,*
> *This invisible activity, this sense.*
> *(OP, 113)*

(III) STEVENS AND FREUD

> *Not as a god, but as a god might be*
> —"Sunday Morning"

In "The Noble Rider and the Sound of Words," Stevens cites "Boileau's remark that Descartes had cut poetry's throat" and suggests substituting Freud's name for that of Descartes. Stevens had particularly in mind *The Future of an Illusion,* which he calls "inimical to poetry" because it advocates "a surrender to reality" (NA, 14–15). Like Nabokov, another aesthete and illusionist *par excellence* who displays considerable irritation at the drop of Freud's name, Stevens adopts a somewhat cantankerous tone in registering his objections, but this is misleading: in both cases the dissent is intellectual and not merely temperamental. Indeed, upon inspection, the quarrel between the American poet and the founder of psychoanalysis delineates itself quite logically into a pair of rival columns. On the left hand side, under Stevens' banner, value adheres to the imagination and to the irrational element which nourishes it; on Freud's side of the ledger, the voice of reason counsels us sternly to brave the terror of existence without recourse to place-bos or narcotics in the form of fond wishes, fairy tales, daydreams, imaginings. Both would agree that religious beliefs, having lost all credibility, amount to illusion, and neither would dispute the other's definition of the word. Freud puts it for both of them when he stresses that "illusionment need not necessarily be false—that is to say, unrealizable or in contradiction to reality."[7] The crucial point is that, whether they prove erroneous or accurate in the long run, illusions derive "from human wishes" and flourish with a complete disregard for scientific verification. Precisely so, Stevens would say. No, it is over the ground of value not meaning—over the worth and neces-sity of fictions, as Stevens prefers to call them—that the two writers engage in their tug-of-war.

At the center of Freud's enterprise is an identification of the rational intellect with civilization itself. Our instincts, though we must be kind to them, are not to be trusted. Like a child come of age, the culture as a whole must, by an act of rational choice and enlightened will, renounce such pleasure-promising instincts as stand in the path of the civilizing impulse, the progress of science translated into the exigen-cies of the social world. Science conceives of itself as the archenemy of illusions and, by extension, of the imagination which contrives them, often enough as part of a self-delusion, a neurotic soap opera of the psyche.

At the heart of Stevens' mystery is the conviction that the zero degree of reality does not provide nourishment enough for the human spirit upon which we who pursue happiness have no choice but to depend. Stevens exalts the mind's illusion-making capacity even as Freud admonishes against it. Nor would the poet shrink from recog-nizing, and accepting, a religious aspect to the poetics he propounds. "After one has abandoned a belief in god, poetry is that essence which takes its place as life's re-demption," he writes in his "Adagia," a Nietzschean compendium of epigrams (OP, 158), thus providing the perfect prose trot to these lines from "The Man with the Blue Guitar":

> The earth, for us, is flat and bare.
> There are no shadows. Poetry
>
> Exceeding music must take the place
> Of empty heaven and its hymns,
>
> Ourselves in poetry must take their place,
> Even in the chattering of your guitar.
> (CP, 167)

Stevens says much the same thing in the rambunctious high spirits of "A High-Toned Old Christian Woman" where he opposes a wink to the devout widow's wince. In that poem's terms, peristyle and saxophones—a conjunction of images that combines Greek aestheticism and jazz "primitivism"—differ from the nave and "windy citherns" of an outmoded Christianity not so much in their desired goal as in their effectiveness in reaching it. "We agree in principle," Stevens tells the old woman, about the need to "project a masque / Beyond the planets." Where we take our separate paths, he adds, tweaking her pious nose, is in our attitudes toward "bawdiness"; far from unholy, as madame would have it, it in fact helps one trace a route to the sublime, to a paradise renewed (CP, 59).

For organized religion, then, Stevens has as little respect as Freud. Heaven is haunted, we are told more than once, and "The darkened ghosts of our old comedy" (CP, 56) must go the way of that "old catastrophe," the crucifixion (CP, 67). But Freud aspires to an Utopian nowhere; he brandishes his sword at the gate and banishes the ghosts from the ghostly paradise and into a world of forced labor. Stevens, on the contrary, envisions a sensuous New Jerusalem in Eden's stead, an imagined land where spirit and sense will replace spirits and shadows. Where Freud, under no illusions as to the discontents reality generates, resolutely stands as realism's champion, Stevens' visionary mission leads him to wonder quite candidly whether he has "lived a skeleton's life. / As a disbeliever in reality," as he writes in the late poem "As You Leave the Room." The doubt endures a momentary existence: the "elevation" the poet experiences is, he maintains, "Part of a major reality, part of / An appreciation of a reality" (OP, 117). Yet speaking for Freud, we can seize upon that flicker of doubt and say that the imagination's high priest must, by the very nature of things, lapse into the domain of the unreal or, at least, the unreasonable. Stevens accepts this danger in stride. If, after all, the imagination alone can furnish a satisfactory response to the dilemma of reality, and if the imagination remains a natural instinct rather than a culturally acquired value, so be it. Like a religion, indeed, "poetry must be irrational" (OP, 162).

As I have mapped it out, the conflict between Freud and Stevens seems made to order for the perennial university symposia which pit culture and reason against nature and instinct in a philosophical debate of universal application.

But perhaps the most interesting feature of Stevens' quarrel with Freud is that, in the bold strokes I have drawn to summarize the confrontation, neither party is being completely fair to himself; their attitudes are far more complex than the positions the logic of the argument compels them to take. In fact, each is as it were heroically ambivalent about the very articles of his faith; the uneasy relations between reality and the imagination call forth paradoxical responses from both authors. It is that area of overlap to which I want to give some attention, for reasons that will, I hope, become clear in the process.

Consider Freud first. The opinion put forth with such vigor in *The Future of an Illusion* faintly contradicts other of his assumptions and premises. Of this Freud himself seems, one could say, subconsciously cognizant. Beginning with the fourth chapter of his book, he transforms his "monologue" into a putative dialogue with "an opponent who follows my argument with mistrust" (FI, 21). This is a familiar if no less efficient rhetorical device; it is nothing else than the dialectical method employed by Socrates, with whom Freud shares the dual credo that "the unexamined life is not worth living" and that reason is the proper baton to conduct the examination. But the very ease with which Freud adopts an adversary stance—only to knock it down, to be sure—does testify to his sympathetic identification with the rival point of view. It would not be going too far to say that he contains his own enemy, in both senses of *contain:* he has it inside him, like a mutinous id, and he repels its military advance or at least limits it to a slice of mental territory set within well-defined borders. Like Stevens, Freud is an adept nay-sayer, and what he says no to he includes, albeit in a shadowed form.

No one had done more than Freud to present as a legitimate source of knowledge what his own and previous generations dismissed as the irrational. No one succeeded as he did in expanding our sense of reality, conferring ontological and epistemological status to the unconscious, the mythic, the products of fancy and fantasy, wit and "the diseased imagination," whether these manifested themselves in dreams, jokes, and errors, or in texts and tales. From the theatre of illusions came the Oedipal paradigm that Freud made the cornerstone of his new science. To that complex of behavioral patterns he affixed the phrase "the family romance"; the phrase suggests the extent to which Freud cast the character of the Psyche in terms derived from aesthetic (primarily dramatic) categories. (He was also, it should be added, quick to own up to his indebtedness to the poets who, as he put it, got there first.)[8] Freud operated rather like a literary critic in his scrutiny of the psyche's poetic inventions. It is not at all difficult to see why a contemporary of his might have looked upon him as a witch-doctor, for in a quite literal sense he believed himself to be a mindreader. To the degree it provided him with a text to interpret, clues to track down, defenses to "deconstruct," the neurotic imagination was capable of remedy; its concealments themselves would foster revelation, just as poetic figures such as metaphor and irony disguise (or repress) the truth in order to express it in all its intricacy.

How then could the doctor in good conscience attack the system of signs that was all that stood between him and, in Yeats' phrase, "a fabulous, formless darkness"? The obvious answer is that, for Freud, the signs are symptoms, metaphors of malaise. The function of criticism is not to foster an appreciation of illusions and enchantments but to debunk them and to insist that a new script in a new, diagnostic language supercede the old one. Freud would, by writing about a myth, replace it, to extend the parallel with literary criticism, much of which seems determined at present to dispatch into oblivion the kind of writing on which presumably it used to feast. By re-christening poems "texts", which title also designates their own critical writings, literary theorists seem to want to substitute abstruse research for primary imagination, the prose of reason for the uncommon-sense of poetry. To be fair to Freud, he eschews the exaggerations that plague some of our most advanced critics. Like Plato who banished poets from *The Republic* and yet wrote as one, employing parables and elaborate figures to chart out his grasp of the truth and staging the proceedings as a comedy of ideas whose purely formal possibilities (as Oscar Wilde showed in *The Decay of Living* and *The Critic as Artist*) still obtain, Freud was himself a spellbinding poet and masterly mythologizer. What's more, he believed the myth *was* truth; he himself acted the part of the Teiresian proof-giver in demonstrating that our lives enact and reenact, compulsively repeating, parts mythically played by Oedipus and Jocasta and Laius. Inasmuch as his writing often took the form of a refiguring of ancient myth and literary metaphor—one thinks, for example, of his analysis of the three caskets in *The Merchant of Venice*[9]—Freud's procedures have something vital in common with those of modern poets such as Eliot, Rilke, Joyce, and Cocteau, to name but a few who conceived the present in mythic patterns and consciously sought to "update" their sources. Edmund Wilson, in a striking phrase, called Karl Marx "the poet of commodities";[10] as the poet of the psyche, the poet of Cupid and Psyche, Freud likewise speaks the voice of prophecy—with the added virtue that, like Adam's dream, it seems a waking truth.

Certainly the poet no less than the critic owes an obligation to Freud. James Merrill's poetry, which David Kalstone contends is an autobiography-in-verse, would in its general contours and specific details—the weight given to dreams and to the dream-language of the pun, for instance—argue a close affinity with Freud's questioning of reality.[11] It is pertinent too that John Ashbery should publish a poem entitled "Civilization and Its Discontents,"[12] while Kenneth Koch weighs in with "The Problem of Anxiety."[13] And going back a generation, Auden's poetry, from the time of his American sojourn onwards, is virtually predicated on a holy alliance between Kierkegaard and Freud.

By touching thus briefly on the poetic base (and the poetic attractions) of Freud's scientific structures, I think we can discern a latent heroism in his renunciation of an instinctive myth-mindedness. It could even be argued that this constitutes the secret autobiographical message of *The Future of an Illusion,* if we read that work as a poem: in some important way the argument there mirrors the life.

It is as easy to detect the philosopher in Stevens as the poet in Freud. Like Shelley, Stevens grounds his vision in a deep skepticism; his assent is invariably prefaced by denial. In poem after poem Stevens speaks in the accents of the skeptical ironist; he is a rationalist by diction, a metaphysician by temperament. Where Eliot's *Four Quartets* are philosophical in content but structured on the model of a musical composition, Stevens' poems suggest the structure of an argument to go with their philosophical concerns. Reading "Le Monocle de Mon Oncle" or "Sunday Morning" requires one to follow an argument whose terms are metaphorical and whose propositions add up by dint of a definite if parabolic logic. The sense of a dogged progression through contraries is as strong in these poems as it is in *The Future of an Illusion.*

Moreover, Stevens resembles Freud closely in the pronounced approval he gives to Nietzsche's exposé of the tyranny of heaven. From both Stevens and Freud we can derive a clear understanding of the process by which

> The people grow out of the weather;
> The gods grow out of the people.
> (*"Loneliness in Jersey City,"* CP, 210)

Like Freud, Stevens would subscribe to Voltaire's assertion that "man invented god in his own image and god instantly returned the favor." The logic here, incidentally, illustrates nicely Harold Bloom's exposition of the necessary belatedness of all poetic activity. If the primitive mind perceives what it projects, an angry god in a lightning storm; if, from the image of "the fire eye in the clouds," he imagines a deity; then clearly the divinity he beholds must be made in man's own image. Thus, by insisting that man is made in the image of his maker, the religious mythologizer wishes precisely to reverse the priority, to make the belated seem early—an example of Bloom's trope of *metalepsis.* Man's worship is at root an acknowledgement of his weakness in the face of the savage forces of nature; giving birth to a god which he can, by propitiating, control, he has transmuted the very measure of his weakness into an avenue of power, a "shadowed strength" in Bloom's phrase.[14]

Stevens is after a myth of divinity that is original in both senses, that achieves its priority not by a confidence trick but by visionary intelligence. He wants to recover the myth that survives the obsolescence of myths; he knows he must go back to the source to find food for the fictive imagination. As he writes in "The Sense of the Sleight-of-Hand Man,"

> *It is a wheel, the rays*
> *Around the sun. The wheel survives the myths.*
> *The fire eye in the clouds survives the gods.*
> *(CP, 222)*

In pursuing his supreme fiction, in prophesying a savage "chant of paradise" so at odds with Christian austerity, Stevens would deny that he forfeits his right to the title of realist. Or, rather, he would assert that "Realism is a corruption of reality" (OP, 166); he would remind us that a fiction, if believed in, is no longer fiction. Still, in order to command our belief and our allegiance, poetry must be founded on the real; there is that crucial distinction to be made between fiction and falsehood. "The real is only the base," Stevens writes in the "Adagia" (OP, 160). "But it is the base." The imagination must call our attention to what is actually there—"The empty spirit / In vacant space" (CP, 131)—before we can possibly presume to go beyond it.

Where does all this leave us? The confrontation between Stevens and Freud can now, I think, be seen "more truly and more strange." In brief, Stevens would "abstract reality, which he does by placing it in his imagination" (NA, 23); Freud would do the exact reverse. Perhaps one should say "the lateral reverse" and communicate thereby the idea that Freud and Stevens have, in effect, swapped mirrors. Just as Freud's nobility is apparent in his attempt to surmount the "infantilism" of "religious consolations" (FI, 49), so is there nobility in Stevens' ambition to surmount his native rationalism in the name of the sublime. And one somehow wants not merely to navigate between the two points of view but to include them both. It has frequently been observed that with the advance of civilization the prose impulse becomes stronger and the verse impulse correspondingly weaker; that idea is disturbing indeed, not least because poetry has historically brought with it a species of redemptive enchantment of which we today are sorely in need. Rather than succumb to so costly an "advance," Stevens holds out the possibility of a sublime transcendence; to say no to "the pressure of reality," to cancel it out, is to pave the way to that possible yes on which "the future world depends." As a stay against the tide, a possibility preserved, Stevens' defense of "imagination as value" (NA, 133) is exemplary. It seems, finally, a value that the humanist must keep in the forefront of consciousness even as he puts into practice Freud's program of an "education to reality" (FI, 49).[15]

NOTES

1. *The Collected Poems of Wallace Stevens* (New York: Knopf, 1954), p. 59. Further references to this volume will be abbreviated CP and incorporated in the text. I will also use these other abbreviations for parenthetical references to Stevens's work: *Opus Posthumous*. ed. Samuel F. Morse (New York: Knopf, 1957)—OP; *The Necessary Angel* (New York: Random House, 1951)—NA.

2. It is in *The Critic as Artist* that Wilde cites Arnold's formula and argues that his subversion of it ensures results more interesting *and* more accurate. See pp. 83–87 of *The Portable Oscar Wilde*, ed. Richard Aldington (New York: Viking, 1965).

3. For an excellent account of the OuLiPo's procedures, and a list of some of its formal innovations, see Harry Mathews's "OuLiPo" in *World Ways: The Journal of Recreational Linguistics* 9, no. 2 (May 1976): 67–74. In this connection it is worth noting Stevens' remark that "All poetry is experimental poetry" (OP, 161).

4. First published in 1910, this review of Karl Abel's *Über den Gegensinn der Urworte* (1884) may be found in *Character and Culture,* ed. Philip Rieff (New York: Collier Books, 1963, 1972), pp. 44–50.

5. *Sphere: The Form of a Motion* (New York: Norton, 1974), p. 5.

6. See *Wallace Stevens: The Poems of our Climate* (Ithaca, N. Y.: Cornell University Press, 1977), pp. 255–56.

7. *The Future of an Illusion,* trans. James Strachey (New York: Norton, 1961). Further references to this volume will be abbreviated FI and incorporated in the text.

8. See Lionel Trilling, "Freud and Literature," in *The Liberal Imagination* (New York: Scribner's, 1976), p. 34.

9. "The Theme of the Three Caskets." in *Character and Culture,* pp. 67–79.

10. *To the Finland Station* (New York: Doubleday, 1953), pp. 289–91.

11. "Much of Merrill's interest in narrative and everyday experience has been aimed at discovering the charges with which certain objects have become invested for him. He seems in his developed poetry to be asking the Freudian or the Proustian question: what animates certain scenes—and not others—for us?" David Kalstone, *Five Temperaments* (New York: Oxford University Press, 1977). p. 83.

12. In *Rivers and Mountains* (New York: Holt Rinehart and Winston, 1966). pp. 11–15.

13. In *The Burning Mystery of Anna in 1951* (New York: Random House, 1979). pp. 28–36.

14. See Bloom's *Poetry and Repression: Revisionism from Blake to Stevens* (New Haven: Yale University Press, 1976).

15. For a discussion of recent books that treat the implications for theology of the psychoanalyst's articles of faith, see "Freud and God" by Robert Coles in *Virginia Quarterly Review* 57, no. 3 (Summer 1981): 381–400.

"TRANSLATING" FORM: POUND, RILKE, THEIR SCULPTORS AND THE CONTEMPORARY POEM

MICHAEL HELLER

Ezra Pound quoting Gaudier-Brzeska: "works of art attract by a resembling unlikeness." Or say more simply and generally: this leaf *not* that leaf. Enough in the mind to call it leaf or to hear wind and imagine a stirring. What is of interest here are the possibilities—likeliness or unlikeness—of a relation between dissimilars, between stone or material alive on the air and words or a song of words alive on the page and in the hearing.

The dumb show of an art, even a verbal art is its end in silence. If the poem excites the hearing, it is only to bring hearing to a resolute close. If the stone prompts an eye to move across its surfaces, to "take it in," there comes a point, a fullness of seeing in which eye and intellect rest, where response ends in awe. Consider what has been seen or overheard: surfaces and angles of stone, words and expressions, images, terms, chinks and chunks of the discrete. Look at some object or person beside you, immediately the rest of the surroundings diminish. By what magical act will you set object with object, word with word, surface with surface in some organization which succeeds in expressing a wholeness without diminishing any of its parts in the process. Art's silence and wholeness.

And yet, how such silence still manages to speak, how such wholeness and completeness can invoke the incomplete. Consider how one artist's work seems to speak, not so much to its creator but to another artist's work, as though a dialogue were carried on between quite dissimilar works, dissimilar forms. Consider this as a kind of translation; that is, consider two forms, even in two entirely different idioms, attempting to express what commonality there is between them. And this commonality, since its exists as much between works as in works and is thus never defined entirely within any one of them, going by such names as tradition, spirit, zeitgeist.

I am concerned here with two well-known instances of such translation: the work of Ezra Pound and its involvement with Gaudier-Brzeska's and that of Rilke with Rodin's.

I want not simply to recapitulate the well-told stories of how the poets in question were influenced by the sculptors (Both Hugh Kenner's *The Pound Era* and Donald Davie's *The Poet as Sculptor* are exhaustive studies of Pound's connection to sculpture and the other arts.) Rather, I am concerned with how the notions of attraction and of "translating" from one art to another throw light on the problem of form and what such interaction suggests by way of lesson and exemplum for the contemporary poet.

A little backtracking from Kenner's book. Let us reimagine Ezra Pound in his twenties, wandering London before the Great War, an American casting his eye on the overblown optimistic art of the Empire or on that other art (Beardsley and the Rosettis, for example), in such revulsion against its milieu that, but by theatrical decadence, it had become a Tartarian mirror of Victorian respectability.

Now Pound, one of the last to be educated in the classics, was concerned to know "by thirty years of age" as he put it, "what is accounted poetry everywhere . . . to know the dynamic kernel from the shell." By this time, his head was full of snippets ("gists and piths" he was later to call them) of an admittedly idiosyncratic "best" of some half-dozen languages. Pound, as we know, meant to employ these snippets, to rescue and reanimate them from the deader than dead exegesis of scholars.

It was here that Pound encountered Gaudier's work and the ideas behind it as formalized in Gaudier's *Vortex*. It was that work and writing which helped set modern poetry on its present course.

Pound was coming at the act of writing from two similar and self-reinforcing standpoints. First, poetry could be seen as an act of literary translation; that is, one could draw a parallel between a literary artifact in one language with its own set of parameters, stresses, inflections, etc. and its conversion into an equivalently charged piece of English. This translation, Pound sensed, was not dissimilar to what happened when a poet tried to render what is seen or thought or overheard into the vigorous, emotionally charged language of the poem. Second, Pound was reinventing what he called in "The New Method of Scholarship" the notion of the "luminous detail." The "luminous detail" was an alternative way of rendering the meaning of a time, place, or epoch. Instead of the usual fact-heavy accumulations of standard history, Pound proposed that a time or place could be rendered or at least implied by a single heightened fact, a single inimitable gesture such as a work of art. Seen thus, a tomb-scroll opened up all of Egypt, a passage of Homer radiated the psychological makeup of its age. As we know, further support for these notions would come very shortly in Hulme's Imagism and Fenollosa's study of the Chinese ideogram. Yet the one thing all these notions lacked, and which may have caused Pound to wonder what one does with all these gists and piths, was an organizing principle, a methodology by which to transform a collection of "dynamic yet isolated kernels" into a work of art. At this point, Pound's encounter with Gaudier becomes significant.

The meeting of Pound and Gaudier was in no sense a confrontation; rather, it was as though one parallel track had run into another. Gaudier's work suggested a solution to Pound's need for a principle of poetic construction, a principle which in its working out is a major aspect of the anguished history of poetry in our time. Consider, for example, how these sentences from Gaudier's *Vortex* may have spoken to Pound: "Sculptural feeling is the appreciation of masses in relation. Sculptural ability is the defining of these masses by planes." Substitute gists or images for masses, translate the visual-spatial "planes" into their poetic equivalents such as lines or spacing or image-constructs, and one begins to appreciate how Gaudier and Pound nearly resonate with each other's theorizing. Again and again, we see this echoing. Gaudier, for example, in a letter to Pound reaffirming the principles of *Vortex*, writes: I shall derive my emotions solely from the ARRANGEMENT OF SURFACES. I shall present my emotions by the arrangement of my surfaces, the planes and lines by which they are defined." And

Pound (in *Mauberley* later, but looking back to the London period) recalls: "Turned from the eau-forte / Par Jacquemont / to the strait head of Messalina / An art in profile . . . This urge to convey the relation of eyelid and cheekbone / by verbal manifestation." We note that in each of these artists' conception there is the sense of something discrete (call it mass or pith) with an expressive life of its own which it is the artist's business to group into a whole that renders the total artistic meaning.

Pound's purpose in the *Cantos* was to write "a poem containing history." Not another linear textbook of events, but Pound's individuated vision of what History meant to one man in the here and now: how it is that in his magnificent phrase, "all ages are contemporaneous." In this vision, the *Cantos* itself, the "planes and masses" are discrete pieces of history's verbal manifestations: Confucian wisdom, troubadour song, quotations from Jefferson and Adams, politics, economics, on and on—not as anthology of thought or interesting memorabilia, but as plane against plane, mass against mass, time against time—here by direct presentation, there by enjambment or by a phrase mocked in the poet's translation. And always with the eye taught by Gaudier to make beauty in the details, fulfilling something Pound had also overheard in Brancusi, that "every one of the thousand angles of approach to a statue ought to be interesting, it ought to have a life (Brancusi might perhaps permit me to say 'divine' life) of its own." And like Gaudier's work, the mystery of the *Cantos,* its expressive life, is "between" its elements as much as within them, so that it too has a kind of totemic power.

Gaudier-Brzeska (from *Vortex*): "The fair Greek saw himself only. *He* petrified his own semblance." Both Gaudier and Pound (Pound, probably because of Gaudier) saw Greek sculpture as a narcissistic decay of that interest in form which marked the power of Egyptian art. Yet, put the way Gaudier had said it, "The fair Greek saw himself only," one can imagine Rilke's wishful concurrence. For the art to which the German Romantics looked was above all Greek art and in Gaudier's condemnation one finds both the reason and the problems of Romantic art. For in the Romantics, this looking on was not formal in the sense that the artist wished to acquire the technical means of the Greeks, as say Pound wishes in studying the troubadours. Rather, it was an inspired looking, a hopeful looking wherein the Romantic imagination saw the ideal closure of subject in form. Whether either view, that of Gaudier's which saw decadence, or that of the Romantic which saw embodied idealization, is true to the Greeks is another question. What does seem true is that Gaudier's perspective can be set in opposition to the Romantic, especially the classical-romantic tradition as exemplified by Rodin for whom Rilke worked and by whom Rilke felt himself influenced. Also, we can pose an opposition in Pound's way as a poet, his emphasis on the objective notion of the art, and Rilke's, in some respects *the* quintessential subjective poet.

Such an opposition, between objective and subjective, lies at the very center of the problem of form and of those tensions which animate the contemporary poem. The poet, leaping into the modern and postmodern phase of his or her art, may ignore one of these opposing poles only it would seem at great artistic peril. With Pound and Rilke, we see this opposition as problematic—bearing with it a complexity which forces us to rethink the objective/subjective dichotomies. Again, a bit of historical backtracking.

Rilke:

ARCHAIC TORSO OF APOLLO

We did not know his legendary head,
in which the eyeballs ripened. But
his torso still glows like a candelabrum
in which his gaze, only turned low,

holds and gleams. Else could not the curve
of the breast blind you, nor in the slight turn
of the loins could a smile be running
to that middle, which carried procreation.

Else would this stone be standing maimed and short
under the shoulder's translucent plunge
nor flimmering like the fell of breasts of prey

nor breaking out of all its contours
like a star: for there is no place
that does not see you. You must change your life.

Is it not an accident—blessed accident—that some division, some separate solitary path leads one of us to the form alive in the air and another to the form shaped in speech or in print? And yet, do not these utterances, by their different means, do they not converge in the perceiver? Is he not lifted, crushed, anguished, overjoyed in the apprehension? Is it not, as Rilke insists, that life must change "breaking out of all contours like a star" before either the song or the stone?

Yet come another way into this: A song of the stone? Before the stone, before the world, honoring, praising? Is it not, in this poem, a way of speaking which intertwines with the stone, gathering in a movement toward further possibility, toward a deepened sense of life. Rilke, before the torso: "You must change your life." Because, of the stone: "there is no place that does not see you." The marble "gazes" back, prompting the utterance, prompting in the observer the desire to alter by act of eye-consciousness, to take "within" one, the movements of the stone, which Rilke thought would modify the soul. Humankind's stone and humankind's song caught in a particular nexus.

Rilke often suggested that the purpose of his art (see, for example, the letters he wrote during the composition of the *Duino Elegies*) was to keep "life open towards death"; not the sense of death as extinction but "imagined as an altogether surpassing intensity." I wonder if we do not all recognize the truth and intention of these words of Rilke's, that far from being a call to morbidity, they ask that we open ourselves to the world, to, in a sense, "give over" to the thing seen. I wonder if we do not all experience this at one time or another, before nature or a work of art or a deeply loved person; do we not, as the artist will say, "die into the form of the other."

I am speaking here metaphorically of course, not so much to bind us to an image as to admit the lack of adequate knowledge and terminology. Consider the thing across the room, the print on the page, the voice on air—these are somehow complete, closed in on themselves, yet they all gesture outward. Now the gesture may not be the artist's first consideration. He may be concerned with arrestment, with "solution," with some rearrangement of the visible or the oral which will ease a tension which really began in his addressing himself to the materials at hand, or to an as yet unspoken or unvisualized image. From the tension and its resolution there emerges the outward gesture.

Now what amazed and enraptured Rilke and the German Romantic movement about classical sculpture was the sheer perfection of its solution (even fragments conveyed its wholeness: "else would this stone be standing maimed and short"), its seeming closedness, along with the power of its outward gesture. It did not ask you to complete *it,* but to complete *yourself,* that is, to discover what it means to face that death-into-another-form of surpassing intensity.

Rilke's poem is a virtual textbook of the struggle within the Romantic imagination. For while this urge for completion, for changing one's life, is universal, it has its peculiar historical *moment* in the Romantics. We know that while the Greeks lived in a world of gods and men and perfected themselves in the glare of the deities, the Romantics, who loved Greek art, had no deities they were accountable to but had instead to confront a mechanical world indifferent to man. Romantic man had first to create his own purpose, his own *raison* of existence. The poem is a paradigm of this situation. First, we have the gaze upon the statue, the taking in of its qualities and suggestions; then, suddenly, the leap inward to another space, another dimension with the last two lines:

for there is no place
that does not see you. You must change your life

The descriptive passages up to that point do not logically entail the conclusion. One can imagine the poem ending with the words "like a star," a praising of the statue. But the Torso, by its seeming wholeness *punishes* the Romantic observer, confronts him with his own sense of uncertain being. It is this wholeness (as Gaudier remarked of the Greek) which the observer would be quite happy to see in himself.

Let us speak again of form. Before all the forms, the poems, and the marble, there is a sense of awe, of "surpassing intensity." There is that miracle, that "resembling unlikeness" which attracts, which alters consciousness, which prompts us as spectators or artists to "die into form."

In sculpture the visual forms twist and play among each other, deferring then fulfilling certain expectations. So too, in poetry, the logical, the linear progression of a thought, a line, or a musical idea is deformed in the interest of making the poem. The problem in both is the subtilization of the deformation so that "unlikeness" is not banality nor exaggeration (though sometimes exaggeration is sought for satiric purposes).

On the other hand, certain problems of the poet and the sculptor appear apposite. If the problem of the sculptor is to enliven inert mass, to force solid and form into outward gesture, the poet's problem is that his words continually point beyond the poem's use of them. An untouched stone has a kind of indifferent, enigmatic beauty;

the enigmatic beauty of simple words is their referential depths quite beside the poet's use: indifference again but this time to the poet's will. (One thinks of the poet using words like "love"or "peace" with their millions of individualized meanings; how does he *mean* one over the many?). All this deformation in the service of a form.

Rilke, Pound, Gaudier-Brzeska, all three at one time or another were interested in the Egyptian cult of the dead, the preparation in this life for the next. Gaudier-Brzeska saw the Egyptian sense of form as a way of man reaching into divinity, connecting with the gods: Rilke's life and work were an open metaphor toward death. Pound, somewhat differently, saw his task as the creation of a "Paradise terrestrial"—to bring the gods to earth. It would not be misleading to see these as reaching symbolically for the same thing.

The capstone of the form, of the arch is, as the Egyptians thought, to carry one from this life into the next. Pound, his being consumed by a surpassingly personal vision of history, sought, as he says in the later *Cantos*, "to make it cohere" to complete the vision. Though his organizing principle, derived from Gaudier, was presentation and juxtaposition, the ultimate purpose was to complete the form, "to make Cosmos" as he defined it. If, like the Hieratic Head of Pound done by Gaudier, or like a cubist painting, it truncates the world of history and tradition (the only world in which the poem can truly live), it is still like those works in the service of a new imaginative wholeness.

If, on the other hand, we consider Rilke looking at the Apollo and reminded of a wholeness which had fled and could only be restored, and then *possibly,* by a transcendent leap of faith, we can see this too as a principle of organization. For it is the rested totalitiy of the Apollo, the work of art perfected to the point where no distinction can be made between content and form, which is what it means to have made Cosmos. Because only gods make perfect objects. And it did become a lesson and a principle of Rilke's that the perfect objects of the world, first its works of art, then the world of Nature itself, drew one toward one's own wholeness: "Transitoriness is everywhere plunging into a profound Being. And therefore all the forces of the here and now are not merely to be used in a time limited way, but so far as we can, instated within these superior significances in which we share. . . . Yes, for our task is to stamp this provisional, perishing earth into ourselves so deeply, so painfully and passionately, that its being may rise again 'invisibly' in us" (Rilke's letter of Nov. 13th 1925 to the Polish translator of the *Elegies*).

The capstone; the form. This life, this term of years, this "life" as an entity, the capstone of death which is the final closure. Pound, toward the end of his life facing the world, struck, if somewhat mellower, the note heard earlier in the young Rilke before the Apollo. As Rilke saw in the Apollo's unity and wholeness a call and challenge to being, so Pound: "the verb is 'see', not 'walk on' / i.e. it coheres all right / even if my notes do not cohere" which is at once a joyous and terrible admission.

And Rilke, at the writing of the *Ninth Elegy,* has begun to echo Pound: "So show him some simple thing, remoulded by age after age, till it lives in our hands and eyes as a part of ourselves. *Tell him things.*" Yet these are resonances, not resolutions. Our problematic concerning form (to use contemporary jargon) contains further implications.

It should be noted that Pound, who disliked Rodin's work, did not think much of Rilke's either. It may have been in part due to Rilke's seemingly easy acceptance of the verse conventions of his day. Pound makes mention of this in his *Guide to Kultur.* "As in English there is a god awful slump . . . so in German . . . And you do NOT get out of such slumps by a Tennyson or a Rilke. . . . Without a rigorous technique NO renaissance." The dislike may have stemmed as well from Pound's antipathy to subjectivity, to psychology and speculation. And yet one feels in reading the early *Cantos* that it is precisely this lack of subjectivity which is their failure, that some study of the self colateral with the study of history is necessary to say something authentic about either. (It is just such an infusion of subjectivity by the way which makes the later *Pisan Cantos* great literature.)

We find ourselves in many ways dissatisfied with much of the art produced today. One reason is that artists seem to have too heartily embraced either the path of early Pound or the private inwardness of early Rilke. Pound's initial notions of a renaissance involved perhaps too much of an attenuation of subjectivity in the service of technique. Today, in poetry, perhaps as a result of Pound's attitudes, we often see a mechanical acceleration of technique in conquest of technique, an historically conscious wave of trend upon trend, until the meaning of a work of art, like Rilke's subjective uncertainty, no longer seems to lie within the work itself. In relation to the techniques of past works of art, the worth of new work is judged not by form-content values but by its novelty. The once necessary overthrow has now become an empty convention, so that much of art, far from trying "to get the modern in," moves toward diminishment rather than enlargement. It is as though Gaudier-Brzeska's manifesto had been rather neatly edited to remove all the implications that the living vortex was given birth in the wedding of expression and technique.

At the other end of the spectrum is the art of unstructured expression—a kind of neodadaism which operates on the idea that there is still a convention of rigid (one might say "bourgeois") formalism such as obtained in the 1910s and 1920s which must be fought against. It is this work which strikes one as romantic in the bad sense of the word, because it offers only chaos to shock one, when it has always been order— new order, in, of, and critical of its age—which is the most radical form the artist can offer. It is this radical form which has the outward gesture that commands us to change our lives.

Form. Rilke, we recall, had written of "the love that consists in this, that two solitudes protect and border and salute each other." He was, of course, speaking of how two individuals might relate maturely together, how the very essence of love was the awareness of solitude, of great space across which lay the other. Some of Rilke's critics, most recently Robert Hass, in his introduction to Stephen Mitchell's translations, have suggested that Rilke's words are a deflection from the intensity of relationships, that this was in keeping with Rilke's "drawing back" whenever he came too close to forming an attachment. The critics continue that this was so for Rilke because, as Hass puts it, his "final confrontation was always with himself." To this one wants to say, possibly. There is, I think, another way of looking at these remarks of Rilke's: they are less concerned with the risks of engagement or how to rationalize keeping one's distance than with profound recognition. The border of solitudes Rilke speaks of is not the space of not knowing but the space of *not being.* Love here involves the awareness of difference rather than sameness; it only superficially resembles the mystical union of two in one, the fictional stuff of romance that has, in our time, been transformed into the dominance of one and the surrender of the other. (Imagine, if you will, the violence of the phrase "I know you.") Rilke, by contrast, seeks to find, against the cultural programming of his time (and ours), what constitutes love and the nature of its interanimation.

For Rilke, love is more dancelike, characterized by uncertainty of possession. This dance is many things, pleasure, poise, give and take, pain and humor—many things—but never actual possession of one partner by the other.

For Rilke then, love is not a violation of boundaries but an awareness of them. Love can violate the boundary only at the cost of violating itself, of transforming that which one loves into something else. In this it is remarkably like hate, for hate too acknowledges possession from a similar point of view; to violate its object is to attempt to transform it into that which is no longer hateful. Thus, with both love and hate, the object is entire. It can be broken or manipulated or made subservient only at the cost of love or hate. The object, once broken or tamed to another's sphere of power and interest, is no longer the object once loved. Thus Rilke, writing about Socrates, portrays a harried Eros "always a little out of breath, sleepless, troubled day and night about the two between whom he trod, to and fro, hither and yon, ceaselessly accosted by both." For Eros must mediate, Eros must deal with two individuals who live and change and who sometimes perceive (or mistake) their union as the melting of two into one.

And when then does Eros rest? In Rilkean terms, Eros rests only when one of the lovers assumes a form in the eyes or gaze of the other. To imagine the other as a form is not to imagine a static block of stone, but to imagine the other as something already perfected—not "ideal"—merely perfect and complete, the very thing which you began by loving and, as with Apollo's broken torso, that insists you change your life. When we properly relate to form, we do not try to change it but allow the form to animate us, to stir us perhaps into change. This is the Rilkean soul-work, indeed a "final confrontation with the self" as Hass puts it, because in its respect for the solitude of others, its affective point is our own egoistic clingings, our desire to lock up and control the object of love. This would be the transformative or, in Rilke's sense, the proper form of love. Eros rests when we acknowledge the presence of the other to be a form for us, to "salute" and tell us (from itself) about ourselves. This recognition would no longer involve form as being merely an instrument of knowledge but as having affect, involving its utter mysteriousness, its gratuitous, concept-breaking characteristics, its inability to be fully comprehended even as it is desired.

Love here is then form, and both love and form are related to our premonitions of death. For change, authentic change which risks everything, not because it is a gambler but because no change is meaningful unless the entire order of oneself is involved, implies this complete remaking of one's form. The *du*, the you of Rilke's last line in the Apollo poem, is a self-address, a command to the self as it exists. And in the transaction with the statue, Rilke has understood the deeper meaning of form.

This deeper meaning can be expressed quite simply: form calls to form. That is, in order to call or be called to, one must see oneself as a form. We could mean by form such terms as "self-conception" or "reference point," or even how we see ourselves. The main thing here is that without such a point there can be no real transformation, just a kind of thrashing about. What Rilke seems to suggest is that to have such a reference point, to be *this* and not *that* is to acknowledge incompleteness. The inmost heart of Rilke's poetry, the *Elegies*, amounts to nothing less than an attempt to abolish, if only in their moment, the this/that distinction, to "stamp this provisional, perishing earth into ourselves so deeply . . . that its being rises again." In this formulation, the statue, or the poem for that matter, does not address the human but what I would call the form of the human, the human addressed as he or she sees his or her own psychic constitution. In this sense, the "call" is not so much something recognizable but that which evokes or suggests conditions to change. There is nothing *gemutlicht* in this transaction, nothing coy or cozy or slyly knowing. The "call" respects the receiver, and to that extent it is uncomfortable. (The precision I'm aiming for here is significant.) For the human (as opposed to the form or self-conception of the human) is dynamic, is capable of enacting change upon its own form. We could say that this is what we mean by working on one's self. The form is the one's "self," and what works on it is what is only loosely nameable as human, something which cannot be contained by a conceptualization but is rather a dynamic potentiality *and actuality*. The total human is ungrounded; it is, if we think of the Buddhist conceptions of mind and space, unoriginated, without attributes, without character. This is the "entity" which makes form possible, for form is an aspect of it, a dimension or attribute which can appear out of it. Form is love in this understanding because it is a communication. In the Buddhist terminology, it is Nirmanakaya, the form of instruction or teaching, the instance of being in the world.

Rilke, in his essay on Rodin, points to this understanding. In speaking of Rodin's attempt to capture the meaning of Balzac in sculpture, Rilke describes Rodin's elaborate preparations and discoveries, the many models and attempts the form of the statue undergoes. Of the final version, Rilke comments, "That was Creation itself, assuming the figure of Balzac that it might appear in visible form." If we are to understand that by Creation we mean all that is humanly possible and discernible, then Balzac's figure is but one form of the human, the modality by which the immense power of creativity is communicated.

In the passage immediately following this discussion, Rilke hints at something equally suggestive. Here he discusses Rodin's methods for maintaining unity not only in a single figure but among groups of figures: "flat marble bands have been left here and there between the figures and between their individual parts, like cross-pieces, uniting one form with another in the background. Nor is this accidental. These blocks prevent *useless vistas which would carry the eye beyond the object into empty space*" (my italics). The point of form, the "illusion" of form, is its inviolate boundedness. Seeing "wholeness," as Rilke saw in the Apollo, is the appropriate response to form; aleatory interpretations do not apply. What punishes—in creative fashion—is the unity, the wholeness.

Pound and form. Pound we might look upon, at least in all but the latter stages of his life, as a kind of Confucianist. The meaning of history for the Confucianist, Joseph Levenson has written, is not in a fulfillment of the end stages of culture but in a kind of "sage-antiquity"; to put it another way, the Chinese classical past provides man's good examples. In Pound, the impulse is to see the art-culture-antiquity nexus as exemplary. Another aspect of the Confucian sense of history is that its emphasis is not on process but on incident. This, too, strikes me as characterizing Pound's poetics up to a point. And indeed, what is remarkable about Poundian poetry is the typology of the formal break that Pound makes with the poetry of his time in order to enact a poetry of historical incident. Pound's method, as Laszlo Gefin points out in *Ideogram,* is paratactic; Pound layers event against event, as the sculptor—Gaudier-Breszka in particular—lays mass against mass. The reader/seer constructs or infers the whole. In other words, the function of the *Cantos* is to restore via ideogramatic technique a catalog of significant history. Again, this history is not processional or developmental but exemplary.

What is most interesting (and most peculiar) is that if we examine the notions of form as formulated by Pound and Rilke, the inescapable conclusion is that Pound is much more traditional in his concept of form, is, if one can use the word without invoking a concert of groans, mimetic. Pound articulates this quite clearly in *Gaudier-Breszka* where he says "Every concept, every emotion presents itself to the vivid consciousness in some primary form." Pound's intentions it would seem—often powerfully exceeded in his work—are to find a kind of rightness or propriety of form, an almost Platonic sense of ideation hinted at in the phrase "primary form." Rilke, as with Holderlin and German Romanticism in general (though, again, one must not easily equate these), is enthralled not so much by the technical perfection of Greek form as by its assurance. The Apollo is not something to be imitated but, in the face of the general European cultural collapse, becomes a focus for the poet/artist of immense longing, of the desire to express, against the very erosions of certainty, a wholeness and integrity.

Were we to carry this analysis a bit farther we might see (again, curiosity of curiosities) that Rilke's work, though coming earlier than Pound's is a kind of critique, not of Pound's form, but of his content. For in Rilke we encounter a modernity which has already understood the failure of the art and institutions which Pound has drawn upon. Yes, Rilke, so-called "traditional" in form (the charge Pound levels against him), anticipates the problem of formlessness (of culture, of thought, of art) in a far more original manner than Pound, the formal avant-gardist. It was this anticipation which moved Robert Musil to recognize in Rilke the poetic voice of the age. All his poetry, Musil was to write, was a matter "of the feeling as totality, on which the world rests like an island. . . . He was in a certain sense the most religious poet since Novalis, but I am not certain whether he had any religion at all. He saw differently. In a new, inner way."

My impression is that the "inner way" for Pound came only with the cage at Pisa. As with all authentic inner ways, it came expectedly and as a confrontation with his entire being. The true meaning of the civilization for which Pound had proselytized comes to him there in all its failure if not its horror. And though its final "sinking in" may have come with his own final period of silence, it is as powerful a source of inspiration, of inner seeking, as Rilke's facing of the Apollo.

To conclude, I would like to hazard a crude formulation and suggest a few of its implications. If Rilke seems, in this piece, the wiser poet, it is because he lived out the content of his poetry. Pound, by contrast, until his later phases, lives out his formal inventiveness, possibly at the expense of content—we remember how much of Pound's poetics are reactions to prevailing conditions of the art.

Our contemporary interest in form—the "language" poets are but an extreme example—often seems to involve a willingness to revel in new discoveries, even new concepts of thought and language, as they occur through the manipulation of the medium of language. The content, as it were, is not a source or inspiration toward action and knowledge but a throwaway, a mark of the power of the work underhand, of its formal inventiveness, to be creative, inventive, spontaneous, in other words, to show forth those contemporary "values" which themselves are already mystifications. In this, the inventiveness nearly mimics the pre–World War II poetry of Pound. Yet Pound's sense of history, as I have tried to show, his desire to prescribe and judge, is theoretical, unlived, and even sentimental.

Now a parallel process is also identifiable in early Rilke; in particular, one thinks of the charms and sentimentalisms of his period work. It is poetry as surely sentimental about its bourgeois origins as is Pound's sentimental version of history. As with Pound in the Pisan cage, Rilke had to outgrow this taking for granted of the unspoken assumptions of his time. It was only when Rilke went beyond, only when, as Musil noted, Rilke's poetry no longer had anything to do "either with philosophy or skepticism or with anything else except experience" that Rilke could speak to his time. Such "experience" is not, one must insist, the manipulation of dead or received counters, nor is it psychologizing; least of all is it a capitulation for their own sake regardless of personal or social cost. This, if nothing else, Rilke (and Europe) have to teach us. For Rilke does not give us so much a picture of *his* experiences as of the experience of relatedness, a way of bringing into the open the new connections and the fictions of connectedness between individuals and their world.

Finally, I would suggest that this sense of Rilke's "experience" is coterminous with poetic responsibility (and license for that matter) and that what the new formalisms endanger is not the status of the old poetries but the poet's connection to meaning and language, and that this in turn leads to both evasion and illusion. Equally illusory, of course, is the self-centered inwardness found in so much confessional and surrealistic work of our time.

The poet as always is left only with his being human and perhaps with the possibility that his poetry, like the figure of Eros described above, is harried, "always a little out of breath . . . troubled about the two," world and human, between whom he or she must continually mediate.

ORPHEUS THE PAINTER: APOLLINAIRE AND ROBERT DELAUNAY

ROSANNA WARREN

In the disposition of its typography, Mallarmé's *Un Coup de dés* raised anew the perennial problem of the relation, in poetry, between the senses of hearing and vision, and between their corresponding arts, music and painting. If Symbolist poetics had seemed (though the issue is complicated)[1] to aspire to the condition of music, *Un Coup de dés* shifted its allegiance toward the pictorial and may be said to be a pivotal text, a turn toward a new poetry which would take its cue from Cubist painting.

Already, in the essays preceding *Un Coup de dés*, "La Musique et les lettres" (1894) and "Crise de vers" (1896), Mallarmé had affirmed the dual and intermediary nature of poetry, which draws lifeblood from both the visual and the auditory. In his letter to Gide concerning *Un Coup de dés* (Fig. 1), Mallarmé insisted on the corporeality of the poem: "The constellation will assume there, in accordance with precise laws and insofar as the printed text permits, fatally the bearing ("l'allure) of a constellation . . . ; for, and this is the whole point of view . . . , the *rhythm of a sentence* concerning an act, or even an object, makes no sense unless it *imitates* them, and, *figured upon the paper*, taken back by the letter from the original printed impression (l'estampe), contrives to *render,* in spite of everything, something of them" (n'en sait rendre, malgré tout, quelquechose); the emphases are mine, and I should probably be struck by lightning for presuming to transpose Mallarmé's syntax. Roger Shattuck has aptly described this attitude as Mallarmé's cratylism.[2] On the other hand, *Un Coup de dés*, that hymn to the conditional and subjunctive moods and to multiple semantic vibration, denies its own textual materiality, and the materiality of the world, "dans ces parages / du vague / en quoi toute realité se dissout" (crudely rendered, "in these latitudes / of the vague / in which all reality dissolves;" this is not the occasion to discuss Mallarmé's undermining of reference through puns and gender manipulations, such as those with both "wave" and "vague"). The poem's typography, Mallarmé suggests in "Crise de vers," should aim "at the total rhythm, which would be the poem silenced, at the white spaces"; in other words, it aims at a spirituality transcending music as well as the pictorial.

Mallarmé's musings on these subjects often crystallize around the word "lieu," a richly suggestive term whose sense, in French, ranges from "place" and "space" to notions of temporality, permission, and reason or motive. Carrying the news—"the astonishing news," as he said—of the new poetics to Oxford in 1894, Mallarmé asks

RIEN

de la mémorable crise
ou se fût
l'événement

Figure 1. Page from "Un Coup de dés," Stéphane Mallarmé, *Oeuvres Complètes*, ed.
Henri Mondor and G. Jean-Aubry, Bibliothèque nouvelle revue française de la Pléiade
(1945), pp. 474–75.

accompli en vue de tout résultat nul
                                        humain

                    N'AURA EU LIEU
              une élévation ordinaire verse l'absence

                                    QUE LE LIEU
        inférieur clapotis quelconque comme pour disperser l'acte vide
                            abruptement qui sinon
                        par son mensonge
                                eût fondé
                            la perdition

    dans ces parages
                    du vague
                            en quoi toute réalité se dissout

"s'il y a lieu d'ecrire," if there is *room* in which to write, a *place* for writing, permission or possibility to write. It is an appropriate question, considering the void left by Victor Hugo's "great going"; but Mallarmé has given the word its full metaphysical cast, and concludes his talk with the Platonic evocation of an ideal city, "un lieu abstrait, supérieur, nulle part situé, ici séjour pour l'homme"; (an abstract, superior place, situated nowhere, man's abode here). I suggest that the poem, the typographical and pictorial phenomenon of *Un Coup de dés,* in which "NOTHING . . . WILL HAVE TAKEN PLACE . . . BUT THE PLACE" (RIEN . . . N'AURA EU LIEU . . . QUE LE LIEU), is itself that transcendent place, or *lieu,* of which Mallarmé spoke in Oxford.

I wish to explore Apollinaire's cultivation of the poetic place, the textual, musical, and pictorial *lieu,* bequeathed by Mallarmé. With the advent of Cubism, painting—which was beginning to examine more consciously its own semiotic nature[3]—became the dominant model for poetic practice. The outstanding poems of the period, by Jacob, Reverdy, Cendrars, Huidobro, and Apollinaire himself, spring largely from procedures and attitudes learned at the Bateau Lavoir. Reciprocally, Cubism's triumph owed much to the enthusiastic promotion it received at the hands of writers, especially Apollinaire, Gertrude Stein, and, later, Pierre Reverdy.

Apollinaire published articles about Picasso from 1905 on and in 1913 assembled his various writings about art in the ambiguously titled *Méditations esthétiques: LES PEINTRES CUBISTES,* whose publisher capitalized the wrong phrase, thus skewing Apollinaire's emphasis. In some ways, Apollinaire understood very little about painting. At least, he rarely seems to have looked at it with much precision. Picasso, Braque, Jacques Villon, and the art dealer and publisher Kahnweiler have all spoken critically of Apollinaire's lack of visual comprehension[4]; his classification of "cubisms" into the "scientific," the "physical," the "orphic," and the "instinctive" was regarded as absurd, and his mystagogic reflections on the fourth dimension ("It figures the immensity of space eternalising itself in all directions at a given moment. It is space itself, the dimension of the infinite.") seemed, to most painters, pure hooey. Worse still, for Picasso and Braque, was Apollinaire's blithe skipping off into the camp of Sonia and Robert Delaunay.

Robert Delaunay's "Orphism" owed to analytic Cubism its freedom in breaking down hierarchies of perspective and volume, and its elevation of abstract geometric elements—triangular wedges, discs, arcs, straight lines—to the roles of major actors. Delaunay's treachery, if such it be considered, was his luscious celebration of hue but relative neglect of value, tone, and volumetric tension; a glorying in primary chromatic play that seemed, to Picasso and Braque, a betrayal of their rites of purification. But Delaunay's "misreading" of Cubism, a deviance which was to prove so fruitful for Paul Klee, also released a new poetry in Guillaume Apollinaire. Apollinaire's art criticism is not criticism at all: it is notes for a new translation of painting into poetry, the visualization of a new poetic space, a zone beyond "Zone."

Apollinaire's poem "Les Fenêtres" and the Calligrammes which closely followed it are inscribed in a long Western tradition of ekphrasis whose genealogy has been admirably traced by Jean Hagstrum, by John Hollander, by Wendy Steiner, and by Albert Cook, among others. I will not rehearse it here. But before turning to Delaunay's paintings, "Les Fenêtres," and to Apollinaire's poem to and for them, I want to recall Lessing's sober separation of the media, visual art into the spatial mode and writing into the temporal, lest Apollinaire's pictorialism seem too facile an enterprise. Pierre Reverdy, when he declared, "Poésie cubiste? Idée ridicule,"[5] was reformulating Lessing and helps remind us that Apollinaire's attempt to render painting into poetry was something of an unnatural act. But then, so is all art.

Delaunay exhibited a series of the window paintings in Berlin in December 1912 with Apollinaire's poem as commissioned catalogue copy. (Fig. 2) Briefly, we should note the shattering of the represented cityscape, Paris, into a self-reflective act of vision, a look through a hypothetical window whose frame is invisible. The totemic figure of the Eiffel tower, symbol of "pure" structure and of the synchronization of world time,[6] has become the constitutive element, its triangle wedge shape organizing the rhythm of the color across the surface. Delaunay's catchword for his painting was "simultaneity," by which he meant the orchestrated contrasts of complementary hues; it is a term to which Apollinaire would give full temporal and metaphorical force.

One of the conversation poems, "Les Fenêtres" first took shape in a cafe with interventions by André Dupuy and André Billy; Apollinaire finished it in the Delaunay studio. *Ut pictura poesis:* how does he translate the paintings? The secret, I believe, is his refusal to describe. Instead, the poem discovers the principle of action in the paintings, and invents an analogous linguistic enactment.

LES FENÊTRES

Du rouge au vert tout le jaune se meurt
Quand chantent les aras dans les forêts natales
Abatis de pihis
Il y a un poème à faire sur l'oiseau qui n'a qu'une aile
Nous l'enverrons en message téléphonique
Traumatisme géant
Il fait couler les yeux
Voilà une jolie jeune fille parmi les jeunes Turinaises
Le pauvre jeune homme se mouchait dans sa cravate blanche
Tu soulèveras le rideau
Et maintenant voilà que s'ouvre la fenêtre
Araignées quand les mains tissaient la lumière
Beauté pâleur insondables violets
Nous tenterons en vain de prendre du repos
On commencera à minuit
Quand on a le temps on a la liberté

Bigorneaux Lotte multiples Soleils et l'Oursin du couchant
Une vieille paire de chaussures jaunes devant la fenêtre
Tours
Les Tours ce sont les rues
Puits
Puits ce sont les places
Puits
Arbres creux qui abritent les Câpresses vagabondes
Les Chabins chantent des airs à mourir
Aux Chabines marronnes
Et l'oie oua-oua trompette au nord

Figure 2. Robert Delaunay, *Simultaneous Windows (2nd Motif, 1st part)*, 1912.
(From the Solomon R. Guggenheim Museum, New York. Photograph by David Heald.)

> *Où les chasseurs de ratons*
> *Raclent les pelleteries*
> *Etincelant diamant*
> *Vancouver*
> *Où le train blanc de neige et de feux nocturnes fuit l'hiver*
> *O Paris*
> *Du rouge au vert tout le jaune se meurt*
> *Paris Vancouver Hyères Maintenon New-York et les Antilles*
> *La fenêtre s'ouvre comme une orange*
> *Le beau fruit de la lumière*

Delaunay's principle, as we have seen, is to break the represented hierarchies of volume and space into abstract elements, the wedge shape and the color contrasts; the paintings also rely on the play between *passage,* the passing of one plane into another, and its opposite manoeuvre, the abrupt meeting of planes along the line Leo Steinberg has called the "arris."[7] *Passage,* as practiced by Cézanne and elaborated by Picasso, involved strenuous discontinuity in the representation of solid volumes, and, because the Delaunay window paintings do not seriously articulate volume, the smokey blurring of planes into one another is a rather weak brand of *passage.* Similarly, the hard edges separating planes hardly make three-dimensional suggestions in Delaunay's windows, and have, consequently, a much lazier time of it than in a Picasso. Still, Delaunay organizes his surface by contrasts in complementary hues and in planar arrangement, and the effect of such contrasts is to disintegrate Renaissance perspectival assumptions about volume, space, and distance.

Apollinaire, for his part, must break the hierarchy of time, that is, sequence. He tries to do this by interruption of the proferred narration, by a new simplified syntax which makes each line an independent unit, and by mixing up verb tenses:

> *Here is a pretty young girl . . .*
> *The unfortunate young man was blowing his nose . . .*
> *You will raise the curtain . . .*

Such narrative and temporal discontinuity is an easy game, however, which never succeeds in simulating real "simultaneity" because even the nonsequiturs are condemned to sequential presentation. The real discovery of the poem is not to have imitated pictorial simultaneity, but to have disrupted and reconstituted syntactic and semantic order through the exploitation of an abstract linguistic element analogous to the colored wedge: the syllable.

Like the wedge in Delaunay's paintings, the syllable defines both *passage* and disjuncture. The very first line announces the theme of *passage:*

> *Du rouge au vert tout le jaune se meurt*
> *(From red to green all the yellow dies out)*

The diphthong [o] in "jaune" mediates between the [u:] in "rouge" and the [ɛ:] in "vert"; but Delaunay prefers contrast to mediation, and the color yellow dies out, in the paintings, in favor of more vibrant complementarities, as the rainbow of vowels disappears into the contrasts of [a], [ã] and [i]:

Quand chantent les arras dans les forêts natales
Abatis de pihis . . .

(When the macaws sing in their native forests
Giblets of pihis)

The poem will continue to advance like this, not primarily by a logic of description or narration, but in the phonetic engendering of one syllable by another, all the while maintaining a strong semantic vibration, an appeal to reference, just as the paintings keep appealing to representation and never entirely lose sight of Paris.

The next lines present the theoretical intention:

Il y a un poème à faire sur l'oiseau qui n'a qu'une aile
Nous l'enverrons en message téléphonique

(There is a poem to be made on the bird which has only one wing
We will send it as a message téléphonique)

Here, technology becomes mythology: the new, winged poem (the ambiguous pronoun in "l'enverrons" [we will send it] confuses bird and poem) to be sent through the new urban telegraph system is a revolutionary communication designed to crack the hierarchies of space and time: therefore, "traumatisme géant" (giant traumatism).

With the anonymous young man and young girl we are on the familiar terrain of Cubist narrative discontinuity; but line ten, "Tu soulèveras le rideau" (You will raise the curtain) introduces a new, heroic pronoun, "you," herald of the theatrical vision which opens as if of its own accord into the mystical present-tense eternity of the poem:

Et maintenant voilà que s'ouvre la fenêtre

(And now the window is opening)

The next lines veer close to description as they evoke, in their sonorities, Delaunay's colors:

Araignées quand les mains tissaient la lumière
Beauté pâleur insondables violets

(Spiders when hands were weaving light
Beauty pallor unfathomable violets)

The metaphor of weaving carries the material into the immaterial and hints at the transcendental nature this poem's *lieu* will assume.

Nous tenterons en vain de prendre du repos
On commencera à minuit
Quand on a le temps on a la liberté

> *(We'll try in vain to rest*
> *We'll begin at midnight*
> *When you have time you have freedom)*

Here Apollinaire redoubles the assault on temporality. As Albert Cook has finely observed, "commencera" (will begin) is doubly future; and the poem transfigures the cliché about having free time, and the cliché names of newspapers, *Le Temps* and *La Liberté*, into a literal and revolutionary declaration.

Its overt narration fractured, the poem lets its new freedom blossom into a cosmic allegorical vision which evolves, in a sustained *passage*, from the sea to the heavens, from green to red, from the material to the immaterial, with a cubistically multiplied solar system in the center:

> *Bigorneaux Lotte multiples Soleils et l'Oursin du couchant*

> *(Winkles Burbot multiple Suns and the sea-urchin of sunset)*

In his book *Figural Choice in Poetry and Art*, Albert Cook has brilliantly registered the reverberations of this line. I would like to point, additionally, to its astonishing juxtaposition with the line which follows:

> *Une vieille paire de chaussures jaunes devant la fenêtre*

> *(An old pair of yellow shoes in front of the window)*

The point of view precipitates us from exterior to interior, from cosmic to domestic space, from red and green to yellow, and produces that "simultaneist" vertigo that Apollinaire admired in his friend's paintings. This effect of juxtaposition is analogous, not to pictorial *passage*, but to its opposite, the articulation of the hard edge, or arris, between planes; it shows that Apollinaire, for all his palaver, was acutely sensitive to the multiple constructive procedures of the painting. When he wrote to his fiancée Madeleine Pagès that he liked this poem "beaucoup, beaucoup," it was to this new articulation, this flexible, clean-cut syntax that he referred.

The visionary pilgrimage continues with a series of semantic eviscerations: like Delaunay's overworked wedges, Apollinaire's phonemes have multiple duties to perform, and in performance they collapse height into depth, vertical into horizontal, space into time:

> *Tours*
> *Les Tours ce sont les rues*
> *Puits*
> *Puits ce sont les places*
> *Puits*
>
> *(Towers*
> *The towers are streets*
> *Wells*
> *Wells are town squares*
> *Well)*

"Tours": the word means towers, circular movements, turns, magic tricks. The poem exploits all senses. Towers melt into streets; wells turn into town squares; but "puits" (wells) is also an unstable syllable, since the same sounds, "puis," mean "then" and launch us back into the sequential narration the poem has denied.

In the newly cleared poetic space an edenic vision rises, time and space delivered up to the play of vowels and especially to the familiar caresses of [a], [ã], and [i]:

> Arbres creux qui abritent les Câpresses vagabondes
> Les Chabins chantent des airs à mourir
> Aux Chabines marronnes
>
> (Hollow trees sheltering vagrant mulattoes
> The octoroon men sing endless tunes
> To brown octoroon women)

In its final phase, the poem enters a phonetic and onomatopoeic delirium in which the goose identifies "utterly" with its cry and in which the word seems truly incarnate, hence untranslatable:

> Et l'oie oua-oua trompette au nord
>
> (And the goose honk-honk trumpets to the north)

Listen now, in the poem's conclusion, to the flight of syllables, their metamorphoses, their undermining of syntactic and semantic order; listen especially to the syllable "ver," which is a color "vert" (green) and a line of verse "vers" but also the preposition "vers" (toward), essential but always suppressed in this poem of transition, of *passage;* "ver" shares also in the name of a city and a season: VancouVER, hiVER. Listen, look—for ear and eye must collaborate intimately—listen to the identity of space and time in the rhyming couples Hyères/hier, Maintenon/maintenant; see how the impossible geographical flight between cities simulates pictorial *passage,* while the syllable "ant" frolics between color in "blanc" (white), space in VANcouver, and time in the suggested but not quite present "mainteNANT."

The poem concludes almost at the place of its beginning, thus in a near cyclical eternity and denial of progression, with the repetition of its first line, "Du rouge au vert tout le jaune se meurt." Like the window, the poem opens "like an orange," offering slices of fruit, the wedges displayed and splayed, in Delaunay's paintings: "La fenêtre s'ouvre comme une orange" (The window opens like an orange). The simile seems to leave us with a figurative incarnation, the fruit. But just as the sea urchin turned into a sunset, the last line takes yet another turn and turns the comparison inside out, transforming matter, the orange, into spirit and light: "Le beau fruit de la lumière." The incarnation proposed was unstable and temporary, and leaves us merely with the echo of a by-now-familiar sound, "er"; "Le beau fruit de la lumiÈRE."

If *Un Coup de dés* set out to be a musical score, but remained, in part, typography and painting—if it wanted to be spirit but could not deny its flesh—"Les Fenêtres" aspires to the condition of painting but remains, in part, music, and spirit. It is Apollinaire's triumph to have endowed poetic music with a new phonetic fleshliness, a new way of irritating sound into sense.

Since a major source of Apollinaire's inspiration lay in painting, most vitally in the work of Picasso and Delaunay, it is not surprising that soon after his pictorial experiment in "Les Fenêtres" he should have pressed his medium still further in the direction of the visual. Huidobro, the Italian Futurists, and the Russian "Rayonists" Larionov and Goncharova were already experimenting in poems and on posters with wildly various and wildly placed typography.[8] In *Calligrammes* Apollinaire formalized those impulses and seemed driven to transform Mallarmé's transcendent *lieu,* the text which is, finally, a sign to be erased into an entirely earthly and incarnate space, a text-picture which literally embodies itself, a *lieu* not so much significant as self-signified. The poem-as-emblem, a familiar creature in the lineage extending from Simmias of Rhodes (ca. 300 B.C.) through George Herbert, gains new life in the post-Symbolist linguistic context.

The first version of *Calligrammes* was a small collection of "idéogrammes lyriques" scheduled to appear in August 1914. It was entitled *Et moi aussi je suis peintre* (And I also am a painter). The outbreak of war interrupted the publication of the book, which did not come out until April 1918, much expanded, with the title *Calligrammes.* If Apollinaire's pictorial ambition declared itself more modestly in the new title— "gramma" in Greek means the line of a drawing as well as an alphabetical letter— that ambition was hardly diluted in the pictorial typography of the poems. The calligrammes, poems shaped like watches, neckties, crowns, fountains, the Eiffel Tower and so forth, seem to break the tenuous equilibrium between image and sound established in *Un Coup de dés* and "Les Fenêtres" and seem to affirm the pictorial materiality, the mere presence, of the text.

Perhaps not surprisingly, in subjecting language to such strains, the calligrammes end up meditating not about the pictorial but about the poetic: in courting the literal, they explore the resources of the symbolic, which refuses to be suppressed. Looking into an alien medium, Apollinaire sees himself reflected; looking into painting, he *hears* poetry. In the calligramme "Coeur couronne et miroir" which juxtaposes three objects on one page, each is an emblem of the poet: the heart is his own, a flame reversed; the crown (disentangled from its image) tells us that "Les Rois qui meurent tour à tour renaissent au coeur des poètes" (Kings dying one by one are reborn in the heart of poets); and the circular mirror, which is a circular sentence, encloses the inscription GUILLAUME APOLLINAIRE. It would appear then that, for this poet at least, painting is a place in which to encounter poetry, that is to say, himself.

Apollinaire formalizes, as well, what might be considered a dual phenomenology of reading. Pondering themes of loss and evanescence, eternal lyric motifs given special poignance by the wartime context of this book, the calligrammes seem to oppose the temporality of reading by presenting each poem as a "simultaneous" shape which can be grasped with the illusion of immediacy. In "La colombe poignardée et le jet d'eau" (Fig. 3), the poet arrests a bird in flight over a spurting fountain and immortalizes in each fugitive emblem the names of the lost: women in the bird, his dispersed male companions in the ejaculating water. Such is the perennial ambition of poets: Horace's *"exegi monumentum aere perennius,"* Shakespeare's "That in black ink my love may still shine bright." Apollinaire's shaped poem, the text-as-*lieu,* rescues not only loves and friends and the erotic moment itself lost to time but also strains to remove the very act of reading from time by encoding it in a visual image. Reading

LA COLOMBE POIGNARDÉE ET LE JET D'EAU

Figure 3. "La colombe poignardée et le jet d'eau," Guillaume Apollinaire, *Oeuvres Poétiques*, ed. Marcel Adema and Michel Décaudin, Bibliothèque nouvelle revue française de la Pléiade (1965), p. 213.

itself, then, could be construed as an erotic act, fatally perishable but solicitous of immortality. On the other hand, the poem can only be deciphered in time; it is only in time that its haunting rhymes and eight-syllable units reveal themselves. All reading of poetry depends on such a dual awareness of a poem's iconic unity and of its musical passage; in the *Calligrammes,* Apollinaire dramatizes and makes explicit what every reader of poetry must perform.

In conclusion, I would like to trace some of the implications of the enterprise by looking briefly at one of the *Calligrammes.* "Il pleut" (Fig. 4) appeared in 1916 in Pierre Albert-Birot's journal *SIC.* Even before reading the poem, we are confronted, visually, by its offense against our habit of reading horizontally. At first glance, "Il pleut" may appear a fairly juvenile exercise: words become rain; sound becomes image. I would like to suggest that its power rises from an opposite impulse: the metamorphosis of image into music.

Most of the lines, rearranged, have a rather conventional prosody. Given the liberties that Apollinaire habitually takes with the final "e" and with the pronunciation of verbs in the third person plural, the lines fall (literally) into fairly regular eight and ten syllable units and into alexandrines. The poem presents an equally traditional lyric subject-matter: the ephemeral nature of love. It is a complaint against time. And with the pressure of this subject, the poem-painting shades into the poem-score, into music.

We can trace this transformation. In the first half-line, "Il pleut des voix de femmes comme si" (It rains voices of women as if), a material reality, the rain, dissolves into sound, the women's voices. In the half-line's complement, "elles étaient mortes même dans le souvenir" (they were dead even in memory), the ambiguous pronoun "elles" could refer either to the voices or to the women: we are witnessing still another dissolution, that of the women themselves into sound and of sound into uncertain memory.

The second line, or line of rain, precipitates memory back into its liquid state, but with such metaphoric intervention that we can no longer trust the materiality of these raindrops: "C'est vous aussi qu'il pleut merveilleuses recontres de ma vie ô gouttelettes" (It's you also that it rains marvelous encounters of my life oh droplets). In the third line, each hemistich evolves from the visual to the auditory: "et ces *nuages* cabrés se prennent à *hennir* tout un *univers* de villes *auriculaires*" (and these clouds start whinnying a whole universe of auricular cities).

The penultimate line contains a chiasm of auditory/emotional/emotional/auditory: "*écoute* s'il pleut tandis que le *regret* et le *dédain* pleurent une ancienne *musique*" (listen if it's raining while regret and contempt weep an ancient music). We should note as well a near-pun in French between the verbs for raining and weeping, "pleuvoir" and "pleurer," reinforcing the line's inner symmetry. If the poem concluded here, it would leave us with a simple resolution in favor of the last word, "musique." But that would be *too* simple a reversal of the apparent pictorial pretensions. It concludes, instead, with a new and precarious balance between the claims of the ear and those of the eye: "écoute tomber les liens qui te retiennent en haut et en bas" (listen to the fall of the ties which hold you high and low). I hope it is not too willful of me to understand "liens" (ties, bonds, ligatures, lines) as an allusion to the lines of verse; this poem which holds and doesn't hold its lines, in defiance of typographical gravity,

IL PLEUT

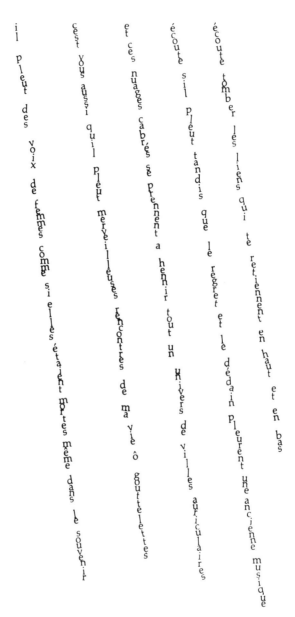

Figure 4. "Il pleut," Guillaume Apollinaire, *Oeuvres Poétiques,* ed. Marcel Adema and Michel Décaudin, Bibliothèque nouvelle revue français de la Pléiade (1965), p. 203.

seems to me an emblem of loss as well as of paradoxical restitution. Love falls from memory, the poem falls out of its prosody, image dissolves into music and music into memory. But the emblem itself, the image, and the idea of form remain and hold us "high and low." It is the profession of an ancient and subtle faith in the resources of poetic form. And this poem, so aggressively situated in the *lieu*, the space, of vision, discovers that it is a space haunted, even consecrated, by music.

NOTES

All translations from the French are by Rosanna Warren.

1. For an erudite and level-headed analysis of the role assigned to music in Symbolism, see Henri Peyre's chapter "Symbolisme, Peinture et Musique," in *Qu'est-ce que le symbolisme?* (Presses Universitaires de France, 1974), pp. 178 ff.

2. In his essay "Apollinaire's Great Wheel," in *The Innocent Eye* (Washington Square Press, 1986), pp. 291 ff., Roger Shattuck describes in loving detail the artistic and literary context from which Apollinaire's Calligrammes emerged and pays particular attention to the connection with Mallarmé.

3. Even before Braque included the letters B-A-L in his painting "Le Portugais" in 1911, Cubist art had been implicitly asserting the conventionality of pictorial signs by incorporating contradictory codes of representation within a single canvas. In recent work on Picasso, such as the lecture delivered at the Museum of Fine Arts in Boston, February 1987, Leo Steinberg even suggests the subtle relevance of de Saussure to such enterprises. Wendy Steiner, for her part, points to the inspiration Jakobson derived from Cubist art, particularly from Braque (*The Colors of Rhetoric* [University of Chicago Press, 1982], p. 195).

4. Francis Steegmuller, Apollinaire's magisterial biographer, has collected a formidable array of such complaints. See his *Apollinaire: Poet among the Painters* (Farrar Straus and Co., 1963), pp. 139 ff.

5. Ibid.

6. I am indebted to Roger Shattuck for this observation, as for so many others. See *The Innocent Eye*, p. 306.

7. For a brilliant, extended discussion of *passage* and its relevance to Cubist historiography, see Leo Steinberg's reply to William Rubin, "The Polemical Part" (*Art in America* [March–April 1979]:114–47). In an earlier essay in the same controversy, Steinberg initiates the use of the term "arris" for the line defining the meeting of planes. These terms are of particular importance in the discussion of Picasso, whose work is so insistently volumetric: "An irregular lattice of arrises emerges as the condition of three-dimensionality in symbolic form." Leo Steinberg, "Resisting Cézanne: Picasso's 'Three Women'" (*Art in America* [November–December 1978]:127, 128).

8. Shattuck, *The Innocent Eye*, 297–300.

SOUL MUSIC:
RELIGION AND POETRY

BARON WORMSER

T. S. Eliot once observed that for most people religious poetry was synonymous with minor poetry. Poetry with religious concerns was assumed to be confining, peculiar, unbalanced. I would like to propose that for those living in the long shadows of the late twentieth century just the opposite is true: genuine religious poetry is likely to be major poetry.

Although I could offer, to support my assertion, various post–World War II American examples beginning with the extraordinary religious poems of Robert Lowell, Anne Sexton, and Thomas Merton and continuing to the present moment in the work of such diverse poets as Gjertrud Schnackenberg, Li-Young Lee, Christopher Jane Corkery, Daniel Mark Epstein, and Reynolds Price, I would rather proceed existentially. Why— to put the question directly—is religious poetry crucial at this time?

The answer to this question is one more question: Do human beings have souls? As I understand it, this question looks each of us in the face every day. My well-adjusted, positivist, therapeutically-inclined reader is likely to ask, "From where is this stare coming? Burger King, the tennis court, the shopping center, the vacation to the south of France, the new Toyota?" Which is to say, are we mere gourmandizing, exercising, purchasing bodies that aspire to be amiable nihilists?

This century has both systematically and absentmindedly impugned the grounds of human dignity. Familial, geographical, economic, cultural, and political bases of identity have been tossed aside like so many shards. What remains in this stolidly apocalyptic setting is the notion that something exists that cannot be taken away. That presence—to the indifference, despair, and contempt of politicos, merchandisers, and theorists—is the soul.

The existence of the soul proclaims something of consequence in each human being. This margin of spirit may be defined for our time as that which man cannot take away from man. It is not of this world because its lineage has nothing to do with cause and effect. The soul, which stands for the spark of being, is a gift. We may say that it is God's, that it is karmic, that it is unknowable. Ecumenicism, after all, need not be trivial; all religions acknowledge the primacy of the soul, that which can be sensed but never seen. The soul proclaims the miracle, not of explanation, that continuous modern miracle, but of presence, the unbidden miracle. The soul is not cozy but rather radical and uncanny. In its creaturely way it is frightening; hence, our common desire to forget it emerges.

If poetry is the music of meaning, then the recognition of the soul is the ground for meaning for poetry in our time. No other notion—identity, nature, language, time (and modernity is the secular worship of time), aestheticism, psychology—can speak as unequivocally for the integrity of each life. In the face of all that opposes human consequentiality, that regiments, belittles, traduces, ignores, and subverts the spiritual, the presence of the soul says quietly that we have been touched by the genius of being. Recognizing this genius, neither inflating it nor sentimentalizing it, is often a painful task. Sustaining the soul is a struggle. The expedient confidence of humanism is shallow because it is a confidence tied to the chimeras of achievement. With human beings nothing is achieved.

Imagine a world in which decades, movements, epochs, isms—all the paraphernalia of self-consciousness—did not matter. Mircea Eliade has noted that in various archaic societies time does not exist in its narrow, marking, differentiating sense. Time only matters as the circular, ritual-informing stuff of life—seasons and days and nights, the habits of the planet. Time in our newsweekly sense is unnecessary because spirit is endless. The crumbs of time do not matter because time is whole. The modern time-spirit, the Zeitgeist, is paltry. Meanings are recognized for what they are—symbolic rather than factual.

Our awareness is becoming more chthonic as our global dilemmas—ecological, military, economic—become more real to us. Our consciousness of the earth is becoming more a part of us, not a romantic affectation or a presentiment but an abiding faith, an ethic tinged with love. This earth-consciousness is bound to become spiritually evocative. For all its lucid benefits, understanding is no substitute for reverence and delight.

The awareness in a poet's work of the soul need not be announced by the use of that word. What I look for is a sense of a larger perspective, an awareness of how spirit informs each aspect of our lives. To be serious about spirit means the hard work of locating spirit in a time and a place. It means the hard work of coming to terms with many concepts and qualities—good and evil, profanity, divinity, sin, eternity, humility, salvation, karma, corruption, bliss, enlightenment, desire, despair, temptation—that have lost their currency in an era which swears allegiance to objective explanations (even as it fails, as it must, to live by these explanations). It means the hard work of indicating the accuracy of the frameworks of existing religions and the urgency of emerging religious notions.

Poets know that everything that is social is fictive. Poetic truth thus tends to be spiritual truth, the awareness of what does not change, what remains "at the still point of the turning world." Poets always must beware—this tendency is easily trivialized.

To say that something is sacred—what a powerful word! How can we be worthy of using this word? All the obeisances, prostrations, vigils, and meditation practices of the religions make eminent sense when one confronts such a word. Like the novice, the poet must earn his or her words.

Poetry is not a substitute for religion. Poetry may be a means of voicing religious concerns, intuitions, or tenets. It may be an offering or a confession. Such a poetry has nothing to do with the self-regarding religion of poetry that various modern poets have espoused. Poetry does not exist unto itself in some *sub specie aeternitatis* dreamland; it must be wedded to something.

Literary historians of our century tend to gloss over or ignore the quarrel between William Carlos Williams and T. S. Eliot. This is a disservice to both men. Williams thought Eliot turncoat, someone who rejected his country and its democratic confusions for the dubious orders of Europe. For his part, Eliot distrusted the genius of vitalism, the wisdom of the momentary perception. Williams was irreligious in the pagan sense; Eliot was, of course, religious in the most traditional sense. It is important to understand the divide between the two men; one cannot have things both ways. The notion that we can be all things to all poets is specious and debasing. The answer to the struggles Williams and Eliot endured is not latitudinarianism.

The primacy of the image in our poetry is ultimately imprisoning because the richness of symbol cannot inform the circumstantial image. However brilliantly adroit the image may be, it must fall short in the sense that it cannot participate in the texture of spiritual meaning. One understands our love of the image as a sign of life and a protest against the grayness and pretension of too many modern situations, but this love can take more profound forms. Moments and their attendant images are terribly slim supports for the drama of human lifetimes. Overreliance on the image indicates a sort of complacency; the travails of articulation are subjugated to the legerdemain of the visual.

Anyone who reads much contemporary verse is bound to ask, "Is there life beyond the lyric?" A consideration of the religious aspects of poetry reminds us that other genres do exist. I am thinking of the exaltation, the parable, the lament, the hymn, the confession, and even the teaching. The word "didactic" is invariably a term of abuse in our society, a synonym for heavy-handedness. It may be that we fear teaching because we do not believe that anyone could have anything to teach, because we are all equal authorities, and because we are taught (!) that poems are to be appreciated rather than learned from. This eudaemonistic approach is—we should remember—at odds with what most people on this planet have thought and practiced at most times. Most societies have cherished poetry, be it spoken or written, as a vessel for a teaching, however modest or far-ranging the teaching may be. But then most societies haven't been mass, pluralistic democracies. Our vaunted equality may be a camouflage for insolence and despair.

To say that poetry lacks a spiritual context today would be an understatement. It is foolish to blame anyone for this, but it is not to say that such a context is not possible. I believe that the context for poetry will change because there is a hunger, which is growing, for legends of the soul. The spiritual nature of humankind has been shamed and overawed, but it has not disappeared. Eliot's affirmation "that the whole of modern literature is corrupted by . . . Secularism, that it is simply unaware of, simply cannot understand the meaning of the primacy of the supernatural over natural life," cannot be brushed aside as reactionary flapdoodle. It is ridiculous to think that the preponderance of Secularism will go on forever. The reduction of poetry's stature has been—as Blake and many others have realized—coincidental with the reduction of spirit's stature. The curious refuges poetry has sought—the salvation of technique or the genius of the Zeitgeist—have been spiritual dodges, ways of staying alive. The great modernists are best seen in this light. The uncompromising wariness of a Frost or an Auden or a Bishop or a Montale seems at once extraordinary and understandable—as does the frustration of a Pound or a Lowell. Their examples are to be cherished.

Along with earth-consciousness, there is a growing consciousness of the teachings of Christ. The sirens of progressive knowledge have lead many people over the past two centuries to compromise Christ, to believe that Christ was historical and thus outmoded. It should go without saying that Christ's example is perpetual. Christians must bend to Christ; they must be broken of their shallow social conceit, their eager bows to whatever idols the era tosses up. A poem is one place to wrestle with Christ. Only a soul or one who seeks his or her soul can do this. For without a soul, nothing is at stake.

The death in life is automatism, the abnegation of the soul. The answer to such a death involves, however, more than lyric spontaneity.

It is very hard for us to be honest about romantic art. How embarrassing we find its excesses! How quick we are to ridicule the genius of a Shelley or a Lizst! This is because we do not recognize such art as a cry of the soul—bewildered, prophetic, ecstatic, despairing, wounded. You don't look for mannerliness and decorum from someone who has been stung. The romantics witnessed the practical annihilation of the soul. With what more tormenting vision can an artist be faced?

Emily Dickinson is as much a heroic poet of this nation as Walt Whitman. Whitman's expansiveness is tremendously appealing, but it rests on the exertions of hope. What Dickinson pursued—the reality of the soul, its movements, its deceptions, its insights, its correspondences—seems in many ways more courageous than Whitman's cosmic embrace. The democratic genius—as our times have endlessly made clear—is easily manipulated and easily satisfied. Whitman, of course, knew this himself. Dickinson, however, sounded a note of more acute defiance: the soul's refusal to submit to the journalistic moment.

At times I am able to intuit how poetry can be healing, how it can knit together what has been riven. I have no desire to analyze or package this intuition. It is like light in dark water—an alert solace.

The social setting of any art is bound to involve some degree of degradation. At times, particularly if the artist can maintain a spiritual perspective as did a Waugh or an Auden, this degradation is slightly (or for that matter, enormously) hilarious; at times it is pathetic. We should not forget that the putative good works of universities, foundations, and workshops are different from the soul-searchings of faith. Nor should we forget which—good works or faith—is foremost.

Summaries of whole centuries, the unfathomable weight of millions of lives, are hateful. Yet to say of modern times that it replaced the soul with the self is not far off a very large mark. Modernity is secular and the modern individual is relentlessly defined in terms of the self, the social accretions that define a time and a place. There is something infinitely sad about all the hullabaloo concerning what is circumstantial. After all, anxiety is endemic to the human condition, but to seek to allay uncertainty with what is palpably ephemeral has been to compound the condition. The self has not been able to bear the fierce weight that governments, economies, ideologies, and technologies have placed upon it. How could it? The temporal self is sturdiest when it is able to behold itself from a spiritual perspective, for then it understands that it need not be everything. It may even begin to understand the illusory nature of that pronoun "I." Identity, like spirit, is something shared rather than possessed. The identity crises and fits of alienation that characterized so many postwar perspectives seem representative of a sort of spiritual splinter that refuses to heal: the soul cries out that it is more than a self; the self, for its part, is uncomfortable when forced into becoming an ersatz soul. Camus was the greatest delineator of this predicament.

Intellectuals too often conceive of religion as primarily ethical. Since ethics have become secularized, this is doubly unfortunate as the popular dilution of ethics may be viewed by the modern secular intellectual as another failing of religion. This is most unfair. The ideal springs from a spiritual perception, a sense of the equality not of rights that may be interpreted variously but of souls that are adamant. Ethics offer insight into human suffering—not in the secular sense of deprivation but in the sense of persistent vice and constant struggle typifying whatever goodness we may approach. An ethics that is not moored to the perils of the soul is fated to wind up as legalistic or bumptiously commonsensical. However well-meant the poem is, the alert reader is unintentionally amused by Arnold's "Dover Beach." Arnold's honesty is, at bottom, a sort of slavishness to temporal concerns. For all his rectitude Arnold is a much more corrupt poet than the supposedly Satanic Baudelaire.

The shortcoming of the natural religion that has characterized much postwar American poetry lies in its exaggerated polarities: confusion and discovery. The continuum of spiritual and social reality, however, cannot be limned in episodic encounters with nature. The absence of a before and an after makes much of this poetry—however heartfelt—inevitably portentous. Epiphanies occur very rarely. The work of spirit is shockingly prosaic.

If anything I have said seems programmatic, let me apologize. I wish to register possibilities. Awareness cannot substitute for achievement, and nothing can substitute for the audacity at the heart of poetry. But it is important to feel that there are other contexts and standards for verse beyond the conventional ones. There are all manner of judgments.

THE ABRUPT EDGE

STANLEY PLUMLY

In robes of green, in garments of adieu

A Brontë postcard—

At the top of the High Street, Haworth Parsonage, of a cold brownstone, stained by two centuries of weather, and behind it, and above—the sky half thick with cloud, half-blue—Haworth Moor, in outline, in too-brilliant a summer green, the high grass caught permanently, it seems, in a wind directly from the sea, while in front of the house and flanking it, gravestones and pines and stunted fir and perhaps some beech trees and a few rooks for heavy punctuation and moor-grass running to the church just below, then starting to the right, out of the picture, the cobblestones that still lead into the village and the Black Bull. . . .

Like most clichés, this one is not hard to imagine, though it changes with memory. What I remember being struck by my first visit to the village of Haworth was the completeness of its world, the circumscription but completeness of the idea of village life, the sense of self-containment and limit that nomadic Americans in particular have trouble relating to. You could live the provincial life here in Haworth or in any number of a thousand little towns like it and not miss much: a concept of the microcosm that even George Eliot, Thomas Hardy, and Agatha Christie share. You could stand on top of the house and count the world and know that the numbers, though small, were perfect. You could see the boundaries, mark where the basic needs of flesh and spirit would be met—the butcher, the baker, the candlestick maker, and God. In a place like Haworth confinement could mean concentration, focus, perspective; you might be forced, in fact, to come to terms with yourself, to know and accept and thrive in limitation.

I remember drifting in this fantasy awhile. Then I walked around, measuring the town's circumference and had lunch at the Black Bull Pub. To come to Haworth, which sits high in the wind above Worth Valley, West Yorkshire, you have to pass through some of the ugliest Lawrencian industrial scab-pockets in England, of dead-black mill and ironworks and smokestack purity. You also pass through some of the most beautiful countryside on earth, great sweeps of the near-moorland climbing away from the road right up to the sky, divided into pasture by stone—green pastures made to lie down in. Haworth is in recess from both extremes, tucked and diminutive, but for the

Brontës it was large enough to be divisible by four: the moor, the parsonage, the graveyard, and the pub. It was their whole world because of the juxtaposition of its parts—the great moor looming against the back of the house, the house pressed (and doubtless oppressed) by the churchyard below, and lower still the twilit, carnal, interior space of the Black Bull. Charlotte and Anne, in the best of their fiction, either longed to leave or rejected Haworth, its Gothic isolation and its proximity to industrial violence and drabness; their brother Branwell—a real-life inspiration for Heathcliff—finally wanted only to disappear and painted himself out of the sibling portrait and drank himself to death at the Bull. Emily came to terms with the contradictions of Haworth by embracing the wildness and darkness of the landscape surrounding the isolated, repressed, and dull safety of the nest. Having survived them all, wife and children, the Brontë preacher-father, in later life, would often show visitors, especially Americans, the room his daughters worked in, now still almost undisturbed, the furniture intact, their books and memorabilia everywhere. He was oddly proud of his daughters, but was still preaching—from Job, remembered one visitor—with his eye on the graveyard: "There the wicked cease from troubling; and the weary be at rest."

I remember standing, not on a house, but on a flat gravestone in order to better see the whole of the place and how the parts of Haworth fit. From high on the horizon the silver and green of the deep moorgrass seemed to pour, like a wind, down on the parsonage right on through to the church and churchyard, and, though it fell in stages and in different lengths, interrupted by fence and path or clump of trees, the grass should have made the transition between territories more natural; instead it heightened the difference. And where the grass ended, the cobblestones picked up the rhythm and carried it on into the town. I began to understand that what ought to provide continuity was in fact underlining the difference between the wild and open moor and the tiny island of church and citizen. Standing there, trying to get perspective, the moor at the top of the land and the milltown of Keighley at the very bottom in the valley, I began to see that a landscape is many scapes, many entities, many walls, invisible sometimes, sometimes visible but permeable. It is no secret that Emily Brontë came to see the open, ocean wilderness of the moor as freedom from the strictures of space and consciousness in her father's house, as liberation from the vacuum of small rooms viewing graves. Yet when she contracted consumption—the poet's disease—she chose to withdraw from her loved long moorland walks and die at the window. Her brother chose the closed space of his own stupor. He could not apparently imagine a life beyond the circle of Haworth or at least did not have the talent to cross and embrace the wild outside. He simply sank deeper into the well of himself. He died against his father, in the town's one pub. He got stuck at the edge.

Standing in a graveyard that seems more attached to the house than to the church is unsettling. Matthew Arnold, not exactly a cup of cheer himself, in an 1855 elegy for Charlotte Brontë entitled "Haworth Churchyard," makes the spatial arrangement clear: "the church / Stands on the Crest of the hill, / Lonely and bleak;—at the side / The parsonage-house and the graves." The graves, as I recall, were rough, with that handmade, hand-dug roughness of the animal, the ground over the bodies still heaped a little, the stones handset, off-center, weathered and natural-looking, the names driven in with a hammer. Many of the names and dates named and dated children or people who, like the Brontë children, did not make it much into or out of their thirties. The cold and the damp and the Yorkshire grim and the black north wind would have made short work of most of us—the weather had the feel of the congenital. Yet the green ground against the black and deeper green of the towering graveyard trees, with the stones lit gray like fieldstones and the rooks calling what sounded like the names of the dead from above, all had a kind of beauty, a sense of ceremony. The humanity of the place felt at one with the nature of the place—loss was piled on loss, yet the spirit felt fed. What the earth pulled down, the branching of the trees and the greening of the grass returned to light. The rooks could be witnesses or angels, depending. The richness went to the root. Death lived here, in rest and in peace, next door, one of the choices.

In ornithology there occurs the phrase *the abrupt edge,* which, according to the birdbooks, is "the edge between two types of vegetation . . . where the advantages of both are most convenient." In the less precipitous sense such edges are gradual, over a distance, sometimes up to miles, where a woodland thins out to shrub and grassland or a hedgerow drifts into ellipsis and disuse and finally pasture. In the more abrupt forest-at-the-edge-of-the-field sense, however, trees will stand isolated in a grove, in open country, or clumped in a thicket by a good river, like islands; closer to home, the protective hedge and shrub corners of a garden will act as a border, while the line of young maples or the understory of pyracantha and azalea will mark the boundary between safety and vulnerability. The advantage of the edge is that it allows the bird to live in two worlds at once, and the more abrupt the more intense the advantage. From a position of height or secrecy, the bird can spy for danger or prey; it can come and go quickly, like a thief. Where the vegetation is more varied, the shade and cover thicker, the insect life rising, the tanager can sweep down from its treetop, the thrush can fly out from the gloom, and the redwing can sit the fencepost all day in the summer sun. The edge is the concept of the doorway, shadow and light, inside and outside, room and warlde's room, where the density and variety of the plants that love the sun and the open air yield to the darker, greener, cooler interior world, at the margin. It is no surprise, then, that the greatest number of species as well as individuals live at the edge and fly the pathways and corridors and trails at the joining of the juxtaposition. That is where the richness is, the thick, deep vegetable life—a wall of life, where the trees turn to meadows, the meadows to columnar, watchtower trees.

A man of sense, coming to a clearing, a great open space, will always wait among the trees, in the doorway, until the coast is clear.

You cannot walk the moors forever. You cannot live in the daylight at the Black Bull. The list of abrupt edges is endless, but for the American Crow and English Rook through to the Wren and Yellow Warbler, the general list is Waterside Vegetation, Isolated Prominence, Mixed Brush and Grass, Margin on Open Country, Broken Openings, Deep Mixed, Deep Conifers, Deep Deciduous. And to negotiate the edge there is the long glide-and-search, the ground hunt, and dash-and-hide. But always there is the return to coloration and safety and the nest. In order for the habitat to be whole it must be divided—inside and outside, tower and open field, island and ocean. Like most principles and techniques of survival, the edge is ultimately a rather domestic arrangement. For birds it is the way the race thrives, the way the day is made, the way work and the rest from work are defined. I have to remember that Emily Brontë wrote her work in her father's house, as I must remember that without the moors there might have been no work to do. If we are fed or inspired in the open, the spirit and the hand must labor in the cloister. Without work to do the edge is meaningless. That is why the Brontë brother had to paint himself out of the picture—he had no work to do, only the night world of further and further withdrawal.

Far from the Yorkshire moors, south, about the year Emily Brontë was born, at the edge of the village of Hampstead, John Keats used to sit out in the summer evenings, claret in hand, and let the day go dark in long, blue, infinite graduations all around him. He was usually with friends, from what would later be known as the Keats circle; based on his own and the reports of others the conversation was exciting and diverting, both at the level of gossip and philosophy. The company was changeable, but Leigh Hunt was often there—or they would all be at Hunt's, in the Vale of Health—and the painter Robert Haydon, and perhaps Joseph Severn, and of course Charles Brown, and Charles Dilke, and later William Hazlitt and Richard Woodhouse, et al. Hampstead is still famous for its Heath, a great wild park now part of London. But then, in the early nineteenth century, it was forest and hill and understory almost exclusively, thick and green and burly, with country paths. The Charles Brown half of the house where Keats was staying was right at the border of the Heath and Hampstead proper, a good place for people to gather. Keats was about to enter his greatest period as a poet, between the awful autumn 1818 of his brother Tom's illness and death and his own contract with tuberculosis, a year-and-a-half later. Keats, a Londoner, was habitually restless, and whenever and wherever he was living in London he had three haunts: the busy commercial area around Fleet Street, the intimacy of tiny Hampstead, and the enclosure and canopy of the Heath itself. He seemed primarily to prefer the place in between the place now known as the Keats House, Keats Grove, Hampstead.

I have thought a lot about John Keats over the past few years. For all his restlessness and planning, he was not the great long-distance walker many of his Romantic contemporaries were, including the unromantic Charles Brown. Keats nearly died an even earlier death from a Brown-instigated weeks-long walking tour of the Lake District and Scottish Highlands, all cold rain and haggis. He once grew so unhappy on the Isle of Wight that he fled, after great expectations, because its isolation turned out to be too much solitude, space, and vista. And he would have been uncomfortable, without question, on the open, empty Yorkshire moors just to be walking. He preferred the walks between near-places—the populated ten miles from the Thames to Hampstead or the much shorter path of "beechen green" between Brown's house and Leigh Hunt's cottage in the Vale. When he lived in Winchester, during the period of "To Autumn," he took the water-meadows walk along the River Itchen every day—from the Cathedral to the St. Cross Abbey and back again, about forty-five minutes one way. He would go out, in other words, only so far, to reveal only so much. He loved intimate, small space, the closed distance. That is why he seemed to love the evenings so much, with friends, at the darkening and blurring edge of worlds, the arcadian sublime of the near-house with the secure green of its grounds opposed to the rich, green space and chaos of the forest and underlife starting across East Heath Road, a chaos he would find compelling.

We cannot read Emily Brontë without an awareness of the impressive graveyard just beyond the Brontë windows. The correlative of the moors is obvious in her work, but the graveyard is the darkness. The weight and gloom and pull of its presence have everything to do with the tone and undertow of *Wuthering Heights,* and, at the last, with the novel's farewell.

> I sought, and soon discovered, the three head-stones on the slope next to the moor: the middle one grey, and half buried in the heath: Edgar Linton's only harmonised by the turf and moss creeping up its foot: Heathcliff's still bare.

> I lingered round them, under the benign sky; watched the moths fluttering among the heath and harebells, listened to the soft wind breathing through the grass, and wondered how any one could ever imagine unquiet slumbers for the sleepers in that quiet earth.

While the moors may have been Emily's freedom, Haworth Churchyard is the place, in the short distance, of simplest riches. The graves are her final emotional resource, the resonance under the work. The graves bring the outside inside, right into the parsonage, into the writing room, through the eye to the mind—they make intimate the space between life and death and give that edge its complexity and richness and its powerful attraction. We cannot read "Ode to a Nightingale" without accounting for the weeks, in the fall of 1818, that Keats spent with Tom in their little rooms above the Bentley's in Well Walk. Keats was ill himself with a very bad sore throat, having just returned from his bone-soaking northern tour with Brown. Tom, though, was dying, and until the end in November Keats would be his nurse. In the gray, tubercular air of the sickroom Keats would himself slowly become marked with the mark of youth that "grows pale, and spectre-thin." It is not hard to imagine Keats, the physician, bending over the sad and wasting body of his brother, knowing somewhere in himself what he was doing and risking.

Severn, Keats's last great friend, was fond of reporting how the poet would suddenly disengage himself from the group, when they were gathered after supper for the evening, at Hunt's or Brown's, and wander off onto the Heath, lost, apparently, in a long thought. Severn would claim of later finding Keats lying on a hillside, scribbling, listening to a thrush. Severn was convinced, against Brown's better-distributed opinion, that it was during these absences, in the early spring of 1819, in the first rush of warm and healthy Hampstead air and green, that Keats started thinking and speculating about the poem that became the nightingale ode. It is a nice story. Brown's version that Keats wrote the poem in a single extended sitting, on a May morning no less, right in front of the house, better fits our vanities of emotion recollected in tranquility. Yet what appeals to me in the Severn story is what appeals to me in the poem itself: the sense of secret, intimate space within or abutting the larger, enclosing, impending mystery of trees and the interlacing, vegetal and floral network of their trunk and root—a wall of green. It takes no scholar of Keats's poetry to notice how much he is impelled and empowered by that mystery and how sensual he finds its attraction though it overwhelms him with its palpable, physical, total information. At the edge of the small room, the small found space out of time, is the immensity and threat and gravity of the other world: all that is not the self, all that would confuse the senses, all that will not suffer the condition of art. When we bend over the face of the dead or the dying, as Keats did, everything opens; suddenly everything seems possible, in a moment. The mind begins to collapse into the imagination, into dimensions of another size and density. Keats's nightingale is a miracle for what it promises: at the crucial, heart-filling moment, at the edge, at the green wall, it sings from the other side. It makes no demands, calls no questions, shows no interest. It simply sings of mortal summer from the depth of the mystery, with full-throated ease.

To write a poem like the "Nightingale" you have to be at the right place at the right time and to know it and to know the difference between whistling and the "plaintive anthem." Keats cannot follow his nightingale, and yet he does—"past the near meadows, over the still stream, / Up the hill-side . . . into the next valley-glades." At one level, his "imaginative leap" is a flight from weariness and fever and fret; at another, it is an understanding, an insighting of his long suffering with Tom. His intimacy with this moment, at the edge of spaces, is to know absolutely, and at last, the distinction and ultimate disinterest between life and art, that edge where nature, beyond the human, the egotistical sublime, does its richest business. My impression of the nightingale ode has always been that the so-called green chaos and the "embalmed darkness" become synonymous at the point at which Keats cannot see the flowers underfoot nor identify the soft incense on the boughs, so he guesses, he says—which is a form of acceptance—

> *Wherewith the seasonable month endows*
> *The grass, the thicket, and the fruit-tree wild;*
> *White hawthorn, and the pastoral eglantine;*
> *Fast fading violets cover'd up in leaves;*
> *And mid-May's eldest child,*
> *The coming musk-rose, full of dewy wine,*
> *The murmurous haunt of flies on summer eves.*

Through the motion and medium of the falling evening dark the abrupt green edge has been blurred and moved to include Keats; rather passively, in his waking dream, he has, in imagination, passed over, passed through the wall, to the place where he can say, meaningfully, that he too has been half in love with easeful death and that now more than ever seems it rich to die. Because he has been so prepared and so patient, the wall has come to him, though his complaint is the familiar complaint of the listener who would hear more, whose fantasy of immortality is the closure of the past: of hungry generations, of emperor and clown, of Ruth among the alien corn. The close of his poem is to leave him back at the edge, in silence in a question, but also in the clearing.

Life, of course, for Keats, will imitate art. He will perfect his vision only to see it end. I have often wondered how such a mimesis happens: how our lives can seem so emphatically plotted and predicated by the poem or story. The obvious answer is that our lives themselves have done the plotting; the materials were there from the start, and the imagination lets us see, forces us to see, who we are and what will become of us. The imaginative leap is a leap from memory, from the edges of experience. The other world, the other side of the green wall, the graveyard, the intimate understory of the Heath, may or may not be the future; they are certainly the simultaneous present—a parallel, disinterested order of a different order, a wholly terrible and powerful otherness enacted at the speed of light. Imagination is the body alchemized, through fire, into spirit. When I lived in Devon I thought of Plath—"The hills step off into whiteness." When I lived in Seattle I thought of Roethke—"The edge is what I have." Both poets confronted the wall in their lives; both were committed to the imagination at the peril of their lives.

In Devon the happiest necessity is walking. The weather is dramatic; the landscape is dramatic. The clouds come in off the ocean in armadas, stacked with rain to the top-sail, tinged with sunlight. The weather is six things in a day. The landscape is in rhythm with the sky: it rolls; it opens; it closes; it runs right up to the edge of the open water, then drops straight down, hundreds of feet. Devon blue is a color; so is Devon green, a luminescent, bristling, gorgeous green of infinite version. As the sky and ocean beat against it, the landscape holds its own by being only more or less domesticated—fisherman and farmer, laborer and shepherd. The land and off-land work. The excitement of the place comes mostly from the melodramatic wind, constant and omnipresent and vocal, a third scape between sky and land, sky and sea. A wind filled with birds and the sounds of birds and the skim from the saltwater. Perhaps the strongest visual link in the Devon countryside is the hedgerow, a history of the common life of the vegetable, animal, and human kingdoms. It runs head-high or higher in seams all over the shire. The trope of knitting, of weaving, is appropriate. If you walked the road between rows in the evening, the sun would light candles on top of the hedge, while in the haw-life underneath, in the bramble and thicket, the sounds, except for the thrush, would be settling into sleep.

In her poem "Wuthering Heights," Sylvia Plath complains that "there is no life higher than the grasstops / Or the hearts of sheep, and the wind / Pours by like destiny. . . ." A short time later, when she takes her own moorland Devon walk, in her poem "Blackberrying," the dimensions of life will substantially increase, though the same claustrophobic fear of closure becoming enclosure will obtain. It is the richness, the fecundity, the almost grotesque fullness of the bramble hedge hugging both sides of the road that disturbs her—"a blackberry alley"—and, at the same time, the pull of the antithetical open ocean at the end of the lane that compels her to go on. She has no place of safety. Having already filled, by the end of the first stanza, her blackberry quota, she must either retreat or go on, though either way is closed. She goes on, to the open end of the lane. Unlike Brontë or Keats, Plath seems to be seeking the edge, an extreme edge, an edge that would, given the opportunity, shut down imagination. Even overhead, as if to blind and mute the sky, "the choughs in black, cacophonous flocks," congregate, like the berries. Theirs is the only voice, protesting, protesting. "Blackberrying," written in 1960, has more and more struck me as a poem certain of suicide, a suicide of that moment when the imagination overloads or precipitously empties and will not work anymore, cannot lift. It can only metaphorize the moment, exactly what Plath does once she reaches the place where "the only thing to come now is the sea." The imagination, or something, seems to shut down, and the brilliant, painful machine takes over. The cliff face, she says, at the edge of the Atlantic, looks out on nothing, "nothing but a great space / Of white and pewter lights, and a din like silversmiths / Beating and beating at an intractable metal." The world of the hedgerow, the green world, is overwhelming, and now the great shining space of the open water and the shout of the sea-wind overload seal off the senses—this time a white wall rather than a green. And though she tries and tries, and ends her career writing pure but nearly anorectic forms, the richness and promise of the edge, closed or open, green as well as white, drive her back into her own perfection and fears so that instead of finding a way through the wall, whatever its texture, she retreats to the child-sized dimensions of the grasstops and dies in a tiny kitchen, with her head in a tiny oven.

The open, light-refracting undifferentiated surface of the ocean may be too alien, too nonhuman a wall, in spite of the human figure of the silversmiths. Yet the ripe hedge is also too thick for Plath, too threatening. Theodore Roethke, in "The Far Field," declares to have learned, half-way through the journey of his poem, "not to fear infinity / The far field, the windy cliffs of forever." Brave words, from a brave man. As we know, by the finish of this wonderful poem, Roethke will have joined, imaginatively, all air and water; at the edge of his far field he will have begun to be absorbed into the natural cycle in order to wind, like a lively Yeatsian spirit, around the waters of the world. Bainbridge Island, where Roethke lived in the Northwest, is just west of Seattle and next to the Olympic Peninsula. In Roethke's time it was much less populated than it is today, which means there were even more trees—big pines and spruce and fir and Pacific yew, a wall of evergreen, standing and mixing with a variable but almost continual wall of mist and fog and rain. An interaction of the green and white, on a landscape of forest just above sea level. Plath might have suffocated in such closeness—at least the white noise of the Devon coast feels separate at the edge.

One of the essential differences between "Blackberrying" and "The Far Field" is that Roethke begins his poem where Plath chooses to end hers. The extreme edge, the apparent dead-end, where the imagination is in trouble, is, in "The Far Field," the condition to be overcome. Roethke starts off by saying that he dreams of journeys repeatedly, yet offers the examples of the cul-de-sac—first with the bat flying into the narrowing tunnel, expressed as a simile, then, extensively, with the speaker driving alone, without luggage, out a long peninsula, in the cold of the year, alternate snow and sleet, no on-coming traffic, and no lights behind . . .

> *The road changing from glazed tarface to a rubble of stone,*
> *Ending at last in a hopeless sand-rut,*
> *Where the car stalls,*
> *Churning in a snowdrift*
> *Until the headlights darken.*

Roethke then sets himself the task of solving this suicidal position—by, in effect, stepping out of his car and addressing the edge of the natural, mortal world, which is not quite yet the abyss. "I suffered for birds," he says, "my grief was not excessive." He makes no secret of the fact that the richness he is about to embrace is ordered in his mind with the thought of his own death, "The dry scent of a dying garden in September, / The wind fanning the ash of a low fire." This poignancy continues outside him, with the wrens bickering and singing in the half-green hedgerows, the flicker drumming from his dead tree in the chicken-yard, and himself lying naked, like a body projected, in the shallows of a coastal river, fingering a shell—then the river turns on itself, becomes two rivers, and returns toward the sea.

At one point, in the middle of his poem Roethke apposes his line about the windy cliffs with "the dying of time in the white light of tomorrow." This image seems to me to be more than simply another effective generalization in his sequence—it has particular emotional content, an especial quality of surrender, as distinguished from Plath's brilliant but combative pewter and silversmith strategy at the close of "Blackberrying." Roethke is yielding to the rest of his journey. Plath has no further to go. I am reminded of another of Plath's telling Devon poems, "Sheep in Fog," that concludes:

> *My bones had a stillness, the far*
> *fields melt my heart.*
>
> *They threaten*
> *To let me through to a heaven*
> *Starless and fatherless, a dark water.*

Here the extremity of the edge threatens by its promise of starlessness and fatherlessness, with no chance of renewal or return. The far fields here become a dark, deadly water of dissolution. It is too simple to say that Plath killed herself and that Roethke died a longer death. The difference is that both poets are animated by similar edges with different results. Roethke reads renewal; Plath reads the perfection of the closed rose "when the garden / Stiffens and odours bleed/ From the sweet, deep throats of the night flower." Is Plath's a spiritual suicide as well? I have said that the edge is where the richness is, the clearing, the open space, the water or the green wall. The bird flies back and forth between worlds because the risk is exactly where the richness is.

Plath's is the art of divestment. Roethke's the art of acquisition. Plath wishes to forget, Roethke to remember. Plath wants more than to disappear into her emblem; she wants to be perfected by it—dissolve into it completely, traceless, like the arrow and dew, as she says in "Ariel," at one with the drive into the cauldron of morning. She wants to melt into the wall. She wants the air emptied behind her. At the point of richness and energy and intensity and the potential of return, she wants only absence, absolutely. She wants to be transformed without the further burden of transcendence. Emily Dickinson speaks of "just the Door ajar / That Oceans are . . . / And that White Sustenance—/ Despair—." Plath's genius and beauty, in those poems at the utter edge, is that she is willing to admit when the imagination is terminal and the body carnal and the spirit slow dissolve. She is willing to yield to the impermeability of the wall itself, willing to melt into it, yet unwilling to admit that once at the edge we cannot stay there: we must go into the openness or density of the other, the natural, the green world, and we must find our way back again. The sustenance of white is the death of the spirit, a flight into oblivion and the absolute, and Plath's greatness lies in her willingness to risk it.

Roethke, though, is dressed "in robes of green, / garments of adieu." He knows he will join, must join, the "silence of water above a sunken tree: / The pure serene of memory in one man." He will give himself up to the world in detail, to the immensity, he says, of change. Roethke's spiritual analogue could never be found, like his mentor's, in a golden bird on a golden bough, the announcement of artifice. Instead, it is in the analogue of the tree, roots in one world, branches in the other, with that oldest symbol of the soul, the wren, the warbler, the brown thrush, hidden in the leaves. Sitting there also, like unconscious life itself, as one in the *wylder ness,* is the green man, who cannot be killed, though we strike him dead. At the edge of his secret position, from the gloom and intimacy and complexity of the root and branching, he beckons that we put off this flesh and be as one with the tree—magical in the natural, green and evergreen—even the shade tree at the grave. His seduction is practically sexual.

Near the end of his exhaustive elegy for Lincoln and the Civil War, Whitman does the most curious thing ever done in an elegy—certainly as antithetically arcadian as a Lycidian elegy could be. He has arrived at Part 14 of his sixteen-part poem. And he is at the edge of the dooryard, at the close of day, at the edge of the swamp, at the edge of a vision.

> *Now while I sat in the day and looked forth,*
> *In the close of the day with its light and the fields of spring,*
>   *and the farmers preparing their crops,*
> *In the large unconscious scenery of my land with its lakes*
>   *and forests,*
> *In the heavenly aerial beauty (after the perturbed winds*
>   *and the storms),*
> *Under the arching heavens of the afternoon swift passing,*
>   *and the voices of children and women.*
> *The many-moving sea-tides, and I saw the ships how they*
>   *sailed,*
> *And the summer approaching with richness, and the fields*
>   *all busy with labor,*
> *And the infinite separate houses, how they all went on,*
>   *each with its meals and minutia of uses . . .*

He continues in this rhythm, and rhapsody, for several more lines ("Be with me, Whitman, maker of catalogues," says Roethke.), setting the scene, taking the long perspective, confusing even the grammar of the sequence, in order, apparently, to create a context for the wild elegiac assumption he is about to make: that by befriending the enemy he can win a victory; that by befriending death he can know it, and its thought, and its sacred knowledge; that by walking—"as walking" he actually says—with the knowledge of death on one side and the thought of death close-walking on the other, as with companions, "as holding the hands of companions," he can understand the night and the green wall of the swamp and the solemn shadowy cedars and the ghostly pines so still. He continues in this rhythm in order to show that "then and there / Falling upon them all and among them all, enveloping me with the rest / Appeared the cloud, appeared the long black trail"—in order to show that life-in-death is whole and in order to prepare for the song outside the cycle, from the other side. The song of the gray-brown thrush, from the swamp. It is this song that will tally with the voice of his own spirit into a hymn of acceptance, a carol of joy—"*Come lovely and soothing death / Undulate round the world, serenely arriving, arriving*"—and it is this song of the soul's tally that will permit Whitman passage to his further and transcendent vision, "long panoramas of vision," far beyond the original object of his concern. His word for the perception of his new understanding will be "askant": or sideways, angular, slant, sublime.

> And I saw askant the armies,
> I saw as in noiseless dreams hundreds of battle-flags,
> Borne through the smoke of the battles and pierc'd with
>   missiles I saw them,
> And carried hither and yon through the smoke, and torn
>   and bloody,
> And at last but a few shreds left on the staffs (and all in
>   silence)
> And the staffs all splinter'd and broken.
>
> I saw battle-corpses, myriads of them,
> And the white skeletons of young men, I saw them,
> I saw the debris and debris of all the slain soldiers of the war,
> But I saw they were not as was thought,
> They themselves were fully at rest, they suffer'd not,
> The living remain'd and suffer'd, the mother suffer'd,
> And the wife and the child and the musing comrade suffer'd,
> And the armies that remain'd suffer'd.

These lines, so rich in repetition and detail, so generous, so empathic, are remarkable for what they posit: an afterlife here on earth in the long reflective moment and realism after death. The corpses are as they were, the corpses are as they were: what a simple and profound act of imagination. Sitting in his dooryard, in the spring, at the edge of the whole green world and ghostly swamp, Whitman has seen beyond the green man, beyond the garments of adieu, beyond grieving, beyond the renewal in the cycle of the leaf. He has heard and understood the song of the bird, who is also in the tree, who wants nothing from us—a song of the joy of the spirit that tallies with our own, that tells us not to be afraid, not to turn away, that this richness too is ours, if we accept it, as we might accept the riches of the dream at the end of the night, and the daydream in the evening, out on the lawn. Whitman has imagined the unimaginable because he has prepared for and listened to the spirit in the wood, the hermit thrush—solitary and secret except at the articulate edge. The lilac as well, Whitman says, with its mastering odor, holds him, and the great western star. But they are merely marvelous. The loud human song, as he calls it, "with the voice of uttermost woe," that is the sound at the edge of our hearing, that is the sound and symbol, in the crisis of imagination, we become.

One early October morning I was being driven by a friend from Billings, Montana, to Sheridan, Wyoming. My first visit: We had the time so she asked if I would like to stop off at the Little Bighorn, which was on the way. I said sure, why not, with no idea. The weather had turned sour, with an intermittent ice-cold drizzle and a black sky. The rain in fact had been falling all night and had given the land more weight, as if it needed it. The tourist season was long over, but the drive into the main area of the Custer Battlefield National Monument was still open. It was on a rise, though not too high. Through the cloud and ceiling of the sky there was little, it seemed, to see, as the landscape diminished into lush endless moorland and into sameness and a gray wall of weather. It was a landscape to get lost in, even on a good day. You could see that much. Yet standing there awhile, within the isolation of the cold rain, staring out at the long undulant ground, I was moved, more moved than I have ever been by a landscape, except the grounds at Gettysburg, which are also mapped and discovered and toured until one day you pass by by accident and see, perhaps, askant. Men had died here, bravely, and had been buried, in pieces, where they lay. Even in the obscurity of the weather you could feel the presence of the power of the dead in battle. You could feel it in the roll and secrecy and totality of the land, which was a series of blindsides and which was nothing else but this one history. It was human, and it was alive. And though the dead could not humble the land, they were now an intimate part of it. Its richness.

So we say life and death, as if that were the edge of ultimate concern to the imagination, when the real edge is between life and more life, memory and wish. The powerful imagination does not work, as every good poem reminds us, unless it comes to an edge, makes its pass, and, one way or another, returns. It surely, in a lifetime, gets harder and harder to get back. And a lifetime can be barely thirty years, as it was for Plath and Emily Brontë and almost for Keats. They were nourished by the very thing that would bring them down. That was their intensity. Plath, at the end, was cold with intensity: so little of the spirit seems to make it back to the woman, the person inside the poet. Roethke lasts longer; still, his *Far Field* is a posthumous book. Whitman writes and rewrites until he is subsumed, body, beard, and great soul, into the organicism of his poems. In the late pictures he looks like a natural object, like part of an oak or a shock of wheat, the green man grown old. It can look like freedom—the open, the far field or the forest-building protective-coloration of the trees or the sublime vision of the afterlife. But the imagination leads only a half-life, a fantasy-life, if it does not come back from the other side, no matter how compelling or consuming. And it will have no life at all if it does not fly, as Keats says, with new Phoenix wings at its desire.

NOTES ON THE CONTRIBUTORS

GLORIA ANZALDUA is the author of *Borderlands/La frontera: The New Mestiza* and edited with Cherrié Moraga *This Bridge Called My Back: Writings of Radical Women of Color.* She currently teaches at the University of California, Santa Cruz.

MARVIN BELL is the author of eight volumes of poetry, a book of essays, and a collection of poems written as correspondence with William Stafford. His *New and Selected Poems* was published by Atheneum in 1987. He lives in Iowa City, where he is Flannery O'Connor Professor of Letters at The University of Iowa, and, as much as possible, in Port Townsend, Washington.

CHARLES BERNSTEIN is the author of fourteen books of poetry, most recently *The Sophist.* His critical essays have been collected as *Content's Dream: Essays 1975–1984.* With Bruce Andrews, he edited $L=A=N=G=U=A=G=E$, which has been anthologized as *The $L=A=N=G=U=A=G=E$ Book.* He lives in Manhattan and is a correspondent for *Sulphur.*

PAUL CHRISTENSEN is the author of *Signs of the Whelming* and *Weights and Measures.* His critical books include *Charles Olson: Call Him Ishmael* and a study of the poet Clayton Eshleman, *Mining the Underworld.* He teaches modern literature at Texas A & M University.

AMY CLAMPITT was born and brought up in rural Iowa, graduated from Grinnell College, and has since lived mainly in New York City. Her poems began appearing in *The New Yorker* and elsewhere in 1978. Her full-length collections include *The Kingfisher, What the Light Was Like,* and, most recently, *Archaic Figure.* She has been writer in residence at the College of William and Mary and visiting writer at Amherst College.

CHERYL CLARKE is the author of several books of poems, including *Narratives: poems in the tradition of black women, Living as a Lesbian,* and *Scarred Rocks.* Her writing appears in *Conditions, IKON, Sinister Wisdom, Heresies, Black Scholar,* and *Callaloo.* She lives in Jersey City, New Jersey.

ALFRED CORN'S books of poetry include *All Roads At Once, A Call in the Midst of the Crowd, The Various Light,* and *Notes from a Child of Paradise.* His critical essays have been collected in *The Metamorphoses of Metaphors: Essays in Poetry and Fiction.* He was a Fulbright Fellow to France, and has received many awards including a special award from the Academy and Institute of Arts and Letters, fellowships from the Guggenheim Foundation, the National Endowment for the Arts, and most recently, the Fellowship of the Academy of American Poets. He has taught at Connecticut College, Yale University, and the School of the Arts at Columbia. He lives in New York City.

DOUGLAS CRASE, the author of *The Revisionist,* received the Witter Bynner Prize for poetry from the American Academy and Institute of Arts and Letters in 1983. His criticism appears in *The Nation.* He was named a MacArthur Fellow in 1987. He lives in New York City.

MICHAEL DAVIDSON teaches at the University of California, San Diego. He is the author of *The Landing of Rochambeau* and *The Analogy of the Ion*. Cambridge University Press will be bringing out his book of criticism, *The San Francisco Renaissance: Poetics and Community at Mid-Century*.

RACHEL BLAU DUPLESSIS, Professor of English at Temple University, is the author of *Writing Beyond the Ending: Narrative Strategies of Twentieth-Century Women's Writing* and *H.D.: The Career of that Struggle*, along with two books of poetry, *Wells* and *Tabula Rosa*. Among her speculative essays on gender and culture are "For the Etruscans," "Language Aquisition," and "Sub Rosa." She is currently editing a Selected Letters of George Oppen, and coediting, with Susan Friedman, a collection of H.D. criticism.

CLAYTON ESHLEMAN'S publications include *Conductors of the Pit: Major Works by Rimbaud, Vallejo, Cesaire, Artaud, and Holan* (Paragon House, 1988) and *Antiphonal Swing: Selected Prose 1962–1987* (McPherson and Co., 1988). He teaches at Eastern Michigan University and edits *Sulfur* magazine.

ALICE FULTON'S first book of poems, *Dance Script with Electric Ballerina*, won the 1982 Associated Writing Programs Award. Her second *Palladium* was selected for the 1985 National Poetry Series. She is the William Wilhartz Assistant Professor of English at The University of Michigan, Ann Arbor.

JONATHAN GALASSI has published two volumes of translations of work by the Italian poet Eugenio Montale, *The Second Life of Art: Selected Essays of Eugenio Montale* and *Otherwise: Last and First Poems*. He is currently preparing an edition of Montale's first three books of poems. A collection of his poems, *Morning Run*, was published in 1988 by Paris Review Editions.

SANDRA GILBERT is the author of many books of criticism; with Susan Gubar, she is the coauthor of *The Madwoman in the Attic* and, most recently, *No Man's Land: The Place of the Woman Writer in the Twentieth-Century; Volume I, The War of the Words*. She is also the author of four volumes of poetry, including the most recent collection, *Blood Pressure*. She is professor of English at Princeton University.

DANA GIOIA is a businessman in New York. His poems and essays appear regularly in *The Hudson Review, Poetry,* and *The New Yorker. Daily Horoscope,* his first collection of poems, appeared in 1986 from Graywolf Press.

JUDY GRAHN is the author of three collections of poetry, *The Work of a Common Woman, The Queen of Wands,* and *The Queen of Swords* as well as two critical works, *Another Mother Tongue: Gay Words, Gay Worlds,* and *The Highest Apple: Sappho and the Lesbian Poetic Tradition.* In 1980, she received a fellowship from the National Endowment for the Arts. She is an independent intellectual, helping to define and expand the borders of "women's poetry" and establishing lesbian poetry as a genre.

EMILY GROSHOLZ has published two collections of poetry, *The River Painter* and *Shores and Headlands.* She is an advisory editor for *The Hudson Review* and is the recipient of an Ingram Merrill Foundation Award for poetry and a John Simon Guggenheim Fellowship for poetry. She is associate professor of philosophy at Pennsylvania State University.

MARILYN HACKER is the author of five collections of poetry: *Presentation Piece,* which received the National Book Award in 1975, *Separations, Taking Notice, Assumptions,* and *Love, Death, and the Changing of the Seasons.* She lives in New York City, and was, from 1982 through 1986, editor of the feminist literary magazine, *13th Moon.*

RACHEL HADAS is the author of three volumes of poetry, most recently *A Son From Sleep.* She has written a comparative study of Frost and Seferis, *Form, Cycle, Infinity.* She teaches English at the Newark campus of Rutgers University and lives in New York City with her husband and son.

SAM HAMILL is editor at Copper Canyon Press in Port Townsend, Washington, and author of several volumes of poetry, including most recently *Fatal Pleasure* and *The Nootka Rose,* as well as translations from Chinese, Japanese, Latin, and Estonian. He has received a National Endowment for the Arts Fellowship, a Pacific Northwest Booksellers' Award, a Guggenheim Fellowship, and a Japan-U.S. Fellowship.

CHARLES HARTMAN has published *Free Verse: An Essay on Prosody* and books of poems, including *Making a Place.* He has received grants from the National Endowment for the Arts and the Ingram Merrill Foundation. He teaches at Connecticut College and lives in Rhode Island.

MICHAEL HELLER'S most recent volume of poetry is *Knowledge.* His essays on the Objectivist poets, *Conviction's Net of Branches,* were published in 1985.

EDWARD HIRSCH is the author of two books of poems: *For the Sleepwalkers,* which won the Lavan Younger Poets Award and the Delmore Schwartz Memorial Award, and *Wild Gratitude,* which won the National Book Critics Circle Award. He teaches in the Creative Writing Program at the University of Houston.

LAURA JENSEN has taught workshops from time to time at Tacoma Community College since 1982 as well as traveling throughout the United States to visit as a poet and to read. Her full-length collections include *Bad Boats, Memory,* and *Shelter.*

IRENA KLEPFISZ was born in 1941 in Warsaw, Poland, and emigrated to the United States at the age of eight. She received the Ph.D. from the University of Chicago in literature. She is a 1988 recipient of a fellowship from the National Endowment for the Arts. Her books include *Keeper of Accounts* and *Different Enclosures: The Poetry Prose of Irena Klepfisz.* She is also a coeditor of *The Tribe of Dina: A Jewish Women's Anthology.* She is currently teaching creative writing and women's studies in the Adult Degree Program of Vermont College, translating Yiddish women writers, and teaching Yiddish in the summer program at Columbia University.

ANN LAUTERBACH grew up in Manhattan, attended the University of Wisconsin and Columbia. She lived in London from 1967–1974. Since her return, she has worked in various art galleries, written art criticism, and taught in the M.F.A. programs at Brooklyn College, Columbia, and the Writers' Workshop in Iowa. She is the recipient of a Guggenheim Fellowship and an Ingram Merrill grant. Her books include *Many Times, But Then,* and *Before Recollection.* She has been a contributing editor of *Conjunctions* magazine since 1982.

DAVID LEHMAN is the editor of three collections: *Beyond Amazement: New Essays on John Ashbery, James Merrill, Essays in Criticism,* and *Ecstatic Occasions, Expedient Forms.* His collection of poems, *An Alternative to Speech,* was published in 1986.

BRAD LEITHAUSER has published two books of poems, *Hundreds of Fireflies* and *Cats of the Temple,* and two novels, *Equal Distance* and *Hence.*

DENISE LEVERTOV is the author of many volumes of poetry, most recently *Candles in Babylon, Oblique Prayers,* and *Breathing the Water.* Her collections of essays include *The Poet in the World* and *Light Up the Cave.* She is professor of English Stanford University.

LARRY LEVIS is the author of *The Wrecking Crew; The Afterlife,* which won the Lamont Award; *The Dollmaker's Ghost,* winner of the Open Competition of the National Poetry Series; and *Winter Stars.* He teaches in the Creative Writing Program at The University of Utah. He has received two National Endowment for the Arts Fellowships in poetry and a Guggenheim Fellowship.

WILLIAM LOGAN teaches at the University of Florida. He is the author of *Sad-faced Men, Difficulty,* and, most recently, *Sullen Weedy Lakes.*

NATHANIEL MACKEY is the author of two chapbooks of poetry, *Four for Trane* and *Septet for the End of Time,* one book of poetry which was a National Poetry Selection, *Eroding Witness,* and a book of prose, *Bedouin Hornbook.* He edits the literary magazine *Hambone* and teaches literature at The University of California, Santa Cruz.

J. D. McCLATCHY is the author of two collections of poems, *Scenes from Another Life* and *Stars Principal.* His essays and reviews appear regularly in *The New York Times Book Review, The New Republic,* and *Poetry.* A collection of his essays, *White Paper,* is forthcoming. He is the poetry editor of *The Yale Review* and has taught at Princeton and Yale. The recipient of Guggenheim and National Endowment for the Arts fellowships, he has also been awarded the Witter Bynner Poetry Prize by the American Academy and Institute of Arts and Letters.

ROBERT McDOWELL'S volume of narrative poetry, *Quiet Money,* appeared in 1987. He is the publisher and chief editor of Story Line Press and coedits, with Mark Jarman, *The Reaper,* a literary quarterly devoted to the resurgence of narrative in contemporary poetry.

JAMES McKEAN, originally from the Pacific Northwest, now lives with his family in Iowa City, where he teaches at The University of Iowa. His first book of poems, *Headlong,* was published in 1987.

ALICIA OSTRIKER is the author of *Stealing the Language: The Emergence of Women's Poetry in America* and a volume of critical essays, *Writing Like a Woman.* Her most recent book of poems, *The Imaginary Lover,* won the William Carlos Williams Prize of the Poetry Society of America. She is a Blake scholar, editor, and professor of English at Rutgers University.

MOLLY PEACOCK currently lives in New York City where she teaches at Friends Seminary. Her books of poetry include *And Live Apart, Raw Heaven,* and *Take Heart.*

STANLEY PLUMLY is the author of several volumes of poetry, including *Out-of-the-Body Travel* and *Summer Celestial.* A frequent contributor to *The American Poetry Review, Antaeus,* and *The Ohio Review,* he is currently putting together a collection of his own essays. In 1989, a new collection of his poems will be published. He teaches at The University of Maryland.

MARGARET RANDALL is an American-born writer, photographer, and teacher, who lived for twenty-three years in Latin America and returned to the United States in 1984. The U.S. Immigration and Naturalization Service has attempted to deport her solely on the basis of her writings, under the ideological exclusion clause of the 1952 McCarran-Walter Act. Among her most recent books are *Risking a Somersault in the Air: Conversations with Nicaraguan Writers, Albuquerque: Coming*

Back to the USA, Women Brave in the Face of Danger, This is About Incest, and *Memory Says Yes.* She is a visiting professor of English at Trinity College in Hartford.

JOAN RETALLACK is the author of the collection of poems *Circumstantial Evidence.* She teaches interdisciplinary seminars in The General Honors Program at The University of Maryland and is an associate of The Institute for Writing and Thinking at Bard College. A commentator for National Public Radio's "All Things Considered," she is currently working on an essay-novel.

JEROME ROTHENBERG is the author of over forty books of poetry including *Poems for the Game of Silence, Poland/1931, A Seneca Journal, Vienna Blood,* and *That Dada Strain.* His *Pre-Faces & Other Writings,* a collection of prose, received the Before Columbus Foundation American Book Award. His anthologies are remarkable assemblages and include *Technicians of the Sacred, Shaking the Pumpkin, America a Prophecy* (with George Quasha), *Revolution of the Word, A Big Jewish Book* (with Harris Lenowitz and Charles Doria), and *Symposium of the Whole* (with Diane Rothenberg).

MARK RUDMAN'S books include *By Contraries and Other Poems, Robert Lowell: An Introduction to the Poetry,* and a translation (with Bohdan Boychuk) of Pasternak's *My Sister—Life* and *The Sublime Malady.* He is presently completing a book of poems, *The Nowhere Steps,* and a translation of Euripides' *The Trojan Women.* He lives in New York City where he teaches in, and is assistant director of, the Graduate Writing Program at New York University.

GRACE SCHULMAN'S books of poems include *Burn Down the Icons* and *Hemispheres.* She is the author of a critical study, *Marianne Moore: the Poetry of Engagement,* editor of *Ezra Pound: A Collection of Criticism,* and cotranslator of *Songs of Cifar and the Sweet Sea,* by Pablo Antonio Cuadra. She is the recipient of a Witter Bynner Grant-in-Aid and of a Present Tense Literary Award for her translation of T. Carmi's *At the Stone of Losses.* She is the poetry editor of *The Nation.* She has taught at Princeton, Columbia, Wesleyan, and Bennington College. She is currently professor of English at Baruch College.

RON SILLIMAN is the author of *The Age of Huts, Ketjak, Paradise,* and *Tjanting.* He edited the anthology of new poetry *In the American Tree,* and his book of criticism, *The New Sentence,* was recently published. He is executive editor of *Socialist Review.*

TIMOTHY STEELE, born in Vermont in 1948, has published two collections of poems, *Uncertainties and Rest* and *Sapphics Against Anger and Other Poems.* He is currently an associate professor in the English Department at California State University, Los Angeles, and his recent honors include a Guggenheim Fellowship and a Peter I. B. Lavan Younger Poets Award from the Academy of American Poets.

GERALD STERN is the author of six volumes of poetry. His most recent book, *Lovesick,* was published in 1987. Harper & Row will be bringing out a collection of essays and a selected poems. He teaches at The Writers' Workshop at The University of Iowa.

DAVID ST. JOHN is the author of three collections of poetry: *Hush, The Shore,* and *No Heaven.* He has received grants and fellowships from the National Endowment for the Arts, the Guggenheim Foundation, and the Ingram Merrill Foundation. In 1984, he was awarded the Rome Fellowship in Literature from The American Academy and Institute of Arts and Letters. He is professor of English at The University of Southern California.

MARY SWANDER is the author of two books of poems, *Succession* and *Driving the Body Back,* which she recently transformed into a play. A native of Carroll, Iowa, she now teaches at Iowa State University. Her awards include the Carl Sandburg Literary Arts Award, a *Nation*/Discovery Award, and a grant from the Ingram Merrill Foundation.

JOHN TAGGART'S books of poems include *Peace on Earth, Dehiscence,* and *Loop.* He has published essays on the poetry and poetics of Duncan, Olson, and Oppen.

LUZ MARIA UMPIERRE is professor of Modern Languages and Intercultural Studies at Western Kentucky University. She is the author of the critical works *Ideologia y novela en Puerto Rico* and *Nuevas aproximaciones criticas a la literatura puertorriquena contemporanea.* She is also the author of four volumes of poems: *Una puertorriquena en Penna, En el pais de las maravillas, Y otras desgracias/And Other Misfortunes,* and *The Margarita Poems.* She is currently working on a book of interviews with Hispanic women writers in the United States.

ROSANNA WARREN is the author of *Each Leaf Shines Separate.* She is writing a literary biography of Max Jacob and teaches comparative literature at Boston University.

C. K. WILLIAMS has published five books of poetry, the last of which, *Flesh and Blood,* won the National Book Critics Circle Award for 1987. His *Poems 1963–1983* was published in the Fall of 1988. He has also published, with Gregory Dickerson, a translation of Sophocles' *Women of Trachis,* and has a translation of Euripides' *Bacchae* forthcoming. He is a professor of English at George Mason University.

BARON WORMSER lives with his family in Mercer, Maine. He is the author of *The White Words* and *Good Trembling.*

INDEX

The manuscript was edited by Lisa Nowak Gerry. The book was designed by Selma Tenenbaum. The typeface for the text and display is Benguiat Book Condensed and Benguiat Bold.

Manufactured in the United States.